Inside Microsoft SharePoint 2013

Scot Hillier
Mirjam van Olst
Ted Pattison
Andrew Connell
Wictor Wilén
Kyle Davis

Published with the authorization of Microsoft Corporation by:
O'Reilly Media, Inc.
1005 Gravenstein Highway North
Sebastopol, California 95472

ISBN: 978-0-7356-7447-9

1 2 3 4 5 6 7 8 9 LSI 8 7 6 5 4 3

Printed and bound in the United States of America.

Microsoft Press books are available through booksellers and distributors worldwide. If you need support related to this book, email Microsoft Press Book Support at *mspinput@microsoft.com*. Please tell us what you think of this book at *http://www.microsoft.com/learning/booksurvey*.

Acquisitions and Developmental Editor: Kenyon Brown

Production Editor: Kara Ebrahim

Editorial Production: Online Training Solutions, Inc. (OTSI)

Technical Reviewers: Wayne Ewington and Neil Hodgkinson

Copyeditor: Online Training Solutions, Inc. (OTSI)

Indexer: Angela Howard

Cover Design: Twist Creative • Seattle

Cover Composition: Ellie Volckhausen

Illustrator: Rebecca Demarest

Contents at a glance

	Introduction	*xvii*
CHAPTER 1	SharePoint 2013 developer roadmap	1
CHAPTER 2	SharePoint development practices and techniques	35
CHAPTER 3	Server-side solution development	71
CHAPTER 4	SharePoint apps	119
CHAPTER 5	Client-side programming	163
CHAPTER 6	SharePoint security	213
CHAPTER 7	SharePoint pages	267
CHAPTER 8	SharePoint Web Parts	309
CHAPTER 9	SharePoint lists	353
CHAPTER 10	SharePoint type definitions and templates	405
CHAPTER 11	SharePoint site provisioning	441
CHAPTER 12	SharePoint workflows	467
CHAPTER 13	SharePoint search	503
CHAPTER 14	SharePoint Enterprise Content Management	541
CHAPTER 15	Web content management	591
CHAPTER 16	Business Connectivity Services	621
CHAPTER 17	SharePoint social enterprise features	673
	Index	*725*

Contents

Introduction . . . .*xvii*

Chapter 1   SharePoint 2013 developer roadmap   1

A brief history of SharePoint. 2

    Understanding the impact of SharePoint Online on the
    SharePoint platform. 3

Examining SharePoint Foundation architecture .4

    Understanding SharePoint farms 6

    Creating web applications 8

    Understanding service applications 12

    Creating service applications in SharePoint Server 2013 14

    Managing sites 15

    Customizing sites 19

    Using SharePoint Designer 2013 23

    Understanding site customization vs. SharePoint development . . .24

Windows PowerShell boot camp for SharePoint professionals 26

    Learn Windows PowerShell in 21 minutes. 26

    The Windows PowerShell Integrated Scripting
    Environment (ISE). 30

    The SharePoint PowerShell snap-in 31

Summary. 34

Chapter 2   SharePoint development practices and techniques   35

Setting up a developer environment. 36

    Deciding between virtual and physical 37

    Understanding hardware and software requirements 38

    Delivering high-quality solutions 40

Automating SharePoint administration by using Windows
PowerShell scripts 42

    Using PowerShell to deploy a custom solution 44

Configuring SharePoint service applications 46

Using debugging tools. 52

    Working with ULS and Windows event logs 53

    Using the Developer Dashboard 54

Using the SharePoint Developer Tools in Visual Studio 2012 55

Choosing a development approach 59

Using the SharePoint APIs 61

    Understanding the server-side object model 62

    Using the client-side object model 63

    Using the REST APIs 67

Summary. 69

Chapter 3 Server-side solution development   71

Understanding the server-side object model 73

Developing farm solutions 76

    Creating a SharePoint project in Visual Studio 77

    Designing your SharePoint solution: Features 79

    Adding declarative elements 81

    Adding a feature receiver 84

    Understanding the SharePoint root directory 86

    Deploying and debugging farm solutions. .89

    Updating farm solutions 94

    Upgrading features 95

Developing sandboxed solutions. 102

    Understanding the sandbox execution environment 104

    Creating a SharePoint project for a sandboxed solution 106

    Deploying and debugging sandboxed solutions 109

    Updating and upgrading sandboxed solutions 113

Summary. 117

Chapter 4 SharePoint apps   119

Understanding the new SharePoint app model .119

    Understanding SharePoint solution challenges 120

    Understanding the SharePoint app model design goals 122

Understanding SharePoint app model architecture. 122

    Working with app service applications 123

    Understanding app installation scopes 124

    Understanding app code isolation 125

    Understanding app hosting models. 126

    Reviewing the app manifest. 130

    Setting the start page URL. 132

    Understanding the app web 134

    Working with app user interface entry points 137

Using the chrome control 144

Packaging and distributing apps 147

    Packaging apps. 147

    Publishing apps 152

    Installing apps. 155

    Upgrading apps 157

    Trapping app life cycle events 158

Summary. 162

Chapter 5   Client-side programming   163

Understanding app designs 163

    Assessing SharePoint-hosted app designs. 164

    Assessing cloud-hosted app designs 164

Introduction to JavaScript for SharePoint developers 165

    Understanding JavaScript namespaces 165

    Understanding JavaScript variables 166

    Understanding JavaScript functions. 167

    Understanding JavaScript closures 168

    Understanding JavaScript prototypes 169

    Creating custom libraries 170

Introduction to jQuery for SharePoint developers. 173

    Referencing jQuery 174

    Understanding the global function 174

    Understanding selector syntax 175

Understanding jQuery methods 175

Understanding jQuery event handling 176

Working with the client-side object model 177

Understanding client object model fundamentals 177

Working with the managed client object model 180

Working with the JavaScript client object model 188

Working with the REST API 195

Understanding REST fundamentals 196

Working with the REST API in JavaScript 200

Working with the REST API in C# 206

Summary 212

Chapter 6   SharePoint security   213

Reviewing authentication and authorization 213

Understanding user authentication 214

Understanding the User Information List 216

Working with users and groups 216

Working with application pool identities 219

Understanding the SHAREPOINT\SYSTEM account 220

Delegating user credentials 221

User impersonation with the user token 221

Securing objects with SharePoint 222

Rights and permission levels 224

Understanding app authentication 224

Understanding app authentication flow 233

Understanding app authorization 234

Managing app permissions 235

Understanding app permission policies 235

Requesting and granting app permissions 236

Requesting app-only permissions 239

Establishing app identity by using OAuth .240

Understanding app principals 242

Developing with OAuth 247

Establishing app identity by using S2S trusts 256

    Architecture of an S2S trust 257

    Configuring an S2S trust. 259

    Developing provider-hosted apps by using S2S trusts 263

Summary. 265

Chapter 7   SharePoint pages   267

SharePoint and ASP.NET 267

    Learning ASP.NET basics. 267

    Understanding how SharePoint relates to IIS web applications . .271

    Understanding the web.config file 272

    Understanding the SharePoint virtual file system 274

    Working with files and folders in SharePoint 275

    Understanding page customization 277

Using pages in SharePoint. 282

    Understanding master pages. 282

    Understanding MDS 287

    Understanding content pages. 289

    Creating a custom branding solution. 296

    Working with application pages 298

Customizing the ribbon. 303

    Understanding the anatomy of the SharePoint ribbon. 303

    Adding a custom ribbon control. 304

Summary. 307

Chapter 8   SharePoint Web Parts   309

Understanding Web Part fundamentals. 309

    Understanding Web Parts 309

    Comparing ASP.NET and SharePoint Web Parts. 310

    Understanding App Parts. 311

    Understanding Web Part zones. 311

    Understanding the Web Part Manager 312

    Understanding static Web Parts 312

    Storing Web Part control description files in the
    Web Part Gallery 313

Developing and deploying Web Parts 313

    Building your first Web Part...............................313

    Deploying and uninstalling a Web Part.....................317

    Deploying a Web Part page with Web Parts.................319

Controlling Web Part rendering................................324

    Overriding the *RenderContents* method 324

    Using *CreateChildControls* *325*

    Responding to events 325

    Combining *CreateChildControls* and *RenderContents* *327*

    Using Visual Web Parts 329

Working with Web Part properties 331

    Persisting Web Part properties 331

    Using custom Editor Parts 333

Exploring advanced Web Part development.......................337

    Using Web Part verbs 337

    Using Web Part connections 340

    Using parallel and asynchronous execution in Web Parts 345

Summary..350

Chapter 9   **SharePoint lists**   **353**

Creating lists 353

Working with fields and field types..............................357

    Performing basic field operations..........................358

    Working with lookups and relationships 361

Understanding site columns.....................................362

Working with content types 366

    Programming with content types..........................368

    Creating custom content types 370

Working with document libraries................................372

    Creating a document library 372

    Adding a custom document template.......................373

    Creating document-based content types 375

    Working with folders......................................378

Creating and registering event handlers 379

Understanding event receiver classes 380

Understanding remote event receivers 381

Registering event handlers. 383

Programming before events 387

Programming after events 388

Querying lists with CAML 389

Understanding CAML fundamentals 389

Querying joined lists 391

Querying multiple lists 392

Throttling queries. 394

Working with LINQ to SharePoint 396

Generating entities with *SPMetal* *396*

Querying with LINQ to SharePoint. 401

Adding, deleting, and updating with LINQ to SharePoint 402

Summary. 404

Chapter 10   SharePoint type definitions and templates   405

Custom field types 405

Creating custom field types 406

Creating custom field controls. 410

JSLink 420

Custom site columns and content types. 428

Creating site columns and content types by using CAML 428

Creating site columns and content types by using the
server-side object model 430

Custom list definitions 433

Summary. 439

Chapter 11   SharePoint site provisioning   441

The GLOBAL site definition 442

Site definitions. 443

Webtemp*.xml 443

ONET.xml for site definitions 445

Feature stapling 448

Order of provisioning when using site definitions 449

Custom site definitions 450

Web templates. 451

elements.xml. 451

ONET.xml for web templates 452

Deploying web templates. 455

Using custom code to create sites 458

Site templates 458

Site provisioning providers 459

Web provisioning events. 461

Web templates and SharePoint apps 463

Summary. 465

Chapter 12 SharePoint workflows   467

Workflow architecture in SharePoint 2013. 467

Installing and configuring a Workflow Manager 1.0 farm 468

Understanding workflow in SharePoint 2013 469

Creating custom workflows for SharePoint 2013 469

Building custom workflows. 470

Custom workflows with Visio 2013 and SharePoint
Designer 2013. 470

Custom workflows with Visual Studio 2012. 476

SharePoint Designer 2013 and web services. 485

Creating custom activities 487

Using tasks in workflows 492

Adding tasks to a workflow 492

Custom task outcomes 494

Workflow services CSOM and JSOM 497

Adding custom forms to workflows 498

Association forms in SharePoint 2013 498

Initiation forms in SharePoint 2013. 500

Summary. 502

Chapter 13 SharePoint search   **503**

    Introducing search-based applications. 504

    Understanding search architecture 506

        Understanding the indexing process 507

        Understanding the query process. 509

    Understanding Keyword Query Language. 510

    Creating no-code customizations 513

        Creating simple link queries. 513

        Extending the Search Center 514

        Using the Content Search Web Part. 523

    Using the client-side API 523

        Using the REST API. 524

        Using the CSOM API 526

    Using the script Web Parts 528

    Improving relevancy. 529

    Enhancing content processing 531

    Creating .NET Assembly Connectors for search .534

        Search-enabling a model 534

        Implementing security in search results. 537

        Crawling the .NET Assembly Connector 539

    Summary. 539

Chapter 14 SharePoint Enterprise Content Management   **541**

    Understanding the Managed Metadata Service Application 541

        Understanding managed metadata 542

        Using managed metadata in a custom solution. 545

        Understanding content type syndication .556

    Document services 559

        Understanding versioning 559

        Understanding Document IDs. 563

        Understanding Document Sets. 567

        Using the Content Organizer. 574

        Understanding Word Automation Services. 578

Records management 584

    In-place records management. 584

    Records archives. 586

    eDiscovery 586

Summary. 589

Chapter 15 Web content management   591

Understanding the WCM features. 591

    Publishing site templates 592

Accessing SharePoint publishing files 594

    Mapping to the SharePoint Master Page Gallery. 594

Page layouts. 595

    Understanding the page model 595

    Creating a new page layout. 597

    Managing the presentation of page fields 597

    Working with edit mode panels 599

    Working with Web Part zones. 600

Understanding device channels. 600

    Working with device channel panels 603

Understanding managed navigation 604

    Working with managed navigation APIs .604

    Creating a navigational term set. 605

Content aggregation 607

    Deciding between the Content Query and
    Content Search Web Parts 609

    Working with display templates 611

Understanding cross-site publishing. 617

    Working with catalogs 617

Summary. 620

Chapter 16 Business Connectivity Services   621

Introduction to Business Connectivity Services. .622

Creating simple BCS solutions 624

Creating External Content Types. 624

Creating External Lists. 627

Understanding External List limitations 628

Understanding BCS architecture 630

Understanding connectors. 631

Understanding Business Data Connectivity 631

Managing the BDC service. 632

Understanding the BDC Server Runtime. .635

Understanding the client cache. 635

Understanding the BDC Client Runtime 635

Introduction to the Secure Store Service. 635

Understanding package deployment. 639

Understanding authentication scenarios 639

Configuring authentication models 639

Accessing claims-based systems 643

Accessing token-based systems 643

Managing client authentication 643

Creating External Content Types 644

Creating operations. 645

Creating relationships 648

Defining filters 649

Using ECTs in SharePoint 2013 651

Creating custom forms 651

Using External Data Columns 652

Using External Data Web Parts 652

Creating a profile page 653

Searching External Systems 654

Supplementing user profiles 655

Using ECTs in Office 2013 655

Understanding Outlook integration. 655

Using Word Quick Parts 656

Creating custom BCS solutions. 656

Using the BDC Runtime object models 656

Using the Administration Object Model .659

Creating custom event receivers..............................662

Creating .NET Assembly Connectors 663

Developing SharePoint apps 668

Summary..671

Chapter 17   SharePoint social enterprise features   673

What's new in SharePoint 2013 673

Understanding social components 674

Working with the social APIs 675

Understanding user profiles 676

Retrieving user profile properties...........................677

Understanding social feeds.......................................689

Retrieving posts from your newsfeed.........................689

Retrieving posts from a site feed............................698

Posting to your personal feed 704

Posting to a site feed.....................................709

Understanding following within SharePoint 2013 710

Following people 712

Understanding Yammer.......................................719

Understanding how Yammer can work with SharePoint.........719

Retrieving followers and followings from Yammer 719

Summary..723

Index   *725*

Introduction

The purpose of this book is to help you design and develop custom business apps and solutions for SharePoint 2013, which includes the two products SharePoint Foundation and SharePoint Server 2013. Our goal is to teach you how to create, debug, and deploy the various components of apps and solutions such as Features, Pages, App Parts, Remote Event Handlers, and Workflows. Once you apply yourself and become comfortable developing with these building blocks, there's no limit to the types of apps and solutions you can create on the SharePoint 2013 platform.

Who this book is for

This book is written for experienced SharePoint developers who are proficient with Microsoft Visual Studio 2012, the Microsoft .NET Framework 4, and who understand the fundamentals of the SharePoint object model. The code samples in this book are written in JavaScript and C# and are intended to represent the spectrum of possible solutions. The primary audience for the book is SharePoint architects and developers looking to master SharePoint 2013 development.

Organization of this book

This book is organized into 17 chapters:

- Chapter 1, "SharePoint 2013 developer roadmap," provides a strategic view of SharePoint development options. The chapter presents the various development models and how they fit into the overall SharePoint development story.

- Chapter 2, "SharePoint development practices and techniques," provides guidance in setting up your development environment. Additionally, the chapter covers related technologies that are important for SharePoint development, such as Windows PowerShell.

- Chapter 3, "Server-side solution development," presents the fundamentals of sandbox and full-trust solution development. The chapter also presents the basics of the server-side object model.

- Chapter 4, "SharePoint apps," covers the new app model in detail. This chapter presents the tools and techniques necessary for developing apps.

- Chapter 5, "Client-side programming," first provides a JavaScript and jQuery primer for SharePoint developers with an emphasis on professional patterns. The second half of the chapter presents the fundamentals of the client-side object model and REST APIs for SharePoint 2013.

- Chapter 6, "SharePoint security," presents the security concepts necessary for successfully developing solutions and apps. This chapter explains the concepts behind user authentication and authorization, in addition to the app principal. This chapter also presents the details behind the claims and OAuth security models.

- Chapter 7, "SharePoint pages," presents techniques and information for working with pages in SharePoint solutions and apps. The chapter covers core concepts such as master pages, content placeholders, and application pages.

- Chapter 8, "SharePoint Web Parts," presents the tools and techniques required to create Web Parts and app parts.

- Chapter 9, "SharePoint lists," presents the information necessary for creating lists and performing operations against them. This chapter contains many code samples for reading and writing, using both server and client technologies.

- Chapter 10, "SharePoint type definitions and templates," covers the techniques for creating field types and field controls. The second part of the chapter covers the new JSLink technology and how it can be used to customize views.

- Chapter 11, "SharePoint site provisioning," shows how to create site templates and site definitions. These templates can be reused in solutions and apps.

- Chapter 12, "SharePoint workflows," presents all the information necessary for developing custom workflows by using the new Workflow Manager engine. Techniques for both the SharePoint Designer and Visual Studio are presented.

- Chapter 13, "SharePoint search," presents architecture and development techniques for Enterprise Search. The chapter details the creation of no-code solutions as well as apps.

- Chapter 14, "SharePoint Enterprise Content Management," presents structure and development techniques for managed metadata, document services, and records management.

- Chapter 15, "Web content management," details the significant improvements made for supporting website development. The chapter presents improvements in data-driven sites, master page creation, and metadata navigation.

- Chapter 16, "Business Connectivity Services," provides the background and tools for creating solutions based on data in external systems. The chapter presents approaches for both solutions and apps.

- Chapter 17, "SharePoint social enterprise features," presents the details of the new social infrastructure. The chapter also shows how to create solutions that utilize social features.

Acknowledgments

The process of writing this book really began two years before the release of SharePoint 2013, when we were fortunate enough to be selected as the team to create the first SharePoint 2013 training materials for Microsoft. We worked through many "Dev Kitchens" with the SharePoint team and got great information from Mike Ammerlann, Rob Howard, Brad Stevenson, Mike Morton, Mauricio Ordonez, and many others. After learning the technologies, we worked with a great team headed by Keenan Newton to deliver training to Microsoft personnel around the country. Later, we worked with Uma Subramanian and the MSDN team to create samples and videos to be deployed online. Thanks to all these people and everyone at Microsoft for the wonderful support and opportunities.

Of course, the book could not possibly have come together without the patience and support of the team at Microsoft Press, starting with our editor, Ken Brown (O'Reilly Media). Although we frustrated him endlessly at times, he maintained focus and drove us all to success. We'd also like to thank Kara Ebrahim (Production Editor, O'Reilly Media), Kathy Krause (Copyeditor, Online Training Solutions, Inc. [OTSI]), Wayne Ewington (Technical Editor), and Neil Hodgkinson (Technical Editor).

Thanks, everyone. It feels great to be done!

Support & feedback

The following sections provide information on errata, book support, feedback, and contact information.

Errata

We've made every effort to ensure the accuracy of this book and its companion content. Any errors that have been reported since this book was published are listed at:

http://aka.ms/InsideSP2013/errata

If you find an error that is not already listed, you can report it to us through the same page.

If you need additional support, email Microsoft Press Book Support at *mspinput@ microsoft.com*.

Please note that product support for Microsoft software is not offered through the addresses above.

We want to hear from you

At Microsoft Press, your satisfaction is our top priority, and your feedback our most valuable asset. Please tell us what you think of this book at:

http://aka.ms/tellpress

The survey is short, and we read every one of your comments and ideas. Thanks in advance for your input!

Stay in touch

Let's keep the conversation going! We're on Twitter: *http://twitter.com/MicrosoftPress*

CHAPTER 1

SharePoint 2013 developer roadmap

Microsoft SharePoint technologies have become increasing popular and have made it into the mainstream of IT infrastructures used by companies and organizations around the world. Today, millions of people work with SharePoint technologies every day, including business users, power users, executives, site administrators, farm administrators, and professional developers.

It is important for you, as a software developer, to view SharePoint technologies as a true platform for professional developers. The key point is that SharePoint technologies serve as a foundation on top of which you can design and implement business solutions. However, getting started can be daunting because there are several different versions of the SharePoint platform, and each version has several different variations.

Over the last decade, most of the companies that have used SharePoint technologies have deployed them as server-side software products on server computers that are under their control. This is a scenario that is often referred to as *SharePoint on-premises*. It is also important to note that the vast majority of SharePoint-related development projects have historically targeted the SharePoint on-premises scenario. However, this is beginning to change, and the change is occurring at a very fast pace.

Over the last few years, Microsoft has shifted the focus of their SharePoint adoption strategy from the original on-premises model to a newer subscription-based model where the SharePoint platform is made available to customers as a cloud-based service hosted in the Microsoft Office 365 environment. The hosted version of the SharePoint platform in the Office 365 environment is known as *SharePoint Online*.

It's clear that Microsoft sees SharePoint Online as the future direction of SharePoint technologies. However, it's also true that a significantly large portion of the existing SharePoint customer base is still using the older SharePoint on-premises model. Microsoft's ongoing effort to move its SharePoint customer base from the original on-premises model to SharePoint Online raises a few important questions:

- Are the SharePoint on-premises model and SharePoint Online just two different variations of the same development platform, or do they represent two entirely different platforms?

- When developing a business solution for SharePoint 2013, is it important to choose between targeting SharePoint on-premises and targeting SharePoint Online?

- Can you write a generic business solution that runs equally well in a SharePoint on-premises environment and in the SharePoint Online environment?

Unfortunately, the answer to each of these questions is "it depends," because they are all dependent upon the scenario at hand. In one scenario, you might be able to write a generic business solution that works in on-premises environments and in SharePoint Online. In another scenario, you might find it necessary to use a development technique that works in on-premises environments but doesn't work at all in SharePoint Online. In a third scenario, you might decide to take advantage of features in the Office 365 environment that are not available in the on-premises environment.

The bottom line is that there are an incredible number of details and techniques that you have to learn if you want to build a level of expertise across the entire SharePoint platform. The goal of this book is to cover the SharePoint 2013 development story from end to end to prepare you to make the correct choices in any SharePoint development scenario you might encounter.

A brief history of SharePoint

Microsoft has released five versions of SharePoint technologies, which are listed in Table 1-1. Each SharePoint release has included an underlying core infrastructure product and a second product that adds business value to the infrastructure. The core infrastructure product has always been free to customers who already have licenses for the underlying server-side operating system, Windows Server. Microsoft makes money on SharePoint technologies in the on-premises model by selling customers server-side licenses as well as client access licenses (CALs).

TABLE 1-1 A brief history of SharePoint

Year	Core infrastructure product	Business value product
2001	SharePoint Team Services	SharePoint Portal Server 2001
2003	Windows SharePoint Services 2.0	Microsoft SharePoint Portal Server 2003
2007	Windows SharePoint Services 3.0	Microsoft Office SharePoint Server 2007
2010	Microsoft SharePoint Foundation 2010	Microsoft SharePoint Server 2010
2013	Microsoft SharePoint Foundation 2013	Microsoft SharePoint Server 2013

SharePoint 2001 introduced an environment that allowed users to create sites, lists, and document libraries on demand based on a data-driven design. The implementation was based on a Microsoft SQL Server database that tracked the creation of sites and lists by adding records to a static set of database tables. This initial version of SharePoint had a couple of noteworthy shortcomings. First, it was cumbersome to customize sites. Second, the files uploaded to a document library were stored on the local file system of a single, dedicated web server, which made it impossible to scale out SharePoint Team Services sites by using a farm of web servers.

SharePoint 2003 was the first version to be implemented on top of the Microsoft .NET Framework and ASP.NET. This version began to open up new opportunities for professional developers looking to extend the SharePoint environment with Web Parts and event handlers. Also in this version, Microsoft altered the implementation for document libraries to store files inside a back-end SQL Server database, which made it possible to scale out SharePoint sites by using a farm of web servers.

SharePoint 2007 introduced many new concepts to the underlying SharePoint architecture, including site columns, content types, and features and solution packages. Microsoft also improved the integration of SharePoint with ASP.NET, which made it possible for .NET developers to extend SharePoint sites by creating familiar ASP.NET components such as master pages, user controls, navigation providers, authentication providers, and custom *HttpModule* components.

SharePoint 2010 was the fourth release of SharePoint technologies. It included Microsoft SharePoint Foundation 2010 and Microsoft SharePoint Server 2010. SharePoint 2010 introduced the new service application architecture and a significant modernization to the user interface experience with the server-side ribbon, model dialogs, and new Asynchronous JavaScript and XML (AJAX) behavior that reduced the need for page post backs. It was also with the SharePoint 2010 release that the Microsoft Visual Studio team released the original version of the SharePoint Developer Tools, which moved SharePoint developers out of the dark ages and into a far more productive era.

SharePoint 2013 is the fifth and most recent release of SharePoint technologies. It includes SharePoint Foundation 2013 and Microsoft SharePoint Server 2013. As you will see, the most significant changes that Microsoft has made to SharePoint 2013 have been done to adapt the SharePoint platform for hosted environments in the cloud, such as SharePoint Online in the Office 365 environment. This is a big change for developers because the SharePoint platform has been split in two. There is the older, familiar SharePoint platform in scenarios in which a company has deployed SharePoint on-premises. And now there is a second SharePoint platform in which developers are called upon to provide business solutions for hosted environments such as SharePoint Online.

Understanding the impact of SharePoint Online on the SharePoint platform

With its first two releases, Microsoft generated revenue from SharePoint technologies by using only the on-premises model. More specifically, Microsoft made money by selling SharePoint Server as a traditional software product that requires the customer to purchase a server-side license for each server and a client access license (CAL) for each user.

Starting in the SharePoint 2007 life cycle, Microsoft began to sell hosted versions of SharePoint that were bundled together with other services such as Microsoft Exchange, under the name of Business Productivity Online Standard Suite (BPOS). In the SharePoint 2010 life cycle, Microsoft changed the name of their bundled hosting service from BPOS to Office 365.

SharePoint 2013 represents the version in which Microsoft got serious about adapting the SharePoint platform for hosted environments such as SharePoint Online. This is evidenced by significant investments on the part of Microsoft to re-architect many core aspects of the SharePoint platform that had been causing scalability issues in SharePoint Online with SharePoint 2010.

Microsoft made one other big decision that is having a profound impact on every developer that works with the SharePoint platform. With SharePoint 2013, Microsoft has introduced a new strategy for developing business solutions based on the new *SharePoint app model*, which is a 180-degree turn from anything that has existed before.

With SharePoint 2013, there are now two separate and distinct styles in which you can develop a business solution. First, there is the original style of SharePoint development based on SharePoint solutions. Second, there is the new style of development based on SharePoint apps. This means that you must decide between creating a SharePoint solution and creating a SharePoint app each time you start a new development project on the SharePoint platform. So which one should you choose? The answer to that question is easy: it depends.

Examining SharePoint Foundation architecture

At its core, SharePoint Foundation 2013 is a provisioning engine—that is, its fundamental design is based on the idea of using web-based templates to create sites, lists, and libraries to store and organize content. Templates are used to create both new websites and various elements inside a website, such as lists, pages, and Web Parts.

SharePoint Foundation is particularly valuable to companies and organizations faced with the task of creating and administering a large number of websites, because it dramatically reduces the amount of work required. Someone in the IT department or even an ordinary business user can *provision* (a fancy word for *create*) a site in SharePoint Foundation in less than a minute by filling in a browser-based form and clicking the OK button. Creating a new page or a new list inside a site is just as easy.

SharePoint Foundation takes care of all the provisioning details behind the scenes by adding and modifying records in a SQL Server database. The database administrator doesn't need to create a new database or any new tables. The ASP.NET developer doesn't need to create a new ASP.NET website to supply a user interface. And the system administrator doesn't need to copy any files on the front-end web server or configure any Internet Information Services (IIS) settings. It all just works. That's the magic of the SharePoint platform.

The architecture of SharePoint Foundation was specifically designed to operate in a web farm environment. Figure 1-1 shows a basic diagram of a simple web farm with two front-end web servers and a database server. In scenarios that have multiple web servers, a network load balancer is used to take incoming HTTP requests and determine which front-end web server each request should be sent to.

SharePoint Foundation 2013 and SharePoint Server 2013 are available only in 64-bit versions. They can be installed on a 64-bit version of Windows Server 2012 or Windows Server 2008 R2. Unlike SharePoint 2010, Microsoft does not support installing SharePoint 2013 on a client operating system such as Windows 7 or Windows 8. However, you can run Windows 8 and enable Microsoft Hyper-V, which will allow you to create virtual machines (VMs) based on Windows Server 2012 or Windows Server 2008 R2. Therefore, you can install SharePoint 2013 on a VM running on Windows 8.

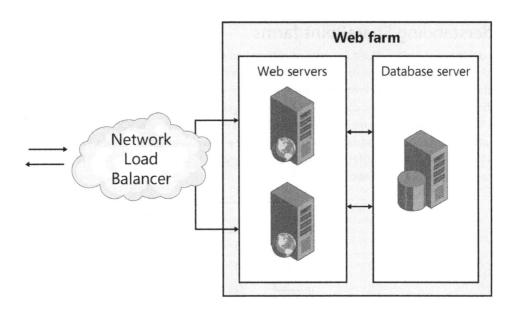

FIGURE 1-1 SharePoint Foundation is designed to scale out by using a farm of web servers.

SharePoint Foundation takes advantage of IIS on front-end web servers to listen for incoming HTTP requests and to manage the server-side worker processes by using the IIS application pool infrastructure. The version of IIS depends upon the operating system. Windows Server 2012 will use IIS 8.0, whereas Windows Server 2008 R2 will use IIS 7.5. The runtime environment of SharePoint Foundation runs within a worker process launched from the IIS application pool executable named w3wp.exe. As shown in Figure 1-2, SharePoint Foundation 2013 is built on .NET Framework 4.5.

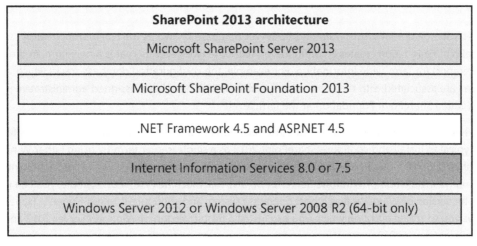

FIGURE 1-2 The SharePoint Foundation runtime loads into an IIS application pool running ASP.NET 4.5.

Understanding SharePoint farms

Every deployment of SharePoint Foundation is based on the concept of a farm. Simply stated, a *SharePoint farm* is a set of one or more server computers working together to provide SharePoint Foundation functionality to clients. For simple scenarios, you can set up an on-premises farm by installing SharePoint 2013 and configuring everything you need on a single server computer or a single VM. An on-premises farm in a typical production environment runs SQL Server on a separate, dedicated database server and can have multiple front-end web servers, as shown in Figure 1-3. As you will learn later in this chapter, a farm can also run one or more application servers in addition to a database server and a set of web servers.

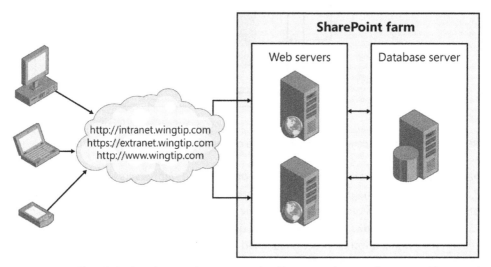

FIGURE 1-3 A SharePoint farm is a set of servers running SharePoint that are all associated by a single configuration database.

Each SharePoint farm runs a single SQL Server database known as the *configuration database*. SharePoint Foundation creates a configuration database whenever it creates a new farm, in order to track important farm-wide information. For example, the configuration database tracks which web servers are associated with the farm, as well as which users have been assigned administrative permissions within SharePoint Foundation at the farm level.

When you are creating a SharePoint 2013 development environment with an on-premises farm, it is typical to install and configure SharePoint 2013 as a single-server farm by using either Windows Server 2012 or Windows Server 2008 R2. You have the option of installing a version of SharePoint 2013 on a native installation of Windows Server or on a virtual machine (VM). For example, you can install a 64-bit version of Windows 8 as a host operating system and configure it to run Hyper-V. Hyper-V allows you to create a VM on which you can install a 64-bit version of Windows Server 2012 and SharePoint Server 2013.

As a SharePoint developer, you must remember that farms come in all different shapes and sizes. Although it is common to write and test your code on a single-server farm, this type of environment is probably not the type of farm in which your code will be deployed. It can be a big mistake to assume that your target SharePoint production environment is just like your development environment.

Many companies that are invested in on-premises SharePoint development categorize their farms into three different types. SharePoint developers write and debug SharePoint solutions in *development farms*. *Staging farms* simulate a more realistic environment and are used to conduct quality assurance testing on SharePoint solutions. For example, the servers in a staging farm should be built without installing developer tools such as Microsoft Visual Studio 2012. After a SharePoint solution or a SharePoint app has been thoroughly tested in a staging farm, it can be deployed in a *production farm*, where its functionality is made available to users.

Working with SharePoint 2013 Central Administration

As a SharePoint developer, you must wear many hats. One hat you frequently wear is that of a SharePoint farm administrator. You should become familiar with the administrative site that SharePoint Foundation automatically creates for each farm. This administrative site is known as *SharePoint 2013 Central Administration*, and its home page is shown in Figure 1-4.

FIGURE 1-4 SharePoint developers should become familiar with SharePoint 2013 Central Administration.

Figure 1-4 shows the home page of SharePoint 2013 Central Administration in an on-premises farm with SharePoint Server 2013 installed. If you only install SharePoint Foundation instead of SharePoint Server 2013, you will not find as many links to administrative pages, because quite a few are only installed with SharePoint Server 2013. Also note that SharePoint 2013 Central Administration is extensible. If you need to create a SharePoint solution for administrative purposes, you canintegrate your work into SharePoint 2013 Central Administration by adding custom links and custom administration pages.

Scenario: Introducing Wingtip Toys

Many of the example configurations and code samples in this book are based on Wingtip Toys, a company that was fictitiously founded in 1882 by Henry Livingston Wingtip. Wingtip Toys has a long and proud history of producing the industry's most unique and inventive toys for people of all ages. Wingtip Toys has set up an intranet using SharePoint internally to provide a means of collaboration between its trinket design scientists, its manufacturing team, and its remote sales force. It has also erected an extranet, using SharePoint to interact with partners and toy stores around the world. Finally, Wingtip Toys has decided to use SharePoint to create its Internet-facing site to advertise and promote its famous line of toys and novelties.

Creating web applications

SharePoint 2013 is built on top of Internet Information Services (IIS). SharePoint 2013 is completely dependent upon IIS because it uses IIS websites to listen for and process incoming HTTP requests. Therefore, you need to understand exactly what an IIS website really is.

An IIS website provides an entry point into the IIS web server infrastructure. For example, the default website that is automatically created by IIS listens for incoming HTTP requests on port 80. You can create additional IIS websites to provide additional HTTP entry points using different port numbers, different IP addresses, or different host headers. In this book's scenario, we'll use host headers to create HTTP entry points for domain names such as *http://intranet.wingtiptoys.com*.

SharePoint Foundation creates an abstraction on top of IIS that is known as a *web application*. At a physical level, a SharePoint web application is a collection of one or more IIS websites configured to map incoming HTTP requests to a set of SharePoint sites. The web application also maps each SharePoint site to one or more specific *content databases*. SharePoint Foundation uses content databases to store site content such as list items, documents, and customization information.

SharePoint Foundation leverages the ASP.NET 4.0 support in IIS to extend the standard behavior of an IIS website. It does this by configuring IIS websites to run SharePoint-specific components in the ASP.NET pipeline by using *HttpModule* objects. This integration with ASP.NET allows SharePoint Foundation to take control over every request that reaches an IIS website that has been configured as a SharePoint web application.

Keep in mind that every SharePoint web application runs as one large ASP.NET application. Consequently, SharePoint Foundation adds a standard ASP.NET web.config file to the root directory of each IIS website associated with a web application. When you create a web application in SharePoint Foundation, it creates an IIS website with a root folder containing a web.config file at the following location:

```
C:\inetpub\wwwroot\wss\VirtualDirectories
```

The fact that there is a one-to-many relationship between a web.config file and SharePoint sites can be counterintuitive for developers who are migrating from ASP.NET. A single SharePoint site is unlike an ASP.NET site because it can't have its own web.config file. That means that a single web.config file in SharePoint Foundation supplies configuration information for every site in a web application. This is true even in scenarios where the number of sites in a web application reaches into the hundreds or thousands.

A SharePoint on-premises farm typically runs two or more web applications. The first web application is created automatically when the farm is created. This web application is used to run SharePoint 2013 Central Administration. You need at least one additional web application to create the sites that are used by business users. The IT staff at Wingtip Toys decided to configure their production farm with three different web applications used to reach employees, partners, and customers, as shown in Figure 1-5.

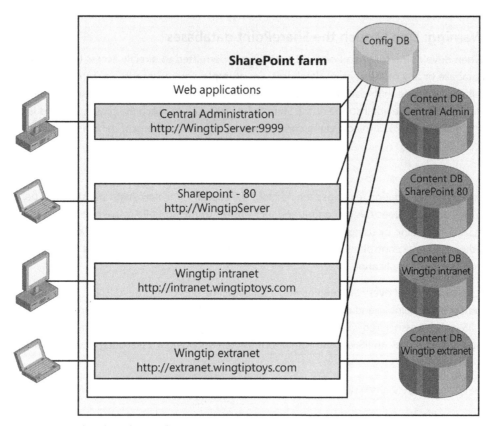

FIGURE 1-5 Each web application has one or more content databases.

Understanding web applications and user authentication

The first thing to understand is that the SharePoint platform itself does not supply the actual code to authenticate users. Instead, the SharePoint platform relies on external user authentication systems such as Windows Server and Active Directory or the built-in support in ASP.NET for forms-based authentication (FBA). After an external system has authenticated a user and created a security token, the SharePoint platform is then able to create a profile around that security token to establish and track the user's identity inside the SharePoint security system.

The manner in which SharePoint authenticates users is configured at the web application level. When you create a SharePoint web application, you have the option of creating it in either claims mode or classic mode. Classic authentication mode is the older style of user authentication that was used in SharePoint 2007, where user identity is tracked by using native Windows security tokens. Though classic mode is still supported in SharePoint 2013 for older scenarios, its use is deprecated and should be avoided. That means new web applications should be configured to use claims-based security.

The claims-based authentication mode was introduced in SharePoint 2010; it allows the SharePoint platform to use a single, unified format for all the security tokens that are created during the user authentication process. More specifically, the user authentication tokens are converted into a special format for caching known as a *FedAuth token*. Within developer circles, a FedAuth token is also commonly referred to as a *claims token*.

Let's walk through the authentication process in a SharePoint web application in a scenario in which the user is authenticated with Windows authentication. The first part of the authentication process involves creating a native Windows security token. In the second part of the authentication process, SharePoint Foundation will convert the Windows security token into a FedAuth token by using a local service known as the *Security Token Service (STS)*.

You also have the option of configuring a web application in an on-premises farm to support forms-based authentication by using an ASP.NET authentication provider. In this style of authentication, SharePoint Foundation once again calls upon the STS to create a FedAuth token for the FBA user during the user authentication process.

In SharePoint 2010, the FedAuth tokens created during the user authentication process are cached in memory on a per–web server basis and can be reused across multiple requests from the same user. SharePoint 2013 further optimizes the caching of FedAuth tokens with a new platform-level service known as the Distributed Cache Service, which can be configured to maintain a farm-wide cache of FedAuth tokens.

SharePoint Foundation's use of claims-based authentication and FedAuth tokens provides another noteworthy point of flexibility. It opens up the number of identity providers that can be integrated with a SharePoint farm to provide user authentication. In addition to supporting Windows authentication and FBA, claims-based security makes it possible to configure a SharePoint web application to authenticate users by using external identity providers that support an XML-based industry standard known as *Security Assertion Markup Language (SAML)*. More specifically, SharePoint 2013 supports identity providers that support the SAML 1.1 specification. Examples of supported providers include Windows Azure Access Control Service (ACS), Windows Live ID, Google Single Sign-on, and Facebook.

Now that you have learned the fundamentals of how web applications provide the support for user authentication, let's examine how you might configure a set of web applications in a real-world scenario. For example, imagine a scenario in which the IT staff at Wingtip Toys must decide how many web applications should be created in their production farm.

The Wingtip Toys IT staff decided to create the first web application for the exclusive use of Wingtip employees, all of whom have their own Active Directory user accounts. Therefore, the first web application was configured for intranet usage by requiring Integrated Windows authentication and by prohibiting anonymous access.

The Wingtip Toys IT staff decided to create a second web application so they could create sites that could be made accessible to external users such as partners and vendors. The key characteristic of these external users is that they will never have their own Active Directory user accounts and, therefore, cannot be authenticated by using Windows authentication. Therefore, the Wingtip Toys IT staff decided to configure the second web application to support user authentication using FBA, so that these external users can be authenticated without any need for Active Directory user accounts.

The Wingtip Toys IT staff decided to create a third web application to host any SharePoint site that requires anonymous access, such as their public website hosted at *http://www.wingtiptoys.com*. Although they configured this web application to allow visitors from the Internet to view their public website anonymously, they also wanted to make logging onto the site an available option so that customers could create member accounts and customer profiles. Therefore, they configured this web application with a trust to Windows Live ID. When customers attempt to log onto the Wingtip Toys public website, they are redirected to the Windows Live ID site and prompted to enter their Windows Live ID credentials. After the customer is authenticated by Windows Live ID, he is then redirected back to the Wingtip Toys public website with an established identity.

Understanding service applications

A SharePoint farm must provide an efficient way to share resources across sites running in different web applications. It must also provide the means for offloading processing cycles for certain types of processes from front-end web servers to dedicated application servers. To meet this requirement, SharePoint Foundation uses an architecture based on *service applications* that was introduced in SharePoint 2010. Service applications are used to facilitate sharing resources across sites running in different web applications and different farms. The service application architecture also provides the means for scaling a SharePoint farm by offloading processing cycles from the front-end web servers over to dedicated application servers in the middle tier.

A key benefit of the service application architecture is that you can treat a service application as a moveable entity. After you create a service application, you can configure it for several different deployment scenarios. In a simple two-tier farms, the service application can be configured to run on one or more of the web servers in the farm, as shown on the left in Figure 1-6. In scenarios that require the ability to scale to thousands of users, the same service application can be configured to run on a dedicated application server such as the one shown on the right in Figure 1-6. In scenarios that require even greater scale, a service application can be configured to run within its own dedicated farm of application servers.

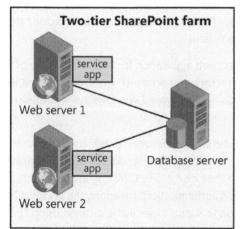 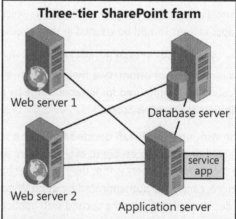

FIGURE 1-6 SharePoint farms run service applications in addition to web applications.

The service application architecture of the SharePoint platform was created with extensibility in mind. Any developer with the proper knowledge and motivation can develop a service application that can be deployed within a SharePoint 2013 farm. However, this is not an easy undertaking. A service application targeting a SharePoint platform must be written to a specific set of requirements. For example, a service application must query the configuration database about its current deployment configuration and adjust its behavior accordingly. A service application must be written in such a way that it can be deployed and configured using nothing more than Windows PowerShell.

When a service application runs across the network on a dedicated application server, it relies on a proxy component that must be written to run on the web server. The service application proxy is created and configured along with the service application. The service application proxy provides value by abstracting away the code required to discover where the service application lives on the network. The service application proxy provides additional value by encapsulating the Windows Communication Foundation (WCF) code used to execute web service calls on the target service application.

The proxy-based design of service applications provides flexibility in terms of deployment and configuration. For example, you can configure a proxy in one farm to communicate with a service application in another farm. The proxy simply consults the configuration database and discovers the correct address for the application server running the service application. The implication here is that the new service application architecture makes it much easier to share resources across farms while still controlling what services are made available and how they are consumed.

As a SharePoint developer creating business solutions, it is unlikely that you would ever find the need or have the proper incentives to develop a custom SharePoint service application. However, you still need to understand how service applications work and how they fit into the high-level architecture of SharePoint Foundation. For example, SharePoint Server 2013 delivers a good deal of its functionality through service applications.

The key point here is that you must learn how to create and configure service applications and service application proxies to properly build out a local on-premises farm for SharePoint development. This can be done most easily by using the Farm Configuration Wizard, which is available in Central Administration. However, using a custom Windows PowerShell script allows you to create service applications and service application proxies with far more control and flexibility than is afforded by the Farm Configuration Wizard.

Building an environment for SharePoint development

If you plan on developing SharePoint solutions or SharePoint apps that will be used within private networks such as a corporate LAN, it makes sense to build out a development environment with a local SharePoint 2013 farm. Critical Path Training provides a free download called the *SharePoint Server 2013 Virtual Machine Setup Guide*, which provides you with step-by-step instructions to install all the software you need and to build out a local SharePoint 2013 farm. You can download the guide from *http://criticalpathtraining.com/Members*.

Creating service applications in SharePoint Server 2013

SharePoint Server 2013 is nothing more than a layer of software that's been written to run on SharePoint Foundation. Every installation of SharePoint Server 2013 begins with an installation of SharePoint Foundation. After installing SharePoint Foundation, the installation for SharePoint Server 2013 then installs its own templates, components, and service applications. The Standard edition of SharePoint Server 2013 only supports a subset of the features and services available in the Enterprise edition of SharePoint Server 2013.

Adding to the complexity is that the feature set of SharePoint Online does not exactly match that of the on-premises version of SharePoint Server 2013. Therefore, you can really break SharePoint 2013 out into four distinct platforms that all vary in some degree from one another:

- SharePoint Foundation 2013

- SharePoint Server 2013 Standard edition

- SharePoint Server 2013 Enterprise edition

- SharePoint Online

To help you understand which service applications are available in each variation of the SharePoint 2013 platform, Table 1-2 lists some of the SharePoint 2013 service applications in addition to the editions of SharePoint 2013 that support each of these service applications.

TABLE 1-2 Service applications included with SharePoint 2013 platform

Name	Foundation	Standard	Enterprise	Online
Access Services	No	No	Yes	Yes
Access Services 2010	No	No	Yes	No
App Management Service	Yes	Yes	Yes	Yes
Business Data Connectivity Service	Yes	Yes	Yes	Yes
Excel Services Application	No	No	Yes	Yes
Machine Translation Service	No	No	Yes	Yes
PerformancePoint Service Application	No	No	Yes	No
PowerPoint Automation Services	No	Yes	Yes	Yes
Managed Metadata Service Application	No	Yes	Yes	Yes
Search Service Application	Yes	Yes	Yes	Yes
Secure Store Service	No	Yes	Yes	Yes
Site Subscription Settings Service	Yes	Yes	Yes	Yes

Name	Foundation	Standard	Enterprise	Online
State Service	Yes	Yes	Yes	Yes
User and Health Data Collection Service	Yes	Yes	Yes	Yes
User Profile Service Application	No	Yes	Yes	Yes
Visio Graphics Service	No	No	Yes	Yes
Word Automation Services	No	Yes	Yes	Yes
Work Management Service Application	No	Yes	Yes	Yes
Workflow Service Application	Yes	Yes	Yes	Yes

Managing sites

Now that you understand the high-level architecture of a SharePoint farm, you need to know how SharePoint Foundation creates and manages sites within the scope of a web application. Let's start by asking a basic question: What exactly is a SharePoint site?

This question has many possible answers. For example, a site is an endpoint that is accessible from across a network such the Internet, an intranet, or an extranet. A site is also a storage container that allows users to store and manage content such as list items and documents. In addition, a site is a customizable entity that allows privileged users to add pages, lists, and child sites as well as install SharePoint apps. Finally, a site is a securable entity whose content is accessible to a configurable set of users.

As a developer, you can also think of a site as an instance of an application. For example, the scientists at Wingtip Toys use a SharePoint site to automate the business process of approving a new toy idea. When Wingtip scientists have new ideas for a toy, they describe their ideas in Microsoft Word documents, which they then upload to a document library in the site. The approval process is initiated whenever a scientist starts a custom approval workflow on one of those documents.

A site can also be used as an integration point to connect users to back-end data sources such as a database application or a line-of-business application such as SAP or PeopleSoft. The Business Connectivity Services that ship with SharePoint 2013 make it possible to establish a read-write connection with a back-end data source. One valuable aspect of the Business Connectivity Services architecture is that this external data often appears to be a native SharePoint list. There are many user scenarios and developer scenarios in which you can treat external data just as you would treat a native SharePoint list.

Understanding the role of site collections

Every SharePoint site must be provisioned within the scope of an existing web application. However, a site can't exist as an independent entity within a web application. Instead, every site must also be created inside the scope of a site collection.

A *site collection* is a container of sites. Every site collection has a top-level site. In addition to the top-level site, a site collection can optionally contain a hierarchy of child sites. Figure 1-7 shows a web application created with a host header path of *http://intranet.wingtiptoys.com* that contains four site collections. The first site collection has been created at the root of the web application and contains just a single, top-level site. Note that the top-level site, the site collection, and the hosting web application all have the same URL.

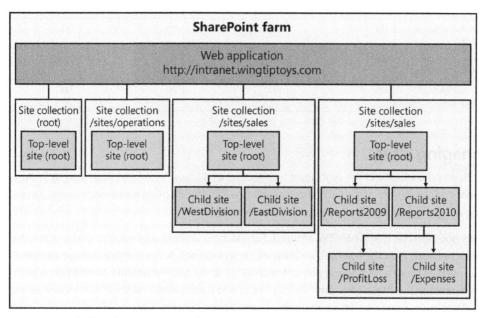

FIGURE 1-7 Each site collection has a top-level site and can optionally contain a hierarchy of child sites.

Only one site collection within a web application can be created at the same URL as the hosting web application itself. The other three site collections shown in Figure 1-7 have been created at URLs that are relative to the host header path of the hosting web application. The site collection created at the relative path of /sites/operations has just a top-level site. The site collection created at the relative path of /sites/sales contains one level of child sites below the top-level site. The last site collection on the right, which has been created at the relative path of /sites/financials, contains a more complex hierarchy with three levels.

When a company begins using SharePoint Foundation or SharePoint Server 2013, one of the first questions that comes up is how to partition sites across site collections. For example, should you create one big site collection with lots of child sites, or should you create many individual site collections? This decision is usually best made after thinking through all the relevant issues discussed in the next few paragraphs. You must gain an understanding of how partitioning sites into site collections affects the scope of administrative privileges, security boundaries, backup and restore operations, and site design.

You could be asking yourself why the SharePoint Foundation architecture requires this special container to hold its sites. For starters, site collections represent a scope for administrative privileges. If you've been assigned as a site collection administrator, you have full administrative permissions within any existing site and any future site created inside that site collection.

Think about the requirements of site management in a large corporation that's provisioning thousands of sites per year. The administrative burden posed by all these sites is going to be more than most IT staffs can deal with in a timely manner. The concept of the site collection is important because it allows the IT staff to hand off the administrative burden to someone in a business division who takes on the role of the site collection administrator.

Let's walk through an example. The Wingtip Toys IT staff is responsible for provisioning new site collections, and one of the Wingtip business divisions submits a request for a new site. Imagine the case where the Wingtip Sales Director has put in a request to create a new team site for his sales staff. A Wingtip IT staff member would handle this request by creating a new site collection with a team site as its top-level site.

When creating the new site collection, the Wingtip IT staff member would add the Wingtip Sales Director who requested the site as the site collection administrator. The Wingtip Sales Director would have full administrative privileges inside the site collection and could add new users, lists, and pages without any further assistance from the Wingtip IT staff. The Wingtip Sales Director could also add child sites and configure access rights to them independently of the top-level site.

A second advantage of site collections is that they provide a scope for membership and the configuration of access rights. By design, every site collection is independent of any other site collection with respect to what security groups are defined, which users have been added as members, and which users are authorized to perform what actions.

For example, imagine that the Wingtip IT staff has provisioned one site collection for the Sales department and a second site collection for the Finance department. Even though some users within the Finance department have administrative permissions within their own site collection, there's nothing they can do that will affect the security configuration of the Sales site collection. SharePoint Foundation sees each site collection as an island with respect to security and permissions configuration.

A third reason for site collections is that they provide a convenient scope for backup and restore operations. You can back up a site collection and later restore it with full fidelity. The restoration of a site collection can take place in the same location where the backup was made. Alternatively, a site collection can be restored in a different location—even inside a different farm. This technique for backing up a site collection and restoring it in another location provides one possible strategy for moving sites and all the content inside from one farm to another.

A final motivation for you to start thinking about in terms of site collections is that they provide a scope for many types of site elements and for running custom queries. For example, the server-side object model of SharePoint Foundation provides you with the capability to run queries that span all the lists within a site collection. However, there is no query mechanism in the SharePoint server-side object model that spans across site collections. Therefore, if your application design calls for running queries to aggregate list data from several different sites, it makes sense to add sites to the same site collection when they contain lists that must be queried together.

Imagine a case in which the West Division of the Wingtip Sales team has four field offices. The Wingtip Sales Director could create a child site for each field office below a site that was created for the West Division. Now assume that each child site has a Contacts list that is used to track sales leads. By using programming techniques shown later in this book, you can execute queries at the scope of the West Division site that would aggregate all the Contacts items found across all of its child sites. You could execute the same query at a higher scope and get different results. For example, if you executed the same query scoped to the top-level site, it would aggregate all the Contacts found throughout the site collection, including both the West Division and the East Division.

Understanding host-named site collections (HNSCs)

The traditional way to manage the URLs of site collections is to create the hosting web application with a host header path such as http://intranet.wingtiptoys.com. The site collections created inside this type of web application are known as path-based site collections because they all must be created with a URL that starts with the same host header path. When you create path-based site collections, you must create the URL for each site collection by starting with the host header path defined by the hosting web application:

- *http://intranet.wingtiptoys.com*

- *http://intranet.wingtiptoys.com/sites/operations*

- *http://intranet.wingtiptoys.com/sites/sales*

- *http://intranet.wingtiptoys.com/sites/financials*

There is a second approach, which provides more flexibility when you are managing the URLs for the site collections with a web application. This approach requires you to create the hosting web application without the traditional host header path. When you create a new web application without the host header path, you then have the ability to create site collections with unique host names. This type of site collection is known as a host-named site collection (HNSC).

Consider the following scenario. Imagine you are required to create a set of site collections using the following domain names:

- *http://operations.wingtiptoys.com*

- *http://sales.wingtiptoys.com*

- *http://financials.wingtiptoys.com*

If you use the older, traditional approach of creating path-based site collections, you would have to create a separate web application to host each of these site collections. However, this approach is going to become problematic because it cannot be scaled due to the fact that you are limited in how many web applications can be created within a single farm. However, if you use an approach based on host-named site collections, you can create all these site collections and many more with unique domain names within a single web application.

Note that the creation of host-named collections can be a little tricky at first. That's because a host-named site collection cannot be created through Central Administration. You must create a host-named site collection by using Windows PowerShell.

Customizing sites

SharePoint Foundation provides many user options for configuring and customizing sites. If you're logged onto a site as the site collection administrator, site administrator, or a user granted Designer permissions, you can perform any site customization options supported by SharePoint Foundation. If you're logged onto a site without administrative privileges in the role of a contributor, however, you won't have the proper permissions to customize the site. Furthermore, if you're logged on as a contributor, SharePoint Foundation uses *security trimming* to remove the links and menu commands that lead to pages with functionality for which you don't have permissions.

If you're logged onto a standard team site as a site administrator, you should be able to locate and open the Site Actions menu by clicking the small gear icon in the upper-right corner of the page, as shown in Figure 1-8. Note that the gear icon of the SharePoint Site Action menu is easy to confuse with the gear icon displayed by Windows Internet Explorer, which provides a menu that can be used to configure browser settings. Remember that the lower gear icon is specific to SharePoint and the one above it is specific to Internet Explorer.

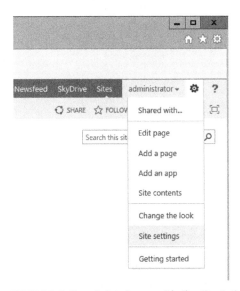

FIGURE 1-8 SharePoint sites provide the Site Actions menu to users with the correct permissions.

The Site Actions menu provides commands that allow you to edit the current page; to create new pages, lists, and document libraries; to view site contents; to change the look and feel of the current site; and to navigate to the Site Settings page shown in Figure 1-9.

SharePoint Foundation Team Site ✏ EDIT LINKS

Site Settings

Home

Documents

Site Contents

✏ EDIT LINKS

Users and Permissions
People and groups
Site permissions
Site collection administrators
Site app permissions

Web Designer Galleries
Site columns
Site content types
Web parts
List templates
Master pages
Themes
Solutions
Composed looks

Site Administration
Regional settings
Site libraries and lists
User alerts
RSS
Sites and workspaces
Workflow settings

Site Collection Administration
Recycle bin
Search Result Sources
Search Result Types
Search Query Rules
Search Schema
Search Settings
Search Configuration Import
Search Configuration Export
Site collection features
Site hierarchy
Portal site connection
Site collection app permissions
Storage Metrics
HTML Field Security
Help settings
SharePoint Designer Settings
Site collection health checks
Site collection upgrade

Look and Feel
Title, description, and logo
Quick launch
Top link bar
Tree view
Change the look

Site Actions
Manage site features
Save site as template
Enable search configuration export
Site Collection Web Analytics reports
Site Web Analytics reports
Reset to site definition
Delete this site

Reporting Services
Manage Shared Schedules
Reporting Services Site Settings
Manage Data Alerts

Search
Result Sources
Result Types
Query Rules
Schema
Search Settings
Search and offline availability
Configuration Import
Configuration Export

FIGURE 1-9 The Site Settings page is accessible to site administrators on any site.

The Site Settings page provides links to pages that allow you to perform various administrative and customization tasks. Notice that the Site Settings page for a top-level site contains one section for Site Administration and a second section for Site Collection Administration. The Site Settings page for child sites doesn't include the section for Site Collection Administration.

Figure 1-9 shows several sections of links, including Users and Permissions, Look and Feel, Web Designer Galleries, Site Actions, Site Administration, and Site Collection Administration, all of which provide links to various other administrative pages for the current site. If you're new to SharePoint Foundation, you should take some time to explore all the administrative pages accessible through the Site Settings page. Also keep in mind that Figure 1-9 shows only the links on the Site Settings page of a team site running within a SharePoint Foundation farm. If the site were running in a SharePoint Server 2013 farm, there would be additional links to even more site administration pages that are not part of the standard SharePoint Foundation installation.

Creating and customizing pages

The support for wiki page libraries and Web Parts is an aspect of SharePoint Foundation that enables business users to make quick changes to the content on pages in a SharePoint site. Business users with no experience in web design or HTML can quickly add and customize webpages. A good example of this can be seen when creating a new SharePoint 2013 team site. As part of the provisioning process, SharePoint Foundation automatically creates a new wiki library at the SitePages path off the root of the site, and it adds a wiki page named Home.aspx. It additionally configures Home.aspx to be the home page of the site, so it becomes the first page users see when navigating to the site.

Customizing the home page is simple for any user who has the proper permissions. The user can enter edit mode by using either the Site Actions menu or the ribbon. When in edit mode, the user is free to simply type text or copy and paste from another application. The Insert tab on the ribbon also makes it easy for the user to add tables, links, and images.

Web Part technology also plays a prominent role in page customization. Web Parts are based on the idea that the SharePoint platform and developers supply a set of visual components that users can add and move around in their pages. Every site collection has a Web Part Gallery, which contains a set of Web Part template files. This set of Web Part template files determines which types of Web Parts can be added to pages within the site collection.

Although earlier versions of SharePoint technologies supported Web Parts, they were not as flexible as SharePoint Foundation because Web Parts could be added only to Web Part pages. Starting with SharePoint 2010, SharePoint Foundation has made it possible to add Web Parts anywhere inside a wiki page. When you're editing the content of a wiki page, you can place the cursor wherever you want and add a new Web Part by using the Insert tab on the ribbon. The new Web Part appears inline along with your other wiki content.

Creating and customizing lists

The Site Actions menu provides an Add A Page menu command for creating new pages and an Add An App menu command for creating new lists and document libraries. If you click the Add An App menu command in the Site Actions menu, SharePoint Foundation displays the Add An App page, which allows you to create a new list or document library, as shown in Figure 1-10.

SharePoint Foundation Team Site   ✏ EDIT LINKS

Site Settings

Home

Documents

Site Contents

✏ EDIT LINKS

Users and Permissions
People and groups
Site permissions
Site collection administrators
Site app permissions

Web Designer Galleries
Site columns
Site content types
Web parts
List templates
Master pages
Themes
Solutions
Composed looks

Site Administration
Regional settings
Site libraries and lists
User alerts
RSS
Sites and workspaces
Workflow settings

Site Collection Administration
Recycle bin
Search Result Sources
Search Result Types
Search Query Rules
Search Schema
Search Settings
Search Configuration Import
Search Configuration Export
Site collection features
Site hierarchy
Portal site connection
Site collection app permissions
Storage Metrics
HTML Field Security
Help settings
SharePoint Designer Settings
Site collection health checks
Site collection upgrade

Look and Feel
Title, description, and logo
Quick launch
Top link bar
Tree view
Change the look

Site Actions
Manage site features
Save site as template
Enable search configuration export
Site Collection Web Analytics reports
Site Web Analytics reports
Reset to site definition
Delete this site

Reporting Services
Manage Shared Schedules
Reporting Services Site Settings
Manage Data Alerts

Search
Result Sources
Result Types
Query Rules
Schema
Search Settings
Search and offline availability
Configuration Import
Configuration Export

FIGURE 1-10 From the Add An App page, you can create new lists and document libraries.

In addition to list templates, the standard collaboration features of SharePoint Foundation also include templates for creating several different types of document libraries. Besides the standard document library type, there are also more specialized document library types for wiki page libraries, picture libraries, and InfoPath form libraries.

What's appealing to SharePoint users is that after they create a new list, it's immediately ready to use. SharePoint Foundation provides instant gratification by including page templates as part of the list template itself, making it possible to create each new list and document library with a set of pages that allow users to add, view, modify, and delete items and documents.

After a list has been created, SharePoint Foundation gives a user the flexibility to further customize it. SharePoint Foundation provides a List Settings page for each list and document library. Figure 1-11 shows a typical List Settings page. It provides a set of links to secondary pages that allow the user to modify properties of a list such as its title and description and to configure other important aspects of the list, including versioning, workflow, and security permissions. The List Settings page also provides links to add and manage the set of columns behind the list.

FIGURE 1-11 The List Settings page allows you to modify list properties and to add columns.

SharePoint Foundation provides many built-in list templates to track information about common business items such as tasks, contacts, and scheduled events. For business scenarios in which the list data that needs to be tracked doesn't conform to a built-in list template, SharePoint Foundation makes it easy for a user to create a custom list with a unique set of columns for these ad hoc situations.

SharePoint Foundation provides a list template named Custom List. When you create a new list from this template, it will initially contain a single column named Title. A user can add columns with just a few mouse clicks. Each added column is based on an underlying field type. SharePoint Foundation supplies a rich set of built-in field types for columns whose values are based on text, numbers, currency, dates, and yes/no values.

Using SharePoint Designer 2013

Microsoft SharePoint Designer 2013 is a specialized site customization tool. It is a rich desktop application that is often easier to use for customizing a site than a browser is. SharePoint Designer 2013 is a free product that can be downloaded from the following URL:

http://www.microsoft.com/en-us/download/details.aspx?id=35491

If you have used a previous version of SharePoint Designer, you might be surprised to find that the editor window for customizing pages no longer supplies a Design View. The Design View feature of the page editor has been discontinued in SharePoint Designer 2013. This means that you only have a Code View editor when working on site pages, master pages, and page layouts.

SharePoint Designer 2013 is primarily designed to assist users who have been granted Designer permissions or have been put in the role of site collection administrator or site administrator. The tool makes it quick and easy to examine the properties and structure of a site and to perform common site tasks such as adding security groups and configuring permissions. Many users will also prefer the experience of SharePoint Designer 2013 over the browser when it comes to creating new lists and adding columns.

SharePoint Designer 2013 also allows a user to perform site customizations that aren't possible through the browser. The ability to create and customize custom workflow logic by using a new set of workflow designers provides a great example. By using SharePoint Designer 2013, an experienced user can create and design complex workflows on targets such as sites, lists, and document libraries.

In Chapter 12, "SharePoint workflows," you will learn that SharePoint Designer 2013 supports the creation of custom workflows in both the new SharePoint 2013 format as well as the older SharePoint 2010 format. You will learn how custom workflows created with SharePoint Designer can be packaged and reused across site collections, web applications, and farms.

Understanding site customization vs. SharePoint development

In one sense, SharePoint Foundation lessens the need for professional software developers because it empowers users to create and customize their own sites. In minutes, a user can create a SharePoint site, add several lists and document libraries, and customize the site's appearance to meet the needs of a particular business situation. An identical solution that has all the rich functionality that Share-Point Foundation provides out of the box would typically take an ASP.NET development team weeks or months to complete.

In another sense, SharePoint Foundation provides professional developers with new and exciting development opportunities. As with any other framework, the out-of-the-box experience with Share-Point Foundation takes you only so far. At some point, you'll find yourself needing to create custom list types and write code for custom SharePoint components such as Web Parts and event handlers. What is attractive about SharePoint Foundation as a development platform is that it was designed from the ground up with developer extensibility in mind.

As you begin to design software for SharePoint 2013, it is critical that you differentiate between *customization* and *development*. SharePoint Foundation is very flexible for users because it was designed to support high levels of customization. As we've pointed out, you no longer need to be a developer to build a complex and highly functional website. Today, many sophisticated users are capable of customizing SharePoint sites for a large number of business scenarios. Site customization has its limitations, however. SharePoint Foundation records every site customization by modifying data within a content database, whether a new list is created or an existing list is customized with new columns and views. All types of site customization that can be performed by using SharePoint Designer 2013 are recorded this way.

The fact that all site customization is recorded as a modification to the content database is both a strength and a weakness for SharePoint Foundation. It is a strength because it provides so much flexibility to users and site administrators doing ad hoc customizations. It is a weakness from the perspective of a professional software developer because customization changes are hard to version and can also be hard or impossible to make repeatable across site collections and farms.

Think about a standard ASP.NET development project in which all the source files you're working with live within a single directory on your development machine. After you've finished the site's initial design and implementation, you can add all the site's source files to a source control management system such as Team Foundation Server.

By using a source control management system, you can formalize a disciplined approach to deploying and updating an ASP.NET site after it has gone into production. You can also elect to push changes out to a staging environment where your site's pages and code can be thoroughly tested before they are used in the production environment.

As a developer, you should ask yourself the following questions: How do I conduct source control management of customization changes? How do I make a customization change to a list definition or a page instance and then move this change from a development environment to a staging environment and finally to a production environment? How do I make a customization change within a site and then reuse it across a hundred different sites? Unfortunately, these questions have tough answers, and usually you'll find that a possible solution isn't worth the trouble.

Fortunately, as a developer, you can work at a level underneath the SharePoint Foundation customization infrastructure. To be more specific, you can create a SharePoint farm solution that allows you to work with the low-level source files to create underlying templates for items such as pages and lists. These low-level source files don't live inside the content database; instead, they live within the file system of the front-end web server.

Working at this level is complex and has a steep learning curve. Even so, this low-level approach lets you centralize source code management and have a more disciplined approach to code sign-off when moving functionality from development to staging to production. This approach also makes versioning and reuse of code far more manageable across multiple sites, web applications, and farms.

For the remainder of this book, we differentiate between customization and development according to these criteria. SharePoint site customizations are updates to a site accomplished by making changes to the content database, generally through the web browser or SharePoint Designer 2013. A site customization never requires the front-end web server to be touched.

SharePoint development, on the other hand, often involves working with farm solutions that include files that must be deployed to the file system of the front-end web server. In Chapter 3, "Server-side solution development," we introduce SharePoint solutions and discuss best practices for how to package a development effort for deployment within a SharePoint 2013 farm. In Chapter 4, "SharePoint apps," we introduce the alternative development approach of creating SharePoint apps. You will learn that the two approaches are quite different.

Windows PowerShell boot camp for SharePoint professionals

SharePoint 2013 is the second version of SharePoint technologies in which Microsoft supports administration through Windows PowerShell scripts. In earlier versions of SharePoint, farm administrators must use a command-line utility named stsadm.exe to run interactive commands from the console window and to write MS-DOS–style batch file scripts to automate common administrative tasks such as creating, backing up, or restoring a new site collection.

SharePoint Foundation still installs the stsadm.exe utility, but it is primarily included to support backward compatibility with pre-existing scripts migrated from earlier versions. Microsoft recommends using the Windows PowerShell support for writing, testing, and executing scripts that automate the same types of administrative tasks that you can accomplish by using stsadm.exe, plus a whole lot more.

The Windows PowerShell support for SharePoint Foundation adds a new required skill for every farm administrator and every developer moving to SharePoint 2010 or SharePoint 2013. You're now required to be able to read, write, and execute Windows PowerShell scripts to automate tasks such as creating a new web application or a new site collection.

Given the expected percentage of readers without any prior experience with Windows PowerShell, we decided to conclude Chapter 1 with a fast and furious Windows PowerShell boot camp. Our goal here is to get you up to speed on Windows PowerShell so that you can start reading, writing, executing, and debugging Windows PowerShell scripts. So fasten your seat belt.

Learning Windows PowerShell in 21 minutes

Working with Windows PowerShell is much easier than writing MS-DOS–style batch files. It's easier because the Windows PowerShell scripting language treats everything as an object. You can create and program against .NET objects as well as COM objects. Furthermore, Windows PowerShell has first-rate support for calling out to EXE-based utilities and passing parameters to execute specific commands.

There are two common ways in which you can use Windows PowerShell. First, you can execute commands interactively by using the Windows PowerShell console window. Second, you can write scripts to automate administration tasks. Then you can execute these scripts either on demand or through some type of scheduling mechanism.

Let's first get familiar with the Windows PowerShell console window. In Windows Server 2012, press the Windows logo key and then type **PowerShell**. In Windows Server 2008 R2, you can launch the Windows PowerShell console window from the following path from the Windows Start menu:

Start\All Programs\Accessories\Windows PowerShell\Windows PowerShell

When the Windows PowerShell console appears, type and execute the following three commands interactively:

1.   Type **cd** and then press Enter. This sets the current location to the root of drive C.

2. Type **cls** and then press Enter. This clears the console window.

3. Type **2 + 2** and then press Enter. This performs a mathematical calculation and displays the result.

If you followed these steps correctly and executed each of the three commands, your console window should look like the one in Figure 1-12.

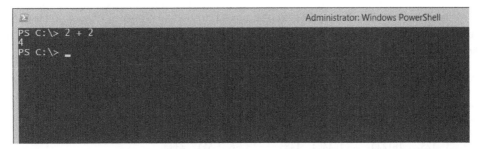

FIGURE 1-12 You can execute commands interactively from the Windows PowerShell console window.

Congratulations! You've just completed your first lesson. Now you know how to execute a command interactively from the Windows PowerShell console window. You simply type the command at the cursor in the Windows PowerShell console window and press Enter.

Windows PowerShell is based on reusable libraries containing functions known as *cmdlets* (pronounced "command lets"). Cmdlets have names that follow the convention of a common verb followed by a noun. For example, the built-in Windows PowerShell libraries provide a cmdlet named *Get-Process*, which returns a collection of objects representing the Windows processes running on the current machine:

```
PS C:\> Get-Process
```

Handles	NPM(K)	PM(K)	WS(K)	VM(M)	CPU(s)	Id	ProcessName
-------	------	-----	-----	-----	------	--	-----------
94	9	2780	13448	99	0.33	6592	conhost
83	9	1588	3652	42	0.03	8188	csrss
130	13	2020	5608	31	0.02	1312	dfssvc
1126	768	1172456	484268	1693	56.23	1176	DistributedCacheService
5261	6161	87624	86352	128	0.88	1636	dns
1197	76	27332	82044	398	11.73	3696	explorer
531	39	9136	34820	183	2.08	5348	iexplore
712	53	46252	56792	598	2.06	1504	Microsoft.ActiveDirectory.WebServices
2045	743	517044	492284	-631	19.44	6748	noderunner
1954	757	557248	503572	-649	17.98	6796	noderunner
461	238	343372	383888	1201	152.95	4828	OWSTIMER
594	39	113076	119668	653	3.03	6676	powershell
867	473	1674072	94884	552	284.56	1852	sqlservr
82	8	1388	5296	38	0.02	2016	sqlwriter
1536	657	378000	210600	1767	8.16	3852	w3wp
1715	794	916880	758228	-1882	29.83	5244	w3wp
1672	657	226404	192840	1772	7.33	5360	w3wp
335	32	32612	36616	547	17.83	2816	WSSADMIN

Pipelining is an important concept to understand when you are executing cmdlets. The basic idea is that every cmdlet returns an object or a collection of objects. Pipelining allows you to take the output results of one cmdlet and pass it as an input parameter to a second cmdlet. The second cmdlet can execute and then pass its output results to a third cmdlet, and so on. You create a pipeline by typing a sequence of cmdlets separated by the | (pipe) character:

```
cmdlet1 | cmdlet2 | cmdlet3
```

Let's examine a common scenario in which you need to create a pipeline of two cmdlets to filter a collection of objects. First you call *Get-Process* to return a collection of objects, and then you use pipelining to pass this collection of objects to the *Where-Object* cmdlet:

```
PS C:\> Get-Process | Where-Object {$_.ProcessName -like "w*"}

Handles  NPM(K)    PM(K)      WS(K) VM(M)   CPU(s)     Id ProcessName
-------  ------    -----      ----- -----   ------     -- -----------
    977     135   173372     180504  1511     4.94   2176 w3wp
    773     123   161220     164464  1485     3.36   5112 w3wp
    270      31    25052      17860   496     0.14   2568 WSSADMIN
```

The *Where-Object* cmdlet takes a predicate expression enclosed in curly braces as a parameter. Inside these curly braces, you can use *$_* to refer to an object as it's being filtered. The predicate expression in this example is *{$_.ProcessName -like "w*"}*. The filter returns all processes whose process name starts with "w".

Windows PowerShell cmdlets such as *Where-Object* use standard Windows PowerShell comparison operators. You should memorize these operators because you'll be using them regularly as you work with Windows PowerShell. Table 1-3 lists some commonly used Windows PowerShell comparison operators.

TABLE 1-3 Commonly used Windows PowerShell comparison operators

Operator	Purpose
-lt	Less than
-le	Less than or equal to
-gt	Greater than
-ge	Greater than or equal to
-eq	Equal to
-ne	Not equal to
-like	Like, using wildcard matches
-notlike	Not like, using wildcard matches

You should understand that Windows PowerShell comparison operators that work with strings are case insensitive by default. However, these operators can be made case sensitive by adding a *c* immediately after the hyphen. For example, *-ceq* represents the case-sensitive *equal-to* operator.

Writing Windows PowerShell scripts

Now that you've seen how to execute cmdlets from the Windows PowerShell console window, it's time to move on to Windows PowerShell scripting. Windows PowerShell scripts are text files that have an extension of .ps1. You can create and edit a Windows PowerShell script by using any text editor, including Notepad.

Before you can begin writing and testing Windows PowerShell scripts, you might be required to adjust the Windows PowerShell script execution policy on your developer workstation. The reason for this step is that Windows PowerShell is configured out of the box to prohibit or to prompt the user during script execution.

You should take note that the installation of SharePoint 2013 actually changes the Windows PowerShell execution policy of the local machine. By default, the Windows PowerShell execution policy is set to restricted, which means that scripts have to be digitally signed before they can be run. However, the installation of SharePoint 2013 lowers the execution policy from restricted to unrestricted, which allows scripts to run even when they are not digitally signed.

On a developer workstation, it's common to disable the default execution constraints so that you can write and test scripts without security errors. You make this adjustment by calling the standard Windows PowerShell cmdlet named *Set-ExecutionPolicy* from the Windows PowerShell console to set the current machine's execution policy to *"bypass"*:

```
Set-ExecutionPolicy "bypass"
```

After you've correctly adjusted the Windows PowerShell execution policy, you can write your first script. Open Notepad and type in the following one-line script:

```
Write-Host "Hello World"
```

Now you need to save the file for the script with a .ps1 extension. First, create a new directory named Scripts on your local drive C. Next, save your new Windows PowerShell script file as c:\Scripts\Script1.ps1. Now that you've saved the Windows PowerShell script file with a .ps1 extension, you can execute the script to test your work.

Let's first execute the script through the Windows PowerShell console window. In the console window, move to the new directory by executing *Set-Location c:\Scripts*. Now you can execute the script by typing **.\Script1.ps1** and pressing Enter. When you do this, the message *Hello World* should appear in the Windows PowerShell console window.

Now let's create a Windows batch file so that you can execute the script without having to use the Windows PowerShell console window. Just create a new text file named RunIt.bat in the same directory as Script1.ps1, and call powershell.exe and pass the -*Command* parameter with the following syntax to execute the script:

```
powershell.exe -Command "& {.\Script1.ps1}"
pause
```

Notice that this example batch file also added a *pause* operation at the end. This can be handy because it keeps the Windows PowerShell console window open so that you can view the output of your Windows PowerShell script.

Finally, you should learn how to directly execute a Windows PowerShell script without any assistance from an MS-DOS batch file. If you right-click a Windows PowerShell script such as Script1.ps1 in Windows Explorer, you'll find a Run With PowerShell menu command. If you execute this command, the Windows operating system takes care of executing the Windows PowerShell script for you.

Executing Windows PowerShell scripts by using the Run With PowerShell command is quick and easy, but it doesn't leave the Windows PowerShell console window open when it's done. If you like using this technique but you still want to display the Windows PowerShell console window afterward, you can simply add the *Read-Host* cmdlet at the bottom of your script, which results in the Windows PowerShell console window remaining open until you press the Enter key:

```
Write-Host "Hello World"
Read-Host
```

The Windows PowerShell Integrated Scripting Environment (ISE)

Although you can use any text editor to write Windows PowerShell scripts, you'll probably prefer to use a powerful new utility, the *Windows PowerShell Integrated Scripting Environment (ISE)*, which is included with the Windows Server operating system.

The Windows PowerShell ISE will be immediately familiar to anyone with experience in Visual Studio. You can type a script in the top window and then press the F5 key to execute the script in debug mode. The Windows PowerShell ISE allows you to debug by setting breakpoints and to single-step through your code. After you've launched the Windows PowerShell ISE, type the following script into the top window and then press F5:

```
$sum1 = 2 + 2
$sum2 = 3 + 4
$sum3 = $sum1 + $sum2
Write-Host $sum3
```

This example shows how to create a new variable in a Windows PowerShell script. You simply create a new variable name, which begins with the $ character. You don't need to define variables before you use them, as you do in C#. Instead, you just create a variable when you begin using it.

Now, let's write a Windows PowerShell control-of-flow construct. In this case, we create a new string array by using the proper Windows PowerShell syntax, and then write a *foreach* loop to enumerate each string:

```
$band = "Paul", "John", "George", "Ringo"

foreach($member in $band) {
  Write-Host $member
}
```

One aspect of Windows PowerShell that will instantly appeal to .NET developers is that you can create and program against any .NET object. For example, imagine you want to create an object from the *DateTime* class of the .NET Framework. You do this by executing the *New-Object* cmdlet and passing the class name and initialization values as parameters:

```
$date = New-Object -TypeName System.DateTime -ArgumentList @(1882,7,4,0,0,0)
$message = "Wingtip Toys, Inc. was founded on " + $date.ToLongDateString()
Write-Host $message
```

The preceding script produces the following output:

```
Wingtip Toys, Inc. was founded on Tuesday, July 04, 1882
```

In addition to creating new .NET objects, Windows PowerShell allows you to call the static methods and static properties of classes in the .NET Framework. You do this by typing the namespace-qualified class name in square brackets, like this: *[System.DateTime]*. After you type the class name, you add the :: operator (two colons) and then the call to a static member:

```
$today = [System.DateTime]::Today
Write-Host $today.ToLongDateString()
Write-Host $today.ToString("MM/dd/yy")
Write-Host $today.AddDays(100).ToString("MMMM d")
```

If you're feeling nostalgic, you can even use Windows PowerShell to create and program against COM objects. For example, let's say you want to write a Windows PowerShell script that launches Internet Explorer and navigates to a specific URL. The Windows operating system provides a built-in COM interface that allows you to launch and control Internet Explorer:

```
$ie = New-Object -ComObject "InternetExplorer.Application"
$ie.Navigate("http://intranet.wingtiptoys.com")
$ie.Visible = $true
```

Windows PowerShell snap-ins for SharePoint

Windows PowerShell installs a set of core libraries containing cmdlets such as *Write-Host, Get-Process,* and *Where-Object*. Environments such as SharePoint Foundation add their own library of custom cmdlets by installing and registering a special type of an assembly DLL known as a *Windows PowerShell snap-in*. When you install SharePoint 2013, a Windows PowerShell snap-in named *Microsoft.SharePoint.PowerShell* is installed. However, this snap-in doesn't automatically load into every Windows PowerShell session. Instead, you have to ensure that the *Microsoft.SharePoint. PowerShell* snap-in is loaded before you begin to call the cmdlets specific to SharePoint.

SharePoint Foundation provides a specialized version of the Windows PowerShell console known as the *SharePoint 2013 Management Shell*. The main difference between the standard Windows PowerShell console window and the SharePoint 2013 Management Shell console has to do with which Windows PowerShell providers get loaded automatically. More specifically, the SharePoint 2013 Management Shell automatically loads the *Microsoft.SharePoint.PowerShell* snap-in, whereas the standard Windows PowerShell console does not. In general, you can't always rely on the SharePoint snap-in *Microsoft.SharePoint.PowerShell* being loaded automatically, so you need to learn how to load it explicitly within a Windows PowerShell script.

Let's say you've just launched the standard Windows PowerShell console window and you attempt to execute one of the cmdlets built into SharePoint Foundation, such as *Get-SPWebApplication*. The call to this cmdlet will fail unless you've already loaded the *Microsoft.SharePoint.PowerShell* Windows PowerShell snap-in. Before calling the *Get-SPWebApplication* cmdlet, you need to load the SharePoint Management Windows PowerShell snap-ins for SharePoint by using the *Add-PSSnapin* cmdlet:

```
Add-PSSnapin Microsoft.SharePoint.PowerShell
Get-SPWebApplication
```

Executing these two cmdlets in sequence displays the current collection of web applications for the current farm, excluding the web application for SharePoint 2010 Central Administration:

```
DisplayName                 Url
-----------                 ---
Wingtip Intranet            http://intranet.wingtiptoys.com/
Wingtip Extranet            http://extranet.wingtiptoys.com/
Wingtip Public Web site     http://www.wingtiptoys.com/
```

Now let's write a Windows PowerShell script to create a new web application. You can do this by calling the *New-SPWebApplication* cmdlet. The call requires quite a few parameters. Note that the following script creates a "classic mode" web application, which is no longer supported through the Central Administration interface in SharePoint 2013:

```
Add-PSSnapin Microsoft.SharePoint.PowerShell -ErrorAction "SilentlyContinue"

$name = "Wingtip Intranet Web App"
$port = 80
$hostHeader = "intranet.wingtiptoys.com"
$url = "http://intranet.wingtiptoys.com"
$appPoolName = "SharePoint Default Appl Pool"
$appPoolAccount = Get-SPManagedAccount "WINGTIP\SP_Content"

New-SPWebApplication -Name $name -Port $port -HostHeader $hostHeader -URL $url '
                     -ApplicationPool $appPoolName '
                     -ApplicationPoolAccount $appPoolAccount
```

Notice that the call to the *New-SPWebApplication* cmdlet in the preceding script breaks across multiple lines for clarity. When you write scripts, however, you must place the entire call to a cmdlet and all its parameters on a single line. That is, of course, unless you know the special trick of using the grave accent (`) to add line breaks within a call to a cmdlet inside a Windows PowerShell script, as shown in the preceding example.

As you can imagine, writing and executing scripts like this can save you quite a bit of time in a production farm because the need to perform the same tasks manually through SharePoint 2013 Central Administration is eliminated. Scripts like this also provide a great way to create consistency in how you create web applications across farms.

We'll finish with one more example. Let's write a script to create a new site collection in the web application created earlier, which has a team site as its top-level site. You can accomplish this by calling the *New-SPSite* cmdlet:

```
Add-PSSnapin Microsoft.SharePoint.PowerShell

$title= "Wingtip Intranet"
$url = "http://intranet.wingtiptoys.com"
$owner = "WINGTIP\Administrator"
$template = "STS#0"

New-SPSite -URL $url -Name $title -OwnerAlias $owner -Template $template
```

When you create a new site collection by using the *New-SPSite* cmdlet, you must specify the URL and title and provide a user account to be configured as the site collection administrator. You can also specify a template by using the *Template* parameter, which is applied on the top-level site. In this example, a template of *STS#0* has been applied to create the top-level site as a standard team site.

Now you've written a script to create a new site collection. The first time you run it, it works great. But what happens when you run it a second time? The second attempt to call the *New-SPSite* cmdlet fails because a site collection already exists at the target URL.

During development, there's a common scenario in which you must continually delete and re-create a site to effectively test and debug your code. Before deleting a site collection, your script should check to determine whether a target site collection already exists at the target URL by using the *Get-SPSite* cmdlet. If the site collection already exists, you can delete it with the *Remove-SPSite* cmdlet:

```
Add-PSSnapin Microsoft.SharePoint.PowerShell

$title= "Wingtip Intranet"
$url = "http://intranet.wingtiptoys.com"
$owner = "WINGTIP\Administrator"
$template = "STS#1"

# delete target site collection if it exists
$targetSite = Get-SPSite | Where-Object {$_.Url -eq $url}
if ($targetSite -ne $null) {
  Remove-SPSite -Identity targetSite -Confirm:$false
}

# create new site collection
New-SPSite -URL $url -Name $title -OwnerAlias $owner -Template $template
```

Remember that cmdlets such as *New-SPSite* return objects that you can program against. For example, imagine you want to update the title of the top-level site after the site collection has been created. A site collection object exposes a *RootWeb* property that allows you to access the top-level site. The site object provides a *Title* property that you can modify with a new title. You must call the site object's *Update* method to write your changes back to the content database:

```
Add-PSSnapin Microsoft.SharePoint.PowerShell

$title= "Wingtip Dev Site"
$url = "http://intranet.wingtiptoys.com"
$owner = "WINGTIP\Administrator"
$template = "STS#0"

# delete target site collection if it exists
$targetSite = Get-SPSite | Where-Object {$_.Url -eq $url}
if ($targetSite -ne $null) {
  Remove-SPSite -Identity targetSite -Confirm:$false
}

$sc = New-SPSite -URL $url -Name $title -OwnerAlias $owner -Template $template
$site = $sc.RootWeb
$site.Title = "My New Site Title"
$site.Update
```

You've just seen an example of writing code against the server-side object model of SharePoint Foundation. Unfortunately, the Windows PowerShell ISE isn't able to provide IntelliSense in the same manner that Visual Studio does. However, the Windows PowerShell ISE still has valuable editing and debugging features that are easy to learn and use. You should become familiar with this tool because it provides a quick way to script out changes to the local farm in your development workstation or in a production environment.

Summary

SharePoint 2013 mainly consists of two products: SharePoint Foundation and SharePoint Server 2013. Having a solid understanding of SharePoint Foundation is essential even for developers who are only building software for SharePoint Server 2013. That's because SharePoint Foundation provides the underlying infrastructure on which SharePoint Server 2013 is built.

SharePoint Foundation represents different things to different people. To users, SharePoint Foundation provides the infrastructure for web-based business solutions that scale from simple team-collaboration sites to enterprise-level applications. To site collection administrators, SharePoint Foundation provides the capability to customize sites by adding lists and document libraries and by customizing many aspects of a site's appearance through the browser or by using a customization tool such as SharePoint Designer 2013.

To a company's IT staff, SharePoint Foundation provides a scalable and cost-effective solution for provisioning and managing a large number of sites in a web farm environment. It also provides a reliable mechanism to roll out applications and to version these applications over time.

To a developer, SharePoint Foundation represents a rich development platform that adds value on top of the underlying ASP.NET platform. Developers build software solutions targeting SharePoint Foundation by using features and components such as Web Parts, event handlers, and workflows. Now that you've studied the SharePoint developer roadmap and made it through our Windows PowerShell boot camp, you're ready to dive into the fundamentals of SharePoint 2013 development.

## CHAPTER 2

SharePoint development practices and techniques

Before you can start building a custom Microsoft SharePoint solution you will have to make sure you set up your development environment correctly. Because the hardware requirements for SharePoint 2013 are again a lot more demanding than they were for SharePoint 2010, setting up a new development environment might well mean that you have to acquire new hardware. There might be quite a bit of time between the moment that you order the hardware, whether from an external vendor or from an internal department, and when you can actually start using the hardware. This means that it's important to start planning your SharePoint customizations early, so that waiting on the hardware will not interfere with your project planning.

When you have gotten the hardware, you will have to install your development environment. It is important to do this meticulously, to follow best practices and to make sure you document the entire configuration. Documentation is important if you have to create a second environment, or if you have to recreate your development environment.

When your SharePoint environment has been set up properly, you will need proper specifications so that you can start designing your solution. You will have to decide what type of solution will best suit your skills, the environment into which the solution will have to be deployed, and the functionality that you have to create. SharePoint 2013 introduces a new development approach, which means that you can now not only create farm solutions and sandboxes solution, but you can also create SharePoint apps. SharePoint 2013 also introduces a third application programming interface (API) by making Representational State Transfer (REST) APIs available that allow you to use simple HTTP requests and responses to perform CRUD (create, read, update, delete) operations on SharePoint data.

All these additions give you more options, but they also require you to make more choices, and it is important to make deliberate and well-informed choices to make sure that you end up with the best solution that you could possibly build for your specific situation and scenario. This chapter talks you through a lot of the choices and can help you make the right decisions.

Setting up a developer environment

Whenever you are looking at building a custom solution for any platform, one of the things you will have to determine is what environment you will use to build your custom solution. This is no different when you want to create a custom solution for SharePoint. Determining the best way to set up your development environment has always been difficult for SharePoint, and SharePoint 2013 adds even more complexity to it, with extended hardware requirements and two new types of servers.

Let's start by looking at the different server roles that you can choose from.

- Domain controller

- Database server

- SharePoint server

  - Web server

  - Application server

- Office Web Apps server

- Windows Azure workflow server

Although it is possible to build a development environment by using a standalone server installation of SharePoint on a single server without a domain controller or separate computer that is running Microsoft SQL Server, for practical reasons you will at least need a domain controller, a database server, and a SharePoint server. For certain types of SharePoint apps you might not need a SharePoint development environment, because these apps can be hosted on a generic web server that doesn't have SharePoint installed on it. However, you should test what your app looks like in a SharePoint environment before you add the app to the production environment, so you should always use some sort of test or development environment.

If your development environment is installed in an existing domain, you don't have to build your own domain controller; you can simply use an existing one. If you are creating your own domain, you will have to create a domain controller as well. You can create a single server and use that as the domain controller, the database server, and the SharePoint server. Be aware, though, that some things don't work on a domain controller and some things have to be configured differently. It is important to keep this in mind while developing and testing custom solutions on your development server.

In SharePoint 2010, Microsoft Office Web Apps came in a separate installation that had to be installed on at least one of the SharePoint servers in the farm. After installation, they could be configured as service applications. In SharePoint 2013, this is no longer the case. Office Web Apps is now its own product. Office Web Apps has to be installed in its own separate farm, and it cannot be installed on a server that also has SharePoint installed on it, because Office Web Apps will completely take over the Internet Information Services (IIS) on the server. You can install Office Web Apps on one or more servers and connect the Office Web Apps farm to the SharePoint farm. Having Office Web Apps installed in its own farm on one or more servers means that it is now more scalable. The Office Web

Apps farm can be connected to one or more SharePoint farms. This means that one Office Web Apps farm can support the SharePoint servers of several developers.

With SharePoint 2010, you automatically got the SharePoint 2010 workflow host, which was based on Windows Workflow Foundation 3. Windows Workflow Foundation was a native part of SharePoint, but the way in which it was implemented meant that customers who were serious about using workflow in SharePoint almost always ran into issues with scalability. SharePoint 2013 uses a new workflow service, which is built on the Windows Workflow Foundation components of the Microsoft .NET Framework 4.5. The new workflow service is called Workflow Manager and, like Office Web Apps, is a separate installation that should be installed on separate servers. After you have created a Workflow Manager farm consisting of one or more servers, you can connect this farm to your SharePoint 2013 farm. As with Office Web Apps, creating a separate workflow farm means that your environment will be a lot easier to scale out and a lot more suitable for use in a serious workflow solution or a large enterprise. Your old SharePoint 2010 workflows will still work, because SharePoint 2013 automatically installs the SharePoint 2010 workflow engine.

To summarize, if you want to have all SharePoint 2013 functionality available to you in your development environment, you will need at least three servers:

- A domain controller/database server/SharePoint server

- An Office Web Apps server

- A Workflow Manager server

You can, of course, have many more: you could split out your domain controller, database server, and SharePoint server; you could have separate SharePoint web and application servers; and you can have as many Office Web Apps and Workflow Manager servers as you want. How many servers you use will mostly depend on the size of the solution that you are building, the type of functionality that you need, and—let's face it—your budget.

Deciding between virtual and physical

An important decision that you have to make when you start to think about your development environment is whether you will be using virtual or physical servers. You could choose to install a supported server operating system (we'll get into more detail on that soon) directly on your computer, either by connecting to an existing domain or turning the computer into a domain controller and installing SQL Server and SharePoint on it. You can no longer install SharePoint on a client operating system such as Windows 7 or Windows 8 as you could with SharePoint 2010. However, unlike Windows 7, Windows 8 does support Hyper-V, which means that you can create your virtual machines in Hyper-V on your Windows 8 computer. The Windows 8 version of Hyper-V is officially called Client Hyper-V.

As long as you only work on a single project, and you only need a single server (so you don't need Workflow Manager or Office Web Apps), you can run your development environment directly on your computer. However, creating your development environment by using virtual servers is a far more flexible solution. You can either host the virtual servers on your own computer or on a server somewhere in the network, or even in the cloud. With today's hardware requirements (especially the memory) and considering the fact that you might need more than one server, running your development environment on your computer won't be a feasible solution for most people, so in a lot of cases development servers are hosted in a network somewhere. If you are using your development environment on a daily basis, it is recommended that you make sure that your servers are hosted somewhere relatively close to you to minimize latency issues and frustrations.

Running the development environment on a virtual server has a few advantages:

- Using virtual servers as a development environment means that you can use a different virtual server for each project you're working on. When a developer works on more than one project, it is better not to have the configuration and custom solutions from these projects in a single environment. Settings or solutions from one project might influence the behavior of the solutions from the second project, which means that you have no way of knowing what is causing problems and you can't determine how the solution will behave in the production environment.

- Another advantage of working with virtual servers is the fact that it's easy to create snapshots and to go back to them. By using snapshots, the developer can run tests and, depending on the outcome of a test, decide to go back to a snapshot of a previous situation. He can then make some changes to the solution and run the same tests again.

  Also, when project work goes on for a long time, environments sometimes get messy from testing different solutions and settings, and going back to a snapshot is a very easy way to clean that up. Using snapshots also means that you can go back to a previous state if a solution that you deployed or a script that you ran messed up your environment.

- Using virtual servers to create development environments also makes it easier to set up a new development environment when a new developer is added to the project. Later on in this chapter we will talk in more detail about having a team of developers work on a single project.

- In most cases, using virtual servers is also a lot cheaper than using physical servers. If you have a large physical server, you can run several virtual servers on it. This means you can save on hardware costs. Also, if you don't need all your servers at the same time, they can share the resources, and if you need a new server, you can very quickly set it up, instead of having to order hardware and wait till it arrives.

Understanding hardware and software requirements

As with every SharePoint version, SharePoint 2013 has its own hardware requirements. Table 2-1 shows an overview of the hardware requirements for SharePoint 2013. As you can see, the amount of memory needed to run a SharePoint Server development environment has again increased significantly. There are a couple of things to note:

- *Single server* means that both SharePoint and its databases are running on the same server.

- A single server development installation of SharePoint Server 2013 is listed as requiring 24 gigabytes (GB) of RAM. However, the amount of RAM it really needs heavily depends on what services you are running in the environment. For instance, if you are actively using search, you probably need 24 GB, or at least something close to that. However, if you are only using web applications and some of the lighter service applications, you can get away with having a lot less memory.

■ The storage on the system drive has to be at least 80 GB. It is very important to note that this does not include the storage that is needed to store the databases that contain the content from your SharePoint environment, and it doesn't include the storage that is needed to store, for instance, the SharePoint logs. Make sure that you have enough storage on your system; storage is cheap, and it's very annoying to have to go into your development server every day to try and free up some storage so that at least your server will keep running.

TABLE 2-1 Hardware requirements for SharePoint 2013

Type of installation	RAM	Processor	Storage on system drive
Single server development installation of SharePoint Foundation 2013	8 GB	64-bit, 4 cores	80 GB
Single server development installation of SharePoint Server 2013	24 GB	64-bit, 4 cores	80 GB
SharePoint server in a SharePoint Server 2013 development environment	12 GB	64-bit, 4 cores	80 GB
Database server in a SharePoint 2013 development environment	8 GB	64-bit, 4 cores	80 GB

SharePoint 2013 also comes with its own software requirements. For a SharePoint 2013 server, the following software is required:

■ The 64-bit edition of Windows Server 2008 R2 Service Pack 1 (SP1) Standard, Enterprise, or Datacenter or the 64-bit edition of Windows Server 2012 Standard or Datacenter

■ Hotfix: The SharePoint parsing process crashes in Windows Server 2008 R2 (KB 2554876)

■ Hotfix: FIX: IIS 7.5 configurations are not updated when you use the ServerManager class to commit configuration changes (KB 2708075)

■ Hotfix: WCF: process may crash with "System.Net.Sockets.SocketException: An invalid argument was supplied" when under high load (KB 2726478)

■ The prerequisites installed by the Microsoft SharePoint Products Preparation Tool

■ Hotfix: ASP.NET (SharePoint) race condition in .NET 4.5 RTM:

  • Windows Server 2008 R2 SP1 (KB 2759112)

  • Windows Server 2012 (KB 2765317)

For a database server in a SharePoint 2013 farm, the following software is required:

- The 64-bit edition of Microsoft SQL Server 2012, or the 64-bit edition of SQL Server 2008 R2 Service Pack 1

- The 64-bit edition of Windows Server 2008 R2 Service Pack 1 (SP1) Standard, Enterprise, or Datacenter or the 64-bit edition of Windows Server 2012 Standard or Datacenter

- Hotfix: The SharePoint parsing process crashes in Windows Server 2008 R2 (KB 2554876)

- Hotfix: FIX: IIS 7.5 configurations are not updated when you use the ServerManager class to commit configuration changes (KB 2708075)

- Hotfix: ASP.NET (SharePoint) race condition in .NET 4.5 RTM:

  - Windows Server 2008 R2 SP1 (KB 2759112)

  - Windows Server 2012 (KB 2765317)

- .NET Framework version 4.5

When setting up your development environment, you should always aim to make sure that it's as much like the production environment as possible.

Delivering high-quality solutions

To deliver high-quality solutions it is best for the development environment to be as much like the production environment as possible. Theoretically this is true for all aspects of the environment: hardware, software, configuration, and data. In most cases, however, the hardware of a development environment cannot be the same as the hardware of a production environment. This is fine, as long as you are aware of the differences and what the impact of them might be on your test results.

So that accurate tests can be performed in a development environment, the software should be the same as the software in the production environment. You should use the same version of Windows Server and SharePoint and a similar version of SQL Server. If the production environment has SharePoint Server installed, make sure the development environment doesn't have SharePoint Foundation installed. If the production server has a Windows service pack installed on it, make sure you install the same service pack in the development environment. It also works the other way around; if the service pack will not be installed in the production environment, do no install it in the development environment either. If one of the environments gets a SharePoint service pack or cumulative update installed on it, make sure all environments get that same service pack or cumulative update installed on them.

The way in which you configure your development server should also be as much like the production environment as possible. The best thing is to try and get access to the build guide for the production environment and use that to set up your development environment.

Examples of settings that are important when configuring your development environment are:

- Using the default SQL instance or different instances

- The authentication type:

    - NT LAN Manager (NTLM)

    - Kerberos

    - Windows claims

    - Security Assertion Markup Language (SAML) claims

- Using host headers on your web application, or Host Header Site Collections

- HTTP or HTTPS

- The number of web applications

- The way in which the farm, application pool, and services accounts are configured and the level of permissions they have. Make sure you have the same number of managed accounts in your development environment as in the production environment.

In order to get accurate test results, it is also very helpful to have representative sample data and test users. The data will help you perform the same type of actions that a user would. If you are able to load enough sample data into your development environment, it will also help you test the scalability of your solution, at least to a certain extent. Most custom solutions perform very well with only a couple of documents, users, or sites, but when there are tens of thousands it might be a completely different story. Even if you can't test on the scale of your production environment, you should always keep in mind what numbers your solution will have to cope with after it's in production. It is always a good idea to at least make sure that you test whether your application will keep working past the list view threshold. The *list view threshold* is a web application setting that can be adjusted in Central Administration that tells SharePoint how many items can be requested from the database in a single query. The default list view threshold is 5,000.

As a developer, you will usually log in with an account that has administrative permissions. It's the only way in which you can properly develop custom full trust solutions. Do make sure that you are not logged on as the SharePoint farm account. When you are testing your solution, it is very important to not only test it using your administrative account, but also with accounts that have Read, Contribute, and Site Owner permissions. A lot of custom SharePoint solutions will work fine when run by an administrator, but need more work when a reader or contributor of a site should be able to work with them as well. For instance, the List view threshold (the throttling feature that specifies the maximum number of list or library items that a database operation, such as a query, can process at the same time) will not be applied if you are logging onto your SharePoint environment as a local administrator, which means that you cannot test the behavior of large lists properly.

Automating SharePoint administration by using Windows PowerShell scripts

Windows PowerShell scripts can be used to automate SharePoint installation and management. When you are using Windows PowerShell scripts to install SharePoint, it is easy to repeat the installation in exactly the same way. This is very useful when you have to create multiple development environments or multiple servers in a production environment, or when a farm has to be rebuilt after a system failure. Be aware that not all steps of the installation can be scripted by using Windows PowerShell, so you will still have to make sure that all steps are documented as well.

Using Windows PowerShell to manage SharePoint is very useful for repeatable tasks. When you use a saved script every time, the chances of human errors causing serious problems during mainte-nance decrease. Windows PowerShell can also be used to fully automate maintenance steps. It would, for example, be possible to create a Windows PowerShell script that creates a new site collection. The next step would be to add a couple of parameters and then automatically start the script. You could, for instance, start the script whenever a new project or customer is added to a Customer Relationship Management (CRM) system.

Though it is often convenient to use Windows PowerShell to install or configure SharePoint, in some cases you don't have a choice because some functionality doesn't show up in the user interface and can only be configured by using Windows PowerShell. Examples of this are the multitenancy features. The multitenancy features are a set of features that allow SharePoint to work as a hosting platform. They allow for operational service management of SharePoint for one or more divisions, organizations, or companies. Using the multitenancy features allows SharePoint to separate data, features, administration, customizations, and operations. In order to set up multitenancy in an envi-ronment, you have to set up site subscriptions, partitioned service applications, tenant administration sites, and (optionally) host header site collections and feature packs. All these features can only be configured by using Windows PowerShell.

If you need to install development environments on a regular basis—for instance, because you are working on different projects, or because you are working on a long-running project and developers are coming and going—it is worthwhile to create a Windows PowerShell script to install a develop-ment environment. Even if you would just use Windows PowerShell to configure SharePoint, this will save you a lot of time. It will also make sure that your development environments are always config-ured in exactly the same way. In addition to the fact that doing a scripted installation is often faster, this approach also allows you to do work on something else while the script is running.

There are two different tools in which you can write and run Windows PowerShell scripts: the Windows PowerShell console window or the Windows PowerShell Integrated Scripting Environment (ISE). To make the Windows PowerShell ISE available on your server, you need to install the Windows PowerShell Integrated Scripting Environment (ISE) Windows feature. You can do this by opening up the Server Manager, clicking Add Features, and selecting the ISE feature.

If you are using the console environment, you can either use the general console environment or the SharePoint 2013 Management Shell. You can access the general console environment by selecting it from the Windows Start menu. If it's not on the first page, you can get to it from the Windows Start menu by simply starting to type **PowerShell**. This will give you the option to select one of the available Windows PowerShell tools and consoles.

Don't pick the 32-bit version (x86); SharePoint is a 64-bit product. You can also go to the Windows Start menu to select the SharePoint 2013 Management Shell. You can find this in the same way as the general console; go to the Start menu, start typing **PowerShell**, and select the SharePoint 2013 Management Console.

These are effectively the same environment, except for the fact that in the SharePoint Management Shell the Microsoft.SharePoint.PowerShell snap-in has already been loaded. If you are using the standard console, you will have to load the snap-in yourself, by using the following command:

```
Add-PSSnapin Microsoft.SharePoint.PowerShell -ErrorAction "SilentlyContinue"
```

You add the *-ErrorAction "SilentlyContinue"* mainly because the console will throw an error if the snap-in has already been loaded. You can ignore this, so it will look nicer if you hide the error. You can also play it safe and check to see whether the snap-in is already loaded before attempting to load it, by using the following:

```
$snap = Get-PSSnapin | Where-Object {$_.Name -eq 'Microsoft.SharePoint.PowerShell'}
if ($snap -eq $null) {
  Add-PSSnapin Microsoft.SharePoint.PowerShell
}
```

If you are creating a larger script, it is probably easier to open up the Windows PowerShell ISE, because this provides a better editing environment. You will have to load the Microsoft.SharePoint.PowerShell snap-in into the ISE as well. You can do this by using exactly the same script used for the console. If you find yourself using the ISE a lot, you can also add the snap-in automatically when the ISE starts, by adding it to the Windows PowerShell profile. The profile is a Windows PowerShell script file that runs every time you start Windows PowerShell. It has a .ps1 extension like any normal Windows PowerShell file, and you can put any valid Windows PowerShell cmdlet in it. The only way in which the profile file differs from a normal script file is in its name and location.

If you want to use the profile, you will first have to figure out whether a profile already exists on the server. You can do this by using the *Test-Path* cmdlet:

```
Test-Path $profile
```

If the profile already exists, the *Test-Path* cmdlet will return *True*; if it doesn't exist, it will return *False*. You can also just run the *$profile* cmdlet and use Windows Explorer to browse to the path that it returns. If the file isn't there, the profile doesn't exist:

```
$profile
```

You can use the *New-Item* cmdlet to create a profile if one doesn't already exist. *-path $profile* passes in the full path, and *-type file* tells the cmdlet that you are trying to create a file:

```
New-Item -path $profile -type file
```

When you open the profile, you will notice that it is completely empty. You can add to it any script that you want to always be executed before you start working on your scripts. This could, for instance, be a command telling Windows PowerShell to always go to a default location:

```
Set-Location C:\scripts
```

Or you can add the Microsoft.SharePoint.PowerShell snap-in:

```
Add-PSSnapin Microsoft.SharePoint.PowerShell -ErrorAction "SilentlyContinue"
```

Using Windows PowerShell to deploy a custom solution

As a developer, you may also find Windows PowerShell very useful for creating a deployment script that can be used to install your custom solution in a SharePoint environment. This will allow you to distribute your custom solution across test, user acceptance, and production environments a lot more easily. It will mean that administrators don't have to perform a lot of manual steps and that you as a developer don't have to describe all these steps in a deployment manual.

When using Windows PowerShell to write a deployment script, you will have to take into account that a previous version of your solution might already be installed in the environment that you are deploying to. This means that you first have to retract and remove the solution before you can install and deploy the solution. Retracting a solution forces SharePoint to delete most of the files it copied during deployment as well as to uninstall features and delete assemblies from the global assembly cache. After you've retracted a solution, you can then remove it, which deletes the solution package file from the configuration database.

One thing to be aware of is that SharePoint doesn't clean up after itself very well when you retract a solution. For instance, SharePoint doesn't explicitly deactivate features before it retracts the solution that they are deployed in. Because of this, it is a best practice to make sure that you deactivate all features in a solution before retracting the solution. Another thing to keep in mind is that SharePoint doesn't always delete all files that were deployed using a solution when the solution is retracted. When it doesn't, this often is for a good reason (for instance, because it could cause errors if the files were to be deleted), but it is something to keep in mind because it can cause quite a bit of cluttering, especially in a development or test environment where solutions are installed and retracted all the time.

You can retract a solution package by using the *Uninstall-SPSolution* cmdlet. When calling *Uninstall-SPSolution*, you should pass the *-Identity* parameter and the *-Local* parameter in the same manner as when calling *Install-SPSolution*. You should also pass the *-Confirm* parameter with a value of *$false* because failing to do so will cause the cmdlet to prompt the user, which can cause problems if the script is not monitored while it runs. After you've retracted the solution, you can then remove it by calling *Remove-SPSolution*, which instructs SharePoint Foundation to delete the solution package file from the configuration database:

```
Add-PSSnapin Microsoft.SharePoint.PowerShell -ErrorAction "SilentlyContinue"
$SolutionPackageName = "WingtipDevProject1.wsp"
Uninstall-SPSolution -Identity $SolutionPackageName -Local -Confirm:$false
Remove-SPSolution -Identity $SolutionPackageName -Confirm:$false
```

These calls to *Uninstall-SPSolution* and *Remove-SPSolution* will fail if the solution package isn't currently installed and deployed. Therefore, it makes sense to add a call to *Get-SPSolution* and conditional logic to determine whether the solution package is currently installed and deployed before attempting to retract or remove it:

```
Add-PSSnapin Microsoft.SharePoint.PowerShell -ErrorAction "SilentlyContinue"
$SolutionPackageName = "WingtipDevProject1.wsp"
$solution = Get-SPSolution | where-object {$_.Name -eq $SolutionPackageName}
# check to see if solution package has been installed
if ($solution -ne $null) {
  # check to see if solution package is currently deployed
  if($solution.Deployed -eq $true){
    Uninstall-SPSolution -Identity $SolutionPackageName -Local -Confirm:$false
    Remove-SPSolution -Identity $SolutionPackageName -Confirm:$false
  }
}
```

Now that you've made sure that there's no old version of your solution installed on the farm, you can add and deploy your solution. Listing 2-1 shows the complete Windows PowerShell script. This script can be used to deploy a solution that cannot be scoped to a web application. Also, the DLL file in this solution will be deployed to the global assembly cache. If a solution can be scoped to a web application, the *–AllWebApplications* parameter can be used to deploy the solution to all web applications, or the *–WebApplication* parameter can be used to specify a specific web application that the solution should be deployed to.

LISTING 2-1 A Windows PowerShell script to uninstall and install a solution

```
Add-PSSnapin Microsoft.SharePoint.PowerShell -ErrorAction "SilentlyContinue"
$solution = Get-SPSolution | where-object {$_.Name -eq $SolutionPackageName}
if ($solution -ne $null) {
  if($solution.Deployed -eq $true){
    Uninstall-SPSolution -Identity $SolutionPackageName -Local -Confirm:$false
  }
  Remove-SPSolution -Identity $SolutionPackageName -Confirm:$false
}
Add-SPSolution -LiteralPath $SolutionPackagePath
Install-SPSolution -Identity $SolutionPackageName -Local -GACDeployment
```

Configuring SharePoint service applications

In SharePoint Server 2010 the concept of service applications was introduced. SharePoint contains several different service applications, and all of them provide a specific piece of functionality to your SharePoint farm if they are enabled. All service applications can be shared across web applications, and some service applications can even be shared across farms. Let's establish the terminology first.

A *service application* itself is the logical container of the service. We use the term *service application* to describe the services architecture in SharePoint. It is also what is exposed in the Central Administration site through the Manage Service Applications page. For most service applications, there can be more than one instance of the service application in a single farm.

The *service instance* is the actual implementation of the service, the binaries. A service instance could include Windows Services, configuration, registry settings, timer jobs, and more. The bits that make up the service instance are deployed to every SharePoint server in the farm.

The *service machine instance* of a particular service application is the server or servers in the farm on which the service for that service application runs. You can check where a service is running and start or stop a service on a particular server by going to the Services On Server page in the Central Administration site. On this page, you can select a server and then start the services you want to run on that particular server. When a service runs on more than one server in the farm, software round-robin load balancing is provided by SharePoint. Not all service applications have an associated service machine instance. Most service applications can have more than one associated service machine instance, but some can only have one. Not all services you see on the Services On Server page are service machine instances of a service application.

The *service application endpoint* is created when you start a service. Starting the service and thus creating a service machine instance creates an Internet Information Services (IIS) virtual application in the SharePoint Web Services IIS website. The virtual application includes a Windows Communication Foundation (WCF) or .asmx web service. This web service is the service application endpoint. Each service application must have its own service application endpoint.

A *service application proxy* (also called *service connection* or *service association*) is a virtual link between a web application and a service application. The service application proxy also enables cross-farm services.

A *proxy group* is a group of service application proxies that are selected for one or more web applications. By default, all service application proxies are included in the default proxy group. When you create a web application, you can do one of the following:

- Select the default proxy group.

- Create a custom proxy group by selecting which service application proxies you want to link to the web application. These service application proxies will then be included in the proxy group.

The custom proxy group for one web application cannot be reused with a different web application.

There are three ways in which you can configure service applications:

- By selecting services when you run the SharePoint Products Configuration Wizard

- By adding services one by one on the Manage Service Applications page in SharePoint 2013 Central Administration

- By using Windows PowerShell

It is not recommended that you use the SharePoint Product Configuration Wizard to configure service applications. Using the wizard will create the service applications with a set of default settings that might not be suitable for your environment. If you use the wizard it is also very easy (as easy as selecting a check box) to create too many service applications. You should always just create the service applications that you need in your farm. Every service application consumes a certain amount of resources, so creating a service application that you don't need means that you are burning valuable resources on your server.

To create a service application from the Manage Service Applications page in Central Administration, you start by clicking the New button on the Manage Service Applications page, as shown in Figure 2-1. Click Managed Metadata Service to create a managed metadata service application.

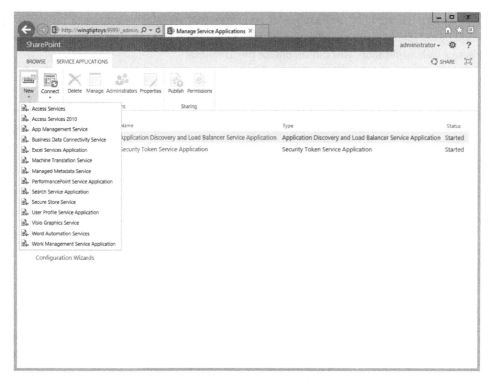

FIGURE 2-1 The Manage Service Applications page in Central Administration

On the next page, you enter a name for the service application and for the database that will store the contents and configuration of the managed metadata service application that you are creating, as shown in Figure 2-2. In this example, the name of the service application is Managed Metadata Service Application. The name of the database is ManagedMetadata. If this is the first service application that you are creating, you will also have to create an application pool that it can use. The name of the application pool in this example is SharePoint Web Services Default. This is the same name that the wizard would have used for the application pool that it creates if you use it to create service applications. In most cases, this application pool can be used for most if not all of your service applications. The account that is used in this example is the WINGTIPTOYS\spservices account. Be aware that the account that you use as the application pool account must be a managed account. Go to the Configure Managed Accounts page in Central Administration to create a new managed account. All managed accounts should be dedicated service accounts. Selecting Add This Service Application To The Farm's Default List means that SharePoint will add the service application to the default proxy group after you click OK.

Figure 2-3 shows the Manage Service Applications page after the managed metadata service application has been created. Creating the managed metadata service application through the Manage Service Applications page also automatically creates the managed metadata service application proxy. Most service applications automatically create their proxy when they are created through the Central Administration user interface. When Windows PowerShell is used to create the service application, you will almost always have to create the service application proxy yourself.

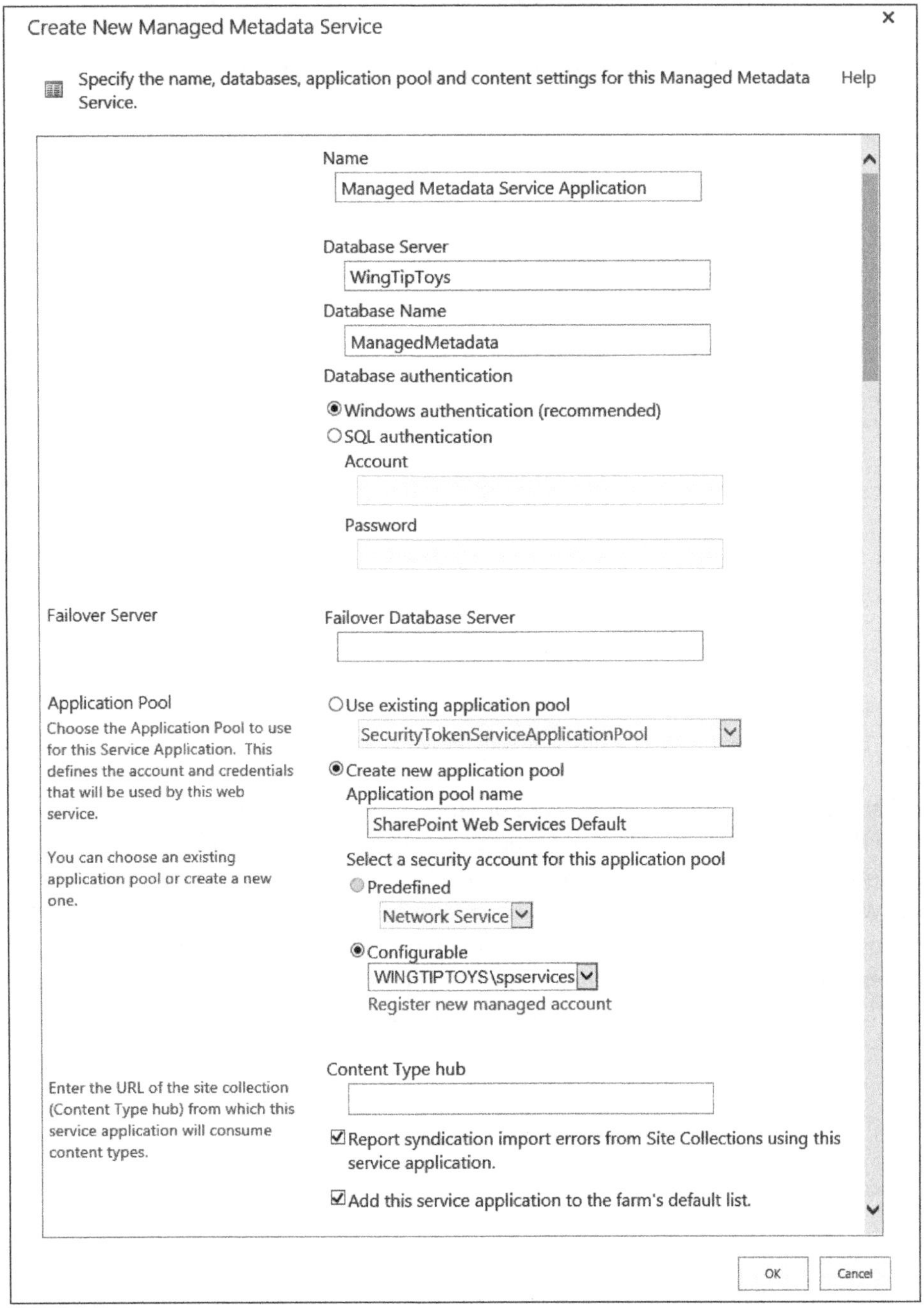

Create New Managed Metadata Service ✕

🔲 Specify the name, databases, application pool and content settings for this Managed Metadata   Help
Service.

Name
Managed Metadata Service Application

Database Server
WingTipToys

Database Name
ManagedMetadata

Database authentication

◉ Windows authentication (recommended)
○ SQL authentication
Account

Password

Failover Server   Failover Database Server

Application Pool   ○ Use existing application pool
Choose the Application Pool to use   SecurityTokenServiceApplicationPool ▾
for this Service Application. This
defines the account and credentials ◉ Create new application pool
that will be used by this web   Application pool name
service.
                                       SharePoint Web Services Default
You can choose an existing
application pool or create a new   Select a security account for this application pool
one.   ○ Predefined
                                          Network Service ▾
                                       ◉ Configurable
                                          WINGTIPTOYS\spservices ▾
                                          Register new managed account

                                  Content Type hub
Enter the URL of the site collection
(Content Type hub) from which this
service application will consume   ☑ Report syndication import errors from Site Collections using this
content types.   service application.

                                  ☑ Add this service application to the farm's default list.

                                                        OK   Cancel

FIGURE 2-2 Creating a Managed Metadata Service Application

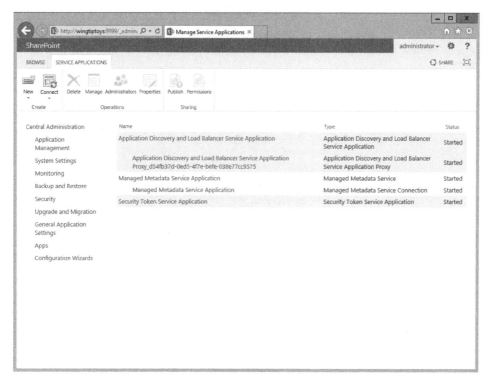

FIGURE 2-3 The Manage Service Applications page with the Managed Metadata Service Application and proxy

Some service applications start their service or services automatically, but for most service applications you will have to go into the Manage Services On Server page in Central Administration (shown in Figure 2-4). For the managed metadata service application, you will have to start the Managed Metadata Web Service on at least one server in the farm. In most development environments you will only have one SharePoint server, so you can start the service only on that server. Starting the service will also create a new IIS virtual application in the SharePoint Web Services IIS website. The name of the virtual application is a GUID, and the application will include the MetadataWebService.svc web service.

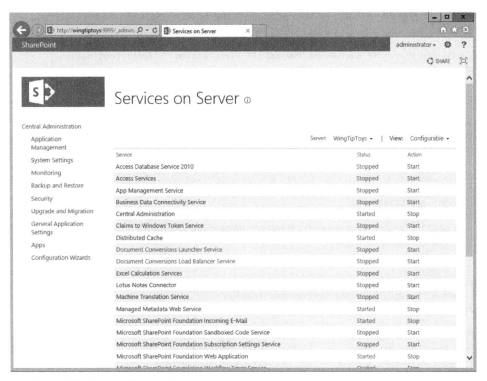

FIGURE 2-4 The Manage Services On Server page

Listing 2-2 shows the Windows PowerShell script that will create the service application, the application pool, and the service application proxy and that will start the managed metadata web service.

LISTING 2-2 A Windows PowerShell script to configure the Managed Metadata Service Application

```
Add-PSSnapin Microsoft.SharePoint.PowerShell -ErrorAction "SilentlyContinue"

$saAppPoolName = "SharePoint Web Services Default"
$appPoolUserName = "WINGTIPTOYS\spservices"

# Gets Application Pool, or creates one
$saAppPool = Get-SPServiceApplicationPool -Identity $saAppPoolName -EA 0
if($saAppPool -eq $null)
{

  Write-Host "Creating Application Pool"
  # Create Application Pool
  $saAppPoolAccount = Get-SPManagedAccount -Identity $appPoolUserName
  $saAppPool = New-SPServiceApplicationPool -Name $saAppPoolName `
    -Account $saAppPoolAccount
}

$mmsInstanceName = "MetadataWebServiceInstance"
$mmsName = "Managed Metadata Service Application"
$mmsDBName = "ManagedMetadata"

Write-Host "Creating Managed Metadata Service Application & proxy"
$mms = New-SPMetadataServiceApplication -Name $mmsName `
    -ApplicationPool $saAppPoolName -DatabaseName $mmsDBName
$proxy = New-SPMetadataServiceApplicationProxy -Name "$mmsName Proxy "`
    -ServiceApplication $mms -DefaultProxyGroup
Write-Host "Starting Managed Metadata Web Service"
Get-SPServiceInstance | where {$_.GetType().Name `
    -eq $mmsInstanceName} | Start-SPServiceInstance
Write-Host "Managed Metadata Service Application successful configured!"
```

Using debugging tools

While creating a custom solution, you can and probably will use Microsoft Visual Studio to debug your code in your development environment if you experience any issues or unexpected behavior. You might even use Visual Studio to do some debugging to simply get a better understanding of what's happening behind the scenes in SharePoint. The Visual Studio Debugger is not the only way to understand and troubleshoot SharePoint and your custom components, though. Other tools that you can use include:

- Unified Logging Service (ULS) and Windows event logs

- The Developer Dashboard

- Fiddler and other network monitoring tools

Working with ULS and Windows event logs

The ULS logs are SharePoint's own dedicated log files. Whenever there is problem with a SharePoint environment, the first place a SharePoint developer or administrator should look for information is in the ULS logs. One of the advantages of the ULS logs is that they can be used for troubleshooting in all types of environments. Regardless of whether problems are occurring in a development environment, in a test or integration environment, or in a production environment, ULS logs should contain valuable pointers to what's happening.

By default, the ULS logs are stored on the file system of every SharePoint server in the *<Program Files Directory>*\Common Files\Microsoft Shared\Web Server Extensions\15\LOGS folder, which is the LOGS folder under the SharePoint root folder. By going into Configure Diagnostic Logging on the Monitoring page in Central Administration, it is possible to specify the folder where the ULS logs are stored. Administrators can change the number of days logs are kept and the total amount of disk space that can be used by the logs. If you are troubleshooting a server that wasn't configured by you and the logs are not in the LOGS folder in the SharePoint root folder, you can browse to the Configure Diagnostic Logging page to find out where the log files are stored on the server. The page can also be used to change the severity of the events that are logged both to the ULS logs and to the Windows event logs. Flood protection can be enabled to make sure that SharePoint events won't flood the Windows event logs.

The ULS logs are text files that are quite difficult to read and that usually contain a lot of data. To more easily read events in the ULS logs and also to search, sort, and filter the ULS logs, the ULS Viewer is a must-have tool for everyone who has to troubleshoot SharePoint. The ULS Viewer can be downloaded from MSDN at *http://archive.msdn.microsoft.com/ULSViewer* and is an .exe file that has to be run on the SharePoint server. It will enable you to start and stop traces and to search through the logs by using a well-organized user interface instead of a text file.

Troubleshooting information for a SharePoint environment can also be found in the Windows event logs. On the server, the Windows event logs can be consulted by opening up the Event Viewer. There is some overlap in the information between the ULS logs and the Windows Event Viewer, but both also contain specific information that can be valuable for finding the source of the problem.

When an error occurs in SharePoint, an error message will be displayed in the user interface that contains what is referred to as a correlation ID. A *correlation ID* is a GUID that uniquely identifies a particular request. The correlation ID is generated by the SharePoint web server that receives the request. Every event that is part of the request is tagged with the same ID, and the ID even persists across different servers in the farm. For instance, if a request was sent to a SharePoint web server, it will be generated on that server and it will mark all entries in the ULS log that are part of the request with that particular correlation ID. If, as part of the request, some managed metadata has to be requested from the Managed Metadata service that runs on a dedicated application server, the same correlation ID can be found in the ULS logs on that application server. You can even use the correlation ID to trace the request on the server that is running SQL Server by using SQL Profiler to filter out requests related to the ID.

When an end user encounters an error in a SharePoint environment, that user will usually see an error message that contains a correlation ID. Even though the ID is of no use to the user himself, users can be asked to include the ID when they place a call to a helpdesk. Having the ID of the user's faulty request can help administrators and developers find out what went wrong with the user's request and help solve the issue.

Correlation IDs aren't just generated for faulty requests; they are generated for all requests. To find the correlation ID for a successful request, you can use the Developer Dashboard.

Using the Developer Dashboard

The Developer Dashboard was introduced in SharePoint 2010 to show performance and tracing information for a SharePoint page in a control on the page itself. In SharePoint 2013, the Developer Dashboard has been dramatically improved. The dashboard is no longer a control on a page; it opens in a separate dedicated window. The dashboard also no longer just contains information about the latest request but contains information about several requests, so that you can compare them if you want to and more easily get an overview. The information on the Developer Dashboard is a lot more detailed than it was in SharePoint 2010. For instance, you can now easily see the SQL requests and the time it took to process them, the different scopes and execution times, service calls, and also all ULS log entries that are related to the selected request. All this can really help you to identify any potential problems related to a request, because you have all the information SharePoint collected about the requests in a single place.

By default, the Developer Dashboard is disabled. You can enable it by using Windows PowerShell. The Windows PowerShell cmdlet only supports *On* or *Off*; the *OnDemand* parameter has been deprecated, although *On* now pretty much acts the way *OnDemand* did in SharePoint 2010; it displays an icon in the upper-right corner that allows you to open up the Developer Dashboard. The Windows PowerShell cmdlet to turn on the Developer Dashboard is displayed in Listing 2-3.

LISTING 2-3 Changing the mode of the Developer Dashboard

```
Add-PSSnapin Microsoft.SharePoint.PowerShell -ErrorAction "SilentlyContinue"
$DevDashboardSettings = [Microsoft.SharePoint.Administration.SPWebService]:: `
ContentService.DeveloperDashboardSettings
$DevDashboardSettings.DisplayLevel = 'On'
$DevDashboardsettings.Update()
```

Figure 2-5 shows the Developer Dashboard after the welcome page of an out-of-the-box team site has been loaded. On the dashboard, you can see different tabs for server information, scopes, SQL info, ULS information, and a lot more. The Server Info tab contains the total execution time for the page, the current user, whether the page is published, and the correlation ID. The SQL tab also shows the execution time for all database queries and for all methods. By using the dashboard you can not only see how long a page took to load just the out-of-the-box functionality on it, but you can also see how long it takes your custom component to load. You can identify whether your code executes any expensive methods or database queries.

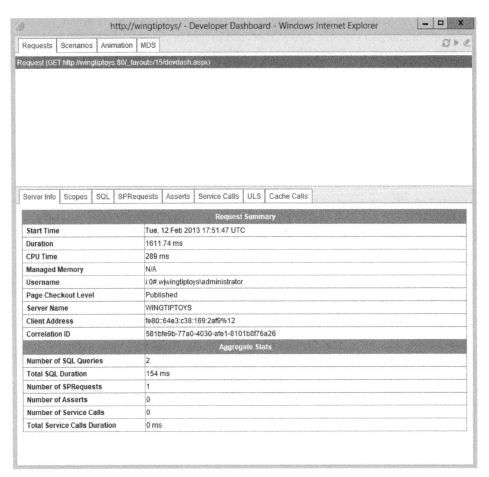

FIGURE 2-5 The Developer Dashboard

To write information from your own custom solution to the Developer Dashboard you can either execute your code in an *OnInit* or *Render* override, or you can wrap your code in an *SPMonitoredScope* block. Only code from farm solutions can send information to the Developer Dashboard; the contents of sandboxed solutions or apps cannot send information to the dashboard.

Using the SharePoint Developer Tools in Visual Studio 2012

The release of SharePoint 2007 was a significant milestone for SharePoint as a development platform because in this version, Microsoft introduced support for features and solution packages. Soon after SharePoint 2007 was released, however, it became clear within Microsoft and throughout the industry that more and better developer productivity tools were needed. With SharePoint 2010, Microsoft extended the developer platform by introducing the SharePoint Developer Tools in Visual Studio 2010. These new tools made developing for SharePoint 2010 much faster and easier because they automated grungy tasks and hid many of the low-level details that developers had to worry about when developing for SharePoint 2007. For example, every SharePoint project in Visual Studio 2010 is created with built-in support to generate its output as a solution package. The SharePoint Developer Tools also integrate commands into the Visual Studio 2010 environment that make it easy to deploy and retract the solution package for a SharePoint project during testing and debugging.

With the introduction of SharePoint 2013 and Visual Studio 2012, Microsoft has further improved the SharePoint Developer Tools. For the project types that were available for SharePoint 2010 there are now also SharePoint 2013 versions. There are also Office add-in project types that can be used to create add-ins for the Microsoft Office 2013 and Office 2010 applications. The biggest change, however, is that the SharePoint Developer Tools in Visual Studio 2012 contain two project types that allow you to create two different types of apps:

- Apps for Office 2013

- Apps for SharePoint 2013

You can find the app for SharePoint 2013 C# in the New Project dialog box within Visual Studio 2012 by navigating to Visual C#\Office/SharePoint\Apps, as shown in Figure 2-6.

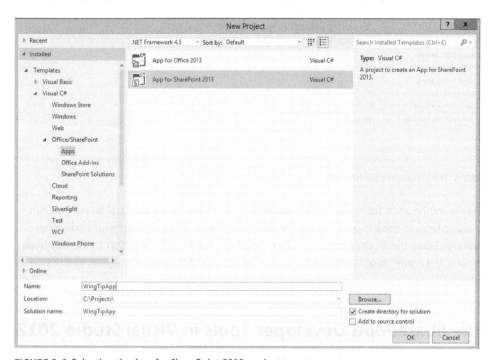

FIGURE 2-6 Selecting the App for SharePoint 2013 project type to create an app

When you click OK you are asked to confirm the name of the app and specify the site to which you want Visual Studio to deploy the app and how you want to host your app, as shown in Figure 2-7.

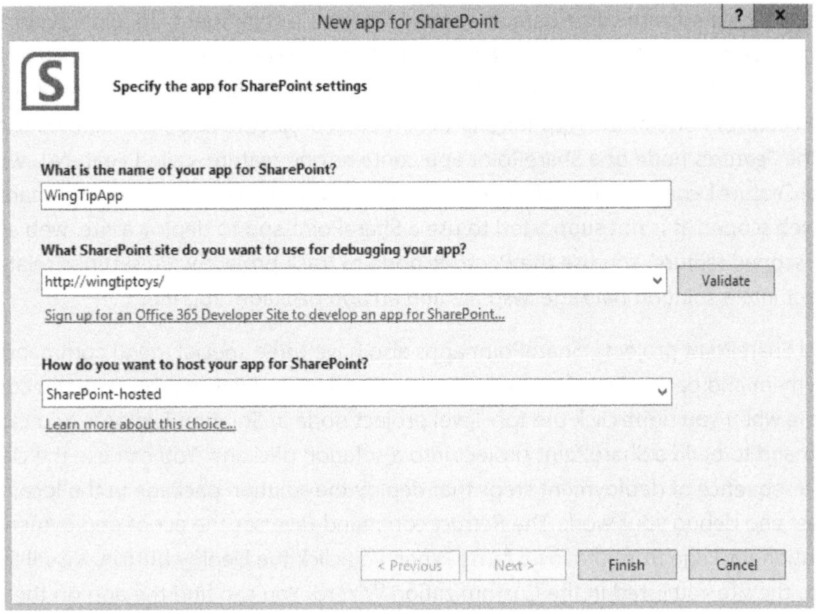

New app for SharePoint

? X

S Specify the app for SharePoint settings

What is the name of your app for SharePoint?

WingTipApp

What SharePoint site do you want to use for debugging your app?

http://wingtiptoys/   ∨   Validate

Sign up for an Office 365 Developer Site to develop an app for SharePoint...

How do you want to host your app for SharePoint?

SharePoint-hosted   ∨

Learn more about this choice...

< Previous   Next >   Finish   Cancel

FIGURE 2-7 Specifying a name, test site URL, and trust level for an app

SharePoint apps will be discussed in detail in Chapter 4, "SharePoint apps." For now, you will create a SharePoint-hosted app, which means that all of the app will be deployed to a SharePoint site. When you click the Finish button in the SharePoint Customization Wizard, Visual Studio takes a few seconds to create and configure the new project. Figure 2-8 shows what the new SharePoint project looks like in Solution Explorer.

FIGURE 2-8 An app's Features node, Package node, and some standard content

A SharePoint app is created with some default content. There is a style sheet, an app icon image, a default page, and several JavaScript files. The AppManifest.xml file contains metadata such as the name and the title of the app, the app icon, and the scopes at which the app needs to have permissions. You use the *Features* node of the App for SharePoint 2013 project to add new features to the app. Notice that the *Features* node of a SharePoint app contains one feature, called Feature1, when the app is created. Feature1 contains the default content and is web scoped. A feature in a SharePoint app can only be web scoped, it is not supported to use a SharePoint app to deploy a site, web application, or farm-scoped feature. You use the *Package* node to track project-wide settings related to building the project into a solution package .wsp file and an app package .app file.

Just like normal SharePoint projects, SharePoint apps also have three special menu commands to support deployment and packaging of the app: *Deploy*, *Package*, and *Retract*. These menu commands are available when you right-click the top-level project node in Solution Explorer. You can run the *Package* command to build a SharePoint project into a solution package. You can use the *Deploy* command to run a sequence of deployment steps that deploy the solution package in the local farm so that you can test and debug your work. The *Retract* command reverses the act of deployment by retracting the solution package from the local farm. When you click the Deploy button, Visual Studio deploys the app to the site you listed in the Customization Wizard. You can find the app on the Site Contents page and in the navigation pane on the left side of the page, under the Recent heading, as shown in Figure 2-9. Clicking the app name or icon will open the app's default.aspx page.

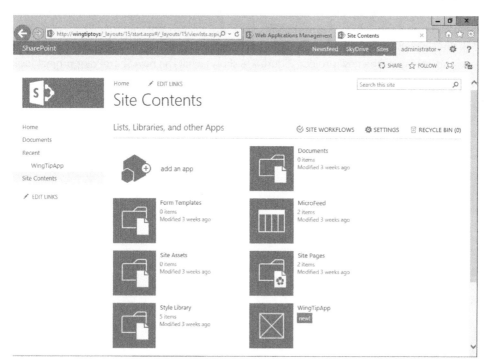

FIGURE 2-9 The WingTip app on the Site Contents page and in the navigation pane on the left side of the page

Choosing a development approach

At least as important as knowing how to create a solution is knowing when to create a solution and what type of solution to create. Even though this is a book about custom development, the best approach when using SharePoint is to use out-of-the-box functionality. Customizations are the number-one cause of problems with SharePoint environments. Knowing this, you have to make sure that when you create a custom solution, the same functionality couldn't be achieved by using out-of-the-box functionality. If you do have to create a custom solution, you have to make sure that you create the right type of solution and that you build the solution in a way that uses the least amount of resources from the SharePoint server.

When you open up Visual Studio, the first thing you have to decide is what type of project you want to create. With the new SharePoint 2013 app model added into the mix, you can now choose between a SharePoint 2013 farm solution, a SharePoint 2013 sandboxed solution, and a SharePoint 2013 app. There isn't one right project type; the best type depends on what kind of customizations you want to build and to what type of environment you want to deploy the customizations.

The best option is always the project type that puts the least amount of load on the SharePoint server. However, the solution also has to be maintainable and upgradable. The solution should not be overly complex, so that it can be maintained by others. The solution design should follow best practices to ensure that it can be upgraded to a next version of SharePoint. Of course, you also have to make sure that the solution can be deployed to the environment that you are creating the customizations for. To summarize, when you create SharePoint customizations, the following things have to be taken into account:

- Put the least possible load on the SharePoint server.

- Keep the customizations as simple as possible.

- Make sure you follow best practices, so the solutions don't block the SharePoint environment from being upgraded.

- Ensure that the solution can be deployed to the target environment.

Because a SharePoint app can't deploy server-side code to the SharePoint server, that will always be the project type that puts the least amount of load on the SharePoint server. Sandboxed solutions can deploy server-side code to the SharePoint server; however, a sandboxed solution can only use a limited amount of server resources before it is shut down. A farm solution can technically use all the resources that are available on the server, and because of that, a farm solution can bring down an entire SharePoint farm. This is not just a theoretical scenario; it actually happens on a regular basis to both small and really large SharePoint environments.

It is likely that the version of the customizations that you are building is not the last version. Either the customizations will be a huge hit and users will ask for more functionality, or they aren't what users were expecting and they need modifications to fit the user's needs. To make the solution easy to maintain, make it as simple as possible. This means that even though your first choice should be to build a SharePoint app, because that would consume the least amount of SharePoint server resources, you shouldn't do it at all costs. If creating an app would create a solution that is significantly more complex, the best solution is probably to build a sandboxed or farm solution.

If the SharePoint environment is successful, it's very likely that at some point the environment will have to be upgraded to the next version of SharePoint. Some SharePoint customizations can block the upgrade of a SharePoint environment. For instance, if a solution makes unsupported changes to the database or to SharePoint files on the file system, it won't be possible to upgrade the environment. Also, when certain customizations such as site definitions are involved, it will be significantly more difficult to move the contents of the SharePoint farm to a cloud-hosted environment. Because Microsoft has positioned the SharePoint app model as the SharePoint customization type of the future, and because almost all parts of the SharePoint app live outside of SharePoint, creating apps is your safest bet when you want to guarantee that your environment can upgrade without being hindered by the customizations.

Using farm solutions means that the solution will have to be upgraded when the SharePoint farm gets upgraded. Sandboxed solutions live in the content database and can only affect the site collection that they are deployed in. This means that the impact they can have on an upgrade to a new version of SharePoint is a lot smaller than for farm solutions. However, sandboxed solutions are deprecated in SharePoint 2013. This means that although both sandboxed solutions that were created for SharePoint 2010 and new sandboxed solutions created for SharePoint 2013 are still fully supported, Microsoft is planning to remove support for sandboxed solutions at some point in the future. This doesn't necessarily have to be in the next release; it could be in the release after that, or an even later release. Investing in large-scale sandboxed solutions is probably not a good idea, though.

If your environment is a cloud-hosted environment such as Office 365, you might not have much of a choice, because you won't be allowed to deploy full trust solutions, and not all customizations can be created by using apps. In those cases, you will probably still want to create new sandboxed solutions. The advice would then be to try and create the solutions in such a way that you can remove the sandboxed solution without the entire site breaking down. When Microsoft then at some point removes the support for sandboxed solutions, at least your existing content is still accessible.

When you are upgrading from SharePoint 2010 to SharePoint 2013, you can choose how you want to upgrade you custom solutions:

- You can deploy your SharePoint 2010 solutions as is. Microsoft has designed SharePoint 2013 to make sure that your solutions keep working. This means that the entire solution should work when a site is in SharePoint 2010 mode. When a site is in SharePoint 2013 mode, most of the solution should work, but some things might not work. Things that don't work are mostly related to functionality that is no longer available in SharePoint. For instance, custom solutions that use the SharePoint 2010 Web Analytics features will not work in a SharePoint 2013 environment, because the Web Analytics Service Application and all related functionality has been removed. In most cases, you will not just deploy your existing solutions as is. The only case in which it makes sense to not make any changes and just deploy an existing SharePoint 2010 solution as is to a SharePoint 2013 environment is when the solution is only there to keep existing SharePoint 2010 sites working in SharePoint 2010 mode in the SharePoint 2013 environment. In all other cases, you will at least want to recompile your solution.

■ The second way to move SharePoint 2010 solutions to a SharePoint 2013 environment is to open the SharePoint 2010 solution in Visual Studio 2012. The solution can then be recompiled against the SharePoint 2013 DLLs. While you are doing this, you can decide to make some minor changes to the solution. You should definitely remove any references to functionality that no longer exists in SharePoint 2013, such as the Web Analytics functionality. Another example of something that will definitely not work in a SharePoint 2013 mode are SharePoint 2010 visual designs. Any master pages and style sheets that were created for SharePoint 2010 will not work in sites that are in SharePoint 2013 mode. Normally SharePoint will just not use the SharePoint 2010 designs in SharePoint 2013 mode sites. However, if you had a stapling feature in SharePoint 2010 that stapled a custom design to sites in the environment, especially if it stapled the design to all sites in the environment by stapling it to the GLOBAL site definition, you will want to remove the stapling feature before moving the solution to SharePoint 2013. Stapling a SharePoint 2010 design to the GLOBAL site definition and deploying it to SharePoint 2013 can make it impossible to create any fully functional sites, either by using out-of-the-box site definitions or custom web templates.

■ The third approach that can be taken when moving solutions from SharePoint 2010 to SharePoint 2013 is to rebuild the solution to use the new SharePoint 2013 functionality where possible. Rebuilding the solution could mean replacing custom features with new out-of-the-box functionality. In a lot of cases, the aim should be to minimize the amount of customizations in an environment, which means that cutting customizations in favor of new out-of-the-box functionality is a very valid change to invest in. Do keep in mind, though, that in order to be able to upgrade existing sites you might need to have certain SharePoint 2010 customizations deployed in your environment, even if you don't want to actively use them anymore in your SharePoint 2013 environment. There are also cases in which a customization can't be replaced by out-of-the-box functionality but could be replaced by SharePoint apps, by an application that runs external to SharePoint and that uses the SharePoint Web Services or the vastly improved SharePoint Client Object Model. This should only be done if replacing the functionality by using a SharePoint app or an external solution doesn't make the solution significantly more complex. If that is not the case, rebuilding functionality as a SharePoint app or as an external service will give you practice and experience in using the new development options, and it will make sure that your solution is easier to deploy in hosted environments. Assuming that the SharePoint app model is here to stay, it will also make sure that your solution becomes more future proof.

Using the SharePoint APIs

In SharePoint 2013, you can now choose from three different APIs: the server-side object model (SSOM), the client-side object model (CSOM), and the REST API. All three APIs give you the option to build customizations for your SharePoint environment. This section will provide an overview of the three different APIs. Each API will then be used extensively in examples throughout the book. For specific detailed coverage of CSOM and REST, see Chapter 5, "Client-side programming."

Understanding the server-side object model

The core server-side object model of SharePoint Foundation is loaded through an assembly named *Microsoft.SharePoint.dll*. When you reference this assembly within a Visual Studio 2012 project, you can start programming against the classes in the server-side object model, such as *SPSite, SPWeb*, and *SPList*. There are two initial requirements for a Visual Studio project that programs against the server-side object model by using the *Microsoft.SharePoint* assembly. First, the project must be configured to use .NET Framework 4 or 4.5 as its target framework. Pay extra attention if you are upgrading a SharePoint 2010 solution, because that will have been built using the .NET Framework 3.5 as its target framework. The second requirement is that your project must have a platform target setting that is compatible with a 64-bit environment, which is essential for properly loading the *Microsoft.SharePoint* assembly.

Another critical requirement for any application or component that is programmed against the server-side object model is that the application or component must be deployed and run on a SharePoint server in the farm in which you want to use the component. The deployment of applications or components that use the SharePoint server-side object model should always be done by using a SharePoint Solution or .wsp file. To deploy the solution, you will need access to at least one SharePoint server in the farm where the solution should be deployed. In most production environments, this means that you will hand off the solution and a document that describes how to deploy the solution to the administrator of the server. In your development environment, Visual Studio will usually do the deployment for you.

You can also create client applications with Visual Studio 2012 that program against the server-side object model. For example, you can create a standard console application that uses the server-side object model to access a site and the elements inside the site, such as lists and items. However, keep in mind that any client application that depends on the *Microsoft.SharePoint* assembly can be run only when launched on a server that has SharePoint installed on it and that is part of a SharePoint farm. This means that it's not likely that you will encounter real-world scenarios that call for creating client applications that use the server-side object model. Even so, creating simple console applications that program against the *Microsoft.SharePoint* assembly in your development environment can be useful, because it gives you a quick and easy way to write and test code as you begin learning the server-side object model.

Most of the SharePoint Foundation APIs reside in *Microsoft.SharePoint.dll*. However, if you are building a custom solution ,using the server-side object model you might also want to use SharePoint Server APIs and functionality. The bulk of the SharePoint Server APIs reside in *Microsoft.Office.Server.dll*; however, this isn't the only available DLL that contains SharePoint Server APIs. For a full list of SharePoint APIs and the DLLs in which you can find them, see the MSDN page *.NET server API reference for SharePoint 2013* at *http://msdn.microsoft.com/en-us/library/jj193058.aspx*.

Using the client-side object model

SharePoint 2010 introduced the SharePoint Foundation client-side object model, which allows developers to use SharePoint content and objects in their client-side solutions. As a developer, you could now create a very simple solution that would be deployed into a SharePoint site or onto a user's desktop and that could read or manage data in a SharePoint site.

In SharePoint 2010, the client-side object model was only available for SharePoint Foundation objects. In SharePoint 2013, however, the client-side object model has again been vastly improved by making a lot of the SharePoint Server objects available through the client-side object model. In SharePoint 2010 there were three client-side object models, and in SharePoint 2013 there are four. SharePoint 2013 allows you to choose between the Managed, Silverlight, Mobile, and JavaScript object models. Each of the four object models provides an object interface to SharePoint functionality that is based on the objects available in the *Microsoft.SharePoint* namespace. All four client-side object models also have support for at least part of the SharePoint Server 2013 functionality, but not all of them include the same SharePoint Server 2013 components.

The four client-side object models also all have their own usages. Each of the four object models presents an object interface in front of a service proxy. Developers write client-side code by using the object model, but the operations are batched and sent as a single XML request to the Client.svc service. When the XML request is received, the Client.svc service makes calls to the server-side object model on behalf of the client. The results of the server-side calls are then sent back to the calling client in the form of a JavaScript Object Notation (JSON) object.

The object model for Microsoft Silverlight can be used to build Silverlight applications, Web Parts, ASP.NET applications, apps for SharePoint and Office, and Silverlight applications for phones that use SharePoint data or SharePoint objects. A Silverlight application is compiled into an .xap file that can pretty much be stored anywhere. Examples of where .xap files can be deployed are a client computer, the file system of a SharePoint server, a list in a SharePoint library, and an external (web) server. The Silverlight client-side object model is contained in assemblies in the LAYOUTS\ClientBin folder. The following DLLs are available:

- Microsoft.SharePoint.Client.Silverlight.dll

- Microsoft.SharePoint.Client.Silverlight.Runtime.dll

- Microsoft.SharePoint.Client.DocumentManagement.Silverlight.dll

- Microsoft.SharePoint.Client.Publishing.Silverlight.dll

- Microsoft.SharePoint.Client.Search.Applications.Silverlight.dll

- Microsoft.SharePoint.Client.Search.Silverlight.dll

- Microsoft.SharePoint.Client.Taxonomy.Silverlight.dll

- Microsoft.SharePoint.Client.UserProfiles.Silverlight.dll

- Microsoft.SharePoint.Client.WorkflowServices.Silverlight.dll

- Microsoft.Office.Client.Policy.Silverlight.dll

- Microsoft.Office.Client.TranslationServices.Silverlight.dll

The Mobile object model can be used to create applications that run on Windows Phones. The Mobile client-side object model is a special version of the Silverlight client-side object model. The Mobile object model contains most of the same functionality as the Silverlight object model. A couple of areas are missing, but when you are creating a Windows Phone application using the Mobile object model you can use the REST APIs to access these areas. The Mobile client-side object model also contains some functionality that is specific to phones, such as APIs that enable a phone app to register for notifications from the Microsoft Push Notification Service. The Mobile client-side object model can be found in the same folder as the Silverlight client-side object model, in the LAYOUTS\ClientBin folder. The DLLs that are available for the Mobile client-side object model are:

- Microsoft.SharePoint.Client.Phone.dll

- Microsoft.SharePoint.Client.Phone.Runtime.dll

- Microsoft.SharePoint.Client.DocumentManagement.Phone.dll

- Microsoft.SharePoint.Client.Publishing.Phone.dll

- Microsoft.SharePoint.Client.Taxonomy.Phone.dll

- Microsoft.SharePoint.Client.UserProfiles.Phone.dll

- Microsoft.Office.Client.Policy.Phone.dll

- Microsoft.Office.Client.TranslationServices.Phone.dll

The Managed object model can be used to create .NET applications that run on Windows operating systems that aren't phones or SharePoint servers. This means that the Managed object model can be used to create applications that run on client computers, or on Windows web servers not running SharePoint. The Managed object model can be found in the ISAPI folder and is contained in the following DLLs:

- Microsoft.SharePoint.Client.dll

- Microsoft.SharePoint.Client.Runtime.dll

- Microsoft.SharePoint.Client.ServerRuntime.dll

- Microsoft.SharePoint.Client.DocumentManagement.dll

- Microsoft.SharePoint.Client.Publishing.dll

- Microsoft.SharePoint.Client.Search.Applications.dll

- Microsoft.SharePoint.Client.Search.dll

- Microsoft.SharePoint.Client.Taxonomy.dll

- Microsoft.SharePoint.Client.UserProfiles.dll

- Microsoft.SharePoint.Client.WorkflowServices.dll

- Microsoft.Office.Client.Education.dll

- Microsoft.Office.Client.Policy.dll

- Microsoft.Office.Client.TranslationServices.dll

- Microsoft.Office.SharePoint.ClientExtensions.dll

The last client-side object model is the JavaScript object model. The JavaScript object model can be used in inline script or in separate .js files. Using the JavaScript client-side object model is an excellent way to add custom SharePoint code to a SharePoint-hosted app. The JavaScript object model is different from the other three in that it is not contained in a set of DLLs. Instead, it is contained in a JavaScript library, inside of .js files. The many .js files that make up the JavaScript client-side object model are located in the LAYOUTS folder. The core SharePoint functionality can be found in SP.js and in SP.Core.js.

Though the four client-side object models don't contain exactly the same functionality, Microsoft has taken great care to ensure that the four models return objects that behave similarly. This means that if you know how to write code against one of the models, you can easily port that code to either of the other three models. Table 2-2 shows some of the main objects supported by each model alongside the related object from the server-side model.

TABLE 2-2 Equivalent objects in the server and client models

Server model	Managed model	Silverlight model	Mobile model	JavaScript model
SPContext	ClientContext	ClientContext	ClientContext	ClientContext
SPSite	Site	Site	Site	Site
SPWeb	Web	Web	Web	Web
SPList	List	List	List	List
SPListItem	ListItem	ListItem	ListItem	ListItem
SPField	Field	Field	Field	Field

As in the standard code you write against the server-side object model, code written for client object models requires a starting point in the form of a context object. The context object provides an entry point into the associated API that can be used to gain access to other objects. When you have access to the objects, you can interact with the scalar properties of the object freely (for example, *Name, Title, Url*, and so on). Listing 2-4 shows how to create a context in each of the models and return an object representing a site collection. After the site collection object is returned, the *Url* property is examined. Code for the server model is included for comparison.

LISTING 2-4 Creating contexts

```
//Server Object Model
SPSite siteCollection = SPContext.Current.Site;
string url = siteCollection.Url;

//Managed Client Object Model
using (ClientContext ctx = new ClientContext("http://intranet.wingtiptoys.com"))
{
    Site siteCollection = ctx.Site;
    ctx.Load(siteCollection);
    ctx.ExecuteQuery();
    string url = siteCollection.Url;
}

//Silverlight Client Object Model
using (ClientContext ctx =
    new ClientContext("http://intranet.wingtiptoys.com"))
{
    Site siteCollection = ctx.Site;
    ctx.Load(siteCollection);
    ctx.ExecuteQuery();
    string url = siteCollection.Url;
}

//Mobile Client Object Model
using (ClientContext ctx =
    new ClientContext("http://intranet.wingtiptoys.com"))
{
    Site siteCollection = ctx.Site;
    ctx.Load(siteCollection);
    ctx.ExecuteQuery();
    string url = siteCollection.Url;
}

//JavaScript Client Object Model
var siteCollection;
function getSiteCollection
{
    var ctx = new SP.ClientContext("/");
    siteCollection = ctx.get_site;
    ctx.load(site);
    ctx.executeQueryAsync(success, failure);
}

function success {
    string url = siteCollection.get_url;
}

function failure {
    alert("Failure!");
}
```

The *ClientContext* class in the Managed, Silverlight, and Mobile object models inherits from the *ClientContextRuntime* class. By using the *ClientContext* class, you can get a valid run-time context by passing in the URL of a site. In addition, this class provides several members that are needed to access data and invoke methods on the server.

The *SP.ClientContext* class in the JavaScript client object model inherits from the *SP.ClientContext-Runtime* class and provides equivalent functionality to the *ClientContext* class found in the Managed, Silverlight, and Mobile client object models. As with the Managed and Silverlight models, you can get a run-time context in the JavaScript model by using the *SP.ClientContext* class and passing a URL. Unlike the other client object models, however, the JavaScript model also allows you to get a run-time context to the current site by using a constructor with no arguments, so the example above could be rewritten as simply *var ctx = new SP.ClientContext*.

All four client-side object models only communicate with the SharePoint server when the code calls the *ExecuteQuery* or *ExecuteQueryAsync* method. This is to prevent the object models from making too many calls to the SharePoint server and from affecting the SharePoint server's health by querying the server too much. This means that when you are writing your code, you have to really think about when the statements that you are writing actually have to be executed on the server. You will want to minimize traffic to the server, but you will need to communicate with the server if you want to request data from, or send data into, the SharePoint environment.

The *ExecuteQuery* method creates an XML request and passes it to the Client.svc service. The client then waits synchronously while the batch is executed and the JSON results are returned. The *Execute-QueryAsync* method, which is used in the Silverlight and Mobile client object models, sends the XML request to the server, but it returns immediately. Designated success and failure callback methods receive notification when the batch operation is complete.

The JavaScript model works like the Managed and Silverlight models by loading operations and executing batches. In the case of the JavaScript model, however, all batch executions are accomplished asynchronously. This means that you must call the *ExecuteQueryAsync* method and pass in the name of functions that will receive success and failure callbacks, as shown earlier in Listing 2-4.

Using the REST APIs

The most lightweight option for performing relatively simple operations on data in SharePoint lists and sites is to use the REST capabilities that are built into SharePoint 2013. The SharePoint 2013 implementation of a REST web service uses the Open Data Protocol (OData) to perform CRUD operations on data in SharePoint. Using REST allows your code to interact with SharePoint by using standard HTTP requests and responses. Table 2-3 shows the mapping between HTTP verbs and data operations.

TABLE 2-3 Mapping between HTTP verbs and data operations

HTTP verb	Data operation
GET	Retrieve
POST	Create
PUT	Update all fields
DELETE	Delete
MERGE	Update specified fields

The Client.svc web service handles the HTTP request and serves a response in either Atom or JSON format.

To access any object on a site by using a RESTful call, the URL you should use will start with the following construction:

```
http://<server>/<site>/_api
```

To access an actual object within the site you simply add the object to the URL:

```
//Access a site collection
http://<server>/<site>/_api/site

//Access a specific site
http://<server>/<site>/_api/web

//Access a list in a specific site
http://<server>/<site>/_api/web/lists('GUID')
```

You can use the querystring syntax to specify parameters for the methods that you call by using a RESTful HTTP request:

```
//Apply a "blank" site site definition to a SharePoint site
http://<server>/<site>/_api/web/applyWebTemplate?template="STS#1"
```

The query strings can become rather complex, but because of that the queries that can be performed are rather powerful as well. You can select, sort, page, filter, and expand data by using a RESTful query. The filtering allows both numeric and string comparisons as well as date and time comparisons. The next example of a RESTful query requests the FirstName, LastName, and Phone-Number columns from a list with a specific GUID and filters the items by items where the FirstName starts with an *a*:

```
http://<server>/<site>/_api/web/lists('GUID')/items?$select=FirstName,LastName,
PhoneNumber$filter=startWith(FirstName, a)
```

Summary

In this chapter, all the basics of developing a custom SharePoint solution have been touched on. The first step is to determine what type of development environment you need to create the solution that you want to create, or to complete the project that you are working on. When you have your hardware and the design of the development environment in place, you can install and configure it manually, but you can also use Windows PowerShell to configure your server. Especially if you need to create multiple development environments, scripting the installation and configuration can save you time and will help to ensure that all development environments are identical.

The next step is to determine a development approach. The best approach for your solution depends on the functionality that you want to build and on the environment that the solution should be deployed to. If the solution has to be deployed to a cloud-hosted environment, creating a farm solution is not an option, because you won't be able to deploy it. The most future-proof approach is to create a SharePoint app. However, some of the functionality that you might want to build might not be able to be created by using a SharePoint app (yet). This forces you to make a decision between creating an app that implements as much of the functionality as possible and creating a farm solution that implements the exact functionality that you are looking for. If you deploying a farm solution, you will have to upgrade it if you want to upgrade your environment, and at some point in the future Microsoft might remove support for farm solutions completely. Although it will be a while before this happens, it should already be a consideration when you are determining the development approach you are going to use for your solution.

After your solution is deployed, you might have to debug it. There are several debugging tools that can be used to debug custom SharePoint solutions. The best tool to use depends on the type of problem you are trying to debug and on what type of environment your solution is in. The ULS and Windows Event Logs, and the Developer Dashboard, can give you valuable information from all types of environments and are all useful tools to help you identify the cause of a problem on your farm.

## CHAPTER 3

Server-side solution development

Microsoft SharePoint 2013 offers a new way to customize your SharePoint environment called the SharePoint app model. However, the approaches you used to customize your SharePoint environment prior to SharePoint 2013 are for the most part still valid. You can still build farm solutions and sandboxed solutions. This chapter walks you through how to create farm and sandboxed solutions and talks about dos and don'ts for both approaches. It also guides you through what's different in SharePoint 2013 compared to SharePoint 2010, both in terms of changes to the tools and object model and in terms of changes to the guidance around using farm and sandboxed solutions.

A farm solution is a solution that will be deployed via the SharePoint Central Administration website or Windows PowerShell. Someone with access to the SharePoint server will upload the solution by using Windows PowerShell, and the solution will be stored in the Farm Solutions store, which is persisted in the SharePoint Configuration Database. This is the database that also stores a lot of the farm settings for the SharePoint farm. It is not a content database, which means that there are no SharePoint site settings and site content stored in it. After the solution has been added to the Farm Solutions store it can be deployed, which means that the files packaged in the solution can be deployed to the right locations and that users and administrators can start using the functionality that was packaged in the solution. Deployment can either be done through Central Administration or via Windows PowerShell. The Windows PowerShell script to upload and deploy a SharePoint solution can be found in Listing 2-1 in Chapter 2, "SharePoint development practices and techniques."

A sandboxed solution is a solution that is uploaded to a site collection's *Solution Gallery*. Sandboxed solutions can be uploaded and activated by site collection administrators. The sandbox solution will also be stored in the content database that the site collection is stored in. A sandboxed solution and its contents will not be deployed to the SharePoint server's file system. The functionality from a sandboxed solution is only available in the site collection or collections where it has been deployed.

To build farm or sandboxed solutions for SharePoint 2013 you use Microsoft Visual Studio 2012 Professional, Premium, or Ultimate, including the SharePoint Developer Tools. As shown in Figure 3-1, the SharePoint Developer Tools can be installed as an optional feature during Visual Studio installation.

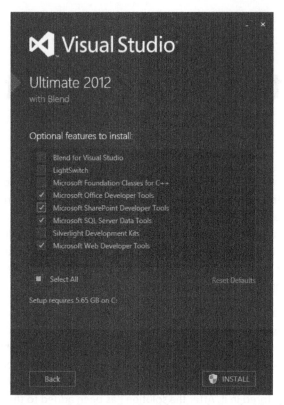

FIGURE 3-1 Selection of optional features during the Visual Studio 2012 installation

The new SharePoint Developer Tools include support for building farm solutions, sandboxed solutions, and SharePoint and Office apps. As in SharePoint 2010, you will need a SharePoint farm on your development server to build farm or sandboxed solutions. The farm can be either a SharePoint Server or a SharePoint Foundation farm. In general the recommendation is to make sure that the SharePoint version that you use in your development environment is the same as the version used in the production environment.

The first time you start Visual Studio after installing it, Visual Studio asks for your default environment settings, as shown in Figure 3-2. The options don't include settings for "SharePoint Development," so you'll have to make do with one of the other options. The options that come closest are either Web Development or Visual C# Development Settings. For this example, we chose Web Development.

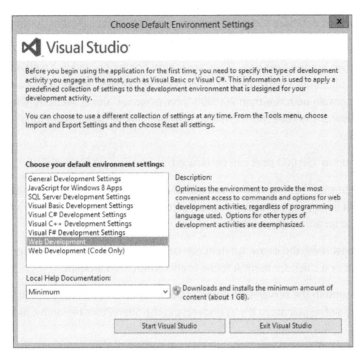

FIGURE 3-2 Choosing the default environment settings for Visual Studio 2012

Visual Studio 2012 is now fully installed; however, Visual Studio 2012 doesn't include the templates for SharePoint and Microsoft Office 2013 development. The Office Developer Tools for Visual Studio 2012 can be downloaded separately from *http://www.microsoft.com/web/handlers/ WebPI.ashx?command=GetInstallerRedirect&appid=OfficeToolsForVS2012GA*. After the installation is complete, you can open Visual Studio and either watch some of the introductory videos or start a new project.

Understanding the server-side object model

SharePoint's high-level architecture is based upon a hierarchy of components:

- The highest level is the *farm*. This is the collection of all physical and logical components that make up an environment.

- At the next level are the most important and most notable physical components, the *servers*. A small development farm can consist of a single server, whereas a large production environment can contain dozens of servers.

- The third level is the *web application*. Web applications are the highest level of logical component. Each web application has its own website in Internet Information Services (IIS). Most farms have between 2 and 10 web applications. Every farm has a Central Administration web application; without it the farm will not be supported or operational.

- The next level is the content database. Content databases are SQL databases that contain all of the data and many of the settings that are stored in site collections.

- Site collections themselves are the next level. They are logical containers within a web application. Within a site collection, a visual design, navigation, workflows, and policies can be shared. A farm should contain no more than 250,000 "non-personal" site collections. On top of the 250,000 non-personal site collections it is also possible to have 500,000 personal sites (also known as *my sites*).

- Within site collections, up to 250,000 sites can be created.

- Sites contain lists and libraries that are used to store files, documents, and items. Examples of libraries are a document library, a pages library, and a picture library. Examples of lists are a tasks list, a calendar, and an announcements list.

- This bring us to the lowest level, the items. An item can be a document, a picture, a page, a task, an announcement, or a calendar item. A folder is also considered an item.

This hierarchy can also be found in the server-side object model, in Microsoft.SharePoint.dll. The names of the objects are pretty self-explanatory if you understand the SharePoint hierarchy, as shown in Table 3-1.

TABLE 3-1 SharePoint server-side object model components and namespaces

SharePoint component	Server-side OM object	Namespace
Farm	SPFarm	Microsoft.SharePoint.Administration
Server	SPServer	Microsoft.SharePoint.Administration
Web application	SPWebApplication	Microsoft.SharePoint.Administration
Content database	SPContentDatabase	Microsoft.SharePoint.Administration
Site collection	SPSite	Microsoft.SharePoint
Site	SPWeb	Microsoft.SharePoint
List/library	SPList	Microsoft.SharePoint
Item	SPItem	Microsoft.SharePoint

The only thing that stands out when you compare the component names to the object names are the *SPSite* and the *SPWeb* objects. A site collection is represented by the *SPSite* object, and a site is an *SPWeb* object.

Listing 3-1 shows an example of how the objects that represent the SharePoint hierarchy can be used in a custom solution. Be aware that the example in Listing 3-1 is iterating through all objects in the farm, which is a very poor practice. The code in the listing only serves as an example to demonstrate the different objects. If you are using the server-side object model in a farm solution, the resources you can use are not limited or controlled by the system. By the time your solution has used all of the available resources, it's likely that you will have also brought down the entire farm. This means that building farm solutions using the server-side object model comes with a lot of power, but also with a lot of responsibility.

Iterating over SharePoint objects such as site collections, sites, lists, or items will seldom cause problems in a development environment. However, if you are creating a solution that iterates over SharePoint objects, try to estimate how many objects you will be iterating over in the production environment. Also consider how that may change over time—for instance, in a year from now. You might very well end up iterating over more objects than you can or should iterate over, especially if your code called synchronously, while a user is waiting for it. In that case, the best way to avoid this would be to build your solution so that you don't need the iteration, maybe using search instead. If that's not an option, you can create a (timer) job that runs at night when there are not as many users using the environment and cache the results in a custom database or XML file.

LISTING 3-1 An example of how to use the main objects that make up the SharePoint hierarchy

```
SPFarm farm = SPFarm.Local;
hierarchyInfo += "Farm: " + farm.Name + "</br></br>";
SPServerCollection servers = farm.Servers;

foreach (SPServer server in servers)
{
    hierarchyInfo += "Server: " + server.DisplayName + "</br>";
}

SPWebService service = farm.Services.GetValue<SPWebService>("");
foreach (SPWebApplication webApplication in service.WebApplications)
{
    hierarchyInfo += "<br>Web Application: " + webApplication.Name + "</br>";

    foreach (SPContentDatabase database in webApplication.ContentDatabases)
    {
        hierarchyInfo += "Content Database: " + database.Name + "</br>";

        foreach (SPSite site in database.Sites)
        {
            hierarchyInfo += "Site Collection: " + site.Url + "</br>";

            foreach (SPWeb web in site.AllWebs)
            {
                hierarchyInfo += "Site: " + web.Title + "</br>";

                foreach (SPList list in web.Lists)
                {
                    if (!list.Hidden)
                    {
                        hierarchyInfo += "List: " + list.Title + "</br>";
                        hierarchyInfo += "Items: " + list.ItemCount + "</br>";
                    }
                }
            }
            web.Dispose();
        }
        site.Dispose();
    }
}
```

In a sandboxed solution, you can only access objects that are within the boundaries of the site collection to which the solution is deployed. This means that you can use one *SPSite* object, the *SPSite* object that represents the site collection that the solution is deployed to. Within that site collection, you can iterate through the *SPWeb*, *SPList*, and *SPListItem* objects. Keep in mind, though, that a sandboxed solution is only allowed to consume a limited amount of resources. These resources are normalized to *Resource Points*. When the Resource Points of a specific site collection have been used up, all sandboxed solutions in that site collection are shut down until the Resource Points are reset. This happens once every 24 hours by default. This makes iterating through objects in a sandboxed solution a risky exercise, because it can quickly consume many of the available Resource Points. If the site collection that the solution is deployed to grows, it might use a lot of memory and cause issues not just for your solution, but also for other sandboxed solutions in that site collection. When you are designing and building a sandboxed solution, it is important to constantly be aware that the solution should minimize resource usage and ensure that the resources used are as predictable as possible, regardless of the size of the environment. The good news, though, is that you can't hurt the entire farm from a sandboxed solution—you will only affect the site collection.

Another thing that is crucial to understand when working with the server-side object model is that the original SharePoint objects are created in unmanaged code, in Component Object Model (COM). Some of the current objects are only wrappers around these COM objects, and because of that, they are not automatically disposed of. If you are using a lot of these objects—for example, when you're iterating through them—you will create a memory leak that can cause serious problems in your environment. The objects that we have to be worried about in the earlier example are the *SPSite* and *SPWeb* objects. We have to dispose of these objects in the solutions.

The code in Listing 3-1 disposes of the *SPSite* and *SPWeb* objects by using *SPSite.Dispose()* and *SPWeb.Dispose()*. It is also possible to leverage *Using* statements to make sure that objects are automatically disposed of. Because not all *SPSite* and *SPWeb* objects should be disposed of, it is important that you gain some understanding of when objects should be disposed of and when they shouldn't. A very extensive article on the subject can be found on MSDN (*http://msdn.microsoft.com/en-us/library/ ee557362.aspx*). This article was written for SharePoint 2010 but is still relevant for SharePoint 2013. There is also a tool that can help, SPDisposeCheck. You can run this tool against your code, or include the SPDisposeCheck rules in the static code analysis tool of your choice (for instance, FXCop) to check your code for memory leaks before you deploy it. Because SPDisposeCheck can occasionally report false positives, you should not just rely on the tool, you should also study the article to gain a good understanding of when objects should be disposed of.

Developing farm solutions

Now it's time to open up Visual Studio and create a new project. In this section, you will create a new Visual Studio project that will contain a SharePoint 2013 farm solution, a feature, some declarative elements, and a feature receiver. After that, you will make some changes to the solution and look at how to upgrade existing solutions and features.

Creating a SharePoint project in Visual Studio

Start a new project by clicking the New Project link on the left side of the screen. The next step is to select a project template. Depending on how you installed Visual Studio, you will be able to select different project templates for different types of projects and different programming languages. The SharePoint project templates are available in Microsoft Visual Basic and Microsoft Visual C#. By default, Visual Basic is selected; if you want to use Visual C# to create SharePoint solutions, you will have to select Visual C# and choose Office | SharePoint. This gives you the option to choose between Apps, Office Add-ins, and SharePoint Solutions. Select SharePoint Solutions and choose the SharePoint 2013 - Empty Project template, as shown in Figure 3-3. By choosing the empty project template you will give yourself maximum flexibility.

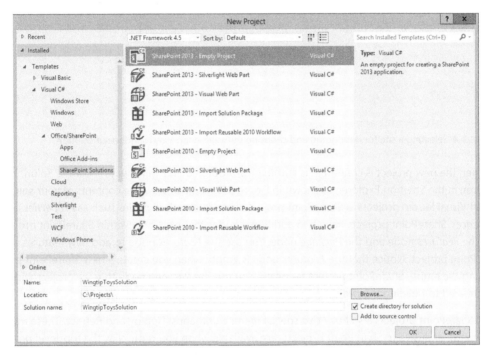

FIGURE 3-3 Creating a new SharePoint 2013 empty project

After you click OK, the SharePoint Customization Wizard starts (see Figure 3-4). From here you can choose a URL of the team site that Visual Studio will use as the URL of the site to which the solution will be deployed, and with which the solution can be debugged. When you enter the URL in the SharePoint Customization Wizard, you must provide the URL to a site that is accessible within the local SharePoint farm. The SharePoint Developer Tools use this site URL when testing and debugging the project. The wizard also allows you to choose between a sandboxed solution and a farm solution. WingtipToysSolution will be deployed as a farm solution to *http://wingtiptoys*. You will find that the solution really is rather empty after creation; it only contains the absolute basics.

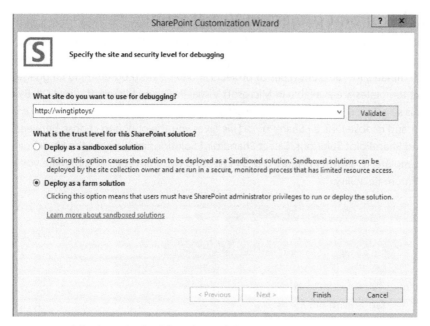

FIGURE 3-4 Selecting a site for debugging and choosing between a farm and sandboxed solution

When the new project is created, it is automatically opened and will always show the Solution Explorer. In the Solution Explorer, as shown in Figure 3-5, you can view the contents of your solution. Like all Visual Studio projects, a SharePoint project contains standard nodes such as *Properties* and *References*. SharePoint projects have two additional nodes that exist only within SharePoint projects: the *Features* node and the *Package* node. You use the *Features* node to add new features to a SharePoint project. Notice that the *Features* node is empty when you create a new SharePoint project by using the empty SharePoint project template. You use the *Package* node to track project-wide settings related to building the project into a SharePoint solution package, or .wsp file.

All SharePoint projects also have two special menu commands: Deploy and Retract. These menu commands, exclusive to SharePoint projects, are available when you right-click the top-level project node in the Solution Explorer. These two menu commands are shown in Figure 3-5. You can use the Deploy command to run a sequence of deployment steps that deploy the solution package to the local farm and the site that you selected in the customization wizard, so that you can test and debug your work. The Retract command reverses the act of deployment by retracting the solution package from the local farm and site.

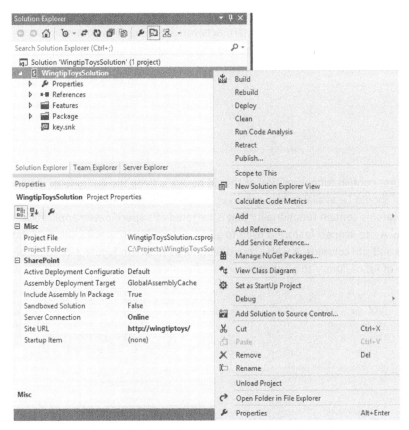

FIGURE 3-5 The Solution Explorer showing an empty SharePoint project

Designing your SharePoint solution: Features

You now have an empty SharePoint project and can start adding files to it. These files will create the actual functionality that the solution will provide. When you start adding SharePoint files into the solution, features will be added to the *Features* node automatically. For most files, a web-scoped feature will be created with the name *Feature 1*. Web-scoped means that the feature can be activated at the lowest level at which features can be activated, which is the subsite or *SPWeb* level. In all cases you will want to rename the feature so that the name of the feature describes what kind of functionality it contains. It is also a best practice to put the scope of the feature in the name. If you were deploying a custom contacts list, for instance, you could call the feature *Web-ContactsList*. A feature also has a title and a description. This is displayed in the user interface after deployment, so it should be something descriptive that will tell the person who is thinking about activating the feature what functionality will be added to the site when the feature is activated.

It is important to design the features that you use to add functionality properly. First of all, you have to determine what type of SharePoint files or artifacts you are creating in your solution, and in what scope these artifacts have to be activated. You can choose between the following scopes:

- Farm
- Web application
- Site
- Web

Farm-scoped features contain functionality that should be available in the entire farm. An example is a web template that should be available for users everywhere to create sites based on it. Web application–scoped features contain functionality that is targeted at a specific web application. An example is a timer job. A site-scoped feature is used to add functionality to specific site collections, such as content types and site columns. A web-scoped feature, as shown in Figure 3-6, could be used to add a custom type of list or library to a subsite.

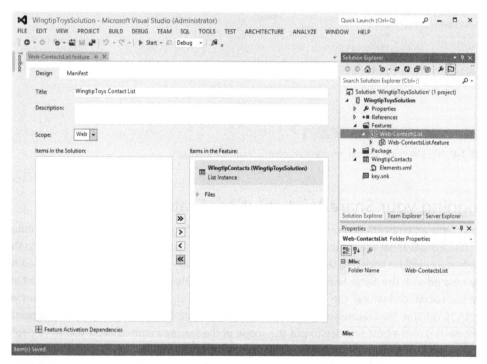

FIGURE 3-6 A solution containing a custom web-scoped feature that contains a list instance

When you are designing your solution and its features, it is important that you create the right amount of features for the right reasons. There is no magic number; as with everything related to SharePoint, the right amount of features *depends on* your solution. You will definitely need different features for functionality that has to be activated at a different scope. This is relatively easy to determine. Some SharePoint artifacts can only be activated at a specific scope. Content types and site columns, for instance can only be activated at the site collection level, so they will always be activated by using a site-scoped feature. Lists are a bit more difficult; they can be activated at the site collection or subsite level. It is up to you to determine whether you want the list to always be created in the root site of a site collection, or whether you want the list to be available on subsites as well. If you want users of subsites to be able to use the list, you can activate it by using a web-scoped feature. Farm-scoped and web application–scoped features can only be managed from Central Administration or by using Windows PowerShell. This means that they can only be activated or deactivated by SharePoint administrators who have access to the server. Site-scoped and web-scoped features can be activated by site collection administrators (site) or site owners (web).

When you have several features that can be activated at the same scope, think about whether you always want the artifacts to be activated and deactivated at the same time, as well as whether they should be updated at the same time, and whether the different artifacts are part of the same piece of functionality, or whether they are completely different things. For instance, site columns and content types, and master pages and style sheets, are often activated at the site collection level. Activating site columns and content types at the same time makes sense, and updates to both are often deployed at the same time. Master pages and style sheets, however, provide a completely different type of functionality (a custom look and feel for the site), and it's likely that when a column is added to the site, the visual design won't change. Similarly, when the visual design changes, that doesn't necessarily mean that the content types on the site collection would have to change. In this case, you would likely create two features:

- *Site-ColumnsAndContentTypes*

- *Site-WingtipToysDesign*

Try to make sure that the feature names have a reasonable length. If names get too long, it can cause problems with deployment.

Adding declarative elements

Let's add a list to the solution. You can do this by right-clicking the project node in the Solution Explorer and clicking Add and New Item. Next you can select the type of item to add to your solution. For this example, choose List and call it **WingtipContacts** (see Figure 3-7).

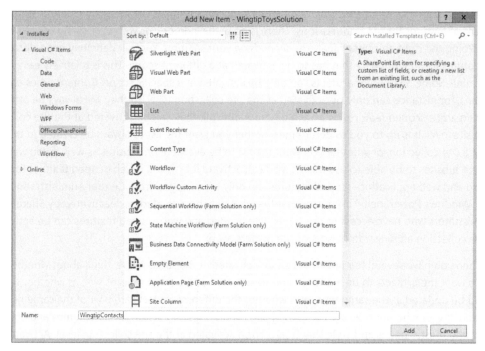

FIGURE 3-7 Adding a new list to the custom SharePoint solution

In the next dialog box, you can choose the display name of the list and whether you want the list to be *customizable* or *non-customizable*. You can also choose what type of list you want to base your custom list on.

If you create a customizable list, you will create a custom list definition and a custom list instance. With the custom list definition, you will be adding a new list template or a new type of list to the site. Users can use this custom list type to create their own list instances based on it. When you create a custom list definition, you choose a list type that you will use as a basis for your custom list type. Using this as a starting point, you can then add, remove, or modify columns and views that are created when a list instance is created based on your custom list definition. A custom list instance is also created when the feature that your list is part of is activated.

If you create a non-customizable list, you are only creating a custom list instance, based on the list type that you select as the basis for your custom list instance in Visual Studio. When the feature that the list instance is part of is activated, the list instance will be created on the site. In this example, you will be creating a non-customizable list, and thus a list instance (see Figure 3-8).

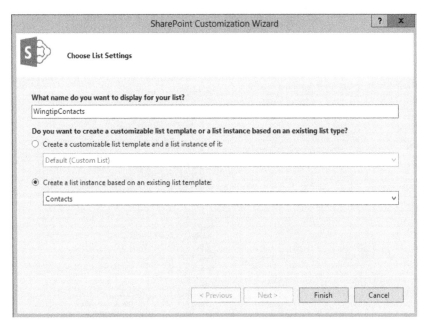

FIGURE 3-8 Creating a non-customizable list and selecting a base list type

After you add the list instance to the solution, a feature will be created. The feature will be called *Feature 1*, and it will be web scoped. The list instance will be added to the feature automatically. Rename the feature to **Web-ContactsList** and leave the scope at Web. If you are creating multiple SharePoint artifacts in the same solution and you want to use multiple features to activate the artifacts in your SharePoint environment, you will have to make sure that you manage your features properly. Whenever a new artifact is added to your solution, SharePoint will add it to a feature. This might not be the right feature, though. And even if you add your artifact to the right feature, it will not be automatically removed from any other features to which it was added, so make sure you actively check all features to make sure that they contain the right artifacts before you deploy your solution.

Figure 3-9 shows the designer view of the WingtipToys contacts list instance. Here you can fill in a title, description, and URL, and choose whether the list should be displayed on the Quick Launch bar on the left side of the screen and whether the list should be hidden or not. The title and description are seen by users who are working with the list, so make sure this is something they can relate to.

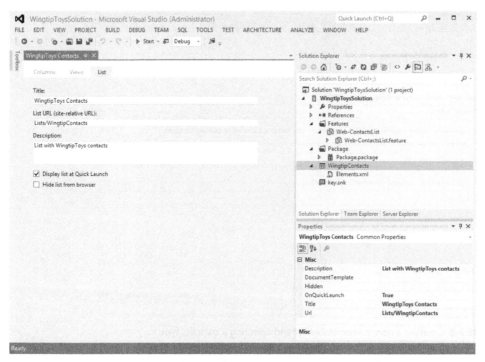

FIGURE 3-9 Solution containing a custom list instance and a single feature

Adding a feature receiver

Every feature can have a feature receiver added to it. You can use a feature receiver to write an event handler that will fire when a feature is activated or deactivated. For both events, you can choose whether to fire the event handler synchronously while the feature is being activated or deactivated, or whether to fire it asynchronously after the feature has been activated or deactivated. The code you write in these event handlers can access the SharePoint server-side object model, and it can use the properties to access and modify the site collection or site on which the feature is activated or deactivated. For example, you can write an event handler that fires during feature activation and performs routine initialization tasks such as creating new lists and adding list items. You can also extend the site by adding pages, navigation links, and Web Part instances.

To create a feature receiver, right-click the feature's top-level node and click Add Event Receiver. When you add an event receiver by using this technique, the SharePoint Developer Tools do quite a bit of work for you behind the scenes. First, they add a source file, which is based on either C# or Visual Basic, depending on the language of the underlying project. If you create a feature receiver for the feature named *Web-ContactsList*, the SharePoint Developer Tools create a C# source file named *Web-ContactsList.EventReceiver.cs*. The SharePoint Developer Tools also add configuration data behind the scenes that hooks up the feature receiver to the feature by adding the *ReceiverClass* and *ReceiverAssembly* attributes to the feature, so that SharePoint recognizes the feature receiver and so that the event handlers added to the feature receiver are executed at the correct times.

The source file created for the feature receiver contains a class definition for the feature receiver that inherits from the *SPFeatureReceiver* class. The feature receiver contains method stubs that are commented out that represent the events that you can handle. You simply uncomment the stubs and add your custom code. The SharePoint Developer Tools also add a special GUID attribute when creating a new feature receiver class, to give it a unique identifier. You shouldn't remove the GUID attribute from a feature receiver class, because the SharePoint Developer Tools use the GUID behind the scenes during the packaging process.

In the following example, you will add code for the *FeatureActivated* and *FeatureDeactivating* methods so that you can run custom C# code whenever the feature is activated or deactivated. Listing 3-2 shows the stubs for the different events for which you can create event handlers. Implementations have been created for the *FeatureActivated* and *FeatureDeactivating* events. When the feature is activated, a custom view is added to the *Project Contacts* list that shows a first name, last name, company, email address, and mobile phone number for a contact. The event handler also makes sure that the list is displayed on the Quick Launch bar on the left side of the screen. When the feature is deactivated, you remove the custom view and also remove the link to the list from the Quick Launch bar. Note that when the feature is deactivated, you can still access the list by browsing to the *Site Contents* page. SharePoint doesn't clean up by deleting the list that was created when the feature was activated. This is a good thing; if SharePoint deleted the list, users might lose data because the feature is deactivated. You should be aware of this yourself as well. Although using an event receiver to clean up after yourself is a good thing in almost all cases, you should make sure not to delete a user's data while cleaning up.

LISTING 3-2 A feature receiver class with implemented event handlers

```
using System;
using System.Runtime.InteropServices;
using System.Security.Permissions;
using Microsoft.SharePoint;
using System.Collections.Specialized;

namespace WingtipToysSolution.Features.Web_ContactsList
{
    /// <summary>
    /// This class handles events raised during feature activation,
    /// deactivation, installation, uninstallation, and upgrade.
    /// </summary>
    /// <remarks>
    /// The GUID attached to this class may be used during packaging
    /// and should not be modified.
    /// </remarks>

    [Guid("05a2eb8a-16e6-4cae-9cb1-4a181c94fd1e")]
    public class Web_ContactsListEventReceiver : SPFeatureReceiver
    {
        string _viewName = "Project Contacts";
```

```csharp
public override void FeatureActivated(SPFeatureReceiverProperties properties)
{
    SPWeb web = properties.Feature.Parent as SPWeb;
    SPList contactsList = web.GetList("/Lists/WingtipContacts");
    contactsList.OnQuickLaunch = true;

    SPViewCollection listViews = contactsList.Views;
    StringCollection viewFields = new StringCollection();
    viewFields.Add("FirstName");
    viewFields.Add("Title");
    viewFields.Add("Company");
    viewFields.Add("Email");
    viewFields.Add("CellPhone");

    listViews.Add(_viewName, viewFields, string.Empty, 30, true, true);
    contactsList.Update();
}


public override void FeatureDeactivating(SPFeatureReceiverProperties properties)
{
    SPWeb web = properties.Feature.Parent as SPWeb;
    SPList contactsList = web.GetList("/Lists/WingtipContacts");
    contactsList.OnQuickLaunch = false;

    SPView listView = contactsList.Views[_viewName];
    contactsList.Views.Delete(listView.ID);
    contactsList.Update();
}


}
}
```

Understanding the SharePoint root directory

The fundamental architecture of SharePoint Foundation relies on a set of template files that are stored in a special directory on the local file system of each SharePoint server. This folder is called the *SharePoint root directory*. On a SharePoint 2007 server, the name of this folder was 12; on a SharePoint 2010 server, it was 14. On a SharePoint 2013 server, the root folder is called 15, but you will find that all SharePoint 2013 servers also contain a 14 folder. This folder is used to make sure that site collections can run in *SharePoint 2010 mode*. When you run in SharePoint 2010 mode, a site collection on SharePoint 2013 looks like a SharePoint 2010 site. This is mainly useful when you are upgrading an environment from SharePoint 2010 to SharePoint 2013. Typically the root directory can be found at the following path:

C:\Program Files\Common Files\Microsoft Shared\Web Server Extensions\15

If you've installed only SharePoint Foundation and not SharePoint Server 2013, the SharePoint root directory contains a stock set of images, templates, features, and pages. If you install SharePoint Server 2013, the SharePoint root directory contains the same stock files for SharePoint Foundation and also a wealth of template files to provide additional functionality beyond that supplied by SharePoint Foundation.

When you are creating a SharePoint solution that is to be deployed as a farm solution, many of the types of template files that you add to your solution will be deployed in specific directories within the SharePoint root directory. Table 3-2 lists some of the more commonly used directories, along with the types of template files they contain.

TABLE 3-2 SharePoint solution file locations in the SharePoint root directory

Path relative to SharePoint root directory	Template file types
/ISAPI	Web services (.svc, .ashx, and .asmx)
/Resources	Resource files (.resx)
/TEMPLATE/ADMIN	Application pages used exclusively in Central Administration
/TEMPLATE/CONTROLTEMPLATES	ASP.NET user controls (.ascx)
/TEMPLATE/FEATURES	Feature files
/TEMPLATE/IMAGES	Images
/TEMPLATE/LAYOUTS	Application pages (.aspx)
/TEMPLATE/LAYOUTS/1033/STYLES	CSS Files (.css)
/TEMPLATE/LAYOUTS/ClientBin	CSOM files (.jz, .xap)

Several SharePoint artifacts that are part of the SharePoint Development Tools are deployed to the SharePoint root directory when a project is deployed, either by using Visual Studio or by using Windows PowerShell. For instance, features and the files that they contain are automatically deployed to the /TEMPLATE/FEATURES folder in the SharePoint root directory. You can also use Visual Studio to add files to the SharePoint root directory in a different way. When you right-click the project name and click Add, you can choose to add a mapped folder (see Figure 3-10). You can map a folder to any subfolder of the SharePoint root directory. When you add a file to a mapped folder in Visual Studio, the file will be deployed to the mapped directory in the SharePoint root directory when the solution isdeployed. The SharePoint Development Tools have made it easy by creating two shortcuts for creating mapped folders to the IMAGES and the LAYOUTS folders.

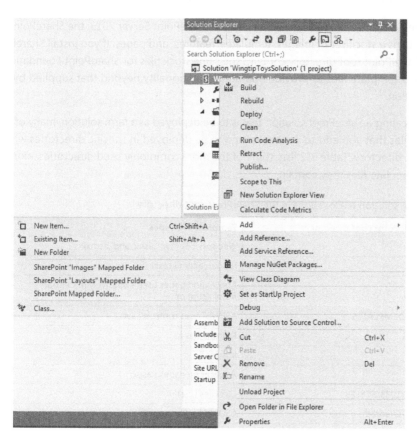

FIGURE 3-10 Adding mapped folders to a SharePoint solution in Visual Studio

You will now add an image to the example solution that you will deploy to the IMAGES directory in the SharePoint root directory. Just right-click the top-level project node in Solution Explorer, expand the Add menu, and click the SharePoint "Images" Mapped Folder command. After you've created the Images folder inside your project, you should be able to observe that the SharePoint Developer Tools automatically created a child folder with the same name as the current project. In this example, the SharePoint Developer Tools created an Images folder inside the project that contains a child folder named WingTipToysSolution, as shown in Figure 3-11. This child folder is added to make sure that you can never accidentally overwrite out-of-the-box SharePoint files or files deployed by using a different custom solution. It is a best practice to always use a namespaced subfolder when deploying files into the SharePoint root directory, and the Developer Tools make this an easy best practice to follow.

FIGURE 3-11 A mapped Images folder used to deploy files to the IMAGES folder in the RootFiles folder.

You can add custom image files to this folder, such as Contacts.png and SiteIcon.png, the ones shown in Figure 3-11. You can add files to a mapped folder by right-clicking the child folder (in this case, the one named WingTipToysSolution) and then clicking Add | Existing Items. When the resulting dialog box opens, you can navigate to the folder on your development workstation that contains the files you want, and select them to be copied into your mapped folder. You can also browse to the files you want to include in the solution by using Windows Explorer. You can then simply copy the files and paste them into the WingtipToysSolution folder by right-clicking the folder and choosing Paste. Mapped folders don't have to be added to features to be deployed; they are automatically deployed when the .wsp solution is deployed.

Deploying and debugging farm solutions

Now that you have a SharePoint project with a list, a feature, a feature receiver, and two images, it's time to package and deploy the solution.

If you expand the *Package* node in a SharePoint project, you'll find an inner node named *Package.package*. If you double-click this node, the SharePoint Developer Tools display the Package Designer. In the lower left-hand corner of the Package Designer are three tabs: Design, Advanced, and Manifest. These tabs allow you to switch back and forth between different views of the project's solution package. The Design view allows you to add features and files to the package. By default, all features and files that don't have the *NoDeployment* property set on them are added to the package by the Developer Tools. The Manifest view reveals the XML that is written into the manifest.xml file when the SharePoint Developer Tools builds the project into a solution package. In most scenarios, a developer doesn't need to inspect or care about the XML that goes into the manifest.xml file. After all, the SharePoint Developer Tools take care of creating the package for you.

In other scenarios, however, a developer will need to directly edit the manifest.xml file. For example, when you need to add an XML element that the SharePoint Developer Tools don't directly support, such as the *ActivationDependencies* element, you have to add it manually to manifest.xml.

If you look at the *Package* node in Solution Explorer in Figure 3-11, you'll notice a source file named Package.Template.xml. If you open this file, you'll find that it has a top-level *Solution* element but no inner elements. All you need to do is add the *ActivationDependencies* element to this file inside the *Solution* element. When the SharePoint Developer Tools generate the manifest.xml file, they merge the XML elements they create behind the scenes with any XML elements you have added to Package.Template.xml. By using this technique, you can call on your knowledge of SharePoint development to supplement what the SharePoint Developer Tools support directly.

When your solution is properly packaged up, you can deploy it. If you right-click the top-level project node inside Solution Explorer to display the shortcut menu, you'll find a Deploy command and a Retract command. You'll use these commands constantly when you test and debug SharePoint projects.

You might be wondering what happens when you execute the Deploy command. The answer is, *it depends*. More specifically, it depends on which deployment configuration your project is using. You can view and modify the available deployment configurations for a SharePoint project on the SharePoint tab of the project properties dialog box, as shown in Figure 3-12. Every new SharePoint project is created with two deployment configurations, Default and No Activation. You can add more deployment configurations if you want something different. However, you can't modify the Default and No Activation configurations. You can only modify deployment configurations you've added.

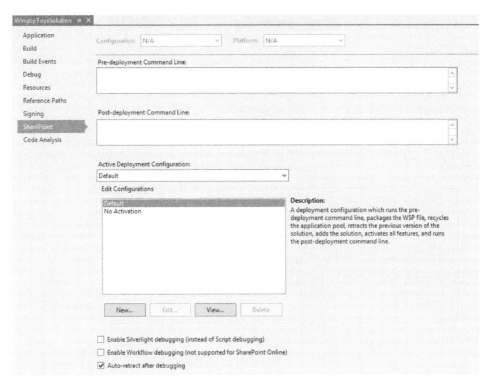

FIGURE 3-12 A SharePoint project's project properties dialog box showing deployment configurations

Notice the two text boxes on the SharePoint tab: Pre-Deployment Command Line and Post-Deployment Command Line. By using these text boxes, you can add command-line instructions that will execute either just before or directly after the active deployment configuration is processed. For example, you can add a command-line instruction to call a custom Windows PowerShell script. This ability to change or modify the deployment configuration for a SharePoint project provides a convenient degree of flexibility. The SharePoint Developer Tools allow you to control the processing that occurs behind the Deploy and Retract commands by using units of execution known as *deployment steps*.

To view the deployment steps within a specific deployment configuration, select that deployment configuration on the SharePoint tab and then click the View button. Figure 3-13 shows the sequence of deployment steps for the Default deployment configuration. First, the target IIS application pool is recycled. Then, any previous deployment of the solution package is retracted and removed. Next, the latest build of the project's solution package is installed and deployed. Finally, any project features that have a Scope setting of either Web or Site are automatically activated.

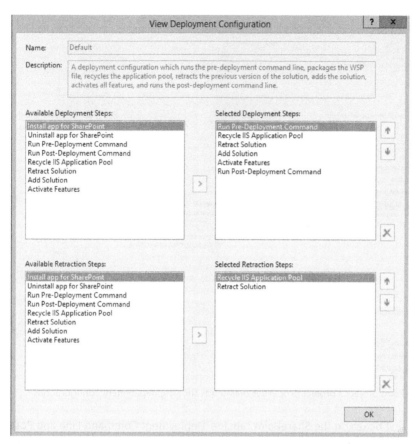

FIGURE 3-13 The deployment steps of the Default deployment configuration

On the left side of the View Deployment Configuration dialog box shown in Figure 3-13, there is a list of available deployment steps that come out of the box with the SharePoint Developer Tools. If you add a new deployment configuration, you can use this screen to add the steps you want in your custom deployment configuration.

To deploy your solution to your development server, all you have to do now is click the Deploy command. However, if you want to deploy your solution on a separate test server or even a production server, you need to get the .wsp solution package and move that to the server you want to deploy it to. When the Deploy or Publish command is run, the .wsp package is created and put in the bin\Debug or bin\Release folder of the project, depending on whether you have your build configuration set to Debug or Release. If you were to deploy your solution to a production environment, you should create a Release build by using Deploy or Publish. However, if you want to deploy to your development server and you want to test and potentially debug your solution, you should create a Debug build. When you've got the package, you can copy it to the server or farm you want to deploy it to and run the Windows PowerShell scripts from Chapter 2 to install it.

Go ahead and deploy your solution to your development environment by clicking the Deploy command. If you want to see how your code is executed, you can debug your solution. You will use debugging to step through the execution of the code-behind in your solution one line at a time. This can be useful if you are seeing issues you can't explain, or if you are seeing results you didn't expect. You can start debugging by pressing F5 or by opening up the Debug menu in Visual Studio 2012 and clicking Start Debugging, or you can attach your project to a process by clicking Attach To Process. Code that is called from the browser usually runs in the w3wp.exe process, so by attaching your project to the w3wp.exe processes, you can browse your SharePoint site as you normally would, and Visual Studio will hold execution when a breakpoint is hit. You can then go into your solution and step through your code to monitor exactly what happens during execution.

For the WingtipToysSolution example, you can use both approaches. Click Start Debugging. The solution will be rebuilt and deployed, and a new browser window will open with the site that you have set as the site the solution should be deployed to. Debugging will have to be enabled in the web.config of the site; if this is not yet the case, Visual Studio 2012 will prompt you about this and will offer to resolve it, as shown in Figure 3-14.

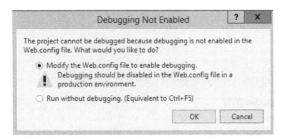

FIGURE 3-14 Visual Studio 2012 offering to enable debugging on the web application

The only code-behind in WingtipToysSolution is in the feature receiver, so you should set a breakpoint in the event receiver code. The breakpoints from Figure 3-15 will be hit when the feature is either activated or deactivated. You can then use F11 and F10, or Step Into and Step Over, to step through the code. You can check the values of individual objects and variables to make sure that these are what you expect them to be.

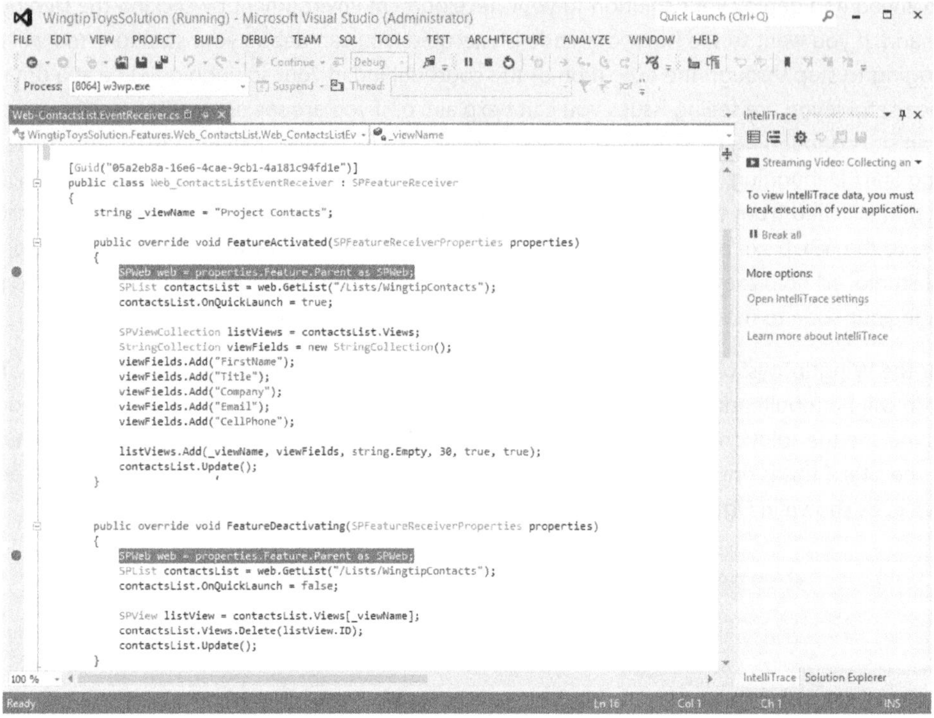

FIGURE 3-15 Debugging event receivers in Visual Studio 2012

Updating farm solutions

After one of your solution packages has been deployed in a production farm, you might need to up-date some of the files that have already been deployed. SharePoint supports the concept of updating a solution package. This technique allows you to replace existing files that have already been de-ployed, as well as to deploy new files that weren't part of the original solution package deployment.

For example, imagine a simple scenario in which WingtipToysSolution.wsp has already been deployed and its feature definition has been activated in several sites. What if, after the fact, Wingtip Toys decides that they want to add a custom document library to the solution as well? SharePoint makes it easy to accommodate this change. You can simply update your Visual Studio project by adding a document library and a feature. Then you can rebuild the solution package and run the *Update-SPSolution* cmdlet to deploy the updated solution:

```
$SolutionPackageName  = "WingtipToysSolution.wsp"
$SolutionPackagePath = "C:\Solutions\WingtipToysSolution.wsp"
Update-SPSolution -Identity $SolutionPackageName
                  -LiteralPath $SolutionPackagePath
                  -Local -GACDeployment
```

As you'll learn in the next section, using the technique of updating a solution provides the means to update a feature definition when you need to upgrade a feature. Updating a solution also provides a simple way to replace files and components with enhanced versions. For example, imagine that you need to fix a bug in the C# code you've written inside the *ActivateFeature* event handler, or you want to replace an existing image of a logo with a new one. You can simply update the code or the image and build a new version of the solution package. When you update the solution, the old copy of WingtipToysSolution.dll in the global assembly cache is replaced with the new copy, and the SharePoint worker process restarts to ensure that the new version gets loaded.

A lot of the things that you can do by updating a solution can also be done by retracting and reinstalling a solution, as long as you are not using the feature upgrade functionality described in the next section. Microsoft considers updating the solution to be a best practice at this point, though, and also enforces it when solutions are deployed to SharePoint Online dedicated environments.

There is currently no Upgrade command available to upgrade solutions directly from Visual Studio 2012. You could solve this by creating a new deployment configuration that doesn't contain the deployment steps for Retract Solution or Add Solution. Then you could add a Post-Deployment Command Line instruction call to a custom Windows PowerShell script that runs the *Update-SPSolution* cmdlet.

Another approach is to either create or find a custom deployment step that adds the functionality you need. This option is possible because the team that created the SharePoint Developer Tools designed deployment steps to be extensible. A developer can create a custom extension for Visual Studio 2012 and the SharePoint Developer Tools that adds custom deployment steps. Within the SharePoint developer community, Visual Studio extensions that extend the SharePoint Developer Tools with a custom deployment step for updating solutions—and much more—are already available.

Upgrading features

SharePoint Foundation supports feature activation at four different levels: site, site collection, web application, and farm. Whenever a feature definition is activated, SharePoint Foundation creates a feature instance that tracks metadata about the underlying feature definition. The feature instance tracks feature properties such as *Id, Title*, and *Version*. The *Version* property of a feature instance represents the current version of the feature definition at the time of activation. After you've pushed a feature definition into a production farm and it has been activated, you might be required to update it to deal with changing business requirements. You can define upgrade actions inside a feature definition that will be processed when a feature instance is upgraded to the new version. Upgrade actions can be created inside the feature.xml file by using declarative XML and can also execute custom event handlers written in C# or Visual Basic.

After you've updated a feature definition in a Visual Studio project such as WingtipToysSolution, you can rebuild the solution package and push the new version out into a production farm or a staging farm by using the *Update-SPSolution* cmdlet. However, pushing out a new version of a feature definition by using *Update-SPSolution* is only half the story.

The farm now has an updated feature definition, but all the existing feature instances are still based on a previous version of the feature definition. You have a couple of different options with regard to how to go about updating existing feature instances. You can either update feature instances one at a time by querying for the ones that need to be updated, or you can update all of them at the same time by running either the SharePoint Products Configuration wizard or PSConfig.

Updating a feature definition with upgrade actions

SharePoint Foundation tracks the version numbers for feature definitions by using a four-part number similar to version numbers for assemblies in the Microsoft .NET Framework. The initial version of the WingtipToys Contacts List feature had a version number of 1.0.0.0. This version number will have to be specified explicitly when the initial version of a feature is created, because by default it will be set to 0.0.0.0. All the sites in which the WingtipToys Contacts List feature has been activated also have version 1.0.0.0 feature instances.

The initial version of the WingtipToys Contacts List feature definition includes a single element manifest named elements.xml. This element manifest is referenced by using an *ElementManifest* element in the feature.xml file:

```
<Feature xmlns="http://schemas.microsoft.com/sharepoint/"
         Title="WingtipToys Contact List"
         Id="593228ab-7fcd-4a81-a4b8-ea77b2cbe1cc"
         Scope="Web">
  <ElementManifests>
    <ElementManifest Location="WingtipContacts\Elements.xml" />
  </ElementManifests>
</Feature>
```

Now you'll begin updating the Wingtip Contacts List feature definition. Start by incrementing the *Version* number. You can do this in the feature's property pane, as shown in Figure 3-16.

The next step is to add a new *ListInstance* element to the feature definition to create a Calendar along with the Contacts list, to store appointments in. You can add the calendar as a separate feature, or you could add the ListInstance XML for the calendar into the Contacts list element.xml file. Neither of these options would allow you to use the feature upgrade framework, though, and both would require you to come up with a solution to update existing instances or sites. Adding the XML into an existing elements.xml is not a recommended approach, but in certain scenarios, adding a different feature can be a valid option. In this case, however, you will want to use the feature upgrade framework, so in order to do that you will add a new element manifest file to the *Contacts List* feature. This element manifest will have to contain the elements that you want to provision during the upgrade process.

FIGURE 3-16 Updating the version number of a feature in the feature's property pane

To create the Calendar list instance, follow the same steps that you did for the Contacts list instance, but this time base your list instance on a Calendar list, instead of a Contacts list. The list instance will automatically be added to the feature, but it will only be created when the feature is activated. This means that the Calendar will not be created on sites that already have the first instance of the feature activated on them. To add the new Calendar list to sites that have the first instance of the feature activated on them, you have to modify the feature.xml file. You can do this by going to the Manifest tab of the feature in Visual Studio 2012 and displaying the Edit options. You can now add an *UpgradeActions* element inside the top-level *Feature* element. The *UpgradeActions* element can optionally contain a *VersionRange* element that defines a *BeginVersion* attribute and an *EndVersion* attribute. If no *VersionRange* is specified, the upgrade action will be applied to all instances of the feature, regardless of their version. Inside the *VersionRange* element (or the *UpgradeActions* element if no *VersionRange* is specified), you should add an *ApplyElementManifests* element with an inner *ElementManifest* element. By making the following modification to the feature.xml file, you can en- sure that SharePoint will inspect the Calendar's elements.xml file during the feature upgrade process for a site and provision the Calendar list (see Listing 3-3). Visual Studio and the SharePoint Developer Tools will merge the changes that you make with the generated feature.xml contents.

LISTING 3-3 Adding an element manifest file to the *UpgradeActions* element in the feature.xml file to upgrade existing feature instances

```xml
<Feature xmlns="http://schemas.microsoft.com/sharepoint/"
         Title="WingtipToys Contact List" Id="593228ab-7fcd-4a81-a4b8-ea77b2cbe1cc"
         ReceiverAssembly="WingtipToysSolution, Version=1.0.0.0, Culture=neutral,
                           PublicKeyToken=d829d679b4cb139f"
         ReceiverClass="WingtipToysSolution.Features.
                        Web_ContactsList.Web_ContactsListEventReceiver"
         Scope="Web"
         Version="2.0.0.0">
  <UpgradeActions>
    <VersionRange BeginVersion="0.0.0.0" EndVersion="2.0.0.0">
      <ApplyElementManifests>
        <ElementManifest Location="ContactsCalendar\Elements.xml" />
      </ApplyElementManifests>
    </VersionRange>
  </UpgradeActions>
  <ElementManifests>
    <ElementManifest Location="WingtipContacts\Elements.xml" />
    <ElementManifest Location="ContactsCalendar\Elements.xml" />
  </ElementManifests>
</Feature>
```

The updated version of feature.xml has two different references to ContactsCalendar\Elements.xml. The first reference is used when an older feature instance is upgraded to version 2.0.0.0. The second reference is used by SharePoint when a user activates the Wingtip Contact list feature definition in a site for the first time, using version 2.0.0.0. In this case, the feature instance is never upgraded, but the feature definition must still provision a Calendar list.

Adding code-behind custom upgrade actions

Earlier in this chapter, you saw how to extend a feature definition with a feature receiver by creating a public class that inherited from *SPFeatureReceiver*. In addition to the event handler methods you added, *FeatureActivated* and *FeatureDeactivating*, you will now add another event handler method, *FeatureUpgrading*, which must be overwritten to execute code during a custom upgrade action. The *FeatureUpgrading* event handler is a bit more complicated than the event handlers for *FeatureActivated* and *FeatureDeactivating*. When you add a feature receiver to a feature, the SharePoint Developer Tools will add *ReceiverAssembly* and *ReceiverClass* attributes to the *UpgradeActions* element, as shown in Listing 3-4. To add upgrade steps, you must add one or more *CustomUpgradeAction* elements inside the *UpgradeActions* element and optionally also inside a *VersionRange* element.

LISTING 3-4 Defining code-behind upgrade actions by adding a *ReceiverAssembly* and a *ReceiverClass* property to the UpgradeActions element and a *CustomUpgradeAction* to the feature.xml file

```
<Feature xmlns="http://schemas.microsoft.com/sharepoint/"
         Title="WingtipToys Contact List"
         Id="593228ab-7fcd-4a81-a4b8-ea77b2cbe1cc"
         ReceiverAssembly="WingtipToysSolution, Version=1.0.0.0, Culture=neutral,
                     PublicKeyToken=d829d679b4cb139f"
         ReceiverClass="WingtipToysSolution.
                     Features.Web_ContactsList.Web_ContactsListEventReceiver"
         Scope="Web"
         Version="2.0.0.0">
  <UpgradeActions
   ReceiverAssembly="WingtipToysSolution, Version=1.0.0.0, Culture=neutral,
     PublicKeyToken=d829d679b4cb139f"
   ReceiverClass="WingtipToysSolution.Features.Web_ContactsList.
   Web_ContactsListEventReceiver">
    <VersionRange BeginVersion="0.0.0.0" EndVersion="2.0.0.0">
      <CustomUpgradeAction Name="UpdateContactsListTitle">
        <Parameters>
          <Parameter Name="NewListTitle">New and improved Contacts</Parameter>
        </Parameters>
      </CustomUpgradeAction>
      <ApplyElementManifests>
        <ElementManifest Location="ContactsCalendar\Elements.xml" />
      </ApplyElementManifests>
    </VersionRange>
  </UpgradeActions>
  <ElementManifests>
    <ElementManifest Location="WingtipContacts\Elements.xml" />
    <ElementManifest Location="ContactsCalendar\Elements.xml" />
  </ElementManifests>
</Feature>
```

As shown in Listing 3-4, a *CustomUpgradeAction* element is defined with the *Name* attribute and a parameter collection, which here contains only a single entry. It is essential to understand that the *FeatureUpgrading* event handler will execute once for each *CustomUpgradeAction* element. If you don't add at least one *CustomUpgradeAction* element, the *FeatureUpgrading* event handler will never fire.

You can add as many *CustomUpgradeAction* elements as you want. When you implement the *FeatureUpgrading* event handler, you can use the parameter named *upgradeActionName* to determine which custom upgrade action is being processed, and you can use the argument-named parameters to retrieve the parameters defined by the currently processing custom upgrade action.

In this case, the only custom upgrade action is named *UpdateContactsListTitle*, and it contains a single parameter, *NewListTitle*. The implementation of the *FeatureUpgrading* event handler in Listing 3-5 uses a C# *switch* statement to execute the correct code for the custom upgrade action, named *UpdateContactsListTitle*. Notice how the implementation must retrieve the value for the *NewListTitle* parameter to properly update the list title.

LISTING 3-5 The *FeatureUpgrading* method, which executes once for each *CustomUpgradeAction* element

```
public override void FeatureUpgrading(SPFeatureReceiverProperties properties,
    string upgradeActionName,
    System.Collections.Generic.IDictionary<string, string> parameters)
{
    // perform common initialization for all custom upgrade actions
    SPWeb web= properties.Feature.Parent as SPWeb;

    if (web != null)
    {
        SPList contactsList = web.GetList("/Lists/WingtipContacts");

        // determine which custom upgrade action is executing
        switch (upgradeActionName)
        {
            case "UpdateContactsListTitle":

                //*** begin code for UpdateContactsListTitle upgrade action
                string newListTitle = parameters["NewListTitle"];
                contactsList.Title = newListTitle;
                contactsList.Update();
                //*** end for UpdateSiteTitle upgrade action

                break;
            default:
                // unexpected feature upgrade action
                break;
        }
    }
}
```

We've now walked through adding an *UpgradeActions* element to the feature.xml file to upgrade a feature instance from version 1.0.0.0 to version 2.0.0.0. Keep in mind that this structure of the *UpgradeActions* element provides a good deal of flexibility to help you deal with future updates. Consider the scenario of pushing out a version 3.0.0.0 update. You might need to upgrade some feature instances that are currently in version 1.0.0.0, in addition to feature instances that are in version 2.0.0.0. You can add multiple *VersionRange* elements to differentiate between these two scenarios. *VersionRange* elements are processed in the order in which they are specified. If *VersionRange* elements overlap, all upgrade actions that apply to a feature instance will be executed. In the following example, the first two actions will both be applied to feature instances that are currently on version 1.0.0.0:

```
<UpgradeActions>

  <VersionRange BeginVersion="1.0.0.0" EndVersion="2.0.0.0">
    <!-- upgrade actions for upgrading from version 1 to 2 -->
  </VersionRange>
```

```
<VersionRange BeginVersion="1.0.0.0" EndVersion="3.0.0.0">
  <!-- upgrade actions for upgrading from version 1 to 3 -->
</VersionRange>

<VersionRange BeginVersion="2.0.0.0" EndVersion="3.0.0.0">
  <!-- upgrade actions for upgrading from version 2 to 3 -->
</VersionRange>

</UpgradeActions>
```

Upgrading feature instances

After you've updated the feature definition, you must then push out the updated files by using the *Update-SPSolution* cmdlet, as shown earlier in the chapter. You're still not done, however, because you still have to make sure that all existing feature instances are updated as well. You can either update feature instances one at a time by querying for the ones that need to be updated, or you can update all of them at the same time by running the SharePoint Products Configuration wizard or PSConfig.

To run the SharePoint Products Configuration wizard, start it by selecting it from the Start menu if you are running Windows Server 2008 R2, or you can select the app tile if you are running Windows Server 2012. After the wizard is started, you can simply click Next until the end. Be aware, though, that running the wizard means that your SharePoint farm will temporarily be offline because the IIS sites and the SharePoint timer job will be reset. Microsoft also uses this approach to update existing features. This is one of the reasons why you always have to run the Configuration wizard or PSConfig after installing a SharePoint Cumulative Update (CU) or Service Pack (SP).

If you prefer a more gracious approach, you will have to put more effort into updating existing feature instances. You must run a query to find all the feature instances that need to be updated, and you must then call the *Upgrade* method on each feature instance to trigger the feature upgrade process. When the *Upgrade* method is called on a feature instance, SharePoint triggers the upgrade actions you've defined in your feature definition.

You can use the server-side object model to query for all the feature instances that require an upgrade. The *SPWebApplication* class exposes a *QueryFeatures* method that accepts the GUID identifier for a feature definition and returns all the associated feature instances. The *QueryFeatures* method has an overloaded implementation, which also allows you to filter the query based on whether the feature instance is up to date with the farm's current version of the feature definition. Here's a simple C# console application that executes a query to retrieve all feature instances requiring upgrade and explicitly calls the *Upgrade* method:

```
// get reference to target web application
Uri webAppUrl = new Uri("http://wingtiptoys");
SPWebApplication webApp = SPWebApplication.Lookup(webAppUrl);

// query web application for feature instances needing an upgrade
Guid featureDefinitionId = new Guid("593228ab-7fcd-4a81-a4b8-ea77b2cbe1cc ");
SPFeatureQueryResultCollection features =
  webApp.QueryFeatures(featureDefinitionId, true);
```

```
// enumerate through feature instances and call Upgrade
foreach (SPFeature  feature in features) {
  feature.Upgrade(true);
}
```

Although the C# code from the console application is easy to read and understand, it doesn't provide a practical way to upgrade feature instances in a production farm. It makes more sense to add
the equivalent code to a Windows PowerShell script. The Windows PowerShell script in Listing 3-6 has
been written to upgrade all the feature instances in the web application at *http://wingtiptoys*.

LISTING 3-6 A Windows PowerShell script that explicitly upgrades feature instances

```
Add-PSSnapin Microsoft.SharePoint.Powershell -ErrorAction "SilentlyContinue"
$WebAppUrl = "http://wingtiptoys"
$featureId = New-Object System.Guid
                    -ArgumentList "593228ab-7fcd-4a81-a4b8-ea77b2cbe1cc"

$webApp = Get-SPWebApplication $WebAppUrl
$features = $webApp.QueryFeatures($FeatureId, $true)

foreach($feature in $features){
  $feature.Upgrade($true)
}
```

Now that you've seen the entire process, let's summarize how feature upgrade works. Remember
that feature upgrade only makes sense in a scenario in which a feature definition has been deployed
and feature instances have already been created. The first step is to update the feature definition
to include one or more upgrade actions. The second step is to rebuild the solution package and
push the updates out into the farm by using the *Update-SPSolution* cmdlet. The final step is to run a
Windows PowerShell script or use another approach to trigger the upgrade process on specific feature
instances, or to run the SharePoint Products Configuration wizard to upgrade all feature instances.
When you trigger the upgrade process, SharePoint begins to process your upgrade actions.

Developing sandboxed solutions

Sandboxed solutions were introduced in SharePoint 2010. They are SharePoint solutions that are
packaged into .wsp files, just like farm solutions. They are deployed into the site collection Solution
Gallery by site collection administrators. When the code from a sandboxed solution is executed, it
runs in a partially trusted environment referred to as the *sandbox*. The sandbox has been designed
to bring greater stability to a SharePoint farm by restricting actions that could cause problems with
performance, security, or other areas. This stability is achieved by limiting the functionality accessible
to custom code solutions through the use of code access security (CAS) policies, by restricting access
to portions of the object model, by limiting the amount of resources that can be used by a sandboxed

solution, and by the fact that the code from a sandboxed solution runs in a different process than the SharePoint farm.

Prior to SharePoint 2010, the vast majority of custom code had to be deployed to the global assembly cache. Because of this, developers often operated with full trust in the SharePoint server not only to call any part of the object model, but also to access databases, web services, directories, and more. The result of this situation was that nearly all code in the farm ran with full trust and potentially with access to all data and functionality in SharePoint and to all resources on the SharePoint servers. The drawback of this approach is that the SharePoint farm was (and is) occasionally destabilized by custom code. In fact, the most common problem that Microsoft sees when they get a support call is poorly behaving custom code.

As an example, consider the case in which an intermediate-level SharePoint developer is writing a Web Part designed to aggregate all sites that a user has access to within the web application to display on the intranet home page. Suppose that the developer building the Web Part is unaware of fact that he should use search to get a list of all sites for a particular user, and instead he loops through all the sites in the web application. The developer will also have to use elevated privileges with the Web Part code to ensure that the Web Part can iterate through all sites without throwing access-denied errors for users who don't have access to all sites. This simple Web Part could easily destabilize the entire farm.

If there are many sites looping, through all of them will take a long time and use a lot of memory. If the developer is unaware that he will have to dispose of all *Microsoft.SharePoint.SPSite* and *Microsoft.SharePoint.SPWeb* objects, he will create a serious memory leak that will quickly destabilize the farm. If this simple Web Part is deployed to the global assembly cache, it will have no limitations on the resources it can consume. If the Web Part is then put on the home page of the portal, it could be hit by potentially thousands of users. It wouldn't be long before the farm was brought to a standstill because of low memory availability. This is not just a made-up example; this has brought down a large farm on its launch day in real life.

Part of the sandboxed solution capability has been deprecated in SharePoint 2013. Although the sandbox is still a great way to create declarative solutions by using Collaborative Application Markup Language (CAML), avoid creating new sandboxed solutions containing a lot of code-behind. Code-behind in sandboxed solutions will still work in SharePoint 2013, but because the sandbox is deprecated, there is no way to tell what will happen in future versions of SharePoint. If you have a choice, it would be better to use a SharePoint app. You don't always have a choice, though, because SharePoint apps have their own limitations, and you can't deploy farm solutions to a hosted environment such as SharePoint Online.

If you have to use code-behind in your sandboxed solution, it's worth trying to build it in a way that allows you to remove the solution without breaking your site. If you use code-behind to configure a site or a list, for instance, removing the solution won't break the configured site or list, so there is no real risk.

The following is a list of supported CAML elements that you can use in your declarative sandboxed solutions:

- *ContentType*
- *CustomAction*
- *Field*
- *ListInstance*
- *ListTemplate*
- *Module*
- *PropertyBag*
- *Receivers*
- *WebTemplate*
- *WorkflowActions*
- *WorkflowAssociation*

Understanding the sandbox execution environment

The sandbox is a separate process in which a SharePoint solution runs in isolation. This separate process exposes a subset of the *Microsoft.SharePoint* namespace that an assembly can call. Additionally, the process runs under a CAS policy that restricts programmatic access to any resource outside the sandbox. Enabling sandboxed solutions in a SharePoint farm is simple and can be done by starting the *SharePoint Foundation User Code Service* on the Central Administration\System Settings\Manage Services On Server page. The User Code Service is responsible for managing the execution of sandboxed solutions across the farm. Each server in the farm that will participate in hosting sandboxed solutions must have the User Code Service enabled. Generally, this service simply runs under the Farm account. If you have installed your SharePoint server by using a standalone installation, the User Code Service will run under the Network Service account. When this service is enabled, you can begin running sandboxed solutions.

Although the User Code Service is responsible for managing the execution of sandboxed solutions throughout the farm, several other components and processes are involved in the system. These components and processes include the *Execution Manager*, the *Worker Service*, and the *Worker Service Proxy*. Figure 3-17 shows an architectural diagram of the sandboxing system.

The sandboxing system uses a component named the Execution Manager to handle the loading and execution of sandboxed solution code. The Execution Manager runs within the IIS application pool and is responsible for making a call out to the User Code Service (SPUCHostService.exe) requesting that a sandboxed solution be loaded.

As stated earlier, the User Code Service can be running on many different servers in the farm. You specify load balancing execution across the servers in the farm through administrative settings in Central Administration\System Settings\Manage User Solutions. By using these options, you can choose to execute the sandboxed solution on the same server where the user request was made or on a dedicated set of servers. In either case, the User Code Service makes a request of the Worker Service (SPUCWorkerProcess.exe) to load the sandboxed solution.

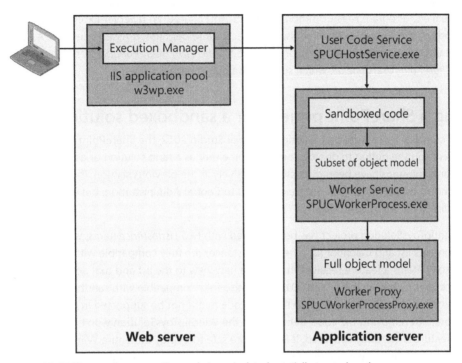

FIGURE 3-17 The sandbox executing code in an isolated, partially trusted worker process

After the assembly of a sandboxed solution is loaded into the Worker Service, its code can be executed. A pool of *AppDomains* is maintained within SPUCWorkerProcess.exe, and an available *AppDomain* is used to execute the request. Only one request at a time is executed in any *AppDomain*, so there won't be conflicts between the solutions.

As mentioned previously, execution of the code is limited to a subset of the *Microsoft.SharePoint* namespace and subject to CAS policy restrictions. Any calls to the SharePoint object model are first filtered against the subset object model to prevent any disallowed calls and then executed against the full object model, which runs in the Worker Service Proxy. When the code execution completes, the results are bubbled back up to the client request, which has been waiting synchronously for the request to complete. The final page is then drawn and delivered to the user.

If you know which processes are supporting the sandbox, you can debug your solutions. In a full-trust solution, you can debug code by attaching to the w3wp.exe process. However, sandboxed solutions are running in a separate process, so you must attach the Visual Studio 2012 debugger to the SPUCWorkerProcess.exe process instead. If you use F5 to debug your solution, Visual Studio will automatically attach to the right process.

The components that make up the sandboxing system can be found in the SharePoint System Directory at C:\Program Files\Common Files\Microsoft Shared\Web Server Extensions\15\UserCode. In this directory, you'll find SPUCHostService.exe, SPUCWorkerProcess.exe, and SPUCWorkerProcessProxy.exe. Along with the executables, you'll also find a web.config file that references the CAS policy restrictions, in the file C:\Program Files\Common Files\Microsoft Shared\Web Server Extensions\15\CONFIG\wss_usercode.config. Finally, this folder also contains a subfolder named Assemblies. The Assemblies folder contains the assemblies *Microsoft.SharePoint.dll, Microsoft.SharePoint.SubsetProxy.dll*, and *Microsoft.SharePoint.UserCode.dll*, which support the object model subset.

Creating a SharePoint project for a sandboxed solution

When you create a new SharePoint solution in Visual Studio 2012, the SharePoint Customization Wizard offers you the option to deploy your solution either as a farm solution or as a sandboxed solution. Farm solutions have been discussed extensively in the previous section. If you choose to create a sandboxed solution, it will not be deployed to Central Administration, but instead it will be deployed directly to a site collection.

The WingtipToysSolution project has been created with two *ListInstance* items, which are used to create a Contacts list and Calendar list. These list instances are fully compatible with the sandbox. The solution also contains a feature receiver that adds a new view to the list and that adds a link to the list to the Quick Launch bar. In SharePoint 2013 this is also fully compatible with sandboxed solutions. In future versions of SharePoint, the feature receiver code might not be supported in a sandboxed solution anymore, but removing the code-behind from the WingtipToysSolution won't break any sites on which the feature is currently activated. It is therefore safe to deploy the entire WingtipToysSolution as a sandboxed solution. If you are building the solution from scratch, though, you might want to try and find a different solution for the feature receiver to avoid possible rework on the solution in the future. To convert the WingtipToysSolution from a farm solution to a sandboxed solution, all you have to do is change the *Sandboxed Solution* property of the project in the project property pane from *False* to *True*.

Now it's time to walk through an example of creating a sandboxed solution. You'll start again by creating an empty SharePoint project, naming it *WingtipToysSandbox*. When you click OK to create the new project, the Visual Studio SharePoint Customization Wizard allows you to select Deploy As A Sandboxed Solution, as shown in Figure 3-18.

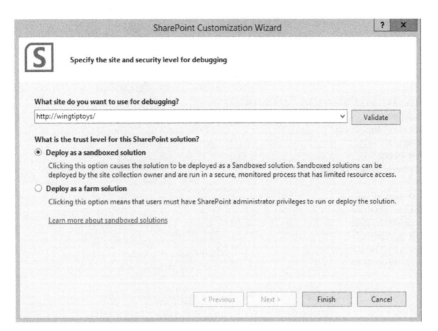

FIGURE 3-18 Creating a sandboxed solution

After you create the project in Visual Studio, you can alter the deployment target by editing the *Sandboxed Solution* property of the project in the project property pane. Along with changing the deployment target, the *Sandboxed Solution* property also determines whether the *System.Security.AllowPartiallyTrustedCallers* attribute appears in the *AssemblyInfo* file. By default, assemblies targeting the sandbox have this attribute and assemblies targeting the farm do not.

From the perspective of Visual Studio, there is no difference between a sandboxed solution and a farm solution. Both solutions are packaged and built in exactly the same manner. The differences are strictly related to the deployment target and the functionality that you can use in the solution. If you do try to use functionality that is not available in a sandboxed solution, Visual Studio will throw an error when it tries to compile the solution.

Now you will add a custom content type and a custom site column to the WingtipToysSandbox solution. The content type is called *Toys* and will be added to a list that will contain a list of toys. The site column that will be added to the content type is *Age Group*, indicating what age group the toys are suitable for. Both the content type and the site column will be added to a site by using a single site collection–scoped feature called *Site-WingtipContentTypes*. Listing 3-7 shows the content type, and Listing 3-8 shows the site column. The structure of the solution and the *Sandboxed Solution* property of the project are displayed in Figure 3-19.

LISTING 3-7 The XML used to create a custom site column

```xml
<?xml version="1.0" encoding="utf-8"?>
<Elements xmlns="http://schemas.microsoft.com/sharepoint/">
  <Field
      ID="{742e3245-a013-4537-82d3-727ddbfb981a}"
      Name="AgeGroup"
      DisplayName="Age Group"
      Type="Choice"
      Required="TRUE"
      Group="WingtipToys Columns">
    <CHOICES>
      <CHOICE>0-1</CHOICE>
      <CHOICE>1-3</CHOICE>
      <CHOICE>3-6</CHOICE>
      <CHOICE>6-9</CHOICE>
      <CHOICE>9-12</CHOICE>
      <CHOICE>12+</CHOICE>
    </CHOICES>
  </Field>
</Elements>
```

LISTING 3-8 The XML used to create a custom content type

```xml
<?xml version="1.0" encoding="utf-8"?>
<Elements xmlns="http://schemas.microsoft.com/sharepoint/">
  <!-- Parent ContentType: Item (0x01) -->
  <ContentType ID="0x01007E6057B85C8A465D9A695CC2E60AB705"
               Name="Toys"
               Group="WingtipToys Content Types"
               Description="Content type used to store information about toys"
               Inherits="TRUE"
               Version="0">
    <FieldRefs>
      <FieldRef ID="{742e3245-a013-4537-82d3-727ddbfb981a}"
                DisplayName="Age Group"
                Required="TRUE"
                Name="AgeGroup" />
    </FieldRefs>
  </ContentType>
</Elements>
```

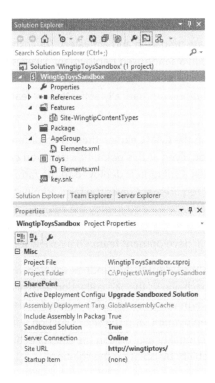

FIGURE 3-19 Solution Explorer and project properties of a sandboxed solution project in Visual Studio

Deploying and debugging sandboxed solutions

When the *Sandboxed Solution* property is set to *True*, selecting Build | Deploy Solution deploys the solution to the site collection's Solution Gallery. This new gallery is the repository for all sandboxed solutions uploaded within the site collection. You can access the gallery from the Site Settings page, in the Galleries area, by using the Solutions link. Figure 3-20 shows the Solution Gallery with the uploaded solution.

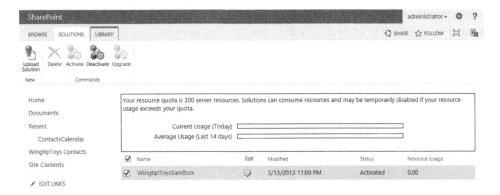

FIGURE 3-20 The Solution Gallery allowing a site collection owner to upload and activate a sandboxed solution

Keep in mind that there is a terminology difference between the two deployment methods. Farm solutions are installed and deployed. Sandboxed solutions are uploaded and activated. The installation step in a farm deployment is similar to the upload step in a sandboxed deployment. Likewise, the deploy step in a farm deployment is similar to the activate step in a sandboxed deployment. The one notable difference is that the activation of a sandboxed solution automatically activates any feature scoped to the level of the site collection.

For the content type and site column elements defined in the CAML earlier, there is no difference in behavior between a sandboxed solution or a farm solution. Even at this point, however, you can notice a significant difference in the deployment process. When a solution is deployed to the farm-level gallery, the farm administrator must become involved. This requirement gives the farm administrator significant control over the solution, but he will also have to make time to deploy the solution and can be called responsible for a solution that is being deployed to the farm. Because of that, he should review the solution, or have someone other than the original development team do a review for him.

A SharePoint solution designed for the sandbox, such as the WingtipToysSandbox solution, doesn't require farm-level deployment. Instead, the sandbox approach allows the site collection administrator to upload the solution and deploy it without involving the farm administrator. The farm administrator is thus relieved from the burden of dealing with solution deployment, and the site collection administrator is empowered to make decisions regarding the functionality available in the site collection. Furthermore, the sandbox is protecting the farm from instability by isolating the solution.

Because a site collection administrator can upload and activate a sandboxed solution, it is very difficult, if not impossible, for a farm administrator to keep track of what sandboxed solution is deployed where. It might be useful for the administrator to know this, though, so that she can identify sandboxed solutions that are deployed in a lot of sites and that might have to be rebuilt as farm solutions to reduce maintenance; or if a farm has to be upgraded to a new version of SharePoint, so that she can warn site collection administrators that their sandboxed solutions might not work anymore after the upgrade.

To solve this problem, you can create a custom solution validator that runs whenever a solution is activated within a site collection. Your custom solution validator can write some information about the activated sandboxed solution to a dedicated list somewhere in the SharePoint environment. Validators can also be used to do some testing on a solution that is being activated and can help you decide whether you want to allow or prohibit a solution. For example, you can decide to allow only sandboxed solutions with assemblies that have been compiled by using your company's private signing key.

To develop a validator, you create a class that inherits from *Microsoft.SharePoint.UserCode. SPSolutionValidator*. The *SPSolutionValidator* class in turn inherits from the *Microsoft.SharePoint. Administration.SPPersistedObject* class, which means that *SPSolutionValidator* can serialize its state into the SharePoint database. The impact of this capability is that you can use a generic *List<string>* collection to store any information you want to support validation. For example, you could use this approach to store information about known bad publishers.

When you inherit from the *SPSolutionValidator* class, you must provide a *System.Runtime. InteropServices.Guid* for your validator that is surfaced as the *ProviderID* property of the validator. Your validator must provide a default constructor that takes no arguments, as well as a constructor that takes a *Microsoft.SharePoint.UserCode.SPUserCodeService* object. In the second constructor, you must set the *Signature* property to a unique value. Listing 3-9 shows a basic validator class with constructors.

LISTING 3-9 A listing showing that a solution validator class must inherit from *SPSolutionValidator*

```
[Guid("D1735DCC-141F-4F1A-8DFE-8F3F48DACD1F")]
public class SimpleSolutionValidator : SPSolutionValidator {
    [Persisted]
    List<string> allowedPublishers;

    private const string validatorName = "Simple Solution Validator";

    public SimpleSolutionValidator() { }
    public SimpleSolutionValidator(SPUserCodeService userCodeService)
        : base(validatorName, userCodeService) {
        this.Signature = 5555;
    }
}
```

After coding the basic class and constructors, you must override the *ValidateSolution* and *ValidateAssembly* methods. *ValidateSolution* is called once for each solution, and *ValidateAssembly* is called once for each assembly within each solution. The *ValidateSolution* method receives a *SPSolutionValidationProperties* object, which contains information about the solution. The *Validate-Assembly* method receives a *SPSolutionValidationProperties* object as well, but it also receives a *SPSolutionFile* object with additional information about the assembly being validated. Listing 3-10 shows the *ValidateSolution* and *ValidateAssembly* methods, which for the sake of this demonstration are simply checking whether the name of any file in the solution or assembly begins with the string *"Bad_"*. If any file begins with this string, the file fails validation.

LISTING 3-10 A solution validator preventing a sandboxed solution from activating by setting the *isValid* property to *false*

```
public override void
  ValidateSolution(SPSolutionValidationProperties properties) {
    base.ValidateSolution(properties);
    bool isValid = true;

    //Check the name of the package
    if (properties.PackageFile.Location.StartsWith("Bad_",
                            StringComparison.CurrentCultureIgnoreCase)) {
        isValid = false;
    }

    //Look at the files in the package
    foreach (SPSolutionFile file in properties.Files) {
        if (file.Location.StartsWith("Bad_",
                                StringComparison.CurrentCultureIgnoreCase))
            isValid = false;
    }

    //set error handler
    properties.ValidationErrorMessage = "Failed simple validation.";
    properties.ValidationErrorUrl =
        "/_layouts/Simple_Validator/ValidationError.aspx?SolutionName="
      + properties.Name;
    properties.Valid = isValid;
}

public override void ValidateAssembly(
    SPSolutionValidationProperties properties, SPSolutionFile assembly) {
    base.ValidateAssembly(properties, assembly);
    bool isValid = true;

    //Check the name of the assembly
    if (assembly.Location.StartsWith("Bad_",
                StringComparison.CurrentCultureIgnoreCase))
        isValid = false;

    //set error handler
    properties.ValidationErrorMessage = "Failed simple validation.";
    properties.ValidationErrorUrl =
            "/_layouts/Simple_Validator/ValidationError.aspx?SolutionName="
        + properties.Name;
    properties.Valid = isValid;
}
```

When a solution fails validation, you can elect to display an error page. The *ValidationErrorMessage* and *ValidationErrorUrl* properties are used to set the values for handling validation errors. Typically, you simply create an application page in the LAYOUTS directory that is called when validation fails.

Before a custom solution validator can be used, it must be registered with the farm. This means that you can't deploy any custom solution validators to a cloud-hosted environment to which you cannot deploy a farm solution. To register the validator with the farm, you use a feature receiver in a farm-level feature. In fact, it's best to package the custom validator, application page, and feature receiver into a single feature. This way, the farm administrator can simply activate a single farm-level feature and the validator will be active. Listing 3-11 shows a feature receiver for registering and un-registering a custom validator.

LISTING 3-11 A feature receiver used to register a solution validator

```
public class FeatureEventReceiver : SPFeatureReceiver {
  public override void
    FeatureActivated(SPFeatureReceiverProperties properties) {
    SPUserCodeService userCodeService = SPUserCodeService.Local;
    SPSolutionValidator validator =
        new SimpleSolutionValidator(userCodeService);
    userCodeService.SolutionValidators.Add(validator);
  }

  public override void
    FeatureDeactivating(SPFeatureReceiverProperties properties) {
    SPUserCodeService userCodeService = SPUserCodeService.Local;
    SPSolutionValidator validator =
        new SimpleSolutionValidator(userCodeService);
    userCodeService.SolutionValidators.Remove(validator.Id);
  }
}
```

If after deployment of your sandboxed solution you want to debug the solution, you can use F5 or open up the Debug menu in Visual Studio 2012 and click Start Debugging. You can also attach your project to the process that the solution runs in by clicking Attach To Process and then selecting the SPUCWorkerProcess.exe process. From that point on, debugging a sandboxed solution is exactly the same as debugging a farm solution. The only difference is the process in which the solution runs.

Updating and upgrading sandboxed solutions

Just as with farm solutions, you might want to make changes to a sandboxed solution after it has been deployed and after features from it have been activated on sites. Sandboxed solutions and the features in them can be upgraded, just like farm solutions and features. The way upgrading the solutions and features works is a bit different for sandboxed solutions, though.

Let's start by creating a feature upgrade action for the *Toys* content type that you created earlier. You will add an extra column to the content type to store the price of the toys. Listing 3-12 shows the XML for the new site column. You have to add a new site column to the solution or a new elements file to the AgeGroup site column to ensure that you can add the column when upgrading existing instances of the feature.

LISTING 3-12 A custom site column

```
<Field
        ID="{f75c27ba-e321-4bbe-a30b-be0e085a5517}"
        Name="ToysPrice"
        DisplayName="Price"
        Type="Currency"
        LCID="1033"
        Decimals="2"
        Required="TRUE"
        Group="WingtipToys Columns">
   </Field>
```

Next you will add the new column to the *Toys* content type. You can add the column to the elements.xml file directly by modifying the XML, or you can use the designer and simply select the new Price column, as shown in Figure 3-21.

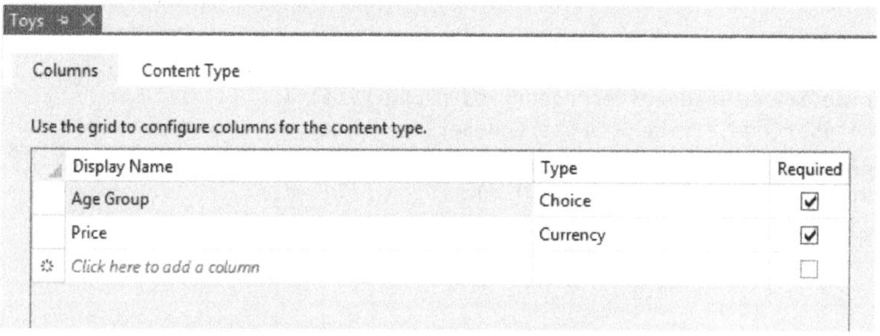

FIGURE 3-21 Using the designer view to add a new site column to a content type in Visual Studio

By doing this you have ensured that new instances of the *Site-WingtipContentTypes* feature will add both columns to the *Toys* content type. However, in order to make sure you can add the new column to existing instances of the feature and content type as well, you have to first increase the version number of the *Site-WingtipContentTypes* feature.

Next you can add *UpgradeActions* to the feature. Just as when you were upgrading a farm solution, you will use a *VersionRange* and an *ApplyElementManifests* element. This time, you will also use the *AddContentTypeField* element to add the new *Price* field to existing instances of the content type. Listing 3-13 contains the complete XML of the *Site-WingtipContentTypes* feature.

LISTING 3-13 A feature that uses the *UpgradeActions* and *AddContentType* elements to add a new content type to existing instances

```xml
<Feature xmlns="http://schemas.microsoft.com/sharepoint/"
  Title="WingtipToysSandbox WingtipToys Content Types"
  Description="This feature contains the WingtipToys
              Content Types and Site Columns"
  Id="d531e843-9706-48d1-bd38-bae81c916ec7"
  Scope="Site"
  Version="2.0.0.0">
  <UpgradeActions>
    <VersionRange EndVersion="2.0.0.0">
      <ApplyElementManifests>
        <ElementManifest Location="Price\Elements.xml" />
      </ApplyElementManifests>
      <AddContentTypeField
        ContentTypeId="0x01007E6057B85C8A465D9A695CC2E60AB705"
        FieldId="{f75c27ba-e321-4bbe-a30b-be0e085a5517}"
        PushDown="TRUE" />
    </VersionRange>
  </UpgradeActions>
  <ElementManifests>
    <ElementManifest Location="AgeGroup\Elements.xml" />
    <ElementManifest Location="Toys\Elements.xml" />
  </ElementManifests>
</Feature>
```

The solution is now ready to be deployed. Upgrading a sandboxed solution is accomplished by creating a new solution (.wsp) file with a different name than the previous version, but with the same solution ID. When you subsequently deploy the new solution version by uploading it into the Solution Gallery of a site collection, SharePoint will recognize that the ID matches an existing solution and prompt you to upgrade the solution. After the solution is upgraded, the old solution is automatically deactivated. Unlike upgrading farm solutions, upgrading sandboxed solutions doesn't require any additional steps such as upgrading feature instances using *SPFeature.Upgrade* or running PSConfig.

Testing the upgrade of your sandboxed solution from Visual Studio requires some additional configuration steps. First you have to create a new *deployment configuration* by opening up the properties of the project and going to the SharePoint tab. Click the New button and call the new deployment configuration **Upgrade Sandboxed Solution**. The previous version of the solution must be in the Solution Gallery when you upload the new version of the solution, so you don't want to retract the solution. All you need is the Add Solution step in the deployment steps, as shown in Figure 3-22. The next step to enable upgrading of your sandboxed solution is to double-click Package and to adjust the name of the package; for instance, by adding *v2* to it.

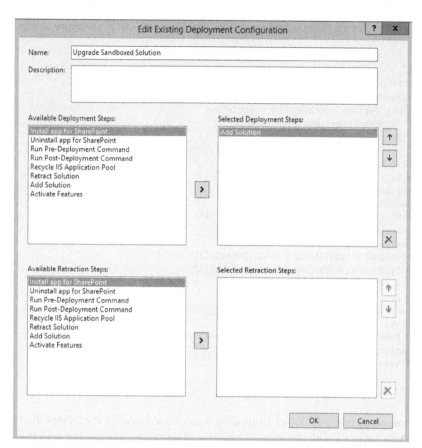

FIGURE 3-22 The deployment steps of the Upgrade Sandboxed Solution deployment configuration

Now you can right-click the project and click Deploy. This will automatically deactivate the previous version of the solution and activate the new version (see Figure 3-23). It will also automatically upgrade all existing instances of the feature in the site collection. Note that this behavior is different from the feature upgrade behavior of a farm solution, where you have to explicitly upgrade existing instances of the feature after a new version of a solution has been deployed.

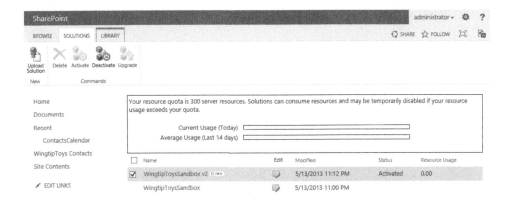

FIGURE 3-23 The Solution Gallery containing the previous and the new versions of the sandboxed solution

Summary

When you are developing SharePoint solutions, there are innumerable options to customize your SharePoint environment. You can add functionality to it by creating farm solutions or sandboxed solutions.

Farm solutions are deployed to Central Administration and are available in the entire farm. Deploying a farm solution requires farm administrator access and access to at least one of the SharePoint servers in the farm. Code from a farm solution can run under full trust permissions and can use as many resources as there are available in the farm. This means that creating farm solutions gives you great power, but with that great power comes great responsibility. A badly built farm solution could bring down an entire SharePoint farm.

Sandboxed solutions are deployed to a site collection's Solution Gallery, and functionality from them is only available in the site collection in which it is deployed. A sandboxed solution can also only access data and objects from within the site collection. The amount of resources that a sandboxed solution can consume is limited by the number of resource points that are assigned to a site collection. Using code-behind in sandboxed solutions is deprecated in SharePoint 2013. This means that although you can still use sandboxed solutions with code-behind in them and they will work fine, if you are creating new sandboxed solutions, the use of code-behind is discouraged. It would be better to try to find an alternative. Sandboxed solutions will provide the developer with less flexibility and power, but they will prevent that developer from bringing down the SharePoint farm.

## CHAPTER 4

SharePoint apps

Let's begin with a bit of history so that you can understand why and how the Microsoft SharePoint app model came about. It was back with SharePoint 2007 that Microsoft first invested in transforming SharePoint technologies into a true development platform by introducing features and farm solutions. With the release of SharePoint 2010, Microsoft extended the options available to developers by introducing sandboxed-solution deployment as an alternative to farm-solution deployment. With SharePoint 2013, Microsoft has now added a third option for SharePoint developers with the introduction of SharePoint apps.

When developing for SharePoint 2013, you must learn how to decide between using a farm solution, a sandboxed solution, or a SharePoint app. To make this decision in an informed manner, you must learn what's different about developing SharePoint apps. As you will learn in this chapter, SharePoint app development has several important strengths and a few noteworthy constraints when compared to the "old school" approach of developing SharePoint solutions for SharePoint 2010.

As you begin to get your head around what the new SharePoint app model is all about, it's helpful to understand one of Microsoft's key motivations behind it. SharePoint 2007 and SharePoint 2010 have gained large-scale adoption worldwide and have generated billions of dollars in revenue, primarily from the companies and organizations that have installed SharePoint on their own hardware in an *on-premises farm*. And whereas previous versions of SharePoint have been very successful products with respect to all these on-premises farms, Microsoft's success and adoption rate in hosted environments such as Microsoft Office 365 have been far more modest.

The release of SharePoint 2013 represents a significant shift in Microsoft's strategy for evolving the product. Microsoft's focus is now on improving how SharePoint works in the cloud, and especially with Office 365. Microsoft's primary investment in SharePoint 2013 has been to add features and functionality that work equally well in the cloud and in on-premises farms.

Understanding the new SharePoint app model

The move from SharePoint solutions development to SharePoint app development represents a significant change in development technique and perspective. However, Microsoft is not making this change just for the sake of making a change; there are very valid technical reasons that warrant such a drastic shift in the future of the SharePoint development platform.

To fully understand Microsoft's motivation for beginning to transition away from SharePoint solutions to the new SharePoint app model, you must first understand the challenges presented by SharePoint solutions development. Therefore, this section begins by describing the limitations and constraints imposed by SharePoint solution development. After that, the discussion turns to the design goals and architecture of the new SharePoint app model and addresses how this architecture improves upon the limitations and constraints imposed by SharePoint solution development.

Understanding SharePoint solution challenges

The first issue with SharePoint solutions development is that most of the custom code written by developers runs within the SharePoint host environment. For example, managed code deployed in a farm solution runs within the main SharePoint worker process (w3wp.exe). Managed code deployed by using a sandboxed solution runs within the SharePoint sandboxed worker process (SPUCWorker-Process.exe).

There are two primary reasons why Microsoft wants to change this behavior to no longer allow custom code to run within the SharePoint environment. The first reason has to do with increasing the stability of SharePoint farms. This one should be pretty obvious. Eliminating any type of custom code that runs within the SharePoint environment results in lower risk, fewer problems, and greater stability for the hosting farm.

The second reason has to do with the ability to upgrade an on-premises farm to newer versions of SharePoint. SharePoint solutions are often developed with full trust and perform complex operations. These solutions are often tightly bound to a particular feature set, which means that they might not move gracefully to the next version of SharePoint. Fearing the necessity of performing a complete rewrite of dozens of solutions, many customers have delayed upgrading their SharePoint farms.

Because many SharePoint customers have postponed the upgrade of their production on-premises farms for months, and sometimes years, until they have had time to update their SharePoint solution code and test it against the new version of Microsoft.SharePoint.dll, it was high on the priority list of issues to address when Microsoft began to design SharePoint 2013.

Another significant challenge with SharePoint solution development has to do with security and permissions. The root issue is that code always runs under the identity and with the permissions of a specific user. As an example, think about the common scenario in which a site administrator activates a feature from a SharePoint solution that has a feature receiver. There is a security issue in that a SharePoint solution with a feature receiver is able to execute code that can do anything that the site administrator can do. There really isn't a practical way to constrain the SharePoint solution code so that it runs with a more restricted set of permissions than the user who activated the feature has.

Most SharePoint professionals are under the impression that code inside a sandboxed solution is constrained from being able to perform attacks. This is only partially true. The sandbox protects the farm and other site collections within the farm, but it does not really protect the content of the site collections in which a sandboxed solution is activated. For example, there isn't any type of enforcement to prohibit the feature activation code in a sandboxed solution from deleting every item and every document in the current site collection.

Another concern with sandboxed solutions is that there's no ability to perform impersonation. Therefore, custom code in a sandboxed solution always runs as the current user. This can be very limiting when the current user is a low-privileged user such as a contributor or a visitor. There is no way to elevate privileges so that your code can do more than the current user can do.

Farm solutions, on the other hand, allow for impersonation. This means that a developer can elevate privileges so that farm solution code can perform actions even when the current user does not possess the required permissions. However, this simply replaces one issue with another.

A farm solution developer can call *SPSecurity.RunWithElevatedPrivileges*, which allows custom code to impersonate the all-powerful SHAREPOINT\SYSTEM account. When code runs under this identity, it executes with no security constraints whatsoever. The code can then essentially do whatever it wants on a farm-wide basis. This type of impersonation represents the Pandora's box of the SharePoint development platform, because a farm solution could perform an attack on any part of a farm in which it's deployed, and it must be trusted not to do so. As you can imagine, this can cause anxiety with SharePoint farm administrators who are much fonder of security enforcement than they are of trust.

In a nutshell, the security issues with SharePoint solutions stem from the fact that you cannot effectively configure permissions for a specific SharePoint solution. This limitation cannot be overcome, because the SharePoint solution development model provides no way to establish the identity of SharePoint solution code independent of user identity. Because there is no way to establish the identity of code from a SharePoint solution, there is no way to configure permissions for it.

The last important challenge of SharePoint solution development centers around installation and upgrade. The installation of farm solutions is problematic because it requires a farm administrator and it often requires restarting Internet Information Services (IIS) on all the front-end web servers, causing an interruption in service. Although the deployment of a sandboxed solution doesn't involve these problems, it raises other concerns. Business users often have trouble finding and uploading sandboxed solutions in order to activate them. Furthermore, a business user is given very little information to indicate whether or not to trust a sandboxed solution before activating it and giving its code access to all the content within the current site collection.

Of all the issues surrounding SharePoint solution development, nothing is more prone to error and less understood than the process for upgrading code from one version of a SharePoint solution to another. Even though Microsoft added support for feature upgrade and assembly version redirection in SharePoint 2010, it is not widely used. The required steps and the underlying semantics of the feature upgrade process have proven to be too tricky for most developers to deal with. Furthermore, the vast majority of professional SharePoint developers have made the decision never to change the assembly version number of the assembly dynamic-link library (DLL) deployed with a SharePoint solution. That's because creating and managing the required assembly redirection entries across a growing set of web.config files is just too difficult and error prone.

You have just read about the most significant challenges with respect to SharePoint solution development. Here is a summary of these challenges:

- Custom code running inside the SharePoint host environment poses risks and compromises scalability.

- Custom code with dependencies on in-process DLLs causes problems when migrating from one version of SharePoint to the next.

- A permissions model for custom code based entirely on the identity of the current user is inflexible.

- User impersonation addresses the too-little-permissions issue but replaces it with the too-many-permissions issue, which is even worse.

- SharePoint solutions lack effective support and easily understood semantics for distribution, installation, and upgrade.

Understanding the SharePoint app model design goals

The SharePoint app model was designed from the ground up to remedy the problems with SharePoint solutions that were discussed in the previous section. This means that the architecture of the SharePoint app model is very different from that of SharePoint solutions, which represent SharePoint's original development platform. This new architecture was built based on the following design goals:

- Apps must be supported in Office 365 and in on-premises farms.

- App code never runs within the SharePoint host environment.

- App code programs against SharePoint sites by using web service entry points to minimize version-specific dependencies.

- App code is authenticated and runs under a distinct identity.

- App permissions can be configured independently of user permissions.

- Apps are deployed by using a publishing scheme based on app catalogs.

- Apps that are published in a catalog are easier to discover, install, and upgrade.

You have now seen the design goals for the new SharePoint app model and you have read about the motivating factors behind them. This should provide you with greater insight and a better appreciation of why Microsoft designed the SharePoint app model the way it did. Now it's time to dive into the details of the SharePoint app model and its underlying architecture.

Understanding SharePoint app model architecture

Microsoft designed the SharePoint app model to work in the Office 365 environment as well as within on-premises farms. However, developing for Office 365 introduces a few important new concepts that will be unfamiliar to many experienced SharePoint developers. One of the new concepts that is essential to the development of SharePoint apps is a *SharePoint tenancy*.

A SharePoint tenancy is a set of site collections that are configured and administrated as a unit. When a new customer establishes an Office 365 account to host its SharePoint sites, the Office 365 environment creates a new tenancy. The customer's business users who access the tenancy are known (not surprisingly) as *tenants*.

When the Office 365 environment creates a new tenancy for a customer, it creates an administrative site collection that is accessible to users who have been configured to play the role of *tenant administrator*. A tenant administrator can create additional site collections and configure the set of services that are available to all the sites running within the tenancy.

The concept of tenancies was first introduced in SharePoint 2010 to support hosting environments such as Office 365. Although the creation and use of tenancies is essential to the Office 365 environment, their use has not been widely adopted in on-premises farms. This is primarily due to the fact that SharePoint farm administrators can create site collections and configure the services available to users within the scope of a web application.

The architecture of the SharePoint app model requires apps to always be installed and run within the context of a specific tenancy. This can be a bit confusing for scenarios in which you want to install SharePoint apps in an on-premises farm that doesn't involve the explicit creation of tenancies. However, SharePoint 2013 is able to support installing and running SharePoint apps in on-premises farms by transparently creating a farm-wide tenancy behind the scenes; this is known as the *default tenancy*.

Working with app service applications

SharePoint 2013 relies on two service applications to manage the environment that supports SharePoint apps. The first service application is the App Management Service, which is new in SharePoint 2013. The second service application is the Site Subscription Settings Service, which was introduced in SharePoint 2010. A high-level view of a SharePoint 2013 farm running these two service applications is shown in Figure 4-1.

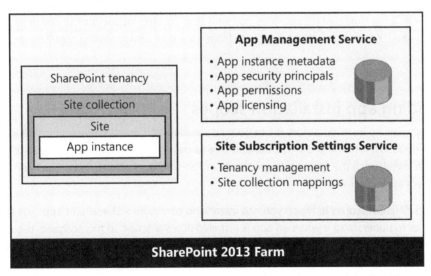

FIGURE 4-1 A SharePoint farm that supports apps requires an instance of the App Management Service and the Site Subscription Settings Service.

The App Management Service has its own database that is used to store the configuration details for apps as they are installed and configured. The App Management Service is also responsible for tracking other types of app-specific configuration data that deals with app security principals, app permissions, and app licensing.

The Site Subscription Settings Service takes on the responsibility of managing tenancies. Each time a new tenancy is created, this service adds configuration data for it in its own database. The Site Subscription Settings Service is particularly important to the SharePoint app model due to the requirement that SharePoint apps must always be installed and run within the context of a specific tenancy.

When you are working within the Office 365 environment, you never have to worry about creating or configuring these two service applications, because they are entirely managed behind the scenes. However, things are different when you want to configure support for SharePoint apps in an on-premises farm. In particular, you must explicitly create an instance of both the App Management Service and the Site Subscription Settings Service.

Creating an instance of the App Management Service is easier because it can be done manually via Central Administration or by using the Farm Creation Wizard. Creating an instance of the Site Subscription Settings Service is a bit trickier because it must be done by using Windows PowerShell. However, when you create an instance of the Site Subscription Settings Service by using Windows PowerShell, it automatically creates the default tenancy, which then makes it possible to install SharePoint apps in sites throughout the farm.

> ### Building an environment for SharePoint app development
>
> If you plan to develop SharePoint apps that will be used within private networks such as corporate LANs, it makes sense to build out a development environment with a local SharePoint 2013 farm. Critical Path Training provides a free download called the *SharePoint Server 2013 Virtual Machine Setup Guide*, which provides you with step-by-step instructions to install all the software you need. You can download the guide from *www.criticalpathtraining.com/Members*.

Understanding app installation scopes

A SharePoint app must be installed before it can be made available to users. When you install a SharePoint app, you must install it within the context of a target web. After the app has been installed, users can then launch the app and begin to use it. The site from which an app has been launched is known as the *host web*.

There are two different scopes in which you can install and configure a SharePoint app. The scenario that is easier to understand is when an app is installed at a *site scope*. In this scenario, the app is installed and launched within the scope of the same SharePoint site. In this scenario, the host web will always be the same site where the app has been installed.

SharePoint apps can also be installed and configured at the *tenancy scope*. In this scenario, an app is installed in a special type of SharePoint site known as an *app catalog site*. After the app has been installed in an app catalog site, the app can then be configured so that users can launch it from other sites. In this scenario, the host web will not be the same site where the app has been installed.

The ability to install and configure apps at tenancy scope is especially valuable for scenarios in which a single app is going to be used by many different users across multiple sites within an Office 365 tenancy or an on-premises farm. A single administrative user can configure app permissions and manage licensing in one place, which avoids the need to install and configure the app on a site-by-site basis. The topic of installing apps will be revisited in greater detail at the end of this chapter.

This book discusses many different scenarios in which SharePoint apps behave the same way, regardless of whether they have been installed in an Office 365 tenancy or in an on-premises farm. Therefore, the book frequently uses the generic term *SharePoint host environment* when talking about scenarios that work the same way across either environment.

Understanding app code isolation

When you develop a SharePoint app, you obviously need to write custom code to implement your business logic, and that code must run some place other than on the web servers in the hosting SharePoint farm. The SharePoint app model provides you with two places to run your custom code. First, a SharePoint app can contain client-side code that runs inside the browser on the user's computer. Second, a SharePoint app can contain server-side code that runs in an external website that is implemented and deployed as part of the app itself.

There are many different ways in which you can design and implement a SharePoint app. For example, you could create a SharePoint app that contains only client-side resources such as webpages and client-side JavaScript code that are served up by the SharePoint host environment. This type of app is known as a *SharePoint-hosted app* because it is contained entirely within the app web. You could write a SharePoint-hosted app that uses Microsoft Silverlight, Microsoft VBScript, Flash, or whatever client-side technology you prefer.

Now imagine that you want to create a second SharePoint app in which you want to write server-side code in a language such as C#. This type of SharePoint app will require its own external website so that your server-side code has a place to execute outside of the SharePoint host environment. In SharePoint 2013 terminology, a SharePoint app with its own external website is known as a *cloud-hosted app*, and the external website is known as the *remote web*. The diagram in Figure 4-2 shows the key architectural difference between a SharePoint-hosted app and a cloud-hosted app.

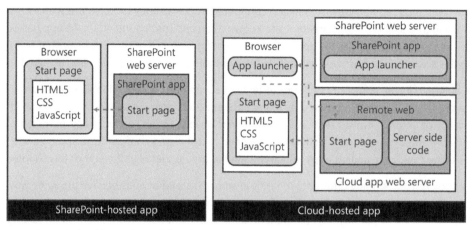

FIGURE 4-2 A cloud-hosted app differs from a SharePoint-hosted app in that it has an associated remote web, which makes it possible for the developer to write server-side code.

From the diagram in Figure 4-2, you can tell that both SharePoint-hosted apps and cloud-hosted apps have a start page that represents the app's primary entry point. With a SharePoint-hosted app, the app's start page is served up by the SharePoint host; however, with a cloud-hosted app, the start page is served up from the remote web. Therefore, the SharePoint host environment must track the remote web URL for each cloud-hosted app that has been installed so that it can redirect users to the app's start page.

There is infrastructure in the SharePoint host environment that creates a client-side JavaScript component known as an *app launcher*, which is used to redirect the user from a page served up by the SharePoint host environment over to the remote web.

When you decide to develop a cloud-hosted SharePoint app, you must often take on the responsibility of hosting the app's remote web. However, this responsibility of creating and deploying a remote web along with a SharePoint app also comes with a degree of flexibility. You can implement the remote web associated with a SharePoint app by using any existing web-based development platform.

For example, the remote web for a cloud-hosted SharePoint app could be implemented by using a non-Microsoft platform such as Java, LAMP, or PHP. However, the easiest and the most common approach for SharePoint developers is to design and implement the remote web for cloud-hosted apps by using ASP.NET web forms or MVC4.

Understanding app hosting models

Thus far, this chapter has discussed how a SharePoint app can be categorized as either a SharePoint-hosted app or a cloud-hosted app. However, the SharePoint app model actually defines three app hosting models, not just two.

Any time you create a new SharePoint app project in Microsoft Visual Studio 2012, you must pick from one of the following three app hosting model:

- SharePoint-hosted
- Provider-hosted
- Autohosted

This chapter has already explained SharePoint-hosted apps. Recall that a SharePoint-hosted app is simply an app that adds its start page and all its other resources into the SharePoint host environment during installation. Now it's time to explain the differences between the other two app hosting models.

A provider-hosted app and an autohosted app are just two variations of the hosting model for a cloud-hosted app. Both types of apps have an associated remote web that is capable of hosting the app's start page and any other resources the app requires. Furthermore, both provider-hosted apps and autohosted apps can and often will host their own custom databases to store app-specific data. The difference between these two different app hosting models involves how the remote web and its associated database are created when an app is deployed and installed.

It makes sense to begin by first examining the hosting model for a provider-hosted app. Imagine a scenario in which a developer has just finished testing and debugging a provider-hosted app that has a remote web with its own custom database. Before the app can be installed in a SharePoint host environment, the developer or some other party must first deploy the website for the remote web to make it accessible across the Internet or on a private network.

The custom database used by the remote web must also be created on a database server and made accessible to the remote web as part of the deployment process. When the remote web and its custom database are up and running, the provider-hosted app can then be installed in a SharePoint tenancy and made available to the customer's users, as depicted in Figure 4-3.

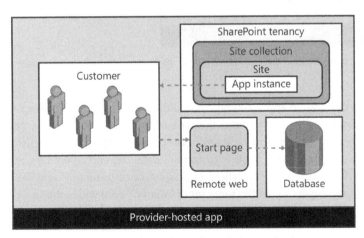

FIGURE 4-3 Many provider-hosted apps have their own database.

After a provider-hosted app has been deployed, the company that developed the app usually assumes the responsibility for its ongoing maintenance. For example, if a company develops a provider-hosted app and deploys its remote web on one or more of its local web servers, it must ensure that those web servers remain healthy and accessible. If it deploys the remote app for its provider-hosted app in a hosting environment such as Windows Azure, it must pay a monthly fee for the hosting services. Furthermore, it will be responsible for backing up the app's database and then restoring it if data becomes lost or corrupt.

Keep in mind that a provider-hosted app can be installed in more than one SharePoint site. Furthermore, a provider-hosted app can be installed in many different SharePoint sites that span across multiple customers and multiple SharePoint host environments. This is a common scenario, and it is known as *multitenancy*. What is critical to acknowledge is that multitenancy introduces several noteworthy design issues and deployment concerns. Let's look at an example.

Think about a scenario involving multitenancy in which a provider-hosted app has been installed by many different customers and the number of users is continually growing larger. All these users will be accessing the same remote web through a single entry point, which is the app's start page, as shown in Figure 4-4.

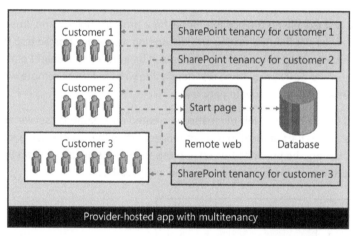

FIGURE 4-4 A provider-hosted app in a multitenant environment must be designed to scale and to isolate data on a customer-by-customer basis.

As you can imagine, a provider-hosted app in this type of multitenant scenario must have a way to scale up as the number of users increases. Furthermore, this type of app should generally be designed to isolate the data for each customer to keep it separate from the data belonging to other customers. You would never want one customer accessing another customer's data. Depending on the customers' industry, there could even be government regulations or privacy concerns that prevent the app from storing data for different customers within the same set of tables or even within the same database.

The important takeaway is that multitenancy introduces complexity. The development of a provider-hosted app that will be used in a multitenant scenario typically requires a design that isolates data on a customer-by-customer basis. As you can imagine, this increases both the time and the cost associated with developing a provider-hosted app.

Now that you have seen some of the inherit design issues that arise due to multitenancy, you will be able to more fully appreciate the benefits of the hosting model for autohosted apps. Autohosted apps offer value because they relieve the developer from having to worry about many of the issues involved with app deployment, scalability, and data isolation.

The first thing to understand about autohosted apps is that they are only supported in the Office 365 environment. Although this constraint might change in future releases, with SharePoint 2013 you cannot install an autohosted app in an on-premises farm. The reason for this is that the hosting model for autohosted apps is based on a private infrastructure that integrates the Office 365 environment with Windows Azure and its ability to provision websites and databases on demand.

The central idea behind the hosting model for autohosted apps is that the Office 365 environment can deploy the remote web on demand when an app is installed. You can also configure an autohosted app so that it creates its own private database during app installation. Again, the Office 365 environment and its integration with Windows Azure is able to create a SQL Azure database on demand and then make it accessible to the remote web.

Autohosted apps offer value over provider-hosted apps because the Office 365 environment transparently handles the deployment of the remote web and potentially the creation of a custom database, as well. Autohosted apps also transfer the ongoing cost of ownership of the remote web and its database from the developer over to the customer who owns the Office 365 tenancy where the app has been installed. Therefore, the app developer doesn't have to worry about babysitting web servers, backing up databases, or coming up with a strategy for scaling up the remote web as the number of users increases.

The benefits of an autohosted app over a provider-hosted app also extend into app design, which can serve to lower development costs. That's because each customer gets his own private database whenever he installs an autohosted app, as illustrated in Figure 4-5. The benefit is that the developer isn't required to add complexity to the app's design and implementation to provide isolation because each customer's data is isolated automatically.

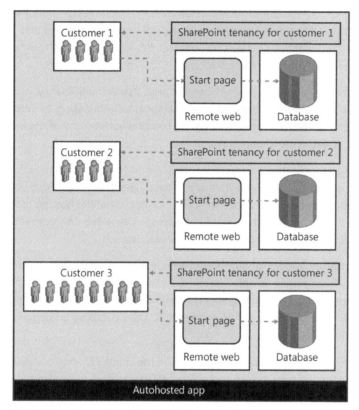

FIGURE 4-5 An autohosted app is able to create its remote web and a database on demand as part of the app installation process.

Reviewing the app manifest

Every SharePoint app requires an XML file called AppManifest.xml, which is known as the *app manifest*. The app manifest contains essential metadata for the app that is read and tracked by the SharePoint host environment when an app is installed. Listing 4-1 presents a simple example of what the app manifest looks like for a SharePoint-hosted app.

LISTING 4-1 An app manifest

```
<App xmlns=http://schemas.microsoft.com/sharepoint/2012/app/manifest
     Name="MySharePointApp"
     ProductID="{b93e8f64-4d14-4c72-be47-3b89f7f5fdf6}"
     Version="1.0.0.0"
     SharePointMinVersion="15.0.0.0" >
```

```
<Properties>
  <Title>My SharePoint App</Title>
  <StartPage>~appWebUrl/Pages/Default.aspx?{StandardTokens}</StartPage>
</Properties>

<AppPrincipal>
  <Internal />
</AppPrincipal>

</App>
```

The app manifest contains a top-level *<App>* element that requires a set of attributes such as *Name, ProductID,* and *Version.* Within the *<App>* element there is an inner *<Properties>* element that contains important child elements such as *<Title>* and *<StartPage>.* The *<Title>* element contains human-readable text that is displayed to the user in the app launcher. The *<StartPage>* element contains the URL that the SharePoint host environment uses in the app launcher to redirect the user to the app's start page.

Listing 4-1 shows the minimal amount of metadata required in an app manifest; however, the app manifest for most real-world apps will contain a good deal more. The app manifest often contains addition metadata to configure other essential aspects of an app, such as app-level events, authentication, permissions, and the SharePoint services that an app requires from the SharePoint host environment. Table 4-1 lists the most common elements you might be required to add to an app manifest.

TABLE 4-1 The elements used in the app manifest file

Element	Purpose
Name	Used to create the URL to the app web.
ProductID	Used to identify the app.
Version	Used to indicate the specific version of the app.
SharePointMinVersion	Used to indicate the version of SharePoint.
Properties\Title	Used to provide text for the app launcher.
Properties\StartPage	Used to redirect the user to the app's start page.
Properties\WebTemplate	Used to supply a custom site template for the app web.
Properties\InstalledEventEndpoint	Used to execute custom code during installation.
Properties\UpgradedEventEndpoint	Used to execute custom code during upgrade.
Properties\UninstallingEventEndpoint	Used to execute custom code during uninstallation.
AppPrincipal\Internal	Used to indicate that there is no need for external authentication. This is what is always used for SharePoint-hosted apps.
AppPrincipal\RemoteWebApplication	Used to indicate that the app is provider-hosted and requires external authentication.
AppPrincipal\AutoDeployedWebApplication	Used to indicate that the app is autohosted and requires external authentication.

Element	Purpose
AppPermissionRequests\AppPermissionRequest	Used to add permission requests that must be granted during app installation.
AppPrerequisites\AppPrerequisite	Used to indicate what SharePoint services must be enabled in the SharePoint host environment for the app to work properly.
RemoteEndpoints\RemoteEndpoint	Used to configure allowable domains for cross-domain calls using the web proxy.

Using the app manifest designer in Visual Studio 2012

When you are working with the app manifest in a SharePoint app project, Visual Studio 2012 provides the visual designer shown in Figure 4-6. This visual designer eliminates the need to edit the XML in the AppManifest.xml file by hand. The designer provides drop-down lists that make editing more convenient and adds a valuable degree of validation as you are selecting the app start page or configuring permission requests, feature prerequisites, and capability prerequisites.

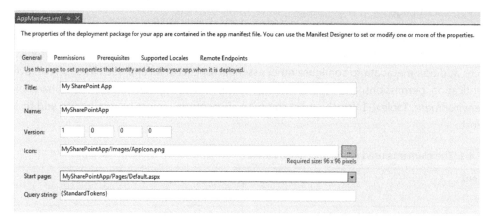

FIGURE 4-6 Visual Studio 2012 provides a visual editor for editing the app manifest.

Although you should take advantage of the visual designer whenever you can to edit the app manifest, it is important to understand that it cannot make certain types of modifications that you might require. Therefore, you should also become accustomed to opening the AppManifest.xml file in code view and making changes manually to the XML within. Fortunately, in times when you need to manually edit the AppManifest.xml file, Visual Studio 2012 is able to provide IntelliSense, based on the XML schema behind the app manifest.

Setting the start page URL

Every app has a start page whose URL must be configured by using the *<StartPage>* element within the app manifest. The SharePoint host environment uses this URL when creating app launchers that redirect the user to the app's start page. For a SharePoint-hosted app, the start page must be located in a child site known as the app web, which will be discussed in more detail later in this chapter. For a cloud-hosted app, the start page will usually be located in the remote web.

When you are configuring the URL within the *<StartPage>* element for a SharePoint-hosted app, you must use a dynamic token named *~appWebUrl*, as demonstrated in the following:

```
~appWebUrl/Pages/Default.aspx
```

This use of the *~appWebUrl* token is required because the actual URL to the app's start page will not be known until the app has been installed. The SharePoint host environment is able to recognize the *~appWebUrl* token during app installation, and it replaces it with the absolute URL to the app web.

In the case of a provider-hosted app, whose start page exists within the remote web, the *<Start-Page>* element can be configured with the actual URL that is used to access the start page where the remote web has been deployed, such as in the following:

```
https://RemoteWebServer.wingtipToys.com/MyAppsRemoteWeb/Pages/Default.aspx
```

When you are debugging provider-hosted apps and autohosted apps, you can use a convenient dynamic token named *~remoteAppUrl* that eliminates the need to hardcode the path to the remote web during the development phase. For example, you can configure the *<StartPage>* element with the following value:

```
~remoteAppUrl/Pages/Default.aspx
```

The reason this works during debugging is due to some extra support in Visual Studio 2012. When you create a new SharePoint app project and select the option for a provider-hosted app or an autohosted app, Visual Studio 2012 automatically creates a second project for the remote web that is configured as the *web project*. Whenever you debug the Visual Studio solution containing these two projects, Visual Studio 2012 performs a substitution to replace *~remoteAppUrl* with the current URL of the web project. After the substitution, the app manifest contains a start page URL that looks like this:

```
https://localhost:44300/Pages/Default.aspx
```

The key point is that Visual Studio 2012 replaces the *~remoteAppUrl* token during a debugging session before the app manifest is installed into the SharePoint host environment. This provides you with a convenience in the debugging phase of a SharePoint app project.

Now think about what happens after you have finished testing and debugging an app and its remote web. Visual Studio 2012 provides a *Publish* command with which you can build a final version of the AppManifest.xml file that will be distributed along with your app. In this case, what will Visual Studio 2012 do with the *~remoteAppUrl* token? The answer is different depending on whether the app is an autohosted app or a provider-hosted app.

When you use the *Publish* command with an autohosted app, Visual Studio 2012 builds a final version of the AppManifest.xml in which the *~remoteAppUrl* token remains within the *<StartPage>* element. This is done because the actual URL to the remote web of an autohosted app will not be known until the app installation process has started and the Office 365 environment has created the remote web. You can tell that the *~remoteAppUrl* token is replaced by Visual Studio 2012 in some scenarios and by the Office 365 environment in other scenarios.

When you use the *Publish* command with a provider-hosted app, the final version of the App-Manifest.xml cannot contain the *~remoteAppUrl* token. You must know the URL to the remote web ahead of time. Therefore, when it is used with a provider-hosted app, the *Publish* command prompts you for several pieces of information, including the actual URL where the remote web will be deployed.

When you are creating the URL for the *<StartPage>* element, it is a standard practice to include a query string that contains another dynamic token named *{StandardTokens}*, as demonstrated in the following example:

```
~remoteAppUrl/Pages/Default.aspx?{StandardTokens}
```

The *{StandardTokens}* token is never replaced by Visual Studio 2012. Instead, this dynamic token remains inside the final version of the app manifest that is installed in the SharePoint host environment. The SharePoint host environment performs a substitution on the *{StandardTokens}* token whenever it creates the URL for an app launcher. This substitution involves replacing the *{StandardTokens}* token with a standard set of query string parameters that are frequently used in SharePoint app development, such as the *SPHostUrl* parameter and the *SPLangauge* parameter, as shown in the following:

```
default.aspx?SPHostUrl=http%3A%2F%2Fwingtipserver&SPLanguage=en%2DUS
```

When you implement the code behind the start page of a SharePoint app, you can generally expect that the page will be passed the two query string parameters named *SPLanguage* and *SPHostUrl*, which are used to determine the language in use and the URL that points back to the host web. In some scenarios, the SharePoint host environment will add additional query string parameters beyond these two.

Understanding the app web

Each time you install a SharePoint app, you must install it on a specific target site. A SharePoint app has the ability to add its own files to the SharePoint host environment during installation. For example, a SharePoint-hosted app must add a start page and will typically add other resources as well, such as a CSS file and a JavaScript file to implement the app's user experience. The SharePoint host environment stores these files in the standard fashion by adding them to the content database associated with the site in which the app is being installed.

Beyond adding basic files such as a start page and a JavaScript file, a SharePoint app also has the ability to create other SharePoint-specific site elements in the SharePoint host during installation, such as lists and document libraries. Let's look at an example.

Imagine that you want to create a simple SharePoint app to manage customers. During installation, the app can be designed to create a customer list by using the standard Contacts list type along with a set of pages designed to provide a snazzy user experience for adding and finding customers. Your app could additionally be designed to create a document library upon installation, so that the app can store customer contracts as Microsoft Word documents, where each Word document would reference a specific customer item in the customers list.

So where does the SharePoint host environment store the content added by an app during installation? The answer is inside a special child site that the SharePoint host environment creates under the site where the app has been installed. This child site is known as the *app web*.

The app web is an essential part of the SharePoint app model because it represents the isolated storage that is owned by an installed instance of a SharePoint app. The app web provides a scope for the app's private implementation details. Note that an app by default has full permissions to read and write content within its own app web. However, a SharePoint app has no other default permissions to access content from any other location in the SharePoint host environment. The app web is the only place an app can access content without requesting permissions that then must be granted by a user.

There is a valuable aspect of the SharePoint app model that deals with uninstalling an app and ensuring that all the app-specific storage is deleted automatically. In particular, the SharePoint host environment will automatically delete the app web for an app whenever the app is uninstalled. This provides a set of cleanup semantics for SharePoint apps that is entirely missing from the development model for SharePoint solutions. When an app is uninstalled, it doesn't leave a bunch of junk behind.

Understanding the app web hosting domain

Now it's time to focus on the start page for a SharePoint-hosted app. As you have seen, the start page for a SharePoint-hosted app is added to the app web during installation. Consider a scenario in which you have installed a SharePoint app with the name MyFirstApp in a SharePoint team site, and that it is accessible through the following URL:

```
https://intranet.wingtip.com.
```

During app installation, the SharePoint host environment creates the app web as a child site under the site where the app is being installed. The SharePoint host environment creates a relative URL for the app web based on the app's *Name* property. Therefore, in this example, the app web is created with a relative path of *MyFirstApp*. If the app's start page, named default.aspx, is located in the app web within the Pages folder, the relative path to the start page is MyFirstApp/Pages/default.aspx. Your intuition might tell you that the app's start page will be accessible through a URL that combines the URL of the host web together with the relative path to the app's start page, as in the following:

```
https://intranet.wingtip.com/MyFirstApp/Pages/default.aspx
```

However, this is not the case. The SharePoint host environment does not make the app web or any of its pages accessible through the same domain as the host web that is used to launch the app. Instead, the SharePoint host environment creates a new unique domain on the fly each time it creates a new app web, as part of the app installation process. By doing so, the SharePoint host environment can isolate all the pages from an app web in its own private domain. The start page for a SharePoint-hosted app is made accessible through a URL that looks like this:

```
https://wingtiptenant-ee060af276f95a.apps.wingtip.com/MyFirstApp/Pages/Default.aspx
```

At this point, it should be clear why you are required to configure the *<StartPage>* element for a SharePoint-hosted app by using the *~appWebUrl* token. The URL to the app web is not known until the SharePoint host environment creates the new domain for the app web during installation. After creating the domain for an app web, the SharePoint host environment can replace the ~appWebUrl token with an actual URL.

Let's examine the URL that is used to access the app web in greater detail. Consider the following URL, which is used to access an app web in an on-premises farm:

```
wingtiptenant-ee060af276f95a.apps.wingtip.com/MyFirstApp
```

The first part of the app web URL (*wingtiptenant*) is based on the name of the tenancy where the app has been installed. This value is configurable in an on-premises farm. In the Office 365 environment, the tenancy name is established when the customer creates a new account, and it cannot be changed afterward.

The second part of the app web URL (*ee060af276f95a*) is known as an *APPUID*. This is a unique 14-character identifier created by the SharePoint host environment when the app is installed. Remember that the APPUID is really an identifier for an installed instance of an app, as opposed to an identifier for the app itself.

The third part of the app web URL (*apps.wingtip.com*) is the *app web hosting domain*. You have the ability to configure this in an on-premises farm to whatever value you would like. Just ensure that you have also configured the proper Domain Name System (DNS) setting for this domain so that it resolves to an IP address pointing to the web servers or servers of your on-premises farms. In Office 365, the app web hosting domain is always *sharepoint.com*.

Now ask yourself this fundamental question: why doesn't the SharePoint host environment serve up pages from the app web by using the same domain as the host web from which the app has been launched? The reasons why the SharePoint host environment serves up pages from the app web in their own isolated domain might not be obvious. There are two primary reasons why the SharePoint app model does this. Both of these reasons are related to security and the enforcement of permissions granted to an app.

The first reason for isolating an app web in its own private domain has to do with preventing direct JavaScript calls from pages in the app web back to the host web. This security protection of the SharePoint app model builds on the browser's built-in support for prohibiting cross-site scripting (XSS). Because JavaScript code running on pages from an app web originates from a different domain, this code cannot directly call back to the host web. More specifically, calls from JavaScript running on app webpages do not run with the same established user identity as JavaScript code behind pages in the host web. Therefore, the JavaScript code running on app webpages doesn't automatically receive the same set of permissions as JavaScript code running on pages from the host web.

The second reason for creating an isolated domain for each app web has to do with processing of JavaScript callbacks that occur on the web server of the SharePoint host environment. Because the SharePoint host environment creates a new unique domain for each app web, it can determine exactly which app is calling when it finds a JavaScript callback originating from a page in an app web.

The key point is that the SharePoint host environment is able to use an internal mechanism to authenticate an app that uses JavaScript callbacks originating from its app web. As a result, the

SharePoint host environment can enforce a security policy based on the permissions that have been granted to the app.

Remember that a SharePoint app has a default set of permissions by which it can access its app web but has no other permissions, by default, to access any other site. The ability of the SharePoint host environment to authenticate an app by inspecting the URL of incoming calls originating from the app web hosting domain is essential to enforcing this default permissions scheme.

Working with app user interface entry points

Every SharePoint app requires a start page. As you know, the URL to the start page is used within an app launcher to redirect the user from the host web to the start page. This type of entry into the user interface of the app is known as a *full immersion experience* because the app takes over the user interface of the browser with a full-page view.

The user interface guidelines of SharePoint app development require the app start page to provide a link back to the host web. This requirement exists so that a user can always return to the host web from which the app has been launched. When you are developing a SharePoint-hosted app, there is a standard master page used in app webs named app.master that automatically adds the required link back to the host web for you.

When you are developing a cloud-based app with the start page in the remote web, you cannot rely on a SharePoint master page to automatically provide the link on the start page to redirect the user back to the host web. Instead, you must use a technique that involves reading the *SPHostUrl* parameter, which is passed to the start page in the query string. This is one of the key reasons why you always want to follow the practice of adding the *{StandardTokens}* token to the start page URL of a cloud-hosted app.

There are several different techniques that you can use in the code behind a start page in the remote web to read the *SPHostUrl* parameter value from the query string and use it to configure the required link back to the host web. For example, you can accomplish this task with server-side C# code or with client-side JavaScript code.

In addition to the required start page, a SharePoint app can optionally provide two other types of entry points, known as *app parts* and *UI custom actions*. Unlike the start page, app parts and UI custom actions are used to extend the user interface of the host web.

Building app parts

An app part is a user interface element that is surfaced on pages in the host web by using an IFrame. After an app with an app part has been installed, a user can then add an app part to pages in the host web by using the same user interface experience that is used to add standard Web Parts.

You implement an app part in Visual Studio 2012 by using a *client Web Part*. This makes most developers ask, "What's the difference between an app part and a client Web Part?" The best way to think about this is that the term "app part" is meant for SharePoint users, whereas the term "client Web Part" is used by developers to describe the implementation of an app part.

Despite having similar names, client Web Parts are very different from the standard Web Parts that are familiar to most SharePoint developers. In particular, a client Web Part cannot have any server-side code that runs within the SharePoint host environment. The implementation of a client Web Part must follow the rules of SharePoint app development.

Client Web Parts are supported under each of the three app hosting models. You implement a client Web Part in a SharePoint-hosted app by using HTML, CSS, and JavaScript. In a cloud-hosted app, you also have the option of implementing the behavior for a client Web Part by using server-side code in the remote web.

At first, many developers assume that a client Web Part is nothing more than an IFrame wrapper around an external webpage. However, the client Web Part provides significant value beyond that. When you configure the URL within a client Web Part, you can use the same tokens as with the start page, such as *~appWebUrl*, *~remoteAppUrl*, and *{StandardTokens}*. Client Web Parts also support adding custom properties, as well. Furthermore, the page behind a client Web Part is often passed contextual security information that allows it to call back into the SharePoint host environment with an established app identity.

When you want to add a new client Web Part to a SharePoint app project, you use the Add New Item command. The Add New Item dialog box in Visual Studio 2012 provides a Client Web Part item template, as shown in Figure 4-7.

FIGURE 4-7 The Add New Item dialog box provides item templates for adding client Web Parts and UI custom actions.

When you add a new project item for a client Web Part, Visual Studio 2012 adds an elements. xml file to the SharePoint app project that contains a *ClientWebPart* element. The following code is a simple example of the XML definition for a client Web Part in a SharePoint-hosted app project that is implemented by using a page inside the app web:

```
<ClientWebPart Name="MyAppPart" Title="My App Part" Description="My description"
               DefaultWidth="300" DefaultHeight="200" >

  <Content Type="html" Src="~appWebUrl/Pages/AppPart1.aspx" />

</ClientWebPart>
```

As you can tell from this example, the content displayed in a client Web Part is configured by assigning a URL to the *Src* attribute of the *<Content>* element. The webpage that is referenced by this URL is usually added to either the app web or to the remote web. However, you can even reference a webpage on the Internet that is neither in an app web nor in a remote web. The only important restriction is that the webpage cannot be returned with the *X-Frame-Options* header in the HTTP response. This is a header used by some websites to prevent its pages from being used inside an IFrame with a type of attack known as *clickjacking*.

Here is something that can catch you off guard when creating a client Web Part in a SharePoint-hosted app: the default behavior of SharePoint 2013 is to add the *X-Frame-Options* header with a value of *SAMEORIGIN* in the HTTP response when it serves up pages from a SharePoint site. The result of this is that a page served up from the app web will not work when you attempt to use it as the page behind a client Web Part. The way to deal with this problem is to add the following directive to the top of any page in the app web referenced by a client Web Part, to suppress the default behavior of adding the *X-Frame-Options* header:

```
<WebPartPages:AllowFraming ID="AllowFraming1" runat="server" />
```

When you develop client Web Parts, you can add custom properties. The real value of custom properties is that they can be customized by the user in the browser in the same way that a user customizes the properties of standard Web Parts. You define a custom property by adding a *<Properties>* element into the *<ClientWebPart>* element and then adding a *<Property>* element within that, as illustrated in Listing 4-2.

LISTING 4-2 Client Web Part properties

```
<Properties>
  <Property
    Name="MyProperty"
    Type="string"
    WebBrowsable="true"
    WebDisplayName="My Custom Property"
    WebDescription="Insightful property description"
    WebCategory="Custom Properties"
    DefaultValue="Some default value"
    RequiresDesignerPermission="true" />
</Properties>
```

After you have added a custom property, you must then modify the query string at the end of the URL that is assigned to the *Src* attribute in the *<Content>* element. You do this by adding a query string parameter and assigning a value based on a pattern by which the property name is given an underscore before it and after it. Thus, for a property named *MyProperty*, you should create a query string parameter and assign it a value of *_MyProperty_*. This would result in XML within the *<Content>* element that looks like the following:

```
<Content
  Type="html"
  Src="~appWebUrl/Pages/AppPart1.aspx?MyPropertyParameter=_MyProperty_"
/>
```

Note that you can use any name you want for the query string parameter itself. It's when you assign a value to the parameter that you have to use the actual property name and follow the pattern of adding the underscores both before and after.

Building UI custom actions

A UI custom action is a developer extension in the SharePoint app model with which you can add custom commands to the host site. The command for a UI custom action is surfaced in the user interface of the host site by using either a button in the ribbon or a menu command in the menu associated with items in a list or documents in a document library. This menu is known as the Edit Control Block (ECB) menu. It is the act of installing an app with UI custom actions that automatically extends the user interface of the host site with ribbon buttons and ECB menu commands.

As in the case of the client Web Part, UI custom actions are supported in each of the three app hosting models. However, a UI custom action is different than the client Web Part because its purpose is not to display content in the host web. Instead, it provides an executable command for business users with which they can display a page supplied by the app. The page that is referenced by a UI custom action can be in either the app web or the remote web.

As a developer, you have control over what is passed in the query string for a UI custom action. This makes it possible to pass contextual information about the item or the document on which the command was executed. This in turn makes it possible for code inside the app to discover information, such as the URL that can be used to access the item or document, by using either the client-side object model (CSOM) or the new Representational State Transfer (REST) API, which is discussed in Chapter 5, "Client-side programming."

Keep in mind that an app will require additional permissions beyond the default permission set in order to access content in the host web. This topic is discussed in Chapter 6, "SharePoint security." This chapter will only discuss how to create a UI custom action that passes contextual information to a page supplied by the app. Chapter 6 also covers what's required to actually use this information to call back into the SharePoint host environment.

In the dialog box shown earlier in Figure 4-7, you can tell that Visual Studio 2012 provides a project item template named UI Custom Action. When you use this item template to create a new UI custom action, Visual Studio 2012 adds a new elements.xml file to your SharePoint app project. When you look inside the elements.xml file you find a *<CustomAction>* element that you can modify to define either an ECB menu item or a button on the ribbon.

Many SharePoint developers already have experience working with custom actions in SharePoint 2007 and SharePoint 2010. The good news is that the manner in which you edit the XML within the *<CustomAction>* element for a SharePoint app project works the same way as it does for a SharePoint solution project. The bad news is that many of the custom actions that are available when developing farm solutions are not available when developing a SharePoint app.

In particular, a SharePoint app only allows for UI custom actions that create ECB menu commands and ribbon buttons. The SharePoint app model imposes this restriction to provide a balance between functionality and security concerns. Furthermore, you are prohibited from adding any custom JavaScript code when you configure the URL for a UI custom action in a SharePoint app. If this restriction were not enforced, JavaScript code from the app could call into the host site without being granted the proper permissions.

Suppose that you want to create a UI custom action to add a custom ECB menu item to all the items in every Contacts list within the host site. You can structure the *<CustomAction>* element to look like that presented in Listing 4-3.

LISTING 4-3 A custom action definition

```
<CustomAction
  Id="CustomAction1"
  RegistrationType="List"
  RegistrationId="105"
  Location="EditControlBlock"
  Sequence="100"
  Title="Send Contact To App">

    <UrlAction Url="~appWebUrl/Pages/Action1.aspx" />

</CustomAction>
```

When you install an app with this UI custom action, it registers an ECB menu command for every item in lists that have a list type ID of 105. This is the ID for the Contacts list type. After the app is installed, the host web will provide a custom menu item on the ECB menu for each item in any Contacts list. An example of what the ECM menu command looks like is shown in Figure 4-8.

FIGURE 4-8 A UI custom action can be used to add a custom menu command to the ECB menu associated with an item or a document.

The default action of a UI custom action is to redirect the user to the page referenced by the URL configured within the *<UrlAction>* element. This makes sense for a scenario in which you want to move the user from the host web into the full-immersion experience of the app in order to do some work. However, this default behavior will provide a distracting user interface experience for a scenario in which a user wants to return to the host web immediately after viewing the page displayed by the app. For these scenarios, you can modify the UI custom action to display the page from the app as a dialog box in the context of the host web. This type of user interface experience is much better because the user can view a page from the app without ever leaving the host web.

Listing 4-4 demonstrates the technique to display the page referenced by a UI custom action as a dialog box, which involves adding three attributes to the *<CustomAction>* element. First, you add the *HostWebDialog* attribute and assign it a value of *true*. Next, you add the *HostWebDialogWidth* attribute and the *HostWebDialogHeight* attribute and assign them values to set the width and height of the dialog box.

LISTING 4-4 Displaying a referenced page

```
<CustomAction
  Id="CustomAction1"
  RegistrationType="List"
  RegistrationId="105"
  Location="EditControlBlock"
  Sequence="100"
  Title="Display more information about this contact"
  HostWebDialog="TRUE"
  HostWebDialogWidth="480"
  HostWebDialogHeight="240" >

    <UrlAction Url="~appWebUrl/Pages/Action1.aspx" />

</CustomAction>
</Elements>
```

Now, let's go into more detail about configuring the *Url* attribute of the *<UrlAction>* element. When you configure the URL, you can use the same familiar tokens that you use with the start page and with client Web Parts, such as *~appWebUrl*, *~remoteAppUrl*, and *{StandardTokens}*, as shown in the following code:

```
<UrlAction Url="~appWebUrl/Pages/Action1.aspx" />
```

However, UI custom actions support several additional tokens beyond what is available for start pages and client Web Parts. These are the tokens that make it possible to pass contextual information about the item or document on which the command was executed. For example, you can pass the site-relative URL to the item or document by using the *{ItemURL}* token:

```
<UrlAction Url="~appWebUrl/Pages/Action1.aspx?ItemUrl={ItemURL}" />
```

In most scenarios, you will also need the absolute URL to the root of the host web, which can be passed by using the *{HostUrl}* token. Note that the *Url* is configured by using an XML attribute, so you cannot use the "&" character when combining two or more parameters together. Instead, you must use the XML-encoded value, which is &amp, as shown in the following example:

```
<UrlAction Url="~appWebUrl/Pages/Action1.aspx?HostUrl={HostUrl}&amp;ItemURL={ItemUrl}" />
```

Note that the SharePoint host environment substitutes values into these tokens by using standard URL encoding. This means that you must write code in the app to use a URL decoding technique before you can use these values to construct a URL that can be used to access the item or document.

Table 4-2 lists the tokens that can be used in UI custom actions, beyond those that are also supported in start pages and client Web Parts. Note that some of the tokens work equally well regardless of whether the UI custom action is used to create an ECB menu item or a button on the ribbon. However, the *{ListId}* and *{ItemId}* tokens work with ECB menu items but not with buttons in the ribbon. Conversely, the *{SelectedListId}* and *{SelectedItemId}* tokens work with buttons on the ribbon but not with ECB menu items.

TABLE 4-2 The extra tokens available for configuring the URL for a UI custom action

Token	Purpose
{HostUrl}	Provides an absolute URL to the root of the host site
{SiteUrl}	Provides an absolute URL to the root of the current site collection
{Source}	Provides a relative URL to the page that hosts the custom action
{ListUrlDir}	Provides a site-relative URL to the root folder of the current list
{ListId}	Provides a GUID-based ID of the current list (ECB only)
{ItemUrl}	Provides a site-relative URL to the item or document
{ItemId}	Provides an integer-based ID of the item or document (ECB only)
{SelectedListId}	Provides a GUID-based ID of the selected list (ribbon only)
{SelectedItemId}	Provides an integer-based ID of the selected item or document (ribbon only)

Using the chrome control

Although apps are isolated from the host web, the end user should feel like the app is just a natural extension of the host web. To achieve a seamless feel, apps should take on some of the styling elements of the host web and provide a navigation system that incorporates a link back to the host web. If you are creating a SharePoint-hosted app, these issues are addressed by the app project template in Visual Studio. However, if you are creating a provider-hosted or autohosted app, the remote web will need some help in achieving these goals. This is the purpose of the chrome control.

With the chrome control, a remote web can use the header elements of a specific SharePoint site (usually the host web) without knowing the styles ahead of time. In addition to styling, the chrome control also provides a link back to the host web. Optionally, the chrome control can define a drop-down list box similar to the Site Settings menu, and a Help menu. Figure 4-9 shows a remote web displaying a table of contacts with the host web chrome visible at the top of the page. The figure also shows the link back to the host web, as well as the drop-down list.

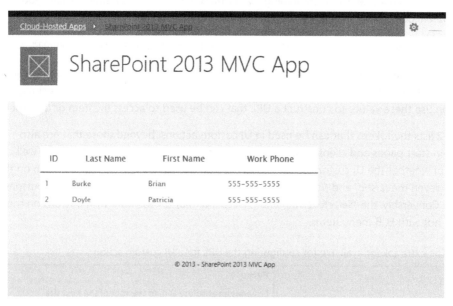

FIGURE 4-9 The chrome control lets the app take on the styling of its parent web.

The chrome control is contained within the sp.ui.controls.js library, which is located in the LAYOUTS directory. The simplest way to use the library is to copy it into the remote web project. The library contains the definition for the *SP.UI.Controls.Navigation* object, which can retrieve the style sheet from the host web for use in the remote web. The *SP.UI.Controls.Navigation* object makes a call to the defaultcss.ashx handler to retrieve the URL for the host web style sheet. The host web style sheet is then downloaded for use by the chrome control. The chrome control then generates a header section for the app into a target *<div>* element, which you specify.

The chrome control relies on four parameters in the query string for its functionality: *SPHostUrl*, *SPHostTitle*, *SPAppWebUrl*, and *SPLanguage*. If your app uses the *{StandardTokens}* query string in the manifest and has an associated app web, then the start page URL will include the *SPHostUrl*, *SPAppWebUrl*, and *SPLanguage* parameters. However, you will need to add the *{HostTitle}* token to include the *SPHostTitle* parameter, as shown in Figure 4-10.

Query string:	{StandardTokens}&SPHostTitle={HostTitle}

FIGURE 4-10 The start page query string can include additional parameters.

You can use the chrome control either programmatically or declaratively. When it is used programmatically, you typically provide a target *<div>* element in the app page and create a library to set the options for the *SP.UI.Controls.Navigation* object. Listing 4-5 presents a complete library for using the chrome control.

LISTING 4-5 Using the chrome control

```
"use strict";

var WingtipToys = window.WingtipToys || {};

WingtipToys.ChromeControl = function () {

    render = function () {
        var options = {
            "appIconUrl": "../Images/AppIcon.png",
            "appTitle": "SharePoint 2013 MVC App",
            "appHelpPageUrl": "../Help?" + document.URL.split("?")[1],
            "settingsLinks": [
                {
                    "linkUrl": "../Contacts/ReadAll?" + document.URL.split("?")[1],
                    "displayName": "Contacts"
                },
                {
                    "linkUrl": "../Welcome/Message?" + document.URL.split("?")[1],
                    "displayName": "Home"
                }
            ]
        };

        var nav = new SP.UI.Controls.Navigation(
                        "chrome_ctrl_placeholder",
                        options
                    );
        nav.setVisible(true);
    },
```

```
    getQueryStringParameter = function (p) {
        var params =
            document.URL.split("?")[1].split("&");
        var strParams = "";
        for (var i = 0; i < params.length; i = i + 1) {
            var singleParam = params[i].split("=");
            if (singleParam[0] == p)
                return decodeURIComponent(singleParam[1]);
        }
    }

    return {
        render: render
    }
}();

$(document).ready(function () {
    WingtipToys.ChromeControl.render();
});
```

When the *ready* event of the document fires, the *render* method of the *WingtipToys.ChromeControl* object is called. This method sets the options for the *SP.UI.Controls.Navigation* object. Notice that the options make it possible for the icon, title, help link, and navigation links to be defined. After it is defined, the *SP.UI.Controls.Navigation* object is instantiated with the options and the identifier of the *<div>* element where the chrome should be rendered.

When using the chrome control declaratively, you set the options directly in the markup of the target *<div>* element. The chrome control will automatically render within the target *<div>* element if it declares the *data-ms-control="SP.UI.Controls.Navigation"*. attribute. Listing 4-6 demonstrates the declarative equivalent of Listing 4-5.

LISTING 4-6 Using the chrome control declaratively

```
<div
    id="chrome_ctrl_container"
    data-ms-control="SP.UI.Controls.Navigation"
    data-ms-options=
        '{
        "appIconUrl": "../Images/AppIcon.png",
        "appTitle": "SharePoint 2013 MVC App",
        "appHelpPageUrl": "../Help?" + document.URL.split("?")[1],
```

```
            "settingsLinks": [
                {
                    "linkUrl": "../Contacts/ReadAll?" + document.URL.split("?")[1],
                    "displayName": "Contacts"
                },
                {
                    "linkUrl": "../Welcome/Message?" + document.URL.split("?")[1],
                    "displayName": "Home"
                }
            ]
        }'>
</div>
```

Packaging and distributing apps

The final section of this chapter examines how SharePoint apps are distributed and deployed into production, as well as how apps are managed over time. First, you will learn about the details of how apps are packaged into redistributable files. After that, you will learn how these files are published and installed to make SharePoint apps available to users. As you will find, the SharePoint app model provides valuable support for managing apps in a production environment and upgrading to newer versions.

Packaging apps

A SharePoint app is packaged up for deployment by using a distributable file known as an *app package*. An app package is a file built by using the zip archive file format and requires an extension of .app. For example, if you create a new SharePoint-hosted app project named MySharePointApp, the project will generate an app package named MySharePointApp.app as its output.

Note that the zip file format for creating an app package is based on the Open Package Convention (OPC). This is the same file format that Microsoft Office began using with the release of Office 2007, for creating Word documents (.docx) and Microsoft Excel workbooks (.xslx).

The primary requirement for an app package is that it contains the app manifest as a top-level file named AppManifest.xml. As discussed earlier in this chapter, the SharePoint host environment relies on metadata contained in the app manifest so that it can properly configure an app during the installation process.

An app package will usually contain an app icon file named AppIcon.png. The AppIcon.png file, like many of the other files in an app package, is paired with an XML file. For the app icon, the file is named AppIcon.png.config.xml. The purpose of this XML file is to assign the AppIcon.png file an identifying GUID.

Understanding the app web solution package

In addition to the AppManifest.xml file, the app package often contains additional files that are used as part of the app's implementation. For example, the app package for a SharePoint-hosted app contains a file for the app's start page along with other resources used by the start page, such as a CSS file and a JavaScript file. These are example of files that are added to the app web as part of the app installation process.

The distribution mechanism used by a SharePoint app to add pages and lists to the app web during installation is a standard solution package, which is a cabinet (CAB) file with a .wsp extension. If this sounds familiar, that's because the solution package file embedded within an app package has the same file format as the solution package files that developers have been using to deploy SharePoint solutions in SharePoint 2007 and SharePoint 2010. The one key difference is that the solution package used by the SharePoint app model to add files to an app web is not a stand-alone file. Instead, it is embedded as a .wsp file within the app package, as shown in Figure 4-11.

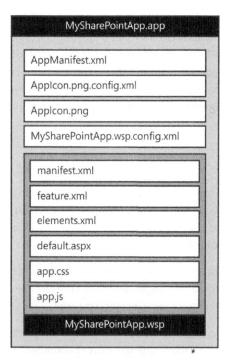

FIGURE 4-11 Elements added to an app web during the installation of an app are packaged in a solution package file that is embedded inside the app package file.

When a user installs a SharePoint app, the SharePoint host environment examines the app package to determine if it contains an inner solution package. It is the presence of an inner solution package within the app package file that specifies to the SharePoint host environment whether it needs to create an app web during installation. If the app package does not contain an inner solution package, the SharePoint host environment installs the app without creating an app web.

The app web solution package contains a single web-scoped feature. The SharePoint host environment activates this feature automatically on the app web immediately after the app web is created. This feature is what makes it possible to add declarative elements such as pages and lists to the app web as the app is installed.

An app web solution package cannot contain a .NET assembly DLL with server-side code. Therefore, you can say that the app web solution package embedded inside an app package is constrained because it must be a fully declarative solution package. This is different from the solution packages for farm solutions and sandboxed solutions, which can contain assembly DLLs with custom .NET code written in either C# or VB.NET.

Keep in mind that the installation of a SharePoint app doesn't always result in the creation of an app web. Some apps are designed to create an app web during installation, and some are not. A SharePoint-hosted app is the type of app that will always create an app web during installation. This is a requirement because a SharePoint-hosted app requires a start page that must be added to the app web.

However, things are different with a cloud-hosted app. Because a cloud-hosted app usually has a start page that is served up from a remote web, it does not require the creation of an app web during installation. Therefore, the use of an app web in the design of a provider-hosted app or an autohosted app is really just an available option as opposed to a requirement, as it is with a SharePoint-hosted app.

When you design a provider-hosted app or an autohosted app, you have a choice of whether to create an app web during installation to store private app implementation details inside the SharePoint host. Some cloud-hosted apps will store all the content they need within their own external database and will not need to create an app web during installation. Other cloud-hosted apps can be designed to create an app web during installation for scenarios in which it makes sense to store content within the SharePoint host environment for each installed instance of the app.

Packaging host web features

This chapter has already discussed client Web Parts and UI custom actions. As you recall, these two types of features are used to extend the user interface of the host web, as opposed to many of the other types of elements in an app that are added to the app web. For this reason, the XML files containing the definitions of client Web Parts and UI custom actions are not deployed within a solution package embedded within the app package. Instead, the XML files that define client Web Parts and UI custom actions are added to the app package as top-level files.

Consider an example SharePoint app named MyAppParts that contains two client Web Parts. The contents of the app package for this app will contain a top-level elements.xml file for each of the client Web Parts and a top-level feature.xml file for the feature that hosts them. When Visual Studio 2012 creates these XML files and builds them into the output app package file, it adds a unique GUID to each file name to avoid naming conflicts, as illustrated in Figure 4-12.

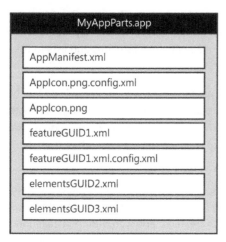

FIGURE 4-12 The XML files that define client Web Parts and UI custom actions are packaged as top-level files within the app package.

The feature that hosts client Web Parts and UI custom actions is a web-scoped feature known as a *host web feature*. The SharePoint host environment is able to detect a host web feature inside an app package during app installation and activate it in the host web. When an app with a web host feature is installed at tenancy scope, that feature will be activated in more than one site.

Packaging for autohosted apps

When it comes to packaging a SharePoint app for distribution, autohosted apps are more complicated and deserve a little extra attention. The extra complexity is required because the app package for an autohosted app must contain the resources required to create an ASP.NET application on demand to deploy the remote web. An autohosted app can also be designed to create a SQL Azure database as well during the app installation process.

When you create a new autohosted app, Visual Studio 2012 creates two projects. There is one project for the app itself and a second web project for an ASP.NET application to implement the remote web. For example, if you create a new autohosted app using the name MyAutoHostedApp, Visual Studio 2012 creates an app project named MyAutoHostedApp and an ASP.NET project named MyAutoHostedAppWeb and adds them to a single Visual Studio solution.

What is important to understand is that the app package built for the MyAutoHostedApp project must contain all the necessary files to deploy the ASP.NET project named MyAutoHostedAppWeb. This is a requirement because the installation of this app package must provide the Office 365 environment with the means to provision the remote web as a Windows Azure application. This is what makes it possible for an autohosted app to create its own remote web during the installation process.

Visual Studio 2012 relies on a packaging format that Microsoft created especially for the Windows Azure environment, by which all the files and metadata required to deploy an ASP.NET application are built into a single zip file for distribution. This zip file is known as a *web deploy package*. When used within the SharePoint app model, the web deploy package is embedded within the app package of an autohosted app for distribution.

When Visual Studio 2012 builds the web deploy package for an autohosted app, it creates the file by combining the app package name together with a web.zip extension. For example, an app package named MyAutohostedApp.app will have an embedded web deploy package named MyAutohostedApp.web.zip.

Now consider the scenario in which an autohosted app has an associated SQL Azure database. The Office 365 environment must create this database on demand during app installation. Therefore, the app package must contain the resources required to create a SQL Azure database containing standard database objects, such as tables, indexes, stored procedures, and triggers.

The SharePoint app packaging model takes advantage of a second packaging format that Microsoft created for Windows Azure known as a *Data Tier Application package.* In this packaging format, the metadata required to automate the creation of a SQL Azure database is defined in XML files that are built into a zip file with an extension of .dacpac. The name of the Data Tier Application package is typically based on the name of the database. For example, a SQL Azure database named MySqlDatabase will have an associated Data Tier Application package named MySqlDatabase.dacpac. If you look inside a Data Tier Application package, you can locate a file named model.xml, which defines the database objects that need to be created.

Figure 4-13 shows the layout of an app package for an autohosted app that will trigger the Office 365 environment to create a remote web and a SQL Azure database as part of the app installation process. Remember that the web deploy package is required in an autohosted app package, whereas the Data Tier Application package is optional.

FIGURE 4-13 An autohosted app package contains a web deploy package to create the remote web and a Data Tier Application package to create a SQL Azure database.

When you create an autohosted app, Visual Studio 2012 automatically creates the web project and takes care of setting up all that's required to build the web deploy package into the app package. However, you have to take a few extra steps to create a SQL database project and configure it to properly build the Data Tier Application package into the app package.

The first step is to create a new SQL database project in Visual Studio 2012 and add it to the same solution that contains the autohosted project. Next, on the Properties page of the SQL database project, go to the Project Settings tab and change the target platform setting to SQL Azure. This is the step that changes the project output to a Data Tier Application package. After this, you must build the SQL database project at least once to build the Data Tier Application package.

The final step is to configure the app project to reference the Data Tier Application package. You can accomplish this by using the property sheet for the autohosted app project. You will find a project property named *SQL Package*. After you configure the *SQL Package* property to point to the Data Tier Application package (.dacpac) file, you have made the necessary changes so that Visual Studio 2012 can begin building the Data Tier Application package into the app package file.

Publishing apps

The app package is a distributable file that's used to publish SharePoint apps. After the app package has been published, it is available for users to install. In the case of SharePoint-hosted apps and autohosted apps, the app package contains all the resources required to deploy the app during the installation process. However, provider-hosted apps require the developer to deploy the remote web independently of the publication process and the installation process.

You publish a SharePoint app by uploading its app package file to one of two different places. First, you can publish an app by uploading its app package to the public Office Store. This is the right choice to make your app available to the general public, including users with SharePoint tenancies in Office 365.

The second way to publish a SharePoint app is by uploading the app package to a special type of site known as an app catalog site. This is the option to use when you want to make the app available only to users within a specific Office 365 tenancy or within a specific on-premises farm.

Publishing SharePoint apps to the Office Store

To publish an app to the public Office Store, the developer must first create a *dashboard seller account*. You can create this type of account by navigating to *https://sellerdashboard.microsoft.com* in your browser and logging on with a valid Windows Live ID. After you have logged on, you can create a new dashboard seller account that is either an individual account or a company account.

A very appealing aspect of publishing apps to the Office Store with a dashboard seller account is that it provides assistance with the management of licensing as well as collecting money from customers through credit card transactions. When you create a dashboard seller account, you are able to create a second payout account from which you supply Microsoft with the necessary details, so when it collects money from customers purchasing your apps, it can transfer the funds you have earned to either a bank account or a PayPal account.

After you have gone through the process of creating a dashboard seller account, it takes a day or two for this new account to be approved. When your account has been approved, you can then begin to publish your apps in the Office Store. The Office Store supports publishing three types of apps: SharePoint apps, Apps for Office, and Windows Azure Catalog Apps.

You publish a SharePoint app by uploading its app package file and filling in the details associated with the app. For example, the publishing process for the Office Store requires you to provide a title, version number, description, category, logo, and at least one screen shot that shows potential customers what your app looks like.

When you publish a SharePoint app, you can also indicate via the seller dashboard whether your app is free or must be purchased. If you publish an app for purchase, you can specify the licensing fee for each user or for a specified number of users. There is even an option to configure a free trial period for an app that has an associated licensing fee.

After you have uploaded an app and provided the required information, the app must then go through an approval process. The approval process involves checking the app package to ensure that it only contains valid resources. There are also checks to validate that the app meets the minimum requirements of the user experience guidelines. For example, there is a check to ensure that the start page for the app contains the required link back to the host web.

After the app has been approved, it is then ready for use and is added to the public Office Store, where it can be discovered and installed by SharePoint users.

Publishing apps to an app catalog

What should you do if you want to publish an app but you don't want to publish it to the Office Store? For example, imagine a scenario in which you don't want to make an app available to the general public. Instead, you want to publish the app to make it available to a smaller audience, such as a handful of companies who are willing to pay you for your development effort. The answer is to publish the app to an *app catalog site*.

An app catalog site contains a special type of document library that is used to upload and store app package files. Along with storing the app package file, this document library also tracks various types of metadata for each app. Some of this metadata is required, whereas other metadata is optional.

In the Office 365 environment, the app catalog site is automatically added when a tenancy is created for a new customer. However, this is not the case in an on-premises farm. Instead, you must explicitly create the app catalog site by using the Central Administration site or by using Windows PowerShell. Furthermore, the app catalog is created at web application scope, so you must create a separate app catalog site for each web application.

You must have farm administrator permissions within an on-premises farm to create an app catalog site. You begin by navigating to the home page of Central Administration. On the home page, there is a top-level Apps link. When you click the Apps link, you will be redirected to a page with a group of links under the heading of App Management. Within this group of links, locate and click the link titled Manage App Catalog.

The first time you click the Manage App Catalog link, you are redirected to the Create App Catalog page, which you can use to create a new app catalog site, as shown in Figure 4-14. Note that the app catalog site must be created as a top-level site within a new site collection. On the Create App Catalog page, you can select the target web application that will host the new app catalog site.

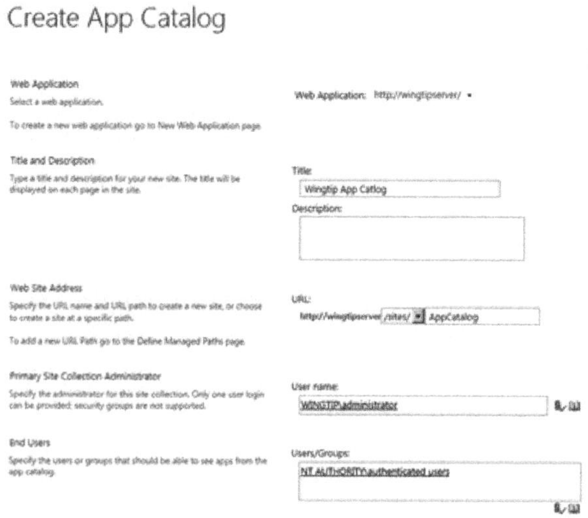

FIGURE 4-14 Central Administration provides the Create App Catalog page, which makes it possible for you to create an app catalog site within a specific web application.

Note that you can also use the Create App Catalog page to configure user access permissions to the app catalog site. Remember that providing users with access to the app catalog site is what makes it possible for them to discover and install apps of their own. You must provide read access to users if you want them to have the ability to discover apps and install them at site scope. However, you might decide against configuring user access to the app catalog site if you plan to install apps at tenancy scope.

After you have created the app catalog site within an on-premises farm, you should navigate to it and inspect what's inside. You will find that there is a document library called *Apps for SharePoint* that is used to publish SharePoint apps. There is a second document library called *Apps for Office* that is used to publish apps created for Office applications such as Word and Excel.

You publish a SharePoint app by uploading its app package to the *Apps for SharePoint* document library. The SharePoint host environment is able to automatically fill in some of the required app metadata such as the Title, Version, and Product ID by reading the app manifest while the app package is uploaded. However, there is additional metadata that must be filled in manually or by some other means. A view of apps that have been published in the *Apps for SharePoint* document library is presented in Figure 4-15.

		Site	Name	App Version	Edit	Product ID	Metadata Locale	Is Default Locale	Modified	Enabled
✓	☐									

▲ Product ID : {B93E8F64-4D14-4C72-8E47-3889F7F5FDF6} (1)

| | ☐ | My SharePoint App | MySharePointApp ⊞ | ⋯ | 1.0.0.0 | 🗊 | {B93E8F64-4D54-4C72-8E47-3889F7F5FDF6} | English - 1033 | Yes | Yesterday at 8:41 PM | Yes |

▲ Product ID : {4F144A8E-6F6E-4823-8BCB-D699C46F7901} (1)

| | ☐ | SharePoint App Rest Demo | SharePointAppRestDemo ⊞ | ⋯ | 1.0.0.0 | 🗊 | {4F144A8E-6F6E-4823-8BCB-D699C46F7901} | English - 1033 | Yes | Yesterday at 8:39 PM | Yes |

FIGURE 4-15 The *Apps for SharePoint* document library tracks the app package file and associated metadata for published apps.

You will also notice that the app catalog site supports the management of app requests from users. The idea here is that a user within a site can request an app from the Office Store. The app catalog administrator can view this request and decide whether to purchase the app or not. If the app request seems appropriate, the app catalog administrator can purchase the app and make it available for site-scope installation. Alternatively, the app catalog administrator can make the app available to the requester by using a tenancy-scoped installation.

Installing apps

After an app has been published, it can be discovered and installed by a user who has administrator permissions in the current site. The Site Contents page contains a tile labeled *Add An App*. Clicking this tile redirects the browser to the main page for installing apps. This page displays apps that have been published to the app catalog site. Remember that an Office 365 tenancy has a single app catalog site, but on-premises farms have an app catalog site for each web application. Therefore, you will not find apps that have been published to an app catalog site in a different web application.

A user requires administrator permissions within a site to install an app. If you are logged on with a user account that does not have administrator permissions within the current site, you will not be able to view apps that have been published in the app catalog site. This is true even when your user account has been granted permissions on the app catalog site itself.

After you locate an app you want to install, you can simply click its tile to install it. The app installation process typically prompts you to verify whether you trust the app. A page appears that displays a list of the permissions that the app is requesting, along with a button allowing you to grant or deny the app's permission request. You must grant all permissions that the app has requested to continue with the installation process. There is no ability to grant one requested permission to an app while denying another. Granting permissions to an app during installation is always an all-or-nothing proposition.

After the app has been installed, you will find a tile for it on the Site Content page. This tile represents the app launcher that a user can click to be redirected to the app's start page. The app title also displays an ellipse you can click to display menu for app management, as illustrated in Figure 4-16.

FIGURE 4-16 When an app has been installed, it can be launched and managed through its tile, which is displayed on the Site Content page.

Recall from earlier in the chapter what happens during app installation. Some apps require an app web. When this is the case, the app web is created as a child site under the current site where the app has been installed. If the app contains host feature elements such as client Web Parts and UI custom actions, these user interface extensions will be made available in the host site, as well.

Installing apps at tenancy scope

You have seen that the app catalog site provides a place where you can upload apps in order to publish them. When an app has been published in the app catalog site, a user within the same Office 365 tenancy or within the same on-premises web application can discover the app and install it at site scope. However, the functionality of an app catalog site goes one step further. It plays a central role in installing apps at tenancy level.

You install an app at tenancy scope by installing it in an app catalog site. Just as with a site-scoped installation, you must first publish the app by uploading it to the *Apps for SharePoint* document library in the app catalog site. After publishing the app, you should be able to locate it on the Add An App page of the app catalog site and install it just as you would install an app in any other type of site. However, things are a bit different after the app has been installed in an app catalog site. More specifically, the app provides different options in the menu that is available on the Site Content page, as shown in Figure 4-17.

FIGURE 4-17 After an app has been installed in an app catalog site, it provides a Deployment menu, with which you can make the app available for use in other sites.

As shown in Figure 4-17, an app that has been installed in an app catalog site has a Deployment menu command that is not available in any other type of site. When you click the Deployment menu command, you are redirected to a page on which you can configure the app so that you can make it available to users in other sites.

You have several different options when you configure an app in an app catalog site to make it available in other sites. One option is to make the app available to all sites within the scope of the app catalog site. Or you can be more selective and just make the app available in sites that were created by using a specific site template or sites created under a specific managed path. There is even an option to add the URLs of site collections one by one, if you need fine-grained control.

After you configure the criteria for a tenancy-scoped app installation to indicate the sites in which it can be used, you will find that the app does not appear in those sites instantly. That's because the SharePoint host environment relies on a timer job to push the required app metadata from the app catalog site to all the other sites. By default, this timer job is configured to run once every five minutes. During your testing you can speed things up by navigating to the Central Administration site and locating the timer job definition named App Installation Service. The page for this timer job definition provides a Run Now button that you can click to run the job on demand.

Upgrading apps

The upgrade process designed by the SharePoint app model provides a much better experience compared to the upgrade process used with SharePoint solutions. When apps are published, the Office Store and app catalog sites always track their version number. When an app is installed, the SharePoint host environment detects this version number and records it for the installed app instance.

Take a simple example. Imagine you have uploaded version 1.0.0.0 of an app. After that, the app is installed in several sites via site-scoped installation. The SharePoint host environment remembers that each of these sites has installed version 1.0.0.0 of the app.

Now, imagine that you want to further develop your app. Maybe you need to fix a bug, improve its performance, or extend the app's functionality. After you have finished your testing, you decide to update the version number to 2.0.0.0 and to publish the new version in the same app catalog site where you installed the original version.

One important aspect of the upgrade process of the SharePoint app model is that an updated version of an app is never forced upon the user who installed the app. Instead, the user is notified that a new version of the app is available. This user can then decide to do nothing or to update the app to the new version. Figure 4-18 shows the notification that the SharePoint host environment adds to the app tile on the Site Contents page.

My SharePoint App
An update for this app is available.

FIGURE 4-18 The tile for an app displays a notification when an updated version has been published to the Office Store or to the app catalog site.

The notification depicted in Figure 4-18 contains an update link that a user can click to be redirected to a page with a button that activates the upgrade process. What actually occurs during the upgrade process differs depending on whether the app is a SharePoint-hosted app or a cloud-hosted app.

When you are working on an updated version of a SharePoint-hosted app, you have the ability to change some of the metadata in the app manifest and to add new elements into the app web. For example, you could add a new page named startv2.aspx to the app web and then modify the app manifest to use this start page instead of the start page that was used in original version of the app. You could also add other, new app web elements such as JavaScript files, lists, and document libraries. Many of the techniques used to upgrade elements in the app web are based on the same techniques developers have been using with feature upgrade in SharePoint solutions.

When it comes to updating a cloud-hosted app, things are different. That's because most of the important changes to the app's implementation are made to the remote web and not to anything inside the SharePoint host environment. If you are working with a provider-hosted app, you must roll out these changes to the remote web before you publish the new version of the app to the Office Store or any app catalog site.

It's equally important that the updated version of the remote web must continue to support customers who will continue to use the original version of the app. Remember; there is nothing that forces the user to accept an update. You should expect that some customers will be happy with the original version and will be opposed to upgrading to a new version of an app.

After you have pushed out one or more updates to a provider-hosted app, you must begin to track what version each customer is using. One technique to accomplish this task is to provide a different start page for each version of the app. Many provider-hosted apps will go a step further and store the current version of app in a customer profile that is tracked in a custom database behind the remote web.

Trapping app life cycle events

One favorable aspect of the SharePoint app model for developers is the ability to design a cloud-hosted app with custom server-side code that is automatically executed when an app is installed, upgraded, or uninstalled. By taking advantage of the ability to add code behind these three app life cycle events, you can program against the host web and the app web with logic to initialize, update, and clean up site elements in the SharePoint environment. These app life cycle events also provide the necessary triggers for updating the custom database used by provider-hosted apps and autohosted apps.

The architecture of app events is based on registering app event handlers in the app manifest that cause the SharePoint host environment to call out to a web service entry point in the remote web. Due to the architecture's reliance on a server-side entry point, app events are not supported in SharePoint-hosted apps. Therefore, you can only use the app events in autohosted apps and provider-hosted apps.

It's relatively simple to add support for app events to the project for an autohosted app or a provider-hosted app. The property sheet for the app project contains three properties named *Handle App Installed*, *Handle App Uninstalling*, and *Handle App Upgraded*, as shown in Figure 4-19.

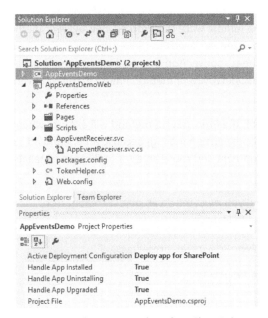

FIGURE 4-19 The property sheet for a SharePoint app project provides three properties that you can use to add support for app event handling.

The default value for each of these app event properties is *false*. The first time you change one of these properties to a value of *true*, Visual Studio 2012 adds a web service entry point into the web project with a name of AppEventReceiver.svc. Visual Studio 2012 also adds the required configuration information into the app manifest file, as well. If you enable all three events, the *<Properties>* element within *<App>* element of the app manifest will be updated with the following three elements:

```
<InstalledEventEndpoint>~remoteAppUrl/AppEventReceiver.svc</InstalledEventEndpoint>
<UninstallingEventEndpoint>~remoteAppUrl/AppEventReceiver.svc</UninstallingEventEndpoint>
<UpgradedEventEndpoint>~remoteAppUrl/AppEventReceiver.svc</UpgradedEventEndpoint>
```

After you have enabled one or more of the app events, you can then begin to write the code that will execute when the events occur. You write this code in the code-behind file named App-EventReceiver.svc.cs. If you examine this file, you will find that Visual Studio 2012 has created a class named *IRemoteEventService* (shown in the following code), which implements a special interface that the SharePoint team created for remote event handling:

```
public class AppEventReceiver : IRemoteEventService {
  public SPRemoteEventResult ProcessEvent(RemoteEventProperties properties) {}
  public void ProcessOneWayEvent(RemoteEventProperties properties) { }
}
```

The *IRemoteEventService* interface is used with app events and also with other types of remote event handlers, as well. There are two methods named *ProcessEvent* and *ProcessOneWayEvent*. The SharePoint host environment makes a web service call that executes the *ProcessEvent* method when it needs to inspect the response returned from the remote web. The *ProcessOneWayEvent* method is called for cases in which the SharePoint host environment needs to trigger the execution of code in the remote web but doesn't need to inspect the response. App events always trigger to the *ProcessEvent* method, so you can leave the *ProcessOneWayEvent* method empty in the AppEvent-Receiver.svc.cs file.

If you have registered for the *AppInstalled* event, the *ProcessEvent* method will execute whenever a user is installing the app. It is critical to supply robust error handling, because an unhandled exception will be returned to the SharePoint host environment and cause an error in the app installation process.

When you implement the *ProcessEvent* method, you must return an object created from the *SPRemoteEventResult* class, as demonstrated in the following:

```
public SPRemoteEventResult ProcessEvent(RemoteEventProperties properties) {
  // return an SPRemoteEventResult object
  SPRemoteEventResult result = new SPRemoteEventResult();
  return result;
}
```

The *SPRemoteEventResult* class was designed to allow code in the remote web to relay contextual information back to the SharePoint host environment. For example, imagine that you have detected that the installer's IP address is located in a country that you do not want to support. You can tell the SharePoint host environment to cancel the installation process and pass an appropriate error message, as shown here:

```
SPRemoteEventResult result = new SPRemoteEventResult();
result.Status = SPRemoteEventServiceStatus.CancelWithError;
result.ErrorMessage = "App cannot be installed due to invalid IP address";
return result;
```

The *ProcessEvent* method passes a parameter named *properties*, which is based on a type named *RemoteEventProperties*. You can use this parameter to access important contextual information such as the URL of the host web and the security access token required to call back into the SharePoint host environment. Listing 4-7 shows that the *properties* parameter also provides an *EventType* property, with which you can determine which of the three app events has caused the *ProcessEvent* method to execute.

LISTING 4-7 Handling events

```
public SPRemoteEventResult ProcessEvent(RemoteEventProperties properties) {

    // obtain context information from RemoteEventProperties property
    string HostWeb = properties.AppEventProperties.HostWebFullUrl.AbsolutePath;
    string AccessToken = properties.AccessToken;

    // handle event type
    switch (properties.EventType) {
      case RemoteEventType.AppInstalled:
        // add code here to handle app installation
        break;
      case RemoteEventType.AppUpgraded:
        // add code here to handle app upgrade
        break;
      case RemoteEventType.AppUninstalling:
        // add code here to handle app uninstallation
        break;
      default:
        break;
    }

    // return an SPRemoteEventResult object
    SPRemoteEventResult result = new SPRemoteEventResult();
    return result;

}
```

Note that debugging app event handlers can be especially tricky to set up, and in many situations it doesn't work at all. That's because the SharePoint host environment must be able to call back into the remote web. For cases in which you have installed the app into an Office 365 tenancy for testing, it is a web server in the Office 365 environment that will be issuing the call to the remote web. This web server hosted in the Office 365 environment must be able to locate and access the web server hosting the remote web. Therefore, attempting to debug an app event handler for which the remote web is configured to use a host name such as localhost or to use a host domain name that only resolves to the proper IP address inside your testing environment will not work.

Summary

This chapter provided you with an introduction to SharePoint apps. You learned about the pain points of SharePoint solution development and the design goals that influenced how the architecture of the SharePoint app model was created. You also learned many details about app hosting models, user interface design, publishing, installation, and upgrading. Now it's time to move ahead and begin learning about how to write code in an app that accesses the SharePoint host environment by using the CSOM and the new REST API.

## CHAPTER 5

Client-side programming

The Microsoft SharePoint 2013 app model does not support running server-side code within the SharePoint host environment. As a result, SharePoint developers cannot use the server-side application programming interface (API) in apps. Instead, app developers must use the client-side API, which consists of the client-side object model (CSOM) and the Representational State Transfer (REST) API.

This chapter demonstrates the use of CSOM and REST in the various app designs. Along the way, it introduces the required technical concepts necessary to understand the app designs and the best practices for developing them. The chapter starts with a short JavaScript primer followed by a review of the various patterns for creating reusable and maintainable libraries in JavaScript. It then covers the fundamentals of the CSOM and REST object models.

Because app security is covered in Chapter 6, "SharePoint security," the examples in this chapter steer clear of situations that involve advanced app authentication. Instead, this chapter focuses on the fundamentals necessary to successfully develop apps against CSOM and REST. The patterns and principles presented in this chapter are subsequently applied in samples throughout the book.

Understanding app designs

When you are developing apps, you can program CSOM and the REST API by using either C# or JavaScript. C# is used in remote webs associated with provider-hosted or autohosted apps. JavaScript can run in the browser in SharePoint-hosted, provider-hosted, or autohosted apps. The combination of languages and APIs results in the 12 different permutations shown in Table 5-1.

TABLE 5-1 App designs

Language	API	SharePoint-hosted	Provider-hosted	Autohosted
JavaScript	CSOM	Supported	Cross-Domain Calls	Cross-Domain Calls
JavaScript	REST	Supported	Cross-Domain Calls	Cross-Domain Calls
C#	CSOM	Not Supported	Supported	Supported
C#	REST	Not Supported	Supported	Supported

Although the choices outlined in Table 5-1 offer a lot of flexibility, you will find that some app designs are much more natural choices than others. For example, if you want to do most of your development in C#, you will find that CSOM in a provider-hosted or autohosted app is the most straightforward design. On the other hand, if you mostly want to create SharePoint-hosted apps for Microsoft Office 365, JavaScript against the REST API will be the easiest design. The following sections discuss these designs in detail.

Assessing SharePoint-hosted app designs

SharePoint-hosted apps can never use C# code and must use always use JavaScript. Developers can use either REST or CSOM (also known as the JavaScript Object Model, JSOM). For most development, REST is preferred over JSOM. REST is an Internet standard that many technologies—such as jQuery—already use. Your app code is simply more "standard" when you use REST. REST techniques with JavaScript are covered in the section "Working with the REST API in JavaScript" later in this chapter.

Though REST is more of a standard than JSOM, there are legitimate advantages to using JSOM over REST. The most important advantage is that JSOM is currently a superset of REST functionality. There are some operations that can't be performed in REST. However, most of the basic operations—such as list operations—are fully supported in REST. The second advantage of JSOM is that it currently has much better documentation than the REST API. This is because it has been around since 2010. The REST documentation will catch up over time, but right now it is often frustrating to do anything beyond list operations. Finally, JSOM payloads are smaller than REST payloads. Some non-scientific Fiddler analysis has shown REST payloads to be as much as twice the size of JSOM payloads. JSOM techniques are covered in the section "Working with the JavaScript client object model" later in this chapter.

Assessing cloud-hosted app designs

Cloud-hosted apps (meaning both provider-hosted and autohosted) can use JavaScript or C# against both the CSOM and REST APIs. However, it is important to understand when to use each approach. The most important consideration in this regard is the architecture of your SharePoint farm and whether it is completely on premises, completely in the cloud, or a hybrid.

When working with apps hosted completely in the cloud, you often have to work with OAuth tokens. The *TokenHelper* class, which is included in the Microsoft Visual Studio 2012 project template, makes this much easier. So immediately you can see that C# is a better choice than JavaScript where tokens are important. When working with apps hosted completely on premises, you do not have the benefit of using OAuth. However, you can still make use of the *TokenHelper* class, which supports additional functionality for server-to-server (S2S) authentication. The *TokenHelper* class, OAuth, and S2S are covered in detail in Chapter 6.

When you have concluded that C# is the way to go, you'll discover that writing CSOM code is much easier than REST. CSOM can be used synchronously in the managed object model, which makes the code very simple and straightforward. CSOM techniques are covered in the section "Working with the managed client object model" later in this chapter. REST calls, on the other hand, have some serious drawbacks. First, they require asynchronous round trips to the server to acquire the *FormDigest* from SharePoint as part of the authentication process. Second, you have to create POST messages by hand in code, which can be messy. Both of these concerns are demonstrated in the section "Working with the REST API in C#" later in this chapter.

When working in hybrid environments, you may have the situation in which a call from a SharePoint Online app must be made back to an on-premises farm. In this case, the use of the *TokenHelper* class will likely be precluded by a firewall. In this situation, the best approach is to use either the REST or JSOM *cross-domain library*. These libraries allow cross-domain calls directly from JavaScript, which will allow the call to made regardless of an intervening firewall. The cross-domain libraries are covered in detail in Chapter 6.

Introduction to JavaScript for SharePoint developers

JavaScript takes on increased importance in app development. Therefore, this section presents a brief overview of the JavaScript language and its key characteristics from the perspective of an experienced SharePoint programmer. Although you have probably written some JavaScript, you might not have taken the time to understand JavaScript at the level necessary to be successful in writing SharePoint apps. If you are a JavaScript expert, you can certainly skip this section. If you have only used JavaScript casually in your past SharePoint solutions, you should read this section thoroughly and pay special attention to the discussion in the section "Creating Custom Libraries."

Understanding JavaScript namespaces

As a SharePoint developer, you have probably written at least some JavaScript in a webpage; thus, you understand that JavaScript code is made up of functions. These functions can be written directly into the webpage by using script tags or referenced in separate library files. If you are more of a casual JavaScript developer, however, you might not be aware that simply writing a named function places that function in the *global namespace*. The global namespace is the container into which all variables and functions are placed by default. In the browser, this container is the *window* object. Cluttering the global namespace with functions can easily lead to naming conflicts and "spaghetti" code.

In addition to the global namespace, you can define your own custom namespaces. Namespaces in JavaScript are essentially just containing objects defined within the global namespace. By using custom namespaces, you can isolate your code from other JavaScript in the page. This is essential for preventing naming conflicts. Custom namespaces are one of the few things that should be defined within the global namespace. Most variables and functions are generally defined within a custom namespace. The following code shows how to define a custom namespace:

```
var Wingtip = window.Wingtip || {};
```

In the sample code, a new namespace named *Wingtip* is defined. The code sets a global variable named *Wingtip* to either reference an existing global variable or create a new one if it does not exist already. This is the standard approach to creating namespaces because this line of code can exist in several different libraries without causing a naming conflict. The first library loaded with this code present establishes the namespace definition for those loaded later.

Understanding JavaScript variables

Variables in JavaScript can be declared either in a namespace or within a function. Unlike C# variables, JavaScript variables are not declared by using a data type keyword. Instead, JavaScript uses the *var* keyword to define a variable. Although it is not strictly required, variables should always be declared by using the *var* keyword. This is important because when it is not used, the variable is automatically defined within the global namespace. When the *var* keyword is used outside of a function, the associated variable is always defined within the global namespace. When it is used within a function, the associated variable is scoped to the function only. The following code shows an example of a global variable, global function, and local variable:

```
<script type="text/JavaScript">
    var myGlobalVar = "This is a global variable";
    function myGlobalFunction() {
        alert("This function is defined in the global namespace");
        for (var i=0; i<5; i++) {
            alert("This variable is local to the function: " + i);
        }
    }
</script>
```

Variables can be defined within a custom namespace by simply referencing the namespace when using the variable. The code that follows shows how to create a variable within a custom namespace. The section "Creating custom libraries" later in this chapter expands upon this idea significantly to show how to encapsulate code and keep it out of the global namespace:

```
var Wingtip = window.Wingtip || {};
var window.Wingtip.myNamespaceVar = "This is a variable defined within a namespace";
```

Although JavaScript does not have specific data type keywords, a declared variable does have a type based on the value it holds. Variable types can be examined by using the *typeof* operator. The *typeof* operator returns one of the following values when applied to a variable or function parameter:

- *undefined*

- *string*

- *number*

- *Boolean*

- *function*

- *object*

Because JavaScript is very loose with rules concerning variable and object definitions, you should be sure to always use *strict* JavaScript in your apps. Strict JavaScript is an improved version of JavaScript that can be enabled by adding the line *"use strict"* at the top of any library or function. Strict JavaScript will prevent you from making many common mistakes in your code.

The following lists some of the key restrictions enabled by strict JavaScript.

- Cannot use a variable without declaring it
- Cannot write to a read-only property
- Cannot add properties to non-extensible objects
- Cannot illegally delete functions and variables
- Cannot define a property more than once in an object literal
- Cannot use a parameter name more than once in a function
- Cannot use reserved words, *eval*, or arguments as names for functions and variables
- The value of *this* in a function is no longer the *window* object
- Cannot declare functions inside of statements
- Cannot change the members of the *arguments* array

Understanding JavaScript functions

When writing functions, you need to understand that the function signature consists of the function name, parameters, and scope. In C# programming against the SharePoint server-side API, the calling code should match the function signature by passing in parameters that are typed appropriately. Furthermore, an error is thrown when the calling code does not match the function signature. In JavaScript, however, no error is thrown when the list of parameters passed to a function does not match the function signature. Instead, all parameters are available within a function through the *arguments* array. Consider the following JavaScript function:

```
function Add(){
    var sum = 0;
    for (var i=0; i<arguments.length; i++) {
        sum += arguments[i];
    }
    return sum;
}
```

The *Add* function definition does not include any parameters. Instead, the function looks through the *arguments* array and simply adds together the values contained within it. Because of this, the following calls to the *Add* function will all succeed:

```
var sum1 = Add();
var sum2 = Add(7);
var sum3 = Add(7,11);
var sum4 = Add(7,11,21,36);
```

Functions in JavaScript are actually objects. As such, they can be assigned to a variable. The variable referencing the function can then be invoked as if it were the name of the function. A function can also be defined without a name, making it an *anonymous* function. The following code shows an example of an anonymous function assigned to a variable named *talk* and then invoked:

```
var talk = function() {
    alert("hello there!");
};
talk();
```

Understanding JavaScript closures

Because anonymous functions can be assigned to a variable, they can also be returned from other functions. Furthermore, the local variables defined within the containing function are available through the returned anonymous function. This concept is called a *closure*. Consider the following code, which returns an anonymous function from a containing named function:

```
function echo (shoutText) {
    var echoText = shoutText + " " + shoutText;
    var echoReturn = function() { alert(echoText); };
    return echoReturn;
}
```

Because the return value from the named function is an anonymous function, the code that follows can be used to invoke the returned function. When the returned function is invoked, the browser displays the text "Hello! Hello!":

```
echo("Hello!")();
```

What is interesting in this example is the fact that the anonymous function is using the local variable *echoText* within its body, and the local variable is available even after the function returns. This is possible because the returned value is essentially a pointer to the anonymous function defined within the named function, which means that the local variables do not go out of scope after the named function completes. This is the essence of a closure in JavaScript.

At first glance, closures might appear to be more of a curiosity than a useful construct. However, closures are essential to the process of creating encapsulated JavaScript that is maintainable. Consider the following code:

```
function person (name) {
    var talk = function() { alert("My name is " + name); };
    return {
        speak:talk
    };
}
```

In the preceding example, an anonymous function is assigned to the local variable *talk*. The return value of the function is an object that has a key *speak*, which references the value *talk*. By using this type of closure, the function can be invoked by using method syntax, which returns the message "My name is Brian Cox":

```
person("Brian Cox").speak();
```

Notice how the code that invokes the function appears almost as if it is object oriented. Even though JavaScript is clearly not object oriented, by using closures you can create functions that look and feel more familiar to C# developers and significantly improve maintainability. This concept results in several development patterns that are investigated in the section "Creating custom libraries" later in this chapter.

Understanding JavaScript prototypes

A JavaScript object is really just an unordered collection of key-value pairs. Objects can be created with the key-value pairs defined at the moment the object is created. The keys are then used to access the values. The following code shows a simple *customer* object with a *name* property defined:

```
customer = {Name: "Brian Cox"};
alert("My name is " + customer["Name"]);
```

Every JavaScript object is based on a *prototype*, which is an object that supports the inheritance of its properties. With prototypes, you can define the structure of an object and then use that structure to create new object instances. Listing 5-1 shows an example of defining a prototype and creating an object from it.

LISTING 5-1 Creating an object from prototypes

```
var human = Object.create(null);

Object.defineProperty(human, "name",
                          {value: "undefined",
                           writable: true,
                           enumerable: true,
                           configurable: true}
                          );

var customer = Object.create(human);

Object.defineProperty(customer, "title",
                          {value: "undefined",
                           writable: true,
                           enumerable: true,
                           configurable: true}
                          );

customer["name"] = "Brian Cox";
customer["title"] = "Developer";
alert("My name is " + customer["name"]);
alert("My title is " + customer["title"]);
```

In Listing 5-1, a null *human* prototype is created and then a single *name* property is defined. The *human* prototype is then used to create an instance called *customer*. The *customer* prototype is then modified to contain a *title* property. If you call a property on an object but the property does not exist, JavaScript will look for the property by following the *prototype chain* up the inheritance tree. In this case, the *name* property of the *customer* is defined in the *human* prototype.

Using prototypes is very efficient when you are creating large numbers of objects because the functions do not need to be created for each instance. This behavior results in development patterns that are presented in the next section.

Creating custom libraries

Even though the function-based nature of JavaScript makes it deceptively easy to get started, most developers who are new to the language simply write global functions directly in the webpage. This practice, however, is seriously flawed because naming conflicts will inevitably arise between functions in libraries. Furthermore, writing reams of functions in the global namespace is simply unmaintainable. This section examines several approaches for creating custom libraries that are efficient and maintainable.

Understanding the singleton pattern

The singleton pattern creates a single instance of an object that encapsulates code within it. The singleton pattern is a straightforward implementation of an object designed to encapsulate code and keep it out of the global namespace. As an example, consider the following code that sets up a custom namespace and then defines a singleton:

```
"use strict";

var Wingtip = window.Wingtip || {};
Wingtip.Customer = {

    name: "Brian Cox",
    speak: function() { alert("My name is " + this.name); }

};
```

Within the *Customer* object, each member is added by declaring a publicly accessible key, followed by the definition of a function or object as the value. Note the use of the *this* keyword within the *speak* function to reference the *name* member object. Calling code might interact with the publically accessible members as shown in the following code:

```
Wingtip.Customer.speak();
```

The singleton pattern does a nice job of encapsulating code into the *Customer* object outside of the global namespace. Additionally, the calling code is straightforward, readable, and maintainable. The entire *Customer* definition could subsequently be packaged into a separate file (for example, wingtip.customer.js) and reused across several apps. The obvious disadvantage of this pattern is that you can only have one customer. In a typical SharePoint app, you are going to need to create many customer instances.

Understanding the module pattern

The module pattern and its variants use a function instead of an object as the basis for encapsulation. The advantage of the module pattern is that it can support private members, public members, and multiple instances; the exact support is based on the pattern variant you use.

The standard module pattern uses a self-invoking function as the container. The standard module pattern can be regarded as an improved version of the singleton pattern because it still only supports one instance. Listing 5-2 shows an example of the module pattern.

LISTING 5-2 The module pattern

```
"use strict";

var Wingtip = window.Wingtip || {};
Wingtip.Customer = function () {

    //private members
    var name = "Brian Cox",
        talk = function() {alert("My name is " + name);};

    //public interface
    return {
        fullname: name,
        speak: talk
    }

}();
```

In Listing 5-2, notice that the function definition is followed by a set of parentheses. It is these parentheses that make the function self-invoking. The return value is an object whose key-value pairs reference the private members, which effectively creates a public interface for the library. The following code shows how the module is called:

```
alert(Wingtip.Customer.fullname);
Wingtip.Customer.speak();
```

Note that the return value doesn't have to actually provide a key-value pair for every one of the private members. When the return value reveals only a subset of the members, the pattern is said to be a variant of the module pattern known as the *revealing module pattern*. The revealing module pattern allows for the definition of private members that are inaccessible through the public interface. Listing 5-3 shows an example that uses *get* and *set* functions to access the *name* member.

LISTING 5-3 The revealing module pattern

```
"use strict";

var Wingtip = window.Wingtip || {};
Wingtip.Customer = function () {

    //private members
    var name,
        setname = function(n) { name = n; },
        getname = function() { return name; },
        talk = function() {alert("My name is " + name);};

    //public interface
    return {
        set_name: setname,
        get_name: getname,
        speak: talk
    }

}();
```

If the parentheses are removed from the function, it is no longer self-invoking. To make use of the module, you must create an instance referenced by a new variable. Using this variant of the module pattern, you can create multiple customer instances for use, which should feel very familiar to C# developers. The following code shows how to create an instance if the module were not self-invoking:

```
var customer1 = new Wingtip.Customer();
customer1.set_name("Brian Cox");
customer1.speak();
```

Understanding the prototype pattern

Unlike previous patterns, the prototype pattern does not rely on closures to achieve its functionality. Instead, it relies on the inheritance of the prototype chain. The prototype provides a means of defining members in a single place for use by many instances. Every object in JavaScript has a prototype property with which you can expand to include new members. This sets up a very interesting pattern that you can use to define a prototype that can be used to create instances later. If you're a C# developer, this feels a lot like defining a class from which instances are created. The following code shows an example of the prototype pattern:

```
"use strict";

var Wingtip = window.Wingtip || {};
Wingtip.Customer = function (n) {
    this.name = n;
};

Wingtip.Customer.prototype.speak = function() {
    alert("My name is " + this.name);
}
```

The prototype pattern begins with the definition of a function. This function often accepts initialization parameters, which are stored in variables defined within the prototype by using the *this* keyword. The initial function definition acts as the constructor for new instances, which means that the variables defined within it are also defined for each instance as part of the prototype.

The prototype associated with a function can easily be extended by referencing the prototype property and adding a new member. In the example, a *speak* function is added to the prototype. As an alternative, you can also define the prototype as an object containing many functions, as shown in the following code:

```
"use strict";

var Wingtip = window.Wingtip || {};
Wingtip.Customer = function (n) {
    this.name = n
};
Wingtip.Customer.prototype = {
    get_name: function() { return this.name; },
    set_name: function(n) { this.name = n; },
    speak: function() { alert("My name is " + this.name); }
};
```

The prototype pattern can also be combined with the module pattern by simply defining a self-invoking function in the prototype. Additionally, defining members separately is not required; you could simply define all members in the constructor, as shown in the code that follows. In summary, you can create hybrid patterns by combining several concepts together:

```
"use strict";

var Wingtip = window.Wingtip || {};
Wingtip.Customer = function (n) {
    this.name = n;
    this.speak = function() { alert("My name is " + this.name); };
};
```

After the prototype is defined, you can create instances by using the *new* keyword. Each instance inherits the definition of the function prototype. The code that follows shows how to create an instance and invoke a function. The resulting code has a decidedly object-oriented feel that should make C# programmers comfortable:

```
var customer1 = new Wingtip.Customer("Brian Cox");
customer1.speak();
```

Introduction to jQuery for SharePoint developers

In the same way that developers can build and reuse their own JavaScript libraries, third parties have created JavaScript libraries that can simply be referenced and used in app development. Although there are many third-party libraries available on the Internet, one library, jQuery, is so popular that it has almost become synonymous with JavaScript itself.

The reason for the popularity of jQuery is that it does two very important things extremely well: it makes it easy to select elements from the document object model (DOM) and then perform operations on the selected elements. jQuery is so important that Microsoft has included it in the app project template in Visual Studio 2012. Therefore, SharePoint app developers must understand how to use the jQuery library. The following sections present a brief introduction to jQuery from a SharePoint app developer perspective. Readers who want complete coverage of the library should visit the jQuery website at *http://www.jquery.com*.

Referencing jQuery

To include any JavaScript library in an app, you must reference it by using a script tag. The script tag refers to the location of the library so that it can be downloaded. In the Visual Studio app project template, the jQuery library is included as a file and referenced in the *Default.aspx* page, as shown in the following code:

```
<script type="text/javascript" src="../Scripts/jquery-1.6.2.min.js"></script>
```

Along with directly hosting the jQuery library in your app, you can also choose to use a content delivery network (CDN). A CDN hosts the jQuery library in the cloud so that it is always available. Referencing a CDN can improve performance of public-facing apps because the library is downloaded in parallel and cached. The same version of the library can then be used across several different apps. The following code shows how to reference the Microsoft CDN for jQuery:

```
<script src="http://ajax.aspnetcdn.com/ajax/jquery/jquery-1.8.0.min.js" type="text/javascript">
</script>
```

Understanding the global function

The jQuery library is encapsulated in a single function named *jQuery*, which is known as the *global function*. By using the global function, you can easily select elements from the DOM, which is fundamental to any JavaScript solution. To select DOM elements, the global function is invoked and selector syntax is passed. The following code shows the traditional method of selecting elements in JavaScript by using the *getElementById* method, contrasted with the jQuery approach:

```
var elem1 = document.getElementById("displayDiv");
var elem2 = jQuery("#displayDiv");
```

In the preceding code, the jQuery selector syntax uses the hash sign to indicate that the selector corresponds to the ID of the desired element. You can simplify this code even further because the jQuery library uses the $ symbol as an alias for the global function. Therefore, the following code is equivalent:

```
var elem1 = document.getElementById("displayDiv");
var elem2 = $("#displayDiv");
```

Understanding selector syntax

At first, it might seem that selecting DOM elements by using jQuery is not that exciting. The power of jQuery, however, lies in the fact that the selector syntax is identical to that used in cascading style sheets (CSS). This means that you can use a rich, familiar selector syntax to reference any part of the DOM, which becomes a powerful and efficient way to manipulate the DOM elements. Table 5-2 shows common selection operations and how to accomplish them in jQuery.

TABLE 5-2 jQuery selector syntax

Operation	Example	Description
Select elements by type	$("p")	Selects all paragraph elements in the page
Select elements by ID	$("#container")	Selects the element whose *ID* is "container"
Select elements by class	$(".emphasis")	Selects all elements with a *class* attribute of "emphasis"
Select elements by type and ID	$("div#displayDiv")	Select the div element whose *ID* is "displayDiv"
Select elements by ancestor and descendant	$("div#displayDiv p")	Select all paragraph elements within the *div* whose *ID* is "displayDiv", regardless of where they are inside the *div* element
Select elements based on their parent	$("div#displayDiv > p")	Select all paragraph elements that are children of the *div* whose *ID* is "displayDiv"
Select the first child of a parent	$("ul#displayList > li:first")	Select the first list item element in the unordered list whose *ID* is "displayList"
Select the last child of a parent	$("ul#displayList > li:last")	Select the last list item element in the unordered list whose *ID* is "displayList"
Select elements by attribute	$("input[name='firstName']")	Select the *input* element whose name attribute is "firstName"

After you understand the common selection operations, you can move ahead to combine them in order to create more sophisticated selectors. The jQuery library also supports a number of extensions that provide yet more capabilities. A complete description of supported selectors is available on the jQuery website at *http://api.jquery.com/category/selectors/*.

Understanding jQuery methods

After you have selected DOM elements, you will want to manipulate them. This is where jQuery methods come into play. The jQuery library has a tremendous number of methods that perform all kinds of useful DOM manipulations. These manipulations are always performed on the collection of elements returned from the jQuery global function. Table 5-3 shows some commonly used jQuery methods.

TABLE 5-3 Common jQuery methods

Method	Example	Description
Read the HTML within an element	`var x = $("#displayDiv").html();`	Returns the inner HTML of the element whose *ID* is "displayDiv"
Modify the HTML within an element	`$("#displayDiv").` `html("<p>Hello</p>")`	Sets the inner HTML of the element whose *ID* is "displayDiv"
Read the text of an element	`$("ul#displayList > li:first").` `text();`	Returns the text of the first list item in the unordered list whose *ID* is "displayList"
Modify the text of an element	`$("ul#displayList > li:first").` `text("Item 1");`	Sets the text of the first list item in the unordered list whose *ID* is "displayList"
Read the value of a style property	`var x = $("#displayDiv").` `css("marginTop");`	Returns the value of the "margin-top" CSS property for the element whose *ID* is "displayDiv"
Set the value of a style property	`$("#displayDiv").` `css("marginTop","5px");`	Sets the value of the "margin-top" CSS property for the element whose *ID* is "displayDiv" to "5px"
Add a CSS class to an element	`$("#displayDiv").` `addClass("emphasis")`	Adds the CSS class named "emphasis" to the element whose *ID* is "displayDiv"
Remove a CSS class from an element	`$("#displayDiv").` `removeClass("emphasis")`	Removes the CSS class named "emphasis" from the element whose *ID* is "displayDiv"
Hide an element	`$("#displayDiv").hide()`	Hides the element whose *ID* is "displayDiv"
Show an element	`$("#displayDiv").show()`	Shows the element whose *ID* is "displayDiv"
Toggle the display of an element	`$("#displayDiv").toggle()`	Hides the element whose *ID* is "displayDiv" if it is visible; otherwise, shows it

jQuery supports many methods for manipulating DOM elements beyond what is shown in Table 5-3. The complete reference of supported methods is available at *http://api.jquery.com/ category/manipulation*. Furthermore, jQuery methods can be chained together so that you can perform several operations in a single line of code. The following code changes the inner HTML of an element, adds a class, and then displays the result, all in a single line:

```
$("displayDiv").html("<p>Hello</p>").addClass("emphasis").show();
```

Understanding jQuery event handling

Along with selecting and manipulating elements, you can use jQuery to attach event handlers to DOM elements. By handling events in jQuery, you can keep your JavaScript code out of the webpage and contained within custom libraries. This approach makes your code much more maintainable and isolated than using a more traditional approach to bind events to DOM elements.

The basic approach for binding events is to select the target DOM element by using the global function and then bind the event. The code to run in response to the event can be defined directly in the binding as an anonymous function. The following code shows a simple example of binding the click event of all paragraph elements:

```
$("p").click( function (e) {
    alert($(e.target).text());
});
```

Notice in the preceding code that the function handling the click event is defined in line with the binding. Additionally, notice how the element that caused the event can be determined by selecting *e.target* within the function. Complete documentation for the events supported by the jQuery library is available at *http://api.jquery.com/category/events*.

Of all the events available in jQuery, the most important is the *ready* event of the *document* object. This event fires when the DOM is ready for selection and manipulation. The SharePoint-hosted app project template in Visual Studio 2012 automatically adds this event handler into the *Apps.js* library of the app to act as the starting point. This is a pattern that you should follow in your apps as well.

Working with the client-side object model

SharePoint 2010 introduced the client-side object model (CSOM) as a way to program against a Windows Communication Foundation (WCF) endpoint in SharePoint by using a style that mimicked server-side API development. Prior to the introduction of CSOM, SharePoint developers had only a limited set of web services available for use from client-side code. With the introduction of CSOM, developers had a way to access a significant portion of core SharePoint functionality from C# (called the Managed Client Object Model), JavaScript, and Silverlight. Although the Silverlight CSOM is still available in SharePoint 2013, its primary role is for creating mobile apps, so this chapter focuses on the managed and JavaScript implementations of CSOM.

Understanding client object model fundamentals

The managed and JavaScript client object models are maintained in separate libraries, which are located under the SharePoint system directory. The managed client object model is contained in the assemblies *Microsoft.SharePoint.Client.dll* and *Microsoft.SharePoint.ClientRuntime.dll*, which can be found in the ISAPI folder. The JavaScript client object model is contained in the library *sp.js*, which is located in the LAYOUTS folder. Although each of the models provides a different programming interface, each interacts with SharePoint through a WCF service named Client.svc, which is located in the ISAPI directory. Figure 5-1 shows a basic architectural diagram for the client object models.

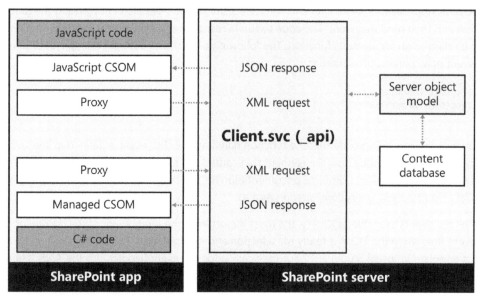

FIGURE 5-1 An overview of the client object model architecture

In SharePoint 2013, CSOM has been greatly expanded to include functionality from workloads outside of SharePoint Foundation. By using CSOM, app developers now have client-side access to Enterprise Search, Business Connectivity Services, Managed Metadata, Social, and much more. This additional functionality is made available through separate assemblies and libraries that can be referenced in your apps.

Each of the object models presents an object interface in front of a service proxy. Developers write client-side code by using the object model, but the operations are batched and sent as a single XML request to the Client.svc service. When the XML request is received, the Client.svc service makes calls to the server-side object model on behalf of the client. The results of the server-side calls are then sent back to the calling client in the form of a JavaScript Object Notation (JSON) object.

Understanding contexts

As in the standard code you write against the server-side object model, CSOM requires a starting point in the form of a context object. The context object provides an entry point into the associated API that can be used to gain access to other objects. When you have access to the objects, you can interact with the scalar properties of the object freely (for example, *Name*, *Title*, *Url*, and so on). Listing 5-4 shows how to create a context in each of the models and return an object representing asite collection. When the site collection object is returned, the *Url* property is examined.

LISTING 5-4 Creating contexts

```
//Managed Client Object Model
string appWebUrl = Page.Request["SPAppWebUrl"];
using (ClientContext ctx = new ClientContext(appWebUrl))
{
    Site siteCollection = ctx.Site;
    ctx.Load(siteCollection);
    ctx.ExecuteQuery();
    string url = siteCollection.Url;
}

//JavaScript Client Object Model
var siteCollection;
var ctx = new SP.ClientContext.get_current();
siteCollection = ctx.get_site();
ctx.load(siteCollection);
ctx.executeQueryAsync(success, failure);

function success() {
    var url = siteCollection.get_url();
}
function failure() {
    alert("Failure!");
}
```

The *ClientContext* class in the managed object model inherits from the *ClientContextRuntime* class. By using the *ClientContext* class, you can get a valid runtime context by passing in the URL of a site. In Listing 5-4, the URL of the app web is retrieved from the *SPAppWebUrl* querystring parameter. This URL is always available to the remote web and can be used to create a client context in scenarios where the SharePoint app is using the "internal" security principal. Scenarios that use OAuth tokens for app authentication are covered in Chapter 11, "SharePoint site provisioning."

The *SP.ClientContext* object in the JavaScript client object model inherits from the *SP.ClientContext-Runtime* object and provides equivalent functionality to the *ClientContext* class found in the managed client object model. As in the managed model, you can get a runtime context in the JavaScript model by using the *SP.ClientContext* class and passing a URL. In Listing 5-4, the context is created by using the *get_current* method, which returns a client context for the app web.

Loading and executing operations

The *ClientContextRuntime* class used by the managed client defines two methods for loading objects: *Load* and *LoadQuery*. You use these load methods to designate objects that should be retrieved from the server. The *Load* method specifies an object or collection to retrieve, whereas you use the *Load-Query* method to return collections of objects by using a Language-Integrated Query (LINQ) request.

Executing the *Load* or *LoadQuery* method does not cause the client to communicate with the server. Instead, it adds the load operation to a batch that will be executed on the server. In fact, you can execute multiple load methods (as well as other operations) before calling the server. Each operation is batched waiting for your code to initiate communication with server. To execute the batched operations, your code must call the *ExecuteQuery* method in managed code or the *ExecuteQueryAsync* method in JavaScript. The *ExecuteQuery* method creates an XML request and passes it to the Client.svc service synchronously. The *ExecuteQueryAsync* method sends the request asynchronously. Designated success and failure callback methods receive notification when the asynchronous batch operation is complete.

The sample code in Listing 5-4 uses the *Load* method to request an object representing the current site collection. When an object is returned, you can generally access any of the scalar properties associated with the object. In cases for which you do not want to return all of the scalar properties for a given object, you can designate the properties to return. In the managed object, properties are designated by providing a series of lambda expressions. In the JavaScript object model, properties are designated by name. This technique helps to minimize the amount of data sent between the client and server. The following code shows how to request only the *Title* and *ServerRelativeUrl* properties for a web object:

```
//Managed CSOM references properties via lambda expressions
ctx.Load(site, s=>s.Title, s=>s.ServerRelativeUrl);

//JavaScript CSOM references properties by name
ctx.Load(site, "Title", "ServerRelativeUrl");
```

Working with the managed client object model

Because the managed client object model is supported by Microsoft IntelliSense, is checked at compile time, and functions synchronously, many developers choose to develop apps that use remote webs and the managed CSOM to communicate with SharePoint. Using the managed client object model is a simple matter of setting a reference to the assemblies *Microsoft.SharePoint.Client.dll* and *Microsoft.SharePoint.ClientRuntime.dll*, adding a *using* statement for the *Microsoft.SharePoint.Client* namespace, and writing code. This section details how to perform basic operations with the managed client object model.

Returning collections

When working with the client object models, you will quite often be interested in returning collections of items such as all the lists in a site or all of the items in a list. Collections of items can be returned by using either the *Load* or *LoadQuery* method. When specifying the items of a collection to return, you can use the *Load* method along with a LINQ query formatted by using *method* syntax. Additionally, you can use the *LoadQuery* method with a LINQ query formatted by using *query* syntax. Listing 5-5 shows how to return all of the list titles in a site for which the *Title* is not *NULL*.

LISTING 5-5 Returning collections by using LINQ

```
string appWebUrl = Page.Request["SPAppWebUrl"];
using (ClientContext ctx = new ClientContext(appWebUrl))
{
    //Method Syntax
    ctx.Load(ctx.Web,
            w => w.Lists.Include(l => l.Title).Where(l => l.Title != null));
    ctx.ExecuteQuery();

    foreach (List list in ctx.Web.Lists)
    {
        Response.Write(list.Title);
    }

    //Query Syntax
    var q = from l in ctx.Web.Lists
            where l.Title != null
            select l;

    var r = ctx.LoadQuery(q);
    ctx.ExecuteQuery();

    Response.Write("<ul>");
    foreach (var i in r)
    {
        Response.Write("<li>");
        Response.Write(i.Title);
        Response.Write("</li>");
    }
    Response.Write("</ul>");
}
```

Handling errors

Because of the disconnected nature of the client object model, error handling is especially important. You might see errors thrown when you attempt to access an object or value that has not yet been retrieved from the server. You might also see errors if you create a query that is not meaningful in the current context, such as trying to retrieve list items before loading the associated list. Finally, you must deal with errors that happen in the middle of batch operations on the server. All of these situations mean that you must pay special attention to error handling in your CSOM solutions.

If you attempt to access a scalar property that has not been retrieved, you will receive a Property-OrFieldNotInitializedException error. If you make a request to the server that is deemed invalid, you will receive a ClientRequestException error. If your LINQ query is invalid, you will receive an Invalid-QueryExpressionException error. General errors thrown on the server during execution of a request will result in a ServerException error. Listing 5-6 shows code that generates the various runtime errors you might see when working with the managed client object model.

LISTING 5-6 Handling request errors

```
string appWebUrl = Page.Request["SPAppWebUrl"];
using (ClientContext ctx = new ClientContext(appWebUrl))
{
    try
    {
        //Fails because the object was not initialized
        //Requires Load() and ExecuteQuery()
        Response.Write(ctx.Web.Title);
    }
    catch (PropertyOrFieldNotInitializedException x)
    {
        Response.Write("<p>Property not initialized. " + x.Message + "</p>");
    }

    try
    {
        //Fails because Skip() and Take() are meaningless
        //in the context of a list collection
        ctx.Load(ctx.Web, w => w.Lists.Skip(5).Take(5));
        ctx.ExecuteQuery();
    }
    catch (InvalidQueryExpressionException x)
    {
        Response.Write("<p>Invalid LINQ query. " + x.Message + "</p>");
    }

    try
    {
        //Fails because InvalidObject is a meaningless object
        InvalidObject o = new InvalidObject(ctx, null);
        ctx.Load(o);
        ctx.ExecuteQuery();
    }
    catch (ClientRequestException x)
    {
        Response.Write("<p>Bad request. " + x.Message + "</p>");
    }

    try
    {
      //Fails because the list does not exist
        //The failure occurs on the server during processing
        ctx.Load(ctx.Web,w=>w.Lists);
        List myList = ctx.Web.Lists.GetByTitle("Non-Existent List");
        myList.Description = "A new description";
        myList.Update();
        ctx.ExecuteQuery();
    }
```

```
        catch (ServerException x)
        {
            Response.Write("<p>Exception on server. " + x.Message + "</p>");
        }
    }
```

After you have looked over the errors that can occur during operations, the ServerException error should stand out as noteworthy. This is because the ServerException error is thrown when an operation fails on the server. Furthermore, the failing operation could be in the middle of a large batch of operations, which can lead to unpredictable behavior. The fundamental challenge with the batch model embodied in the client object model is that you need a way to respond to errors that happen on the server so that the remainder of the batch operations can finish processing. The ServerException error is thrown on the client after the batch has failed, which gives you no opportunity to correct the error.

Fortunately, CSOM provides a mechanism for sending error-handling instructions to the server along with the batch operations. You can use the *ExceptionHandlingScope* object to define a *try-catch-finally* block that embodies server-side operations. If errors occur during processing on the server, they are handled on the server by the code embodied in the *ExceptionHandlingScope* object. Listing 5-7 shows how exception-handling scopes are implemented in the managed client object model.

LISTING 5-7 Handling errors in a scope

```
string appWebUrl = Page.Request["SPAppWebUrl"];
using (ClientContext ctx = new ClientContext(appWebUrl))
{
    //Set up error handling
    ExceptionHandlingScope xScope = new ExceptionHandlingScope(ctx);

    using (xScope.StartScope())
    {
        using (xScope.StartTry())
        {
            //Try to update the description of a list named "My List"
            List myList = ctx.Web.Lists.GetByTitle("My List");
            myList.Description = "A new description";
            myList.Update();
        }
```

```
using (xScope.StartCatch())
{
    //Fails if the list "My List" does not exist
    //So, we'll create a new list
    ListCreationInformation listCI = new ListCreationInformation();
    listCI.Title = "My List";
    listCI.TemplateType = (int)ListTemplateType.GenericList;
    listCI.QuickLaunchOption = Microsoft.SharePoint.Client.QuickLaunchOptions.On;
    List list = ctx.Web.Lists.Add(listCI);
}
using (xScope.StartFinally())
{
    //Try to update the list now if it failed originally
    List myList = ctx.Web.Lists.GetByTitle("My List");
    if(myList.Description.Length==0)
    {
        myList.Description = "A new description";
        myList.Update();
    }
}
}

//Execute the entire try-catch as a batch!
ctx.ExecuteQuery();
}
```

The most important aspect of the code shown in Listing 5-7 is that the *ExecuteQuery* method is called only once, and it appears after the code in the exception-handling scope. This means that all of the operations defined in the exception-handling scope are sent to the server in a single batch. Initially, the server tries to update the description of the target list. If this operation fails, the exception-handling scope assumes it is because the list does not exist. Therefore, the exception-handling scope creates a new list with the correct name. Finally, the description is updated for the newly created list.

The exception-handling scope provides a powerful way for you to deal with errors that occur during batch processing, but it does require some additional planning. For example, the code in Listing 5-7 assumes that any failure is the result of a nonexistent list. However, there are other reasons why the operation could fail, such as the end user not having the rights to update the list. Fortunately, the *ExceptionHandlingScope* method provides properties that help you to understand exactly what went wrong on the server. The *ServerErrorCode*, *ServerErrorValue*, and *ServerStackTrace* properties can all be used to analyze the server error and make a decision about how to proceed.

Creating, reading, updating, and deleting

In the conditional scope shown in Listing 5-7, a new list is created if the user has the appropriate permissions. Creating new lists and items by using the managed client object model is done with the creation information objects. By using the *ListCreationInformation* and *ListItemCreationInformation* objects, you can define all of the necessary values for a list or item and then send that data with the batch back to the server. Listing 5-8 shows how to use these objects to create a new list and list item.

LISTING 5-8 Creating a list and list item

```
string appWebUrl = Page.Request["SPAppWebUrl"];
using (ClientContext ctx = new ClientContext(appWebUrl))
{
    //Create a new list
    ListCreationInformation listCI = new ListCreationInformation();
    listCI.Title = "My List";
    listCI.Description += "A list for use with the Client OM";
    listCI.TemplateType = (int)ListTemplateType.GenericList;
    listCI.QuickLaunchOption = Microsoft.SharePoint.Client.QuickLaunchOptions.On;
    List list = ctx.Web.Lists.Add(listCI);
    ctx.ExecuteQuery();

    //Create a new list item
    ListItemCreationInformation listItemCI = new ListItemCreationInformation();
    ListItem item = list.AddItem(listItemCI);
    item["Title"] = "New Item";
    item.Update();
    ctx.ExecuteQuery();
}
```

If you would like to return items from a list by using CSOM, you must write Collaborative Application Markup Language (CAML) queries. CAML queries are created for the managed client object model via the *CamlQuery* object. This object has a *ViewXml* property that accepts a CAML query designating the items to return. Listing 5-9 demonstrates running a CAML query against a list.

LISTING 5-9 Using CAML to return list items

```
string appWebUrl = Page.Request["SPAppWebUrl"];
using (ClientContext ctx = new ClientContext(appWebUrl))
{
    //Read the Site, List, and Items
    ctx.Load(ctx.Web);

    List myList = ctx.Web.Lists.GetByTitle("My List");
    ctx.Load(myList);

    StringBuilder caml = new StringBuilder();
    caml.Append("<View><Query>");
    caml.Append("<Where><Eq><FieldRef Name='Title'/>");
    caml.Append("<Value Type='Text'>New Item</Value></Eq></Where>");
    caml.Append("</Query><RowLimit>50</RowLimit></View>");

    CamlQuery query = new CamlQuery();
    query.ViewXml = caml.ToString();
    ListItemCollection myItems = myList.GetItems(query);
    ctx.Load(myItems);
```

```
        ctx.ExecuteQuery();
        Response.Write("<p>Site: " + ctx.Web.Title + "</p>");
        Response.Write("<p>List: " + myList.Title + "</p>");
        Response.Write("<p>Item Count: " + myItems.Count.ToString() + "</p>");
    }
```

Updating through the managed client object model is straightforward. In most cases, you will simply set the value of a property and then call the appropriate *Update* method. Listing 5-10 presents samples of updating the site, list, and list item from Listing 5-9.

LISTING 5-10 Update operations

```
//Update the Site, List, and Items
ctx.Web.Description = "Client OM samples";
ctx.Web.Update();

myList.Description = "Client OM data";
myList.Update();

foreach (ListItem myItem in myItems)
{
    myItem["Title"] = "Updated";
    myItem.Update();
}

ctx.ExecuteQuery();
Response.Write("<p>Site: " + ctx.Web.Description + "</p>");
Response.Write("<p>List: " + myList.Description + "</p>");
Response.Write("<p>Item Count: " + myItems.Count.ToString()+ "</p>");
```

Deleting objects with the managed client object model involves calling the *DeleteObject* method. This method is the same across most objects that can be deleted. The following code shows how to delete the list created earlier:

```
myList.DeleteObject();
ctx.ExecuteQuery();
```

Along with lists, you'll also want to work with libraries. Document libraries are handled in the managed client object model much as lists are handled. Of course, the major difference is in handling documents. Fortunately, uploading documents to libraries by using the managed client object model is very similar to doing so using the server object model; you must upload the document using the URL of the folder in which you want to store the document. Listing 5-11 shows a full set of create, read, update, and delete operations around a file and a document library.

LISTING 5-11 Working with document libraries

```
string appWebUrl = Page.Request["SPAppWebUrl"];
using (ClientContext ctx = new ClientContext(appWebUrl))
{
    //Get site
    Web site = ctx.Web;
    ctx.Load(site);
    ctx.ExecuteQuery();

    //Create a new library
    ListCreationInformation listCI = new ListCreationInformation();
    listCI.Title = "My Docs";
    listCI.Description = "A library for use with Client OM";
    listCI.TemplateType = (int)ListTemplateType.DocumentLibrary;
    listCI.QuickLaunchOption = Microsoft.SharePoint.Client.QuickLaunchOptions.On;
    List list =site.Lists.Add(listCI);
    ctx.ExecuteQuery();

    //Create a document
    MemoryStream m = new MemoryStream();
    StreamWriter w = new StreamWriter(m);
    w.Write("Some content for the document.");
    w.Flush();

    //Add it to the library
    FileCreationInformation fileCI = new FileCreationInformation();
    fileCI.Content = m.ToArray();
    fileCI.Overwrite = true;
    fileCI.Url = appWebUrl + "/My%20Docs/MyFile.txt";
    Folder rootFolder = site.GetFolderByServerRelativeUrl("My%20Docs");
    ctx.Load(rootFolder);
    Microsoft.SharePoint.Client.File newFile = rootFolder.Files.Add(fileCI);
    ctx.ExecuteQuery();

    //Edit Properties
    ListItem newItem = newFile.ListItemAllFields;
    ctx.Load(newItem);
    newItem["Title"] = "My new file";
    newItem.Update();
    ctx.ExecuteQuery();

    //Delete file
    newItem.DeleteObject();
    ctx.ExecuteQuery();
}
```

Working with the JavaScript client object model

The JavaScript client object model is really only a viable choice in SharePoint-hosted apps where C# code is not allowed and the pages have an associated SharePoint context. The SharePoint 2013 app project template for SharePoint-hosted apps provides some initial template code to implement a welcome message. This code is a good place to see the fundamentals of JSOM in action. Listing 5-12 comes from the app project template for a SharePoint-hosted app.

LISTING 5-12 Visual Studio 2012 app project template code

```
'use strict';

var context = SP.ClientContext.get_current();
var user = context.get_web().get_currentUser();

$(document).ready(function () {
    getUserName();
});
function getUserName() {
    context.load(user);
    context.executeQueryAsync(onGetUserNameSuccess, onGetUserNameFail);
}
function onGetUserNameSuccess() {
    $('#message').text('Hello ' + user.get_title());
}
function onGetUserNameFail(sender, args) {
    alert('Failed to get user name. Error:' + args.get_message());
}
```

The code in Listing 5-12 creates two variables in the global namespace named *context* and *user*, to reference objects needed globally. The *context* variable is used to set up the SharePoint context on the client side so that calls can be made back to the Client.svc endpoint. and the *user* variable references the current app user. Note that this template code violates the best practice of encapsulating code in a separate namespace. Therefore, it is best to simply delete all of the template code when creating your own apps.

To populate the variables, a call is made to the *load* method to specify that the scalar properties should be loaded, and then a call to the *executeQueryAsync* method is made to make an asynchronous call to the Client.svc endpoint. In the app project code, the round trip populates not only information about the app web, but also information about the current user. Combining operations in this way makes CSOM programming more efficient. Two callback functions, which the template code names *onGetUserNameSuccess* and *onGetUserNameFail*, are passed. The first callback function is called if the round trip completes without errors. The second callback function is called if errors occur.

Returning collections

The JavaScript client object model supports both a *load* and *loadQuery* method. The *loadQuery* method can be used to store a collection into a variable other than the one referencing the desired collection. In either method, you can use query strings to request that collections be included in the returned results. Listing 5-13 illustrates how to use the JavaScript client object model to return all of the list titles in the app web along with the field names and descriptions for each list.

LISTING 5-13 Returning collections with JavaScript

```javascript
"use strict";

var Wingtip = window.Wingtip || {}

Wingtip.Collections = function () {

    //private members
    var site,
        listCollection,

        getListCollection = function () {
            var ctx = new SP.ClientContext.get_current();
            site = ctx.get_web();
            ctx.load(site);
            listCollection = site.get_lists();
            ctx.load(listCollection,
                'Include(Title,Id,Fields.Include(Title,Description))');
            ctx.executeQueryAsync(success, failure);
        },

        success = function () {

            var html = [];

            //List Information
            html.push("<ul>");
            var listEnumerator = listCollection.getEnumerator();
            while (listEnumerator.moveNext()) {

                //List Title
                html.push("<li>");
                html.push(listEnumerator.get_current().get_title());
                html.push("<ul>");

                //Field Names
                var fieldEnumerator =
                    listEnumerator.get_current().get_fields().getEnumerator();
                while (fieldEnumerator.moveNext()) {
                    html.push("<li>");
                    html.push(fieldEnumerator.get_current().get_title());
                    html.push("</li>");
                }

                html.push("</ul></li>");
            }
            html.push("</ul>");
```

```
                //Show results
                $("#displayDiv").html(html.join(''));
        },

        failure = function (sender, args) {
            alert(args.get_message());
        }

    //public interface
    return {
        execute: getListCollection
    }
}();

$(document).ready(function () {
    Wingtip.Collections.execute();
});
```

Handling errors

Just like the managed client object model, the JavaScript client object model must deal with the
potential for server-side errors during the round trip. Because the JavaScript client object model can
only make asynchronous calls, the basic error-handling pattern involves the definition of success and
failure callback methods. However, you can also use error scopes in your JavaScript. Listing 5-14 shows
how to set up error scopes in JavaScript. The sample performs the same functionality as presented in
Listing 5-7, wherein managed code was used.

LISTING 5-14 JavaScript CSOM error scopes

```
"use strict";

var Wingtip = window.Wingtip || {}

Wingtip.ErrorScope = function () {

    //private members
    var site,

    scope = function () {

        //Get Context
        var ctx = new SP.ClientContext.get_current();

        //Start Exception-Handling Scope
        var e = new SP.ExceptionHandlingScope(ctx);
        var s = e.startScope();

        //try
        var t = e.startTry();
```

```
        var list1 = ctx.get_web().get_lists().getByTitle("My List");
        ctx.load(list1);
        list1.set_description("A new description");
        list1.update();

        t.dispose();

        //catch
        var c = e.startCatch();

        var listCI = new SP.ListCreationInformation();

        listCI.set_title("My List");
        listCI.set_templateType(SP.ListTemplateType.announcements);
        listCI.set_quickLaunchOption(SP.QuickLaunchOptions.on);

        var list = ctx.get_web().get_lists().add(listCI);

        c.dispose();

        //finally
        var f = e.startFinally();

        var list2 = ctx.get_web().get_lists().getByTitle("My List");
        ctx.load(list2);
        list2.set_description("A new description");
        list2.update();

        f.dispose();

        //End Exception-Handling Scope
        s.dispose();

        //Execute
        ctx.executeQueryAsync(success, failure);

        },

    success = function () {
        alert("Success");
    },

    failure = function (sender, args) {
        alert(args.get_message());
    }

    //public interface
    return {
        execute: scope
    }
}();


$(document).ready(function () {
    Wingtip.ErrorScope.execute();
});
```

Creating, reading, updating, and deleting in the JavaScript client object model

Creating, reading, updating, and deleting list items by using the JavaScript client object model is more complex than with the managed client object model. The additional complexity comes from not only the asynchronous calls, but also the need to properly encapsulate the JavaScript so that it's separated from the global namespace. Listing 5-15 shows the basic structure of a JavaScript library used to perform create, read, update, and delete (CRUD) operations on a contacts list contained in a SharePoint-hosted app.

LISTING 5-15 CSOM library structure

```
"use strict";

var Wingtip = window.Wingtip || {};
Wingtip.Contacts;
Wingtip.ContactList = function () {

    //private members
    var createItem = function (lname, fname, wphone) {
    },
    readAll = function () {
    },
    readAllSuccess = function () {
    },
    updateItem = function (id, lname, fname, wphone) {
    },
    removeItem = function (id) {
    },
    success = function () {
        readAll();
    },
    error = function (sender, args) {
        alert(args.get_message());
    }

    //public interface
    return {
        createContact: createItem,
        updateContact: updateItem,
        deleteContact: removeItem
    }

}();

$(document).ready(function () {
    Wingtip.ContactList.createContact("Cox", "Brian", "555-555-5555");
    alert("Contact Created!");
    Wingtip.ContactList.updateContact(1, "Cox", "Brian", "111-111-1111");
    alert("Contact Updated!");
    Wingtip.ContactList.deleteContact(1);
    alert("Contact Deleted!");
});
```

Before examining the implementation details for the CRUD operations, take some time to study the structure of the library. Listing 5-15 contains the definition of a namespace object and a self-invoking function, which should be familiar from other examples in this chapter. In this case, however, a new property named *Wingtip.Contacts* is also defined. This property is used to hold a reference to the list items between asynchronous calls to the SharePoint server. Within the self-invoking function, all of the CRUD operations are defined, but only the create, update, and delete functions are revealed through the public interface of the library. These functions are called from some example code contained in the *ready* event handler.

Creating new contacts is done in the *createItem* function. This function uses the *SP.ListItemCreationInformation* object to define a new list item. The first name, last name, and phone number are set on the new item, and the item is added to the list. Note that in a contacts list, the *"Title"* field is actually the last name of the contact. Listing 5-16 presents the code for adding a new item.

LISTING 5-16 Creating new items

```
createItem = function (lname, fname, wphone) {
    var ctx = new SP.ClientContext.get_current();
    var list = ctx.get_web().get_lists().getByTitle("Contacts");
    ctx.load(list);
    var listItemCreationInfo = new SP.ListItemCreationInformation();
    var newContact = list.addItem(listItemCreationInfo);
    newContact.set_item("Title", lname);
    newContact.set_item("FirstName", fname);
    newContact.set_item("WorkPhone", wphone);
    newContact.update();
    ctx.executeQueryAsync(success, error);
}
```

After each create, update, or delete operation, the list is read and redrawn. The *readAll* function reads every item in the list by using a CAML query and then creates an HTML table to hold the contacts. The HTML is rendered in a div via jQuery. Listing 5-17 demonstrates how the list is read and drawn. Note the use of the *Wingtip.Contacts* property to reference the list data between asynchronous calls to the server.

LISTING 5-17 Rendering the list items

```
readAll = function () {
    var ctx = new SP.ClientContext.get_current();
    var query = "<View><Query><OrderBy><FieldRef Name='Title'/>" +
                "<FieldRef Name='FirstName'/></OrderBy></Query>" +
                "<ViewFields><FieldRef Name='ID'/><FieldRef Name='Title'/>" +
                "<FieldRef Name='FirstName'/><FieldRef Name='WorkPhone'/></ViewFields></
View>";
    var camlQuery = new SP.CamlQuery();
    camlQuery.set_viewXml(query);
    var list = ctx.get_web().get_lists().getByTitle("Contacts");
    ctx.load(list);
    Wingtip.Contacts = list.getItems(camlQuery);
    ctx.load(Wingtip.Contacts, 'Include(ID,Title,FirstName,WorkPhone)');
    ctx.executeQueryAsync(readAllSuccess, error);
},

readAllSuccess = function () {
    var html = [];
    html.push("<table><thead><tr><th>ID</th><th>First Name</th>");
    html.push("<th>Last Name</th><th>Title</th></tr></thead>");

    var listItemEnumerator = Wingtip.Contacts.getEnumerator();

    while (listItemEnumerator.moveNext()) {
        var listItem = listItemEnumerator.get_current();
        html.push("<tr><td>");
        html.push(listItem.get_item("ID"));
        html.push("</td><td>");
        html.push(listItem.get_item("FirstName"));
        html.push("</td><td>");
        html.push(listItem.get_item("Title"));
        html.push("</td><td>");
        html.push(listItem.get_item("WorkPhone"));
        html.push("</td><td>");
    }

    html.push("</table>");
    $('#displayDiv').html(html.join(''));
}
```

Updating list items is accomplished by using the *updateItem* function. This function retrieves the item to be updated by its ID in the list. The new values for the fields are applied to the list item and the item is updated. After the round trip to the server, the table is redrawn with the new values for the list item visible. Listing 5-18 shows the code for updating items.

LISTING 5-18 Updating list items

```
updateItem = function (id, lname, fname, wphone) {
    var ctx = new SP.ClientContext.get_current();
    var list = ctx.get_web().get_lists().getByTitle("Contacts");
    ctx.load(list);
    var listItem = list.getItemById(id);
    listItem.set_item("Title", lname);
    listItem.set_item("FirstName", fname);
    listItem.set_item("WorkPhone", wphone);
    listItem.update();
    ctx.executeQueryAsync(success, error);
}
```

Deleting list items is done by using the *removeItem* function. The function retrieves the item to delete by its ID. The *deleteObject* method is then called to remove the designated item from the list. After the item is removed asynchronously, the table is redrawn with the remaining list items. Listing 5-19 presents the code for deleting items.

LISTING 5-19 Deleting list items

```
removeItem = function (id) {
    var ctx = new SP.ClientContext.get_current();
    var list = ctx.get_web().get_lists().getByTitle("Contacts");
    ctx.load(list);
    var listItem = list.getItemById(id);
    listItem.deleteObject();
    ctx.executeQueryAsync(success, error);
}
```

Working with the REST API

If you are planning to create apps that are based primarily on JavaScript, you will be interested in the Representational State Transfer (REST) API. Making REST calls from JavaScript is considerably easier than making the equivalent CSOM calls. Furthermore, several libraries such as jQuery provide additional support for REST calls. All of this makes the REST API an attractive approach for app development.

Understanding REST fundamentals

Remote Procedure Call (RPC) is a software architecture that uses a generated client-side proxy to communicate with a remote web service. Simple Object Access Protocol (SOAP) is the protocol that is used along with the RPC architecture in classic SharePoint web services. When developers think about making RPCs to SharePoint, they most often think about calling into a SOAP web service to perform tasks such as retrieving user profile information, running a search, or interacting with a list.

REST is a software architecture that uses uniform resource identifiers (URIs) to specify operations against a remote service. Open Data Protocol (OData) is the protocol that is used along with REST to access many cloud-based services. Although SharePoint developers are most familiar with the RPC/SOAP approach, the REST/OData approach has become important when developing cloud-based solutions.

REST-based (known more commonly as "RESTful") solutions use standard HTTP *GET, POST, PUT,* and *DELETE* verbs to perform CRUD operations against a remote source. Support for the standard HTTP verbs provides easy cross-platform data access and makes REST ideally suited for cloud-based apps. The OData protocol returns results in either the Atom Publishing Protocol (AtomPub) or JSON.

SharePoint 2010 introduced support for RESTful access to list data through the listdata.svc web service. In SharePoint 2013, the listdata.svc service is still available, but it should not be used for any new development. Instead, the client.svc service has been expanded to include significant support for RESTful operations. Nearly all of the APIs available through CSOM have a corresponding RESTful endpoint. Additionally, the client.svc endpoint can be reached through the alias *_api*, which makes forming appropriate URIs more natural. Figure 5-2 presents a basic architectural diagram of the SharePoint 2013 REST infrastructure.

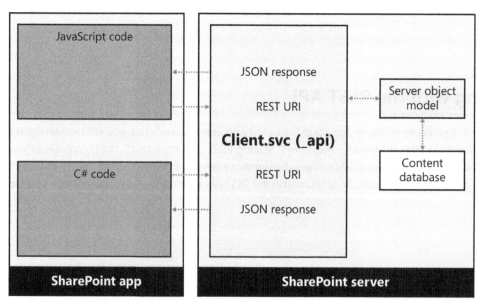

FIGURE 5-2 An overview of the SharePoint 2013 REST architecture

The essential task required to use the REST capabilities in SharePoint 2013 is to create the correct URI. One of the nice things about REST is that you can enter URIs directly in the browser and immediately see the result of the HTTP *GET* operation. By using this approach, you can experiment with the URIs quite easily to ensure that they return the desired results. For a SharePoint site collection located at wingtip.com, Listing 5-20 shows the returned XML from the URI *http://wingtip.com/_api/site*, which returns the site collection properties.

LISTING 5-20 Site collection properties

```xml
<?xml version="1.0" encoding="utf-8" ?>
<entry xml:base="http://wingtip.com/_api/" xmlns="http://www.w3.org/2005/Atom"
 xmlns:d="http://schemas.microsoft.com/ado/2007/08/dataservices"
 xmlns:m="http://schemas.microsoft.com/ado/2007/08/dataservices/metadata"
 xmlns:georss="http://www.georss.org/georss" xmlns:gml="http://www.opengis.net/gml">
 <id>http://wingtip.com/_api/site</id>
 <category term="SP.Site"
  scheme="http://schemas.microsoft.com/ado/2007/08/dataservices/scheme" />
 <link rel="edit" href="site" />
 <link rel="http://schemas.microsoft.com/ado/2007/08/dataservices/related/EventReceivers"
  type="application/atom+xml;type=feed"
  title="EventReceivers" href="site/EventReceivers" />
 <link rel="http://schemas.microsoft.com/ado/2007/08/dataservices/related/Features"
  type="application/atom+xml;type=feed" title="Features" href="site/Features" />
 <link rel="http://schemas.microsoft.com/ado/2007/08/dataservices/related/Owner"
  type="application/atom+xml;type=entry" title="Owner" href="site/Owner" />
 <link rel="http://schemas.microsoft.com/ado/2007/08/dataservices/related/RecycleBin"
  type="application/atom+xml;type=feed" title="RecycleBin" href="site/RecycleBin" />
 <link rel="http://schemas.microsoft.com/ado/2007/08/dataservices/related/RootWeb"
  type="application/atom+xml;type=entry" title="RootWeb" href="site/RootWeb" />
 <link rel="http://schemas.microsoft.com/ado/2007/08/dataservices/related/
UserCustomActions"
  type="application/atom+xml;type=feed" title="UserCustomActions"
  href="site/UserCustomActions" />
 <title />
 <updated>2012-08-27T12:14:20Z</updated>
  <author>
   <name />
  </author>
  <content type="application/xml">
   <m:properties>
    <d:AllowDesigner m:type="Edm.Boolean">true</d:AllowDesigner>
    <d:AllowMasterPageEditing m:type="Edm.Boolean">true</d:AllowMasterPageEditing>
    <d:AllowRevertFromTemplate m:type="Edm.Boolean">true</
d:AllowRevertFromTemplate>
```

```
    <d:AllowSelfServiceUpgrade m:type="Edm.Boolean">true</d:AllowSelfServiceUpgrade>
    <d:AllowSelfServiceUpgradeEvaluation
      m:type="Edm.Boolean">true</d:AllowSelfServiceUpgradeEvaluation>
    <d:CompatibilityLevel m:type="Edm.Int32">15</d:CompatibilityLevel>
    <d:Id m:type="Edm.Guid">eb53c264-14db-4989-a395-b93cbe8b178c</d:Id>
    <d:LockIssue m:null="true" />
    <d:MaxItemsPerThrottledOperation m:type="Edm.Int32">5000</d:MaxItemsPerThrottledOpe
ration>
    <d:PrimaryUri>http://wingtip.com/</d:PrimaryUri>
    <d:ReadOnly m:type="Edm.Boolean">false</d:ReadOnly>
    <d:ServerRelativeUrl>/</d:ServerRelativeUrl>
    <d:ShowUrlStructure m:type="Edm.Boolean">true</d:ShowUrlStructure>
    <d:UIVersionConfigurationEnabled
      m:type="Edm.Boolean">false</d:UIVersionConfigurationEnabled>
    <d:UpgradeReminderDate m:type="Edm.DateTime">1899-12-30T00:00:00</
d:UpgradeReminderDate>
    <d:Url>http://wingtip.com</d:Url>
  </m:properties>
 </content>
</entry>
```

The main entry point for RESTful URIs is through the _api endpoint, which is referenced through either the site collection or site. Using the site collection or site URI as the root establishes the context for the RESTful operation. The following code shows a typical entry point:

```
http://wingtip.com/_api
```

Following the root reference is the namespace, which refers to the workload that you want to reference, such as search or taxonomy. Table 5-4 shows some sample namespaces in URIs. If the functionality you are invoking resides in SharePoint Foundation, no namespace is required. If the functionality resides in one of the many other available namespaces, it can be difficult to determine the exact URI without some form of documentation.

TABLE 5-4 Namespace sample URIs

Sample URI	Description
http://wingtip.com/_api/	SharePoint Foundation namespace
http://wingtip.com/_api/search	Enterprise search namespace
http://wingtip.com/_api/sp.userProfiles.peopleManager	User profiles namespace

The namespace in the URI is followed by a reference to the object, property, indexer, or method target that you want to invoke. Objects can include site collections, sites, lists, and list items. After an object is referenced, you can go on to reference the properties, indexers, and methods of the object. Table 5-5 shows several sample URIs referencing objects, properties, indexers, and methods.

TABLE 5-5 Object sample URIs

Sample URI	Description
http://wingtip.com/_api/site	Site collection object
http://wingtip.com/_api/web	Site object
http://wingtip.com/_api/site/url	Site collection URL property
http://wingtip.com/_api/web/lists	Site lists collection
http://wingtip.com/_api/web/lists('25e2737d-f23a-4fdb-ad5a-e5a94672504b')	Site lists collection indexer
http://wingtip.com/_api/web/lists/getbytitle('Contacts')	Site lists collection method
http://wingtip.com/_api/web/lists/getbytitle('Contacts')/items	List items collection

The RESTful URI ends with any OData query operators to specify selecting, sorting, or filtering. The *$select* operator is used to specify what fields to return from the query of a collection, such as list items or fields. The *$order* operator specifies the sort order of the results. In general, if you do not provide a *$select* operator in your URI, all items in the collection are returned, with the exception of any field or property that might be particularly large. The *$select* operator also supports returning projected fields from related lookup lists by using the *$expand* operator. Table 5-6 shows several sample URIs selecting items to return.

TABLE 5-6 Selecting and sorting items

Sample URI	Description
http://wingtip.com/_api/web/lists/getbytitle('Modules')/items	Select all fields in Modules list.
http://wingtip.com/_api/web/lists/getbytitle('Modules')/items? *$select=Title*	Select *Title* field in Modules list.
http://wingtip.com/_api/web/lists/getbytitle('Modules')/items? *$select=Title,Instructor/FullName&$expand=Instructor/FullName*	Select the *Title* and *Instructor* fields from the Modules list. The *Instructor* field is a lookup from another list, so expand the selection to include the *FullName* field from the list used as a lookup.
http://wingtip.com/_api/web/lists/getbytitle('Modules')/items? *$select=Title&$order=Modified*	Select *Title* field in Modules list and sort by the modified date.

You use the *$filter* operator to filter the results of the RESTful operation. The RESTful URI can include numeric comparisons, string comparisons, and date/time functions. Table 5-7 shows sample URIs that filter returned collections.

TABLE 5-7 Filtering items

Sample URI	Description
http://wingtip.com/_api/web/lists/getbytitle('Contacts')/items?$filter=FirstName eq 'Brian'	Return the item from the Contacts list, for which the FirstName is equal to "Brian"
http://wingtip.com/_api/web/lists/getbytitle('Contacts')/items?$filter=startswith(FirstName,'B')	Return all items from the Contacts list, for which the FirstName starts with the letter B
http://wingtip.com/_api/web/lists/getbytitle('Contacts')/items?$filter=month(Modified) eq 8	Return all items from the Contacts list modified in August

The *$top* and *$skip* operators are used to implement paging for results. The *$top* operator specifies how many results to return. You can use the *$skip* operator to pass over a specified number of items. Table 5-8 lists a few examples using these operators.

TABLE 5-8 Paging items

Sample URI	Description
http://wingtip.com/_api/web/lists/getbytitle('Contacts')/items?$top=5	Return the first five items in the Contacts list
http://wingtip.com/_api/web/lists/getbytitle('Contacts')/items?$top=5&$skip=5	Return the second page of results, with five results on each page
http://wingtip.com/_api/web/lists/getbytitle('Contacts')/items?$sort=Title&$top=5&$skip=5	Return the second page of results, sorted by Last Name (Note: The Title field in a contacts list actually contains the last name)

Working with the REST API in JavaScript

When you choose to use JavaScript with your app, you will find that by using the REST API, you can write cleaner code than with CSOM. Furthermore, you will find built-in support for REST in the jQuery library, which makes it much easier to use than CSOM. This section details the fundamental operations necessary to work with the REST API through JavaScript.

Performing basic operations

The section "Working with the JavaScript client object model" earlier in this chapter explained the SharePoint-hosted app project template code in CSOM. As a starting point for understanding REST, Listing 5-21 shows that CSOM code rewritten by using the REST API. Comparing the two implementations reveals that the REST version is more compact.

LISTING 5-21 Welcoming the current user

```
$(document).ready( function () {
    $.getJSON(_spPageContextInfo.webServerRelativeUrl + "/_api/web/currentuser",
    function(data) {
        $("#message").text('Hello ' + data.d.Title);
    });
});
```

As discussed in the section "Understanding jQuery event handling" earlier in this chapter, the function *ready* is called when the jQuery library is loaded. The RESTful URI in Listing 5-22 is created by using the *_spPageContextInfo* object to retrieve a reference to the *webServerRelativeUrl* property. This property returns a URL, which can be concatenated with *_/api* to form the root of the URI. The *_spPageContextInfo* object is added to the ASPX pages in your app by the *SPWebPartManager* control, which means that you can depend on using it to form RESTful URIs in your apps.

The rewritten code makes use of the *jQuery.getJSON* method to retrieve information about the current user. As the name implies, the data returned from the call is in JSON format. JSON format is easy to transform into a JavaScript object, which simplifies your coding. Notice how easily the *Title* property for the current user is retrieved from the JSON results.

The *jQuery.getJSON* method is a shorthand Asynchronous JavaScript and XML (AJAX) function that simplifies RESTful calls where JSON is returned. For more control over the call, you can use the *jQuery.ajax* method. Listing 5-22 shows the equivalent call made by using the *jQuery.ajax* method.

LISTING 5-22 Using the *jQuery.ajax* method

```
$(document).ready( function () {
    $.ajax(
        {
            url: _spPageContextInfo.webServerRelativeUrl +
                "/_api/web/currentuser",
            type: "GET",
            headers: {
                "accept": "application/json;odata=verbose",
            },
            success: function (data) {
                $("#message").text('Hello ' + data.d.Title);
            },
            error: function (err) {
                alert(JSON.stringify(err));
            }
        }
    );
});
```

Performing CRUD in REST

Much like CSOM CRUD operations, CRUD operations in REST should be encapsulated by using one of the JavaScript library patterns. When you create your RESTful libraries, they can have a structure that is very similar to the ones created for CSOM. Listing 5-23 demonstrates a basic library structure for encapsulating RESTful CRUD operations on a contacts list.

LISTING 5-23 REST library structure

```
"use strict";

var Wingtip = window.Wingtip || {};
Wingtip.ContactList = function () {

    //private members
    var createItem = function (lname, fname, wphone) {
    },
    readAll = function () {
    },
    readAllSuccess = function (data) {
    },
    updateItem = function (id, lname, fname, wphone) {
    },
    removeItem = function (id) {
    }

    //public interface
    return {
        createContact: createItem,
        updateContact: updateItem,
        deleteContact: removeItem
    }

}();

$(document).ready(function () {
    Wingtip.ContactList.createContact("Cox", "Brian", "555-555-5555");
    alert("Contact Created!");
    Wingtip.ContactList.updateContact(1, "Cox", "Brian", "111-111-1111");
    alert("Contact Updated!");
    Wingtip.ContactList.deleteContact(1);
    alert("Contact Deleted!");
});
```

The library structure in Listing 5-23 is similar to the structure used for the CSOM library presented in Listing 5-15. The primary difference between this REST library and the CSOM library is that no additional variable is required to reference objects between round trips to the server. Of course, the implementation details will be drastically different.

Creating new items is done by constructing a URI that refers to the collection to which the new items are to be added, and using the *POST* verb to send an object containing the data for the new item. Whenever a RESTful operation changes a SharePoint resource, the request must include a form digest. The form digest is a security validation that guarantees that the app page has not changed since it was delivered from the server. The easiest way to obtain the form digest is simply to read it from the form digest control on the app page. Listing 5-24 shows how to create a new item in a list by using this technique.

LISTING 5-24 Creating new items in a list

```
createItem = function (lname, fname, wphone) {
    $.ajax({
        url: _spPageContextInfo.webServerRelativeUrl +
            "/_api/web/lists/getByTitle('Contacts')/items",
        type: "POST",
        data: JSON.stringify(
            {
                '__metadata': {
                    'type': 'SP.Data.ContactsListItem'
                },
                'Title': lname,
                'FirstName': fname,
                'WorkPhone': wphone
            }),
        headers: {
            "accept": "application/json;odata=verbose",
            "X-RequestDigest": $("#__REQUESTDIGEST").val()
        },
        success: function () {
            readAll();;
        },
        error: function (err) {
            alert(JSON.stringify(err));
        }
    });
}
```

Along with the form digest, the create operation must also include the type metadata for the item that is being created. The type metadata is unique to the list and can be discovered by examining the metadata returned from a read operation. For list items, the type metadata generally follows the pattern *SP.Data*, concatenated with the name of the list, concatenated with *ListItem*. In Listing 5-25, the type metadata is *SP.Data.ContactsListItem*.

Reading items is a straightforward operation that uses a RESTful URI to request the items. This URI is called by using an HTTP *GET* verb. In the sample library, all successful calls to create, update, or delete an item result in redrawing the list in an HTML table. Listing 5-25 shows how to retrieve the list items and render a simple HTML table to display them.

LISTING 5-25 Reading items and presenting them in an HTML table

```
readAll = function () {
    $.ajax(
        {
            url: _spPageContextInfo.webServerRelativeUrl +
                "/_api/web/lists/getByTitle('Contacts')/items/" +
                "?$select=Id,FirstName,Title,WorkPhone" +
                "&$orderby=Title,FirstName",
            type: "GET",
            headers: {
                "accept": "application/json;odata=verbose",
            },
            success: function (data) {
                readAllSuccess(data);
            },
            error: function (err) {
                alert(JSON.stringify(err));
            }
        }
    );
},

readAllSuccess = function (data) {
    var html = [];
    html.push("<table><thead><tr><th>ID</th><th>First Name</th>" +
            "<th>Last Name</th><th>Title</th></tr></thead>");

    var results = data.d.results;

    for(var i=0; i<results.length; i++) {
        html.push("<tr><td>");
        html.push(results[i].ID);
        html.push("</td><td>");
        html.push(results[i].FirstName);
        html.push("</td><td>");
        html.push(results[i].Title);
        html.push("</td><td>");
        html.push(results[i].WorkPhone);
        html.push("</td></tr>");
    }
    html.push("</table>");
    $('#displayDiv').html(html.join(''));
},
```

Updating items is accomplished by creating a RESTful URI that refers to the item that will be updated. Just like item creation, item updating also requires the request to include a form digest. The URI is then invoked by using a *PUT*, *PATCH*, or *MERGE* verb. When a *PUT* operation is used, you must specify all writable properties in the request. When a *PATCH* or *MERGE* operation is used, you can specify only the properties you want to change. Although *MERGE* and *PATCH* accomplish the same task, the *PATCH* operation is considered more standard. Listing 5-26 shows how to update a list item by using the *PATCH* operation.

LISTING 5-26 Updating items

```
updateItem = function (id, lname, fname, wphone) {
    $.ajax(
        {
            url: _spPageContextInfo.webServerRelativeUrl +
                "/_api/web/lists/getByTitle('Contacts')/getItemByStringId('" +
                id + "')",
            type: "POST",
            contentType: "application/json;odata=verbose",
            data: JSON.stringify(
                {
                    '__metadata': {
                        'type': 'SP.Data.ContactsListItem'
                    },
                    'Title': lname,
                    'FirstName': fname,
                    'WorkPhone': wphone
                }),
            headers: {
                "accept": "application/json;odata=verbose",
                "X-RequestDigest": $("#__REQUESTDIGEST").val(),
                "IF-MATCH": "*",
                "X-Http-Method": "PATCH"
            },
            success: function (data) {
                readAll();
            },
            error: function (err) {
                alert(JSON.stringify(err));
            }
        }
    );
},
```

When performing updates on list items, you can use ETags for concurrency control. *ETags* are version numbers assigned at the list-item level. This number determines whether the list item was altered by another process since your code last read the data. You can find the ETag for a list item by reading it from the metadata. Listing 5-25 could be updated to display ETag values by reading them with the following code:

```
results[i].__metadata.etag
```

ETag values are sent during an update operation via the *IF-MATCH* header. If the ETag sent in the update process is different from the ETag currently assigned to the list item, the update will fail. If you want to force an update regardless of ETag values, you can pass *IF-MATCH:**, which is the approach taken in Listing 5-26.

Deleting an item is accomplished by first constructing a URI that references the target item to delete. The URI is invoked by using an HTTP *DELETE* verb. The delete operation must provide a form digest and an ETag value. Listing 5-27 shows the implementation of a delete operation.

LISTING 5-27 Deleting items

```
removeItem = function (id) {
    $.ajax(
        {
            url: _spPageContextInfo.webServerRelativeUrl +
                "/_api/web/lists/getByTitle('Contacts')/getItemByStringId('" +
                id + "')",
            type: "DELETE",
            headers: {
                "accept": "application/json;odata=verbose",
                "X-RequestDigest": $("#__REQUESTDIGEST").val(),
                "IF-MATCH": "*"
            },
            success: function (data) {
                readAll();
            },
            error: function (err) {
                alert(JSON.stringify(err));
            }
        }
    );
},
```

Working with the REST API in C#

Using the REST API from a C# application is certainly possible, but it is easily the least attractive of all the programming options. You will find that retrieving form digests, parsing out properties, and creating payloads can be tedious and messy. This section details the steps necessary to work with the REST API in C#.

Performing basic operations

In the section "Working with the REST API in JavaScript" earlier in this chapter, the SharePoint-hosted app project template code was rewritten to use REST. As a starting point to understanding how to use REST in C#, Listing 5-28 shows the same code rewritten in a provider-hosted app. The code runs within the *Page_Load* event and welcomes the user to the app.

LISTING 5-28 Welcoming the current user

```
protected void Page_Load(object sender, EventArgs e)
{
    //Construct URI
    string appWebUrl = Page.Request["SPAppWebUrl"];
    Uri uri = new Uri(appWebUrl + "/_api/web/currentuser");

    //Perform GET operation
    HttpWebRequest restRequest = (HttpWebRequest)WebRequest.Create(uri);
    restRequest.Credentials = CredentialCache.DefaultCredentials;
    restRequest.Method = "GET";
    HttpWebResponse restResponse = (HttpWebResponse)restRequest.GetResponse();

    //Parse out Title
    XDocument atomDoc = XDocument.Load(restResponse.GetResponseStream());
    XNamespace ns = "http://schemas.microsoft.com/ado/2007/08/dataservices";
    message.Text = "Hello " + atomDoc.Descendants(ns + "Title").First().Value;
}
```

The code in Listing 5-28 begins by constructing a URI to request the current user object from the REST API. The URI is invoked by using the *HttpWebRequest* object, which uses the HTTP *GET* verb and returns the data in AtomPub format. Finally, the *Title* property is extracted from the returned XML document by using LINQ-to-XML. You can see that the mechanics of using the REST API are the same in C# as they are in JavaScript, but the implementation is not as clean.

Performing CRUD in C#

Performing CRUD operations with C# against the REST API can be a bit challenging. This is because you must go through an extra step to retrieve a form digest and because you must create the proper XML payloads manually. Fortunately, you can encapsulate the basic CRUD functionality in a static class to make it easier. Listing 5-29 shows a basic class structure for encapsulating CRUD operations against the REST API. In keeping with previous examples, the class targets a contacts list in the app.

LISTING 5-29 A class for REST operations

```
namespace Wingtip
{
    public static class Contacts
    {
        public static string AppWebUrl;
        public static void CreateItem(string LastName,
                                      string FirstName,
                                      string WorkPhone){}
        public static List<TableRow> ReadAll(){}
        public static void UpdateItem(string ID,
                                      string LastName,
                                      string FirstName,
                                      string WorkPhone){}
        public static void RemoveItem(string ID){}
        private static string GetFormDigest(){}
    }
}
```

The structure of the static class in Listing 5-29 is similar to that of libraries that were shown previously in JavaScript, which contained methods for creating, reading, updating, and deleting. When using C# against the REST API, however, there are two new elements to consider. First, a static variable *AppWebUrl* is added to make the root URL of the app available to all the methods. Second, a *private* method named *GetFormDigest* is added to retrieve the form digest when necessary.

When you use C# against the REST API, it will always be from a remote web. Therefore, you don't have the luxury of the form digest control being present on the app page. Because of this, you must make a separate RESTful call back to SharePoint solely to retrieve a form digest that can be used in the CRUD operations. Listing 5-30 shows the implementation of the *GetFormDigest* method, which returns the form digest as a string.

LISTING 5-30 Retrieving the form digest

```
private static string GetFormDigest()
{
    Uri uri = new Uri(AppWebUrl + "/_api/contextinfo");
    HttpWebRequest restRequest = (HttpWebRequest)WebRequest.Create(uri);
    restRequest.Credentials = CredentialCache.DefaultCredentials;
    restRequest.Method = "POST";
    restRequest.ContentLength = 0;

    HttpWebResponse restResponse = (HttpWebResponse)restRequest.GetResponse();
    XDocument atomDoc = XDocument.Load(restResponse.GetResponseStream());
    XNamespace d = "http://schemas.microsoft.com/ado/2007/08/dataservices";
    return atomDoc.Descendants(d + "FormDigestValue").First().Value;
}
```

Creating new items in C# requires the same basic approach as in JavaScript. A URI is constructed that refers to the collection to which the new items are to be added, and the *POST* verb is used to send an XML chunk containing the data for the new item. In C#, you must create the XML manually and substitute in the new values. Listing 5-31 shows the code to create a new item in the contacts list.

LISTING 5-31 Creating new items in a contacts list

```
public static void CreateItem(string LastName, string FirstName, string WorkPhone)
{
    Uri uri = new Uri(AppWebUrl +
    "/_api/web/lists/getByTitle('Contacts')/items");

    string itemXML = String.Format(@"
        <entry xmlns='http://www.w3.org/2005/Atom'
         xmlns:d='http://schemas.microsoft.com/ado/2007/08/dataservices'
         xmlns:m='http://schemas.microsoft.com/ado/2007/08/dataservices/metadata'>
          <category term='SP.Data.ContactsListItem'
           scheme='http://schemas.microsoft.com/ado/2007/08/dataservices/scheme' />
            <content type='application/xml'>
              <m:properties>
                <d:FirstName>{0}</d:FirstName>
                <d:Title>{1}</d:Title>
                <d:WorkPhone>{2}</d:WorkPhone>
              </m:properties>
            </content>
        </entry>", FirstName, LastName, WorkPhone);

    HttpWebRequest restRequest = (HttpWebRequest)WebRequest.Create(uri);
    restRequest.Credentials = CredentialCache.DefaultCredentials;
    restRequest.Method = "POST";
    restRequest.Headers["X-RequestDigest"] = GetFormDigest();
    restRequest.Accept = "application/atom+xml";
    restRequest.ContentType = "application/atom+xml";
    restRequest.ContentLength = itemXML.Length;
    StreamWriter sw = new StreamWriter(restRequest.GetRequestStream());
    sw.Write(itemXML);
    sw.Flush();

    HttpWebResponse restResponse = (HttpWebResponse)restRequest.GetResponse();
}
```

Reading items is fairly straightforward. You can simply create the URI referencing the items to return and make the call. Listing 5-32 illustrates the implementation of the *ReadAll* method for the sample. In this case, the method returns a collection of type *TableRow*, which is subsequently added to an ASP.NET *Table* control to display the items.

LISTING 5-32 Reading list items

```
public static List<TableRow> ReadAll()
{
    Uri uri = new Uri(AppWebUrl +
                "/_api/web/lists/getByTitle('Contacts')/items/" +
                "?$select=Id,FirstName,Title,WorkPhone" +
                "&$orderby=Title,FirstName");

    HttpWebRequest restRequest = (HttpWebRequest)WebRequest.Create(uri);
    restRequest.Credentials = CredentialCache.DefaultCredentials;
    restRequest.Method = "GET";

    HttpWebResponse restResponse = (HttpWebResponse)restRequest.GetResponse();
    XDocument atomDoc = XDocument.Load(restResponse.GetResponseStream());
    XNamespace a = "http://www.w3.org/2005/Atom";
    XNamespace d = "http://schemas.microsoft.com/ado/2007/08/dataservices";

    List<TableRow> rows = new List<TableRow>();
    foreach (var entry in atomDoc.Descendants(a + "entry"))
    {
        TableRow r = new TableRow();
        TableCell c1 = new TableCell();
        c1.Text = entry.Descendants(d + "Id").First().Value;
        TableCell c2 = new TableCell();
        c2.Text = entry.Descendants(d + "FirstName").First().Value;
        TableCell c3 = new TableCell();
        c3.Text = entry.Descendants(d + "Title").First().Value;
        TableCell c4 = new TableCell();
        c4.Text = entry.Descendants(d + "WorkPhone").First().Value;
        r.Cells.Add(c1);
        r.Cells.Add(c2);
        r.Cells.Add(c3);
        r.Cells.Add(c4);
        rows.Add(r);
    }
    return rows;
}
```

Updating items is also done by using the same basic approach presented with JavaScript. A URI is constructed that refers to the item to be updated. The XML chunk containing the new property values must be created and a form digest must be added to the headers. Additionally, the *PATCH* method is used to allow only the desired properties to be updated. Finally, the corresponding ETag value must be supplied or an asterisk used to force an update. Listing 5-33 shows the complete implementation of the method to update items in the contacts list.

LISTING 5-33 Updating items in a contacts list

```
public static void UpdateItem(string ID, string LastName, string FirstName, string
WorkPhone)
{
    Uri uri = new Uri(AppWebUrl +
    "/_api/web/lists/getByTitle('Contacts')/items(" + ID + ")");

    string itemXML = String.Format(@"
        <entry xmlns='http://www.w3.org/2005/Atom'
         xmlns:d='http://schemas.microsoft.com/ado/2007/08/dataservices'
         xmlns:m='http://schemas.microsoft.com/ado/2007/08/dataservices/metadata'>
          <category term='SP.Data.ContactsListItem'
           scheme='http://schemas.microsoft.com/ado/2007/08/dataservices/scheme' />
            <content type='application/xml'>
              <m:properties>
                <d:FirstName>{0}</d:FirstName>
                <d:Title>{1}</d:Title>
                <d:WorkPhone>{2}</d:WorkPhone>
              </m:properties>
            </content>
        </entry>", FirstName, LastName, WorkPhone);

    HttpWebRequest restRequest = (HttpWebRequest)WebRequest.Create(uri);
    restRequest.Credentials = CredentialCache.DefaultCredentials;
    restRequest.Method = "POST";
    restRequest.Headers["X-RequestDigest"] = GetFormDigest();
    restRequest.Headers["IF-MATCH"] = "*";
    restRequest.Headers["X-Http-Method"] = "PATCH";
    restRequest.Accept = "application/atom+xml";
    restRequest.ContentType = "application/atom+xml";
    restRequest.ContentLength = itemXML.Length;
    StreamWriter sw = new StreamWriter(restRequest.GetRequestStream());
    sw.Write(itemXML);
    sw.Flush();

    HttpWebResponse restResponse = (HttpWebResponse)restRequest.GetResponse();
}
```

Deleting items is a simple operation compared to the other methods. To delete an item, a URI is constructed that refers to the item to be deleted. A form digest is sent in the headers, and the *DELETE* verb is used to indicate that the target item should be deleted. There is no XML chunk to create for this operation. Listing 5-34 shows the implementation details for deleting items from the contacts list.

LISTING 5-34 Deleting items from a contacts list

```
public static void RemoveItem(string ID)
{
    Uri uri = new Uri(AppWebUrl +
    "/_api/web/lists/getByTitle('Contacts')/items(" + ID + ")");

    HttpWebRequest restRequest = (HttpWebRequest)WebRequest.Create(uri);
    restRequest.Credentials = CredentialCache.DefaultCredentials;
    restRequest.Method = "DELETE";
    restRequest.Headers["X-RequestDigest"] = GetFormDigest();
    restRequest.Headers["IF-MATCH"] = "*";
    restRequest.Accept = "application/atom+xml";
    restRequest.ContentType = "application/atom+xml";

    HttpWebResponse restResponse = (HttpWebResponse)restRequest.GetResponse();
}
```

Summary

Client-side programming against SharePoint 2013 apps is a new paradigm for all SharePoint developers. Even though previous versions of SharePoint supported some of the capabilities found in SharePoint 2013, most developers concentrated on writing server-side code. With the introduction of the app model, SharePoint developers must now become experts in client-side programming.

There are four options for client-side programming: JavaScript against CSOM, JavaScript against REST, C# against CSOM, and C# against REST. When creating SharePoint-hosted apps, you will find that JavaScript against the REST API is generally the best choice. When creating provider-hosted or autohosted apps, you will likely find that C# against CSOM is the best fit. In any case, as a SharePoint developer, you will need to focus on client-side programming much more than you have in the past.

## CHAPTER 6

SharePoint security

Let's begin with a basic question: what is a *security principal*? In a common scenario in a Windows network environment, a security principal can be a user with an account in Active Directory. But the concept of a security principal goes far beyond that. A security principal can also be a user with an account in some other type of identity management system such as Microsoft ASP.NET forms-based authentication (FBA), Microsoft Account, or Facebook.

There are also common scenarios in which a security principal will not have a one-to-one mapping to a human being. For example, an Active Directory security group is a type of security principal, as is an FBA role. A computer becomes a first-class security principal when it is added to an Active Directory domain. In this chapter, you will also see that a Microsoft SharePoint app can also play the role of a first-class security principal, as well.

SharePoint 2010 includes support for authenticating users and providing them with controlled access to SharePoint resources. However, the security infrastructure becomes more complex in SharePoint 2013 due to the new requirements to add support for authenticating apps and managing app permissions. The goal of this chapter is to explain how security works for both users and apps in SharePoint 2013.

Reviewing authentication and authorization

A computer security system performs two basic functions: authentication and authorization. Although you probably already understand these two concepts, this section will provide a quick review, because fully understanding them is critical to all the other material in this chapter.

A security system uses *authentication* to determine the identity of a caller. The first part of the authentication process attempts to map the caller to an existing security principal. For example, authentication could map the caller to a user account in an Active Directory domain. When the authentication process is successful, the system establishes the caller's identity by creating a security token that contains attributes of the security principal in question.

For example, the Windows operating system creates a special type of security token known as a *Windows security token* when it authenticates a user. A Windows security token is an in-memory data structure that contains the user's logon name and a list of security groups in which the user is a member.

If the authentication process asks the question, "Who are you?", the *authorization* process asks, "What can you do?" The authentication process must occur before the authorization process. This is because you must determine the caller's identity before you can determine what the caller can do.

Before the authorization process can begin, the authentication process must create a security token that maps the caller to a security principal. During the authorization process, the system examines information inside the security token to determine whether the caller should be allowed access to the resource(s) being requested.

Understanding user authentication

Every version of SharePoint has provided support for authenticating users and configuring user permissions. However, SharePoint 2013 is the first version to add support for authenticating apps. This chapter will first discuss user authentication in detail before proceeding to discuss app authentication.

The first thing to understand is that the SharePoint platform itself does not supply the actual code to authenticate users. Instead, the SharePoint platform relies on external user authentication systems such as Windows Server and Active Directory or the built-in support in ASP.NET for FBA. After an external system has authenticated a user and created a security token, the SharePoint platform is then able to create a profile around that security token to establish and track the user's identity inside the SharePoint security system.

Let's quickly revisit how user authentication has evolved in SharePoint over the last decade. SharePoint 2003 was pretty limited because it only offered support for Windows authentication. This meant that each and every authenticated user required an Active Directory account.

SharePoint 2007 took a step ahead by adding support for ASP.NET FBA. The new support for FBA was welcomed by developers and system integrators, especially for common scenarios such as extranets and publically facing Internet sites for which it was impractical to create and maintain an Active Directory account for each user or site member.

However, it was with SharePoint 2010 that Microsoft really changed how user authentication works, with the introduction of claims-based security. Prior to SharePoint 2010, the SharePoint platform tracked user identity by using the security token created by the underlying authentication system. For example, SharePoint 2007 tracks user identity via two types of security tokens: Windows security tokens, which are created by Windows Server; and FBA security tokens, which are created by the ASP.NET runtime.

With claims-based security, the SharePoint platform moved to a single, unified format for the security tokens that are created during the user authentication process. More specifically, the user authentication process creates security tokens by using an XML-based standard known as Security Assertion Markup Language (SAML). Within developer circles, this type of security token is commonly referred to as a *SAML token*.

Let's walk through the authentication process in a SharePoint environment configured for claims-based security. In this scenario, the user is authenticated by using either Windows security or FBA. The first part of the authentication process essentially remains unchanged with respect to the fact that it creates a Windows security token or an FBA token. The end of the authentication process is where things are different. This is because any Windows security token or FBA token must be converted into a SAML token.

Every SharePoint web server runs a local service known as the Security Token Service (STS). The STS is responsible for converting Windows security tokens and FBA tokens into SAML tokens as the final part of the authentication process. In SharePoint 2010, these SAML tokens are cached in memory on a per–web server basis and can be reused across multiple requests from the same user. SharePoint 2013 further optimizes the caching of SAML tokens with the Distributed Cache Service, which can be configured to maintain a farm-wide cache of SAML tokens.

SharePoint's adoption of claims-based security and SAML tokens has another significant effect: it has dramatically increased the number of identity providers that can be integrated with a SharePoint farm. In addition to supporting Windows authentication and FBA, claims-based security makes it possible for a SharePoint farm to authenticate users by using external identity providers such as Windows Azure Access Control Service (ACS), Windows Account, Google, and Facebook.

Configuring web applications

The manner in which SharePoint authenticates users is configured at the web application level. When you create a web application in a SharePoint farm, you have the option of creating it in either claims mode or classic mode. A web application created in claims mode authenticates users as described in the previous section. The important point is that a SAML token is created during the user authentication process to establish user identity.

SharePoint's support for creating classic-mode web applications is provided for backward compatibility, and creating a web application in this mode should be avoided except for rare scenarios in which a SharePoint farm contains content migrated from earlier versions that rely on older custom components that need to be rewritten before they can support running within a claims-mode web application.

The bottom line is that you should avoid creating classic-mode web applications in SharePoint 2013 except for scenarios in which you are forced into it to support legacy components. With SharePoint 2013, Microsoft has deprecated the use of classic-mode web applications and removed the ability to create them through Central Administration. The only way to create a classic-mode web application is by using Windows PowerShell.

A significant reason to avoid the use of classic-mode web applications is that they do not support installing and running SharePoint apps. All of Microsoft's design and testing of the SharePoint app model assumes that apps are always installed on sites hosted by claims-mode web applications. For the remainder of this chapter you can assume that any discussion of a web application is referring to a claims-mode web application.

Understanding the User Information List

SharePoint stores and maintains a *user information profile* for authenticated users at the site collection level. There is only one user information profile per user that extends across all the sites for a site collection. User profile information is maintained in a hidden list known as the *User Information List*. You can view this list by browsing to the URL *http://[sitecollection]/_catalogs/users/simple.aspx*. Here you will find basic information, such as logon names and display names for the users. Because the User Information List is just a standard SharePoint list, it can be accessed by using the *SPList* object. Of course, you must have the appropriate permissions to access the list, because it is a securable object that can be seen only by site collection administrators.

The User Information List maintains only a subset of information about users. If you are using SharePoint Server and have the User Profile Service application configured to import profiles, then this information will be used to fill in the User Information List. Two timer jobs, *User Profile to SharePoint Full Synchronization* and *User Profile to SharePoint Quick Synchronization*, run to copy information from the user profiles to the User Information List. User profiles are updated either through synchronization with an external repository such as Active Directory Domain Services (AD DS) or when the user manually enters information into the profile.

Working with users and groups

There are two types of security principals within SharePoint: *users* and *groups*. The SharePoint object model defines the *SPPrincipal* class, which provides the base functionality for assigning permissions to a principal. The SharePoint object model subsequently defines two classes that derive from *SPPrincipal*: *SPUser* and *SPGroup*. These two classes extend this base class with their own unique methods and properties for working with users or groups.

The request of an authenticated user runs under the context of an *SPUser* object and carries a security token. When you create an object reference to an *SPSite*, SharePoint creates an instance of the *SPUserToken* and the *SPUser*. This always happens in the context of the site collection, and it is the user who creates the instance reference that SharePoint uses for authorization. As code attempts to access resources, SharePoint checks this user's security token against access-control lists (ACL) to determine whether it should grant or deny access.

A SharePoint object can either use its own ACL or inherit the ACL of a parent object. By default, most items within the SharePoint object model inherit the parent's ACL. For example, a newly created document library inherits the ACL of its parent site; and a newly created document automatically inherits the ACL of its parent document library. However, it's also possible to configure any document with its own unique ACL to give it an access control policy that differs from other documents within the same document library. This can be done through either the user interface or custom code. To return the parent object containing the ACL used by any securable object in SharePoint, retrieve its *FirstUniqueAncestorSecurableObject* property.

It is important to note that SharePoint manages users and groups and enforces authorization at the scope of the site collection. Rights assigned to a user in one site collection never affect what the user can do in another site collection. It is by design that SharePoint treats each site collection as its own independent item with respect to authorization and access control.

The SharePoint object model tracks user identities by using the *SPUser* class. If you want to access the *SPUser* object for the current user, you use the *CurrentUser* property of the *SPWeb* object associated with the current site. The following simple example shows you how to return the current user using server and client APIs:

```
//Server-Side Object Model
SPUser currentUser = SPContext.Current.Web.CurrentUser;

//JavaScript Client Object Model
var ctx = new SP.ClientContext.get_current();
var user = ctx.get_web().get_currentUser();
ctx.load(user);
ctx.executeQueryAsync(success, failure);

//REST Interface
$.ajax(
{
    url: _spPageContextInfo.webServerRelativeUrl +
        "/_api/web/currentUser",
    type: "GET",
    headers: {
        "accept": "application/json;odata=verbose",
    }
});
```

The current user is always the user who was authenticated when the *SPSite* site collection object was created. If your code is running in the SharePoint website context, this is the authenticated user. If your code is running in the context of a console application, the current user is the user whose Windows principal was used to create the initial *SPSite* reference. You cannot switch the security context of the site collection or its objects after it is created; it is always the user principal who first accessed the site collection that is the current user.

Assigning permissions directly to users is usually not a scalable and maintainable solution, especially across large enterprises with many users and sites. Not only does it complicate user maintenance, as ACLs grow larger they can decrease the performance of SharePoint significantly. This is not an issue unique to SharePoint; it is the same issue solved by AD DS users and groups for any other application. SharePoint solves the problem in the same way—by defining groups.

SharePoint supports the creation of groups within a site collection to ease the configuration of authorization and access control. Groups are never created in the context of the site—they are always created in the context of the site collection and *assigned* to a site. For example, assume that there is a site located at /wingtiptoys/sales, and that the /wingtiptoys/sales site reference is the current context returned from *SPContext.Current.Web*. Given this environment, *SPWeb.Groups* would return the group collection of the sales site. This would be a subset of the groups available in the site collection, which is available through the *SPWeb.SiteGroups* property. The following code shows how to list the groups available to a given site:

```
//Server-Side Object Model
SPWeb site = SPContext.Current.Web;
SPGroupCollection groups = site.Groups;

//JavaScript Client Object Model
var ctx = new SP.ClientContext.get_current();
var groups = ctx.get_web().get_siteGroups();
ctx.load(groups);
ctx.executeQueryAsync(success, failure);

//REST Interface
$.ajax(
{
    url: _spPageContextInfo.webServerRelativeUrl +
        "/_api/web/siteGroups",
    type: "GET",
    headers: {
        "accept": "application/json;odata=verbose",
    }
});
```

Groups cannot be added to a site directly—they must be added to the site collection. If you try to add a group to the site's *Groups* collection, you'll get an exception stating, "You cannot add a group directly to the Groups collection. You can add a group to the SiteGroups collection." This situation occurs because *SPGroup* is always *created* at the Site Collection level and *assigned* to the site. However, this still does not associate the group with the site, nor would it be useful within the site without any permissions. To add the group to the site, create a new *SPRoleAssignment* by associating an *SPRoleDefinition* with the *SPGroup*, and then add that role assignment to the site, as in the following code sample:

```
// Server-Side Object model
SPWeb site = SPContext.Current.Web;
site.SiteGroups.Add("WingtipToysSuperUsers",site.CurrentUser,
site.CurrentUser,"A group to manage Wingtip Toys Security");
SPGroup secGroup = site.SiteGroups["WingtipToysSuperUsers"];
SPRoleAssignment roleAssignment = new SPRoleAssignment(secGroup);
SPRoleDefinition roleDefinition = site.RoleDefinitions["Full Control"];
roleAssignment.RoleDefinitionBindings.Add(roleDefinition);
site.RoleAssignments.Add(roleAssignment);

//JavaScript Client Object Model
var ctx = new SP.ClientContext.get_current();
var createInfo = new SP.GroupCreationInformation();
createInfo.set_title("WingtipToysSuperUsers");
createInfo.set_description("A group to manage Wingtip Toys Security");
var newGroup = ctx.get_web().get_siteGroups().add(createInfo);
ctx.load(newGroup);
var roleDefBinding = SP.RoleDefinitionBindingCollection.newObject(ctx);
var roleDef = ctx.get_web().get_roleDefinitions().getByType("Full Control");
roleDefBinding.add(roleDef);
var roleAssignments = ctx.get_web().get_roleAssignments();
roleAssignments.add(newGroup, roleDefBinding);
ctx.executeQueryAsync(success, failure);
```

As with *Groups* and *SiteGroups*, multiple collections can be used to access site users. Table 6-1 lists user-related properties of the *SPWeb* site object and when to use them.

TABLE 6-1 *SPWeb* user properties

Property	Description
AllUsers	Used to access any user who has accessed the site as a member of a domain group that is a site member, or any user who is explicitly a member of the site. For example, the user Terry Adams (WINGTIP\terrya) may be a member of the WINGTIP\sales group. If WINGTIP\sales has access to the Sales site and Terry has visited the site (as a member of the WINGTIP\sales group), he would gain access through the *AllUsers* collection. Because it is the largest collection of users available (being a combination of the SiteUsers, Users, and group memberships), you generally use the *AllUsers* collection when you want to access a user.
CurrentUser	Returns the current user who created the reference to the *SPSite* site collection. This is generally the user who is accessing the SharePoint website.
SiteUsers	Used to access the collection of users in the site collection. This is a subset of the *AllUsers* collection.
Users	The smallest collection of users, containing only the users explicitly added to a SharePoint site.

Working with application pool identities

The application pool identity plays a large role in SharePoint applications. Besides running the web application, this account is used as the Windows account that connects to the SharePoint Content and Configuration databases, and it is the Windows account used when running code in the *SPSecurity.Run WithElevatedPrivileges* method. When you create a new web application through the SharePoint Central Administration application, you should create it to run inside a new or existing application pool, separate from the Central Administration application pool. Moreover, application pools for web applications that are accessible to users should be configured with a domain account that is not as privileged as the user account for the Central Administration application pool. For example, there is no reason why SharePoint code running within any application pool other than the Central Administration application pool would ever need to create a new content database or configure database security permissions.

Consider what happens when you create a new web application through the SharePoint Central Administration application. When you do this, you get to determine whether SharePoint creates a new application pool for this web application or uses an existing application pool. If you tell SharePoint to create a new application pool, you must supply the name and password of a valid Windows user account. When SharePoint creates the new content database, it grants this user account the SPData-Access role for that content database. SharePoint also grants the database roles public and WSS_Content_Application_Pools to this user account in the configuration database. You should note that user accounts that provide application pool identities must also be added to the local group named WSS_WPG, so that they have the proper permissions to access SharePoint system files and specific locations within the Windows Registry and IIS Metabase.

Understanding the SHAREPOINT\SYSTEM account

The SHAREPOINT\SYSTEM account is an identity to which SharePoint maps internally when code is running under the identity of the hosting application pool. The SHAREPOINT\SYSTEM account is not recognized by Windows because it exists only within the content of the SharePoint runtime environment. This enables SharePoint to use a statically named account for system-related activity regardless of which Windows user account has been configured for the hosting application pool.

For example, if you switch the application pool from WINGTIPTOYS\SP_WorkerProcess1 to WINGTIPTOYS\SP_WorkerProcess2, code running as system code still acts and is audited as the SHAREPOINT\SYSTEM account. However, it is also important to remember that SHAREPOINT\SYSTEM is not recognized by the Windows security subsystem. Therefore, code in SharePoint running as system code is recognized by any resource outside of SharePoint under the identity of the hosting application pool when it attempts to access external resources, such as the local file system or a Microsoft SQL Server database.

Escalating privileges

The *SPSecurity* class provides a static method named *RunWithElevatedPrivileges*, which enables server-side code to execute as system code running under the identity of SHAREPOINT\SYSTEM. This allows code to run in an escalated security context to perform actions as the system. This method should be used with care and should not expose direct access to system resources; rather, it should be used when you need to perform actions on behalf of the system. The method is simple. You can either create a delegate to a public void method or simply write code within an inline delegate. The signature looks like the following:

```
SPSecurity.RunWithElevatedPrivileges(delegate
{
  // Code runs as the SHAREPOINT\SYSTEM user
});
```

Code within the delegate runs under the SHAREPOINT\SYSTEM security principal. As covered in the section "Working with application pool identities" earlier in this chapter, this account uses the application pool identity when passing credentials to external resources, but it uses the system account internally. To modify SharePoint content under the system credentials, you need to create a new *SPSite* site collection that generates a new security context for objects referenced from the site, as in the following example. You cannot switch the security context of the *SPSite* after it has been created, but must instead create a new *SPSite* reference to switch user contexts. The following code uses the system credentials to add a list item using the profile data of the current web user:

```
SPSecurity.RunWithElevatedPrivileges(
  delegate {
    using (SPSite site = new SPSite(web.Site.ID)) {
      using (SPWeb web2 = site.OpenWeb) {
        SPList theList = web2.Lists["visitors"];
        SPListItem record = theList.Items.Add();
```

```
        record["User"] = SPContext.Current.Web.CurrentUser;
        record.Update();
      }
    }
);
```

Delegating user credentials

Within application code running in the SharePoint web application, the code runs under the credentials of the application pool while impersonating the calling user. This condition enables SharePoint
to secure objects, including sites, lists, and list items, by using the calling user's identity. Identity is
configured automatically through the web.config setting *<identity impersonate="true" />*. This is true
for both the web application and web service endpoints. When calling web services, you can use this
identity to authenticate to remote endpoints by setting the credentials to the default credentials.
Note that to pass credentials to back-end services, the SharePoint server must be set up with the
rights to delegate credentials in AD DS. For web service requests to the same box, delegation is not
required. The following code example uses the credentials of the current user to authenticate a web
request against a web data source:

```
WebRequest xmlReq = WebRequest.CreateDefault(xmlUri);
xmlReq.Credentials = CredentialCache.DefaultCredentials;
```

In addition to the current user's credentials, you can access the application pool identity by using
the *SPSecurity* method *RunWithElevatedPrivileges*:

```
SPSecurity.RunWithElevatedPrivileges(delegate {
  WebRequest xmlReq = WebRequest.CreateDefault(xmlUri);
  // Uses the app pool credentials:
  xmlReq.Credentials = CredentialCache.DefaultCredentials;
});
```

User impersonation with the user token

There are two primary ways to create a security context associated with an *SPSite*. One is to use
the current Windows or claims identity, which is the default method whether you are accessing the
site from the SharePoint web application or an administrative console. This is also the method used
with the *SPSecurity.RunWithElevatedPrivileges* delegate—the current principal, which happens to be
SHAREPOINT\SYSTEM, is used to create the site security context.

The other way to create an *SPSite* security context is by using an *SPUserToken* object. The *SPUser-
Token* is the token created upon authentication. It references the principal of the user from the identity store with its groups and roles. In the case of a Windows identity, this token is used to query AD DS
for the *TokenGroups* property. These tokens time out after 24 hours, making them a good candidate
for system code that needs to impersonate users in the case of workflow actions or post-processing
of list data that happens slightly after the original action (not days later). This token timeout value can
be set by using the Windows PowerShell console. When the user token is used in the constructor of

SPSite the code can make changes to the SharePoint object model just as if the actual user were making the changes.

You can request the token for any user in the system by using the *UserToken* property of the *SPUser* class. If the current user is not the user requested, SharePoint builds the token independently from the user's Security ID and group membership. You can then pass this token to the *SPSite* constructor to create a new impersonated security context.

For example, consider an event receiver attached to a custom list that will fire when new items are created. Each time a new item is created, the code will create an announcement with the credentials of the user in a separate Announcements list. To create the item under the impersonated security context, simply obtain a user token from the *SPUser* profile that created the object and pass that into the *SPSite* constructor. When the item is inserted into the Announcements list, it will be as if the impersonated user created the item, even though the event receiver is running under the identity of SHAREPOINT\SYSTEM:

```
public override void ItemAdded(SPItemEventProperties properties) {
  DisableEventFiring();
  string CompanyName = properties.ListItem["Company"].ToString();
  properties.ListItem["Company"] = FormatStringValue(CompanyName);
  properties.ListItem.Update();

  SPUserToken token =
    properties.OpenWeb.AllUsers[properties.UserLoginName].UserToken;

  using( SPSite site = new SPSite(properties.SiteId, token) )
  {
      using(SPWeb web = site.OpenWeb(properties.WebUrl))
      {
        SPListItem announcement = web.Lists["Announcements"].Items.Add();
        announcement["Title"] = properties.ListItem["Company"].ToString();
        announcement["Body"] = "A new company was added!";
        announcement.Update();
      }
  }
}
```

Within this code sample, we are using the *AllUsers* property of the site. Users are available through a reference to the site (the *SPWeb* class). Three user collections are available within the site, and choosing which one to use may be confusing. See Table 6-1, earlier in this chapter, for a description of the options and guidance on when to use each one.

Securing objects with SharePoint

The *SPWeb*, *SPList*, and *SPListItem* classes in SharePoint inherit from the abstract class *SPSecurable-Object*, which encapsulates the functionality necessary to secure them from unauthorized access. Table 6-2 lists the members of the *SPSecurableObject* class.

TABLE 6-2 *SPSecurableObject* members

Member	Description
BreakRoleInheritance	Creates a unique role that does not inherit from the parent object
CheckPermissions	Checks to see if the current user has a given set of permissions
DoesUserHavePermissions	Indicates whether a user has a specified set of permissions
GetUserEffectivePermissionInfo	Returns detailed information about the permissions for a specified user in the current context
GetUserEffectivePermissions	Gets the effective permissions for a specified user in the current context
ResetRoleInheritance	Removes unique permissions and inherits from the parent
AllRolesForCurrentUser	Returns the roles for the current user
EffectiveBasePermissions	Gets the effective permissions for a specified user in the current object
FirstUniqueAncestorSecurableObject	Gets the object where inherited role assignments are defined
HasUniqueRoleAssignments	Indicates whether the object has unique role assignments or inherits from a parent object
ReusableAcl	Gets the access control list for the object
RoleAssignments	Gets the role assignments for the object

SPSecurableObject provides a method for checking whether permissions exist, as well as a method for demanding that the permissions exist. The first method, *DoesUserHavePermissions*, is used to query for permissions and returns a Boolean value, whereas the second method, *CheckPermissions*, throws a security exception if the permission does not exist. Because this interface is common throughout the object model, it is easy to learn how to use it throughout your code. For example, to check whether the current user has permissions to view list items, you can call the *DoesUserHave-Permissions* method of the *SPWeb* class, passing in the *ViewListItems* permission flag, as follows:

```
//Server-Side object model
SPWeb web = SPContext.Current.Web ;
if (web.DoesUserHavePermissions(SPBasePermissions.ViewListItems){
    // Enumerate lists
}

//JavaScript Client Object Model
var deferred = $.Deferred();
var ctx = new SP.ClientContext.get_current();
var permSet = new SP.BasePermissions();
permSet.set(SP.PermissionKind.viewListItems);
var flag = ctx.get_web().doesUserHavePermissions(permSet);
ctx.executeQueryAsync(success, failure);
```

The *SPList* is also an *SPSecurableObject*, which means that you can apply the same principles to checking permissions on lists. To check the user's permission to view list items within a specific list, call the list's *DoesUserHavePermissions* method. Likewise, the same method is available in other objects, such as the *SPListItem* class, which can be used to ensure that the user has permissions to the item or document.

Rights and permission levels

Rights within SharePoint are defined by permissions within the *SPBasePermissions* enumeration. This enumeration is a flags-based enumeration in which multiple permissions can be combined to create a permission set. *SPBasePermissions* are aggregated into roles with the *SPRoleDefinitions* within the site context, in which permissions are role-based. You will most likely assign a role when assigning permissions to a security principal; when validating rights for an action on a particular object, you will check the permission itself. To assign roles to a security principal, use the *SPRoleDefinition* class. Bydefault, each site creates the following role definitions, exposing them through the web's *Role-Definition* property: *Full Control, Design, Contribute, Read,* and *Limited Access*. These roles, along with their aggregated permissions, are listed in Table 6-3. Permissions are stored in the ACL for each *SPSecurableObject* and cached in the binary *ReusableAcl* property. The ACL defines permissions for all users in the site collection on each object. These permissions are always accessed from the object (remember that object references always are accessed through the user and always contain permission information).

TABLE 6-3 Default SharePoint site roles

Site role	SPBasePermissions
Full Control	FullMask
Design	ViewListItems, AddListItems, EditListItems, DeleteListItems, ApproveItems, OpenItems, ViewVersions, DeleteVersions, CancelCheckout, ManagePersonalViews, ManageLists, ViewFormPages, Open, ViewPages, AddAndCustomizePages, ApplyThemeAndBorder, ApplyStyleSheets, CreateSSCSite, BrowseDirectories, BrowseUserInfo, AddDelPrivate WebParts, UpdatePersonalWebParts, UseClientIntegration, UseRemoteAPIs, CreateAlerts, EditMyUserInfo
Contribute	ViewListItems, AddListItems, EditListItems, DeleteListItems, OpenItems, ViewVersions, DeleteVersions, ManagePersonalViews, ViewFormPages, Open, ViewPages, Create SSCSite, BrowseDirectories, BrowseUserInfo, AddDelPrivateWebParts, Update PersonalWebParts, UseClientIntegration, UseRemoteAPIs, CreateAlerts, EditMyUserInfo
Read	ViewListItems, OpenItems, ViewVersions, ViewFormPages, Open, ViewPages, CreateSSCSite, BrowseUserInfo, UseClientIntegration, UseRemoteAPIs, CreateAlerts
Limited Access	ViewFormPages, Open, BrowseUserInfo, UseClientIntegration, UseRemoteAPIs

Understanding app authentication

From the very beginning of the design phase, Microsoft created the SharePoint 2013 app model so that apps could be authenticated and recognized as first-class security principals. The obvious benefit here is that app permissions can be configured independently of user permissions. To achieve this goal, however, Microsoft had to build new infrastructure into SharePoint 2013 that is capable of authenticating incoming calls from apps and tracking app identity.

If you already have a firm understanding of how SharePoint authenticates users, you should not assume that anything is the same with respect to how it authenticates apps. The authentication mechanisms used for apps are completely different. SharePoint 2013 supports three different types of app authentication:

- Internal app authentication

- External app authentication using OAuth

- External app authentication using S2S high-trust

Note that app authentication is supported only in scenarios in which an app is calling to the SharePoint host environment by using the client-side object model (CSOM) or the REST API. SharePoint 2013 does not support app authentication in any other endpoints beyond these. This means it is not possible to develop and deploy a set of custom web service entry points that support app authentication.

Whenever the SharePoint host environment receives an incoming call that targets either CSOM or the REST API, it must decide how to authenticate the call. First, the SharePoint host environment must determine whether the call was initiated by a user or by an app. If the call was initiated by an app, the SharePoint host environment must also determine whether to use internal authentication or external authentication.

The SharePoint host environment inspects an incoming request to see what type of security token has been passed. If an incoming call contains a special type of security token used for app authentication known as an *access token*, the SharePoint host will know the call was made by an app. In this scenario, the SharePoint host environment authenticates the caller by using external app authentication.

If the SharePoint host environment sees a SAML token in an incoming request, it knows that there is already an authenticated user associated with the call. However, at this point the SharePoint host environment cannot yet assume that call was initiated by a user as opposed to an app. The SharePoint host environment must additionally inspect the target URL to determine whether the call was initiated by a user or by an app.

If an incoming request with a SAML token maps to a target URL within a domain associated with an app web, the SharePoint host environment will assume that the call was made by an app. In this scenario, the SharePoint host environment uses internal authentication to authenticate the app and establish its identity. If an incoming request with a SAML token does not map to a target URL within a domain associated with an app web, the SharePoint host environment will know that the call was not made by an app, and it will initialize the call context by using just the user's identity.

The diagram in Figure 6-1 shows four different scenarios for CSOM and REST API calls that target a SharePoint 2013 site. The first call (at the top) is a client-side CSOM or REST API call that has been executed from a page in the host web. The SharePoint host environment authenticates this type of call by using standard user authentication, which results in the creation of a SAML token.

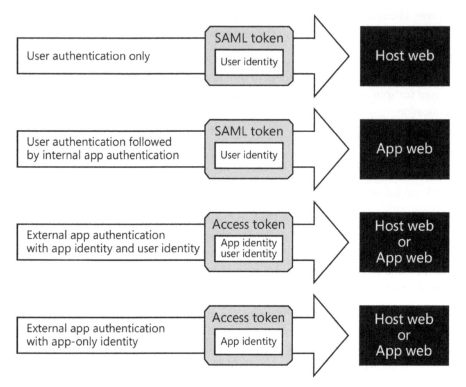

FIGURE 6-1 The SharePoint environment inspects the security tokens that are passed with incoming calls to determine which type of authentication to use.

The second call in Figure 6-1 (second down from the top) is similar to the first call in that the SharePoint host environment uses the standard user authentication process to create a SAML token with the user's identity. However, the second call is treated differently because it targets the domain of an app web. The fact that this call targets an app web is what leads the SharePoint host environment to authenticate the calling app by using internal app authentication.

The third and fourth calls in Figure 6-1 both carry an access token instead of a SAML token. When the SharePoint host environment sees an access token in an incoming CSOM or REST API call, it can assume that it should authenticate the app by using external authentication. The difference between the third call and the fourth call involves whether the access token carries a user identity along with the app identity. The third call is an example of the more common scenario in which the access token includes the identity of the current user in addition to the identity of the app. The fourth call shows an example of an access token that contains an app identity but no user identity. The use of this type of access token containing an app-only identity is not as common but is useful in specific scenarios, which will be described later in this chapter.

Using internal authentication

The most common scenario in which the SharePoint host environment uses internal authentication involves client-side calls that are initiated from pages in an app web. The SharePoint host environment creates an isolated domain whenever it creates an app web during app installation. The cross-site scripting (XSS) restrictions in the browser ensure that CSOM and REST API calls made from pages in the app web target endpoints within the same domain. This makes it possible for the SharePoint host environment to map an incoming call that targets an app web domain to a specific installed instance of an app.

When the SharePoint host environment has determined that an incoming call targets a URL that maps to a specific app, it uses internal authentication to initialize the call context with the app's identity. Because this scenario involves an incoming call with a SAML token, the SharePoint host environment can further initialize the call context with the user's identity in addition to the app's identity.

SharePoint-hosted apps always use internal authentication. That's because all the pages for a SharePoint-hosted app must be added to an app web. This means that the SharePoint host environment can always use internal authentication to authenticate any CSOM or REST API call from a SharePoint-hosted app.

The app manifest for a SharePoint-hosted app should be configured to support internal authentication. This is accomplished in the app manifest by adding an *<AppPrincipal>* element with an inner *<Internal>* element:

```
<AppPrincipal>
  <Internal />
</AppPrincipal>
```

Using the cross-domain library

SharePoint-hosted apps are not the only type of app that can use internal authentication. A second scenario in which internal authentication is used involves client-side calls initiated from a cloud-hosted app using the *cross-domain library*. The cross-domain library is a JavaScript library included with SharePoint 2013 with which a cloud-hosted app can issue client-side calls to the SharePoint host environment from pages in the remote web.

The cross-domain library has been added to SharePoint 2013 to address the scenario in which a cloud-hosted app calls back into the SharePoint host environment by using client-side calls instead of server-side calls. For example, your user interface design might favor client-side calls over server-side calls to give pages in the remote web more of a Web 2.0 look and feel.

Note that CSOM and REST API calls that are executed by using the cross-domain library must be routed through the app web of the calling app. Although cloud-hosted apps do not usually require an app web, this is a scenario in which they do. Therefore, you must configure a cloud-hosted app to create an app web if you plan to use the cross-domain library.

The cross-domain library is contained in the JavaScript file SP.RequestExecutor.js, which is located in the LAYOUTS directory. The cross-domain library can be used when a remote web needs to access data in an app web, but barriers such as a firewall prevent the normal approach of calling back through CSOM with an OAuth token. The cross-domain library works in concert with several components to make cross-site calls possible. Figure 6-2 shows the complete architecture.

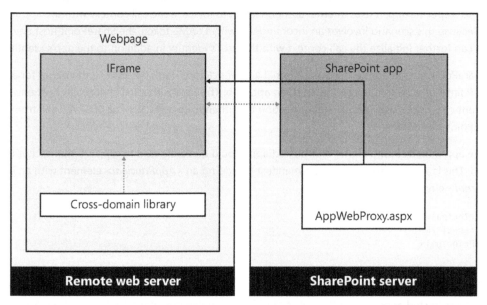

FIGURE 6-2 The cross-domain architecture uses a JavaScript library and ASPX page to facilitate communication.

At the heart of the cross-domain call architecture is the AppWebProxy.aspx page, which provides the functionality to execute the object model commands requested by the remote web on the target app web. Because the AppWebProxy.aspx page is located in the LAYOUTS directory, its location is well known to every remote web. The remote web loads the *SP.RequestExecutor* object and initializes it with the URL of the target app web. At this point, the *SP.RequestExecutor* object creates a hidden *IFrame* within the remote web and loads the AppWebProxy.aspx page from the target app web. The *SP.RequestExecutor* object uses the HTML5 *postMessage* API to send commands from the remote web to the AppWebProxy.aspx page, which in turn executes them against the target app web. Any response passes back across the *IFrame* to the remote web.

When the cross-domain library is first invoked, the user of the remote web will likely not be signed in to the target app web. In this case, the cross-domain library returns a 401 unauthorized response. The library subsequently redirects the user to the SharePoint logon page. After the user logs on, the cross-domain library attempts the original call again.

For a remote web to access an app web by using the cross-domain library, the target app web must explicitly permit the call. If the app is using the Internal principal, the *AllowedRemoteHostUrl* attribute must be set in the app manifest. If you are creating a provider-hosted or autohosted app, the domain you register for OAuth authentication will automatically be trusted for calls to the cross-domain library. The app must also be provided with specific permission grants in the app manifest, just as it would for any OAuth calls. Finally, the app web associated with the remote web needs to provide the URL to the target app web as a querystring parameter in the *<StartPage>* element of the manifest.

In many cases, the target app web and the app web associated with the remote web will be the same. This is the scenario in which the remote web wants to call back into the associated app web but is blocked by a firewall. The target app web can be different, however. All that is required is that the target app web allows the remote web to make the call and the app web associated with the remote web requests for the appropriate permission grants. The following code shows some typical settings for app webs that might or might not be in the same manifest, depending upon your scenario:

```
<AppPrincipal>
  <Internal AllowedRemoteHostUrl="http://crossdomain.wingtip.com/" />
</AppPrincipal>
<Properties>
  <Title>Cross Domain App</Title>
  <StartPage>
    ~remoteAppUrl/Welcome/Message?{StandardTokens}&amp;SPSourceAppUrl=
    http://app-4d277429be4d8d.apps.wingtiptoys.com/cloudhosted/CrossDomainSourceApp
  </StartPage>
</Properties>
```

The simplest way to start using the cross-domain library is to add it directly to the remote web project. After that, an instance of the *SP.RequestExecutor* object can be initialized. The URL for the target app web is retrieved from the querystring passed to the remote web and used in the initialization process. After the initialization process is complete, RESTful requests can easily be made to the target app web. Listing 6-1 shows a sample that reads list items from a contacts list in the target app web.

LISTING 6-1 Reading list items across domains

```
"use strict";

var WingtipToys = window.WingtipToys || {};
WingtipToys.CrossDomain = function () {

    load = function () {
        var appweburl = getQueryStringParameter("SPSourceAppUrl");
        var executor = new SP.RequestExecutor(appweburl);

        executor.executeAsync(
        {
            url:
            appweburl +
            "/_api/web/lists/getByTitle('Contacts')/items/" +
                        "?$select=Id,FirstName,Title,WorkPhone,Email" +
                        "&$orderby=Title,FirstName",
            method: "GET",
            headers: { "Accept": "application/json;odata=verbose" },
            success: successHandler,
            error: errorHandler
        })
    },

    successHandler = function (data) {
        //Take action on returned data
    },

    errorHandler = function (data, errorCode, errorMessage) {
        //Handle the error
    },

    getQueryStringParameter = function (paramToRetrieve) {
        //Get querystring value and return it
    }

    return {
        load: load
    }

}()



$(document).ready(function () {
    Wingtip.CrossDomain.load();
});
```

Using the web proxy

The web proxy is a server-side proxy that can make calls to services in other domains and return them to an app. The web proxy differs from the cross-domain library in that it supports calling any endpoint, not just those contained in an app web. The web proxy is ideal for accessing multiple data sources and creating mashed-up displays in your apps.

You access the web proxy through the *SP.WebRequestInfo* object, which is available in the sp.js library. To use the web proxy, you instantiate and initialize the *SP.WebRequestInfo* object with a RESTful URI. The proxy is then invoked, which creates an asynchronous RESTful call. The returned XML can then be processed to extract the desired values. Listing 6-2 shows part of a custom library that makes a call to the publically available MusicBrainz API to search for songs based on the name of an artist.

LISTING 6-2 Using the web proxy

```
"use strict";

var WingtipToys = window.WingtipToys || {};
WingtipToys.ResponseDocument;

WingtipToys.SongViewModel = function () {

    var load = function (artist) {

            var ctx = SP.ClientContext.get_current();
            var request = new SP.WebRequestInfo();

            request.set_url(
                "http://www.musicbrainz.org/ws/2/recording?query=artist:" + artist
                );
            request.set_method("GET");
            window.WingtipToys.ResponseDocument = SP.WebProxy.invoke(ctx, request);

            ctx.executeQueryAsync(onSuccess, onError);

    },

    onSuccess = function () {
        var xmlDoc = $.parseXML(window.WingtipToys.ResponseDocument.get_body());
        //Process XML to extract values
    },

    onError = function (err) {
        alert(JSON.stringify(err));
    };

    return {
        load: load
    };
}();
```

For cross-domain calls to succeed by using the web proxy, the app must explicitly declare that a domain is trusted. This is accomplished by setting the *<RemoteEndpoint>* element in the app manifest. The following code shows how the element is set for the MusicBrainz sample:

```
<RemoteEndpoints>
    <RemoteEndpoint Url="http://www.musicbrainz.org"/>
</RemoteEndpoints>
```

Using external authentication

There are many scenarios in which a cloud-hosted app makes CSOM and REST API calls to a SharePoint host that cannot be authenticated by using internal authentication. In these scenarios, the app must be configured to use external authentication. The key difference with external authentication is that the app must include an access token when calling to the SharePoint host environment.

There are two ways in which you can configure an app to use external authentication. The first is based on *OAuth authentication*, which is the only type of external authentication supported in the Microsoft Office 365 environment. The second way is based on server-to-server authentication, which is only supported in on-premises farms.

OAuth authentication requires integration with Windows Azure ACS. That means that the remote web of the app requires access to Windows Azure ACS running in the cloud to acquire access tokens. However, this is relatively simple to set up, because the required integration between the Office 365 environment and Windows Azure ACS is automatically configured for you. Your primary requirement when configuring OAuth authentication is to register an app security principal that will have an identifying GUID known as a *client ID*. The details of how to configure OAuth authentication as well as how to implement an app to acquire access tokens from Windows Azure ACS will be discussed later in this chapter.

Server-to-server (S2S) authentication doesn't require an app to access Windows Azure ACS or any other authentication service in the cloud. The only computers involved in the S2S authentication process are the web server running the remote web and a SharePoint web server in an on-premises farm. This makes this form of external authentication ideal for scenarios in which you want to avoid dependencies on servers across the Internet where everything needs to run inside a single, private network.

S2S authentication is configured by establishing a trust between the web servers in an on-premises SharePoint farm and the web server running the remote web of a provider-hosted app. This trust is created by using an X.509 certificate with a public/private key pair. At a high level, S2S authentication is based on the app creating an access token and signing it with the private key. Web servers in the SharePoint farm then authenticate these access tokens by using the public key.

At this point, you should have a high-level understanding of how external authentication works. External authentication can be configured by using either OAuth authentication or S2S authentication. In either case, the remote web passes an access token that allows the SharePoint host environment to authenticate the app and establish the app's identity.

Although an access token is required to contain information about the app's identity, it can optionally contain information about the identity of the current user, as well. Therefore, some access tokens carry information about the identity of both the app and the current user, whereas other access tokens only carry information about the identity of the app.

Understanding app authentication flow

Now that you have learned about the fundamental differences between internal authentication and external authentication, it's time to walk through the authentication flow used by the SharePoint host environment.

Remember that app authentication is only supported in endpoints based on CSOM and the REST API. Therefore, the SharePoint host environment uses only standard user authentication for any request that is not based on CSOM or the REST API. This includes scenarios for page requests from both the host web and the app web.

When the SharePoint host environment processes a CSOM call or a REST API call, it must do more work to determine which type of authentication to use. The diagram in Figure 6-3 shows a flow chart that details the complexity and the factors that the SharePoint host environment uses to choose the correct type of authentication.

The first question the SharePoint host environment asks after starting the authentication process for a CSOM or REST API call is whether the call carries a SAML token with a user identity. If the incoming call does carry a SAML token, the next question is whether the request targets an app web or not. If the call does not target an app web, then the SharePoint host environment uses standard user authentication and sets up the call context with just the user identity. Note that this is exactly what SharePoint does for any request that does not target a CSOM or REST API endpoint.

When an incoming call with a SAML token targets the domain of an app web, the SharePoint host environment determines that it must authenticate the app that is associated with that app web. It then uses internal authentication to authenticate the app and it sets up the call context with the app identity as well as with the user identity it finds in the SAML token.

When an incoming call carries an access token instead of a SAML token, the SharePoint host environment determines that the call is from an app and that it must use external authentication to authenticate it. The SharePoint host environment starts the external authentication process by determining whether the access token is an OAuth token or an S2S token and then validating the authenticity of the access token.

After the access token has been validated, the SharePoint host environment can then extract information about the identity of the app. The SharePoint host environment also inspects the access token to see if it carries information about the identity of the current user. If it does, the SharePoint host environment sets up the call context with both the app identity and the user identity. If the access token does not contain information about the identity of a user, it sets up the call context only with the app identity.

The last scenario involves a request that carries neither a SAML token nor an access token. In this case, the SharePoint host environment can establish neither app identity nor user identity. This leads to the SharePoint host environment setting up the call context by using anonymous access. A call executing under anonymous access will experience an access denied error in all scenarios except the case in which the site has been configured to allow CSOM and REST API calls from an anonymous user.

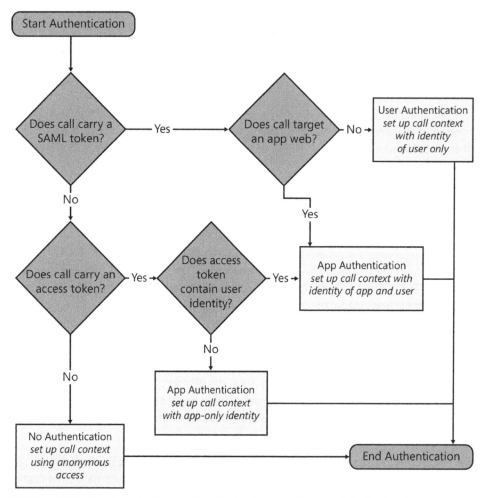

FIGURE 6-3 This flowchart details the authentication flow that the SharePoint host environment uses to process incoming calls that target CSOM and REST API endpoints.

Understanding app authorization

This chapter has already explained the various ways in which SharePoint 2013 is able to authenticate apps. The process of app authentication is what makes it possible to establish an app identity and to map incoming calls from an app to a unique ID for the app, which is tracked in the App Management Service database known as the app identifier. This, in turn, makes it possible for the SharePoint host environment to create and track app permissions by associating each one with an app identifier.

Managing app permissions

When you begin to think about app identity and app permissions, you should keep in mind that an app must be installed before it can be used and that the installation of an app creates a new app instance. For example, if you install the same SharePoint app into two different Office 365 tenancies, you will create two separate app identities as opposed to creating a single app identity that is recognized across tenancy boundaries.

SharePoint 2013 uses app identifiers that are made by combining a GUID that identifies the app instance together with the unique identifier for the hosting tenant. Each time the SharePoint host environment creates an app permission, it must tag this permission with an app identifier to map it back to an installed instance of an app.

Note that much of the Microsoft documentation on app security often uses the generic term "realm" in place of the SharePoint-specific term "tenancy." When you hear someone talking about the hosting realm for an app, he is really just talking about the tenancy in which the app was installed. The realm identifier is really just the identifier for the current tenancy.

When you install a SharePoint-hosted app, the app identifier is created and configured automatically as part of the app installation process. After a SharePoint-hosted app has been installed, the SharePoint host environment is able to use internal authentication to map CSOM and REST API calls from pages in the app web to an existing app identifier. The process of internal authentication was discussed in depth earlier in this chapter.

Managing app identifiers becomes more complicated with apps that use external authentication. In certain scenarios, you must explicitly create the app identifier by registering an app principal before the app is installed. It is the act of registering the app principal that actually creates the app identifier. The details of when and how to register app principals will be covered later in this chapter; however, you now have the required background to begin learning about how SharePoint 2013 manages app permissions.

Understanding app permission policies

Now it's time to discuss what happens after a call from an app has been authenticated and mapped to an app identifier. That's the point in time when the SharePoint host environment inspects permissions on the target object to determine whether the calling app should be able to succeed in what it is attempting to do. If the SharePoint host environment does not find that the correct set of permissions has been granted to the app, an access denied error will be returned to the caller.

As you might expect, an app must be granted the appropriate app permission to read or modify an object in a SharePoint site such as a list or a list item. Moreover, the default authorization policy for apps requires the current user to have the appropriate permissions as well. Let's look at a simple example to illustrate how the default app authorization policy works.

Imagine that an app has been granted write access to the host web. This means that it has the required permissions to create a new list item in the host site. However, for the app to create a new list item by using CSOM or the REST API, the current user requires the permissions to create a new list item, as well. When the app is launched by a site administrator, it can succeed in creating a list in the host web. If the app is launched by a user without write permissions, such as a visitor, an attempt by the app to create a new list item will fail with an access denied error.

A key point here is that the default app authorization policy used for calls from apps checks user permissions as well as app permissions. Therefore, you need to understand how the SharePoint host environment manages user permissions as well as app permissions before you can fully understand how the app authorization process works. For this reason, this chapter will review how user permissions are managed for those readers who require this background. After that, the chapter will then focus on creating and managing app permissions. As you will see, the way in which the SharePoint host environment manages app permissions is significantly different from the way it manages user permissions.

Requesting and granting app permissions

The SharePoint host environment configures a set of default permissions for an app to provide it with full control over its app web. This means that an app which creates an app web during installation always has a place to create new lists and document libraries without having to request additional permissions.

In many scenarios, the default permissions granted to an app will not suffice. Think about the common scenario in which an app is required to create a new list in the host site. In such a scenario, an app will require additional permissions beyond the default app permissions.

An app acquires additional permissions by using *permission requests*. A permission request is an XML-based element that the app developer adds to the app manifest file. When a user or administrator attempts to install a SharePoint app that contains one or more permissions requests, the SharePoint host environment displays a prompt asking the installing user to grant or deny the permissions that the app has requested.

Figure 6-4 shows the dialog box that the SharePoint host environment uses to prompt the person who is installing an app with permission requests. The user must either click the Trust It button to grant the app's permission requests or click the Cancel button to deny them.

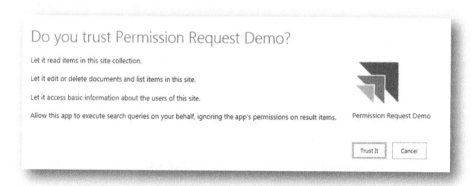

FIGURE 6-4 The user is prompted to grant or deny permission requests when an app is installed.

If the user clicks the Cancel button to deny the app's permission requests, the SharePoint host environment aborts the installation. In other words, you must grant all the permissions requested by an app to install it. It is not possible to selectively grant some permissions an app has requested while denying other permission requests. Granting permission requests during app installation is an all-or-nothing proposition.

It is also important to note that a user must possess any permissions that are granted to an app. For example, an app might request write capabilities on the site collection or the tenancy in which the host web is located. The user must also possess write permissions on the hosting site collection or the hosting tenancy in order to grant that permission to an app during installation. Therefore, you can encounter scenarios in which a site administrator cannot install an app because the app is requesting permissions that the installing user does not possess.

If the installing user clicks the Trust It button to grant the app's permission requests, the SharePoint host environment tracks these permissions in one or more of the SharePoint databases. The permissions that are specific to a site or a site collection are stored in the content database associated with the hosting site collection. Other types of permissions that are scoped above the site-collection level are stored in the App Management Service database.

Permission requests are created by adding *<AppPermissionRequest>* elements into the App-Manifest.xml file within the scope of a top-level *<AppPermissionRequests>* element. Each *<App-PermissionRequest>* element must contain the *Scope* attribute and the *Right* attribute, as shown in the following code:

```
<AppPermissionRequests>

  <AppPermissionRequest
    Scope="http://sharepoint/content/sitecollection/web"
    Right="Read" />

  <AppPermissionRequest
    Scope="http://sharepoint/content/sitecollection/web/list"
    Right="Write" />

</AppPermissionRequests>
```

The *Scope* attribute is used to define the type of object for which the permissions are being requested. The value of the *Scope* attribute is a URI that contains several distinct parts. Consider the URI value of the *Scope* attribute from the previous listing:

```
http://sharepoint/content/sitecollection/web
```

The first part of the *Scope* URI defines the *Product*, which in this example is *sharepoint*. In some scenarios, an app might need to request permissions from another Microsoft product such as *exchange* or *lync*.

The second part of the *Scope* URI defines the *permission provider*, which in this example is *content*. SharePoint 2013 provides several other permission providers such as *search*, *social*, and *bcs*.

The final part of the *Scope* URI defines the *target object type*, which in this example is *sitecollection/web*. This is the target object type used to define the host web. Note that this *Scope* URI will also include any child sites below the host web.

The *Right* attribute defines the type of permission you are requesting. The SharePoint Foundation platform defines four common rights, which include *Read, Write, Manage,* and *FullControl*. The various teams that have created SharePoint 2013 have tried to use these four basic rights as consistently as possible. However, some permission providers have added addition rights beyond these four. For example, the search permission provider defines the *QueryAsUserIgnoreAppPrincipal* right:

```
<AppPermissionRequest
  Scope="http://sharepoint/search"
  Right="QueryAsUserIgnoreAppPrincipal"
/>
```

You can encounter scenarios in which the *Scope* attribute does not provide enough control to specify a certain type of object. For example, imagine that you have an app that needs the *Manage* right on all document libraries in the host web. The *Scope* attribute will let you define a more general target object type for all lists, including document libraries as well as all the other list types:

```
<AppPermissionRequest
  Scope="http://sharepoint/content/sitecollection/web/list"
  Right="Manage"
/>
```

However, the app that requests permissions with this *Scope* URI is requesting the *Manage* right on every type of list, which is more permissions than the app actually needs. You can add a *<Property>* element into an *<AppPermissionRequest>* element to filter the object type beyond what is possible by using the *Scope* URI alone. Here's an example of adding the *BaseTemplateId* property with a value of *101* to filter the permission request to just document libraries:

```
<AppPermissionRequest
  Scope="http://sharepoint/content/sitecollection/web/list"
  Right="Manage" >

  <!-- add filter property to permission request -->
  <Property Name="BaseTemplateId" Value="101" />

</AppPermissionRequest>
```

In certain cases, you are not required to make direct edits to the AppManifest.xml file to add permission requests. The *Permissions* tab of the app Manifest Designer supplied by Microsoft Visual Studio 2012 makes it easy to add and configure permissions requests without having to work with the XML elements directly. Figure 6-5 shows what the Permissions tab looks like when you are configuring permission requests.

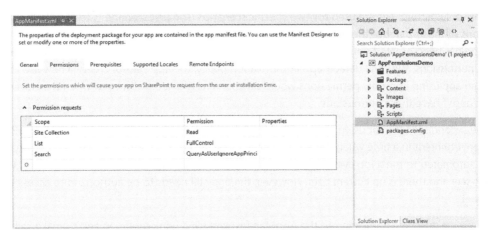

FIGURE 6-5 The Permissions tab of the app manifest designer specifies requested rights for the app.

There are several different types of permissions that an app can request in SharePoint 2013. Table 6-4 provides a listing of the more common ones that can be used in app development in SharePoint 2013.

TABLE 6-4 Permission types in SharePoint 2013

Object type	Scope URI	Rights
Tenancy	*http://sharepoint/content/tenant*	Read, Write, Manage, FullControl
Site collection	*http://sharepoint/content/sitecollection*	Read, Write, Manage, FullControl
Host web	*http://sharepoint/content/sitecollection/web*	Read, Write, Manage, FullControl
Lists	*http://sharepoint/content/sitecollection/web/list*	Read, Write, Manage, FullControl
Search	*http://sharepoint/search*	QueryAsUserIgnoreAppPrincipal
BCS	*http://sharepoint/bcs/connection*	Read
Taxonomy	*http://sharepoint/taxonomy*	Read, Write
Social core	*http://sharepoint/social/core*	Read, Write, Manage, FullControl
User profiles	*http://sharepoint/social/tenant*	Read, Write, Manage, FullControl
News feed	*http://sharepoint/social/microfeed*	Read, Write, Manage, FullControl

Requesting app-only permissions

For certain scenarios, the authorization system for SharePoint apps makes it possible for an app to call into the SharePoint host environment with an app identity but not a user identity. This relaxes the rules of app authorization because only the app needs permissions to access an object instead of both the app and the current user. In such a scenario, calls from an app are authorized by using *app-only permissions*.

App-only permissions are used for two specific scenarios. The first scenario is to elevate the permissions of the app above the permissions of the current user. For example, consider the case in which the app has been granted permissions to create a new list but the current user doesn't possess the same permissions. With the default app authorization policy, the app cannot create a new list. However, an app using app-only permissions would be able to create a new list even when the current user doesn't have those permissions.

The second scenario for using app-only permissions involves an app that accesses the SharePoint host environment in a time when there is no current user. Imagine a scenario in which an app has been automated to run a job every night at midnight to update a set of documents in the host web. In this scenario there is no current user. However, the app still needs to be authorized to access the host web.

You must make a modification to the AppManifest.xml file if you require an app to make calls that are authorized by using app-only permissions. The way this is accomplished is by adding the *Allow-AppOnlyPolicy* attribute to the *<AppPermissionRequests>* element in the app manifest:

```
<AppPermissionRequests AllowAppOnlyPolicy="true" >

  <AppPermissionRequest
    Scope="http://sharepoint/content/sitecollection/web"
    Right="Manage" />

</AppPermissionRequests>
```

Adding the *AllowAppOnlyPolicy* attribute to the *<AppPermissionRequests>* element alone is not enough to execute calls from an app run with the app-only policy. You must additionally create an access token with an app identity but not a user identity. The details of how to create an app-only access token will be covered in the next section of this chapter.

It is worth noting that running with app-only permissions is only possible when external authentication is being used. Executing calls from an app with app-only permissions is not possible when internal authentication is used. Therefore, running with app-only permissions is not possible from SharePoint-hosted apps. Calls from a SharePoint-hosted app will always require app permissions and user permissions to succeed.

Establishing app identity by using OAuth

OAuth is a standard Internet protocol for authentication and authorization that provides a cross-platform mechanism for managing app identity and app permissions. Although the original version, OAuth 1.0, is still being used by some software companies, a second version, OAuth 2.0, was created to simplify development while still providing app authentication and specific authorization flows for web apps, desktop applications, and mobile devices.

Today the OAuth 2.0 protocol is used by software companies such as Microsoft, Google, Facebook, and Salesforce.com. When Microsoft began to design the external authentication infrastructure for provided-hosted apps and autohosted apps in Office 365, it made a decision to build its implementation on top of the OAuth 2.0 protocol. More specifically, it decided that access tokens used for external authentication in the Office 365 environment would be created in accordance with the OAuth 2.0 specification.

Microsoft's implementation of OAuth 2.0 is built on top of the Windows Azure ACS. ACS is a cloud-hosted service on the Internet that is sponsored by Microsoft. The SharePoint host environment in Office 365 has been configured with a trust to ACS. This allows ACS to act as a security token service (STS) that creates access tokens that can be authenticated by Office 365. In most cases, the access tokens created by ACS will contain both an app identity and a user identity. However, ACS is also capable of creating access tokens with only an app identity for scenarios in which an app requires app-only permissions.

Note that the OAuth 2.0 specification provides a way to add permissions into an access token. However, this aspect of the OAuth specification not used in the SharePoint 2013 implementation. SharePoint 2013 makes use of OAuth for app authentication but not for any type of authorization or permissions management. Instead, it tracks and manages app permissions independently of the app authentication scheme in use so that app permissions work the same way as you switch between internal app authentication and external app authentication using either OAuth or S2S authentication.

Understanding where OAuth fits in

At a high level, it is fair to say that OAuth is primarily used for external app authentication in the Office 365 environment, whereas S2S authentication is used for external app authentication in on-premises farms. A common question is whether a company can use OAuth in on-premises farms. The answer to this question is—of course—it depends.

Although it is technically possible to configure OAuth support for external app authentication in an on-premises farm, you have to remember that the OAuth implementation in SharePoint 2013 is tightly coupled to Windows Azure ACS. The technical requirements for configuring OAuth support in an on-premises farm include obtaining an Office 365 tenancy from Microsoft and synchronizing user accounts between the on-premises farm and this Office 365 tenancy. Additional configuration is required to create trusts so that the local on-premises SharePoint farm and the remote web can both communicate with Windows Azure ACS.

The key takeaway is that OAuth is only supported in scenarios in which it is acceptable to have dependencies on Microsoft-hosted authentication servers in the cloud. OAuth cannot be used in a scenario in which you are required to avoid dependencies outside the LAN in which you are hosting an on-premises SharePoint farm and the remote web for a provider-hosted app.

Understanding OAuth terms and concepts

The OAuth 2.0 protocol defines a flow for app authentication, which involves the following four participants:

- Content owners
- Client app

- Content server

- Authentication server

Content owners represent the users who can grant access to the content in a site. In a SharePoint 2013 environment, a content owner has permissions to access objects such as sites, lists, and items, and can consequently grant these same permissions to an app.

The client app represents that part of a website that runs across the network. In a SharePoint 2013 environment, the client app is the portion of the app that runs in the remote web.

The content server is the web server that hosts the site with content. In a SharePoint 2013 environment, the content server is a web server hosted within the Office 365 environment that provides access to SharePoint sites within an Office 365 tenancy for a specific customer.

The authentication server is a server that creates access tokens used for app authentication. The authentication server must be trusted by both the content server and the client app. In a SharePoint 2013 environment, the authentication server is always Windows Azure ACS.

Understanding app principals

The SharePoint 2013 implementation of the OAuth protocol requires any app using external authentication to have an associated security principal known as an *app principal*. You can think of an app principal as a type of security account similar to a user account. The app principal for a cloud-hosted app in the Office 365 environment must be registered within the context of an Office 365 tenancy. A key point is that the app principal is similar to a user account because it is used to establish an identity during the app authentication process.

When you register an app principal within the context of an Office 365 tenancy, the SharePoint host environment tracks it in the App Management Service database. As part of the same registration process, the Office 365 environment also forwards information about the new app principal to Windows Azure ACS. This makes it possible for Windows Azure ACS to keep its configuration data for app principals in sync with each Office 365 tenancy.

The profile for an app principal contains five important properties:

- Client ID

- Client secret

- Title

- App host domain

- Redirect URL

The client ID is a GUID that is used to identify the app principal associated with a cloud-hosted app. Note that the client ID is sometimes referred to as the *app ID*. Don't be confused into thinking that the client ID and the app ID are different. They are just two terms that are used to refer to the same thing.

The client secret (also known as the *app secret*) is a security key created by using a Base64-encoded string that is used to perform symmetric encryption. The client secret is shared between the client app, the hosting Office 365 tenancy, and Windows Azure ACS. The client secret is an integral part of the app authentication process because it facilitates communication among these three parties in a way that makes it possible for messages to be encrypted and authenticated.

The title is a human-readable string for the app principal that is displayed to users within the Office 365 tenancy.

The app host domain is the base URL for the domain in which the remote web is hosted. The registration of the app host domain is important because it makes it possible for both the hosting Office 365 tenancy and Windows Azure ACS to ensure that calls from the remote web of an app have originated from the well-known URL.

The redirect URL is a property that is used in scenarios in which external applications and external websites need to request permissions on the fly. This property is optional. You can register an app principal without a redirect URL. The scenario in which a redirect URL is used will be covered later in this chapter.

Deploying the remote web by using Secure Sockets Layer

Note that the remote web associated with an app in a production environment should always be deployed by using Secure Sockets Layer (SSL). The reason for this is that SSL significantly lowers the risk of an attack by which the attacker calls to the Office 365 host environment pretending to originate from the app host domain when in fact it is being made from some other domain.

Registering app principals

When it comes to registering the app principal for an autohosted app, things are pretty easy. That's because the app principal is registered transparently behind the scenes as part of the app installation process.

When it comes to registering the app principal for a provider-hosted app, there are extra steps involved. The app principal must be explicitly registered by a user that possesses administrative permissions within the hosting Office 365 tenancy.

There are several ways in which you can register an app principal for a provider-hosted app in an Office 365 tenancy. The easiest way to do so is to use a standard application page named AppReg-New.aspx that was added to SharePoint 2013, as shown in Figure 6-6. As you can see, the AppReg-New.aspx page uses the terms *App Id* and *App Secret* instead of client ID and client secret. However, you have already learned that these are just different terms that refer to the client ID and the client secret.

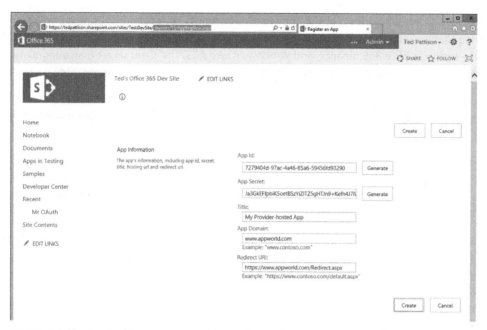

FIGURE 6-6 The AppRegNew.aspx page can be used to register an app principal for a provider-hosted app.

A second way to register an app principal for a provider-hosted app in the Office 365 environment involves using the *SharePoint Online Windows PowerShell Library*. This is a Windows PowerShell library that you install on a local computer that provides cmdlets with which you can create a remote connection to your Office 365 tenancy. After you have established an authenticated connection, the SharePoint Online Windows PowerShell Library provides additional cmdlets with which you can manage various aspects of your Office 365 tenancies, including creating and managing app principals.

Understanding app authentication flow in Office 365

The OAuth 2.0 protocol involves passing various types of security tokens between Windows Azure ACS, the hosting Office 365 tenancy, and the remote web. The following list shows the different types of security tokens that are passed between the participants when authenticating an app by using OAuth:

- Context token

- Refresh token

- Access token

- Authorization code

The context token is a security token that's used to pass contextual information such as the identity of the current user, the URL of the host web, and the ID of the current tenancy. The context token is created by Windows Azure ACS and initially passed to the SharePoint host environment. The

SharePoint host environment is then able to pass the context token to the remote web, where it can be accessed and used by server-side code in the remote web.

The refresh token is included within the context token that is passed to the remote web. The value of the refresh token is that it can be used by code in the remote web to obtain an access token from Windows Azure ACS.

When a refresh token is created, it's good for a period of six months, whereas an access token is only good for 12 hours. Therefore, it often makes sense for an app to store refresh tokens in a database from which they can be retrieved and reused to create access tokens on demand.

The access token is what the server-side code in the remote web actually needs to execute authenticated calls back to the SharePoint host environment by using CSOM or the REST API. Therefore, the remote web requires code to explicitly call into Windows Azure ACS and obtain access tokens when needed. After the code in the remote web has retrieved an access token, it must pass the access token in an HTTP header each time it makes a CSOM or REST API call by using programming techniques that will be discussed later in this chapter.

An authorization code is a special type of security token used in a scenario in which an external website that has never been installed as a SharePoint app wants to acquire permissions on the fly to call into a SharePoint site. The use of authorization codes will be explained later in this chapter.

Now that you have learned about the different types of security tokens, you can understand how the app authentication flow works in a typical scenario with a cloud-hosted app that has been installed in an Office 365 tenancy. Figure 6-7 shows 10 different stages within the OAuth authentication flow as security tokens are passed back and forth between the Office 365 tenancy, Windows Azure ACS, and the remote web of the cloud-hosted app.

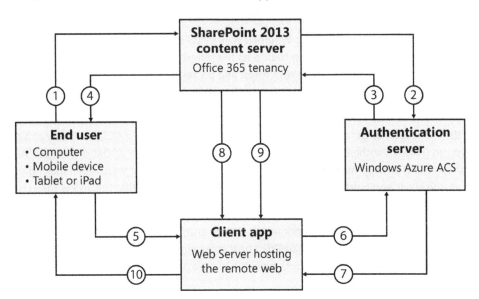

FIGURE 6-7 The authentication flow for an external app involves SharePoint, Azure, the app itself, and the end user.

Let's begin with stage 1, when the user first accesses a page in a SharePoint site within an Office 365 tenancy. The user is authenticated and a SAML token is created that contains information about the user identity such as the user's logon name.

In stage 2, the user navigates to the Site Contents page in which the SharePoint host environment must display a tile that the user can employ to launch the app. When the SharePoint host environment needs to create a tile with an app launcher, it must first call to Windows Azure ACS and request creation of a context token.

When the SharePoint host environment calls to Windows Azure ACS to create a context token, it passes information about the current user, the host web, and the current tenancy. Windows Azure ACS needs this information because it must add information about the current user, the host web, and the current tenancy inside the context token. In stage 3, Windows Azure ACS creates the context token and returns it to the SharePoint host environment.

In stage 4, the SharePoint host environment has the context token returned from Windows Azure ACS. The SharePoint host environment makes use of the context token by adding it into the JavaScript code for the app launcher on the Site Contents page.

Stage 5 occurs when the user clicks the tile for the app on the Site Contents page and launches the app. The JavaScript code behind the app launcher redirects the user to the app's start page in the remote web by using an HTTP *POST* request. When the HTTP *POST* request is executed, the context token is passed to the remote web by using a form variable named *SPAppToken*.

In stage 6 the client app retrieves the context token from *SPAppToken* in the incoming request to the state page. The client app is then able to read what's inside the context token to obtain information about the current user, the host web, and the current tenancy. The client app also has the ability to extract the refresh token from the context token.

Stage 6 is where the client app calls to Windows Azure ACS to request an access token. When requesting an access token, the client app must pass the refresh token. In stage 7, Windows Azure ACS creates the access token from the refresh token and passes it back to the client app. Note that Windows Azure creates an access token that has both the identity of the app as well as the identity of the current user.

After the client app has obtained an access token from Windows Azure ACS, it is finally at a point at which it can make an authenticated call to the host web by using either CSOM or the REST API. Stage 8 shows the client app making a CSOM or REST API call on the host web. When making this type of call, the client app must include explicit programming to ensure that the access token is passed in each call using an HTTP header.

In Stage 9, the SharePoint host environment is able to authenticate the call from the app by using the access token. As long as the SharePoint host environment is able to determine that the authenticated app and the current user both have the proper permissions, it returns content back to the client app.

In the final stage, stage 10, the client app is able to return a page from the remote web that displays content from the host web that was retrieved during stages 8 and 9. At this point, you have seen the end-to-end flow of authentication that's used in an OAuth scenario.

Developing with OAuth

There are three important requirements to keep in mind when developing cloud-hosted apps that will be installed within an Office 365 tenancy. First, the app manifest file must be properly configured to indicate whether the app is a provider-hosted app or an autohosted app. Second, the web.config file in the ASP.NET project for the remote web must be configured to track the client ID and the client secret. Finally, you must write server-side code that creates and manages access tokens.

The app manifest file for a provider-hosted app must be configured with a *<RemoteWebApplication>* element that contains an inner *ClientId* attribute that tracks the GUID identifying an app principal:

```
<AppPrincipal>
  <RemoteWebApplication ClientId="00000000-0000-0000-0000-000000000001" />
</AppPrincipal>
```

If you are developing an autohosted app, on the other hand, the app manifest should be configured with an *<AutoDeployedWebApplication>* element. The *<AutoDeployedWebApplication>* element is different from the *<RemoteWebApplication>* element because it does not contain an attribute for a client ID:

```
<AppPrincipal>
  <AutoDeployedWebApplication/>
</AppPrincipal>
```

The next aspect of configuring a cloud-hosted app for use in the Office 365 environment is configuring the web.config file of the remote web with two settings that are set the same, regardless of whether you are developing a provider-hosted app or an autohosted app. In particular, you must add two *appSettings* variables into the web.config file to track the client ID and the client secret. These *appSettings* variables must be named *ClientId* and *ClientSecret*:

```
<configuration>
  <appSettings>
    <add key="ClientId" value="00000000-0000-0000-0000-000000000001" />
    <add key="ClientSecret" value="rdYuzdeP9LX67rJJLTDjL1E5pvqbrLe4VTs2apITF4g=" />
  </appSettings>
</configuration>
```

At this point, you might be wondering what these two *appSettings* variables are for. As it turns out, these two variables are used by a utility class named *TokenHelper* that Visual Studio 2012 automatically adds to ASP.NET projects that will be used to implement a remote web. The last step in getting up and running with OAuth is learning how to program with the *TokenHelper* class to create access tokens and to pass these access tokens when making CSOM and REST calls back to the SharePoint host environment.

Programming with the *TokenHelper* class

If you plan on developing cloud-hosted apps, you must learn to work with the *TokenHelper* class. The *TokenHelper* class provides a public set of static methods for working with several different types of security tokens including context tokens, refresh tokens, and, most importantly, the access tokens.

Let's start with a simple example. The following code shows an implementation for the *Page_Load* method. This code is very similar to the "hello world" code snippet that Visual Studio 2012 automatically adds to the start page of a cloud-hosted app that uses OAuth. This code has been written to retrieve the context token passed by the SharePoint host environment and then to obtain an access token from Windows Azure ACS:

```
protected void Page_Load(object sender, EventArgs e) {

  // get context token from incoming HTTP form variable
  var contextToken = TokenHelper.GetContextTokenFromRequest(Page.Request);

  // get host web URL from incoming query string parameter
  var hostWeb = Page.Request["SPHostUrl"];

  // call to Window Azure ACS to acquire access token
  using (var clientContext =
          TokenHelper.GetClientContextWithContextToken(hostWeb,
                                                contextToken,
                                                Request.Url.Authority)) {

    // Make CSOM call to SharePoint host passing access token
    clientContext.Load(clientContext.Web, web => web.Title);
    clientContext.ExecuteQuery();

    // display site title on start page
    Response.Write(clientContext.Web.Title);
  }
}
```

Now that you have seen a simple example of using the *TokenHelper* class, it's time to explain how to program against this class in a bit more detail. When a user is redirected from a host web in an Office 365 tenancy to the start page in the remote web, the SharePoint host environment passes several important pieces of data to the app's remote web by using an HTTP *POST* operation.

For example, the SharePoint host environment passes several querying string parameters, including one named *SPHostUrl*, which contains the base URL of the host web. When you are writing server-side code behind the start page for a cloud-hosted app, you can retrieve the host web URL by using the following code:

```
string urlHostWeb = Request.QueryString["SPHostUrl"]
```

In addition to query string parameters, the SharePoint host environment also passes several form parameters when posting to the start page in the remote web, including one named *SPAppToken*, which contains the context token. You can access the context token as a raw string by using the following code:

```
string contextTokenString = Request.Form["SPAppToken"]
```

As you have already seen, you can retrieve the context token by using a *TokenHelper* method named *GetContextTokenFromRequest*. When you make the call to *GetContextTokenFromRequest*, you pass the ASP.NET *Request* object as the one and only parameter value:

```
// when calling GetContextTokenFromRequest, you must pass the ASP.NET Request object
string contextTokenString = TokenHelper.GetContextTokenFromRequest(Request);
```

The code demonstrates passing the context token as a raw string when calling *GetClientContextWithContextToken*. The implementation of this method extracts the refresh token from the context token and then uses it to call to Windows Azure ACS to obtain an access token. After the access token has been returned, the *GetClientContextWithContextToken* method uses it to initialize a CSOM session with a special client context that automatically passes the access token when sending a request to execute CSOM commands on the SharePoint host environment.

If you need to read information from inside the context token, you can convert the context token string to a strongly typed object by calling the *TokenHelper* method *ReadAndValidateContextToken*:

```
string remoteWebUrl = Request.Url.Authority;
string contextTokenString = TokenHelper.GetContextTokenFromRequest(Request);

SharePointContextToken contextToken;
contextToken = TokenHelper.ReadAndValidateContextToken(contextTokenString, remoteWebUrl);
```

The call to *ReadAndValidateContextToken* returns a *SharePointContextToken* object that makes the information inside the context token accessible to your code through simple properties. The code in Listing 6-3 demonstrates the type of information that you can read from the context token.

LISTING 6-3 Accessing information within the context token

```
string remoteWebUrl = Request.Url.Authority;
string contextTokenString = TokenHelper.GetContextTokenFromRequest(Request);

SharePointContextToken contextToken;
contextToken = TokenHelper.ReadAndValidateContextToken(contextTokenString, remoteWebUrl);

// ID of the current user on behalf of which the current call is executing
string nameId = contextToken.NameId;

// Client ID of the app principal used for external authentication
string clientId = contextToken.ActorToken.ActorToken.Id;

// ID of the hosting tenancy in Office 365
string realm = contextToken.Realm;

// Environment ID for Office 365
string targetPrincipalName = contextToken.TargetPrincipalName;

// ID of the authentication server which is Windows Azure ACS
string issuer = contextToken.Issuer;

// URL used when communicating with Windows Azure ACS
string  securityTokenServiceUri = contextToken.SecurityTokenServiceUri;

// time when context token became valid
DateTime validFrom = contextToken.ValidFrom;

// time when context token expires
DateTime validTo = contextToken.ValidTo;

// refresh token
string refreshToken = contextToken.RefreshToken;

// caching key for caching refresh tokens and access tokens
string cacheKey = contextToken.CacheKey;
```

If you look toward the end of Listing 6-3, you can see that the code demonstrates how to retrieve both the refresh token and the cache key from the context token. The refresh token is what the app must pass to Windows Azure ACS to obtain an access token. Although you do not have to work directly with refresh tokens in all scenarios, it can be helpful to store refresh tokens in a database, where they are good for 6 months, to retrieve access tokens. Remember that an access token is only good for 12 hours.

Recall that all refresh tokens and the majority of access tokens contain information about one specific user. Therefore, any scheme you design to cache or store refresh tokens and/or access tokens must ensure that caching is user-specific when required. It would be bad to use the refresh token associated with one user to retrieve an access token for a different user.

The context token contains a special string value named *cacheKey*. The cache key holds a string value that will always be unique for the combination of current user, host web site, and app. The idea is that you can use the *cacheKey* as a dictionary lookup key when caching or storing access tokens in memory or refresh tokens inside a database.

Working with access tokens

At this point, you have already seen the code required to execute CSOM commands by using OAuth. Executing a REST API call by using OAuth is different because you must work directly with access tokens in your code. Listing 6-4 shows the code required to retrieve an access token. After the access token has been acquired, it must be converted into a string and added as an HTTP header before the REST API call is made.

LISTING 6-4 Making a simple REST API call by using OAuth

```
// get context token as a SharePointContextToken object
string remoteWebUrl = Request.Url.Authority;
string contextTokenString = TokenHelper.GetContextTokenFromRequest(Request);
SharePointContextToken contextToken;
contextToken = TokenHelper.ReadAndValidateContextToken(contextTokenString,
                                                       remoteWebUrl);

// retrieve host web information
string hostWebUrl = Request.QueryString["SPHostUrl"];
Uri hostWebUri = new Uri(hostWebUrl);
string hostWebAuthority = hostWebUri.Authority;

// get access token by passing context token and host web authority
OAuth2AccessTokenResponse accessToken = TokenHelper.GetAccessToken(contextToken,
                                                       hostWebAuthority);

// get access token as a Base64 encoded string
string accessTokenString = accessToken.AccessToken;

// prepare HttpWebRequest to execute REST API call
HttpWebRequest request1 =
  (HttpWebRequest)HttpWebRequest.Create(hostWebUrl.ToString() + "/_api/Web/title");

// add access token string as Authorization header
request1.Headers.Add("Authorization", "Bearer " + accessTokenString);

// execute REST API call and inspect response
HttpWebResponse response1 = (HttpWebResponse)request1.GetResponse();
StreamReader reader1 = new StreamReader(response1.GetResponseStream());
XDocument doc1 = XDocument.Load(reader1);
string SiteTitle = doc1.Root.Value;
```

Let's step through some of the code in Listing 6-4. There is a call to the *TokenHelper* method *Get-AccessToken*, which retrieves an access token from Windows Azure ACS. When you call *GetAccessToken*, you must pass a strongly typed context token and the authority of the host web:

```
// get access token by passing context token and host web authority
OAuth2AccessTokenResponse accessToken = TokenHelper.GetAccessToken(contextToken,
                                                                   hostWebAuthority);

// get access token as a Base64 encoded string
string accessTokenString = accessToken.AccessToken;
```

When passing the second parameter for the host web authority, you must pass the URL of the host web but without the protocol in front. For example, the host web authority is a string such as *tenancy01.sharepoint.com*, as opposed to the host web URL, which has the protocol at the beginning with a value such as *https://tenancy01.sharepoint.com*.

You can see that calling *GetAccessToken* returns a strongly typed object of type *OAuth2Access-TokenResponse*. However, you must usually work with the access token in its raw form as a Base64-encoded string. You retrieve the string for the access token by reading the *AccessToken* property of the *OAuth2AccessTokenResponse* object.

The code in Listing 6-4 demonstrates creating an *HttpWebRequest* object and adding the string-based access token as an HTTP header named *Authorization*. You should take note that the *Authorization* header value is created by combining the word "Bearer" together with the access token, with a blank space between them:

```
string restUri = hostWeb + "/_api/Web/title";
HttpWebRequest request1 = (HttpWebRequest)HttpWebRequest.Create(restUri);

// add access token to Authorization header
request1.Headers.Add("Authorization", "Bearer " + accessTokenString);
```

JavaScript Object Notation Web Tokens

OAuth security tokens such as context tokens, refresh tokens, and access tokens are created by using the JSON Web Token (JWT) standard. A JWT is created in a text-based, human-readable format by using JavaScript Object Notation (JSON), which allows you to read the information inside:

```
{ "token_type":"Bearer",
  "access_token":"eyJ0eXAiOiJKV1QiLCJhbGciOiJSUzI1NiIsIng1dCI6Ik5HVEZ2k5HVE2ZEst...",
  "expires_in":"43199",
  "not_before":"1355269661",
  "expires_on":"1355312861",
  "resource":"00000003-0000-0ff1-ce00-000000000000/tenancy01.sharepoint.com@23d..." }
```

> Although JWTs are initially created in a human-readable form, they must be converted into a Base64-encoded format before they are passed across the network. After a security token has been converted into a Base64-encoded format, it loses any trace of human readability:
>
> eyJ0eXAiOiJKV1QiLCJhbGciOiJIUzI1NiJ9.eyJhdWQiOiJmOWIONmIwZiO4YjM2LTQ2ODYtYW
> Y5MiOwMmRhODY3NGNiYzEvbG9jYWxob3N0OjQ0MzA0QDIzZDkOOWFlLWIzNzEtNGJmMS1iNzVmL
> Tg5ZjAwMjk5NDY1ZiIsImlzcyI6IjAwMDAwMDAxLTAwMDAtMDAwMC1jMDAwLTAwMDAwMDAwMDAwM
> EAyM2Q5ND1hZS1iMzcxLTRiZjEtYjc1Zi040WYwMDI5OTQ2NWYiLCJuYmYiOjEzNTUyNjk2NTgsI
> mV4cCI6MTM1NTMxMjg1OCwiYXBwY3R4c2VuZGVyIjoiMDAwMDAwMDMtMDAwMC0wZmYxYxLWN1MDAtM
> DAwMDAwMDAwMDAwQDIzZDkOOWFlLWIzNzEtNGJmMS1iNzVmLTg5ZjAwMjk5NDY1ZiIsImFwcGNOe
> CI6IntcIkhNY2h1S2V5XCI6XCJnK2k1UVFLYjZnMnNt

Working with app-only access tokens

In the majority of scenarios, an access token will carry the identity of the current user in addition to the identity of the app itself. However, there are scenarios for which it makes sense to create an access token that contains an app identity but no user identity. This type of security token is known as an app-only access token.

As discussed earlier in the chapter, there are two primary scenarios in which you should use app-only access tokens. The first scenario involves a requirement to elevate the permissions for an app so that they are not constrained by the permissions of the current user. For example, an app-only access token makes it possible for an app to create a list in the host web even when the current user lacks the permissions to do so.

The second scenario in which it makes sense to create app-only access tokens is during a time when there is no current user. This might be the case if an app runs a batch job every night at midnight to update a set of document in the host web. In this scenario, the app is running but not in the context of any specific user. However, the app is still required to create an access token to make CSOM or REST API calls against the host web.

You can retrieve an app-only access token by calling the *TokenHelper* method named *GetAppOnly-AccessToken*. This method accepts three parameters, including the target principal name, the host web authority, and the realm that identifies the hosting tenancy in Office 365:

```
// get app-only access token as a strongly typed object
OAuth2AccessTokenResponse appOnlyAccessToken =
  TokenHelper.GetAppOnlyAccessToken(contextToken.TargetPrincipalName,
                        hostWebAuthority,
                        contextToken.Realm);

// get access token in a string form to pass across the network
string appOnlyAccessTokenString = appOnlyAccessToken.AccessToken;
```

After you have obtained the app-only access token from Windows Azure ACS and converted it into its string format, you can use it to set up the *Authorization* header, just as you do with standard access tokens. If you want to execute CSOM commands by using app-only permissions, you must first obtain the string value for an app-only access token. You can pass the app-only access token string when calling the *GetClientContextWithAccessToken* method to establish a new CSOM session, which executes its commands by using app-only permissions:

```
ClientContext appOnlyClientContext =
            TokenHelper.GetClientContextWithAccessToken(hostWebUrl,
                                                appOnlyAccessTokenString);
```

The SHAREPOINT\APP account

When the SharePoint host environment authenticates an app by using an access token containing a user identity, it uses the user identity to initialize the calling context. However, things are different when the SharePoint host environment authenticates a call from an app that has passed an app-only access token. When the SharePoint host environment authenticates a CSOM or REST API call with an app-only access token, it initializes the calling context with a special SharePoint system account named SHAREPOINT\APP.

Acquiring permissions on the fly by using authorization code

So far, this chapter has discussed authentication and authorization scenarios involving SharePoint apps that have been installed into a specific SharePoint tenancy. SharePoint 2013 provides another option, which can be used by standard websites that were not developed as SharePoint apps. This allows any type of website on the Internet to request permissions to access a SharePoint 2013 site on the fly.

Although this approach does not involve creating or installing a SharePoint app, it does require you to preregister an app principal within the scope of the target tenancy where the permissions will be requested. Enabling this capability for an external website to request permissions on the fly is the primary scenario in which you must register an app principal with a redirect URL.

For example, imagine that you have developed an ASP.NET website whose base URL is *https://appserver.wingtip.com*, and you want this website to be able to request permissions from a SharePoint site in Office 365 on the fly. First, you need to register an app principal in the scope of the host tenancy for the SharePoint site. When registering the app principal you must set the redirect URL to point to a page in the ASP.NET website such as *https://appserver.wingtip.com/RedirectAccept.aspx*.

After you have registered the app principal with the proper redirect URL, the next step involves writing code in the external website to create the authorization URL. This step is greatly simplified if you add the *TokenHelper* class that is also used in the remote web of a cloud-hosted app. The *Token-Helper* class provides a method named *GetAuthorizationUrl*.

The code in Listing 6-5 demonstrates how to call the *GetAuthorizationUrl* method in an external website. This method accepts three parameters: the URL of the host web, the permission being requested (for example, *Web.Read*), and a redirect URL. The redirect URL is important because it is what the SharePoint host environment uses to call back to the external website if a user with sufficient permissions grants the permission request.

LISTING 6-5 The code required to generate a permission request by using an authorization URL.

```
string urlHostWeb = "https://tenancy01.sharepoint.com/";
string urlRedirectAccept = "https://AppServer.wingtip.com/ RedirectAccept.aspx";
string urlAuthorization = TokenHelper.GetAuthorizationUrl(urlHostWeb,
                                        "Web.Read",
                                        urlRedirectAccept);


// redirect
Response.Redirect(urlAuthorization, true);
```

The *GetAuthorizationUrl* method parses together a URL that targets a standard SharePoint 2013 application page named *OAuthAuthorize.aspx*. The authorization URL also includes query string parameters to pass a GUID for the client ID, the requested permissions, and the redirect URL. As shown in Listing 6-5, you can redirect the user to the authorization URL automatically by calling *Response.Redirect*.

When the user is redirected to the authorization URL within the host web, the SharePoint host environment responds by displaying a page with which the user can either grant or deny the permission request. Just as in the case of a permission request in a SharePoint app, a user must possess any permissions that are granted in a permission request. If the user grants the permission request, the SharePoint host environment responds by passing an authorization code back to the external website by using an HTTP *POST* operation that targets the page configured as the redirect URL. Listing 6-6 shows an example of code behind the redirect page that has been written to retrieve the authorization code and use it to create an access token. The authorization code is passed from the SharePoint host environment to the redirect page by using a query string parameter named *code*.

```
string authorizationCode = Request.QueryString["code"];
string targetPrincipalName = "00000003-0000-0ff1-ce00-000000000000";  // Office 365 ID
string targetRealm = "79597708-fc2e-4c79-acfa-710bb435db25";          // tenancy ID
string urlHostWeb = "https://tenancy01.sharepoint.com/ ";             // host web
string urlRedirectAccept = "https://AppServer.wingtip.com/RedirectAccept.aspx";
Uri uriRedirectAccept = new Uri(urlRedirectAccept);

ClientContext context =
  TokenHelper.GetClientContextWithAuthorizationCode(urlHostWeb,
                                                    targetPrincipalName,
                                                    authorizationCode,
                                                    targetRealm,
                                                    uriRedirectAccept);

context.Load(context.Web);
context.ExecuteQuery();
context.Dispose();
```

After you have retrieved an authorization code, you can pass it in a call to the *GetClientContext-WithAuthorizationCode* method or an overloaded implementation of the *GetAccessToken* method. Thecode in Listing 6-6 demonstrates calling the *GetClientContextWithAuthorizationCode* method to create a CSOM client context with an access token that makes it possible for the website to make CSOM calls on the host web.

Establishing app identity by using S2S trusts

In this chapter, you have learned that SharePoint 2013 supports external app authentication by using both OAuth and S2S trusts. Although OAuth is primarily intended for use in the Office 365 environment, the S2S trust infrastructure was specifically designed to work in on-premises farms with provider-hosted apps.

Using an S2S trust for external app authentication is similar to using OAuth in the sense that code in the remote web passes an access token when calling to the SharePoint host environment. However, the manner in which the access token is created and the parties involved are very different.

One significant difference from using OAuth is that an S2S trust does not require any communications with Windows Azure ACS or any other authentication server in the cloud. The only servers involved in an S2S trust are the web server that hosts the remote web and the web servers of an on-premises SharePoint 2013 farm. Therefore, all of the servers required with an S2S trust can all run within the same LAN or private network.

A second significant difference involves authenticating the current user. When using OAuth, the SharePoint host environment authenticates the current user and then passes this user's identity to the remote web by using the context token.

Things work very differently when using an S2S trust. The SharePoint host environment doesn't pass the identity of the current user to the remote web. In fact, the SharePoint host environment doesn't pass a context token at all. The context token, which is a central figure in OAuth, doesn't even exist in the authentication flow of an S2S trust.

When a provider-hosted app is configured to authenticate by using an S2S trust, its remote web takes on the responsibility of authenticating the current user independently of any user authentication that has taken place in the SharePoint host environment. After the remote web has authenticated the current user, it can then create an access token that contains both the app identity and the identity of the current user.

When you are using OAuth, the remote web must call to Windows Azure ACS to acquire an access token. However, a provider-hosted app using an S2S trust can create an access code on its own by using the *TokenHelper* class.

After the remote web for a provider-hosted app has created an S2S access token, it can then pass the access token to the SharePoint host environment when executing CSOM command or REST API calls. The programming aspects of passing the access token string using the Authentication header in a provider-hosted app by using an S2S trust work the same way as with OAuth.

High-trust configurations vs. full-trust configurations

A provider-hosted app using an S2S trust is often referred to as a high-trust configuration. The term "high trust" is used to imply that the provided-hosted app authenticates the current user independently of the SharePoint host environment. When the provider-hosted app makes a CSOM or REST API call, the SharePoint host environment cannot verify the identity of the current user. Therefore, the SharePoint host environment must trust that the provider-hosted app has properly authenticated the user and passed the true identity of the current user in the access token.

Do not confuse the term "high trust" with "full trust." Code that runs with full trust, such as server-side code in a farm solution, runs without security restrictions. Full-trust code can do whatever it wants to do. This is very different from a provider-hosted app running at high trust, which is constrained by whatever set of permissions has been granted to the app.

Architecture of an S2S trust

The architecture of an S2S trust is based on a X.509 certificate, which contains a public/private key pair. The public and private keys are used to perform asymmetric encryption. The critical underlying concept is that the provider-hosted app uses the private key to sign the access token. The SharePoint host environment uses the public key to verify that the access token has been created and signed by a party that possesses the private key. This, in turn, makes it possible for the SharePoint host environment to authenticate calls from a provider-hosted app that is configured to use an S2S trust.

Figure 6-8 shows the high-level architecture of an S2S trust. Unlike in a scenario involving OAuth, the remote web does not need to communicate with Windows Azure ACS to acquire access tokens. Instead, it is able to create access tokens on its own, which must be signed with the private key. One important observation is that the remote web requires access to the private key at runtime whenever it needs to create an access token.

A second requirement for an S2S trust is that the hosting SharePoint farm must be configured with a special type of secure token service known as a *trusted security token issuer*. You will learn how to configure a trusted security token issuer using a public key file and a Windows PowerShell script later in this chapter.

Let's follow the stages of the S2S authentication flow that are shown in Figure 6-7. In stage 1, the user navigates to a SharePoint site and is prompted to log on. When the user supplies a valid set of credentials and logs on, the SharePoint host environment creates a SAML token to track the user's identity. However, the identity of the user is never passed to a provider-hosted app using an S2S trust.

In stage 2, the user navigates to the Site Settings page and sees the tile for a provider-hosted app, which has been configured to use an S2S trust. When the user clicks this tile, the SharePoint host environment uses an app launcher to redirect the user to the start page in the remote web.

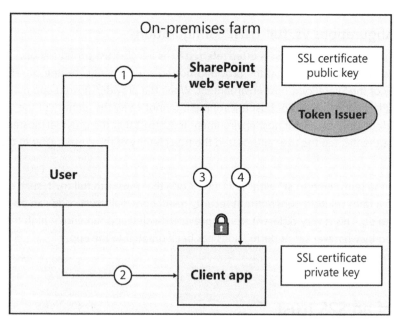

FIGURE 6-8 An S2S trust is based on a public/private key pair that allows apps to create access tokens that carry a digital signature.

When the SharePoint host environment redirects the user to the start page of a provider-hosted app with an S2S trust, it passes many of the same query string parameters as in an OAuth scenario, such as the *SPHostUrl* parameter. However, the SharePoint host environment does not pass a context token. This means that the SharePoint host environment passes nothing to indicate who the user is. This puts the responsibility on the remote web to authenticate the user.

Stage 3 occurs after the user has been authenticated and there is a need to create an access token. When code in the remote web creates an access token by using the *TokenHelper* class, it adds information into the access token about the identity of the app and the identity of the current user. Next, the remote web must acquire the value of the private key file to sign the access token. After the remote web has created and signed the access token, it can pass the access token by using the *Authorization* header each time it executes a CSOM command or a REST API call.

In stage 4, the SharePoint host environment uses external authentication to authenticate a call from a provider-hosted app that is using the S2S trust. For this to work, the hosting SharePoint farm must first be configured with a trusted security token issuer that is based on the public key. During the external authentication process, the SharePoint host environment inspects the access token and uses the trusted security token issuer to verify its authenticity.

Configuring S2S trusts for Microsoft products

The infrastructure for configuring S2S trusts within a SharePoint 2013 farm wasn't just created exclusively for custom app development. When configuring a SharePoint 2013 farm, it is sometimes necessary to create S2S trusts for Microsoft products such as Microsoft Exchange 2013 and Workflow Manager. Configuring an S2S trust makes it possible for these Microsoft products to call into the SharePoint host environment with a distinct app identity and with a set of preconfigured permissions.

Configuring an S2S trust

The first step in configuring an S2S trust for a provider-hosted app is generating a public/private key pair by creating an X.509 certificate. To obtain an X.509 certificate for use on production servers, it is recommended that you go through an established certification authority (CA) that has experience creating professional-grade certificates. For development and other scenarios with lower security concerns, you can create the required X.509 certificate with a public/private key pair by using two command-line tools named makecert.exe and certmgr.exe that are available on any web server on which SharePoint 2013 has been installed.

The Windows PowerShell script shown in Listing 6-7 demonstrates how to create an X.509 certificate with a public/private key pair. You use the makecert.exe tool to create a certificate file named appserver.wingtip.com.cer that contains both the public key and the private key. Use the certmgr.exe tool to register the certificate with IIS so that it can be used to enable SSL on an IIS website.

LISTING 6-7 A Windows PowerShell script creating an X.509 certificate with a public/private key pair

```
$makecert = "C:\Program Files\Microsoft Office Servers\15.0\Tools\makecert.exe"
$certmgr = "C:\Program Files\Microsoft Office Servers\15.0\Tools\certmgr.exe"

# specify domain name for SSL certificate (optional)
$domain = "appserver.wingtip.com"

# create output directory to create SSL certificate file
$outputDirectory = "c:\Certs\"
New-Item $outputDirectory -ItemType Directory -Force -Confirm:$false | Out-Null

# create file name for SSL certificate files
$publicCertificatePath  = $outputDirectory + $domain + ".cer"
$privateCertificatePath = $outputDirectory + $domain + ".pfx"

Write-Host "Creating .cer certificate file..."

& $makecert -r -pe -n "CN=$domain" -b 01/01/2012 -e 01/01/2022 -eku 1.3.6.1.5.5.7.3.1
            -ss my -sr localMachine -sky exchange -sy 12
            -sp "Microsoft RSA SChannel Cryptographic Provider"  $publicCertificatePath

Write-Host "Registering certificate with IIS..."
& $certmgr /add $publicCertificatePath /s /r localMachine root

# get certificate to obtain thumbprint
$publicCertificate = Get-PfxCertificate -FilePath $publicCertificatePath
$publicCertificateThumbprint = $publicCertificate.Thumbprint

Get-ChildItem cert:\\localmachine\my |
  Where-Object {$_.Thumbprint -eq $publicCertificateThumbprint} |
  ForEach-Object {
    Write-Host "  .. exporting private key for certificate (*.PFK)"
    $privateCertificateByteArray = $_.Export("PFX", "Password1")
    [System.IO.File]::WriteAllBytes($privateCertificatePath, $privateCertificateByteArray)
    Write-Host "  Certificate exported" -ForegroundColor Gray
  }
```

There is code at the end of the Windows PowerShell script in Listing 6-7 that exports the certificate's private key to a password-protected file named appserver.wingtip.com.pfx. This means that the remote web requires access to this PFX file and the password in order to retrieve the private key to sign access tokens.

After you have created the .cer file with the public key, you must copy it to a web server in the hosting SharePoint farm to create a trusted security token issuer. The Windows PowerShell script in Listing 6-8 shows how to create the trusted-security token issuer by using a Windows PowerShell cmdlet for SharePoint named *New-SPTrustedSecurityTokenIssuer*. Note that a trusted security-token issuer is registered with an identifying GUID. You should record this GUID because it must be used from the provider-hosted app.

LISTING 6-8 A Windows PowerShell script for SharePoint to register a trusted security-token issuer

```
Add-PSSnapin "Microsoft.SharePoint.PowerShell"

$issuerID = "11111111-1111-1111-1111-111111111111"
$targetSiteUrl = "http://wingtipserver"
$targetSite = Get-SPSite $targetSiteUrl
$realm = Get-SPAuthenticationRealm -ServiceContext $targetSite

$registeredIssuerName = $issuerID + '@' + $realm

$publicCertificatePath = "C:\Certs\appserver.wingtip.com.cer"
$publicCertificate = Get-PfxCertificate $publicCertificatePath

Write-Host "Create token issuer"
$secureTokenIssuer = New-SPTrustedSecurityTokenIssuer '
                        -Name $issuerID '
                        -RegisteredIssuerName $registeredIssuerName '
                        -Certificate $publicCertificate '
                        -IsTrustBroker
```

Although this example demonstrates registering a trusted-security token issuer by using a public key from a .cer file, SharePoint 2013 also supports registering one by using a metadata endpoint exposed by the provider-hosted app. This is typically the way registering is done when the app is a product such as Exchange 2013 or Workflow Manager.

After you have registered a trusted security-token issuer, the next step is to register an app principal. This can be done by using the AppRegNew.aspx page in exactly the same way you would register an app principal for an app that uses OAuth. You can also register the app principal for an S2S trust by using a Windows PowerShell cmdlet for SharePoint named *Register-AppPrincipal*, as shown in Listing 6-9.

LISTING 6-9 Registering the app principal for an S2S trust with *Register-AppPrincipal*

```
# register an app principal for a provider-hosted app using an S2S trust
$appDisplayName = "My S2S High Trust App"
$clientID = "22222222-2222-2222-2222-222222222222"

$targetSiteUrl = "https://intranet.wingtip.com"
$targetSite = Get-SPSite $targetSiteUrl
$realm = Get-SPAuthenticationRealm -ServiceContext $targetSite

$fullAppPrincipalIdentifier = $clientID + '@' + $realm

Write-Host "Register new app principal"
$registeredAppPrincipal = Register-SPAppPrincipal '
                        -NameIdentifier $fullAppPrincipalIdentifier '
                        -Site $targetSite.RootWeb '
                        -DisplayName $AppDisplayName'
```

There are a few scenarios in which the *Register-SPAppPrincipal* cmdlet does not provide enough control to properly configure an app principal. More specifically, the *Register-SPAppPrincipal* cmdlet does not allow you to configure an app domain for the remote web nor a redirect URI. For scenarios in which you need to configure an app principal with an app domain and/or a redirect URI, you can write a Windows PowerShell script for SharePoint that uses the *SPAppPrincipalManager* class in the server-side object model, as shown in Listing 6-10.

LISTING 6-10 Registering an app principal by using the *SPAppPrincipalManager* class

```
Add-PSSnapin "Microsoft.SharePoint.PowerShell"

# set initialization values for new app principal
$appDisplayName = "App Principal for My High Trust App"
$clientID = "33333333-3333-3333-3333-333333333333"
$appHostDomainUrl = "http://localhost:43002/"
$appRedirectUrl = $appHostDomainUrl + "redirect.aspx"

# provide site inside target tenancy (aka realm)
$targetSiteUrl = "http://wingtipserver"

# get App Principal Manager
$web = Get-SPWeb $targetSiteUrl
$appPrincipalManager = [Microsoft.SharePoint.SPAppPrincipalManager]::GetManager($web)

# initialize creation parameters for App Principal host domain
$applicationEndPointAuthorities = new-object System.Collections.Generic.List[string]
$applicationEndPointAuthorities.Add($appHostDomainUrl);

# initialize creation parameters for App Principal security credentials
$symmetricKey = New-Object System.Security.SecureString;
$datetimeNow = [System.DateTime]::Now

$credential = [Microsoft.SharePoint.SPAppPrincipalCredential]::CreateFromSymmetricKey($sy
mmetricKey,

                                                      $datetimeNow,
                                                      $datetimeNow)

# create new object for App Principal creation parameters
$creationParameters =
New-Object Microsoft.SharePoint.SPExternalAppPrincipalCreationParameters(
                                    $clientID,
                                    $appDisplayName,
                                    $applicationEndPointAuthorities,
                                    $credential)
# assign redirect Uri to creation parameters
$creationParameters.RedirectAddresses.Add( (New-Object System.Uri $appRedirectUrl) )

# create app principal
$appPrincipal = $appPrincipalManager.CreateAppPrincipal($creationParameters)
```

Developing provider-hosted apps by using S2S trusts

Before you begin to develop a provider-hosted app with an S2S trust, you should first complete the following steps.

1. Create a .cer certificate file containing a public/private key pair.

2. Use the .cer file to register a trusted security token issuer.

3. Register an app principal with a client ID to help track app identity.

4. Export the private key to a password-protected .pfx file.

5. Make the .pfx file accessible on the server running the remote web.

After you have completed these steps, it is relatively simple to create a new provider-hosted app with Visual Studio 2012 and configure it to use an S2S trust. The first step is to update the app manifest with the client ID of an app principal that has already been registered:

```
<AppPrincipal>
  <RemoteWebApplication ClientId="22222222-2222-2222-2222-222222222222" />
</AppPrincipal>
```

The next step is to update the web.config file of the remote web with four *appSettings* variables that track the IDs of the trusted security token issuer and the app principal as well as the file path and password required to extract the private key from the .pfx file at run time. Note that these four *appSettings* variables are used by Microsoft-supplied code in the *TokenHelper* class. The information in these four variables is used each time the *TokenHelper* class creates an S2S access token:

```
<appSettings>
  <add key="ClientId" value="22222222-2222-2222-2222-222222222222" />
  <add key="ClientSigningCertificatePath" value="C:\Certs\appserver.wingtip.com.pfx" />
  <add key="ClientSigningCertificatePassword" value="Password1" />
  <add key="IssuerId" value="11111111-1111-1111-1111-111111111111" />
</appSettings>
```

At this point, you have seen all the steps required to configure an S2S trust. All that's left to do is to write the code to create access tokens and to pass them to the SharePoint host environment in the *Authentication* header. The code in Listing 6-11 demonstrates how to create an S2S access token by calling the *GetS2SAccessTokenWithWindowsIdentity* method of the *TokenHelper* class. After you have created an S2S access token string, you can add it as an *Authorization* header by using exactly the same code you would use in an app that uses OAuth.

LISTING 6-11 Creating an S2S access token

```
string hostWebUrl = Request.QueryString["SPHostUrl"];
Uri hostWebUri = new Uri(hostWebUrl);
WindowsIdentity currentUser = Request.LogonUserIdentity;

string accessTokenString =
      TokenHelper.GetS2SAccessTokenWithWindowsIdentity(hostWebUri, currentUser);

// prepare HttpWebRequest to execute REST API call
HttpWebRequest request1 =
   (HttpWebRequest)HttpWebRequest.Create(hostWebUrl.ToString() + "/_api/Web/title");

// add access token string as Authorization header
request1.Headers.Add("Authorization", "Bearer " + accessTokenString);

// execute REST API call and inspect response
HttpWebResponse response1 = (HttpWebResponse)request1.GetResponse();
StreamReader reader1 = new StreamReader(response1.GetResponseStream());
XDocument doc1 = XDocument.Load(reader1);
string SiteTitle = doc1.Root.Value;
```

Calling *TrustAllCertificates*

While you are working in a development environment, it is common to use test certificates as opposed to production-grade certificates. The *TokenHelper* class provides a static method named *TrustAllCertificates*, which can be called if you need to relax the rules used in the certificate verification process.

```
TokenHelper.TrustAllCertificates();
```

A call to *TrustAllCertificates* can be helpful to get things working in a development environment where you are using test certificates. However, any calls to *TrustAllCertificates* should be removed before your code goes into production.

Summary

This chapter explained the concepts, configuration details, and programming techniques associated with app authentication and app permission management. You learned that SharePoint 2013 authenticates CSOM and REST API calls from apps by using either internal authentication or external authentication. SharePoint-hosted apps use internal authentication, whereas external authentication is used by cloud-hosted apps that have server-side code running inside the remote web.

The chapter also explained how SharePoint 2013 manages app permissions and enforces a security policy that by default requires both the app and the current user to possess the required permissions to accomplish a specific task. In certain scenarios, you can execute calls with app-only permissions so that your code is not constrained by the permissions of a specific user.

The security model for SharePoint apps often requires you to add permission requests to the app manifest file. Permission requests are the mechanism that your app uses to acquire the permissions it needs to read and modify content in the host web.

The second half of the chapter discussed configuration details and programming techniques that are specific to OAuth and S2S trusts. You saw that OAuth and S2S trusts both require you to write code to obtain access tokens and to pass them to the SharePoint host environment by using the *Authorization* header. However, you also learned that there is quite a difference between the way that OAuth and S2S trusts work behind the scenes.

## CHAPTER 7

SharePoint pages

One of the most fundamental aspects of Microsoft SharePoint or any web-based system, for that matter, is the pages. *Pages* in SharePoint are an important foundation of the infrastructure and of custom solutions, whether those solutions are farm solutions, sandboxed solutions, or SharePoint apps. Pages are used for a variety of scenarios, for instance, presenting information or hosting logic. Users need pages to display their content, applications need pages to render their UIs, and SharePoint needs pages to render lists, libraries, and so on.

This chapter explains how SharePoint works with pages. It begins with a discussion of the infrastructure and plumbing that is done with Microsoft ASP.NET and Microsoft Internet Information Services (IIS) to build the SharePoint virtual file system. This is an important area to know and can affect how you design and develop your solutions. Next, this chapter explains the different kinds of pages in SharePoint and how SharePoint uses the master page concept. You learn about features such as delegate controls, the Minimal Download Strategy (MDS), and the SharePoint ribbon.

SharePoint and ASP.NET

SharePoint is built on top of Microsoft .NET Framework 4.5 and ASP.NET, and it uses much of the ASP.NET core functionality. SharePoint uses the Web Forms technology and not frameworks such as the ASP.NET Model-View-Controller (MVC) framework. Understanding how SharePoint uses ASP.NET is fundamental if you are aspiring to do advanced SharePoint development. The next few sections review how a SharePoint site is hosted as an ASP.NET application in IIS and how SharePoint uses the ASP.NET framework to build its hierarchies of site collections, sites, and pages.

Learning ASP.NET basics

Before you enjoy the magic of SharePoint and the power of ASP.NET, it's a good idea to review some ASP.NET basics. Many books are written on this topic, and if you're not familiar with ASP.NET, you might want to have access to one or two of these books. Having a good understanding of ASP.NET makes your life as a SharePoint developer a lot easier.

Understanding ASP.NET and IIS

ASP.NET is a hugely popular server-side web application framework, based on Microsoft .NET, which you use to create fast, dynamic, and robust web applications. ASP.NET applications are typically hosted on the Windows Server operating system in IIS. One IIS website can contain one or more ASP.NET applications, each one hosted in a *virtual directory*, and the virtual directories are hierarchal, located within the IIS website. Each virtual directory is usually mapped to the physical path of the web server. The name of the virtual directory becomes a part of the URL of the site. Typically, all virtual directories share the same application pool. An *application pool* is the process that executes the code (the *w3wp.exe* process). The IIS website can also contain an *application*, which is a special form of virtual directory in which a separate or dedicated application pool is used, usually to ensure process isolation. Several IIS websites can share the same application pool and still have application isolation thanks to the .NET *AppDomain* provided by the .NET Framework.

The configuration for an ASP.NET application is stored in the configuration file called Web.config. This configuration file is very much like any other .NET application .config file, but it contains specific settings for ASP.NET. By default, each virtual directory or application in IIS can have its own Web.config file to override or set location specific settings. You learn more about the Web.config file and SharePoint in just a bit.

Using ASP.NET Web Forms

There are multiple ways to use ASP.NET to serve content and respond to requests. The most conventional way is by using .aspx pages, which is what SharePoint uses, but there are a plethora of alternatives, such as using ASP.NET MVC or the new ASP.NET Razor view engine. In the past, most SharePoint development focused on .aspx pages and the concept called Web Forms. *Web Forms* are composed of two components: the UI and the code-behind. Each component typically resides in two different files. The UI resides in the .aspx file, and the code-behind resides in .aspx.cs when working with C#, or .aspx.vb when working with Microsoft Visual Basic. The code-behind class contains the implementation of the object for the page, inheriting from the *System.Web.UI.Page* class.

The UI component of a Web Form consists of typical HTML controls (or *tags*) and Web Forms controls, also called *server-side controls*. Listing 7-1 shows a typical ASP.NET .aspx page.

```
<%@ Page Language="C#" AutoEventWireup="true"
    CodeBehind="MyWebForm.aspx.cs" Inherits="Pages.ASPNET.MyWebForm" %>
<!DOCTYPE html>
<html xmlns="http://www.w3.org/1999/xhtml">
<head runat="server">
    <title></title>
</head>
<body>
    <form id="form1" runat="server">
    <div>
        <asp:Label ID="theLabel" runat="server" />
    </div>
    </form>
</body>
</html>
```

The .aspx page contains a combination of traditional HTML tags and Web Forms controls. The first line contains the *page directive*, which tells the compiler that this is an ASP.NET page and should be compiled. It also tells the parser the name of the code-behind file and what *Page* class this file should inherit from.

The elements within the page marked with the attribute *runat="server"* are processed and parsed on the server before being sent to the client. In Listing 7-1, the Web Forms control *asp:Label* represented a simple label control. To write dynamic content to this label, you can use the *Page* object of the page, implemented in the code-behind shown in Listing 7-2. The code-behind file is a C# file with the extension .aspx.cs.

LISTING 7-2 Code-behind for an ASP.NET Web Forms page that sets the value of a server-side control

```
namespace Pages.ASPNET
{
    public partial class MyWebForm : System.Web.UI.Page
    {
        protected void Page_Load(object sender, EventArgs e)
        {
            theLabel.Text = "Hello ASP.NET!";
        }
    }
}
```

The code-behind contains a class for the specific page referenced in Listing 7-2, inheriting from *System.Web.UI.Page*. In this case you use a method—the *Page_Load* method—to set the value of the label control. This method is added by Microsoft Visual Studio 2012 when you create the page, and is executed when the page is loaded.

If this Web Form was a part of a Visual Studio solution and you chose to publish it, Visual Studio would compile the .aspx.cs file into a .NET assembly. To run the Web Form, you would need to deploy the .aspx file to an IIS site and the assembly file into a folder called /bin on that IIS site. When a user requested this Web Forms .aspx page, the ASP.NET parser would read the .aspx file parse and convert the HTML and Web Forms controls into a control-tree, which represents the hierarchy of the controls. Next, it would create a source file with a new class that derived from the class specified in the page directive. Then it would compile this source file to an in-memory assembly that would be used to execute requests for this specific Web Form. The in-memory assembly lives as long as the IIS application pool is running or until the .aspx file is changed. If the file is changed, or rather the date and time stamp on the file is changed, the ASP.NET runtime will notice that, causing a recompile of the page.

Using ASP.NET master pages

To create a consistent look, feel, and behavior for all the pages in your web application, ASP.NET uses a concept called master pages. A *master page* defines the outline of a page and contains placeholder controls. These placeholder controls are then used by the pages that are using the master page (known as *content pages*) to build the complete page. For instance, the master page can define the navigation of the website, the footer, and other common features, whereas the content page defines the actual content and logic for the particular page.

A master page is very similar to a standard .aspx page. Instead of having the .aspx file name extension, however, a master page uses the .master extension. The page directives are replaced by a *master directive*, which contains one or more content placeholders. Suppose you converted the .aspx page in Listing 7-2 to one master page and one content page. Listing 7-3 shows the implementation of the master page and Listing 7-4 shows the content page.

LISTING 7-3 A master page that contains one PlaceHolder control that can be used by pages that are using the master page

```
<%@ Master Language="C#" AutoEventWireup="true"
   CodeBehind="MyMaster.master.cs" Inherits="Pages.ASPNET.MyMaster" %>
<!DOCTYPE html>
<html xmlns="http://www.w3.org/1999/xhtml">
<head runat="server">
   <title></title>
</head>
<body>
   <form id="form1" runat="server">
   <div>
       <asp:ContentPlaceHolder ID="mainContentArea" runat="server">
       </asp:ContentPlaceHolder>
   </div>
   </form>
</body>
</html>
```

Listings 7-3 and 7-4 have two main differences from the original .aspx page in Listing 7-1. First, there is a master directive at the top instead of a page directive. A master directive works in the same way as the page directive for the .aspx page, and in this case, the master page also has a code-behind page with the extension .master.cs. The second difference is the area in which the label control previously was located. This is now replaced by a *ContentPlaceHolder* control with the name *mainContentArea*.

To use this master page file on your Web Form, you need to add a new attribute to the page directive, clear out the redundant controls, and add a Content control, in which you place the label control. Listing 7-4 shows the result of the content page.

LISTING 7-4 A Web Forms page that uses a master page and uses the Content control to add content to the PlaceHolder defined in the master page

```
<%@ Page Language="C#"
    MasterPageFile="~/MyMaster.master" AutoEventWireup="true"
    CodeBehind="MyWebForm.aspx.cs" Inherits="Pages.ASPNET.MyWebForm" %>
<asp:Content ID="Content1" ContentPlaceHolderID="mainContentArea" runat="server">
    <asp:Label ID="theLabel" runat="server" />
</asp:Content>
```

In the page directive, you added the *MasterPageFile* attribute and pointed it to the master page in the ASP.NET application root; the rest of the attributes are left intact. All the HTML and ASP.NET controls are replaced by a single content control, in which you added the label control.

You just read a quick introduction to how ASP.NET pages work and how master pages are used to separate the UI from the page logic. SharePoint relies on this ASP.NET Web Forms concept, and it is very important that you understand Web Forms before you develop pages for SharePoint.

Understanding how SharePoint relates to IIS web applications

This section focuses on SharePoint, specifically on how SharePoint relates to ASP.NET and IIS. All content within SharePoint is hosted inside a SharePoint Web Application. Note that a SharePoint Web Application is not the same as an IIS web application. A *SharePoint Web Application* is a boundary for a lot of configurations such as authentication settings, databases, and security policies. A SharePoint farm has at least one web application, which is the one hosting Central Administration, and most farms have at least two web applications: Central Administration and one or more web applications hosting SharePoint content.

When a web application is created in SharePoint, a new IIS website is also created. This IIS website is the host and entry point for all SharePoint site collections and sites within that web application. All the ASP.NET settings for the IIS website will be used by all sites in the web application. Examples of settings are authentication methods and cache settings. If you're familiar with ASP.NET, you know that ASP.NET stores a lot of configuration information in Web.config, which is stored in each ASP.NET application. The Web.config file exists in the file system of the server, typically in C:\inetpub\wwwroot\wss\virtualdurectories\<id> for SharePoint Web Applications. A SharePoint Web Application can also use multiple IIS websites through a technique called *extending SharePoint Web Applications*. Extending a SharePoint Web Application is of interest when you need to have different configuration settings for the same web application, because extending a SharePoint Web Application creates an additional IIS website, which has its own set of configurations.

Understanding the Web.config file

As mentioned earlier in this chapter, the configuration for an ASP.NET application is stored in the Web.config file. SharePoint is no different in this aspect. When a new SharePoint web application is provisioned and the IIS website is created, SharePoint creates the Web.config file and adds all the required settings to it so that SharePoint can work. Without a correctly configured Web.config file, SharePoint will not work. Usually you should avoid making changes to Web.config, but there are a few exceptions, which you learn about later in this chapter. Although you might want to modify Web.config, doing so could cause problems in addition to the lack of supportability. For instance, a SharePoint farm typically consists of more than one web server, so any changes made to the Web.config file requires you to make sure that the Web.config files are in sync on all machines. And if you add another web server to your SharePoint farm, SharePoint creates a new Web.config file, ignoring any customizing you might have handled on other machines. ASP.NET developers, and to some degree SharePoint developers, historically have stored configuration data in Web.config, however, this is very risky. There are plenty of other good ways to store configuration settings, such as by using SharePoint lists, property bags on farms, site collections, and site levels, or by using custom configuration objects in SharePoint.

SharePoint actually configures quite a lot in the Web.config file. In addition to using the standard configuration Section groups in Web.config, SharePoint has its own Section group named *SharePoint* and another called *microsoft.sharepoint.client*. Listing 7-5 shows the different sections that are specific to SharePoint in Web.config.

LISTING 7-5 Settings specific to SharePoint in Web.config

```
<configuration>
  <configSections>
    <sectionGroup name="SharePoint">
      <section name="SafeControls"/>
      <section name="RuntimeFilter"/>
      <section name="WebPartsLimits"/>
      <section name="WebPartCache"/>
      <section name="WebPartWorkItem"/>
      <section name="WebPartControls"/>
      <section name="SafeMode"/>
      <section name="MergedActions"/>
      <section name="PeoplePickerWildcards"/>
      <section name="WorkflowServices"/>
      <section name="BlobCache"/>
      <section name="OutputCacheProfiles"/>
      <section name="ObjectCache"/>
      <section name="MediaAssets"/>
      <section name="ApplicationAuthentication"/>
    </sectionGroup>
  </configSections>
  <microsoft.sharepoint.client>
    <serverRuntime/>
  </microsoft.sharepoint.client>
  <SharePoint>
    <SafeMode/>
    <WebPartLimits/>
    <WebPartControls/>
    <SafeControls/>
    <PeoplePickerWildCards/>
    <WorkflowServices/>
    <MergedActions/>
    <BlobCache/>
    <ObjectCache/>
    <OutputCacheProfiles/>
    <MediaAssets/>
    <RuntimeFilter/>
  </SharePoint>
</configuration>
```

Some of these customizations are of interest because they help you understand how SharePoint actually works; for instance, later in this chapter, we discuss the SafeMode and the SafeControls sections. Most of these sections should be manually configured, but there are a few exceptions. For instance, the SharePoint BLOB cache is handled by the *BlobCache* section. By default, it is turned off, and to turn it on, you need to modify Web.config. Some of these sections are discussed in more detail later in this chapter, such as the *SafeMode* and *SafeControls* section, and some are discussed in other chapters.

Tip After working with your web application for a while, you might notice that in the IIS virtual directory for the website are many Web.config .bak files, sometimes hundreds. This is normal on a developer's machine. Every time SharePoint needs to make a change to the Web.config file, SharePoint automatically creates a backup file before making the configuration changes. On your developer machine, you can delete these files.

As a developer, one of the first things you will want to do is configure the Web.config file for debugging and turn off the SharePoint friendly error message page. If you're using Visual Studio 2012 and start debugging your first farm solution on a web application, Visual Studio will ask you if this should be done automatically. If you choose to opt out or manually debug it yourself, you need to modify the Web.config file in three different places:

- The *debug* attribute of the */configuration/system.web/compilation* element should be set to *true*.

- The *mode* attribute of the */configuration/system.web/customErrors* element should be set to *off*.

- The *CallStack* attribute of the */configuration/SharePoint/SafeMode* element should be set to *true*.

The first modification tells the compiler to compile assemblies in debug mode, and the second modification makes sure that the yellow ASP.NET error page is shown instead of the user-friendly SharePoint error page. The final modification tells SharePoint to propagate any error messages up the call stack.

Understanding the SharePoint virtual file system

When the IIS website receives a user request, it must find out which page to render. This request is sent through the ASP.NET pipeline. The pipeline contains a set of HTTP modules that the request will go through before eventually ending up in an HTTP handler. Each HTTP module subscribes to one or more events in the ASP.NET pipeline and acts on events such as authentication, request mapping, and request execution. The HTTP handlers are responsible for the actual processing of the request, for instance, the request of a Web Forms .aspx page or a web service .asmx file.

SharePoint adds its own set of HTTP modules and handlers when the Web.config is created for a SharePoint web application. Most importantly, SharePoint adds the *SPRequestModule*. It is in this module that SharePoint does the majority of hooks into the ASP.NET pipeline. This module is also responsible for the SharePoint virtual file system.

The root directory of the IIS website for a SharePoint Web Application does not contain a lot of files. Basically, it consists of the Web.config file and a couple of directories. So where is SharePoint storing all the files and pages in the SharePoint sites? SharePoint is built to host thousands of sites and pages and to handle all this on a large scale and synchronized over a multitude of servers, so these files cannot be stored in the file system. The site collections, sites, lists, list items, and pages are stored in databases, called *content databases*. Any page within a site will have an entry in one of the content databases. To build a file system with these databases, SharePoint uses an ASP.NET feature called *virtual path provider*. Instead of using the default ASP.NET virtual path provider, which maps a request to the corresponding file in the file system, SharePoint has its own virtual path provider, implemented in the internal *SPVirtualPathProvider* class.

This virtual path provider is responsible for finding the correct page among the databases connected to the web application. However, some pages, called *application pages,* are not served through the content databases, and these reside in the file system. These physical files are stored in the SharePoint root and are served through one of the IIS virtual directories. The most common of these IIS virtual directories is the _layouts\ folder, which is mapped to the Template\Layouts folder in the SharePoint Root. In previous versions of SharePoint, this part was straightforward, but in SharePoint 2013, this mapping is getting a bit trickier. The _layouts virtual directory is mapped to the SharePoint 2010 \Template\Layouts folder, whereas the _layouts\15\ virtual directory is mapped to the SharePoint 2013 \Template\Layouts folder. The reasoning behind this is to not break compatibility when you're updating a site collection or solution from SharePoint 2010 to SharePoint 2013. This virtual directory is also mapped to the root of each site collection so that the directory can always be reached through \~sitecollection_layouts. You learn later in this chapter about how to create and deploy application pages.

When the request is handled by the SharePoint module and the SharePoint virtual path provider, the virtual path provider first tries to find out whether the request targets one of the files in the file system, which exists in one of the virtual directories. If the request does, that file will be used when processing the request. If the request does not belong to any virtual directory, it is assumed to exist in one of the content databases, and the SharePoint virtual path provider will locate the file within one of the content databases.

Working with files and folders in SharePoint

SharePoint provides several application programming interfaces (APIs) that can be used to work with pages, files, and folders in the SharePoint virtual file system. The most common ones are the server-side API and the client-side object model (CSOM), introduced in SharePoint 2010. There are also alternatives such as WebDAV and the new Representational State Transfer (REST) APIs. Which model you choose largely depends on what you are building: a server-side component, a SharePoint app, a companion application, and so on.

The server-side object model is the method that gives you the most flexibility when working with files and folders. Creating a new document library on a SharePoint site is a good example of this and illustrates some of the interesting aspects of SharePoint. The following snippet will create a new document library in the current site:

```
SPWeb currrentWeb = SPContext.Current.Web;
currentWeb.Lists.Add(
    "Specifications",
    "Library for specifications documents",
    SPListTemplateType.DocumentLibrary);
```

In this preceding code, you're adding a new list of the type *DocumentLibrary*; a *document library* is just a special version of a SharePoint list. When this library is created, SharePoint provisions a folder in the root of the site (*SPWeb*) with the name as specified in the code. It also provisions a subfolder called Forms and a set of files in that folder. The Forms folder is hidden from the users, but it can be seen in SharePoint Designer, for example, as shown in Figure 7-1. The files in this Forms folder are used by SharePoint when users are uploading, adding, or modifying the properties of those files. There is also one file per public view of the folder. These views are normal content pages on the SharePoint site and can be modified by using the UI, SharePoint Designer, or code. You examine how these content pages works in the "Understanding content pages" section later in this chapter.

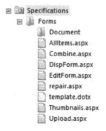

FIGURE 7-1 Every document library has a hidden folder called Forms.

Files and folders within a SharePoint site can exist in a library or outside a library. For instance, when a SharePoint Team site is provisioned, its home page is located in a library called Site Pages at the address /SitePages/Home.aspx, but it also provisions a few files directly at the root of the site. There are a few important differences between files inside a library and files provisioned outside of a library. Files outside of a library cannot have any file properties; these files don't have versioning and you can't control permissions.

To work with files and folder by using the server-side object model, you use the *SPFile* and *SPFolder* objects. Files are retrieved by using the web relative URL:

```
SPWeb currrentWeb = SPContext.Current.Web;
SPFile defaultFile = currentWeb.GetFile("default.aspx");
SPFile homeFile = currentWeb.GetFile("SitePages/Home.aspx");
```

The first retrieved file fetches a file existing directly in the root of the web, which is not in a document library, and the second file fetches a file existing in the *Site Pages* document library. If you specify a URL to a file that does not exist, you do not get an exception or a *null* value returned. Instead, a normal *SPFile* object is returned but with the property *Exists* set to *false*.

After you have the *SPFile* object, you can perform operations on the file, such as read, update, and delete. To delete a file, you use the *Delete* method, and to retrieve its contents, you use *OpenBinary* or *OpenBinaryStream*. You can programmatically add a new file to the site in several ways. You could read a file from the file system, or you could read a file from a memory stream, which could be a result of a file upload, for example. The sample code in Listing 7-6 illustrates how to dynamically create an .aspx page in memory and then add it to a document library.

```
string title = "A dynamically generated HTML page";
StringBuilder sb = new StringBuilder();
sb.Append("<%@ Page %>");
sb.Append("<html>");
sb.Append("<head>");
sb.AppendFormat("<title>{0}</title>", title);
sb.Append("</head>");
sb.Append("<body>");
sb.AppendFormat("<h1>{0}</h1>", title);
sb.Append("</body>");
sb.Append("</html>");

SPWeb web = SPContext.Current.Web;
SPList sitePages = web.Lists.TryGetList("Site Pages");
if(sitePages != null)
{
    sitePages.RootFolder.Files.Add(
        "demo.aspx",
        System.Text.Encoding.UTF8.GetBytes(sb.ToString())
    );
}
```

The source code of the .aspx page is created by using the .NET object *StringBuilder*, and in this case you're just adding an ASP.NET page directive, some HTML, and simple heading text. After the data for the file is created, you retrieve the Site Pages library. To get this library, you first need to get the *SPList* object of the library. Notice that I use the *TryGetList* method, which returns *null* if the list cannot be found and does not throw an exception. You use this list object to retrieve the root folder of the library, the *RootFolder* property, and then with that folder access the *Files* collection and use the *Add* method to add the file. You must specify the URL of the file; in this case, you use the overload of the *Add* method that takes a byte array so that the *StringBuilder* object is converted to a string and then to a byte array.

Most of these operations are also accessible when using the CSOM, the REST API, or WebDAV operations, which allow you to work with files and folders in companion applications, such as apps for Windows 8 and Windows Phone 8. It also allows you to access, modify, and provision new files in the host web from a SharePoint app.

Understanding page customization

Suppose you have a page or file that should exist in all or many of your sites in your set of thousands of sites, and the page is not an application page. Having thousands of copies of that page would cause both performance and storage issues in addition to complex upgrade scenarios. SharePoint handles this through a process called *page customization*. When a page is created in SharePoint as a result of a site being created or a Feature being activated, that page can exist in the physical file system, and only a reference is created in the content database. The file existing in the file system is a *template file* for the files existing in the sites. In earlier versions of SharePoint, this template file was referred to as a *ghosted* file. Such a file solves a lot of potential problems. You have only one copy of the file to process, maintain, and update.

Understanding uncustomized pages

A page is called *uncustomized*, or ghosted, when the actual file (the template file) resides in the file system and is referenced from a site. For instance, when you create a new site collection, a set of files are added to it. One file that is always provisioned is the master page. Because this file is provisioned to every site collection you create, you could have thousands of these; it would be a bad idea to create a new copy of the file and its contents into every site collection. Thus, SharePoint creates a reference in the site collection and the virtual file system that points to the file on the disk. An uncustomized file does not have to be an .aspx file; it can be any kind of file type.

An uncustomized file gives you several benefits, both from a development perspective and from a farm maintenance perspective. As long as the page is uncustomized, any updates in the file on the file system are reflected in the site collections. Assume the opposite: if you had a copy in every site collection or site, any update to that file would have to be done in all the sites, requiring you to create either Feature upgrades or Windows PowerShell scripts, introducing upgrade complexity. Because the file resides only in the file system, the content databases contain fewer BLOBs, which saves you space in the content databases. Uncustomized .aspx pages also have the benefit of being compiled at the first request time, compared to customized pages, which aren't. Historically, this has been a point of performance discussions, but with current hardware and compilers, this is less of an issue.

Worth noticing here is that uncustomized pages can be created only by using full trust solutions. If you are building a sandboxed solution or SharePoint app, all pages you provision will be customized. Only full trust solutions have access to the file system.

Understanding customized pages

When a page is provisioned from a SharePoint app or a sandboxed solution, or when it is uploaded to SharePoint by the user or programmatically, that page and its contents are stored only in the content database. These pages are called *customized* (or *unghosted*). If you modify an uncustomized page, for example, you modify the uncustomized master page of a site collection, and the file becomes a customized page; its contents are from now on stored only in the content database. When building SharePoint apps or sandboxed solutions, all of the assets in your solution will be customized.

Even though it has been changed, a previously uncustomized page will always keep a reference to its template file. As a site owner, you always have the possibility of reverting the page to its original state and discarding all customizations.

Restoring a customized page that has a template file to its uncustomized state can be done programmatically, and you can check the customization status of a page at any time. You can do it by using SharePoint Designer 2013 or by using the server-side API. To revert the file to its uncustomized state by using SharePoint Designer, you select the file, right-click it, and then select Reset To Site Definition. Figure 7-2 shows a file that has been modified from its uncustomized state.

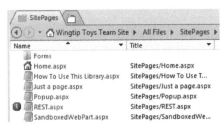

FIGURE 7-2 A page that is customized from its uncustomized state displays a blue information icon in SharePoint Designer 2012.

To check a file's customization state and eventually restore it to its uncustomized state by using the server-side API, you use the following code—for example, in a Web Part or the code-behind of the page:

```
SPFile file = SPContext.Current.Web.GetFile("SitePages/Home.aspx");
if (file.CustomizedPageStatus == SPCustomizedPageStatus.Customized)
{
    file.RevertContentStream();
}
```

On the first line of the preceding code, you grab the file from the current *SPWeb* instance, using the site relative URL. On the second line of the code, the *CustomizedPageStatus* property is evaluated to determine whether the retrieved page has the status set to *Customized*. If it does, the *RevertContent-Stream* method is called on the file object to restore its state to uncustomized. All customizations in the file are lost, and the file contents of the template file are now to be used instead.

Note that the *SPCustomizedPageStatus* enumeration actually has three values: *Uncustomized*, *Customized*, and *None*. At this point, you might know what the first two enumeration values mean, but what does the third one *None* mean? A file or page with the *CustomizedPageStatus* set to *None* implies that the file has been created dynamically or uploaded to SharePoint and does not have any corresponding template file. This file or page cannot be reverted to its original state. A page added by using SharePoint apps or sandboxed solutions always has this status set to *None*. For instance, the pages that you dynamically created in Listing 7-6 do not have a template file and thus cannot be restored.

Note When a site collection is updated from SharePoint 2010 mode to SharePoint 2013, the site collection administrator can perform a Health Check, which checks the health of the site collection according to a set of rules. One of these rules checks whether any pages in the site collection are customized and can be restored to their uncustomized state.

Understanding Safe Mode parsing

Earlier in this chapter, you learned that uncustomized pages are compiled the first time they are used, whereas customized pages are not. Recall from the discussion of ASP.NET basics that one of the core features of ASP.NET is that pages are compiled at the first request to improve performance and resource utilization. Uncustomized pages are parsed and compiled in direct mode by the standard ASP.NET parser. The benefit of this is, of course, performance, and only one compiled copy is needed because uncustomized files share the same template file. However, what happens to customized pages then?

You can have hundreds of thousands, if not millions, of customized pages in SharePoint. Compiling every single one of them would cause a huge memory footprint. SharePoint has a concept called *Safe Mode parsing*, which is used for customized pages or pages without a template file, such as pages supplied by a SharePoint app. These pages are not compiled but instead *parsed* on every request. They are parsed in *Safe Mode*, as opposed to direct mode. Customized pages are not required to be compiled because there are a couple of restrictions set on them:

- Inline code is not allowed. Having that would require compilation and would introduce severe security holes.

- All controls in the page must be registered as safe in the Web.config file. This allows farm administrators to have control over which controls can be used in a web application.

The Safe Mode parsing not only protects your servers from running out of memory but also serves as a security barrier. Only code admitted to the servers by the farm administrators are allowed to run in compiled or direct mode. A site owner cannot upload a file through the UI or modify a file with in-line code by using SharePoint Designer and have that file execute on the server. SharePoint Designer is so smart that it does not allow you to save pages containing inline code. However, users can add controls that are registered as safe in these customized pages.

By default, most of the ASP.NET and the SharePoint controls and Web Parts are registered as safe. All controls that are registered as safe can be found in Web.config under the *SafeControls* element in the *SharePoint* section. If you're building your own farm solution and add custom controls or Web Parts, these custom controls or Web Parts must be registered as safe. Visual Studio 2012 will do the work for you in most cases, such as add a Web Part. But if you're creating a custom control, you need to make sure that it is registered as safe. There are two ways to do this. The preferred option is to either use an existing SharePoint Project Item or add a new empty SharePoint Project Item and then modify its properties. In the SharePoint Project Item Properties window is a collection called *Safe Control Entries*. To add a new safe control registration, click Add, and then modify the *Namespace* property of that new safe control, as shown in Figure 7-3. All added safe controls will then be added to the solution manifest file.

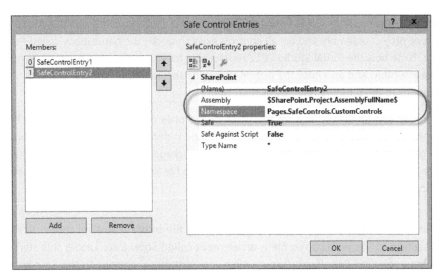

FIGURE 7-3 You can use Visual Studio 2012 to add custom safe control entries by modifying the *Safe Control Entries* property of the SharePoint Project Item.

You can also add your safe controls directly to the solution manifest file by using the Package Designer in Visual Studio 2012. Open the Manifest tab, and then expand the Edit Options at the bottom. Listing 7-7 shows how you can edit the solution manifest file XML to create a custom safe control entry.

LISTING 7-7 Manually modifying the solution manifest file to add a custom safe control

```
<Solution xmlns="http://schemas.microsoft.com/sharepoint/">
  <Assemblies>
    <Assembly
      Location="$SharePoint.Project.AssemblyFileName$"
      DeploymentTarget="GlobalAssemblyCache">
      <SafeControls>
        <SafeControl
          Assembly="$SharePoint.Project.AssemblyFullName$"
          Namespace="Pages.CustomControls"
          TypeName="*"/>
      </SafeControls>
    </Assembly>
  </Assemblies>
</Solution>
```

The package manifest modification in Listing 7-7 adds a new *SafeControl* entry to the Web.config file for the current project assembly and for all controls existing under the namespace called *Pages. CustomControls*. Note how the Visual Studio 2012 replaceable tokens are used to avoid entering the full name of the assembly, and also note the option to modify the assembly name and versions without making changes to the package manifest modification.

All custom-added safe control entries are merged with the ones created by the SharePoint Project Item into the solution manifest file. After the solution package is deployed to a web application, the entries are merged with the Web.config. When the solution package is retracted, the retraction process makes sure that any safe control entries in the Web.config file are removed. You do not need to change this manually in the Web.config file.

 Note Safe Mode parsing is controlled in the Web.config file of the web application. In the *SharePoint* section of the Web.config file is an element called *SafeMode*. Under this element is another element called *PageParserPaths*, which can contain exceptions to the Safe Mode parsing. Using *PageParserPath* elements, you have to option to use direct mode parsing on specific folders or sites and therefore bypass the security imposed by Safe Mode parsing. You can do these overrides for any virtual URL except for pages hosted in SharePoint App Webs. You typically don't need to and should not modify the Safe Mode parsing settings, because of security risks.

Using pages in SharePoint

The page rendering system in SharePoint is based on ASP.NET Web Forms. This has its benefits and drawbacks. It is a well-known and proven programmable model, but it does not have all of the flexibility of more modern frameworks such as the ASP.NET MVC framework. SharePoint uses and extends the Web Forms pattern, and it is really important to understand how pages are rendered by using master pages. SharePoint pages can be divided into two major categories: site pages and application pages. In this section, you learn about how to create master pages and both site and application pages, and how to package these customizations into deployable solutions.

Understanding master pages

Master pages were introduced with ASP.NET more than a decade ago. As described earlier in this chapter, master pages can best be described as a template with a set of placeholders in which content and logic can be inserted. Master pages allow you to have a similar UI for all pages within a site collection. Note that we said *Site Collection* here. In SharePoint, master pages are stored on a per–Site Collection basis, in a specific gallery called the Master Page Gallery (/_catalogs/masterpage) in the root web of the site collection. Depending on how you deploy your solution, the master page within a gallery could be a file on the SharePoint sever file system or exist as a customized file in only a specific site collection. Refer to the preceding discussion about customized and uncustomized files.

Understanding SharePoint 2013 default master pages

SharePoint 2013 comes with a set of master pages; some are new to the 2013 version, and some are in the product for compatibility with previous versions. There was a huge difference in the master pages between SharePoint 2007 and SharePoint 2010, and the SharePoint 2010 master pages (v4.master) were built specifically to handle the visual upgrade scenario in which the sites were updated from SharePoint 2007 to SharePoint 2010, but the SharePoint 2007 UI was used. In SharePoint 2013, this visual upgrade option is no longer available. The upgrade mechanism is far better, and you can actually run the whole site collection in SharePoint 2010 mode instead of just emulating the 2010 UI. You can create trial site collections, which essentially are an exact copy of your site collections, and test how they look when upgraded to SharePoint 2013. This allows you to fix the UI and other issues before upgrading the original site to SharePoint 2013.

In SharePoint 2013, two new master pages are provisioned in addition to those provided by Share-Point 2010. These are the default master pages provisioned in sites in SharePoint 2013:

- **seattle.master**   New default SharePoint 2013 master page

- **oslo.master**   New alternative SharePoint 2013 master page

- **v4.master**   SharePoint 2010 default master page

- **minimal.master**   SharePoint 2010 minimal master page

The main differences between the master pages seattle.master and oslo.master are that when you're using oslo.master, the top navigation pane is replaced with the left navigation pane, and the side bar on the left disappears, giving you more real estate for content on the page. The built-in feature called Change The Look, or Design Gallery, takes advantage of these two master pages. The design you choose determines which master page is used.

Dissecting the seattle.master file

As just described, the default master page in SharePoint 2013 is called seattle.master. The SharePoint 2013 master page is one of the core pieces in the UI and interaction of SharePoint, and you need to understand how it is constructed and works. A poorly crafted custom master page can potentially break the UI in a lot of ways. We recommend that you always start with the seattle or oslo master pages when you're building a master page that will be used for intranet/collaboration scenarios. If you're building a public-facing website, it's a different story—you have much more flexibility.

The best way to understand the SharePoint 2013 master page is by examining it. Listing 7-8, which shows parts of seattle.master, highlights some of the features of the master page that you should understand as a SharePoint developer or designer. If you worked with SharePoint 2010, you will find some aspects are familiar and others are new. First, SharePoint 2013 has been built with web standards in mind, and you will find that the generated HTML is much more compliant with modern web browsers. Support for Windows Internet Explorer 7 is not available in SharePoint 2013. But before going further into the details, review the outline shown in Listing 7-8.

LISTING 7-8 Outline of seattle.master showing some of the content placeholders and delegate controls

```
<%@ Master Language="C#" %>
<!DOCTYPE html PUBLIC "-//W3C//DTD XHTML 1.0 Strict//EN"
 "http://www.w3.org/TR/xhtml1/DTD/xhtml1-strict.dtd">
<SharePoint:SPHtmlTag dir=" ID="SPHtmlTag" runat="server">
 <head runat="server">
   <SharePoint:PageTitle runat="server">
     <asp:ContentPlaceHolder id="PlaceHolderPageTitle" runat="server">
       <SharePoint:ProjectProperty Property="Title" runat="server" />
     </asp:ContentPlaceHolder>
   </SharePoint:PageTitle>
   <SharePoint:AjaxDelta ID="DeltaPlaceHolderAdditionalPageHead"runat="server">
     <asp:ContentPlaceHolder ID="PlaceHolderAdditionalPageHead" runat="server" />
       <SharePoint:DelegateControl runat="server"
         ControlId="AdditionalPageHead" AllowMultipleControls="true" />
     <asp:ContentPlaceHolder ID="PlaceHolderBodyAreaClass" runat="server" />
   </SharePoint:AjaxDelta>
 </head>
 <body>
   <SharePoint:SharePointForm runat="server" >
     <asp:ScriptManager ID="ScriptManager" runat="server"  />
     <div id="suiteBar"> </div>
     <div id="s4-ribbonrow"> <div>
     <div id="s4-workspace">
       <div id="s4-bodyContainer">
         <div id="s4-titlerow"> <div>
         <div id="contentRow">
           <div id="sideNavBox"> </div>
           <div id="contentBox">
             <div id="notificationArea"></div>
             <SharePoint:AjaxDelta runat="server">
               <asp:ContentPlaceHolder ID="PlaceHolderMain" runat="server" />
             </SharePoint:AjaxDelta>
           </div>
         </div>
       </div>
     </div>
   </SharePoint:SharePointForm>
 </body>
</SharePoint:SPHtmlTag>
```

One of the things you might have noticed when looking at the code in Listing 7-8 is that the standard HTML tags <HTML>, <TITLE>, and <FORM> that were used in previous master pages for SharePoint (v4.master) are now replaced with SharePoint-specific web controls: *SPHtmlTag*, *PageTitle*, and *SharePointForm*, respectively. The latter two are required because of MDS.

You might also have noticed that the master page contains a lot of content placeholders, which you learned about earlier. The content placeholders are paramount, and there are a total of 34 of them in the seattle.master, though only a few are shown in Listing 7-8. When building your custom master page, you must not forget to include all of these content placeholders, because various features in SharePoint are dependent on them, and omitting one might break your whole site. If you do not want to show the content placeholder and its content, just add the *Visible* attribute to the control and set its value to *false*, or place the placeholder in a control or an element that has its *Visible* attribute set to false. The content placeholders make it easy for page developers to insert their own content and controls into the pages.

Using delegate controls

What if you want to insert something on all pages in the farm or in just one site? SharePoint has the answer for that: delegate controls, which are declared by using the *DelegateControl* control. *Delegate controls* allow you to add one or more web controls to a specific location in all pages on a farm, in a web application, in a site collection, and at the site level. Delegate control locations and characteristics are specified in the master page. A delegate control can allow only one control to be rendered or multiple controls to be rendered by using the *AllowMultipleControls* property. There are several predefined delegate controls in the SharePoint 2013 master pages, some of which existed in SharePoint 2010. SharePoint itself uses delegate controls heavily.

To add a custom control to a delegate control, you need to create a feature in a SharePoint solution, the scope of which determines where the delegate control should be applied. One of the most common delegate control locations to use is the *AdditionalPageHead* delegate control location. This location is in the head element definition of the master page, and it allows multiple controls. This delegate control could be used to insert a client-side script on all pages, perhaps based on some server-side condition. To understand this, you will build a quick delegate control that shows the name of the current server as a SharePoint notification message. First, you need to create a new Visual Studio SharePoint 2013 farm solution. Note that delegate controls can be used only by farm solutions. The control that you're going to add is created as an ASP.NET *WebControl* and is implemented as shown in Listing 7-9.

LISTING 7-9 A simple *WebControl* that shows the name of the current server via the SharePoint notification message

```
public class ServerNameControl: WebControl
{
  protected override void OnPreRender(EventArgs e)
  {
    string script = string.Format("SP.UI.Notify.addNotification('Current server: {0}');",
      System.Environment.MachineName);
    ScriptManager.RegisterStartupScript(this.Page, typeof(ServerNameControl),
      "currentServer", script, true);
  }
}
```

All this custom web control does is create a JavaScript string that uses the *SP.UI.Notify.addNotification* method to show the name of the current machine. This script is then registered with the *ScriptManager*. To connect this control to the delegate control *AdditionalPageHead* in the master page, you need to add an Empty element SharePoint Project Item to the solution and add the following Collaborative Application Markup Language (CAML):

```
<Elements xmlns="http://schemas.microsoft.com/sharepoint/">
 <Control Id="AdditionalPageHead"
   ControlAssembly="$SharePoint.Project.AssemblyFullName$"
   ControlClass="Pages.DelegateControl.DemoControl"
   Sequence="100"/>
</Elements>
```

This elements manifest contains a *Control* element that uses the *Id* attribute to tell SharePoint which delegate control to connect to. In this case, you're using a web control, and you need to specify the control assembly and class name. Finally, the *Sequence* attribute is used to tell SharePoint in which order to add the controls. For delegate controls, which allow only one single control, the control with the lowest sequence number is chosen. The *Control* element also supports using a control template (.ascx file) instead of a web control. To use a control template, you need to specify the *ControlSrc* attribute instead of the *ControlAssembly* and *ControlClass*. When the empty element SharePoint Project Item was added, Visual Studio automatically added a feature to the solution with the scope set to Web. You can change this scope to the scope of your choice.

You need to do one final task before you can deploy and test this delegate control: make the web control a safe control, as discussed earlier in this chapter, in the "Understanding Safe Mode parsing" section. Right-click the SharePoint Project Item you created, and then click Safe Control Entries. Add a new entry and modify the namespace so that it matches the namespace where you created the control.

Now it's time to test the delegate control. Deploy the solution and browse to the site where you deployed it. When browsing between pages, you should see a notification message displaying the name of the current server, as shown in Figure 7-4.

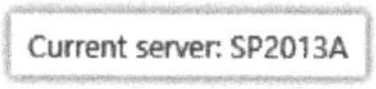

Current server: SP2013A

FIGURE 7-4 A notification message from the delegate control that is added to all pages within a site

Referencing master pages in SharePoint

You've learned how to reference master pages in ASP.NET by using the *MasterPageFile* Page directive and the name of the master page file. If you review the source code of a SharePoint page, you might notice that it is not referencing a master page by its name directly. Instead SharePoint uses dynamic tokens to specify the master page file:

```
<%@Page MasterPageFile="~masterurl/default.master" %>
```

The *~masterurl/default.master* is a dynamic token that during runtime is replaced with the default master page of the site. The default master page URL is stored in the *MasterUrl* property of the *SPWeb* object as a server relative full path to the master page. There is also another secondary master page dynamic token called *~masterurl/custom.master*. This token is mapped to the *CustomMasterUrl* of the *SPWeb* object. The custom master URL is not used by content pages by default in SharePoint, except when using publishing sites, and you are free to use it if you need an alternative master page for your customizations and pages. Both the *MasterUrl* and *CustomMasterUrl* are by default using the seattle.master and have the value of */_catalogs/masterpage/seattle.master.*

Understanding MDS

Another control that makes the master page even more interesting is the *AjaxDelta* control. This is a brand new control in SharePoint 2013, and it is used to mark regions in the master page that can be updated dynamically when using MDS. You could say that it resembles ASP.NET *UpdatePanels*, but the *AjaxDelta* control is smarter.

SharePoint 2013 has been optimized for performance in several ways. One of the focus areas has been client-side code and perceived performance, specifically the way in which SharePoint 2013 renders pages. The order and way that JavaScripts and other client-side assets have been optimized gets users working with the UI faster. Second, the introduction of MDS improves the interface so that subsequent page reloads after the first page is rendered are much faster. This speed is achieved by a combination of client-side JavaScript and server-side code that calculates which parts of the page have changed so that only those changed pieces are sent back to the client. We will now walk through how MDS works, and explain how you can take advantage of it and what you need to think of as a developer when working with sites using MDS.

Improving performance with MDS

If you've worked with SharePoint 2013, you might have noticed that the page URLs on team sites is very different from page URLs in previous versions of SharePoint. When browsing to a site by using MDS, users are redirected to a page at */_layouts/15/start.aspx*:

```
http://wingtiptoys/_layouts/15/start.aspx
```

This is a page requiring very few calculations and renders fast. It will, while displaying a friendly "Working on it" message, load the real home page of the site being visited. The Home page is loaded dynamically by using a JavaScript object called the *DeltaManager*, implemented in start.js. This JavaScript object makes an asynchronous call to the actual page requested by using an extra set of query string parameters. The HTTP request could look like this:

```
http://wingtiptoys/SitePages/Home.aspx?AjaxDelta=1&isStartPltl=1365200007233
```

The *AjaxDelta=1* parameter tells SharePoint that this is an MDS request, and only the delta parts of the page should be returned. The second parameter is the current time stamp and indicates that this is the initial MDS request sent. When the result of the MDS request is returned, the *DeltaManager* updates the delta parts of the page and, at the same time, changes the URL and appends the relative path to the current page:

```
http://wingtiptoys/_layouts/15/start.aspx#/SitePages/Home.aspx
```

The *DeltaManager* not only handles content updates in the delta parts, it also loads and executes any new JavaScripts sent back in the MDS response. The perceived performance by the user is improved because of faster page transitions and because the used bandwidth is reduced as a result of only the deltas sent over the wire. The MDS response could also result in a full reload of the page if any incompatibles with MDS are found in the page, and you learn more details about later in this section.

> **More Info** For more in-depth information about the MDS request and response, go to the following blog post by Wictor Wilén: *http://www.wictorwilen.se/sharepoint-2013---introduc-tion-to-the-minimal-download-strategy-mds*.

Understanding the MDS feature

MDS is implemented as a web-scoped SharePoint Feature and can be enabled or disabled on sites. The Feature is called *Minimal Download Strategy*, and its folder name is *MDSFeature*. By default, it is enabled on team sites, wiki sites, blog sites, and elsewhere, as shown in Figure 7-5. It is not enabled and will not work on any publishing sites.

FIGURE 7-5 MDS is a web-scoped Feature that can be enabled or disabled on demand.

The enabled MDS feature turns on or off a property on the *SPWeb* object called *EnableMinimal-Download*. When that property is set to *true,* SharePoint tries to use MDS when browsing between pages.

Working with MDS requirements and compliance

You've examined the outline of the default SharePoint 2013 seattle.master master page, and you should have seen the presence of the *AjaxDelta* controls. These controls are one of the requirements for MDS. They mark the areas where content can be changed dynamically—that is, during a page transition, the contents of the *AjaxDelta* controls can be replaced, whereas the markup that is not in an *AjaxDelta* control is persistent between page navigations.

All pages that are requested by using MDS must be derived from the SharePoint *DeltaPage* class. This base class is a requirement for doing the necessary delta calculations, and most of the default SharePoint pages inherit from this class. Pages not inheriting from this class force a full reload of the page. Not only are the pages required to derive from this base class, but all controls present on the requested pages must be MDS-compliant. Being MDS-compliant means that the controls or Web Parts have been explicitly marked with the *MdsCompliantAttribute* and the *IsCompliant* property set to *true*. If the *DeltaPage* detects any control without this attribute or with the *IsCompliant* property set to *false*, it returns a message to the client *DeltaManager* that a full page reload is required. The

MdsCompliantAttribute can be set on classes or on an assembly, making all controls within that assembly compliant or not compliant. The attribute is used as follows:

```
[MdsCompliant(true)]
public class MdsCompliantWebPart: WebPart {
 ...
}
```

The client *DeltaManager* object always sends information about the current master page and its version in the MDS request. The *DeltaPage* uses this information to determine if the master page has been changed, which requires a full reload of the page.

A special control called *PageRenderMode* can be inserted on any page to control the MDS status. It can be used to disable MDS for a specific page if required. This control is, for instance, inserted into master pages that are converted as a result of using the Design Manager. To prohibit a page from being rendered by using MDS, insert the following snippet into any page or master page:

```
<SharePoint:PageRenderMode runat="server" RenderModeType="Standard"/>
```

Understanding content pages

Up until now, you've focused on master pages and how pages are rendered. Now it's time to review the most common type of page in SharePoint: content pages, also known as site pages. As you learned earlier in the chapter, content pages are pages where the actual content of the website resides; they are editable by the site owners and members by using either a browser or SharePoint Designer. Content pages can be created by users, but many are automatically created when a site is created. For instance, as shown earlier, the view, edit, and add forms for lists and libraries are created for you. They are normal content pages and can be customized as such. This section explains how to create a new content page and how to package it into a solution for deployment.

Creating a content page

You are going to build a simple content page by using the default SharePoint 2013 master page, based on the knowledge you've gathered so far. This is how you would create a simple content page by using one of the content placeholders in the master page:

```
<%@Page MasterPageFile="~masterurl/default.master"%>
<asp:Content ContentPlaceHolderId="PlaceHolderMain" runat="server">
<h1>This is the simplest Content page ever</h1>
</asp:Content>
```

You specify the default master page dynamic token to give you the default master page on the site, which is seattle.master unless changed. Next, you specify one *asp:Content* control with the attribute *ContentPlaceHolderId* set to *PlaceHolderMain*. This control contains some simple HTML markup that will be replaced in the specified content placeholder in the master page. This page can now be added to a SharePoint site as previously done. You can create the page directly in SharePoint Designer 2013, or you can even create it in Notepad and upload it to a document library. You will also learn how to provision a page by using a SharePoint feature, which is the preferred way of adding content pages.

Deploying a content page

So far, you've learned how to use the server-side API to add a new file, and you've learned that pages can be added by using SharePoint Designer 2013 or by uploading them to a library. Most often you will want to package your solution into a SharePoint solution package (a WSP file), or if you're building a SharePoint app, you will want to create an app package. Both of these ways of packaging solutions use basically the same approach when deploying pages. In this section, you build a WSP package by using Visual Studio 2013, add a custom content page to the solution, and then finally deploy the page to SharePoint. You start doing this by using a farm solution and then later explore what it looks like in a sandbox solution and an app scenario.

Create a new, empty SharePoint 2013 project and choose to deploy it as a farm solution. After the project is created, add a Module SharePoint Project Item and name it **Pages**. When the Module SharePoint Project Item is added to the project, it includes one elements manifest file (Elements.xml) and one sample file (Sample.txt). You cannot add a content page to a Module SharePoint Project Item with any out-of-the-box feature and template in Visual Studio, but you can either copy the file you created in the previous example into this SharePoint Project Item or just rename the sample file to a desired file name for the content page. For instance, rename it to **SimpleContentPage.aspx**. Visual Studio displays a warning when you edit the file name extension, but you can ignore this because you want to edit the file name extension. Then all you need to do is copy and paste the contents from the simple page in the previous sample into the file. Note that if you had the file open before changing the extension of the file, you need to close and reopen the file so that Visual Studio can load the correct editor.

Now consider the elements manifest file, which controls how the page should be deployed and provisioned in the site. The manifest file uses CAML to describe what you want to do. In this case, the *Module* element is used to specify which files to provision to a site, how to provision them, and where they should be provisioned. After adding the simple page or renaming the default sample file, the CAML should look like Listing 7-10.

LISTING 7-10 The default Module SharePoint Project Item elements manifest file after adding a content page

```
<Elements xmlns="http://schemas.microsoft.com/sharepoint/">
  <Module Name="Pages">
    <File Path="Pages\SimpleContentPage.aspx"
       Url="Pages/SimpleContentPage.aspx" />
  </Module>
</Elements>
```

You can tell from the code that Visual Studio has automatically updated the *File* element with the name of the content page. Also notice that the relative path to the pages contains a reference to a folder with the name of the Module SharePoint Project Item. To change the target location of the deployed file, update the *Url* attribute of the *File* element. For instance, to deploy the file to the root of the site, change the *File* element:

```
<File Path="Pages\SimpleContentPage.aspx" Url="SimpleContentPage.aspx" />
```

When you added the Module SharePoint Project Item to the Visual Studio project, Visual Studio automatically created a SharePoint Feature for you under the *Features* node in Solution Explorer. You can rename the Feature name and you can modify the Feature's properties by double-clicking it. You should give the Feature a more appropriate name than the one generated by default. The default scope of the Feature is *Web*, which means that this Feature can be enabled on any website and the file will be provisioned on the sites where it's enabled. For a *Module* element, you could also set the scope to *Site*, which allows you to deploy this module only to a site collection and the page to be provisioned on the root web of that site collection. Your Solution Explorer should look something like the one in Figure 7-6 after you rename the Feature.

 Tip For full CAML references and more about the options for the *Module* and *File* elements, go to the MSDN website and look at the SharePoint Features schema: *http://msdn. microsoft.com/en-us/library/ms414322.aspx*.

FIGURE 7-6 Visual Studio Solution Explorer displays the Module SharePoint Project Item.

If you now deploy this solution to SharePoint either by using the F5 debugging method or the Deploy Solution method, you can browse to the site and the URL you specified as the target URL for the content page, and you should be able to get there. Because this is a farm solution, you can also browse to any other site and enable the Feature and see the page being provisioned. The SharePoint solution that you've just built does not contain any artifacts that require server-side code, and you can easily change this solution into a sandboxed solution by selecting the *Project* node in Solution Explorer and then switching to the Properties Window by pressing F4. In this window, change the *Sandboxed Solution* property to *True* to make the project a sandboxed solution, which you can deploy to a specific site collection on your on-premises farms or in a cloud service, such as Microsoft Office 365 and Microsoft SharePoint Online.

When you deployed the solution as a farm solution and activated the Feature on a site, the page was provisioned as an uncustomized page. When you deploy by using a sandboxed solution, the page is provisioned as a customized page. If you're building a SharePoint app and deploying pages to the app web, the same syntax and methodology is used.

Note When you inactivate the Feature, any files provisioned by using the *Module* element will remain provisioned. If you retract the solution from SharePoint, any uncustomized pages provisioned through the *Module* element will throw an exception. The template file is removed from the file system, but the content page still remains in the site. To fix this, you should programmatically implement code that cleans this up when the Feature is deactivated. A similar sample of this is provided in Chapter 8, "SharePoint Web Parts."

Creating a Web Part page

A specific type of content page, called a Web Part page, is perhaps the most common type of content page in SharePoint. The *Web Part page* allows the users to add content to the pages directly in the web UI. The content can be Web Parts or wiki content. To create a Web Part page, you need to perform some modifications to the page directive. You might have noticed in the previous sample (Listing 7-10), that if you browse back and forth between the simple page and other pages in a team site, the simple page does not use MDS and requires a full page reload. This is because the page does not have a base class; specifically, it does not have a base class that derives from the *DeltaPage* class. To build a Web Part page that can use MDS, you need to choose the correct base class and specify it in the page directive. SharePoint 2013 has two base classes for Web Part pages:

- *WebPartPage*

- *WikiEditPage*

Both of these page classes exist in the *Microsoft.SharePoint.WebPartPages* namespace. The *WebPartPage* class is the base class for all content pages. It's a page type specifically created for hosting Web Parts, which you learn about in Chapter 8. The *WikiEditPage* inherits from the *WebPartPage* and has support for handling wiki content. The default team site Start page is based on the *WikiEditPage*. The *WikiEditPage* can be used only in libraries that have the content type *Wiki Page* enabled because it is storing the wiki content in a field called *Wiki Content*. The *WebPartPage* is used by the forms for lists and libraries. Both of these two page types inherit from the *DeltaPage*, which was discussed in the section "Minimal Download Strategy requirements and compliance" earlier in this chapter. There are many more page classes defined in the various SharePoint assemblies that are specifically built to handle different scenarios. Publishing pages are one of those page classes and are discussed later in the chapter, in the "Understanding publishing pages" section. Depending on your needs, you can also create your own custom page class and make that inherit from any one of these base classes.

If you want to use the *WikiEditPage* as the base class and the standard SharePoint 2013 master page, the page implementation would look like this:

```
<% @Page Language="C#" MasterPageFile="~masterurl/default.master" Inherits="Microsoft.
SharePoint.WebPartPages.WikiEditPage, Microsoft.SharePoint,
Version=15.0.0.0, Culture=neutral, PublicKeyToken=71e9bce111e9429c" %>
<asp:Content ContentPlaceHolderId="PlaceHolderMain" runat="server">
 <h1>This is the simplest MDS Content page ever</h1>
</asp:Content>
```

You need to deploy this wiki-based Web Part page into a document library with the *Wiki Page* content type. The default team site template has a library called *Site Contents* that has this *Wiki Page* content type enabled by default. To properly deploy the file, you could use an elements manifest like this:

```
<Elements xmlns="http://schemas.microsoft.com/sharepoint/">
 <Module Name="Pages" Url="SitePages">
   <File Path="Pages\SimpleContentPage.aspx"
     Url="SimpleContentPage.aspx" Type="GhostableInLibrary" />
 </Module>
</Elements>
```

In the preceding elements manifest are two changes to the previous sample, which are apparent in Listing 7-10. The first change is the addition of a *Url* attribute to the *Module* element. This allows you to specify a base URL for all files within that *Module*, and all *Url* attributes on the *File* elements are relative to that base URL. The second change is a new attribute on the *File* element called *Type*, with the value *GhostableInLibrary*. This attribute tells SharePoint that you would like to make the file that is added to the library an uncustomized file.

If you now deploy this solution to a site, you will note that it looks exactly the same as the simple page that was built in the "Deploying a content page" section, but browsing to and from the page reveals that the page uses MDS. This page can't still be edited in the UI, because there's just static content within it.

To make the page a real Web Part page that can be edited in the UI, you must add one or more Web Part zones and/or a wiki field. A *Web Part zone* is a container control that allows users to dynamically add controls into it. These controls must be Web Parts, which are discussed more in Chapter 8 along with the zones. Web Parts are also configurable by the user in the web interface. Each Web Part has a set of properties and optionally a set of custom properties that can be changed. The Web Part zone is responsible for persisting the Web Parts added to a zone and its properties. The *wiki zone* is a special form of control that allows HTML markup to be mixed with Web Parts. The wiki zone can be used only on pages inheriting from the *WikiEditPage* because it requires some extra plumbing.

To create a new Web Part page and define two zones, add a new file to the *Module* element in the previous sample, and make sure that *Type* is set to *GhostableInLibrary* and that the new file is deployed to the *Site Pages* library or to a document library. Listing 7-11 shows a page inheriting from the *WebPartPage* class, which contains HTML markup and two Web Part zones, one on the left side and one on the right side.

LISTING 7-11 Editable content pages that are created by creating pages inheriting from the *WebPartPage* class and that contain Web Part zones

```
<% @Page Language="C#" MasterPageFile="~masterurl/default.master"
 Inherits="Microsoft.SharePoint.WebPartPages.WebPartPage, Microsoft.SharePoint,
    Version=15.0.0.0, Culture=neutral, PublicKeyToken=71e9bce111e9429c" %>
<%@ Register Tagprefix="WebPartPages"
 Namespace="Microsoft.SharePoint.WebPartPages"
 Assembly="Microsoft.SharePoint,
 Version=15.0.0.0, Culture=neutral, PublicKeyToken=71e9bce111e9429c" %>
<asp:Content ContentPlaceHolderId="PlaceHolderMain" runat="server">
<h1>This is a Web Part page with zones</h1>
<div>
  <div style="float:left;width:50%">
    <WebPartPages:WebPartZone ID="left" Title="Left" runat="server">
    </WebPartPages:WebPartZone>
  </div>
  <div style="float:right;width:50%">
    <WebPartPages:WebPartZone ID="right" Title="Right" runat="server">
    </WebPartPages:WebPartZone>
  </div>
</div>
</asp:Content>
```

When the updated solution with the new Web Part page is deployed, you can browse to the page and click the Edit button on the ribbon. In edit mode are the two Web Part zones, which can be used to add Web Parts, as shown in Figure 7-7.

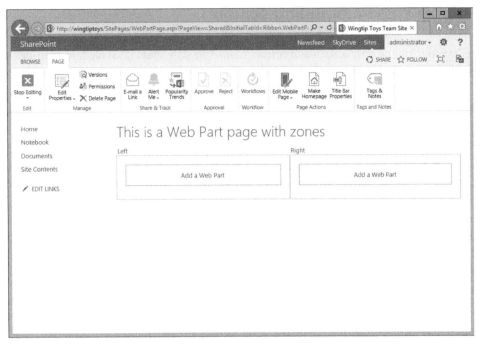

FIGURE 7-7 Web Part pages can be edited directly in the browser and are an easy way for users to customize their sites.

You should now be familiar with the concept of content pages and how you create, package, and deploy them. Most of the methods discussed work in all deployment models: farm solutions, sandboxed solutions, and even SharePoint apps. If you need to further customize the content pages, you can create your own base classes as long as they derive from the *WebPartPage* class or at least the *System.Web.UI.Page* class. This option is available only in farm solutions but provides many possibilities for customizing your pages.

Understanding publishing pages

For more advanced scenarios, when you require even more control of the content and layout in the pages, you can use the SharePoint Server 2013 set of Features. Use the Publishing Features in SharePoint Server to create content pages, called *publishing pages*, by using templates, called *page layouts*. These are more advanced content pages than those discussed earlier in this chapter, but all the content pages share the same base classes—the *WebPartPage* class and the *DeltaPage* class. Although the publishing pages inherit from the *DeltaPages*, they do not take advantage of MDS, because none of the publishing controls are marked as MDS-compliant. In Chapter 15, "Web content management," the Publishing Features of SharePoint are discussed in more detail.

Creating a custom branding solution

One of the most common customizations of any SharePoint installation is branding of the UI. This customization might be simple, such as a custom cascading style sheet (CSS) file that overrides the default SharePoint style sheets, or something more advanced, such as a heavily customized master page and lots of design artifacts. In the next sections, you learn how you to create a reusable solution that deploys a custom master page.

Creating a custom master page

To create a custom master page, you have several options ranging from using a copy of the default master pages to starting with a blank solution and building your own master page. Which approach you take often varies depending on your requirements. For instance, if you're building a collaborative intranet solution, it is often a good idea to start from one of the default master pages and customize that to your needs, whereas if you're building a public-facing Internet site, you often start from an HTML mockup and convert that into a master page. SharePoint Server 2013 introduces a new feature called *Design Manager* that can help you do this automatically. It's a very interesting feature that allows you to convert an ordinary HTML page into a SharePoint master page.

In the following sample, you deploy a copy of the default seattle.master page. You also create a scoped site collection Feature that modifies the default master page to the custom master page when activated, and then when deactivated, restores the original master page settings.

Start by creating a new farm solution project, and add a *Module* element named **SiteBranding**. Visual Studio 2012 automatically creates a Feature for you when the SharePoint Project Item is added, so make sure to change the scope of that Feature from Web to Site. To add the default seattle.master to the module, you copy and paste the original file from the SharePoint root into the *SiteBranding* SharePoint Project Item, and then rename it to something appropriate. You then need to make sure that this module deploys the files to the Master Page Gallery by setting the *Url* attribute of the *Module* element to _catalogs/masterpage. You also need to set some properties of the master page file. To tell SharePoint that it is a master page, you set the content type of the item to the master page *content type id*, and to make the master page available to the SharePoint 2013 UI, you set the *UIVersion* to *15*. Finally, you set the title of the page by using the *Title* property. Listing 7-12 shows the required modifications to the elements manifest.

LISTING 7-12 Master page provisioned into the Master Page Gallery, with content type and *UIVersion* specified

```
<Elements xmlns="http://schemas.microsoft.com/sharepoint/">
 <Module Name="SiteBranding" Url="_catalogs/masterpage">
  <File Path="SiteBranding\CustomBranding.master"
    Url="SiteBranding/CustomBranding.master"
    Type="GhostableInLibrary">
    <Property Name="ContentTypeId" Value="0x010105" />
    <Property Name="UIVersion" Value="15" />
    <Property Name="Title" Value="Custom Branding master page" />
  </File>
 </Module>
</Elements>
```

Adding a feature receiver

The project now deploys only the master page to the Master Page Gallery with the correct set of properties, but to make this master page the default master page, you need to write some code. This activation code will be implemented as a Feature receiver on the site collection–scoped Feature. Listing 7-13 shows the feature activation, which sets the master page on all the sites within the site collection.

LISTING 7-13 Feature activation, which automatically configures the new master page on all sites within the site collection

```
public override void FeatureActivated(SPFeatureReceiverProperties properties)
{
    SPSite site = properties.Feature.Parent as SPSite;
    if (site != null)
    {
        SPWeb rootWeb = site.RootWeb;
        string masterurl = rootWeb.ServerRelativeUrl;
        if (!masterurl.EndsWith("/"))
        {
            masterurl += "/";
        }
        masterurl += "_catalogs/masterpage/SiteBranding/CustomBranding.master";
        // iterate through all the webs in the site collection
        foreach (SPWeb web in site.AllWebs)
        {
            web.Properties["OldMasterUrl"] = web.MasterUrl;
            web.MasterUrl = masterurl;
            web.Update();
            web.Dispose();
        }
    }
}
```

The *FeatureActivated* method is called when the Feature is activated on a site collection, and it builds a URL to the custom master page, which is deployed into the Master Page Gallery of the root web of the site collection. The method then goes through all the sites in the site collection and sets the *MasterUrl* property of the *SPWeb* object to the URL of the custom master page. At the same time, the code is also storing the old value of the *MasterUrl* property into the property bag of the *SPWeb* object so that the old value can be used when you deactivate the Feature and restore the settings of the site. Also note that you're using the *AllWebs* property of the *SPSite* object, which requires properly disposing of all the *SPWeb* objects to avoid memory leaks.

When the Feature is deactivated, you need to restore the master page settings on all the sites. Listing 7-14 shows the *FeatureDeactivating* method of the Feature receiver.

LISTING 7-14 The deactivated Feature resetting the master page customization

```
public override void FeatureDeactivating(SPFeatureReceiverProperties properties)
{
    SPSite site = properties.Feature.Parent as SPSite;
    if (site != null)
    {
        // iterate through all the webs in the site collection
        foreach (SPWeb web in site.AllWebs)
        {
            if(!String.IsNullOrEmpty(web.Properties["OldMasterUrl"])) {
                web.MasterUrl = web.Properties["OldMasterUrl"];
                web.Update();
            }
            web.Dispose();
        }
    }
}
```

The *FeatureDeactivating* method looks very similar to the *FeatureActivating* method. It will go through all the subwebs and reset the master page to the original value.

Working with application pages

SharePoint not only has content pages, which as you know are mainly used for users to consume and work with, but also has another page type called *application pages*. These differ from content pages in several ways. Content pages lives in the sites and in the content databases, as previously discussed, whereas the application pages live outside the content databases and in the IIS virtual directory called *_layouts*, which is one of the reasons application pages are called layout pages. The main purpose of application pages is for administration, and they have no customization options. For instance, the Home page of a site can be different from one site to another, but settings pages should look exactly the same independent of the site you're in, except for the actual settings values. This IIS virtual directory called *_layouts* exists in the root of each site collection, thanks to the virtual file system, but all of these virtual *_layouts* folders are mapped to the same physical file location, TEMPLATE\LAYOUTS under the SharePoint root.

Understanding application page anatomy

Application pages are just like content pages based on the *DeltaPage* base class, which means that they can use MDS. Application pages have two specific derived base classes:

- *UnsecuredLayoutsPageBase*

- *LayoutsPageBase*

These two base types are defined in the *Microsoft.SharePoint.WebControls* namespace. The *Layouts-PageBase* inherits from the *UnsecuredLayoutsPageBase*, and the main difference between the two is that the *LayoutsPageBase* has built-in logic for checking permissions. The *UnsecuredLayoutsPageBase* has a set of overridable methods and properties that, for example, allows you to configure whether the application page permits anonymous users. All custom applications should derive from one of these two base types, and typically *LayoutsPageBase* is used.

Creating an application page

Application pages can be deployed through custom solutions and are often used to provision administrative pages. Because deploying application pages involves adding files to the file system, they are available only in farm solutions. All application pages are also deployed to all sites and site collections, so there is no granularity.

Visual Studio 2013 and the SharePoint tools contain an item template for application pages that can be used to create new application pages. To add a new application page, select the *Project* node in Solution Explorer, right-click Add, and then click New Item. In the Add New Item dialog box, select the Application Page (Farm Solution Only) template, name it, and then click Add. Visual Studio adds the required references to your project, adds a new SharePoint Mapped folder to the Layouts folder if it is not already present, and then creates a subfolder within that mapped folder to which it adds your custom application page, as shown in Figure 7-8.

FIGURE 7-8 Custom application pages are added to the Layouts folder in the Visual Studio project.

The custom application page has one .aspx file and a code-behind file. The code-behind file specifies that the custom application page inherits from *LayoutsPageBase*. Notice that the *Page* directive in the .aspx file does not have a typical *MasterPageFile* attribute. Instead, it has another attribute called *DynamicMasterPageFile*. This attribute allows you to use the dynamic tokens to specify master pages, *~masterurl/default.master* or *~masterurl/custom.master*, which you learned about earlier in this chapter. Another and perhaps more important aspect of Application pages is that SharePoint has a built-in safeguard for specific application pages that makes sure the pages are rendered even when the master page fails to render. It does this by falling back on the default master page (seattle.master). To protect an application page, you set the *RequiresHighAvailablilty* property, inherited from *UnsecuredLayoutsPageBase*, to *true* in the constructor of the custom application page.

Now you will modify this custom application page so that it renders some information about the current site collection. In the .aspx, Web Forms page controls and markup are added to the content placeholders. The item template defines four of the content placeholders by default, but you can add or remove them as necessary. This is how the markup looks for a sample custom application page that shows some more details of the site collection:

```
<asp:Content ID="Main" ContentPlaceHolderID="PlaceHolderMain" runat="server">
<fieldset>
 <legend>Site Information</legend>
 Content database name: <asp:Label ID="contentDatabase" runat="server" />
 <br />
 Is Evaluation site: <asp:Label ID="isEvalSite" runat="server" />
</fieldset>
</asp:Content>

<asp:Content ID="PageTitle" ContentPlaceHolderID="PlaceHolderPageTitle" runat="server">
Site Information
</asp:Content>

<asp:Content ID="PageTitleInTitleArea" ContentPlaceHolderID="PlaceHolderPageTitleInTitleArea"
 runat="server" >
Site Information
</asp:Content>
```

The content placeholder *PlaceHolderMain* is used for the body of the page. It contains two *Label* controls that are set in the code-behind. You use *PageTitle* and *PageTitleInTitleArea* to display the name of the page. The code-behind for the page looks like this:

```
public partial class CustomApplicationPage : LayoutsPageBase
{
 protected void Page_Load(object sender, EventArgs e)
 {
   contentDatabase.Text = SPContext.Current.Site.ContentDatabase.Name;
   isEvalSite.Text = SPContext.Current.Site.IsEvalSite.ToString();

 }
}
```

In the *Page_Load* method, the two *Label* controls are set with values from two site collection properties: one displays the name of the content database in which the site collection is stored, and the other one shows whether the site is an upgrade evaluation site. After the project is deployed, you need to browse to the page. The only way to get to the page is to manually enter its URL into the browser, but you'll fix this. The URL to the page is the name of the site or web, to which you append *_layouts/15*, and then append the name of the folder created by Visual Studio and the name of the application page. The page should look like Figure 7-9.

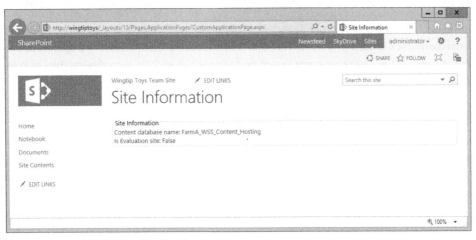

FIGURE 7-9 Custom application pages are deployed to the virtual _layouts_ directory and can be accessed from any site within the farm.

Securing the application page

A user who knows the actual URL of the application page and is a visitor to the site has access to application pages, unless the site has been configured otherwise. More specifically, the permission level called *View Application Pages* is required to give users access to application pages, and the Visitors group has that permission level by default. You cannot set permissions on application pages as you can do on content pages in document libraries. Fortunately, the built-in logic in *LayoutsPageBase* allows you to specify required permissions for the application page.

The *LayoutsPageBase* has a Boolean property called *RequireSiteAdministrator*. By default, this property is set to *false*, and if it is set to *true*, only site collection administrators are allowed to view the page. If you want more fine-grained permissions, you use a property called *RightsRequired* that specifies a *SPBasePermissions* object with the required permissions. If you want only users who have the permission level *View Web Analytics Data* to be able to access the application page, you need to override the *RightsRequired* property:

```
protected override SPBasePermissions RightsRequired
{
  get
  {
    return SPBasePermissions.ViewUsageData;
  }
}
```

After redeploying the solution, users without the View Web Analytics Data permission level will get the Access Denied page for the site. To view this page, users need both the View Web Analytics Data permissions and the View Application Pages permissions. The property *RequireDefaultLayoutsRights* has the default value set to *true*. This means that the permissions check that is done will use the permissions specified in *RightsRequired* and View Application Pages. To use only the *RightsRequired* permissions, you need to override the *RequireDefaultLayoutsRights* and make sure it returns *false*.

You should be aware of one more aspect regarding permissions for application pages. By default, the permission check is done in the ASP.NET event *OnLoadComplete*. You can change this to either handle the check in the *OnPreInit* event or not do the check at all. This is configured by using the *RightsCheckMode* property, which is an enumeration of type *RightCheckModes*.

Adding navigation support to the application page

Application pages are not part of the navigation unless you make them available. There are several ways to accomplish this, and your approach depends on what you need. For instance, one application page might be accessible through a link in a custom Web Part, or another might be accessible through the ribbon (you examine this later in the chapter, in the "Customizing the ribbon" section). Most often, application pages are configured so that they are a part of the site settings navigation.

To make the custom application page a part of the site navigation, you use a custom action, which is an extension to the UI. *Custom actions* are defined declaratively by using CAML in an elements manifest file. Custom actions are very versatile and configurable and can be used to add links, scripts, menu items, and so on. In this scenario, where you want to add a link into site settings under the Site Collection Administration group, you start by adding a new empty Element SharePoint Project Item to the solution. In the elements manifest file, Elements.xml, the following CAML is added to create the link:

```
<Elements xmlns="http://schemas.microsoft.com/sharepoint/">
 <CustomAction Title="Site Information" Id="CustomSiteInformation"
   Location="Microsoft.SharePoint.SiteSettings" GroupId="SiteCollectionAdmin"
   Rights="ViewUsageData">
   <UrlAction Url="~site/_layouts/15/Pages.ApplicationPages/CustomApplicationPage.aspx"/>
 </CustomAction>
</Elements>
```

The *CustomAction* element defines the custom action and is given a *Title*, which is what will be displayed as the link. The location of the link is determined by the *Location* and *GroupId* attribute. In this case, you specify the location of the Site Settings page, and the group is Site Collection Administration. (For a full reference of the possible *Location* and *GroupId* values, refer to the Microsoft MSDN website at *http://msdn.microsoft.com/en-us/library/bb802730.aspx*.) Even though specifying the required permissions is not required, you do the check in the application page. Hiding the link from users who cannot access the page is a good convention. You do this by using the *Rights* attribute, in which you specify the same permissions you implemented in the preceding code-behind. Finally, you need to specify the URL for the application page by using the *UrlAction* element. Note that the URL is specified with *~sitecollection*, which indicates that you should use the current site collection as the base for the URL. If you wanted to refer to site-scoped properties, you would use the *~site* token instead.

Customizing the ribbon

The ribbon menu introduced in Microsoft Office 2007 made its way into SharePoint 2010 and has continued to evolve in SharePoint 2013. The ribbon menu is customizable and, in many cases, is the preferred location for UI customizations because the ribbon is available on most pages, accessible, adapted for touchscreen-enabled interfaces, and gives the users a great user experience.

The SharePoint ribbon can be customized by using custom actions, and the customization can be done by using farm solutions, sandboxed solutions, and SharePoint apps. Using farm solutions gives you the most flexibility and allows you to add everything from custom contextual tabs to new groups and even remove controls and groups. Sandboxed solutions allows you to add new controls to existing groups, and SharePoint apps allows you to customize the ribbon on both the host and app web.

Understanding the anatomy of the SharePoint ribbon

Before you dive into customizing the ribbon, it is essential to know its different components, all of which are customizable. Figure 7-10 shows the different parts of the ribbon.

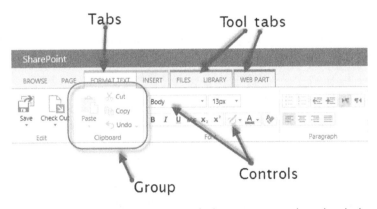

FIGURE 7-10 The ribbon menu consists of tabs, groups, controls, and tool tabs.

The tabs are the top-level element of the ribbon, and each tab has one or more groups. Tabs can be contextual and only appear when a specific Web Part or other component is selected. For instance, if you're working on a Publishing page and choose an image, the Image tool tab will appear. Each group contains one or more ribbon controls. These are some of the available controls:

- *Button*

- *CheckBox*

- *ComboBox*

- *DropDown*

- *FlyoutAnchor*

- *GalleryButton*

- *Label*

- *SplitButton*

- *TextBox*

- *ToggleButton*

Each tab, group, and control can be associated with one or more actions. For instance, the *Toggle-Button* control has one action that is executed when the control is loaded, which can be used to set its state, and another action that is fired when the user clicks the control. The events are implemented as JavaScript functions.

The SharePoint ribbon also adapts to the size of the screen, just as the Office ribbon does. Each group and control has an associated group template that defines how it should scale. If you are building your own tabs, you must define your own group template and scalings. But if you are adding a group or control to an existing tab, you should use the template defined by that tab.

The default ribbon components are defined in the Cmdui.xml file that is located in the SharePoint root in the \Template\Global\XML folder. If you're going to customize the ribbon, we recommend that you take a look at this one but do not modify it.

Adding a custom ribbon control

There are several ways to customize the ribbon. You can use the server-side object model, which is available only for farm solutions, and you can use CAML and a declarative approach. Custom ribbon controls most often also involve a lot of JavaScript code, especially if you're using some of the more advanced controls such as the *GalleryButton* or *ComboBox*.

You are going to create a simple ribbon extension that will contain a *Button* control that will report the customization status of the current page. First you need to find out the location, and specifically the ID, of the Ribbon group where you want to place the *Button* control. The easiest way to do this is to use the Internet Explorer Developer Tools and locate the element ID of the group (see Figure 7-11). You use this ID for two tasks: first, you use it in the elements manifest to specify the location; and second, you use it to find out which template alias to use. The template alias is connected to the group template and defines how the control should handle rendering when the ribbon is resized. To get the correct template alias, you open the Cmdui.xml file and search for a *Group* element with the ID equal to the ID located by using the Internet Explorer Developer Tools. Review any of the child controls of that *Group* element and inspect the *TemplateAlias* attribute. The group might use multiple different template aliases. You have to test to find out which one suits your needs.

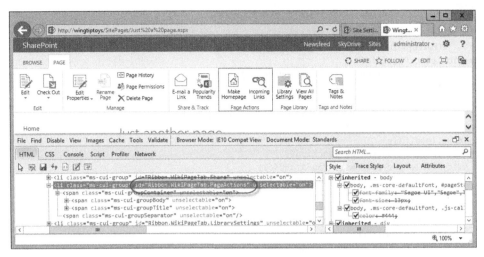

FIGURE 7-11 Internet Explorer Developer Tools can be used to find out the IDs of ribbon tabs, groups, and controls.

In this case, you want to add a custom button to the Page Actions group. Using the Internet Explorer Developer Tools, you can tell that that group has an ID of *Ribbon.WikiPageTab.PageActions*. Using the Cmdui.xml file, you learn that the controls of the Page Actions group are using a template alias called *o2*. Now you have the necessary information to proceed and build the button.

In a new or existing project, which could be a farm solution or a sandboxed solution, add a new *Empty* element. You will use this elements manifest and declare a new *CustomAction*, but instead of adding an *UrlAction* element as you did previously, you will add another element called *CommandUI-Extension*. Another difference from the previous sample shown in the "Adding navigation support to the application page" section, is that you specify the *Location* attribute of the *CustomAction* to *CommandUI.Ribbon*. It takes quite a few lines of CAML to construct and define the ribbon control, as illustrated in Listing 7-15.

LISTING 7-15 The complete CAML required to declare the custom ribbon button

```
<Elements xmlns="http://schemas.microsoft.com/sharepoint/">
  <CustomAction Location="CommandUI.Ribbon" Id="CustomRibbonExtension" Sequence="1000">
    <CommandUIExtension>

      <CommandUIDefinitions>
        <CommandUIDefinition Location="Ribbon.WikiPageTab.PageActions.Controls._children">
          <Button Id="CustomRibbonButton" Alt="Page information" Sequence="1000"
            Command="CheckPageInfo" LabelText="Page information" TemplateAlias="o2"
            Image16by16="/_layouts/15/images/sytelshs.png"
            Image32by32="/_layouts/15/images/styleshh.png"/>
        </CommandUIDefinition>
      </CommandUIDefinitions>
```

```
    <CommandUIHandlers>
        <CommandUIHandler Command="CheckPageInfo" CommandAction="javascript:
function checkPageInfo() {
  var context = SP.ClientContext.get_current();
  var list = context.get_web().get_lists().getById(
    new SP.Guid(_spPageContextInfo.pageListId));
  var item = list.getItemById(_spPageContextInfo.pageItemId);
  var file = item.get_file()
  context.load(file)
  context.executeQueryAsync(function() {
    switch(file.get_customizedPageStatus()) {
      case SP.CustomizedPageStatus.none:
        alert('Page has never been cached'); break;
      case SP.CustomizedPageStatus.uncustomized:
        alert('Page is cached and not customized'); break;
      case SP.CustomizedPageStatus.customized:
        alert('Page is cached and customized'); break;
    }
  },function() {
      alert('An error occurred')
  })
}
checkPageInfo();
"/>
    </CommandUIHandlers>
  </CommandUIExtension>
 </CustomAction>
</Elements>
```

As revealed in the preceding CAML, the *CommandUIExtension* element has two child elements: *CommandUIDefinitions* and *CommandUIHandlers*. *CommandUIDefinitions* contains the definition of the UI, such as tabs, groups, and controls, and *CommandUIHandlers* contains the commands that the different controls act upon. In this case, you're adding only one definition element, *CommandUIDefinition*, and you specify the location in the ribbon for that element by using the *Location* attribute. Here you use the ID that you previously extracted by using the Internet Explorer Developer Tools, and because you want to add a button as a child to the group, you must append *Controls._children* to that ID to specify the location.

Next you define the actual *Button* control. Each control requires a unique ID, a sequence, and a template alias; some controls have additional required attributes. For this *Button* control, you specify a label, alternative text, and two images that will be used at different scalings, and you add the template alias that you found in the Cmdui.xml file. Finally, you add a command to the control. The value of the *Command* attribute should point to a *CommandUIHandler* element, defined in *CommandUI-Handlers*. This tells SharePoint to trigger the handler when a user clicks the button.

The handler is defined in a *CommandUIHandler* element. In this case, you define one handler that has a *Command* attribute equal to the *Command* attribute of *Button* control, and then you specify a block of JavaScript in the *CommandAction* attribute. *CommandAction* could also contain a URL, which would redirect the user to the specified URL instead of executing JavaScript. If you're building a SharePoint app and adding a ribbon extension to it, you must specify a URL here; you cannot use JavaScript.

The JavaScript in the handler uses the JavaScript client-side object model and retrieves the customization status of the current page. If it succeeds, it displays a JavaScript alert box with the current status of the page.

When this project is deployed to SharePoint, either as a farm solution or sandboxed solution, and you browse to a wiki page, the button is displayed, as shown in Figure 7-12. Clicking the button should report the customization status of the current page.

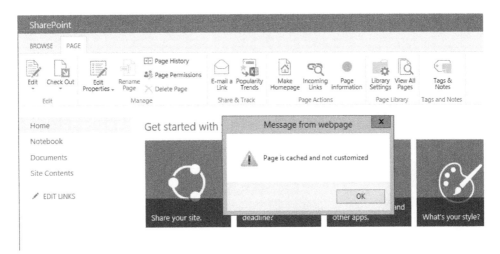

FIGURE 7-12 The custom ribbon extension is displayed in the Page Actions group.

You've completed the ribbon sample. Ribbon customizations can be far more advanced; you can declare custom tabs, and Web Parts can have contextual tabs. If you need to create more advanced client-side code by using JavaScript, you can use the Ribbon Page Components model, which allows for very dynamic ribbon extensions.

Summary

This chapter provided a quick ASP.NET recap and discussed the details of the SharePoint virtual file system. You learned how to create and deploy different kinds of pages in SharePoint, and you learned how to create a quick ribbon extension. The chapter covers the basic knowledge a SharePoint developer needs, whether you are a professional developer or are building custom solutions by using SharePoint Designer. Any kind of project will contain some form of deployed pages, for example, SharePoint-hosted apps. You will use a lot of what you learned in this chapter in Chapter 8, which focuses on Web Parts—one of the original cornerstones of SharePoint.

## CHAPTER 8

SharePoint Web Parts

If you ask any Microsoft SharePoint developer what they built first for SharePoint, the vast majority will answer "a Web Part." Web Parts are one of the fundamental building blocks of SharePoint and, in combination with site pages, allow users to customize SharePoint in many different and interesting ways.

In this chapter, you first review Web Part fundamentals and their relationship to ASP.NET. and then you examine the different pieces that together build the Web Part framework. The chapter covers building Web Parts by using Microsoft Visual Studio 2012 and explains how to package Web Parts for use in sites. You continue the development process by learning about some of the options you have when developing the UI and interacting with Web Parts, and you learn about how to personalize and customize your Web Part.

The last part of this chapter discusses some of the more advanced Web Part development scenarios such as Web Part connections, which allows the end-users to combine the powers of multiple Web Parts to create their own dashboards or mashups. The chapter ends by taking a look at asynchronous and parallel execution of Web Parts, which might be needed to improve the performance of your Web Parts.

Understanding Web Part fundamentals

Your Web Part journey begins by reviewing the history of Web Parts and how ASP.NET uses Web Parts. To understand how Web Parts are developed, used, and managed in ASP.NET and SharePoint, you need to learn about the required components so that your Web Parts work as expected. Even though you might be familiar with Web Parts from ASP.NET or your earlier SharePoint experience, this section should be a valuable read. If you have been working with Web Parts only in SharePoint, you might find this section particularly interesting.

Understanding Web Parts

This chapter starts by discussing what a Web Part is but doesn't go into the details yet; there is plenty of time for that in the remainder of this chapter! Web Parts are one of the more important features of SharePoint, and without Web Parts, SharePoint might not have been as successful as it is. Web Parts are not unique to SharePoint, because every portal platform has similar concepts that are called different names, such as *portlets* or *widgets*.

Web Parts can be described as applications within the portal or page. They can be self-contained or cooperate with other Web Parts, they can display information, and they can ask for information from users. Users can add Web Parts to pages, selecting different Web Parts from a gallery and creating their own unique pages and experiences. The Web Parts themselves can have different configurations, even for different users. SharePoint uses Web Parts a lot; each list view, and each list form or document library, is displayed through a Web Part—a List Viewer Web Part.

Comparing ASP.NET and SharePoint Web Parts

Web Parts is not a SharePoint-specific concept but rather an ASP.NET concept; they first appeared in ASP.NET 2.0. But the Web Part concept was created much earlier, before SharePoint existed, by the Digital Dashboard Resource Kit. The Web Part concept was then inherited by SharePoint 2001 and eventually was ported to the Microsoft .NET Framework 1.1. ASP.NET 2.0 refined the implementation and made the Web Part concept a part of ASP.NET 2.0. When SharePoint 2007 was released based on ASP.NET 2.0, the default Web Part implementation was based on the ASP.NET 2.0 Web Part framework.

A Web Part is essentially a specific derivative of the *System.Web.UI.WebControls.WebControl* control, as illustrated in Figure 8-1. All custom Web Parts must derive from the abstract *WebPart* class, defined in the *System.Web.UI.WebControls.WebParts* namespace. The *WebPart* class also implements some specific interfaces that define the Web Part (*IWebPart*) and define the behavior of the Web Part (*IWebEditable* and *IWebActionable*).

FIGURE 8-1 This Visual Studio class diagram shows a simplified view of the *WebPart* class inheritance.

Just like any control in .NET, Web Parts can have properties. There is a difference between the properties of normal web controls and the properties of Web Parts. The values of a Web Part property can be modified and persisted by users provided that the Web Part has a parent control that is a Web Part zone. The property values can be persisted on a page or per-user basis. You learn more about Web Part properties and zones later in this chapter, in the "Understanding Web Part zones" section.

SharePoint contained the first implementation of Web Parts in the .NET Framework, using the SharePoint-specific class *WebPart*, in the *Microsoft.SharePoint.WebPartPages* namespace. This is the same class name that is used by the ASP.NET *WebPart* class, which might be a bit confusing. The SharePoint class was created before ASP.NET implemented the Web Part framework, and the SharePoint implementation still exists for backward compatibility. Many of the out-of-the-box Web Parts in SharePoint use this class as the base class. It is worth noting that when ASP.NET implemented the Web Part framework and SharePoint 2007 was released, the SharePoint *Web Part* class was reengineered to be derived from the ASP.NET *Web Part* class.

A common question among SharePoint developers is which Web Part implementation to use: the SharePoint or the ASP.NET implementation. In most cases, the ASP.NET Web Part implementation is the recommended starting point. The SharePoint Web Part implementation contains a lot of internal (to SharePoint and Microsoft) functionality for caching and manipulating how the Web Parts are stored and managed. But there are a few scenarios where the SharePoint implementation can be of value for all developers. Whereas the ASP.NET Web Part implementation has not changed in ASP.NET 4.0, the SharePoint 2013 Web Part implementation has been updated with some new features, for example, features for better management of Composed Looks, which is the new theming engine in SharePoint 2013.

One important aspect to keep in mind with regard to the SharePoint Web Part implementation is that the SharePoint sandbox supports only the ASP.NET implementation of Web Parts. Even though code-based sandboxed solutions are deprecated in SharePoint 2013, there might be scenarios when you would like to create a sandboxed Web Part. If that is the case, you must use the ASP.NET Web Part implementation as the base for your Web Part.

Understanding App Parts

Web Parts are available only in farm or sandboxed solutions, not in SharePoint apps. If you need to build a Web Part–similar experience for hosted scenarios, you should look into the App Part or Client Web Part concepts, which are not discussed in this chapter. A Client Web Part can be provisioned by a SharePoint app into the host web. This is an ASP.NET Web Part called *ClientWebPart* that renders an *iframe* element with a page from the SharePoint app, and allows for a customizable set of parameters. You can read more about App Parts in Chapter 4, "SharePoint apps."

Understanding Web Part zones

For Web Parts to be fully functional, they must exist in a Web Part zone. The *Web Part zone* is an ASP.NET control called *WebPartZone*. The Web Part zone defines a region in the page where Web Parts can be hosted, and the responsibility of the Web Part zone control is to lay out the Web Parts. SharePoint uses its own derivative of the ASP.NET *WebPartZone* control. It has the same class name *WebPartZone* and is defined in the *Microsoft.SharePoint.WebPartPages* namespace. The following code shows adding a zone to a Web Part page, as discussed in Chapter 7, "SharePoint pages":

```
<WebPartPages:WebPartZone runat="server" ID="zone"
   Title="The Zone" LayoutOrientation="Horizontal"/>
```

The Web Part zone determines how the Web Parts are rendered on the page. Table 8-1 shows some of the more common configuration properties for the SharePoint Web Part zone. The *ID* property should be treated carefully. After a Web Part zone is used on a page and a Web Part is added to that zone, the *id* of the zone is used when storing the Web Part state in SharePoint. If you remove the zone or change its *id* without removing the Web Parts, the saved Web Part state will be orphaned in the SharePoint databases. But after you change the *id* back to its original value or add another zone with the same *id* as the previous zone, the Web Parts are once again available.

TABLE 8-1 Common SharePoint *WebPartZone* properties

Property name	Description
ID	The ID of the Web Part zone.
Title	The title of the Web Part zone.
LayoutOrientation	Determines in which direction the Web Parts should be rendered; *Horizontal* or *Vertical* (default).
AllowLayoutChange	Boolean value that indicates whether the users are allowed to add, remove, or close Web Parts in the zone, or change specific layout properties of the Web Parts. Default is *true*.
AllowCustomization	Boolean value that indicates whether the users are allowed to modify the properties of Web Parts.
AllowPersonalization	Boolean value that indicates whether the users are allowed to personalize the Web Parts in the zone.
PartChromeType	Defines the chrome for the zone. Allowed values are *Default*, *TitleAndBorder*, *None*, *TitleOnly*, and *BorderOnly*.

Understanding the Web Part Manager

One of the most important components of the Web Part framework is the Web Part Manager. The Web Part Manager is responsible for serializing and deserializing the Web Parts and their properties from persisted storage. ASP.NET implements the *WebPartManager* object, and SharePoint has its own derivative of that object called the *SPWebPartManager* (defined in the *Microsoft.SharePoint.WebPart-Pages* namespace). The SharePoint Web Part Manager is responsible for retrieving and storing the Web Part data in the SharePoint content databases.

A Web Part Manager object is required on all Web Part pages. As described in Chapter 7 in the context of the master page, SharePoint adds the *SPWebPartManager* to the default master pages. You should also add this if you're creating your own master page. When a page is loaded, the Web Part Manager loads the Web Part from the persisted storage, including its state and the shared or personal settings of the Web Part, and populates the Web Part zones.

Understanding static Web Parts

Web Parts are essentially ASP.NET web controls and can be used as such. You don't need to add a Web Part to a Web Part zone; a Web Part can be added to a page directly just like any ASP.NET control. When a Web Part is added to a page outside of a Web Part zone, that Web Part is referred to as a *static Web Part*. Static Web Parts do not have all the unique features that Web Parts located in Web Part zones have. For instance, a static Web Part cannot be customized or personalized; a zone and a Web Part Manager are required to persist the properties of the Web Part.

Storing Web Part control description files in the Web Part Gallery

At this point, you are familiar with the components required to get the Web Part framework to function and render properly. But how do users discover and add Web Parts to pages? In SharePoint, Web Parts that should be available to users to select from should be published to the Web Part Gallery. The *Web Part Gallery* is a specific catalog in SharePoint located in the root web of all site collections (*/_catalogs/wp/*). The Web Part Gallery can be found in the user interface by going to Site Settings and choosing Web Parts in the Web Designer Galleries.

This gallery contains Web Part control description files. These files are often referred to as the Web Parts themselves, but they are more like templates of the Web Parts. A Web Part control description file is an XML file containing a reference to the Web Part type and assembly, and a set of default values for the Web Part's properties. When a Web Part is added to a zone by using a Web Part control description file, the Web Part Manager imports the XML file and instantiates a new instance of the Web Part type. The Web Part Gallery also adds metadata to the Web Part control description file, such as a description, group, and recommended settings. You examine these files more when you build a Web Part later in this chapter, in the "Building your first Web Part" section.

The Web Part Gallery contains two types of XML files: one having the .dwp extension and one having the .webpart extension. The .dwp format is the former format of the Web Part control description files and uses the version 2 (SharePoint 2003) schema for Web Parts, whereas the .webpart files use version 3 of the schema (SharePoint 2007 and newer versions). Version 3 of the schema is the newest version, and you should use it in your projects; you will use it throughout the samples in this chapter.

Developing and deploying Web Parts

Now it's time to build some Web Parts. The Microsoft Office and SharePoint tools in Microsoft Visual Studio 2012 are excellent for building Web Parts and give you a lot of aid to properly implement them. In this section, you build a Web Part from the very beginning, deploy it to the Web Part Gallery, and then verify that it works as expected. The chapter also describes how you can provision Web Part pages prepopulated with Web Parts.

Building your first Web Part

In this sample, you focus on how to create a Web Part by using Visual Studio 2012 and how to properly deploy it to a site collection. You first need to create a new Visual Studio 2012 solution. When choosing the Visual Studio project, you have two options: create an empty project, SharePoint 2013 - Empty Project; or use the predefined Visual Web Part project, SharePoint 2013 - Visual Web Part. The Visual Web Part is discussed in the "Using Visual Web Parts" section later in this chapter, so in this case you start with the empty project, which provides more opportunity to discuss the different parts of a Web Part solution in more detail. As is typical when creating a SharePoint project in Visual Studio, the wizard asks which trust level you would like to use. In this sample, choose a farm solution, because code-based sandboxed solutions are deprecated, and you can do a lot more interesting things with farm solutions.

Next, you need to add a Web Part to this project. The preferred way is to use the Visual Studio SharePoint Project Item for this. Visual Studio 2012 has three Web Part item templates:

- Web Part

- Visual Web Part

- Silverlight Web Part

The difference between the Visual Web Part and the Web Part SharePoint Project Item is that the Visual Web Part uses an .ascx user control to build the UI for the Web Part, and the nonvisual Web Part SharePoint Project Item requires you to build your control hierarchy and rendering. The Visual Web Part does not deploy an .ascx file to SharePoint, which was the initial case with Visual Studio 2010. Instead Visual Studio 2012 compiles the .ascx file and merges it with your code-behind file. The Visual Web Part is the preference if you like to have more separation between the user interface and the logic in your Web Part.

This sample uses the nonvisual Web Part SharePoint Project Item. After you add the project item to the project, Visual Studio adds a few files to the project, as shown in Figure 8-2. The new project item creates a new node in Solution Explorer with the name of the Web Part. Under that node, it will add three files:

- **Elements.xml**   The element manifest for the Web Part containing a *Module* element to deploy the Web Part control description file to the Web Part Gallery

- **WebPart1.cs**   The actual Web Part implementation

- **WebPart1.webpart**   The Web Part control description file that will be deployed to the Web Part Gallery

If you don't have a site-scoped Feature in your project, Visual Studio will also add a new Feature to the project. Web Parts must be deployed through a site-scoped Feature because the Web Part Gallery exists only on the site collection level in the root web.

FIGURE 8-2 The Visual Studio solution adds a Web Part project item.

Implementing the Web Part

Examining the Web Part class file reveals that it derives from the ASP.NET *WebPart* class. This is the default, and recommended, method for creating a new Web Part. The generated class file contains an override for the *CreateChildControls* method (which is discussed in more detail later in this chapter, in the "Using *CreateChildControls*" section). Now you need to make sure that the Web Part writes a Hello message to the current user. Listing 8-1 shows how a new *LiteralControl* object is added to the *Controls* collection of the Web Part and how the current user's name is retrieved by using the *SPContext* object.

LISTING 8-1 A Web Part that writes a line of text containing the current user's display name

```
namespace WingTipWebParts.WebPart1
{
  [ToolboxItemAttribute(false)]
  public class WebPart1: WebPart
  {
    protected override void CreateChildControls()
    {
      this.Controls.Add(
        new LiteralControl(
          String.Format("Hello {0}!", SPContext.Current.Web.CurrentUser.Name)));
    }
  }
}
```

Microsoft Visual Studio also automatically adds a safe control entry for this Web Part. You can locate it if you right-click the Web Part project item in Solution Explorer, click Properties, and select the safe control entry's property, as shown in Figure 8-3.

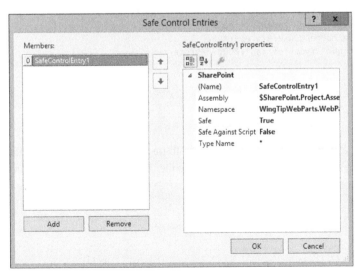

FIGURE 8-3 Visual Studio automatically adds safe control entries for the Web Parts that are added through a Web Part project item.

Examining the Web Part control description file

The next file to examine is the Web Part control description file, or the .webpart file. This file is also automatically generated when the Web Part SharePoint Project Item is added to the project. This file will be added to the Web Part Gallery to provide users with an easy and user-friendly way to locate the Web Part when they want to edit Web Part pages. This template file allows you to specify a title and description for the Web Part, in addition to other default property values that will be used when adding the Web Part to a page.

Listing 8-2 shows the .webpart file after modifying the *Title* and *Description* properties and after adding one of the Web Part default properties—*Height*. The Web Part control description file is divided into two sections. The first one, under the *metaData* element, defines which Web Part type to use and also includes the default error message that should be shown if an error occurs when the Web Part Manager imports the file. The second part, under the *data* element, defines all the property values that should be used for the Web Part instance when the instance is added to a page from the Web Part Gallery. Each property has a name, a type, and a value. Notice that this value is only the start value; after the Web Part is added to a page, any changes in the .webpart file will not be reflected in the Web Parts. Think of the .webpart file as a template or configuration of a Web Part instance.

LISTING 8-2 Modified Web Part control description file

```
<webParts>
  <webPart xmlns="http://schemas.microsoft.com/WebPart/v3">
    <metaData>
      <type name="WingTipWebParts.WebPart1.WebPart1,
        $SharePoint.Project.AssemblyFullName$" />
      <importErrorMessage>$Resources:core,ImportErrorMessage;</importErrorMessage>
    </metaData>
    <data>
      <properties>
        <property name="Title" type="string">Hello user!</property>
        <property name="Description" type="string">
          Says hello to the current user</property>
        <property name="Height" type="string">200px</property>
      </properties>
    </data>
  </webPart>
</webParts>
```

If this was a Web Part that you didn't want the users to add to pages, for example, you wanted it to be added to pages by using only code, you could delete this file. The Web Part would still work but would not be available for selection in the Web Part Gallery.

Understanding the element manifest

The element manifest is responsible for deploying the Web Part control description file to the Web Part Gallery. The file contains a *Module* element, which you already examined in Chapter 7, targeted at the Web Part Gallery. The *List* attribute of the *Module* element is set to 113, which is the ID of the Web Part Gallery list template and defined in the global Onet.xml file, and the *Url* attribute points to the actual Web Part Gallery URL at *_catalogs/wp*.

The *Module* element contains a *File* element that represents the Web Part control description file. Typically you don't need to change anything here unless you want to change the file name of the deployed .webpart file (the *Url* attribute). However, under the *File* element is one *Property* element with the *Name* attribute set to *Group*. This specific element defines in which group in the Web Part Gallery the Web Part should be available. By default, the element is set to *Custom*, and you should always change this value to something more appropriate. For instance, use your project, company, or customer name, or use one of the default categories. Listing 8-3 shows the Web Part control description file with a modified *Group* property.

LISTING 8-3 The element manifest containing a *Module* element that provisions the Web Part control description file to the Web Part Gallery

```
<Elements xmlns="http://schemas.microsoft.com/sharepoint/" >
 <Module Name="WebPart1" List="113" Url="_catalogs/wp">
   <File Path="WebPart1\WebPart1.webpart"
     Url="WingTipWebParts_WebPart1.webpart" Type="GhostableInLibrary">
     <Property Name="Group" Value="Wingtip" />
   </File>
 </Module>
</Elements>
```

Deploying and uninstalling a Web Part

At this point, you are ready to deploy your first Web Part. You can use F5 debugging to deploy the solution and automatically activate the feature on the site you specified when the project was created. Visual Studio will start a new instance of your web browser and go to the Home page of the site. If you edit that page and choose to add a new Web Part by using the ribbon menu, you will discover that the Web Part Gallery and Web Part are deployed into the category called Wingtip, which was the group specified in the element manifest. In the Parts pane, the title, defined in the Web Part control description file, is visible, and to the far right both the title and description are visible after the Web Part is selected. Figure 8-4 shows this simple Web Part in the Web Part Gallery. Click Add to add the Web Part to the page.

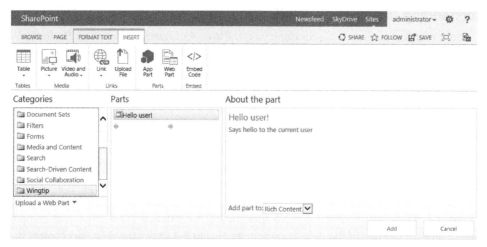

FIGURE 8-4 There is one Web Part Gallery per site collection, and that gallery contains Web Parts organized by category.

When the Web Part is added to the page, the page reloads and the Web Part is rendered. The page displays the title of the Web Part and renders the contents as specified in the implementation of the custom Web Part class, as shown in Figure 8-5.

FIGURE 8-5 A custom Web Part displays the name of the current user.

You've learned how to build a very simple Web Part as a farm solution, and you've learned about the different pieces needed to properly provision the Web Part so that it is available from the Web Part Gallery. This Web Part doesn't use any restricted APIs or anything that is scoped outside of the site collection, so you can change the *Sandboxed Solution* property of the project so that the project is targeted for sandboxed deployment; you can just redeploy it and it will work.

When you're using Visual Studio and perform F5 debugging, after you stop your debugging session, the solution by default is retracted, but not completely. If you added one of your Web Parts to a page during the debugging session, that Web Part will still be on that page and produce an error message, because SharePoint cannot find the assembly and control, which was retracted when the debugging session ended. Also, the Web Part control description file provisioned to the Web Part Gallery will still be there. SharePoint does not automatically remove items provisioned by the *Module* element when the solution is retracted. So users editing a page will still believe that they can use the Web Part, and when they try to add it, they will get an error message stating that "The operation could not be completed because the item was removed from the gallery." It is good practice to mitigate this by using a Feature receiver on your Web Part Features. You do this by adding a new event receiver to the Web Part, which you learned to do in previous chapters, and then implementing the *FeatureDeactivating* of the Feature receiver, as illustrated in Listing 8-4. Note that this event will fire only when the Feature is deactivated, not when it is uninstalled, so you should deactivate the feature before uninstalling.

LISTING 8-4 The *FeatureDeactivating* method of the Feature receiver, used to remove the Web Part templates from the Web Part Gallery

```
public override void FeatureDeactivating(SPFeatureReceiverProperties properties)
{
 SPSite site = properties.Feature.Parent as SPSite;
 if (site != null)
 {
   SPList gallery = site.RootWeb.GetCatalog(SPListTemplateType.WebPartCatalog);
   foreach (SPListItem item in gallery.Items.Cast<SPListItem>().ToArray())
   {
     SPFile file = item.File;
     using (XmlReader reader = XmlReader.Create(file.OpenBinaryStream()))
     {
       XDocument doc = XDocument.Load(reader);
       var typeName = from element in doc.Descendants()
         where element.Name.LocalName == "type"
         select element.Attribute("name");
       if (typeName.Count() == 1)
       {
         Type type = Type.GetType(typeName.First().Value);
         if (type.Assembly.FullName == this.GetType().Assembly.FullName)
         {
           item.Delete();
         }
       }
     }
   }
 }
}
```

The Feature deactivation code in Listing 8-4 reads the XML definition for all the Web Part control description files and takes a look at the type of the control in the file by using a Linq-to-XML query. This requires you to add using statements for *System.Linq*, *System.Xml*, and *System.Xml.Linq* in your code file. The code compares this control type with the type of the current assembly and, if they are the same, removes the template file. This ensures that any Web Parts from the current assembly are removed.

Deploying a Web Part page with Web Parts

In Chapter 7, you focused on how to deploy site pages and learned briefly about Web Part pages. Typically, you want to deploy Web Part pages, or wiki pages that contain a default set of Web Parts. You now examine two approaches: the first is a purely declarative approach, and the second uses an object called *SPLimitedWebPartManager*. Finally, you learn about the special case when you have a wiki page.

Deploying Web Parts by using a declarative approach

One approach to deploying Web Parts is to use a declarative approach. The benefit of the declarative method is that it works both with farm solutions as well as sandboxed solutions. To deploy a Web Part page with a Web Part, you start by deploying the page by using a *Module* element, just as you did in Chapter 7. You need to add a new .aspx page to the *Module* SharePoint Project Item. Listing 8-5 shows the source for the Web Part page, which contains two zones, one on the left side and one on the right.

LISTING 8-5 A custom Web Part page with two zones, named Left and Right.

```
<%@Page Language="C#" MasterPageFile="~masterurl/default.master"
 Inherits="Microsoft.SharePoint.WebPartPages.WebPartPage, Microsoft.SharePoint,
 Version=15.0.0.0, Culture=neutral, PublicKeyToken=71e9bce111e9429c" %>
<%@ Register Tagprefix="WebPartPages" Namespace="Microsoft.SharePoint.WebPartPages"
 Assembly="Microsoft.SharePoint, Version=15.0.0.0, Culture=neutral,
 PublicKeyToken=71e9bce111e9429c" %>
<asp:Content ID="Content1" ContentPlaceHolderId="PlaceHolderMain" runat="server">
<div>
<div style="float:left;width:50%">
  <WebPartPages:WebPartZone ID="left" Title="Left" runat="server">
  </WebPartPages:WebPartZone>
</div>
<div style="float:right;width:50%">
  <WebPartPages:WebPartZone ID="right" Title="Right" runat="server">
  </WebPartPages:WebPartZone>
</div>
</div>
</asp:Content>
```

Next, you modify the element manifest for the *Module* SharePoint Project Item. Assume you want to deploy this page to a team site and the *Site Pages* library. To do this, you specify a *Url* attribute pointing to that library on the *Module* element, as illustrated in Listing 8-6; you update the *File* element with a modified *Url* attribute so that the page will be provisioned in the root of that library; and you set the *Type* property.

The next modification to the element manifest is adding a new element as a child to the *File* element: the *AllUsersWebPart* element. This element is used to add a Web Part to a specific zone. Listing 8-6 shows how the *AllUsersWebPart* is given a unique ID in addition to the name of a Web Part zone and the order within that zone. The contents of the element is identical to the data in the Web Parts control description file deployed to the Web Part Gallery. Note that that XML is enclosed in CDATA tags because the contents of the *AllUsersWebPart* must be text data.

```
<Elements xmlns="http://schemas.microsoft.com/sharepoint/">
 <Module Name="PageModule" Url="SitePages">
   <File Path="PageModule\WebPartPage.aspx" Url="WebPartPage.aspx"
Type="GhostableInLibrary">
     <AllUsersWebPart ID="LeftWebPart" WebPartOrder="0" WebPartZoneID="Left">
       <![CDATA[
       <webParts>
         <webPart xmlns="http://schemas.microsoft.com/WebPart/v3">
           <metaData>
             <type name="WingTipWebParts.WebPart1.WebPart1,
               $SharePoint.Project.AssemblyFullName$" />
             <importErrorMessage>$Resources:core,ImportErrorMessage;</importErrorMessage>
           </metaData>
           <data>
             <properties>
               <property name="Title" type="string">Hello user!</property>
               <property name="Height" type="string">200px</property>
             </properties>
           </data>
         </webPart>
       </webParts>
       ]]>
     </AllUsersWebPart>
   </File>
 </Module>
</Elements>
```

The *File* element can have zero or more *AllUsersWebPart* elements, which means that you can de-ploy a complete dashboard of Web Parts. Just make sure that all Web Parts have unique IDs. You can use this method to deploy your Web Parts or the out-of-the-box Web Parts.

Just as you learned about removing the Web Part control description file from the Web Part Gallery, you should consider removing the custom provisioned pages. Remember that any customizations that the user has made to the pages will be lost if you decide to remove the pages.

Deploying a Web Part by using *SPLimitedWebPartManager*

If you need to work with existing pages, or you want a more programmatic and dynamic approach to deploying Web Parts, you could use the *SPLimitedWebPartManager* object. This is a special object that gives you access to a limited set of operations on the Web Part Manager object, specifically when no *HttpContext* is present, such as in a Feature receiver activated through Windows PowerShell. You can use the *SPLimitedWebPartManager* to add, edit, and remove Web Parts in addition to connecting and disconnecting them, which is discussed in the "Using Web Part connections" section later in this chapter.

The *SPLimitedWebPartManager* object works only with Web Part pages, which have Web Part zones. You should not use it on wiki pages. Listing 8-7 shows site-scoped Feature activation code that retrieves a Web Part page from the root web, the same page created in Listing 8-6, and adds a new Image Web Part to the zone with the ID equal to *"Right"*.

LISTING 8-7 Web Parts added programmatically when a feature is activated by using a Feature receiver

```
public override void FeatureActivated(SPFeatureReceiverProperties properties)
{
 SPSite site = properties.Feature.Parent as SPSite;
 if (site != null)
 {
   SPFile page = site.RootWeb.GetFile("SitePages/WebPartPage.aspx");
   using (SPLimitedWebPartManager manager =
     page.GetLimitedWebPartManager(PersonalizationScope.Shared))
   {
     ImageWebPart image = new ImageWebPart();
     image.ImageLink = "_layouts/15/images/homepage.gif";
     image.ChromeType = PartChromeType.None;
     manager.AddWebPart(image, "Right", 0);
   }
 }
}
```

The *SPLimitedWebPart* manager must always be created from a *SPFile* object and with a person-alization scope. The personalization scope can either be *Shared* or *User*. The *shared scope* means that you're editing the state of the page that is shared among all users, whereas the *user scope* is for the current user only.

To add a Web Part to a zone by using *SPLimitedWe bPartManager*, you only need to create the Web Part control and initialize the properties with the values you need for your solution. Then you use the *AddWebPart* method to add the Web Part to a zone by using the zone ID and the order num-ber in the zone. Using *0* (zero) as the zone index adds the Web Part as the first Web Part in that zone.

Deploying Web Parts to wiki pages

Wiki pages are a special version of Web Part pages that have a wiki zone in which you can alternate wiki content and Web Parts. To insert a Web Part into a wiki zone, adding the Web Part to a hidden Web Part zone and inserting special markup into the wiki zone that references the Web Part in the hidden zone is required. Fortunately, a helper method does all of this for you. Listing 8-8 shows how to insert a Web Part into a wiki zone.

```
SPFile homepage = web.GetFile("SitePages/Home.aspx");
WikiEditPage.InsertWebPartIntoWikiPage(
 homepage,
 new ImageWebPart()
 {
   ImageLink = "_layouts/15/images/homepage.gif",
   ChromeType = PartChromeType.None
 },
 0);
```

The file retrieved in this case is the Home page of a team site. Using the static method *InsertWeb-PartIntoWikiPage* of the *WikiEditPage* class, you specify the page, the Web Part, and the desired insertion position for the Web Part. The position in this case is not the order of the Web Parts but rather the position in the markup of the wiki zone.

Deploying Web Parts by using client-side code

When working with Web Parts, you're not restricted to using only Collaborative Application Markup Language (CAML) or full trust code; you also have the option of using the client-side object model (CSOM), and in SharePoint 2013, even the Representational State Transfer (REST) APIs. These options are very useful when you want to build SharePoint apps or remote applications for hosted services such as SharePoint Online.

The *SPLimitedWebPartManager* has its own REST endpoint, and it can be used to retrieve and edit Web Parts. To get a list of all the Web Parts, the following REST Uniform Resource Identifier (URI) could be used:

```
http://wingtiptoys/_api/web/getfilebyserverrelativeurl('/SitePages/WebPartPage.aspx')
/getlimitedwebpartmanager(1)/WebParts
```

The preceding URI retrieves the page by its server relative URL and then retrieves the limited Web Part Manager, passing in *1* as a parameter, which indicates the shared scope. Finally, the URI retrieves all the Web Parts on that page. To retrieve data about one specific Web Part, you retrieve the ID from the REST *GET* query and pass that into the following URI, replacing the GUID with your ID:

```
http://wingtiptoys/_api/web/getfilebyserverrelativeurl('/SitePages/WebPartPage.aspx')
/getlimitedwebpartmanager(1)/WebParts
/GetById('6c5ee333-cf88-4c32-a192-3152c4f10f8c')/WebPart
```

Controlling Web Part rendering

You just built a very simple Web Part that rendered a simple piece of text on a page. Now you learn how to control the rendering and create a good user experience. There are several approaches to this, and different methods are favored by different developers. The methods discussed here aren't specific to SharePoint but rather reflect standard ASP.NET control development.

Overriding the *RenderContents* method

One of the simplest approaches for rendering the Web Part contents, which gives you full control of the generated output, is to override the *RenderContents* method. The *RenderContents* method takes a *HtmlTextWriter* object as an argument, and you use this object to render the exact HTML that you would like your Web Part to show. Listing 8-9 shows how to override this method and write an HTML heading.

LISTING 8-9 A Web Part overriding the *RenderContents* method to create the UI

```
using Microsoft.SharePoint;
using System.Web.UI;
using System.Web.UI.WebControls.WebParts;

namespace WebParts.Rendering.OverrideRenderContents
{
  public class OverrideRenderContents : WebPart
  {
    protected override void RenderContents(HtmlTextWriter writer)
    {
      writer.RenderBeginTag(HtmlTextWriterTag.H1);
      writer.Write("Hello " + SPContext.Current.Web.CurrentUser.Name);
      writer.RenderEndTag();
    }
  }
}
```

The overwritten *RenderContents* method uses the *HtmlTextWriter* and its methods to render HTML content. You use the *RenderBeginTag* to render the start tag of an *H1* element and then write normal text. Finally, you must end the *H1* element by using the *RenderEndTag* method. This is a straightforward method that allows you to have full control of the generated HTML.

It is very important to note that you override only the *RenderContents* method and not the *Render* method. The *Render* method renders the necessary chrome that a Web Part needs to be functional, and is responsible for calling the *RenderContents* method. The chrome of a Web Part is, for instance, the top bar and title of the Web Part and the Web Part menu.

Using *CreateChildControls*

Another approach to rendering the Web Part contents is to override the *CreateChildControls* method. This is also the method that Visual Studio suggests when you create a Web Part project item, and this method should be the starting point for the vast majority of your Web Parts. Instead of working with the HTML elements directly through the *HtmlTextWriter*, you build a control tree of ASP.NET and HTML controls. The default implementation of the *RenderContents* method will traverse the control tree and render each control and its child controls in the order in which they are added to the control tree. The *WebPart* has a property called *Controls* that is inherited from the *System.Web.UI.Control* object. This property is a collection of *Control* objects, and this collection of objects is the control tree. In Listing 8-10, you build exactly the same Web Part as you built in Listing 8-9, but this time you do so by adding ASP.NET controls to the control tree.

LISTING 8-10 Web Part overriding the *CreateChildControls* method to build the control tree and UI

```
using Microsoft.SharePoint;
using System.Web.UI.HtmlControls;
using System.Web.UI.WebControls.WebParts;

namespace WebParts.Rendering.OverrideCreateChildControls
{
  public class OverrideCreateChildControls : WebPart
  {
    protected override void CreateChildControls()
    {
      HtmlGenericControl heading = new HtmlGenericControl("h1");
      heading.InnerText = "Hello " + SPContext.Current.Web.CurrentUser.Name;
      this.Controls.Add(heading);
    }
  }
}
```

First, you need to create the *H1* element, and you do this by using the *HtmlGenericControl* and passing in the element name. The inner text of the element is set by using the *InnerText* property. Then, you need to add this control to the Web Parts control tree by using the *Add* method of the *Controls* property. When this Web Part is rendered on a page, the default *RenderContents* implementation traverses the control tree and renders the added *HtmlGenericControl*.

Responding to events

One benefit of using the ASP.NET controls is having the abstraction layer over the actual HTML, which lets ASP.NET control the generated HTML. Another benefit of using ASP.NET controls is that you can take advantage of ASP.NET Web Forms features such as events, callbacks, and view state.

It's time to examine a more advanced scenario in which you expect the users to enter data and want the Web Part to act upon that data. Listing 8-11 shows a Web Part that has a text box in which the users can view and edit the title of the current site (*SPWeb*). It also has a button that updates the title of the web when clicked. You extend this sample by adding a validation control that makes sure that the user doesn't specify an empty title, and you add a *Label* control that shows an indication that the web title has been updated.

LISTING 8-11 Web Part that has a button in the UI and uses server-side code to respond to click events

```
using Microsoft.SharePoint;
using System;
using System.Web.UI.WebControls;
using System.Web.UI.WebControls.WebParts;

namespace WebParts.Rendering.EventHandlersWebPart
{
 public class EventHandlersWebPart : WebPart
 {
    protected Button button;
    protected TextBox textBox;
    protected Label message;
    protected RequiredFieldValidator validator;

    protected override void CreateChildControls()
    {
      textBox = new TextBox();
      textBox.Text = SPContext.Current.Web.Title;
      textBox.ID = "titleTextBox";
      this.Controls.Add(textBox);

      button = new Button();
      button.Text = "Update Title";
      button.Click += button_Click;
      this.Controls.Add(button);

      message = new Label();
      this.Controls.Add(message);

      validator = new RequiredFieldValidator();
      validator.ControlToValidate = textBox.ID;
      validator.ErrorMessage = "You must supply a title";
      this.Controls.Add(validator);
    }

    void button_Click(object sender, EventArgs e)
    {
      SPContext.Current.Web.Title = textBox.Text;
      SPContext.Current.Web.Update();
      message.Text = "Title updated";
    }
 }
}
```

In the Web Part, you define the four controls—the text box, button, validation control, and message—as protected members. In *CreateChildControls*, you instantiate every one of these controls, set properties on them, and then add them to the control tree. In the text box, you set the default value to the title of the current site, and you also need to specify an ID for that control. That ID is required by the validation control so that the validation control knows which control to validate. You give the button a title and then do something interesting: you add a custom event handler, which should be invoked whenever the button is clicked. This is an ASP.NET feature that will do a post-back to the page when the button is clicked and then invoke the event handler specified on the *Click* event.

The event handler for the *Click* event is implemented in the *button_Click* method, and it takes the value from the text box and sets it as the new title for the current web. It will also update the message control to notify the user that the title has been updated.

The drawback with this method is that each control is rendered one after the other, meaning that you have less control of the look and feel of the Web Part. Of course, you could add even more ASP.NET controls such as *HtmlTable*, *HtmlTableRow*, and *HtmlTableCell* to control the rendering. If you have a more advanced UI for your Web Part, adding controls will result in a lot of controls and a large control tree, which impacts the server-side processing in terms of CPU and memory usage. In many cases, it also results in code that is really hard to follow.

Combining *CreateChildControls* and *RenderContents*

One way to improve the rendering if you require more styling of your Web Parts is to combine the *CreateChildControls* and *RenderContents* methods. You define the controls that require interaction in *CreateChildControls* and control the layout in the *RenderContents* method. Listing 8-12 shows how to alter the previous Web Part by overriding the *RenderContents* method, and then render out the four controls in an HTML table. This approach also separates the logic a bit from the design.

LISTING 8-12 Using *RenderContents* and the *CreateChildControls* method to have better control of the UI

```
protected override void RenderContents(System.Web.UI.HtmlTextWriter writer)
{
  writer.RenderBeginTag(System.Web.UI.HtmlTextWriterTag.Table);

  writer.RenderBeginTag(System.Web.UI.HtmlTextWriterTag.Tr);
  writer.RenderBeginTag(System.Web.UI.HtmlTextWriterTag.Td);
  writer.Write("Site title: ");
  writer.RenderEndTag();

  writer.RenderBeginTag(System.Web.UI.HtmlTextWriterTag.Td);
  textBox.RenderControl(writer);
  validator.RenderControl(writer);
  writer.RenderEndTag();
  writer.RenderEndTag();

  writer.RenderBeginTag(System.Web.UI.HtmlTextWriterTag.Tr);
  writer.RenderBeginTag(System.Web.UI.HtmlTextWriterTag.Td);
  button.RenderControl(writer);
  writer.RenderEndTag();

  writer.RenderBeginTag(System.Web.UI.HtmlTextWriterTag.Td);
  message.RenderControl(writer);
  writer.RenderEndTag();
  writer.RenderEndTag();

  writer.RenderEndTag();
}
```

In the *RenderContents* method, you render an HTML table with rows and columns (*Tr* and *Td* tags, respectively). In the table cells in which you want the controls to be rendered, you use the *RenderControl* of those controls you added and pass in the *HtmlTextWriter* object. In this way, you can create a more appealing UI without adding a lot of objects to the control tree, which is shown in Figure 8-6.

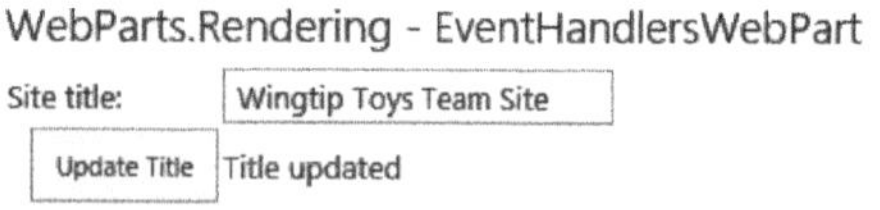
WebParts.Rendering - EventHandlersWebPart
Site title:
Wingtip Toys Team Site
Update Title
Title updated

FIGURE 8-6 Override the *RenderContents* method of the Web Part to have more control over the Web Part rendering.

Using Visual Web Parts

In all examples in this chapter, you must create objects or write one tag at a time to generate the UI. As soon as you have more than a handful of controls, getting an overview of what the interface actually looks like is difficult. If you've previously worked with ASP.NET, you are likely used to a more visual approach when building controls and pages. Fortunately, Visual Studio 2012 provides another Web Part project item called a Visual Web Part. A *Visual Web Part* is essentially a user control (.ascx) that you use to build the UI so that you can mix HTML content with server-side controls. It even allows you to do this in a design surface. Figure 8-7 shows you how the design surface might look when you create a Visual Web Part with the same functionality as in the Web Part in Listing 8-12.

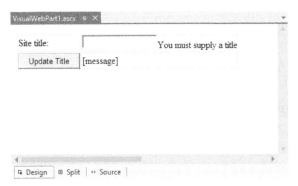

FIGURE 8-7 Visual Web Parts allow you to create the UI by using the design mode in Visual Studio 2012.

Each time you save the .ascx file in Visual Studio 2012, a partial class file is generated from the .ascx file that builds the control tree from the HTML content and the server-side controls. Figure 8-8 shows you the Visual Web Part SharePoint Project Item and the generated file that has the extension of .ascx.g.cs.

FIGURE 8-8 A Visual Web Part uses a control template when building the UI, and Visual Studio automatically generates a .cs file for the control template when saved.

The code in the user control file (.ascx) looks like the code in Listing 8-13, but the page directives that are automatically added by Visual Studio are omitted in the listing. The content is a mix of HTML tags and ASP.NET server-side controls, and this approach gives much better separation of the UI design from the business logic in the code-behind file, which you examine next.

LISTING 8-13 The contents of the Visual Web Part .ascx file, allowing for a combination of HTML markup and ASP.NET server-side controls

```
<table>
 <tr>
   <td>
     Site title:
   </td>
   <td>
     <asp:TextBox ID="siteTitle" runat="server"/>
     <asp:RequiredFieldValidator ID="rfv" ControlToValidate="siteTitle"
       ErrorMessage="You must supply a title" runat="server"/>
   </td>
 </tr>
 <tr>
   <td>
     <asp:Button runat="server" Text="Update Title" OnClick="button_Click" />
   </td>
   <td>
     <asp:Label runat="server" ID="message"/>
   </td>
 </tr>
</table>
```

Using Solution Explorer in Visual Studio 2012, you can expand the Visual Web Part SharePoint Project Item and drill down to the .ascx.g.cs file and open it. In that file is the precompiled implementation of the markup you wrote in the user control. You should not modify this file; if you do, any modifications will be overwritten every time you save the user control (.ascx) file.

Each Visual Web Part has a code-behind file, which should contain the logic for the Web Part. Listing 8-14 shows you how the *Page_Load* method is modified to set the initial values of the server-side controls. It also shows the server-side event handler for the button click event, *button_Click*, which looks exactly the same as in the previous implementation of this Web Part, seen in Listing 8-11.

LISTING 8-14 The server-side code of a Visual Web Part user control

```
protected void Page_Load(object sender, EventArgs e)
{
 siteTitle.Text = SPContext.Current.Web.Title;
}
protected void button_Click(object sender, EventArgs e)
{
 SPContext.Current.Web.Title = siteTitle.Text;
 SPContext.Current.Web.Update();
 message.Text = "Title updated";
}
```

In Listing 8-13 and Listing 8-14, the Visual Web Part contains fewer lines of code and an easier-to-follow implementation. Visual Web Parts are a good starting point if you need to build a Web Part that has a rich UI because they allow you to work with the UI in a much easier way. Worth noticing is that even though you have good control of the actual markup rendered, all HTML markup will be precompiled into ASP.NET objects and a control tree, and you should thoroughly consider the performance implications of such a solution. Every control that ASP.NET needs to keep track of adds to the amount of CPU and RAM used, and the View State might grow larger. For a Web Part that is extensively used throughout a farm, this could cause a performance bottleneck.

Working with Web Part properties

So far this chapter has discussed the rendering of Web Parts and how you can provision Web Parts to the Web Part Gallery so that users can add and remove Web Parts from pages. But one of the core pieces in the Web Part framework is that all Web Part instances can have properties that can be modified by the users and that are persisted (in the case of SharePoint, the persistent storage is the content databases). This section covers how to make Web Part properties persistent and how to make them editable by users through the UI. It also examines more deeply how to customize the edit interface for Web Part properties, specifically by using Editor Parts.

Persisting Web Part properties

To add a property to a Web Part that can be persisted, you first need to add a property and then mark that property by using the *Personalizable* attribute:

```
[Personalizable]
public string Text { get; set; }
```

When SharePoint, or rather the Web Part Manager, sees this attribute on a Web Part property, it serializes and persists the value of the attribute. When rendering the page where the Web Part is placed, the Web Part Manager deserializes the value and sets the property on that Web Part. To set this value, either you could use the programmatic approach, which is to use *SPLimitedWebPartManager*, or you could set the default value by using the Web Part control description file, which is done by adding a new *property* element to the *properties* element:

```
<properties>
 <property name="Text" type="string">This is some random text</property>
</properties>
```

Remember that this default value is used only if the Web Part is added through the Web Part Gallery, not if it is added to a page through code. For properties that require a value, it is always good to also set the default value in the constructor of the Web Part.

By default, any property that is using the *Personalization* attribute can be personalized because the default personalization scope of the attribute is set to *User* scoped. When the personalization scope is set, *User* users are allowed to override the persisted value when personalizing the Web Part, and the value of the property will persisted on a per-user basis. To prohibit this behavior, you can set the personalization scope to *Shared*. Properties with a *Shared* personalization scope can be edited only in the shared view of the page:

```
[Personalizable(PersonalizationScope.User)] // same as [Personalizable]
public string Property { get; set; }
[Personalizable(PersonalizationScope.Shared)] //
public string SharedOnlyProperty { get; set; }
```

To allow the users to actually edit the properties from the web UI, you need to declare another couple of attributes on the property. The following snippet shows how a typical Web Part property could look:

```
[Personalizable]
[WebBrowsable]
[WebDisplayName("Text content")]
[WebDescription("Text displayed in Web Part")]
[Category("Wingtip")]
public string Text { get; set; }
```

First, you use the *Personalizable* attribute to tell the Web Part Manager that the property value should be persisted, in this case by using the *User* personalization scope. Then you add another couple of attributes that tell SharePoint how you want to enable editing in the web interface. The *WebBrowsable* attribute tells SharePoint that you would like the users to be able to edit the property and to generate a default input interface for this property. In this case, the property is of the type *string*, so a text box will be rendered as the input field. The *WebDisplayName* attribute allows you to specify a user-friendly display name for the property, and *WebDescription* allows you to provide a description. Finally, the *Category* attribute allows you to specify a name for the category in which you want the property to be visible. If you omit the *Category* attribute, the property will end up in the *Miscellaneous* category.

The UI generated for editing the property is based on the type of the property. The types in Table 8-2 are natively supported by SharePoint. Figure 8-9 shows you how the edit interface looks for the standard types.

TABLE 8-2 Common SharePoint *WebPartZone* properties

Property type	Edit interface generated
string or char	Text box
bool	Check box
int, byte, sbyte, short, ushort, uint, long, ulong, double, float, or decimal	Text box that validates that the value is numeric
DateTime	Text box that requires a valid date value or date and time value
Unit	Text box that requires a valid unit (for example, 30px, 30pt)
Enumerations	Drop-down list box with available enumeration values

As long as the value of the property type can be represented by and converted to a string, you have another option, which is to use the *TypeConverter attribute* to specify which converter object type to use. The property value is editable through a text box and only values that can be converted by using the specified *TypeConverter* are allowed to be stored. This is, for instance, how a property that has the *Guid* type could be made editable:

```
[Personalizable]
[WebBrowsable]
[Category("Wingtip")]
[TypeConverter(typeof(GuidConverter))]
public Guid VanityGuid { get; set; }
```

The *TypeConverter attribute* specifies that the *Guid* property should be converted from and to a string representation that uses the *GuidConverter* type converter class from the *System.Component-Model* namespace. This property is shown in Figure 8-9.

FIGURE 8-9 Web Part properties can be editable through the web interface if they are of types that SharePoint recognize.

Using custom Editor Parts

Although in most cases, the default generated user interface for Web Part properties might be sufficient, in some cases you will want to have more control over how the properties are edited. For instance, you might have dependencies between properties, you might want to add validation rules, or you might need to load data from another source. Luckily, these scenarios have been considered!

You are going to create a Web Part that has a property that contains the title of a list in the current site and shows the number of items in that list. Listing 8-15 shows how you could implement that property and the *CreateChildControls* for such a Web Part. Worth noting is that the code specifically sets the *WebBrowsable* attribute to *false*. Not having the *WebBrowsable* attribute present is the same thing as specifying it as *false*, but in this case, you do it to explicitly show in the source code that you do not want the standard generated interface for that property.

LISTING 8-15 A Web Part with one personalizable property that cannot be edited in the web interface

```
public class CustomWebPart : WebPart
{
 [Personalizable]
 [WebBrowsable(false)]
 public string ListTitle { get; set; }

 protected override void CreateChildControls()
 {
   if (!String.IsNullOrEmpty(ListTitle))
   {
     SPList list = SPContext.Current.Web.Lists.TryGetList(ListTitle);
     if (list != null)
     {
       this.Controls.Add( new LiteralControl(
         String.Format("The list '{0}' contains {1} items",
           ListTitle, list.ItemCount)));
       return;
     }
   }
   this.Controls.Add(new LiteralControl("List not found or selected"));
 }
}
```

To create a custom user interface to edit the Web Part properties, you need to create an Editor Part. An *Editor Part* is a specialized control that can retrieve from and set property values on a Web Part. To create an Editor Part, you create a normal C# class file and choose to inherit from the *Editor-Part* class, which is a part of ASP.NET:

```
class CustomWebPartEditorPart: EditorPart { }
```

You build the UI of the Editor Part in exactly the same way you build it by using a Web Part. The most common approach is to use the *CreateChildControls* method to build a control tree. For this sample, you want the user to choose one list from the current site by using a drop down list. The *CreateChildControls* method of the Editor Part could look like the code in Listing 8-16.

LISTING 8-16 The *CreateChildControls* method of the Editor Part

```
protected DropDownList dropDown;
protected override void CreateChildControls()
{
  this.Title = "Custom properties";

  this.Controls.Add(new LiteralControl("List:"));

  dropDown = new DropDownList();

  SPContext.Current.Web.Lists.Cast<SPList>().
    Where(l => !l.Hidden).
    Select(l => l.Title).ToList().
    ForEach(t => dropDown.Items.Add(
      new ListItem(t, t)));

  this.Controls.Add(dropDown);
}
```

The *DropDownList* object is defined as a protected object in the class so that it is available for all methods in the class; you will need it later. The first thing you do in the *CreateChildControls* method is to set the title of the Editor Part by using the *Title* property. Although doing this is not necessary, it is a good practice. Next, you add descriptive text before you create the actual drop-down list. The drop-down list box is populated with the titles of all the lists in the current site, and then it is added to the control tree.

After building the Editor Part UI, you need to implement two abstract methods: *SyncChanges* and *ApplyChanges*. The *SyncChanges* method synchronizes the properties from the Web Part to the Editor Part, and *ApplyChanges* applies the property values to the Web Part. The implementation of both methods is in Listing 8-17.

LISTING 8-17 Implementation of the abstract *SyncChanges* and *ApplyChanges* methods in the Editor Part

```
public override void SyncChanges()
{
    EnsureChildControls();
    CustomWebPart wp = this.WebPartToEdit as CustomWebPart;
    dropDown.SelectedValue = wp.ListTitle;
}
public override bool ApplyChanges()
{
    EnsureChildControls();
    CustomWebPart wp = this.WebPartToEdit as CustomWebPart;
    wp.ListTitle = dropDown.SelectedValue;
    return true;
}
```

Both methods start by calling the *EnsureChildControls* method, which is important. The *EnsureChildControls* method, which is defined in the *System.Web.UI.Control* class, makes sure that the *CreateChildControls* method is called before proceeding. In this case, you rely on the fact that the drop-down list box is created and has values; if the *EnsureChildControls* method wasn't called, you could potentially get a null reference exception in the methods. Next, the code retrieves a reference to the Web Part that is using the Editor Part, which is done by using the *WebPartToEdit* property, which is then type-converted to the needed Web Part type. The *SyncChanges* method copies the Web Part property values into the Editor Part controls, and *ApplyChanges* copies the property values in the other direction, and set the values on the Web Part. The *ApplyChanges* method must return *true* when it successfully copies the values from the Editor Part to the Web Part and, if anything fails, should return *false*, prohibiting the Web Part from persisting the change.

You have done everything you need to do to implement a custom property editing interface by using an Editor Part. You next must connect this Editor Part to the Web Part by overriding the *CreateEditorParts* method in the Web Part. The *CreateEditorParts* method is defined in the *IWebEditable* interface, which the *WebPart* class implements. Listing 8-18 shows how the *CreateEditorParts* method should be overridden in this case.

LISTING 8-18 Implementation of the *IWebEditable CreateEditorParts* method in the Web Part

```
public override EditorPartCollection CreateEditorParts()
{
  List<EditorPart> editors = new List<EditorPart>();
  EditorPart editorPart = new CustomWebPartEditorPart();
  editorPart.ID = this.ID + "_editorPart";
  editors.Add(editorPart);
  return new EditorPartCollection(editors);
}
```

In this overridden method, you start by creating a *List<EditorPart>* object to which you will add the custom Editor Part classes. It is possible to have more than one Editor Part. Then you create a new instance of the Editor Part, and before you add the object to the list, you must set the *ID* of the Editor Part. Finally, you convert the list of Editor Parts to an *EditorPartCollection* object and return that.

The end result of this custom Editor Part looks like Figure 8-10. You've just learned how you can create a complete custom editor interface for your Web Part properties and implement logic, validation, and data retrieval.

FIGURE 8-10 Custom Editor Parts are always listed at the top of all Editor Parts.

Exploring advanced Web Part development

This last part of the chapter explains some of the more advanced Web Part development concepts. When used properly, these can give that little extra specialness to your Web Parts. You start by examining Web Part verbs and how to extend the default Web Part menu. You then learn about the Web Part Connections feature, which really shows the strengths in the Web Part framework and allows the user to build even more advanced Web Part pages. Finally, this chapter examines the case in which you are executing, for instance, web service requests in your Web Part, and it shows you how to do this asynchronously to improve performance. The chapter also explains how to take advantage of the .NET Framework 4.0+ parallel features to boost the performance of your Web Parts.

Using Web Part verbs

All Web Parts have a menu in the upper-right corner containing a set of menu options, also known as *Web Part verbs*, such as Minimize, Delete, Close, Export, and Edit (My) Web Part. The menu options shown depend on the Web Part, the user's permissions, settings on the Web Part, and whether the user is in edit mode. If none of the verbs are present, no menu is shown. The default verbs are added by the Web Part zone. For a specific Web Part, you can control some of the built-in verbs. The *WebPart* class has a set of properties that can be used to control this, which are listed in Table 8-3. You use these properties to configure your own Web Parts either by overriding the property or by specifying the property in the Web Part control description file:

```
<property name="AllowClose" type="bool">False</property>
```

TABLE 8-3 Web Part properties to control the Web Part menu

Property name	Purpose
AllowClose	Set to *false* to prohibit closing of the Web Part.
AllowConnect	Set to *false* to prohibit Web Part connections.
AllowEdit	Set to *false* to prohibit the users from editing the Web Part.
AllowHide	Set to *false* to prohibit hiding the Web Part.
AllowMinimize	Set to false to prohibit minimizing the Web Part.
AllowZoneChange	Not directly tied to the Web Part menu but related. Set to *false* to prohibit changing Web Part zone for the Web Part.

The Web Part framework allows you to add custom verbs to a Web Part. You can do this through the *IWebActionable* interface, which the *WebPart* class implements. There are two types of verbs that you can add: client-side verbs, which execute a JavaScript function on the client, or server-side verbs, which execute code on the server. Using both client-side and server-side verbs can be a very good way to add options to your Web Part. For instance, consider how you could implement a Web Part verb that allows you to shift between a basic mode and a detailed mode of a Web Part. To persist the selected display state, you use a property on the Web Part, which is defined as follows:

```
[Personalizable]
public bool ShowDetails { get; set; }
```

To add verbs to a Web Part menu, you must override the *Verbs* method of the *IWebActionable* interface. The default Web Part implementation returns an empty *WebPartVerbCollection*. Listing 8-19 shows how a server-side verb is being added to a Web Part. To create a new verb, the *WebPartVerb* class is used, and the constructor determines whether the verb is a server-side or client-side verb. There is also a constructor that allows you to define a verb that executes both client-side and server-side code.

LISTING 8-19 Overriding the *Verbs* property of a Web Part to extend the Web Part menu with new verbs

```
public override WebPartVerbCollection Verbs
{
 get
 {
   List<WebPartVerb> verbs = new List<WebPartVerb>();
   WebPartVerb detailsVerb = new WebPartVerb(this.ID + "_details", toggleDetails);
   detailsVerb.Text = "Show details";
   detailsVerb.Checked = this.ShowDetails;
   verbs.Add(detailsVerb);
   return new WebPartVerbCollection(base.Verbs, verbs);
 }
}
```

The overridden *Verbs* method creates a new *WebPartVerb* object by using the constructor that creates a server-side verb. The first parameter to the constructor is a unique ID for this *Verb*, constructed from the ID of the Web Part, and the second parameter is the name of the delegate method, shown in Listing 8-20, which should be invoked when the verb is selected on the Web Part menu. You must also set the *Text* property of the Web Part verb, which is the displayed text on the menu. In this case, you also use the *Checked* property of the verb; this is a property that can be used to indicate a checked state. Finally, you create a new *WebPartVerbCollection* object by using a *List<WebPartVerb>* containing the custom verbs. This implementation also uses the constructor of the *WebPartVerbCollection* that can take another *WebPartVerbCollection* object and merge it with the new verbs. This is done just in case the code inherits from another custom Web Part that has its own set of custom verbs.

LISTING 8-20 A server-side verb callback that automatically updates a personalizable property of the current Web Part

```
private void toggleDetails(object sender, WebPartEventArgs eventArgs)
{
  this.ShowDetails = !this.ShowDetails;
  SPFile file = SPContext.Current.File;
  using (var manager = file.GetLimitedWebPartManager(PersonalizationScope.User))
  {
    DetailsWebPart wp = manager.WebParts[this.ID] as DetailsWebPart;
    wp.ShowDetails = this.ShowDetails;
    manager.SaveChanges(wp);
  }
}
```

The *toggleDetails* delegate method that is invoked when the verb is selected on the Web Part menu changes the value of the *ShowDetails* property. Then the delegate method retrieves the current Web Part page and uses the *SPLimitedWebPartManager* to update this property change, because in this case you want to persist this property change.

Implementing a client-side Web Part verb is very similar to implementing a server-side verb. The difference is that you aren't specifying a delegate method but rather a JavaScript string to execute:

```
WebPartVerb clientVerb = new WebPartVerb(this.ID + "_clientVerb", "alert('Client-side Verb')");
clientVerb.Text = "Client-side Verb";
verbs.Add(clientVerb);
```

The constructor determines that the verb is a client-side Web Part verb because it is being passed a string as the second argument. The string passed into the constructor must be a valid JavaScript snippet that can be evaluated. If you're adding this code snippet to the same verb collection that contains the server-side verb, the Web Part menu would look like Figure 8-11.

FIGURE 8-11 The Web Part menu for a Web Part can be customized with custom actions, called verbs.

Using Web Part connections

One of the really interesting features of Web Parts is their ability to connect to each other. One Web Part can connect to one or more other Web Parts and then send information from the single Web Part to the others. This feature is very useful when building Web Part pages and dashboards, and by using it, the user can filter information in other Web Parts. Many of the default Web Parts in SharePoint 2013 support connections, and if you're using the Server edition of SharePoint 2013, you also get access to a set of specific filter Web Parts that can be used to filter the contents of other Web Parts.

A Web Part connection always has one provider and one consumer Web Part. The provider Web Part sends information to the consumer Web Part. *Filter Web Parts*, for instance, are provider Web Parts, and they send filtering information to the consuming Web Part. A Web Part can either be a consumer, a provider, or both. The connection set between a provider and a consumer needs a contract that both the provider and consumer understand. This contract is defined as a .NET Framework interface, which is implemented by the provider Web Part and used by the consumer Web Part. A provider Web Part can support multiple contracts, which means that it can implement multiple connection interfaces. The consumer can consume multiple contracts, but it cannot consume multiple connections of the same type. The Web Part framework comes with a set of predefined contracts that can be used to connect custom Web Parts to the out-of-the-box Web Parts, such as the XSLT List View Web Part:

- ■ *IWebPartField* Sends one cell or field of data

- ■ *IWebPartRow* Sends one row of data

- ■ *IWebPartTable* Sends a full table of data

- ■ *IWebPartParameters* Sends one cell or field of data based on a parameter

The default connection interfaces are very generic and are based on callbacks in the interface. These interfaces allow the consumer to call back into a method in the provider and retrieve the required data instead of just retrieving data from the provider.

Web Part connections are a part of the ASP.NET Web Part infrastructure, even though connections existed in SharePoint prior to ASP.NET 2.0. Web Part connections prior ASP.NET, or SharePoint Web Part connections, worked in similarly to the ASP.NET connections except regarding some important aspects. The connections that were used in earlier versions of SharePoint had the concept of client-side connections, which is not available in the ASP.NET Web Part infrastructure. Connections before ASP.NET could also connect across pages, which the today's connections cannot.

To understand the details of Web Part connections and how to build consumers and providers, you will create one provider Web Part that allows you to select one list from the lists available in the current site, and one consumer Web Part that reads the chosen list from the provider Web Part and shows details about the list. After you build these two Web Parts, you learn about how to connect them by using the UI and the *SPLimitedWebPartManager*, and how to connect them declaratively in a SharePoint Feature.

Building a provider Web Part

The very first task you need to perform is building the provider. This is a simple Web Part that hosts a drop-down list box, with the visible lists in the current site. Whenever a list is selected in the drop-down list box, the code gets the ID, a *Guid*, for the list and stores it in a local variable. Listing 8-21 shows the full implementation of such a Web Part.

LISTING 8-21 The base Web Part implementation for the provider Web Part

```
public class ListChooserWebPart : WebPart
  protected Guid selectedList;
  protected DropDownList dropDown;
  protected override void CreateChildControls()
  {
    this.Controls.Add(new LiteralControl("Choose list:<br/>"));
    dropDown = new DropDownList();
    SPContext.Current.Web.Lists.Cast<SPList>().
      Where(l => !l.Hidden).ToList().
      ForEach(list => dropDown.Items.Add(
        new ListItem(list.Title, list.ID.ToString())));

    if (selectedList == Guid.Empty)
    {
      selectedList = Guid.Parse(dropDown.Items[0].Value);
    }
    dropDown.SelectedValue = selectedList.ToString();
    dropDown.AutoPostBack = true;
    dropDown.SelectedIndexChanged += (s,e) => {
      selectedList = Guid.Parse(dropDown.SelectedValue);
    };
    this.Controls.Add(dropDown);
  }
}
```

The Web Part creates a *DropDownList* object and populates the drop-down list box with all the available and visible lists in the current site. The drop-down list box is also configured to automatically do a postback whenever its list is changed. It uses a lambda expression that is fired when the list is changed, and it stores the current ID of the list.

To be able to use this Web Part as a provider Web Part, you need to define a contract that the consumer can use. This contract is created by using an *interface*. In this case, all you need to expose to the consumer is the ID of the selected list. Listing 8-22 shows the interface you need as the connection contract.

LISTING 8-22 A custom contract, or connection interface, that will be used to connect provider and consumer Web Parts

```
public interface IListProvider
{
  Guid ListID {get;}
}
```

After you have the interface defined, you must implement that interface in the provider Web Part. First, make sure the interface is listed in the class definition:

```
public class ListChooserWebPart : WebPart, IListProvider
```

Next, implement the property that the interface is exposing. You had already stored the list ID in a local variable, so you need only to return that value:

```
public Guid ListID
{
 get
 {
   return selectedList;
 }
}
```

The final task you need to perform on the provider Web Part is to create a connection provider endpoint. This must be a method that returns an object implementing the connection interface type. In most cases, this is the Web Part itself. This method must be marked with the *ConnectionProvider* attribute, as in the following snippet. The attribute allows you to specify a display name for the connection. You can optionally add a unique ID. In this case, also declare that this connection allows multiple consumers by using the *AllowsMultipleConnections* property:

```
[ConnectionProvider("List", AllowsMultipleConnections = true)]
public IListProvider SetListConnection()
{
 return this;
}
```

This code is all you need to build the connection provider Web Part. But to test it, you need to build a consumer that uses this connection contract.

Building a consumer Web Part

The consumer Web Part does not need to implement the connection interface—it just needs to have a consumer connection endpoint, very much like the provider connection endpoint. This must be a method that takes the connection interface as an argument, and it has to be marked with the *ConnectionConsumer* attribute. Listing 8-23 shows how this could be implemented in a consumer Web Part. The consumer connection endpoint, the *GetListConnection* method, stores the reference in a local variable to the connection provider.

```
IListProvider provider;

[ConnectionConsumer("List")]
public void GetListConnection(IListProvider listProvider) {
 provider = listProvider;
}
```

After the consumer connection endpoint is in the consumer Web Part, you can use the connection information in the Web Part. Listing 8-24 implements the *CreateChildControls* method for the consumer Web Part. The method does a check whether the Web Part has a connection. If it does not, it renders an error message, and if it is connected, you use the information sent to the Web Part by the provider and generate the Web Part UI. Remember to always implement a check to determine whether the Web Part is connected. When you add the Web Part to a page, the Web Part will not be connected until you connect it.

LISTING 8-24 *CreateChildControls* using information sent from the provider Web Part to create the UI of the consumer Web Part

```
protected override void CreateChildControls()
{
 if (provider == null)
 {
   this.Controls.Add(new LiteralControl("Not connected!"));
 }
 else
 {
   try
   {
     SPList list = SPContext.Current.Web.Lists[provider.ListID];
     this.Controls.Add(new LiteralControl("You selected: " + list.Title));
   }
   catch (Exception)
   {
     this.Controls.Add(new LiteralControl("List not found..."));
   }
 }
}
```

Connecting Web Parts

You just created one provider Web Part and one consumer Web Part that understand each other through using the connection interface. Now it is time to connect these Web Parts. It can be done in the web interface or by using SharePoint Designer 2013. In the web interface, you connect Web Parts by editing the page and choosing to edit either the consumer or the provider Web Part. If any compatible consumer or provider is found, a Connections menu option is available on the Web Part menu, as shown in Figure 8-12.

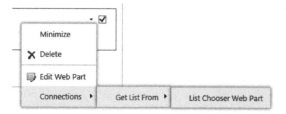

FIGURE 8-12 You connect Web Parts by using the Web Part menu and choosing either the consumer or the provider Web Part.

You can also create a connection in a programmatic way; for instance, by using a Feature receiver. Recall how you previously added Web Parts by using a Feature receiver. (You can refer to Listing 8-7 to review how you did this.) You can use *SPLimitedWebPartManager* not only to add Web Parts to a page but also to connect them together by using the *SPWebPartConnection* object. Listing 8-25 shows an excerpt from a Feature receiver and how the provider and consumer Web Parts are added to the page and then connected.

LISTING 8-25 Web Part connections added through code by using *SPLimitedWebPartManager*

```
SPFile page = site.RootWeb.GetFile("SitePages/WebPartPage2.aspx");
using (SPLimitedWebPartManager manager =
 page.GetLimitedWebPartManager(PersonalizationScope.Shared))
{
ListChooserWebPart.ListChooserWebPart provider =
  new ListChooserWebPart.ListChooserWebPart();
provider.ID = "Provider";
manager.AddWebPart(provider, "Left", 0);

ListInfoWebPart.ListInfoWebPart consumer = new ListInfoWebPart.ListInfoWebPart();
consumer.ID ="Consumer";
manager.AddWebPart(consumer, "Right", 0);

SPWebPartConnection connection = new SPWebPartConnection()
{
  ProviderID = "Provider",
  ConsumerID = "Consumer",
  ID = "Connection"
};
manager.SPWebPartConnections.Add(connection);
manager.SaveChanges(provider);
manager.SaveChanges(consumer);
}
```

The Web Parts are created and added to the Web Part zone, and you must be sure to set their IDs. Then you create a new object of type *SPWebPartConnection*. That object is populated with the ID of both the provider and consumer Web Parts in addition to its own unique ID. In the case where you have multiple consumer or provider endpoints, you must also specify the name of the endpoints. Finally, you add that connection to the limited Web Part Manager and save the Web Parts.

If you prefer to do this declaratively, you use basically the same approach. Assume you deploy a Web Part page by using the *Module* element, and the consumer and provider Web Parts by using the *AllUsersWebPart* element, as child elements to a *File* element. Then you connect the Web Parts by using the *WebPartConnection* element, which also must be a child element of the *File* element:

```
<WebPartConnection
  ProviderID="Provider"
  ConsumerID="Consumer"
  ConsumerConnectionPointID=""
  ProviderConnectionPointID=""
  ID="Connection"/>
```

Just as you did in the Feature receiver, you need to specify the ID of the consumer and provider and give the connection and ID. You also must specify the endpoint IDs when declaratively creating connections. In this case, you leave the endpoint names empty, because you have only one endpoint on both the Web Parts.

You've just explored one of the more interesting features of the Web Part framework. By creating connectable Web Parts, you give your users a lot of power to build their own dashboards or mashups by using Web Part pages and Web Parts.

Using parallel and asynchronous execution in Web Parts

Once in a while, you are required to build a Web Part that performs some long-running operations, such as reading data from databases or web services. If you don't have the possibility of moving this executing to the client side or outside of SharePoint, you need to make sure that you implement the server side thoroughly and use good code patterns and practices. The .NET Framework 4.0 and .NET Framework 4.5 introduce a lot of new features for executing code in parallel or asynchronously, and some of those features can be used in SharePoint development. The following sections describe how to take advantage of these features.

Using parallel execution

One of the options you have with .NET Framework 4.0 is to execute code in parallel. By using the *Parallel* class in the *System.Threading.Tasks* namespace, you can do work in parallel. Even though parallel execution does not reduce stress on the system—most likely the opposite—it can, if used correctly, improve perceived performance. This means that if you have the resources available, you can execute logic in parallel so that the end users receive their information faster.

When building Web Parts, there is often the need to do several lookups, web service calls, or queries to lists or the search index. These tasks were often done synchronously in the Web Parts, and the total time to load the Web Part was the sum of all the tasks. By using parallel execution, you can initiate each query or call so that each runs in parallel, and use the resources on the server more efficiently. The time it takes to perform the tasks is equal to the longest running task.

Consider this simple example. In Listing 8-26 are parts of a Web Part that calculates the total number of tasks from a specific list in each site assigned to the current user in the current site collection. If there are a large number of sites, all these CAML queries typically would be executed one after another. By using the *ForEach* method on the *Parallel* class, the code can, in parallel, walk through all the sites in the site collection and do the CAML query.

LISTING 8-26 Example of using the .NET Framework 4.0 *Parallel* object to execute code in parallel

```
long totaltasks = 0;
string queryText =
"<Where><Eq><FieldRef Name='AssignedTo' LookupId='True' /><Value Type='UserMulti'>" +
SPContext.Current.Web.CurrentUser.ID +
"</Value></Eq></Where>";
Parallel.ForEach(SPContext.Current.Site.AllWebs, web =>
{
SPList list = web.Lists.TryGetList("Shared Tasks");
if (list != null)
{
   SPQuery query = new SPQuery();
   query.Query = queryText;
   SPListItemCollection tasks = list.GetItems(query);
   Interlocked.Add(ref totaltasks, (long)tasks.Count);
}
web.Dispose();
});
```

A couple of things are important to notice in the code. First, you need to dispose the *SPWeb* objects, and for easier reading, any exception handling has been omitted. Second, you cannot simply increment the *totaltasks* variable; you must use the atomic *Interlocked.Add* method to increment the value of the variable, because each parallel execution will run on its own thread.

 Warning You have to be very careful when using the parallel features in .NET Framework 4.0 and SharePoint. All objects executing in parallel have to be thread-safe, and most of the SharePoint objects are not. For instance, you will get exceptions if you try to perform parallel execution on all the lists in one single web.

Using asynchronous execution

Many of these long-running operations consist of calls to external sources, which means that Share-Point is idling, waiting for the data to return from the external source. In this case, you can take advantage of asynchronous features in ASP.NET. Even though a lot of features in ASP.NET 4.5 create asynchronous methods and pages, not all of them can be used in SharePoint 2013 because of its configuration.

There are options for building asynchronous Web Parts, however, by using the asynchronous page tasks. Asynchronous page tasks are an ASP.NET 2.0 feature but still a valid option. To illustrate this, you'll walk through the creation of a Web Part that reads OData (Open Data Protocol) from an external source. If one or more of these Web Parts are on a page, each request to the data source runs sequentially for each Web Part, one at a time. For instance, if the request takes one second and you have four Web Parts, the page load time will be at least four seconds. This demonstration uses the OData Northwind test service to retrieve product information. You can find this test service at *http://services.odata.org/Northwind/Northwind.svc/*.

First, you add three properties to the Web Part that allows you to specify how many products you want to retrieve and how to sort them. You also make these personalizable through the web UI. The UI will be a bulleted list with the product names, and you will also add a *Label* control that shows any error messages:

```
[Personalizable, WebBrowsable]
public string OrderBy { get; set; }
[Personalizable, WebBrowsable]
public int Items { get; set; }
[Personalizable, WebBrowsable]
public bool SortAscending { get; set; }

protected BulletedList products;
protected Label errorMessage;
```

The Web Part control description file is also updated with these properties so that you have default values on the properties. A good convention is also to set default values in the constructor of the Web Part in case a user programmatically adds this Web Part to a page and forgets to set any values on the properties:

```
<property name="Items" type="int">10</property>
<property name="OrderBy" type="string">UnitPrice</property>
<property name="SortAscending" type="bool">true</property>
```

To load the products from the Northwind test service, create a local method called *LoadProducts*, shown in Listing 8-27. This method ensures that the UI controls are present, and then constructs a REST query by using the Web Part properties. Finally, it uses the *WebClient* object to download the OData XML and parse it.

LISTING 8-27 Implementation of loading product information from the OData Northwind test service and populating a drop-down list box with the product names

```
void LoadProducts()
{
  EnsureChildControls();
  errorMessage.Text = String.Empty;
  products.Items.Clear();

  string restUrl = String.Format("http://services.odata.org/Northwind/Northwind.svc/"
    +"Products?$top={0}&$orderby={1}+{2}",
    Items, OrderBy, SortAscending ? "asc" : "desc");

  using (WebClient client = new WebClient())
  {
    try
    {
      client.Encoding = System.Text.Encoding.UTF8;
      string data = client.DownloadString(restUrl);

      XNamespace ns = "http://schemas.microsoft.com/ado/2007/08/dataservices";
      XElement element = XElement.Parse(data);
      var names = element.Descendants(ns + "ProductName").Select(d => d.Value);
      names.ToList().ForEach(n => products.Items.Add(new ListItem(n)));
    }
    catch (WebException we)
    {
      errorMessage.Text = we.Message;
    }
  }
}
```

The REST query is sent to the Northwind test service endpoint, and the code is using Linq-to-XML to retrieve the product names from the returned data. Each product name is then added to the bulleted list. If any error message is returned from the REST call, such as time-outs or invalid queries, this error will be written in the error message label.

In this case, you build the UI by overriding the *CreateChildControls* method, and it is in this method that you register—not start—the asynchronous call. You could also register the asynchronous call in any postback event handlers, or even as late as in the *OnPreRender* method. This is because of how the asynchronous execution is implemented in ASP.NET. If an ASP.NET page has a registered asynchronous task, the thread that the page is executing on will be returned to the thread pool after the *OnPreRender* method. This is to prohibit running all these tasks sequentially on the same thread and blocking other threads from executing. Then the ASP.NET framework picks up one new thread from the thread pool for each asynchronous task, executes the tasks, and waits for them to finish or time out. After all the asynchronous tasks are complete, a new primary thread is retrieved from the thread pool, and the page execution continues on that thread. This process means that you cannot start any external calls in the *RenderContents* method, and you cannot use any of the results from the asynchronous tasks until after the *OnPreRender* has executed.

The *CreateChildControls* method for the Northwind products Web Part, shown in Listing 8-28, initializes the two controls and then registers the asynchronous task. Also notice how you added the *SPMonitoredScope* class to create a monitored scope. It is a good practice to use monitored scopes so that you can use, for instance, the Developer Dashboard to monitor performance of methods and sections in your Web Parts. When running this Web Part at a later time, you can view in the Developer Dashboard that nearly no time was spent in the *CreateChildControls*. You can use this as an exercise and change the implementation of this method from asynchronous to synchronous to compare the difference.

LISTING 8-28 Asynchronous tasks can be created to prohibit execution of long-running operations on the main thread

```
private Action asyncTask;
protected override void CreateChildControls()
{
  using (SPMonitoredScope scope = new SPMonitoredScope("Async CreateChildControls"))
  {
    products = new BulletedList();
    this.Controls.Add(products);
    errorMessage = new Label();
    errorMessage.ForeColor = System.Drawing.Color.Red;
    this.Controls.Add(errorMessage);

    asyncTask = new Action(LoadProducts);

    PageAsyncTask task1 = new PageAsyncTask(OnBegin, OnEnd, OnTimeOut, null, true);
    this.Page.RegisterAsyncTask(task1);
  }
}
```

After creating the controls, you declare an *Action* delegate for the product loader method. It is this delegate that will be executed asynchronously. Asynchronous page tasks are created by instantiating a new object of the class *PageAsyncTask*. The constructor of this object takes five arguments. The first one is the begin handler and is the method that will be executed to start the asynchronous execution. The second and third are two methods that are used when the execution ends and when it times out. The fourth argument can be used to send parameters to the task, and the fifth one indicates, in this case, that you can run this task in parallel with other tasks. Finally, you register the task with the page, so that it can start the asynchronous task later in the page life cycle.

The three methods *OnBegin*, *OnEnd*, and *OnTimeOut*, which you added to the *PageAsyncTask*, are implemented in Listing 8-29. The *OnBegin* method uses the *Action* delegate that was previously created and calls its *BeginInvoke* method to start the execution. This method returns an *IAsyncResult* object, which is used by the framework to keep track of the status of the asynchronous operation. The *OnEnd* method is called when the execution completes successfully, within the time-out limits, and the *OnTimeOut* method will be called if the asynchronous call times out.

LISTING 8-29 Asynchronous page tasks, which must contain methods to start, end, and handle the time-out of the task

```
public IAsyncResult OnBegin(object sender, EventArgs e, AsyncCallback callback,
  object data)
{
 return asyncTask.BeginInvoke(callback, data);
}
public void OnEnd(IAsyncResult result)
{
 asyncTask.EndInvoke(result);
}
public void OnTimeOut(IAsyncResult result)
{
 errorMessage.Text = "Operation timed out...";
}
```

The default time-out value for asynchronous operations in ASP.NET is 45 seconds, but SharePoint lowers this time-out to 7 seconds. This is configured in the Web.config file of the SharePoint Web application in the *pages* element:

```
<pages asyncTimeout="7"/>
```

You should usually not edit this value, but if you know that your asynchronous operation can take longer time than 7 seconds, or you don't want those long time-outs, you can set a temporary longer or shorter value in your Web Part. You do this by changing the settings of the *AsyncTimeout* property of the ASP.NET *Page* object:

```
this.Page.AsyncTimeOut = new TimeSpan(0,0,15);
```

Now you're all set with your asynchronous Web Part. To see any visible benefits from the asynchronous operations, you should add two or more of these Web Parts to a page and then monitor the requests by using the Developer Dashboard.

Summary

This chapter covered one of the historically most predominant features of SharePoint—Web Parts. Web Parts have come a long way since their initial implementation and now are a part of the ASP.NET framework. This chapter discussed the Web Part framework and its important aspects, and how you can take advantage of its features. After covering the fundamentals, you created Web Parts by using Visual Studio 2012. This chapter explained all the different aspects you need to keep in mind to use Web Parts to create a deployable solution.

You explored in depth how to render the UI of Web Parts and how to make them customizable by using Web Part properties. It is the personalized properties that make Web Parts unique and so easy to work with. By taking advantage of these properties, you can create Web Parts that your users will love to use.

Finally, you examined some of the more advanced Web Parts development topics, such as extending the Web Part menu with verbs and how to make Web Parts connectable by using Web Part connections. Both of these features are very interesting if you want to make easy-to-use and reusable Web Parts for your organization or customers. The last part of the advanced topics section discussed parallel and asynchronous execution of Web Parts, which is essential to know when you're dealing with long-running calls and operations.

## CHAPTER 9

SharePoint lists

One of the greatest strengths of Microsoft SharePoint is that it enables users to create lists and to customize them for specific business scenarios. Users can create a new custom list and add whatever columns are required for their current business needs. All the details of how SharePoint tracks the schema definition for columns in a list and how it stores list items in the content database are handled behind the scenes. This approach allows business users to rapidly create light business applications with no involvement from the IT department.

Although lists make it easy to create simple no-code solutions, they are also the foundation of many SharePoint solutions and apps. Developers often rely on lists as the primary data source for solutions and apps because they can be easily accessed through the application programming interface (API) and also provide a ready user interface that supports full create, read, update, delete (CRUD) operations. All this makes the SharePoint list a critical piece of infrastructure and one that developers should know well.

Creating lists

When a user creates a new list, SharePoint allows the user to select a list template from a collection available in the current site. Table 9-1 shows a listing of commonly used list templates supplied by SharePoint Foundation. Each list has both a type and an identifier, which are used to identify classes of lists in solutions and apps. This table is just a small sampling of the available lists. In SharePoint Server Enterprise, for example, there are more than 50 different list types available.

TABLE 9-1 Common list templates and IDs

Template name	Template type	Template type ID
Custom List	*GenericList*	100
Document Library	*DocumentLibrary*	101
Survey	*Survey*	102
Links List	*Links*	103
Announcements List	*Announcements*	104
Contacts List	*Contacts*	105
Calendar	*Events*	106
Tasks List	*Tasks*	107

Template name	Template type	Template type ID
Discussion List	*DiscussionBoard*	108
Picture Library	*PictureLibrary*	109
Form Library	*XMLForm*	115
Wiki Page Library	*WebPageLibrary*	119

As you can imagine, there are many ad hoc scenarios in which creating a list does not require the assistance of a developer. Users who are skilled in SharePoint site customization are more than capable of creating lists and configuring them to achieve a desired goal. At the same time, however, there are definitely scenarios in which it makes sense to automate the creation of lists by using a SharePoint solution. This is especially true when the process for creating a specific set of lists must be repeatable across different sites or different farms.

New lists can be created in solutions or apps using a feature that contains a *ListInstance* element. The *ListInstance* element sets the attributes *TemplateType* and *FeatureId* to identify the list template and the list feature, respectively. The list template type is an identifying number such as one of those listed in Table 9-1. The feature ID is obtained from the Feature.xml file of the feature that defined the list template schema. For example, the following *ListInstance* element will create a new Contacts list:

```
<ListInstance
  TemplateType="105"
  FeatureId="00bfea71-7e6d-4186-9ba8-c047ac750105"
  Title="Customers"
  Description="Wingtip customers list "
  Url="Lists/Customers"
  OnQuickLaunch="TRUE" >
</ListInstance>
```

Chapter 3, "Server-side solution development," introduced the fundamentals of server-side solution development along with the Visual Studio 2012 list designer, which is used to create new lists in solutions and apps. The list designer is valuable because it saves developers from having to figure out the required template types and feature IDs for lists. Additionally, the list designer results in a purely declarative solution, which is preferred because it will work in all types of solutions and apps.

Although creating lists declaratively is useful, you also have the option of creating lists programmatically. You can use either the server-side object model (SSOM), the client-side object model (CSOM), or the Representational State Transfer (REST) interface to create lists. Listing 9-1 shows a sample of each approach.

LISTING 9-1 Creating lists programmatically

```
//Server-Side Object Model
SPWeb site = SPContext.Current.Web;
string ListTitle = "Contacts";
string ListDescription = "Wingtip customers list";
Guid ListId = site.Lists.Add(ListTitle, ListDescription, SPListTemplateType.Contacts);
SPList list = site.Lists[ListId];
list.OnQuickLaunch = true;
list.Update();

//Client-Side Object Model
var ctx = new SP.ClientContext.get_current();
var createInfo = new SP.ListCreationInformation();
createInfo.set_title("Contacts");
createInfo.set_templateType(SP.ListTemplateType.contacts);
var newList = ctx.get_web().get_lists().add(createInfo);
ctx.load(newList);
ctx.executeQueryAsync(success, failure);

//REST interface
$.ajax({
    url: _spPageContextInfo.webServerRelativeUrl +
        "/_api/web/lists",
    type: "POST",
    contentType: "application/json;odata=verbose",
    data: JSON.stringify(
        { '__metadata': { 'type': 'SP.List' },
          'Title': 'Contacts',
          'BaseTemplate': 105
        }),
    headers: {
        "accept": "application/json;odata=verbose",
        "X-RequestDigest": $("#__REQUESTDIGEST").val()
    }
});
```

Looking at the declarative and code-based options for creating lists can be a bit overwhelming. With four different approaches, developers could easily become confused as to which is the best approach. The declarative approach is simple because it uses tools integrated into Visual Studio 2012. However, the declarative approach does have a noteworthy disadvantage: There is no graceful way to handle conflicts. For example, suppose that a user attempts to activate a feature with the *ListInstance* element in a site that already contains a list with the same title. The feature activates successfully, but the feature's attempt to create the list silently fails due to the conflict, leaving the functionality of the feature in an unpredictable state. For apps, this is generally not a problem because each app instance can create its own set of lists.

Developers clearly have more control when creating a list programmatically. Developers can, for example, query the *Lists* collection of the current site to see if there is an existing list with the same title before attempting to create a new list. If there is a list with a conflicting title, you can delete that list or change its title to ensure that your code can create the new list with the desired title successfully.

Another advantage of using code to create lists instead of using the declarative *ListInstance* element is that you have more control over configuring list properties. Listing 9-2 demonstrates how to configure a list to appear on the Quick Launch bar, support attachments, and allow versioning.

LISTING 9-2 Configuring lists programmatically

```
//Server-Side Object model
Guid ListId = site.Lists.Add(ListTitle, ListDescription, SPListTemplateType.Contacts);
list = site.Lists[ListId];
list.OnQuickLaunch = true;
list.EnableAttachments = false;
list.EnableVersioning = true;
list.Update();

//Client-Side Object Model
var ctx = new SP.ClientContext.get_current();
var list = ctx.get_web().get_lists().getByTitle("Contacts")
ctx.load(list);
var.list.set_onQuickLaunch(quickLaunch);
list.set_enableAttachments(attachments);
list.set_enableFolderCreation(folders);
list.set_enableVersioning(versions);
ctx.executeQueryAsync(success, failure)

//REST Interface
$.ajax({
    url: _spPageContextInfo.webServerRelativeUrl +
        "/_api/web/lists/getByTitle('" + title + "')",
    type: "POST",
    contentType: "application/json;odata=verbose",
    data: JSON.stringify(
        { '__metadata': { 'type': 'SP.List' },
          'OnQuickLaunch': quickLaunch,
          'EnableAttachments': attachments,
          'EnableVersioning': versions
        }),
    headers: {
        "accept": "application/json;odata=verbose",
        "X-RequestDigest": $("#__REQUESTDIGEST").val(),
        "IF-MATCH": "*",
        "X-Http-Method": "PATCH"
    }
});
```

Working with fields and field types

Each SharePoint list contains a collection of fields that define what users see as columns. A field can be created inside the context of a single list. These are the types of fields that we will discuss first. However, a field can also be defined within the context of a site, which makes it possible to reuse it across multiple lists. These types of fields are known as site columns, and they will be introduced in the "Understanding site columns" section later in the chapter.

Every field is defined in terms of an underlying field type. Table 9-2 shows a list of field types that SharePoint Foundation displays to users when they are adding a new field to a list by using the Create Column page. Note that in addition to the field types included with SharePoint Foundation, there are extra field types installed by SharePoint Server 2013. Additionally, it's possible to develop custom field types in a SharePoint solution to extend the set of field types available for use within a farm. Custom field types are covered in Chapter 10, "SharePoint type definitions and templates."

TABLE 9-2 SharePoint Foundation field types

Field type	Display name
Text	Single Line Of Text
Note	Multiple Lines Of Text
Choice	Choice
Integer	Integer
Number	Number
Decimal	Decimal
Currency	Currency
DateTime	Date And Time
Lookup	Lookup
Boolean	Yes/No
User	Person Or Group
URL	Hyperlink Or Picture
Calculated	Calculated

At a lower level, SharePoint classifies lists by using base types. Standard lists have a base type of 0, whereas document libraries have a base type of 1. There also are less frequently used base types for discussion forums (3), vote or survey lists (4), and issue lists (5). The base type defines a common set of fields, and all list types configured to use that base type automatically inherit those fields.

For example, all five base types define a field named *ID*. This field enables SharePoint to track each item in a list behind the scenes with a unique integer identifier. All five base types also define fields named *Created*, *Modified*, *Author*, and *Editor*. These fields allow SharePoint to track when and by whom each item was created and last modified.

Performing basic field operations

Every list contains special fields named *Title*, *LinkTitle*, and *LinkTitleNoMenu*. The *Title* field contains text that represents the list item. The *LinkTitle* field and the *LinkTitleNoMenu* field are computed fields based on the value in the *Title* field and cannot be edited. The *LinkTitle* field is used to render the Edit Control Block (ECB) menu shown in Figure 9-1.

This field is special for lists because it contains the value that is rendered inside the Edit Control Block (ECB) menu shown in Figure 9-1. Though the *Title* field contains the value rendered inside the ECB menu, it is not actually the field that SharePoint uses to create the ECB menu within a view. Instead, SharePoint uses a related field named *LinkTitle*, which reads the value of the *Title* field and uses it to render the ECB menu. The *LinkTitleNoMenu* field can be used to display the value of the *Title* field in a hyperlink that can be used to view an item.

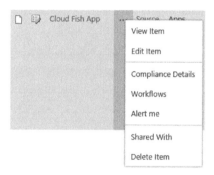

FIGURE 9-1 The Edit Control Block menu

Each field in a list has an internal name as well as a display name. After a field has been created, its internal name can never be modified. However, the display name can be modified. For example, the out-of-the-box Contacts list modifies the display name of the *Title* field to "Last Name". As a result, the Last Name column provides the ECB menu in a Contacts list.

The display name of the *Title* field can be modified directly in the browser or through code. As an example, imagine that you need a list to track product categories, so you create a new list by using the custom list template. The *SPList* class provides a *Fields* collection, from which you can retrieve the *Title* field. After you have obtained an *SPField* reference to the *Title* field, you can modify its display name by using the *Title* property of the *SPField* class and then save your changes by calling the *Update* method. Listing 9-3 shows how to accomplish this modification by using different approaches.

LISTING 9-3 Modifying a field programmatically

```
//Server-Side Object Model
SPList list = SPContext.Current.Web.Lists["ProductCategories"];
SPField fldTitle = list.Fields.GetFieldByInternalName("Title");
fldTitle.Title = "Category";
fldTitle.Update();

//Client-Side Object Model
var ctx = new SP.ClientContext.get_current();
var field = ctx.get_web().get_lists().getByTitle("ProductCategories")
            .get_fields().getByInternalNameOrTitle("Title");
ctx.load(field);
field.set_title("Category");
field.update();
ctx.executeQueryAsync(success, failure);

//REST Interface
$.ajax(
  {
    url: _spPageContextInfo.webServerRelativeUrl +
         "/_api/web/lists/getByTitle('ProductCategories')" +
         "/fields/getByInternalNameOrTitle('Title')",

    type: "POST",
    contentType: "application/json;odata=verbose",
    data: JSON.stringify(
      { '__metadata': { 'type': 'SP.Field' },
        'Title': "Category"
      }),
    headers: {
      "accept": "application/json;odata=verbose",
      "X-RequestDigest": $("#__REQUESTDIGEST").val(),
      "IF-MATCH": "*",
      "X-Http-Method": "PATCH"
    }
  });
```

Now that we have covered the basics of fields and field types, let's write the code required to add a few custom fields to a new list. The *Fields* collection supports an *Add* method that can easily be used to add new fields. Additionally, the *AddFieldAsXml* method allows you to structure an XML chunk to define the new field. These different approaches are shown in Listing 9-4 using the various APIs.

LISTING 9-4 Adding fields to a list programmatically

```
//Server-Side Object Model
list.Fields.Add("ProductDescription", SPFieldType.Text, false);

//JavaScript Client Object Model
var xmlDef = "<Field DisplayName='ProductDescription' Type='Text'/>";
var ctx = new SP.ClientContext.get_current();
var field = ctx.get_web().get_lists().getByTitle("Products")
            .get_fields().addFieldAsXml(xmlDef, false,
             SP.AddFieldOptions.addToNoContentType);
field.update();
ctx.load(field);
ctx.executeQueryAsync(success, failure);

//REST Interface
$.ajax(
    {
        url: _spPageContextInfo.webServerRelativeUrl +
            "/_api/web/lists/getByTitle('Products')/fields",
        type: "POST",
        contentType: "application/json;odata=verbose",
        data: JSON.stringify(
            { '__metadata': { 'type': 'SP.Field' },
              'Title': 'ProductDescription',
              'FieldTypeKind': SP.FieldType.text
            }),
        headers: {
            "accept": "application/json;odata=verbose",
            "X-RequestDigest": $("#__REQUESTDIGEST").val()
        }
    }
);
```

Note that the previous code avoids using spaces when creating the field names. If you create a field with a space in its name, SharePoint creates the internal name by replacing each space with _x0020_. This means that calling the *Add* method and passing a name of "List Price", for example, would create a field with an internal name of *List_x0020_Price*. Most developers prefer to create fields by using a name without spaces.

The properties of the field, such as *DefaultValue*, represent common properties that are shared across all field types. However, specific field types have associated classes that inherit from *SPField*. Examples of these field type classes include *SPFieldBoolean*, *SPFieldChoice*, *SPFieldCurrency*, *SPField-DateTime*, *SPFieldDecimal*, *SPFieldNumber*, *SPFieldText*, *SPFieldUrl*, and *SPFieldUser*. Although the REST API lets you use an endpoint against the underlying type, when you are using the server-side or client-side object model you must convert a field to one of these specific field types. The following code shows an example:

```
//Server-Side Object Model
SPList list = SPContext.Current.Web.Lists["Products"];
SPFieldCurrency fld =
```

```
          (SPFieldCurrency)list.Fields.GetFieldByInternalName("ListPrice");
fld.MinimumValue = 0;
fld.MaximumValue = 10000;
fld.Update();

//JavaScript Client Object Model
var ctx = new SP.ClientContext.get_current();
var field = ctx.get_web().get_lists().getByTitle("Products")
            .get_fields().getByInternalNameOrTitle("ListPrice");
var fieldAsNumber = ctx.castTo(field, SP.FieldNumber);
fieldAsNumber.set_minimumValue(0);
fieldAsNumber.set_maximumValue(10000);
fieldAsNumber.update();
ctx.load(field);
ctx.executeQueryAsync(success, failure);
```

Working with lookups and relationships

SharePoint Foundation supports lookup fields, which make it possible for users to update a field value by using a drop-down menu populated by the field values in another list. For example, imagine that you want to add a field to a list of products that lets the user pick a product category. You can accomplish this by adding a new lookup field to the products list. Listing 9-5 shows how to do this by using both the server-side and client-side object models.

LISTING 9-5 Establishing list relationships programmatically

```
//Server-Side Object Model
string LookupFieldDisplayName = "Category";
SPList LookupList = site.Lists["Product Categories"];
Guid LookupListID = LookupList.ID;
list.Fields.AddLookup(LookupFieldDisplayName, LookupListID, true);
SPFieldLookup fldLookup = (SPFieldLookup)list.Fields["Category"];
fldLookup.Indexed = true;
fldLookup.RelationshipDeleteBehavior = SPRelationshipDeleteBehavior.Restrict;
fldLookup.Update();

//JavaScript Client Object Model
var ctx = new SP.ClientContext.get_current();
var xmlDef = "<Field DisplayName='Category' Type='Lookup'/>";
var field = ctx.get_web().get_lists().getByTitle("Products").get_fields()
            .addFieldAsXml( xmlDef, false, SP.AddFieldOptions.addToNoContentType);
var lookupField = ctx.castTo(field, SP.FieldLookup);
lookupField.set_lookupList({GUID});
lookupField.set_lookupField("Title");
lookupField.set_relationshipDeleteBehavior(SP.RelationshipDeleteBehavior.restrict);
lookupField.update();
ctx.executeQueryAsync(success, failure)
```

When a list is used as a lookup, it can have a relationship that allows you to prevent users from deleting any item in the lookup list that is currently being used by any item in the master list. This is accomplished by setting the *RelationshipDeleteBehavior* property to *restricted delete*. Under this setting, attempting to delete an item from the lookup list that is in use will then result in an error. In some scenarios, however, it makes more sense to create a relationship with *cascading delete* behavior. When a user deletes an item in the lookup list under this setting, all the list items that have been assigned that lookup will be deleted as well.

Though there is definite value in the support for defining list relationships, it is important that you don't overestimate what it really does. It cannot be used to create the same level of referential integrity that can be achieved between two tables in a Microsoft SQL Server database. That means that it does not really prevent the possibility of orphaned items, such as when you have products that are not assigned to an existing product category. The value of creating the relationship with delete behavior simply relieves you of additional development work, such as writing an event handler to achieve something such as cascade delete behavior.

Understanding site columns

As you have seen, SharePoint supports the creation of fields within the scope of a list. SharePoint also supports the creation of site columns, which are fields created within the scope of a site. The advantage of a site column is that it represents a field that can be reused across multiple lists.

Every site within a site collection contains its own site columns gallery. When you add a site column to a site columns gallery, that site column is available for use within the current site, as well as in all the child sites in the site hierarchy below it. When you add a site column to the site column gallery of a top-level site in a site collection, it is available for use throughout the entire site collection. For this reason, site columns are generally added to the site columns gallery of top-level sites instead of child sites.

SharePoint automatically adds a standard set of site columns to the site columns gallery of every top-level site by using a hidden feature. Table 9-3 shows a small sampling of this standard set of site columns that are always available for use in every SharePoint site.

TABLE 9-3 Sampling of site columns

Internal name	Display name	Field type
ID	ID	*Counter*
Title	Title	*Text*
LinkTitle	Title	*Computed*
LinkTitleNoMenu	Title	*Computed*
Author	Created By	*User*
Created	Created	*DateTime*

Internal name	Display name	Field type
Editor	Modified By	*User*
Modified	Modified	*DateTime*
FirstName	First Name	*Text*
HomePhone	Home Phone	*Text*
CellPhone	Mobile Number	*Text*
WorkPhone	Business Phone	*Text*
EMail	E-Mail	*Text*
HomeAddressStreet	Home Address Street	*Text*
HomeAddressCity	Home Address City	*Text*
HomeAddressStateOrProvince	Home Address State Or Province	*Text*
HomeAddressPostalCode	Home Address Postal Code	*Text*
WorkAddress	Address	*Note*
WorkCity	City	*Text*
WorkFax	Fax Number	*Text*
WorkState	State/Province	*Text*
WorkZip	ZIP/Postal Code	*Text*
StartDate	Start Date	*DateTime*
Birthday	Birthday	*DateTime*
SpouseName	Spouse	*Text*

As you can see, the standard set of site columns includes the common fields that the SharePoint Foundation base types add to every list, such as *ID*, *Title*, *Author*, *Created*, *Editor*, and *Modified*. It also includes site columns that are used by standard list types such as Announcements, Contacts, Calendar, and Tasks.

SharePoint Foundation adds more than 400 site columns into the site column gallery of every top-level site. However, many of these site columns are hidden, including quite a few that are included only for backward compatibility with earlier versions. Site administrators can view the site columns that are not hidden by using a standard application page named mngfield.aspx, which is accessible via the Site columns link in the Galleries section of the Site Settings page of a top-level site.

When you need to add a new field to a list, you should determine whether there is already an existing site column that meets your needs. In general, it is preferable to reuse an existing site column instead of creating a new field inside the scope of a list. This is especially true in scenarios where multiple lists require a field with common properties. By updating a site column, you can automatically push your changes to any list within the current site collection that contains a field based on that site column. The use of site columns also makes writing queries easier because you can standardize field names across multiple lists.

The *SPWeb* class provides a *Fields* collection that makes it possible to enumerate through the site columns in the site column gallery for the current site. It is important to understand that the site columns available for use in a site include the site columns in the local site column gallery as well as the site columns in the galleries of all parent sites. The *SPWeb* class provides a second collection property named *AvailableFields*, which allows you to enumerate through all site columns that can be used in the current site. Listing 9-6 shows how to retrieve a site column from the *AvailableFields* collection.

LISTING 9-6 Retrieving columns programmatically

```
//Server-Side Object Model
SPField fld = SPContext.Current.Web.AvailableFields.GetFieldByInternalName("Title");

//JavaScript Client Object Model
var ctx = new SP.ClientContext.get_current();
var column = ctx.get_web().get_availableFields().getByInternalNameOrTitle("Title");
ctx.load(column);
ctx.executeQueryAsync(success, failure)

//REST Interface
$.ajax(
{
    url: _spPageContextInfo.webServerRelativeUrl +
        "/_api/web/availableFields/getByInternalNameOrTitle('" + internalFieldName +
"')",
    type: "GET",
    headers: { "accept": "application/json;odata=verbose", }
});
```

When should you access site columns through the *Fields* collection rather than the *AvailableFields* collection? The first observation is that accessing the *Title* field through the *Fields* collection works only when your code is executed in the context of a top-level site. This code will fail when executed within the scope of a child site. Therefore, accessing site columns through the *AvailableFields* collection can offer more flexibility. However, you should note that you cannot modify a site column that has been accessed through the *AvailableFields* collection. If you plan to modify a site column, you must access it by using the *Fields* collection in the context of the site where it exists.

In addition to using the standard site columns provided by SharePoint Foundation, you can also create your own manually by using the browser or with code by using the server-side object model. You will find that writing the code for creating a new site column is just like writing the code for creating a new field in a list. The main difference is that you call the *Add* method on the *Fields* collection of a site instead of the *Fields* collection of a list. Listing 9-7 demonstrates how to create a new site column in the current site. You could also choose to add the site column to the root site of the current site collection so that it would be available to all sites. This can even be done by using client-side code from an app, as long as the app has the *Manage* permission for the host site collection.

LISTING 9-7 Creating a site column programmatically

```
//Server-Side Object Model
SPWeb site = SPContext.Current.Web;
site.Fields.Add("EmployeeNumber", SPFieldType.Text, true);
SPField fld = site.Fields.GetFieldByInternalName("EmployeeNumber");
fld.Title = "Employee Number";
fld.Group = "Wingtip Toys";
fld.Update();

//JavaScript Client Object Model
var xmlDef = "<Field DisplayName='EmployeeNumber' Type='Text'/>";
var ctx = new SP.ClientContext.get_current();
var field = ctx.get_web().get_fields().addFieldAsXml(
           xmlDef, false, SP.AddFieldOptions.addToNoContentType);
ctx.load(field);
field.set_group("Wingtip Toys");
field.updateAndPushChanges(false);
ctx.executeQueryAsync(success, failure)

//REST Interface
$.ajax(
{
    url: _spPageContextInfo.webServerRelativeUrl +
         "/_api/web/fields",
    type: "POST",
    contentType: "application/json;odata=verbose",
    data: JSON.stringify(
    { '__metadata': { 'type': 'SP.Field' },
      'Title': 'EmployeeNumber',
      'FieldTypeKind': 2,
      'Group': 'Wingtip Toys'
    }),
    headers: {
      "accept": "application/json;odata=verbose",
      "X-RequestDigest": $("#__REQUESTDIGEST").val()
    }
});
```

A significant benefit to using site columns is that they can be used to update multiple lists at once. Imagine a scenario where you have created 10 different lists within a site collection that contain fields based on the site choice column named *EmployeeStatus*. What would you need to do if you wanted to add a new choice value to the *EmployeeStatus* site column and make it available for use in any of those lists? The answer is that you can simply add the new choice value to the site column and then call the *Update* method with a value of *true* to push your changes to all the lists within the current site collection that contain fields based on the site column. Listing 9-8 shows the approach.

LISTING 9-8 Adding choices programmatically

```
//Server-Side Object Model
SPWeb site = SPContext.Current.Site.RootWeb;
SPFieldChoice fld =
        (SPFieldChoice)site.Fields.GetFieldByInternalName("EmployeeStatus");
fld.Choices.Add("Contractor");
fld.Update(true);

//JavaScript Client Object Model
var ctx = new SP.ClientContext.get_current();
var column = ctx.get_web().get_fields().getByInternalNameOrTitle("EmployeeStatus");
ctx.load(column);
var choiceColumn = ctx.castTo(column, SP.FieldChoice);
ctx.load(choiceColumn);
choiceColumn.set_choices("Contractor");
choiceColumn.updateAndPushChanges(true);
ctx.executeQueryAsync(success, failure)
```

Working with content types

SharePoint 2013 supports a flexible and powerful mechanism for designing lists known as a *content type*. A content type is an entity that uses site columns to define a schema of fields for an item in a list or a document in a document library. It's important to understand that content types, like site columns, are defined independently outside the scope of any list or document library. A content type defines a field collection that is reusable across multiple lists or multiple document libraries. Furthermore, content types can be updated to make sweeping changes to many lists at once, such as ascenario in which you need to add a new field to accommodate changing business requirements.

Every site within a site collection contains a *content types gallery*. The content types gallery for a site can be viewed and administered through an application page named mngctype.aspx, which is accessible through the Site Content Types link in the Galleries section of the Site Settings page.

Content type visibility behaves just as it does for site columns. When you add a content type to the content types gallery of a specific site, that content type is available for use within the current site, as well as in all the child sites in the site hierarchy below it. When you add a content type to the content types gallery of a top-level site, it is available for use throughout the entire site collection.

SharePoint Foundation automatically adds a standard set of content types to the content types gallery of every top-level site. Table 9-4 shows a partial listing of the standard content types that SharePoint Foundation makes available within every site. This table lists each content type with its ID and name along with the name of its parent content type.

TABLE 9-4 A partial listing of the standard SharePoint Foundation content types

ID	Name	Parent
0x01	*Item*	*System*
0x0101	*Document*	*Item*
0x0102	*Event*	*Item*
0x0104	*Announcement*	*Item*
0x0105	*Link*	*Item*
0x0106	*Contact*	*Item*
0x0108	*Task*	*Item*
0x0120	*Folder*	*Item*
0x010101	*Form*	*Document*
0x010102	*Picture*	*Document*
0x010105	*Master Page*	*Document*
0x010108	*Wiki Page*	*Document*
0x010109	*Basic Page*	*Document*
0x012002	*Discussion*	*Folder*
0x012004	*Summary Task*	*Folder*

Content types are defined based upon the principles of inheritance. Every content type that you can create or use inherits from another content type. SharePoint Foundation provides a special hidden content type named *System*, which exists at the very top of the inheritance hierarchy above *Item*. However, as a developer, you will never deal directly with the *System* content type or program against it. Therefore, the *Item* content type can be considered the parent of all other content types in SharePoint.

Each content type has a string-based ID that begins with the ID of its parent content type. The *Item* content type has an ID based on the hexadecimal number 0x01. Because every content type inherits from *Item*, all content types have an ID that begins with 0x01. For example, the *Document* content type, which inherits from *Item*, has an ID of 0x0101. Content types that inherit from *Document* have IDs that begin with 0x0101, such as *Form*, which has an ID of 0x010101, and *Picture*, which has an ID of 0x010102.

If you create a new content type through the browser or code, SharePoint will create a new content type ID for you. SharePoint creates a content type ID by parsing together the base content type ID, followed by 00 and a new GUID. For example, if you create a new content type that inherits from *Document*, SharePoint will create a content type ID that looks something like the following:

0x010100F51AEB6BBC8EA2469E1617071D9FF658

The inheritance-based architecture of content types yields quite a bit of power. For example, consider what happens if you add a new site column to the *Document* content type in the content types gallery of a top-level site. You would effectively be adding the site column to all the content types that inherit from *Document*, which provides a simple and effective way to add a new field to every document library in a site collection.

Content types go beyond defining a set of fields. A content type can also define behaviors with event handlers and workflow associations. For example, consider what would happen if you register an event handler on the *Document* content type in the content types gallery of a top-level site. You would effectively be registering the event handler on every document in the site collection, including those documents based on derived content types such as *Form*, *Picture*, *Master Page*, *Wiki Page*, and *Basic Page*.

Programming with content types

The *SPWeb* class provides a *ContentTypes* collection that makes it possible to enumerate through the content types in the content types gallery of the current site. Following the same pattern as for site columns, you can also use a second collection named *AvailableContentTypes*, which allows you to enumerate the aggregation of content types in the content types gallery of the current site and all parent sites. Listing 9-9 shows how to retrieve a content type when you know its name or ID.

LISTING 9-9 Retrieving a content type programmatically

```
//Server-Side Object Model
SPWeb site = SPContext.Current.Web;
SPContentType ctype = site.ContentTypes["WingtipToysProduct"];

//JavaScript Client Object Model
var ctx = new SP.ClientContext.get_current();
var ctype = ctx.get_web().get_contentTypes().getById("0x010100F51AEB6BBC8EA2469E1617071D9
FF658");
ctx.load(ctype);
ctx.executeQueryAsync(success, failure);

//REST Interface
$.ajax(
{
    url: _spPageContextInfo.webServerRelativeUrl +
        "/_api/web/contentTypes/getById('0x010100F51AEB6BBC8EA2469E1617071D9FF658')",
    type: "GET",
    headers: {
        "accept": "application/json;odata=verbose",
    }
});
```

When would you want to access a content type through the *ContentTypes* collection rather than the *AvailableContentTypes* collection? The first observation is that the line of code that accesses the content type through the *ContentTypes* collection will fail if it is ever executed within the context of a child site. Therefore, accessing content types with the *AvailableContentTypes* collection is more flexible if you need to write code that might execute in the context of a child site. This behavior is similar to the behavior of site columns.

However, another important point is that a content type that has been retrieved through the *AvailableContentTypes* collection is read-only and cannot be modified. Therefore, you must retrieve a content type by using the *ContentTypes* collection inside the context of the site where it exists if you need to modify it. Remember that all the standard SharePoint Foundation content types are added to the content types gallery of each top-level site.

Each content type is made up of a set of site columns. Although each content type defines a collection of site columns, it doesn't just track a collection of site columns by using *SPField* objects as you might expect. Instead, it tracks each site column by using an *SPFieldLink* object. You can think of an *SPFieldLink* object as a layer on top of an *SPField* object that the content type can use to customize default property values of the underlying site column.

Consider a scenario in which you might want to add the standard site column named Company to an existing content type. This is accomplished by adding a new field to the collection of field links. Listing 9-10 adds the site column to an existing content type, and then pushes the change to every list and document library that uses it.

LISTING 9-10 Adding site columns to a content type programmatically

```
//Server-Side Object Model
SPContentType ctype = site.ContentTypes["WingtipToysProduct"];
SPField companyField = site.Fields.GetFieldByInternalName("Company");
ctype.FieldLinks.Add(new SPFieldLink(companyField));
ctype.Update(true, false);

//JavaScript Client Object Model
var ctx = new SP.ClientContext.get_current();
var field = ctx.get_site().get_rootWeb().get_fields()
        .getByInternalNameOrTitle("Company");
var ctype = ctx.get_site().get_rootWeb().get_contentTypes()
        .getById("0x010100F51AEB6BBC8EA2469E1617071D9FF658");
ctx.load(ctype);
ctx.load(field);
var createInfo = new SP.FieldLinkCreationInformation();
createInfo.set_field(field);
var fieldLink = ctype.get_fieldLinks().add(createInfo);
ctype.update (true);
ctx.load(fieldLink);
ctx.executeQueryAsync(success, failure);
```

Note that the call to *Update* in the server-side code passes a second parameter with a value of *false*. This second parameter requires some explanation. There are some content types in the standard set of content types added by SharePoint Foundation that are defined as read-only content types. If you do not pass a value of *false* for the second parameter, the call to *Update* fails when it attempts to modify one of these read-only content types. When you pass a value of *false*, the call to *Update* succeeds because it ignores any failures due to the inability to update read-only content types.

Creating custom content types

You will never create a content type from scratch. Instead, you always select an existing content type to serve as the base content type for the new content types you are creating. For example, you can create the most straightforward content type by inheriting from the content type named *Item*. This automatically provides your new content type with the standard fields and behavior that are common across all content types. Alternatively, you can elect to inherit from another content type that inherits from the *Item* content type, such as *Announcement*, *Contact*, *Task*, or *Document*. Beyond creating a new content type manually by using the browser, you can also do it declaratively with Collaborative Application Markup Language (CAML), or programmatically.

Adding a new content type declaratively is straightforward when you are using Visual Studio 2012. Simply select the option to add a new item to your app or solution and select Content Type. A wizard then walks you through selecting from the available content types from which to inherit. You can then easily add existing site columns to the content type. If you need a custom site column, it can also be added as a new item. The end result is an Elements.xml file containing the declarative definition of the new content type, as shown in the following code:

```xml
<?xml version="1.0" encoding="utf-8"?>
<Elements xmlns="http://schemas.microsoft.com/sharepoint/">
  <!-- Parent ContentType: Document (0x0101) -->
  <ContentType ID="0x010100FD82D89E067A4B0C8D0E7474FA662E70"
               Name="FinancialDocument"
               Group="Financial"
               Description="Financial Content Type"
               Inherits="TRUE"
               Version="0">
  - <FieldRefs>
      <FieldRef ID="{a93bbb3e-2a86-4763-bfb5-9c86849d1630}"
               DisplayName="Amount"
               Required="FALSE"
               Name="Amount" />
    </FieldRefs>
  </ContentType>
</Elements>
```

To create a new content type with server-side code, you must call the *SPContentType* class constructor, passing three parameters. The first parameter is the *SPContentType* object associated with the parent content type you want to inherit from. The second parameter is the target content types collection, which should typically be the *ContentTypes* collection of a top-level site. The third parameter is the string name of the content type to be created. After you have created an *SPContentType* object and initialized its properties, such as *Description* and *Group*, you must call the *Add* method on the *ContentTypes* property of the target site to actually save your work in the content database. The following code shows how this works:

```
SPWeb site = SPContext.Current.Site.RootWeb;
string ctypeName = "FinancialDocument";
SPContentType ctypeParent = site.ContentTypes["Document"];
SPContentType ctype = new SPContentType(ctypeParent, site.ContentTypes, ctypeName);
ctype.Description = "A new content type";
ctype.Group = "Financial Content Types";
site.ContentTypes.Add(ctype);
```

When creating a new content type by using CSOM, the process is similar to the server-side example. When creating a new content type by using REST, the process uses a *POST* method but requires the same basic information. Listing 9-11 shows each approach.

LISTING 9-11 Creating content types programmatically

```
//JavaScript Client Object Model
var ctx = new SP.ClientContext.get_current();
var parent = ctx.get_web().get_contentTypes().getById("0x0101");
ctx.load(parent);
var createInfo = new SP.ContentTypeCreationInformation();
createInfo.set_name("FinancialDocument");
createInfo.set_description("A new content type");
createInfo.set_parentContentType(parent);
var newCtype = ctx.get_site().get_rootWeb().get_contentTypes().add(createInfo);
ctx.load(newCtype);
ctx.executeQueryAsync(success, failure)

//REST Interface
$.ajax({
    url: _spPageContextInfo.webServerRelativeUrl +
        "/_api/site/rootWeb/contentTypes",
    type: "POST",
    contentType: "application/json;odata=verbose",
    data: JSON.stringify({
        '__metadata': { 'type': 'SP.ContentType' },
        'Name': contentTypeName,
        'Description': description,
        'Id': {
            '__metadata': { 'type': 'SP.ContentTypeId' },
            'StringValue': createCTypeId(parentId)
            }
    }),
    headers: {
        "accept": "application/json;odata=verbose",
        "X-RequestDigest": $("#__REQUESTDIGEST").val()
        }
});
```

Working with document libraries

A document library is really just a specialized type of list. The main difference between a document library and other types of lists is that a document library is designed to store documents instead of merely list items. Every item in a document library is based on a file stored inside the content database. You can add extra fields to a document library just as you can to a standard list. This is a common practice because the fields in a document library allow you to track document metadata that is stored outside the document file.

Document libraries have an underlying base type of *1*, which defines several document-related fields. For example, SharePoint tracks the name of each file in a document library by using a field named *FileLeafRef*, which has a display name of Name. There is a second field named *FileRef*, with a display name of URL Path, which contains the file name combined with its site-relative path. There is another field named *FileDirRef*, with a display name of Path, which contains the site-relative path without the file name.

The ECB menu works differently in document libraries than in standard lists. More specifically, SharePoint populates the ECB menu for a document by using the file name instead of the *Title* field. SharePoint uses a related field named *LinkFilename*, which reads the file name from the *FileLeafRef* field and uses it to render the ECB menu. There is a third related field named *LinkFilenameNoMenu*, which can be used to display the file name in a hyperlink that can be used to navigate to the View Properties page associated with a document.

You can program against a document library by using the *SPList* class just as you would with any other type of list. The server-side object model also provides the *SPDocumentLibrary* class, which inherits from *SPList*. *SPDocumentLibrary* extends *SPList* with additional functionality that is specific to document libraries. After you obtain an *SPList* reference to a document library from the *Lists* collection of a site, you can convert the *SPList* reference to an *SPDocumentLibrary* reference to access the extra methods and properties that are only available with document libraries, as shown in the following code:

```
SPDocumentLibrary DocLib = (SPDocumentLibrary)site.Lists["Product Proposals"];
```

Creating a document library

You can create a document library declaratively by creating a *ListInstance* element with a *TemplateType* value of 101 and the GUID that identifies the *DocumentLibrary* feature provided by SharePoint. The following code shows a sample in CAML:

```
<ListInstance
  TemplateType="101"
  FeatureId="00bfea71-e717-4e80-aa17-d0c71b360101"
  Url="ProductProposals"
  Title="Product Proposals"
  Description=""
  OnQuickLaunch="TRUE" />
```

If you prefer to create document libraries by using code, you can do so just as you do when creating a standard list. The only difference is that you pass a list template parameter with an *SPList-TemplateType* enumeration value of *DocumentLibrary*. Refer to the code in the section "Creating lists" earlier in this chapter for details.

Adding a custom document template

One unique characteristic of document libraries is that they provide support for document templates. For example, you can create a document template by using Microsoft Word that allows users to create documents that already contain the company letterhead; or you can create a document template using Microsoft Excel that allows users to create documents for expense reports that have a structure predefined by the accounting department. A user can then create a new document from a document template by using the New Document menu on the Documents tab of a document library.

A document library is initially configured with a generic document template. However, you can update it to utilize a custom document template. One approach is to upload the custom document template file by using a *Module* element. SharePoint contains a special folder named *Forms* inside the root folder of each document library. The Forms folder is the proper location in which to upload the document template for a document library. The following code shows the declarative CAML necessary to define a document template within a *Module* element:

```
<Module Name="ProductProposalTemplates" Url="ProductProposals" List="101" >
  <File Path="ProductProposalTemplates\Proposal.dotx"
        Url="Forms/Proposal.dotx"
        Type="GhostableInLibrary" />
</Module>
```

The *Url* attribute of the *Module* element contains the site-relative URL of the document library, which in this case is *ProductProposals*. This is required so that the files inside this *Module* element are provisioned relative to the root of the document library instead of the root of the site. You should also notice that the *Module* element includes a *List* attribute with a value of 101, which is required to indicate that the target location exists inside the scope of a document library. The *Url* attribute of the *File* element contains a path to provision the document template file in the Forms folder. The *Type* attribute is configured with a value of *GhostableInLibrary*, which tells SharePoint to provision the template within a document library.

As an alternative to using a declarative *Module*, you can upload the document template programmatically. In the server-side object model, the *SPFolder* object provides a *Files* collection property with an *Add* method, which makes it possible to upload a copy of the document template file. When you call the *Add* method on a *Files* collection object to create a new file such as a document template, you can pass the contents of the file by using either a byte array or an object based on the *Stream* class, as shown in the following code:

```
SPDocumentLibrary DocLib = (SPDocumentLibrary)site.Lists[DocLibID];
SPFolder formsFolder = DocLib.RootFolder.SubFolders["Forms"];
formsFolder.Files.Add("Specification.dotx", {Stream Object});
DocLib.DocumentTemplateUrl = @"ProductSpecifications/Forms/Specification.dotx";
DocLib.Update();
```

When using the client-side object model or REST interface through JavaScript, you must create a mechanism for selecting and reading the document template into a variable. This is accomplished by using an *input* element of type *file* and the *FileReader* object. The following code snippet shows some HTML and JavaScript for selecting files:

```
<input id="inputFile" type="file" />
<input id="uploadButton" type="button" value="Upload" class="app-button"/>

$("#uploadButton").click(function () {
    var buffer;
    var error;
    var file = document.getElementById("inputFile").files[0];
    var filename = document.getElementById("inputFile").value;

    var reader = new FileReader();
    reader.onload = function (e) {
        buffer = e.target.result;
    };
    reader.onerror = function (e) {
        error = e.target.error;
    };
    reader.readAsArrayBuffer(file);
});
```

The *input* element of type *file* creates a control that allows users to browse for and select files. The *FileReader* object can read the selected files into a buffer by referencing the *files* collection of the control. The *FileReader* reads the selected file asynchronously and fires the *onload* event when finished. The *FileReader* should use the *readAsArrayBuffer* method, which returns an array that is compatible with both the client-side object model and REST. At this point, the buffer containing the file can be retrieved from the *result* property. The contents of the buffer can be used with the client-side object model to upload the file into the Forms folder, as shown in the following code:

```
var ctx = new SP.ClientContext.get_current();
var createInfo = new SP.FileCreationInformation();
createInfo.set_content(buffer);
createInfo.set_overwrite(true);
createInfo.set_url("template.dotx");
var files =
ctx.get_web().getFolderByServerRelativeUrl("ProductSpecifications/Forms").get_files();
ctx.load(files);
files.add(createInfo);
ctx.executeQueryAsync(success, failure);
```

Note that the JavaScript client object model can only upload files up to 1.5 megabytes (MB) in size. If you need to upload larger files, then you must use the REST interface. The REST interface supports uploading documents as large as 2 gigabytes (GB). The following code shows the endpoint to use for uploading with the REST interface:

```
$.ajax({
    url: _spPageContextInfo.webServerRelativeUrl +
        "/_api/web/GetFolderByServerRelativeUrl(' ProductSpecifications/Forms ')/Files" +
        "/Add(url='template.dotx', overwrite=true)",
    type: "POST",
    data: buffer,
    processData: false,
    headers: {
        "accept": "application/json;odata=verbose",
        "X-RequestDigest": $("#__REQUESTDIGEST").val(),
        "content-length": content.length
    }
});
```

After the document template is uploaded, you must write code to configure the *DocumentTemplateUrl* property of the document library. This code ensures that the template is used for the creation of new documents. The following code shows how to do this with server-side and client-side code:

```
//Server-Side Object Model
SPWeb site = SPContext.Current.Web;
SPDocumentLibrary libProposals;
libProposals = (SPDocumentLibrary)site.Lists["Product Proposals"];
string templateUrl = @"ProductProposals/Forms/Proposal.dotx";
libProposals.DocumentTemplateUrl = templateUrl;
libProposals.Update();

//JavaScript Client-Side Object Model
var ctx = new SP.ClientContext.get_current();
var library = ctx.get_web().get_lists().getByTitle('ProductSpecifications')
ctx.load(library);
library.set_documentTemplateUrl('ProductSpecifications/Forms/Proposal.dotx');
library.update();
ctx.executeQueryAsync(success, failure);
```

Creating document-based content types

You can create custom content types for tracking documents. This design approach provides the same type of advantages as creating content types for standard lists. For example, you can create a content type that defines a custom set of site columns for tracking document metadata and then reuse that content type across many document libraries. If you design document libraries by using custom content types, you also have the ability to add new columns to a content type and push the changes to many document libraries at once. Custom content types for document libraries generally inherit from the *Document* content type. One unique aspect of content types that inherit from the *Document* content type is that they add support for document templates.

After you have created a new content type, your next step is to upload a copy of the document template file. Uploading a file for the content type document template is done in the same way as for a document library. However, the tricky part is knowing where to upload this file. SharePoint creates a dedicated folder for each site content type in the virtual file system of the hosting site within a special folder named _cts. When you create a new content type, SharePoint automatically creates a new folder for it at _cts/[Content Type Name]. This is the location where you should upload the document template.

After you have uploaded a copy of the document template file, you can then configure the content type to use it by modifying its *DocumentTemplate* property. In order to properly set the document template, you must know the content type ID and the name of the file to use. Listing 9-12 shows how this is accomplished for a content type named "Invoice".

LISTING 9-12 Setting a document template URL programmatically

```
//Server-Side Object Model
SPWeb site = SPContext.Current.Site.RootWeb;
SPContentType ctype = site.ContentTypes["Invoice"];
ctype.DocumentTemplate("Invoice.docx");

//JavaScript Client-Side Object Model
var ctx = new SP.ClientContext.get_current();
var ctype = ctx.get_web().get_contentTypes().getById("0x0101adbc123")
ctx.load(ctype);
ctype.set_documentTemplate("Invoice.docx");
ctype.update();
ctx.executeQueryAsync(success, failure);

//REST Interface
$.ajax({
    url: _spPageContextInfo.webServerRelativeUrl +
        "/_api/web/contentTypes/getById('0x0101adbc123')",
    type: "POST",
    contentType: "application/json;odata=verbose",
    data: JSON.stringify({
        '__metadata': { 'type': 'SP.ContentType' },
        'DocumentTemplate': 'Invoice.docx'
    }),
    headers: {
    "accept": "application/json;odata=verbose",
    "X-RequestDigest": $("#__REQUESTDIGEST").val(),
    "IF-MATCH": "*",
    "X-Http-Method": "PATCH"
    }
});
```

After the content types are created and the templates defined, the content types can be used in a document library. To add new content types to a document library, the *ContentTypesEnabled* property must be set to *true*. After that, new content types can be added to the collection as shown in Listing 9-13.

LISTING 9-13 Adding content types to a library programmatically

```
//Server-Side Object Model
SPWeb site = SPContext.Current.Site.RootWeb;
SPDocumentLibrary DocLib = (SPDocumentLibrary)site.Lists["FinancialDocuments"];
DocLib.ContentTypes.Add(site.AvailableContentTypes["Invoice"]);

//JavaScript Client-Side Object Model
var ctx = new SP.ClientContext.get_current();
var library = ctx.get_web().get_lists().getByTitle("FinancialDocuments");
ctx.load(library);
var ctype = ctx.get_web().get_contentTypes().getById('0x0101adbc123');
ctx.load(ctype);
library.get_contentTypes().addExistingContentType(ctype);
ctx.executeQueryAsync(success, failure);

//REST Interface
$.ajax(
{
    url: _spPageContextInfo.webServerRelativeUrl +
        "/_api/web/lists/getByTitle('FinancialDocuments')" +
        "/contentTypes/addAvailableContentType('0x0101adbc123')",
    type: "POST",
    contentType: "application/json;odata=verbose",
    headers: {
        "accept": "application/json;odata=verbose",
        "X-RequestDigest": $("#__REQUESTDIGEST").val(),
        }
});
```

There is a dual aspect to programming documents in a document library. Though you can program against a document library by using an *SPList* object, you can also program against a document by using an *SPListItem* object. However, each document is also represented in the server-side object with an *SPFile* object. That means you can program against a document in a document library as either an *SPListItem* or *SPFile* object. You can obtain the file associated with an item through the *File* property by using either server-side or client-side code.

The *SPListItem* object can be used to read or update fields just as you would read or update fields for an item in a standard list. The *SPFile* object, on the other hand, can be used to control other aspects of the document, such as versioning, check-in, and checkout, as well as reading from and writing to the document's content.

When the server-side object model is used, the contents of the document can be accessed through the *SPFile.OpenBinaryStream* method. When the managed client object model is used, the contents can be accessed through the *File.OpenBinaryDirect* and *File.SaveBinaryDirect* methods. When the REST API is used, the contents are accessed by referencing the file followed by the *$value* method, as shown here:

```
http://site/_api/web/GetFileByServerRelativeUrl('filepath')/$value
```

Working with folders

Many document libraries contain folders in addition to documents. Folders, like files, are stored as items within a document library and show up as *SPListItem* objects in the *Items* collection. This can be confusing if you are expecting a classic treeview structure within the library. Instead of navigating a tree, you can inspect a *SPListItem* property named *FileSystemObjectType* before attempting to process an item as an *SPFile* object, as shown in Listing 9-14.

LISTING 9-14 Identifying folder items

```
//Server-Side Object Model
SPWeb site = SPContext.Current.Site.RootWeb;
SPDocumentLibrary DocLib = (SPDocumentLibrary)site.Lists["FinancialDocuments"];
foreach (SPListItem item in docLib.Items) {
  if (item.FileSystemObjectType == SPFileSystemObjectType.File) {
    // process item as document
    SPFile file = item.File;
  }
}

//JavaScript Client Object Model
var enumerator = listItems.getEnumerator(); //Returned from async call
while (enumerator.moveNext()) {
    var listItem = enumerator.get_current();
    if (listItem.get_fileSystemObjectType() === SP.FileSystemObjectType.file) {
        //process item as document
    }
}

//REST interface
var results = data.d.results; //Returned from async call
for (var i = 0; i < results.length; i++) {
    if (results[i].FileSystemObjectType === SP.FileSystemObjectType.file) {
        //process item as document
    }
}
```

One last point to keep in mind is that discovering documents by enumerating through the *Items* collection of a document library finds all documents without regard to whether they exist in the root folder or in folders nested below the root folder. If you would rather enumerate through only the documents in the root folder of a document library, you can use a different approach by using the *SPFolder* and *SPFile* classes. Listing 9-15 shows how to access only documents located in the root folder of the library.

LISTING 9-15 Accessing the root folder programmatically

```
//Server-Side Object model
SPWeb site = SPContext.Current.Site.RootWeb;
SPDocumentLibrary DocLib = (SPDocumentLibrary)site.Lists["FinancialDocuments"];
foreach (SPFile file in docLib.RootFolder.Files) {
  // program against file using SPFile class
}

//JavaScript Client Object Model
var ctx = new SP.ClientContext.get_current();
var list = ctx.get_web().get_lists().getByTitle("FinancialDocuments");
ctx.load(list);
var files = list.get_rootFolder().get_Files();
ctx.load(files);
ctx.executeQueryAsync(success, failure);

//REST interface
$.ajax(
{
    url: _spPageContextInfo.webServerRelativeUrl +
        "/_api/web/lists/getByTitle ('FinancialDocuments')/rootFolder/files",
    type: "GET",
    headers: {
        "accept": "application/json;odata=verbose",
            }
});
```

Creating and registering event handlers

SharePoint supports event notification on host objects such as sites, lists, content types, and apps. This support is valuable to developers because it makes it possible to write event handlers, which are methods that are executed automatically in response to actions such as creating a new list, updating an item in a list, and deleting a document.

Events can be separated into two main categories: before events and after events. *Before events* fire before the corresponding event action occurs and before SharePoint Foundation has written any data to the content database. A key point is that a before event is fired early enough that it supports the cancellation of the event action that triggers it. Therefore, before events are often used to perform custom validations.

After events fire after the event action has completed and after SharePoint has written to the content database to commit the event action. After events do not support cancelling the event action. Instead, after events are used to execute code in response to an event action. A common example is sending out email notifications to let all the members of a site know when a new document has been uploaded.

SharePoint uses a special naming convention for events. Before events are based on methods whose names end with *ing*. For example, before events have names such as *WebAdding*, *WebDeleting*, *ItemAdding*, and *ItemUpdating*. The methods for after events have names that end with *ed*, such as *WebProvisioned*, *WebDeleted*, *ItemAdded*, and *ItemUpdated*.

Each event handler is executed under a specific synchronization mode. The two supported synchronization modes are synchronous and asynchronous. Before events are always executed under a synchronization mode of synchronous. A key point is that synchronous event handlers have a blocking nature because they run on the same thread that is processing the event action.

By default, SharePoint executes after events under a synchronization mode of asynchronous. The main difference is that asynchronous event handlers execute on a separate thread so they do not block the response that is sent back to the user. Imagine a scenario where a user uploads a new document and an after event responds by sending out a series of email notifications to more than 100 users. The asynchronous nature of an after event doesn't require the user who has uploaded the document to wait while the code in the event handler is sending out email messages. The response page is returned to the user while the after event continues to execute.

Although SharePoint Foundation executes after events asynchronously by default, you have the option of configuring an after event to run as a synchronous event. Configuring an after event to run synchronously can be a useful technique in a scenario where code executed by the after event makes an update to an item that must be seen immediately.

Understanding event receiver classes

Event handling with the server-side object model in SharePoint solutions is based on event receiver classes. You create a new event receiver class by inheriting from one of the following event receiver base classes that are defined inside the *Microsoft.SharePoint* assembly:

- *SPItemEventReceiver*
- *SPListEventReceiver*
- *SPEmailEventReceiver*
- *SPWebEventReceiver*
- *SPWorkflowEventReceiver*

The *SPItemEventReceiver* class provides event handling support for when users add, modify, or delete items in a list or documents in a document library. The *SPListEventReceiver* class provides event handling support for when users create and delete lists, as well as when users modify a list's fields collection. The *SPEmailEventReceiver* class provides event handling support for when users send email messages to an email-enabled list.

The *SPWebEventReceiver* class provides event handling support for when users create new child sites within a site collection. The *SPWebEventReceiver* class also provides event handling support for when users move or delete sites, including both child sites and top-level sites. The *SPWorkflowEventReceiver* class provides event handling support for when users start a workflow instance as well as event handling support to signal when a workflow instance has completed or has been postponed.

After you have created a class that inherits from one of the event receiver base classes, you implement the event receiver class by overriding methods that represent event handlers. As an example, Listing 9-16 creates an event handler for an announcements list. The event handler adds a notice and tracking number to each announcement when it is added to the list. Furthermore, the handler prevents the deletion of any items from the list.

LISTING 9-16 Server-side event handler

```
public class ItemReceiver : SPItemEventReceiver
{
    public override void ItemAdding(SPItemEventProperties properties)
    {
        properties.AfterProperties["Body"] += "\n ** For internal use only ** \n";
    }

    public override void ItemAdded(SPItemEventProperties properties)
    {
        properties.ListItem["Body"] +=
            "\n Tracking ID: " + Guid.NewGuid().ToString() + " \n";
        properties.ListItem.Update();
    }

    public override void ItemDeleting(SPItemEventProperties properties)
    {
        properties.Cancel = true;
        properties.Status = SPEventReceiverStatus.CancelWithRedirectUrl;
        properties.ErrorMessage = "Items cannot be deleted from this list.";
    }
}
```

Understanding remote event receivers

Event handling in apps is based upon a completely different architecture known as *remote event receivers*. Remote event receivers are similar in concept to the standard event handlers except that the receiver is a remote service endpoint instead of an assembly. Remote event receivers support events at the web, app, list, and list-item level, which can be both synchronous and asynchronous.

Remote event receivers can be added to an app through either the Add New Item dialog box or the Properties dialog box. If the remote event receiver is to handle anything other than app life cycle events, it should be added to the app by using the Add New Item dialog box. If the remote event receiver is to handle one of the app life cycle events, it is added by setting one of the event properties for the app, as shown in Figure 9-2 and detailed in Chapter 4, "SharePoint apps."

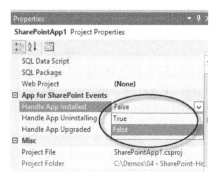

FIGURE 9-2 Setting an app life cycle event

If the remote event receiver is added through the Add New Item dialog box, you will be further prompted to select the event scope and event types to handle. After the scope and type are defined, Visual Studio will automatically add a new web project to your app to handle the events. This web project is automatically set as the associated remote web for the app so that it will start during the debugging process.

Remote event receivers implement the *IRemoteEventService* interface. This interface consists of two methods: *ProcessEvent* and *ProcessOneWayEvent*. You use the *ProcessEvent* method to handle synchronous events and the *ProcessOneWayEvent* method to handle asynchronous events. The new web project comes with template code that implements the *IRemoteEventService* interface and uses the *TokenHelper* class to retrieve a CSOM *ClientContext* for calling back into SharePoint. Listing 9-17 implements a remote event handler for an announcements list similar to what is shown in Listing 9-16.

LISTING 9-17 Remote event receiver

```
public class AnnouncementsReceiver : IRemoteEventService
{
    public SPRemoteEventResult ProcessEvent(RemoteEventProperties properties)
    {
        SPRemoteEventResult result = new SPRemoteEventResult();
        switch (properties.EventType)
        {
            case SPRemoteEventType.ItemAdding:
                result.ChangedItemProperties.Add("Body", "\n ** For internal use only **
\n");
                break;
            case SPRemoteEventType.ItemDeleting:
                result.ErrorMessage = "Items cannot be deleted from this list";
                result.Status = SPRemoteEventServiceStatus.CancelWithError;
                break;
        }
        return result;
    }
```

```
public void ProcessOneWayEvent(RemoteEventProperties properties)
{
    HttpRequestMessageProperty requestproperty =
    (HttpRequestMessageProperty)OperationContext.Current.
    IncomingMessageProperties[HttpRequestMessageProperty.Name];
    string contexttokenstring = requestproperty.Headers["x-sp-accesstoken"];
    if (contexttokenstring != null)
    {
        SharePointContextToken contexttoken =
        TokenHelper.ReadAndValidateContextToken(
        contexttokenstring, requestproperty.Headers[HttpRequestHeader.Host]);
        Uri sharepointurl = new Uri(properties.ItemEventProperties.WebUrl);
        string accesstoken = TokenHelper.GetAccessToken(
        contexttoken, sharepointurl.Authority).AccessToken;
        using (ClientContext clientcontext =
        TokenHelper.GetClientContextWithAccessToken(
        sharepointurl.ToString(), accesstoken))
        {
            if (properties.EventType == SPRemoteEventType.ItemAdded)
            {
                List list =
                clientcontext.Web.Lists.GetByTitle(
                properties.ItemEventProperties.ListTitle);
                clientcontext.Load(list);
                ListItem item =
                list.GetItemById(properties.ItemEventProperties.ListItemId);
                clientcontext.Load(item);
                clientcontext.ExecuteQuery();
                item["Body"] += "\n Tracking ID: " + Guid.NewGuid().ToString() + "
\n";
                item.Update();
                clientcontext.ExecuteQuery();
            }
        }
    }
}
```

Registering event handlers

After you create an event receiver, you must bind one or more of its event handler methods to a host object by using event registration. The types of objects that support event registration include site collections, sites, lists, content types, and documents. Note that only certain types of event handlers are supported by each type of host object. For example, you can register a *ListAdded* event handler with a site collection or a site, but that event type is not supported by host objects such as lists, content types, or documents. Likewise, you can register an *ItemUpdating* event handler with a list, content type, or document, but that event type is not supported by site collections or sites.

The simplest and most common technique for registering an event handler is to use a declarative *Receivers* element in a CAML file. Listing 9-18 shows the CAML for registering the event receiver in Listing 9-16.

LISTING 9-18 Registering an event receiver

```xml
<?xml version="1.0" encoding="utf-8"?>
<Elements xmlns="http://schemas.microsoft.com/sharepoint/">
  <Receivers ListTemplateId="104" Scope="Web">
    <Receiver>
      <Name>ItemReceiverItemAdding</Name>
      <Type>ItemAdding</Type>
      <Assembly>$SharePoint.Project.AssemblyFullName$</Assembly>
      <Class>AnnouncementHandler.ItemReceiver.ItemReceiver</Class>
      <SequenceNumber>10000</SequenceNumber>
    </Receiver>
    <Receiver>
      <Name>ItemReceiverItemDeleting</Name>
      <Type>ItemDeleting</Type>
      <Assembly>$SharePoint.Project.AssemblyFullName$</Assembly>
      <Class>AnnouncementHandler.ItemReceiver.ItemReceiver</Class>
      <SequenceNumber>10000</SequenceNumber>
    </Receiver>
    <Receiver>
      <Name>ItemReceiverItemAdded</Name>
      <Type>ItemAdded</Type>
      <Assembly>$SharePoint.Project.AssemblyFullName$</Assembly>
      <Class>AnnouncementHandler.ItemReceiver.ItemReceiver</Class>
      <SequenceNumber>10000</SequenceNumber>
      <Synchronization>Synchronous</Synchronization>
    </Receiver>
  </Receivers>
</Elements>
```

The registration file for a remote event receiver is nearly identical to the one used for a server-side event receiver. The only difference is that the file adds a *Url* element that refers to the endpoint of the remote event receiver. This is the endpoint that is invoked when the event occurs. Listing 9-19 shows the registration CAML for the remote event receiver described in Listing 9-17.

LISTING 9-19 Registering a remote event receiver

```xml
<?xml version="1.0" encoding="utf-8"?>
<Elements xmlns="http://schemas.microsoft.com/sharepoint/">
  <Receivers ListTemplateId="10000">
    <Receiver>
      <Name>AnnouncementsReceiverItemAdding</Name>
      <Type>ItemAdding</Type>
      <SequenceNumber>10000</SequenceNumber>
      <Url>http://webs.wingtiptoys.com/AnnouncementsReceiver.svc</Url>
    </Receiver>
    <Receiver>
      <Name>AnnouncementsReceiverItemDeleting</Name>
      <Type>ItemDeleting</Type>
      <SequenceNumber>10000</SequenceNumber>
      <Url>http://webs.wingtiptoys.com/AnnouncementsReceiver.svc</Url>
    </Receiver>
    <Receiver>
      <Name>AnnouncementsReceiverItemAdded</Name>
      <Type>ItemAdded</Type>
      <SequenceNumber>10000</SequenceNumber>
      <Url>http://webs.wingtiptoys.com/AnnouncementsReceiver.svc</Url>
    </Receiver>
  </Receivers>
</Elements>
```

Although registering event handlers declaratively by using a *Receivers* element works in the majority of scenarios, there are a few cases for which it doesn't suffice. For example, you cannot register an event handler on a host object such as a content type or an individual document by using a declarative *Receivers* element. These types of event registration must be accomplished by using code.

Host object types that support events such as *SPContentType* expose a collection property named *EventReceivers*. The *EventReceivers* collection property exposes an *Add* method that has five different overloaded implementations. The most straightforward implementation of the *Add* method accepts three parameters: the event type, the four-part assembly name, and the namespace-qualified name of the event receiver class. Listing 9-20 shows an example of implementing the *FeatureActivated* method for a site collection–scoped feature that registers an event handler on the *Item* content type by using an event receiver class named *ItemContentTypeEvents*.

LISTING 9-20 Registering an event receiver by using a feature receiver

```
public override void FeatureActivated(SPFeatureReceiverProperties properties) {
  SPSite siteCollection = (SPSite)properties.Feature.Parent;
  SPWeb site = siteCollection.RootWeb;

  // retrieve content type
  SPContentType ctypeItem = site.ContentTypes["Item"];

  // register event handler for content type
  string ReceiverAssemblyName = this.GetType().Assembly.FullName;
  string ReceiverClassName = typeof(ItemContentTypeEvents).FullName;
  ctypeItem.EventReceivers.Add(SPEventReceiverType.ItemDeleting,
                        ReceiverAssemblyName,
                        ReceiverClassName);

  // push updates to all lists and document libraries
  ctypeItem.Update(true, false);
}
```

Though calling the *Add* method with these three parameters provides the easiest approach for registering an event handler, it provides the least flexibility. For example, you cannot assign registration properties for receiver data or synchronization. To obtain more control, you can register the event handler by calling another implementation of the *Add* method, one that takes no parameters and returns an *SPEventReceiverDefinition* object, as shown in the following code:

```
SPContentType ctypeItem = site.ContentTypes["Item"];
string ReceiverAssemblyName = this.GetType().Assembly.FullName;
string ReceiverClassName = typeof(ItemContentTypeEvents).FullName;

// register event handler by creating SPEventReceiverDefinition object
SPEventReceiverDefinition def = ctypeItem.EventReceivers.Add();
def.Type = SPEventReceiverType.ItemDeleting;
def.Assembly = ReceiverAssemblyName;
def.Class = ReceiverClassName;
def.SequenceNumber = 100;
def.Data = "MyData";
def.Update();

// push updates to all lists and document libraries
ctypeItem.Update(true, false);
```

Remote event receivers support the same type of server-side registration by using a different overload of the *Add* method. In this case, an additional parameter is passed that specifies the *Url* of the remote event receiver endpoint. The general form of the registration is shown in the following code:

```
string serviceUrl= "http://webs.wingtiptoys.com/AnnouncementsReceiver.svc";
string siteUrl= "http://intranet.wingtiptoys.com";
using (SPSite site = new SPSite(siteUrl))
```

```
{
   using (SPWeb web = site.RootWeb)
   {
      SPList list = web.Lists["Announcements"];
      list.EventReceivers.Add(SPEventReceiverType.ItemAdded, serviceUrl);
   }
}
```

Programming before events

When you write the event handler implementation for a before event, you have the ability to cancel the user action that triggered the event. In server-side event handlers, you can accomplish this by assigning a value of *true* to the *Cancel* property of the event handler parameter named properties, as shown in Listing 9-16. In remote event receivers, you can assign the value of *CancelWithError* to the *SPRemoteEventResult* object, as shown in Listing 9-17. When canceling the event action, you can also use the *ErrorMessage* property to assign a custom error message that will be displayed to the user.

When you cancel a before event, SharePoint responds by short-circuiting the user's request and canceling the event action. The key point here is that before events provide you with a layer of defense against unwanted modifications. Instead of deleting the list as the user requested, SharePoint displays the custom error message in an message box to the user.

In some scenarios, you might decide that the standard error dialog box displayed by SharePoint upon the cancellation of an event action is not sufficient. If you want to create a user experience that is more customized, you can modify the *Status* and *RedirectUrl* properties to redirect the user to a custom error page. These properties are available in both server-side and remote event receivers. The following code shows a sample for each:

```
//Server-Side Event Receiver
public override void ListDeleting(SPListEventProperties properties) {
   if (!properties.Web.UserIsSiteAdmin) {
      properties.Cancel = true;
      properties.Status = SPEventReceiverStatus.CancelWithRedirectUrl;
      properties.RedirectUrl = properties.Web.Site.Url + "/error.aspx";
   }
}


//Remote Event Receiver
public SPRemoteEventResult ProcessEvent(RemoteEventProperties properties)
{
   SPRemoteEventResult result = new SPRemoteEventResult();
   switch (properties.EventType)
   {
      case SPRemoteEventType.ItemDeleting:
         result.Status = SPRemoteEventServiceStatus.CancelWithError;
         result.RedirectUrl = "http://webs.wingtiptoys.com/error.aspx";
         break;
   }
   return result;
}
```

Programming after events

After events cannot be used to cancel an event action. Instead, after events provide the opportunity to execute code in response to an event action, such as a user successfully creating a new list. When programming after events, you must reach back into SharePoint and explicitly retrieve the item to work with. In Listing 9-16, for example, the server-side object model is used to retrieve the recently added announcement.

In remote event handlers, you must take the same basic approach. However, calling back into SharePoint requires passing an OAuth token from the event handler, as shown in Listing 9-17. This process is the same for remote event receivers as it is for any SharePoint app containing a remote web. Chapter 6, "SharePoint security," covers the OAuth security infrastructure and the use of the *TokenHelper* class in detail, so it will not be repeated here.

When programming after events, you must be aware of several situations that can result in unexpected behavior. The first situation concerns the manner in which items are updated. The second situation involves the accidental creation of cascading events. The third situation is the need to call after events synchronously.

When updating list items in an after event, you should use the *UpdateOverwriteVersion* method instead of the *Update* method. You should avoiding calling *Update* in an after event on a list where versioning is enabled because it will generate two versions each time a user adds or updates an item. The *UpdateOverwriteVersion* method is provided for this exact scenario because it updates the most current version instead of generating a new version.

Modifying an item in an after event can trigger another cascading event. Consider the scenario in which an after event updates an item, which triggers the after event, which updates the item that triggers the after event, and so on. If you are not careful, you can create a recursive loop that will run until an error occurs. Here is an example of a flawed implementation of *ItemUpdated* that will experience this problem:

```
public override void ItemUpdated(SPItemEventProperties properties) {
    properties.ListItem["Title"] = properties.ListItem["Title"].ToString();
    properties.ListItem.UpdateOverwriteVersion();
}
```

Whenever you are required to implement an after event in which you update the item that triggered the event, you must disable event firing by modifying the *EventFiringEnabled* property of the event receiver class:

```
public override void ItemUpdated(SPItemEventProperties properties) {
    this.EventFiringEnabled = false;
    properties.ListItem["Title"] = properties.ListItem["Title"].ToString();
    properties.ListItem.UpdateOverwriteVersion();
    this.EventFiringEnabled = true;
}
```

If you do not disable event firing in the *ItemAdded* event handler, it is not as critical because it will not cause a recursive loop. However, it is still recommended because you then avoid triggering an *Update* event and executing *ItemUpdated* unnecessarily when a user adds a new item:

```
public override void ItemAdded(SPItemEventProperties properties) {
  this.EventFiringEnabled = false;
  properties.ListItem["Title"] = properties.ListItem["Title"].ToString();
  properties.ListItem.UpdateOverwriteVersion();
  this.EventFiringEnabled = true;
}
```

The final situation of concern centers on the fact that SharePoint Foundation executes the event handlers for after events such as *ItemAdded* and *ItemUpdated* asynchronously by default. The problem with after events that execute asynchronously revolves around the user seeing inconsistent field values. When a user updates a field value in the browser and saves the changes with a postback, any updates made by an event handler running asynchronously are not guaranteed to be reflected in the page that is sent back to the user. When you configure the event handler for an after event to run synchronously, you guarantee that the event handler's updates are reflected in the page returned to the user. To configure the event handler for an after event to run synchronously, you can add a *Synchronization* element with an inner value of *Synchronous* into the *Receiver* element, which is shown in Listing 9-18.

Querying lists with CAML

Using Collaborative Application Markup Language (CAML) to query lists is one of the oldest data-access techniques in SharePoint development and remains a core developer skill. Chapter 5, "Client-side programming," presented many examples using CAML with the client-side object model, so that information will not be repeated here. Instead, this section will focus on a more detailed examination of CAML using the server-side object model.

Understanding CAML fundamentals

Querying a list for specific items that meet a certain criteria can done by using the *Microsoft.SharePoint.SPQuery* object. The *SPQuery* object exposes a *Query* property that accepts a CAML fragment, which defines the query to perform. A *ViewFields* property defines the fields to return. The following code shows a simple query run against a list:

```
SPQuery query = new SPQuery();
query.Viewfields = @"<FieldRef Name='Title'/><FieldRef Name='Expires'/>";
query.Query =
@"<Where>
  <Lt>
    <FieldRef Name='Expires'/>
    <Value Type='DateTime'><Today/></Value>
  </Lt>
</Where>";
SPList list = SPContext.Current.Web.Lists.TryGetList("Announcements");
SPListItemCollections items = list.GetItems(query);
```

The *ViewFields* property accepts a CAML fragment containing a series of *FieldRef* elements. Each *FieldRef* element has a *Name* attribute that specifies the name of the list field to return from the query. Note that the *Name* attribute must contain the name of the field as it is defined in the schema. xml file for the list definition and not simply the display name of the field.

In order to create a query, you must properly construct a CAML fragment defining the items to return from the list. At the highest level, the CAML fragment may contain *Where*, *OrderBy*, and *GroupBy* elements. Inside of each of these elements, you can use additional CAML elements to specify conditions. Table 9-5 contains a complete list of CAML elements that can be used to create a query, and Listing 9-21 shows the basic form of the CAML query.

LISTING 9-21 CAML query form

```
<Where>
  <Lt>,<Gt>,<Eq>,<Leq>,<Geq>,<Neq>,<BeginsWith>,<Contains>,<IsNotNull>,<IsNull>
    <FieldRef/>
    <Value>[Test Value], Today</Value>
  </Lt>,</Gt>,</Eq>,</Leq>,</Geq>,</Neq>,</BeginsWith>,</Contains>,</IsNotNull>,</IsNull>
  <And>,<Or>
  <Lt>,<Gt>,<Eq>,<Leq>,<Geq>,<Neq>,<BeginsWith>,<Contains>,<IsNotNull>,<IsNull>
    <FieldRef/>
    <Value>[Test Value], Today</Value>
  </Lt>,</Gt>,</Eq>,</Leq>,</Geq>,</Neq>,</BeginsWith>,</Contains>,</IsNotNull>,</IsNull>
  </And>,</Or>
</Where>
<OrderBy>
  <FieldRef/>
</OrderBy>
<GroupBy>
  <FieldRef/>
<GroupBy>
```

TABLE 9-5 CAML elements for querying

Element	Description
And	Groups multiple conditions
BeginsWith	Searches for a string at the beginning of the text field
Contains	Searches for a string within the text field
Eq	Equal to
FieldRef	A reference to a field (useful for GroupBy elements)
Geq	Greater than or equal to
GroupBy	Groups results by these fields
Gt	Greater than
IsNotNull	Is not null (not empty)
IsNull	Is null (empty)
Join	Used to query across two lists that are joined through a Lookup field

Element	Description
Leq	Less than or equal to
Lt	Less than
Neq	Not equal to
Now	The current date and time
Or	Boolean OR operator
OrderBy	Orders the results of the query
Today	Today's date
TodayIso	Today's date in ISO format
Where	Used to specify the Where clause of the query

Querying joined lists

In addition to querying single lists, the *SPQuery* object can be used to query across two lists that are joined by a Lookup field and surfacing projected fields. As an example, consider two lists named *Instructors* and *Modules*. The Instructors list is a simple list that contains contact information for classroom instructors. The Modules list is a custom list that contains information about training modules that will be taught in the classroom. The Modules list is joined to the Instructors list via a lookup field that shows the *FullName* of the instructor. Additionally, the instructor's *Email Address* is available as a projected field. In this way, an instructor can be assigned a Module to teach. Using a *SPQuery* object and CAML, you can create a query that returns fields from both of these lists as shown in Listing 9-22.

LISTING 9-22 Querying joined lists

```
SPWeb site = SPContext.Current.Web;
SPList listInstructors = site.Lists["Instructors"];
SPList listModules = site.Lists["Modules"];

SPQuery query = new SPQuery();
query.Query = "<Where><Eq><FieldRef Name=\"Audience\"/>" +
              "<Value Type=\"Text\">Developer</Value></Eq></Where>";
query.Joins = "<Join Type=\"Inner\" ListAlias=\"classInstructors\">" +
              "<Eq><FieldRef Name=\"Instructor\" RefType=\"Id\" />" +
              "<FieldRef List=\"classInstructors\" Name=\"Id\" /></Eq></Join>";
query.ProjectedFields =
"<Field Name='Email' Type='Lookup' List='classInstructors' ShowField='Email'/>";
query.ViewFields = "<FieldRef Name=\"Title\" /><FieldRef Name=\"Instructor\" />"
+
              "<FieldRef Name=\"Email\" />";

SPListItemCollection items = listModules.GetItems(query);
```

In Listing 9-22, the *Where* clause is created to return training modules that are intended for a developer audience; this is similar to the simple example shown earlier. The *Join* property is new and defines the join between the two lists through the lookup field. Remember that the query is being run on the Modules list, so it must be joined to the Instructors list. The *ListAlias* attribute defines an alias for the Instructors list that can be used in the join clause. The first *FieldRef* element refers to the name of the lookup field in the Modules list and will always have a *RefType* equal to *Id*. The second *FieldRef* in the join clause uses the alias name for the Instructors list and will always have a *Name* equal to *Id*. The *ProjectedFields* property also uses the alias name for the Instructors list and refers to additional fields in the instructors list that should be returned with the query.

Querying multiple lists

Although the *SPQuery* object is good for querying a single list or joined lists, if you want to query multiple lists within a site collection simultaneously, then you can make use of the *Microsoft.Share-Point.SPSiteDataQuery* object. Like the *SPQuery* object, the *SPSiteDataQuery* object has *Query* and *ViewFields* properties. In addition to these fields, the *SPSiteDataQuery* object also has *Lists* and *Webs* properties. The *Lists* property is used to specify the lists within the site collection that should be included in the query. The *Webs* property is used to determine the scope of the query. Listing 9-23 shows a query that returns events from all calendars in the current site collection where the end date is later than today.

LISTING 9-23 Querying multiple lists

```
//Creates the query
SPSiteDataQuery query = new SPSiteDataQuery();

//Builds the query
query.Query = "<Where><Gt><FieldRef Name='EndDate'/>" +
              "<Value Type='DateTime'><Today OffsetDays=\"-1\"/></Value></Gt></Where>";

//Sets the list types to search
query.Lists = "<Lists ServerTemplate='106' />";

//Sets the Fields to include in results
query.ViewFields = "<FieldRef Name='fAllDayEvent' />" +
                   "<FieldRef Name='Title' />" +
                   "<FieldRef Name='Location' />" +
                   "<FieldRef Name='EventDate' />" +
                   "<FieldRef Name='EndDate' />";

//Sets the scope of the query
query.Webs = @"<Webs Scope='SiteCollection' />";

//Execute the query
DataTable table = SPContext.Current.Site.RootWeb.GetSiteData(query);
```

The *Lists* property in Listing 9-23 is a CAML fragment that can take several forms to specify the lists to include in the query. Setting the property to *<Lists ServerTemplate=[value]/>* limits the query to lists of a certain server template. For example, type 106 is a calendar. Table 9-6 shows all of the possible values for the *ServerTemplate* attribute. Setting the property to *<Lists BaseType=[value]/>* limits the query to lists of a certain *BaseType*. Table 9-7 lists the possible vales for the *BaseType* attribute. Setting the property to *<Lists Hidden='true'/>* includes hidden lists in the query. Setting the property to *<Lists MaxListLimit=[value]/>* limits the query to considering no more than the specified number of lists.

The *Webs* property is a CAML fragment that must either be *<Webs Scope='SiteCollection'/>* or *<Webs Scope='Recursive'/>*. *SiteCollection* includes all lists in the site collection, whereas *Recursive* includes only those lists in the current site or subsites beneath the current site.

TABLE 9-6 Server templates

Server template	ID	Description
GenericList	100	Custom list
DocumentLibrary	101	Document library
Survey	102	Survey
Links	103	Links List
Announcements	104	Announcements List
Contacts	105	Contacts List
Events	106	Calendar
Tasks	107	Tasks List
DiscussionBoard	108	Discussion Lists
PictureLibrary	109	Picture library
DataSources	110	Data sources library
WebTemplateCatalog	111	Site template gallery
UserInformation	112	User list
WebPartCatalog	113	Web Part gallery
ListTemplateCatalog	114	List template gallery
XMLForm	115	InfoPath form library
MasterPageCatalog	116	Master Page gallery
WebPageLibrary	119	Wiki Page Library
DataConnectionLibrary	130	Data connection library
WorkflowHistory	140	Workflow History list
GanttTasks	150	Project Tasks list
Meetings	200	Meetings
Agenda	201	Meeting agenda
MeetingUser	202	Meeting attendees
Decision	204	Meeting decisions
MeetingObjective	207	Meeting objectives
Posts	301	Blog posts
Comments	302	Blog comments
Categories	303	Blog categories

Server template	ID	Description
IssueTracking	1100	Issue tracking list
AdminTasks	1200	Central Administration tasks

TABLE 9-7 *BaseType* values

Value	Description
0	Generic list
1	Document library
3	Discussion forum
4	Vote or Survey
5	Issues list

Throttling queries

SharePoint 2013 provides special support for large lists. In particular, SharePoint allows administrators to throttle the number of items returned in a list view in order to prevent performance degradation caused by returning an excessive number of items. Though these throttle settings apply to views created by end users, they also apply to queries executed in custom code.

When you are executing queries, the number of results returned will be determined by the throttle settings for the specified list and the rights of the current user. Throttle settings are set for the web application in Central Administration. Rights for the current user that affect throttling include administration rights on the web front-end server, administration rights in the web application, and auditor rights in the web application.

In the context of list throttling, users who have server administration rights on the web front end where the query is run are known as server administrators. Users granted Full Read (auditors) or Full Control (administrators) through the web application policy in Central Administration are considered super users. Everyone else is simply termed a normal user.

The List View Threshold is set at the web application level and specifies the maximum number of items that can be involved in a database operation at a single time. The default value for this setting is 5,000, which means that results returned from a *SPQuery* or *SPSiteDataQuery* object will be generally limited to 5,000 items for both super users and normal users. Additionally, the List View Lookup Threshold specifies the maximum number of lookup, person/group, or workflow status fields that can be involved in the query. This value defaults to 6. Server administrators are normally not affected by the List View Threshold or List View Lookup Threshold settings.

Both the *SPQuery* and *SPSiteDataQuery* objects have a *QueryThrottleMode* property that can be set to one of the values in the *Microsoft.SharePoint.SPQueryThrottleOption* enumeration. The possible values for the property are *Default*, *Override*, and *Strict*. Setting the *QueryThrottleMode* property to *Default* causes query throttling to be implemented for both super users and normal users based on the List View Threshold and List View Lookup Threshold settings. Server administrators are not affected.

Setting the *QueryThrottleMode* property to *Override* allows super users to return items up to the limit specified in the List View Threshold for the Auditors and Administrators setting as long as the Object Model Override setting is set to "Yes" for the current web application. Normal users are still limited to returning the number of items specified in the List View Threshold and List View Lookup Threshold settings. Server administrators remain unaffected.

Setting the *QueryThrottleMode* property to *Strict* causes the limits specified by the List View Threshold and List View Lookup Threshold settings to apply to all users. In this case, it makes no difference what rights you have in the web application or server. Listing 9-24 shows the *RenderContents* method from a Web Part with configurable throttling returning query results from a list and demonstrating the concepts discussed.

LISTING 9-24 Throttling query results

```
protected override void RenderContents(HtmlTextWriter writer)
{
    SPWeb site = SPContext.Current.Web;
    SPList list = site.Lists[listName];
    SPUser user = SPContext.Current.Web.CurrentUser;
    SPQuery query = new SPQuery();

    //Throttle settings
    if (overrideThrottling)
        query.QueryThrottleMode = SPQueryThrottleOption.Override;
    else
        query.QueryThrottleMode = SPQueryThrottleOption.Strict;

    //Execute query
    query.Query = "</OrderBy>";
    query.ViewFields = "<FieldRef Name=\"Title\" />";
    SPListItemCollection items = list.GetItems(query);

    //Show user role
    if(user.IsSiteAdmin || user.IsSiteAuditor)
        writer.Write("<p>You are a 'Super User'</p>");
    else
        writer.Write("<p>You are a regular user</p>");

    //Is throttling enabled?
    if(list.EnableThrottling)
        writer.Write("<p>Throttling is enabled</p>");
    else
        writer.Write("<p>Throttling is not enabled</p>");

    //Show count of items returned
    writer.Write("<p>" + items.Count + " items returned.</p>");

}
```

Regardless of the value set for the *QueryThrottleMode* property, no results will be throttled if the query is run within the time specified in the Daily Time Window for Large Queries. During this time period, all queries are allowed to run to completion. Additionally, the *EnableThrottling* property of the list can be set to *False* to remove the list from any and all throttling restrictions. The *EnableThrottling* property can only be set by someone with Farm Administrator rights using a Windows PowerShell script similar to the following:

```
$site = Get-SPWeb -Identity "http://wingtip.com/products"
$list = $site.Lists["Toys"]
$list.EnableThrottling = $false
```

Working with LINQ to SharePoint

Though CAML queries have been the workhorse of list querying for some time, CAML does present some challenges. First of all, CAML is not object oriented. As the samples have shown, CAML queries are written as text, so they are vulnerable to simple typographical error. Second, CAML is difficult to construct correctly because the rules are not always clear. Typically, a reference and a lot of trouble-shooting is required to get the query right.

In response to these challenges, Microsoft introduced Language Integrated Query (LINQ) in SharePoint 2010. The LINQ to SharePoint provider is part of the *Microsoft.SharePoint.Linq* namespace and is used as an additional layer on top of CAML. LINQ queries created with the LINQ to SharePoint provider are translated into CAML queries for execution. Though LINQ to SharePoint is not a complete replacement for CAML, it does provide CRUD operations for lists in an object-oriented library.

Because of its full support for CRUD operations and the inherent advantages of LINQ development over CAML, you will generally use LINQ as your primary interface for working with lists through the server-side object model. You will fall back to CAML when using the client-side object model, overriding throttles, or aggregating multiple lists with the *SPSiteDataQuery* object.

Generating entities with *SPMetal*

SharePoint list data is maintained in the content database. This means that the structure of the list and item data is based on relational tables. As a SharePoint developer, however, you do not need to understand the structure of these tables because the object model abstracts the structure into *SPList* and *SPListItem* objects. When you write a LINQ to SharePoint query, you should expect the same experience as when using the object model. List and item data should be abstracted so that you do not have to understand the content database schema.

LINQ to SharePoint provides an object layer abstraction on top of the content database through the use of entity classes. Entity classes are lightweight, object-relational interfaces to the list and item data in the content database. Additionally, entity classes are used to track changes and provide optimistic concurrency during updates.

Entity classes are created by using a command-line utility called *SPMetal*. *SPMetal* is located in theSharePoint system directory at C:\Program Files\Common Files\Microsoft Shared\web server extensions\15\bin. As a best practice, you should update the *PATH* variable in your environment to include the path the *SPMetal*. This way, you can simply run the utility immediately after opening a command window.

Generating entity classes with *SPMetal* can be very simple. At a minimum, you must specify the site for which you want to generate entities and the name of the code file to create. After the code file is created, you can immediately add it to a project in Visual Studio and start writing LINQ queries. The following code shows an example that will generate entity classes for all of the lists and content types in a site:

```
SPMetal /web:http://wingtiptoys.com /code:Entities.cs
```

Though generating entity classes can be quite easy, you will likely want more control over which entities are created and how they are structured. *SPMetal* provides a number of additional arguments that you can use to alter code generation. Table 9-8 lists all of the possible arguments for *SPMetal* and describes them.

TABLE 9-8 *SPMetal* Arguments

Argument	Description
/code:<filename>	Specifies the name of the generated file.
/language:<language>	Specifies the language for the generated code. Can be either csharp or vb.
/namespace:<namespace>	Specifies the namespace for the generated code.
/parameters:<file>	Specifies an XML file with detailed code-generation parameters.
/password:<password>	Specifies credentials to use for data access during the code-generation process.
/serialization:<type>	Specifies the serialization type. Can be either none or unidirectional.
/user:<username>	Specifies credentials to use for data access during the code-generation process.
/useremoteapi	Specifies that the generation of entity classes is to be done for a remote SharePoint site such as SharePoint Online.
/web:<url>	The URL of the SharePoint site for which entities will be generated.

If you examine the code file generated by *SPMetal*, you will see that there are two kinds of classes created. First, a single class is created that inherits from *Microsoft.SharePoint.Linq.DataContext*. The *DataContext* class provides a connection to lists and change tracking for operations. You can think of the *DataContext* class as serving a purpose similar to the *SqlConnection* class in data access code. Second, multiple classes are generated that represent the various content types used by the lists in the site. Using the *DataContext* class together with the entity classes allows you to write LINQ queries.

Listing 9-25 shows a simple LINQ query written to return all training modules contained in the list named Modules by using a *DataContext* class named *Entities*.

LISTING 9-25 A simple LINQ to SharePoint query

```
using (Entities dc = new Entities(SPContext.Current.Web.Url))
{
    var q = from m in dc.Modules
            orderby m.Title
            select m;

    foreach (var module in q)
    {
        moduleList.Items.Add(module.Title);
    }
}
```

Understanding the *DataContext* class

Before performing any LINQ operations, you must connect to a site by using the *DataContext* object. The *DataContext* accepts a URL in the constructor so that you can specify the site where it should connect, which is useful as you move your code from development to production. Of course, the site you specify must actually have the lists and content types for which entities have been generated. Otherwise, your operations will fail. The *DataContext* class also implements *IDisposable* so that it can be coded with a *using* block.

The *DataContext* class provides a *GetList<T>()* method that provides access to each list for which an entity has been generated. You can use this method in LINQ query syntax to easily specify the list against which the query should be run. Along with the method, the *DataContext* also has a property of *EntityList<T>* for each list.

The *Log* property can be used for viewing the underlying CAML created from the LINQ query. Not only is this useful for monitoring and debugging, but it can be used to help create CAML queries for other purposes. The *Log* property accepts a *System.IO.TextWriter* object so you can easily write the log to a file or display it in a Web Part.

The *DataContext* will track changes made to the entity objects so that they can be written back to the content database. The *ObjectTrackingEnabled* property determines whether the *DataContext* will track changes. The property defaults to *True*, but setting it to *False* will improve performance for read-only operations. If the *DataContext* is tracking changes, then the content database can be updated by calling the *SubmitChanges()* method, as discussed in the section "Adding, deleting, and updating with LINQ to SharePoint" later in this chapter.

Using parameters.xml to control code generation

The arguments accepted by *SPMetal* provide a fair amount of control over the entity-generation process, but in practice you will likely want even more control. The highest level of control over entity generation is given by passing a parameters.xml file to *SPMetal* with detailed information about the entities to generate.

The parameters.xml file contains elements that give *SPMetal* specific details about code generation. In particular, it specifies what lists, content types, and fields should be generated in code. The parameters.xml file is passed to *SPMetal* through the */parameters* argument. The following code shows a sample parameters.xml file:

```xml
<?xml version="1.0" encoding="utf-8"?>
<Web Class="Entities" AccessModifier="Public"
  xmlns="http://schemas.microsoft.com/SharePoint/2009/spmetal" >
  <List Name="Instructors" Member="Instructors">
    <ContentType Name="Contact" Class="Instructor">
      <Column Name="FullName" Member="FullName"/>
      <ExcludeOtherColumns/>
    </ContentType>
  </List>
  <List Name="Modules" Member="Modules" />
  <ExcludeOtherLists/>
</Web>
```

The *Web* element is the root of the schema. The *Class* attribute specifies the name of the *DataContext* class to generate, and the *AccessModifier* attribute specifies the access level to the class. The *List* element is a child of the *Web* element and specifies the name of a list for which entities should be generated. The *Member* attribute specifies the name of the property in the *DataContext* that will represent this list. The *ContentType* element is a child of the *List* element and specifies a content type for which an entity should be generated. The *Column* element is a child of the *ContentType* element and specifies a column that should be included in the generated entity. The *ExcludeOtherColumns*, *ExcludeOtherContentTypes*, and *ExcludeOtherLists* elements are used to stop looking for items to include in entity generation. In this way, you can specify the exact set of lists, content types, and columns to include in the generated entities. This is very useful for excluding list, content types, and columns that are present in the development environment, but will not be present in the production environment. Table 9-9 shows the complete schema for the parameters.xml file.

TABLE 9-9 Parameters.xml schema

Element	Child Elements	Attribute	Description
Web	List ExcudeList ExcludeOtherLists IncludeHiddenLists ContentType ExcludeContentType ExcludeOtherContentTypes IncludeHiddenContentTypes	Class (optional)	Name of *DataContext* class.
		AccessModifier (optional)	Specifies accessibility of DataContext and entity classes. May be Internal or Public.
List	ContentType . ExcludeContentType	Name	Name of the list in SharePoint.
		Member (optional)	Name of the *DataContext* property representing the list.
		Type (optional)	Type of the *DataContext* property representing the list.
ContentType	Column ExcludeColumn ExcludeOtherColumns IncludeHiddenColumns	Name	Name of the content type.
		Class (optional)	Name of the generated class.
		AccessModifier (optional)	Accessibility of the generated class.
Column		Name	Name of the column.
		Member (optional)	Name of the generated property for the column.
		Type (optional)	Type of the generated property for the column.
ExcludeColumn		Name	Name of the column to exclude from entity generation.
ExcludeOtherColumns			Excludes all columns not explicitly included.
IncludeHiddenColumns			Includes hidden columns in entity generation.
ExcludeList		Name	Name of the list to exclude from entity generation.
ExcludeOtherLists			Excludes all lists not explicitly included.
IncludeHiddenLists			Includes hidden lists in entity generation.
ExcludeContentType		Name	Name of content type to exclude from entity generation.
ExcludeOtherContentTypes			Excludes all content types not explicitly included.
IncludeHiddenContentTypes			Includes hidden content types in entity generation.

Querying with LINQ to SharePoint

After you have entities generated, then you can begin to write LINQ to SharePoint queries. Writing LINQ to SharePoint queries is very similar to writing LINQ queries for other data sources. You formulate a query by using query syntax, receive the results into an anonymous type, and then use the *IEnumerable* interface to iterate over the results.

LINQ to SharePoint also supports querying across lists that are joined by a lookup field. LINQ to SharePoint makes the syntax much simpler than with CAML. The following code shows the equivalent LINQ query for the CAML shown in Listing 9-22. Note how the join is simply done by using the dot operator to move easily from the Modules list to the joined Instructors list:

```
var q = from m in dc.Modules
        orderby m.ModuleID
        select new { m.Title, Presenter = m.Instructor.FullName, Email = m.Instructor.Email};
```

Not only does the code join two lists together, but you can see that it is also using a projection. The new keyword is creating a new set of anonymous objects whose field names have been set to *Title*, *Presenter*, and *Email*.

LINQ to SharePoint also allows you to perform query composition. Query composition is the ability to run a LINQ query on the results of a LINQ query. For example, the following code shows how to run a new query specifically looking for a training module named *Visual Studio 2012*:

```
var q1 = from m1 in dc.Modules
        orderby m1.ModuleID
        select new { m1.Title, Presenter = m1.Instructor.FullName, Email = m1.Instructor.Email};
var q2 = from m2 in q1
        where m2.Title.Equals("Visual Studio 2012")
        select m2;
```

Finally, LINQ to SharePoint supports a number of extension methods that you can use for aggregation, grouping, and returning specific entities. The methods are often used on the results of the query. The following code, for example, shows how to return the total number of training modules in the query results. The most commonly used extension methods are listed in Table 9-10:

```
var t = (from m in dc.Modules
        select m).Count();
```

TABLE 9-10 Commonly used extension methods

Name	Description
Any()	Returns true if there are any items in the query results.
Average()	Returns the aggregated average value.
Count()	Returns the count of items in the query result.
First()	Returns the first item in the results. Useful if you are expecting a single result.
FirstOrDefault()	Returns the first item in the results. If there is no first item, returns the default for the object type.

Name	Description
Max(), Min()	Return the item with the maximum or minimum value.
Skip()	Skips a certain number of items in the results. Useful when used with Take() for paging.
Sum()	Returns the aggregated sum.
Take()	Allows you to return only a specified number of results. Useful when used with Skip() for paging.
ToList()	Returns the query results into a generic List<T>.

Adding, deleting, and updating with LINQ to SharePoint

Along with querying, you can also add, delete, and update lists with LINQ to SharePoint. Adding and deleting items are accomplished by using methods associated with the *EntityList<T>* property of the *DataContext*. The *InsertOnSubmit()* method adds a single new item to a list. The *InsertAllOnSubmit()* method adds a collection of new items to a list. The *DeleteOnSubmit()* method deletes a single item from a list, and the *DeleteAllOnSubmit()* method deletes a collection of items from a list. The *Recycle-OnSubmit()* method puts a single item into the recycle bin, and the *RecycleAllOnSubmit()* method puts a collection of items in the recycle bin. The following code shows an example of adding a new item to the Modules list:

```
using (Entities dc = new Entities(SPContext.Current.Web.Url))
{
    ModulesItem mi = new ModulesItem();
    mi.Title = "LINQ to SharePoint";
    mi.Id = 301;
    dc.Modules.InsertonSubmit(mi);
    dc.SubmitChanges();
}
```

Updating items in lists is done by simply changing the property values in the item and then calling the *SubmitChanges()* method of the *DataContext*. The following code shows a simple example of an update operation:

```
using (Entities dc = new Entities(SPContext.Current.Web.Url))
{
    var q = (from m in dc.Modules
            where m.Id==1
            select m).First();

    q.Title = "Revised Title for Module 1";
    dc.SubmitChanges();
}
```

When updating items, LINQ to SharePoint uses optimistic concurrency. The provider will check to see whether the items in the list have been changed since your LINQ query was run before it will attempt to update them. If a discrepancy is found for any of the submitted entities, then no changes are committed. All discrepancies must be resolved before any change in the current batch can be committed.

When discrepancies are found during the update process, LINQ to SharePoint throws a *Microsoft.SharePoint.Linq.ChangeConflictException*. Additionally, the *ChangeConflicts* collection of the *DataContext* is populated with *ObjectChangeConflict* objects that contain data about fields in the item causing conflicts. The *SubmitChanges()* method supports overloads that allow you to specify whether update attempts should continue after the first conflict or whether update attempts should stop. The *ChangeConflicts* collection will only be populated with information about failed attempts, so electing to stop after the first failure will not provide complete data on all conflicts. Regardless of whether or not you continue update attempts, remember that no changes will be saved if any conflict occurs. The purpose of continuing update attempts is to completely populate the *ChangeConflicts* collection.

The *ChangeConflicts* collection contains a *MemberConflicts* collection that has the detailed information about the actual values causing the conflict. In particular, the *MemberConflicts* collection is populated with *MemberChangeConflict* objects. These objects each have *OriginalValue*, *CurrentValue*, and *DatabaseValue* properties. The *OriginalValue* is the value of the column when the LINQ query was run. The *CurrentValue* is the value that *SubmitChanges()* is attempting to write to the content database. The *DatabaseValue* is the current value of the column in the database. Trapping the *ChangeConflictException* and using the *MemberChangeConflict* objects allows you to display the conflicts to the end user. The code in Listing 9-26 shows how to iterate the collection, build a list, and bind the list to a grid for display.

LISTING 9-26 A simple LINQ to SharePoint query

```
Try
{
    //Update code
}
catch (Microsoft.SharePoint.Linq.ChangeConflictException x)
{
    conflicts = new List<Conflict>();
    foreach (ObjectChangeConflict cc in dc.ChangeConflicts)
    {
        foreach (MemberChangeConflict mc in cc.MemberConflicts)
        {
            Conflict conflict = new Conflict();
            conflict.OriginalValue = mc.OriginalValue.ToString();
            conflict.CurrentValue = mc.CurrentValue.ToString();
            conflict.DatabaseValue = mc.DatabaseValue.ToString();
            conflicts.Add(conflict);
        }

    }
    conflictGrid.DataSource = conflicts;
    conflictGrid.DataBind();
}
```

Along with displaying the results, you can also resolve conflicts in code. After displaying the results to the end user in a grid, you can allow the user to select whether the pending changes should be forced or lost. The *Resolve()* method of the *MemberChangeConflict* class accepts a *Microsoft.Share-Point.Linq.RefreshMode* enumeration that can have a value of *KeepChanges*, *KeepCurrentValues*, or *OverwriteCurrentValues*. *KeepChanges* accepts every pending change, but gives the highest priority to the current user. *KeepCurrentValues* keeps only the changes made by the current user and loses all other changes. *OverwriteCurrentValues* loses the current changes and sets the values to what is in the database. After calling the *Resolve()* method, you must *SubmitChanges()* again to complete the operation. The following code shows an example of keeping the current changes and losing all other changes:

```
foreach (ObjectChangeConflict cc in dc.ChangeConflicts)
{
    foreach (MemberChangeConflict mc in cc.MemberConflicts)
    {
        mc.Resolve(RefreshMode.KeepCurrentValues);
    }
}
dc.SubmitChanges();
```

Summary

In this chapter, we covered the fundamental architecture of lists and document libraries. You learned about fields, field types, site columns, and content types, as well as how to create them by using the various APIs. This chapter also explored working with documents and document libraries, as well as the event infrastructure provided by SharePoint. You learned about the fundamentals of creating event receiver classes and remote event receivers, and registering event handlers. Finally, the chapter provided detailed information about querying lists with CAML and LINQ. Because lists and libraries are essential data stores in SharePoint, all of these areas are core skills for the SharePoint developer.

## CHAPTER 10

SharePoint type definitions and templates

Microsoft SharePoint is a platform and can be customized in a lot of different ways. In this chapter we'll look at how you can use type definitions and templates to customize SharePoint. The first section focuses on using custom field types. This development strategy offers the greatest level of control when you are initializing field values and performing data validation. By using custom field types, developers can customize the editing experience by extending it with a custom field control. We will also have a look at how to customize fields by using the new *JSLink* property.

The second section of the chapter focuses on developing custom site columns and content types. We will look at how to create site columns and content types by using Collaborative Application Markup Language (CAML) and by using the server-side object model. Although developing CAML-based definitions has a steep learning curve and poses more challenges with testing, debugging, and maintenance, it provides an alternative approach with certain advantages over using the server-side object model. Therefore, we will also discuss the advantages and disadvantages of using both approaches.

The last section of the chapter talks about how to create lists and list instances by using the SharePoint Developer Tools designers and CAML.

Custom field types

In Chapter 9, "SharePoint lists," the basics about fields, site columns, and field types were introduced. You learned that every field and every site column is created in terms of an underlying field type. You also learned about the built-in field types in SharePoint, which include *Text, Note, Boolean, Integer, Number, Decimal, Currency, DateTime, Choice,* and *Lookup.* Now it's time to discuss extending the set of built-in field types by developing *custom field types.* What's important to understand is that when you develop a custom field type, you are really developing a *field type definition.*

A primary motivation for creating custom field types is that it provides the greatest level of flexibility when it comes to initializing and formatting field values. Custom field types are also commonly created to allow complex data validation on user input to prevent inconsistent field values from being saved into SharePoint.

A second motivation for developing a custom field type is that it can be extended with an associated user interface component known as a *field control*. A custom field control complements a custom field type because it allows you to create a rich user interface with an HTML layout, ASP.NET server controls, and code-behind that can be as simple or as complicated as the scenario calls for.

Before we begin, we must point out a few challenges that you might face when developing custom field types. First, custom field types can only be deployed by using a farm solution; they cannot be deployed in a sandbox solution or a SharePoint app. Second, custom field types work great when you are using the browser to look at the standard list view, but usually can't be displayed by using the DataSheet view, and they often cause integration problems with Microsoft Office products such as Microsoft Word or Microsoft Excel. Programming against them can also prove to be challenging.

The area in which custom field types are most commonly used is when a custom solution is created for *publishing sites*. The publishing sites functionality is part of SharePoint Server 2013 Standard edition. The high-level design of a publishing site is based on a scheme in which content authors submit page content through browser-based input forms. The power of developing a custom field type along with a custom field control makes it possible to provide content authors with a very rich editing experience in the browser.

SharePoint 2013 also introduces a new JavaScript approach that allows you to customize the way fields are displayed on the page. You can do this by using the *JSLink* property of a field. Fields aren't the only things that can use *JSLink* in SharePoint 2013; the property is also available for *SPForm*, *SPView*, Web Parts and *SPContentType*. You can use the *JSLink* property to specify a JavaScript file that contains client-side script to modify the behavior of the object (the field, Web Part, or form) and the way in which it is displayed.

Creating custom field types

When creating a custom field type in Microsoft Visual Studio 2012, you should start by creating a new SharePoint project based on the empty SharePoint Project template. Inside this project, you will have to add a new public class for each custom field type. You will also have to add a special XML definition file that is required to deploy the project's custom field types.

The downloadable .zip archive of companion code for this book contains a sample SharePoint project named WingtipToysFieldTypes. This project contains working samples of the custom field types and field controls that we are going to examine over the next few pages. You can tell that the project structure of WingtipToysFieldTypes in Figure 10-1 contains the source files for three custom field types named *CustomerFullName, CustomerPhoneNumber* and *CustomerLanguage*.

FIGURE 10-1 The WingtipToysFieldTypes project demonstrates creating custom field types and custom field controls.

Creating classes for custom field types

For each custom field type, you must create a *field type class* that inherits from one of the built-in field type classes, such as *SPFieldText, SPFieldNumber,* or *SPFieldMultiColumn*. The following code snippet shows how each of the custom field type classes in the WingtipToysFieldTypes project inherits from one of these required base classes:

```
public class CustomerFullName : SPFieldMultiColumn {
  // custom field type implementation
}
public class CustomerPhoneNumber : SPFieldText {
  // custom field type implementation
}
public class CustomLanguage : SPFieldText {
  // custom field type implementation
}
```

The first step in implementing a custom field type class is to add two public constructors that are required by SharePoint. The reason why SharePoint requires these two specially parameterized constructors is that it uses them in various scenarios to create instances of the custom field type. When you add these constructors to your field type class, you don't need to supply any actual code inside the curly braces. You just need to define the required parameter list and pass these parameters on to the base class constructor with a matching parameter list:

```
public class CustomerPhoneNumber : SPFieldText {

  public CustomerPhoneNumber(SPFieldCollection fields, string fieldName)
        : base(fields, fieldName) { }

  public CustomerPhoneNumber(SPFieldCollection fields,
                       string typeName, string displayName)
        : base(fields, typeName, displayName) { }

}
```

After you have added these two public constructors, the next step is to override whatever base class methods and properties make sense for your particular scenario. For instance, for the *CustomerLanguage* field type class, you might want to make sure that the default value is English and that the CustomerPhoneNumber should start with +[CountryCode]-(0). Let's first look at the implementation of *DefaultValue*. Because most of Wingtip Toys customers live in the United States, the sales department has decided that the default value for customers' language should be English:

```
public class CustomerLanguage : SPFieldText {
  // constructors omitted for brevity
  // add logic to make sure that English is the default language
  public override string DefaultValue {
    get {
      return "English";
    }
  }
}
```

Now let's have a look at how we can make sure that a phone number is formatted correctly by validating the contents of a field. Field value validation is implemented by overriding a method named *GetValidatedString*, which is always executed prior to SharePoint saving an item that contains a field based on the field type. The *GetValidatedString* method passes a parameter named *value* that you can use to inspect the field value that the user is attempting to save to the content database. If the custom validation logic inside *GetValidatedString* determines that the user input for the field value is not valid, it should be written to throw an exception of type *SPFieldValidationException*. Here is the implementation of the *GetValidatedString* method in the *CustomerPhoneNumber* field type class, which validates that each field value starts with +[CountryCode]-(0):

```
public class CustomerPhoneNumber : SPFieldText {
  // constructors omitted for brevity
  // add validation to ensure proper formatting
  public override string GetValidatedString(object value)
  {
    string input = value.ToString();
    string PN_Regex = @"^\+\d{1,2}\-\(0\)";
    if ((this.Required || !string.IsNullOrEmpty(UserInput)) &
         (!Regex.IsMatch(input, PN_Regex)))
    {
      throw new SPFieldValidationException
          ("Phone Number must be formatted like +[0-99]-(0)..");
    }
    return base.GetValidatedString(value);
  }
}
```

Now let's discuss what happens when this validation code is executed. Imagine a scenario with a list named WingtipToys Customers, which contains a field created from the *CustomerPhoneNumber* field type. What happens when a user attempts to save a customer with a phone number that is formatted in a different way? The *GetValidatedString* method executes and determines that the user input is invalid. At this point, the method throws an exception that cancels the user's request to save the current item and displays an error message to the user, as shown in Figure 10-2.

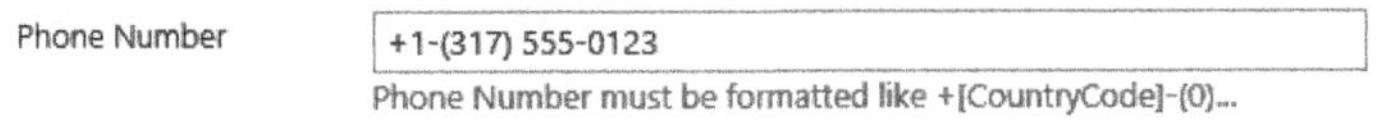

Phone Number	+1-(317) 555-0123

Phone Number must be formatted like +[CountryCode]-(0)...

FIGURE 10-2 Throwing an *SPFieldValidationException* cancels the action to update an item and displays an error message.

Deploying custom field types

Now that you have created a custom field type class, the next step is to create an XML file containing a CAML-based definition for each custom field type that is required for deployment. When you create the XML file to deploy your custom field types, you must create it by using a naming pattern so that the file name starts with *fldtypes* and ends with an *.xml* extension. For example, the WingtipToysField-Types project contains the file fldtypes_WingtipToysFieldTypes.xml. In addition to giving this XML file a special name, you must deploy it to a specific directory inside the SharePoint root directory at the TEMPLATE/XML path.

Let's look at how SharePoint initializes the available set of field types. When SharePoint initializes the worker process for an application pool, it queries the TEMPLATE/XML directory for files that match the of fldtypes*.xml pattern and scans through them to discover the field type definitions deployed within the local farm. From this, you can make two interesting observations about custom field type deployment. First, custom field types are not deployed by using features. Second, custom field types are deployed as an all-or-nothing proposition at farm-level scope. It is not possible to create a custom field type that is only available in a particular site collection or even web application. This also means that custom field types should not be used in a shared environment.

If you look at the TEMPLATE/XML directory on a server in a SharePoint 2013 farm, you will find a system file named fldtypes.xml that defines all the core field types supplied by SharePoint Foundation. The installation of SharePoint Server 2013 deploys several more of these XML files, including fldtypes_hold.xml, fldtypes_publishing.xml, fldtypes_SPRatings.xml, fldtypes_TargetTo.xml, and fldtypes_taxonomy.xml, to supply additional field type definitions. When you are learning how to develop custom field types, it can be very helpful to inspect these XML files to view how the SharePoint team has structured the CAML definitions for the built-in field types.

Each field type definition is created by using a *FieldType* element, which must reside inside a top-level *FieldTypes* element. The WingtipToysFieldType project deploys the definitions for all four custom field types in an XML file named fldtypes_WingtipToysFieldTypes.xml:

```
<FieldTypes>
  <FieldType> <!- CustomerFullName field type definition --> </FieldType>
  <FieldType> <!- CustomerPhoneNumber field type definition --> </FieldType>
  <FieldType> <!- CustomerLanguage field type definition --> </FieldType>
<FieldTypes>
```

When you create the *FieldType* element for a field type definition, you must add several *Field* elements with a *Name* attribute that defines the type of value inside. These *Field* elements are required to provide information about the custom field type, such as its name, its parent type, its display name, the field type class name, and the name of its assembly. The *FieldType* element for the custom field type named *CustomerPhoneNumber* is defined in the following code:

```
<FieldType>
  <Field Name="TypeName">CustomerPhoneNumber</Field>
  <Field Name="ParentType">Text</Field>
  <Field Name="TypeDisplayName">Customer Phone Number</Field>
  <Field Name="TypeShortDescription">Customer Phone Number</Field>
  <Field Name="UserCreatable">TRUE</Field>
  <Field Name="FieldTypeClass">
    WingtipToysFieldTypes.CustomerPhoneNumber,$SharePoint.Project.AssemblyFullName$
  </Field>
</FieldType>
```

Note that there are several more optional attributes that you can use when creating custom field type definitions. For example, you can add optional named attributes, such as *ShowInListCreate*, *ShowInDocumentLibraryCreate*, *ShowInSurveyCreate*, and *ShowInColumnTemplateCreate*, which allow you to define whether a custom field type should be displayed or hidden on the Create Column page for scenarios where users are adding new fields to a list or content type:

```
<FieldType>
  <Field Name="TypeName">CustomerLanguage</Field>
  <Field Name="ParentType">Text</Field>
  <Field Name="TypeDisplayName">Customer Language</Field>
  <Field Name="TypeShortDescription">Customer Preferred Language</Field>
  <Field Name="UserCreatable">TRUE</Field>
  <Field Name="ShowInListCreate">TRUE</Field>
  <Field Name="ShowInDocumentLibraryCreate">TRUE</Field>
  <Field Name="ShowInSurveyCreate">TRUE</Field>
  <Field Name="ShowInColumnTemplateCreate">TRUE</Field>
  <Field Name="FieldTypeClass">
    WingtipToysFieldTypes.CustomerLanguage,$SharePoint.Project.AssemblyFullName$
  </Field>
</FieldType>
```

Creating custom field controls

You have now learned the required steps to create and deploy a custom field type. The next step is to extend a custom field type with a custom field control to provide the user with a customized editing experience. You can also create a custom field type without a custom field control. Creating a custom field control is optional. If the editing experience of one of the out-of-the-box field types is sufficient for your custom field type, you will not have to create your own custom field control. For the *CustomerPhoneNumber* field type, the out-of-the-box editing experience that the field inherits from its parent *Text* is used. The custom editing experience of a custom field control is created by using a *rendering template*. To create a rendering template, you must create a new user control and add a control tag based on a special control type named *RenderingTemplate*:

```
<SharePoint:RenderingTemplate>
  <Template>
    <!-- your HTML layout and server controls go here -->
  </Template>
</SharePoint:RenderingTemplate>
```

The WingtipToysFieldTypes project contains a custom field control for all three custom field types that were created earlier in this chapter. The simplest one is the custom field control that extends the *CustomerPhoneNumber* custom field type. The rendering template for this custom field control is defined inside the user control file named WingtipToysFieldTypes.CustomerPhoneNumber.ascx. The rendering template definition has been created by using a *RenderingTemplate* control with an ID of *CustomerPhoneNumberRenderingTemplate*:

```
<SharePoint:RenderingTemplate ID="CustomerPhoneNumberRenderingTemplate"
    runat="server">
  <Template>
    <asp:TextBox ID="CustomerPhoneNrInput" runat="server"
                 MaxLength="25" CssClass="ms-long" />
  </Template>
</SharePoint:RenderingTemplate>
```

The *RenderingTemplate* control ID of *CustomerPhoneNumberRenderingTemplate* is used to determine what rendering template should be loaded and initialized. Inside the *RenderingTemplate* control, there is a *Template* element. This is where you add the HTML layout and ASP.NET controls to produce a custom editing experience. You have the flexibility to create the *RenderingTemplate* control by using a composite of ASP.NET controls and a rich HTML layout involving *div* elements or an HTML table. The *CustomerPhoneNumberRenderingTemplate* simply uses an ASP.NET *TextBox* control.

If you add an item to a Visual Studio project and you select User Control (Farm Solution Only) from the Office/SharePoint category, the user control will be added to a folder with the project name inside a folder called ControlTemplates. This means that the user control will be deployed to TEMPLATE/CONTROLTEMPLATES/[ProjectName]. Unfortunately, user control files that contain a *RenderTemplate* control tag can only be deployed to the TEMPLATE/CONTROLTEMPLATES folder, because SharePoint only inspects the root directory CONTROLTEMPLATES for user control files with rendering templates and not any of its child directories. Because of this, you will manually have to move your user controls from the *ControlTemplates/WingTipToysFieldTypes* folder to the TEMPLATE/CONTROLTEMPLATES folder.

As a general best practice when developing farm solutions, you should avoid deploying custom files from a SharePoint project directly inside one of the standard directories inside the SharePoint root directory, such as IMAGES, LAYOUTS, or CONTROLTEMPLATES. This is to avoid file name conflicts between the files that you deploy and the files that are already deployed by Microsoft and by other custom solutions. However, when developing custom field types, you cannot follow this practice because you must deploy the user control file directly inside the CONTROLTEMPLATES directory.

To increase your level of protection against file name conflicts, it is recommended that you add the project name to the beginning of the file name to make it more likely to be unique. For example, the user control files with rendering templates in the WingtipToysFieldTypes project have names such as WingtipToysFieldTypes.CustomerPhoneNumber.ascx instead of CustomerPhoneNumber.ascx.

After you have created the rendering template, the next step is to create a *field control class*. You can create the field control class in the CustomerPhoneNumber.cs file by inheriting from a base class named *BaseFieldControl* and overriding properties and methods such as *DefaultTemplateName*, *CreateChildControls*, and *Value*:

```
public class CustomerPhoneNumberFieldControl : BaseFieldControl {

  // used to pass the RenderTemplate ID to SharePoint Foundation
  protected override string DefaultTemplateName {}

  // used to obtain references to controls created by the rendering template
  protected override void CreateChildControls() {}

  // used to read and write values to and from the content database
  public override object Value {}
}
```

When you override the read-only property named *DefaultTemplateName*, your implementation simply needs to return the string-based ID of the rendering template:

```
protected override string DefaultTemplateName {
  get { return "CustomerPhoneNumberRenderingTemplate"; }
}
```

When you have implemented the *DefaultTemplateName* property, the next thing to do is to set up a way to access the controls defined in the rendering template programmatically. You can accomplish this by adding a protected field for each control and overriding *CreateChildControls* to initialize these fields properly. Here is an example of how this is done in the *CustomerPhoneNumberFieldControl* field control class, which has an associated rendering template that contains a single *TextBox* control named *CustomerPhoneNrInput*:

```
public class CustomerPhoneNumberFieldControl : BaseFieldControl {

  protected TextBox CustomerPhoneNrInput;

  protected override void CreateChildControls() {
    base.CreateChildControls();
    CustomerPhoneNrInput =
(TextBox)this.TemplateContainer.FindControl("CustomerPhoneNrInput");
  }
}
```

Note that you will not be instantiating control instances in the *CreateChildControls* method but rather going through a protected property of the base class named *TemplateContainer*, which exposes a *FindControl* method. This technique allows you to obtain references to existing control instances that are created by the control tags inside the rendering template rather than creating new control instances.

The next step is to add the logic to the field control class that is responsible for reading and writing the field's value to and from the content database. You do this by overriding the *Value* property of the *BaseFieldControl* class. The *Value* property is based on the type *System.Object*, which gives you quite a bit of flexibility. You can work with any type of object you want, as long as it supports Microsoft .NET Framework serialization. Fortunately, most of the standard types, arrays, and collections in the base class libraries of the .NET Framework provide automatic support for .NET serialization. The *CustomerPhoneNumberFieldControl* class illustrates a simple example of implementing the *Value* property:

```
public class CustomerPhoneNumberFieldControl : BaseFieldControl {
  protected TextBox CustomerPhoneNrInput;

  public override object Value {
    get {
      this.EnsureChildControls();
      // return control Text property value, which is written to content DB
      return CustomerPhoneNrInput.Text;
    }
    set {
      this.EnsureChildControls();
      // initialize control with current field value retrieved from content DB
      CustomerPhoneNrInput.Text = (string)this.ItemFieldValue;
    }
  }
}
```

As you can tell, the *get* and *set* methods of the *Value* property both begin their implementation with a call to *EnsureChildControls*. The call to *EnsureChildControls* guarantees that the *CreateChildControls* method has already been executed. This is done to ensure that the *CustomerPhoneNrInput* field contains a valid reference so that you can program against the control without getting a null reference exception.

The *get* method of the *Value* property simply returns the string value from the *TextBox* control. The SharePoint runtime will call the *get* method when a user updates an item that contains a column based on this custom field type. SharePoint takes this return value and writes it directly to SharePoint.

SharePoint calls the *set* method when a user opens the item in edit view just before the controls created by your *RenderingTemplate* control are shown to the user. The key point to understand about implementing the *set* method is that the *ItemFieldValue* property provides you with access to the current field value as it is stored in SharePoint. This is what makes it possible for you to initialize the control (or controls) in your *RenderingTemplate*.

At this point, we have walked through the complete implementation of the rendering template and the custom field control class. The only step that remains is to update the custom field type class named *CustomerPhoneNumber* to use the custom field control. You do this by overriding a read-only property named *FieldRenderingControl*. When you override the *get* method of *FieldRenderingControl* in a custom field type class, you must create an instance of the field control class and initialize the *FieldName* property by using the *InternalName* property of the custom field type class. After you have created and initialized an instance of the field control class, you pass it back as the *get* method's return value. This is how a custom field type class informs SharePoint that it wants to load its own custom field control. Listing 10-1 shows the complete *CustomerPhoneNumber* and *CustomerPhoneNumberFieldControl* classes.

LISTING 10-1 Custom field type and custom field control classes

```
using Microsoft.SharePoint;
using Microsoft.SharePoint.WebControls;
using System.Text.RegularExpressions;
using System.Web.UI.WebControls;

namespace WingtipToysFieldTypes
{
    public class CustomerPhoneNumber : SPFieldText
    {
        public CustomerPhoneNumber(SPFieldCollection fields, string fieldName)
            : base(fields, fieldName) { }

        public CustomerPhoneNumber(SPFieldCollection fields,
          string typeName, string displayName)
            : base(fields, typeName, displayName) { }

        public override BaseFieldControl FieldRenderingControl
        {
            get
            {
                BaseFieldControl ctr = new CustomerPhoneNumberFieldControl();
                ctr.FieldName = this.InternalName;
                return ctr;
            }
        }


        // add validation to ensure proper formatting
        public override string GetValidatedString(object value)
        {
            string UserInput = value.ToString();
            string PN_RegularExpression = @"^\+\d{1,2}\-\(0\)";
            if ((this.Required || !string.IsNullOrEmpty(UserInput)) &
                (!Regex.IsMatch(UserInput, PN_RegularExpression)))
            {
                throw new SPFieldValidationException
          ("Phone Number must be formatted like +[CountryCode]-(0)...");
            }
            return base.GetValidatedString(value);
        }
    }

    public class CustomerPhoneNumberFieldControl : BaseFieldControl
    {
        protected TextBox CustomerPhoneNrInput;
        protected override string DefaultTemplateName
        {
            get
            {
                return "CustomerPhoneNumberRenderingTemplate";
            }
        }
```

```
        protected override void CreateChildControls()
        {
            base.CreateChildControls();
            CustomerPhoneNrInput =
    (TextBox)this.TemplateContainer.FindControl("CustomerPhoneNrInput");
        }

        public override object Value
        {
            get
            {
                this.EnsureChildControls();
                return CustomerPhoneNrInput.Text;
            }
            set
            {
                this.EnsureChildControls();
                CustomerPhoneNrInput.Text = (string)this.ItemFieldValue;
            }
        }
    }
}
```

Custom field types with multicolumn values

The custom field type *CustomerFullName* is a field type with multicolumn values. In this case, you will be capturing a first name and a last name in two different text boxes, which are captured and validated as a single field. Multicolumn field types must inherit from *SPFieldMultiColumn*. In most cases, you will also have to specify a custom field control because there aren't any SharePoint out-of-the-box field types that are built up out of several text boxes or other types of input controls. The field control will have to contain a custom *RenderingTemplate* designed to display multiple input controls to the user. Here is an example of the rendering template defined inside WingTipToysFieldTypes. CustomerFullName.ascx:

```
<SharePoint:RenderingTemplate ID="CustomerFullNameRenderingTemplate" runat="server">
  <Template>
    <table class="ms-authoringcontrols" >
      <tr>
        <td>First name:</td>
        <td><asp:TextBox ID="FirstNameInput" runat="server" Width="328px" /></td>
      </tr>
      <tr>
        <td>Last name:</td>
        <td><asp:TextBox ID="LastNameInput" runat="server" Width="328px" /></td>
      </tr>
    </table>
  </Template>
</SharePoint:RenderingTemplate>
```

Now that you have defined the rendering template, you will have to create the logic to move values from these controls back and forth to and from the SharePoint content database as a single multicolumn value. The server-side object model supplies the *SPFieldMultiColumnValue* class type, which makes this possible by using programming syntax similar to dealing with a string array. The *CustomerFullNameFieldControl* class in Listing 10-2 shows how to override the *Value* property with an implementation that reads and writes multicolumn values to and from the content database.

LISTING 10-2 Implementation of a field control class for an *SPFieldMultiColumnValue* type

```
public class CustomerFullNameFieldControl : BaseFieldControl
{
    protected override string DefaultTemplateName
    {
        get
        {
            return "CustomerFullNameRenderingTemplate";
        }
    }
    protected TextBox FirstNameInput;
    protected TextBox LastNameInput;

    protected override void CreateChildControls()
    {
        base.CreateChildControls();
        FirstNameInput =
          (TextBox)this.TemplateContainer.FindControl("FirstNameInput");
        LastNameInput =
          (TextBox)this.TemplateContainer.FindControl("LastNameInput");
    }

    public override object Value
    {
        get
        {
            this.EnsureChildControls();
            SPFieldMultiColumnValue mcv = new SPFieldMultiColumnValue(2);
            mcv[0] = FirstNameInput.Text;
            mcv[1] = LastNameInput.Text;
            return mcv;
        }
        set
        {
            this.EnsureChildControls();
            SPFieldMultiColumnValue mcv =
              (SPFieldMultiColumnValue)this.ItemFieldValue;
            FirstNameInput.Text = mcv[0];
            LastNameInput.Text = mcv[1];
        }
    }
}
```

It would be possible to extend this simple example further to exploit the potential of multicolumn field types. For example, if you were storing an address, you could call to a web service and pass a postal code that would return the associated city. That would allow you to add extra functionality to autopopulate the City text box and to perform validation to ensure that the address is correct.

Custom field types with custom properties

The custom field type named *CustomerLanguage* demonstrates how you can extend a custom field type with one or more *custom properties*. The main idea is that each field instance created from the custom field type gets its own independent property settings. You can create custom properties for a custom field type by adding a *PropertySchema* element to the bottom of the *FieldType* element for a custom field type. You create each custom property by adding *Field* elements inside the *PropertySchema* element. For example, the custom field type *CustomerLanguage* has been defined with five custom properties named *English*, *Spanish*, *French*, *Dutch*, and *German* of which Dutch and German aren't always available:

```
<FieldType>
  <Field Name="TypeName">CustomerLanguage</Field>
  <Field Name="ParentType">Text</Field>
  <Field Name="TypeDisplayName">Customer Language</Field>
  <Field Name="TypeShortDescription">Customer Language</Field>
  <Field Name="UserCreatable">TRUE</Field>
  <Field Name="ShowInColumnTemplateCreate">TRUE</Field>
  <Field Name="FieldTypeClass">
    WingtipToysFieldTypes.CustomerLanguage,WingtipToysFieldTypes,
    Version=1.0.0.0, Culture=neutral, PublicKeyToken=0720027336e99bd9
  </Field>
  <PropertySchema>
    <Fields>
      <Field Name="AvailableInDutch"
             DisplayName="Available in Dutch"
             Type="Boolean">
        <Default>0</Default>
      </Field>
      <Field Name="AvailableInGerman"
             DisplayName="Available in German"
             Type="Boolean">
        <Default>0</Default>
      </Field>
    </Fields>
  </PropertySchema>
</FieldType>
```

After you have added one or more custom properties to a custom field type, SharePoint will automatically add input controls to the page that allow a user to add or update columns based on your custom field type. Figure 10-3 shows what the user sees when adding or updating a field based on the *CustomerLanguage* custom field type. The user can decide whether content is available in Dutch and German.

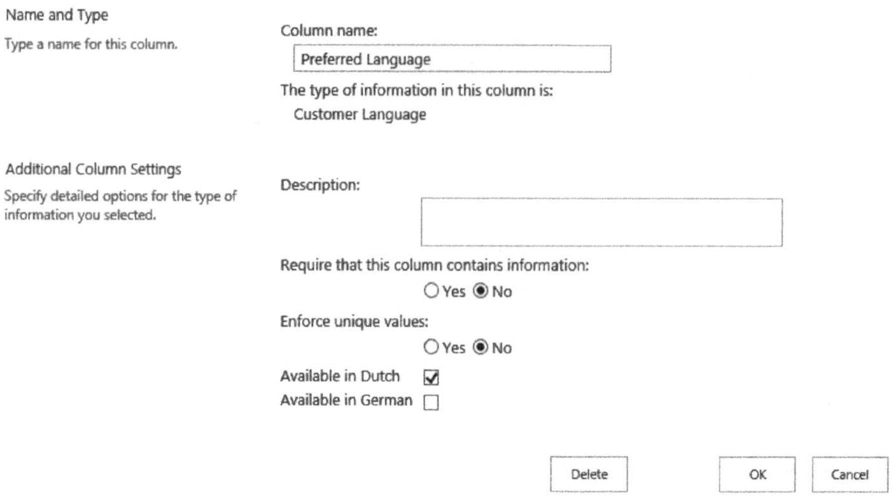

Name and Type

Type a name for this column.

Column name:

Preferred Language

The type of information in this column is:

Customer Language

Additional Column Settings

Specify detailed options for the type of information you selected.

Description:

Require that this column contains information:
  ○ Yes ◉ No

Enforce unique values:
  ○ Yes ◉ No

Available in Dutch ☑

Available in German ☐

[Delete]   [OK]   [Cancel]

FIGURE 10-3 Custom property fields make it possible to parameterize field instances.

After you have extended a custom field type with one or more custom properties, you then must write code to inspect what values the user has assigned to them. In the case of the custom field type named *CustomerLanguage*, there is code in the *CreateChildControls* method of the field control class that initializes a *RadioButtonList* control by adding items for English, Spanish, and French, and by using code to determine whether the options for Dutch and German should be added as well. If the user has set the value for *AvailableInDutch* and *AvailableInGerman* to *true*, the options will be added for the user to select them. Listing 10-3 shows the implementation of the *CustomerLanguage* and *CustomerLanguageFieldControl* classes.

LISTING 10-3 Implementation of the field and field control classes for a field with custom properties

```
public class CustomerLanguage : SPFieldText
{
    public CustomerLanguage(SPFieldCollection fields, string fieldName)
        : base(fields, fieldName) { }

    public CustomerLanguage
      (SPFieldCollection fields, string typeName, string displayName)
        : base(fields, typeName, displayName) { }

    public override BaseFieldControl FieldRenderingControl
    {
        get
        {
            BaseFieldControl ctr = new CustomerLanguageFieldControl();
            ctr.FieldName = this.InternalName;
            return ctr;
        }
```

```csharp
    public override string DefaultValue
    {
        get
        {
            return "English";
        }
    }

}

public class CustomerLanguageFieldControl : BaseFieldControl
{

    protected RadioButtonList CustomerLanguageInput;

    protected override string DefaultTemplateName
    {
        get
        {
            return "CustomerLanguageRenderingTemplate";
        }
    }

    protected override void CreateChildControls()
    {
        base.CreateChildControls();
        CustomerLanguageInput =
          (RadioButtonList)TemplateContainer.FindControl("CustomerLanguageInput");
        if (CustomerLanguageInput != null)
        {
            CustomerLanguageInput.Items.Clear();
            CustomerLanguageInput.Items.Add("English");
            CustomerLanguageInput.Items.Add("Spanish");
            CustomerLanguageInput.Items.Add("French");

            // check to see if Dutch is available
            if (this.Field.GetCustomProperty("AvailableInDutch") != null)
            {
                bool availableInDutch =
                  (bool)this.Field.GetCustomProperty("availableInDutch");
                if (availableInDutch)
                {
                    CustomerLanguageInput.Items.Add("Dutch");
                }
            }

            // check to see if German is available
            if (this.Field.GetCustomProperty("AvailableInGerman") != null)
            {
              bool availableInGerman =
                (bool)this.Field.GetCustomProperty("AvailableInGerman");

                if (availableInGerman)
                {
```

```
                        CustomerLanguageInput.Items.Add("German");
                }
            }
        }
    }

    public override object Value
    {
        get
        {
            this.EnsureChildControls();
            return CustomerLanguageInput.SelectedValue;
        }
        set
        {
            this.EnsureChildControls();
            CustomerLanguageInput.Items.FindByValue
                (ItemFieldValue.ToString()).Selected = true;
        }
    }
}
```

Figure 10-4 shows what the end result looks like if you deploy the WingTipToysFieldTypes solution and configure a list to use the custom fields that you created, but you select the option to indicate that the content isn't available in German.

Title *	Contoso
Full Name	First name: Katie
	Last name: Jordan
Phone Number	+1-(0)(317) 555-0123
Preferred Language	○ English
	○ Spanish
	○ French
	● Dutch

Save   Cancel

FIGURE 10-4 This edit form of a list shows the three custom field types that were created in this chapter.

JSLink

So far in this chapter we have looked at custom field types. Although custom field types provide an incredibly powerful mechanism for creating fields with a custom behavior and look and feel, they also have some significant downsides. The main drawback of custom field types is that they have to be installed by using a farm solution. This means that they can only be used in on-premises SharePoint environments. After they are installed, the custom field types are available throughout the entire environment, whereas you might want to create a custom field for a particular site collection or group of people.

In SharePoint 2013, Microsoft has introduced a new way to customize fields that can be used in both on-premises environments and cloud-based environments such as SharePoint Online 2013. The way fields can be customized by using a sandboxed solution or a SharePoint app is by using the new *JSLink* property that is available on *SPField* objects. It's not just fields that can be adjusted by using *JSLink*. The following objects can use the JSLink property:

- Fields

    - *SPField*

    - *SPFieldAttachments*

    - *SPFieldBoolean*

    - *SPFieldCalculated*

    - *SPFieldChoice*

    - *SPFieldCurrency*

    - *SPFieldDateTime*

    - *SPFieldDecimal*

    - *SPFieldFile*

    - *SPFieldGeolocation*

    - *SPFieldLookup*

    - *SPFieldMultiChoice*

    - *SPFieldMultiLineText*

    - *SPFieldNumber*

    - *SPFieldText*

    - *SPFieldUrl*

    - *SPFieldUser*

    - *TaxonomyField*

    - *OutComeChoiceField*

    - *RelatedItemsField*

- Web Parts

    - *PromotedSitesViewWebPart*

- *BaseXsltListWebPart*
- *ListFormWebPart*
- *TilesViewWebPart*
- Other
  - *SPContentType*
  - *SPForm*
  - *SPView*

As you can tell, the *JSLink* property can be used on a lot of objects. This means that it can help you customize all of these objects. The *JSLink* property itself doesn't actually do that much—it points to a JavaScript file that contains part of the behavior and the look and feel of a particular object.

Because we are talking about modifying fields in this section, we will look at how you can recreate the functionality of the *CustomerPhoneNumber* field type that was created earlier using a custom field type, but now you will be using the *JSLink* property. The *CustomerPhoneNumber* field was a standard text field, but with custom validation rules. These rules apply to the *New* and the *Edit* form of the list, which means that you will have to adjust the *JSLink* properties for these two forms. Note that you will have to adjust both views in order to offer a consistent experience for users, because the *JSLink* property can only be applied to one form at a time.

The first thing you have to do is to create a custom site column whose behavior you will adjust. Start by creating a new Visual Studio project of the type *SharePoint 2013 - Empty Project*. The project will be called **WingtipToysJSLink**. Next, click Add and New Item, and then add a site column. In this example, name the site column **CustomerPhoneNumber2**. You will adjust the display name to **Phone Number (JSLink)**, change the group the column is displayed in to WingtipToys Columns, and add the *JSLink* property, which you will use to point to the JavaScript file that you will create. The contents of the elements.xml file for the CustomerPhoneNumber2 column are shown in Listing 10-4.

LISTING 10-4 The contents of the elements.xml file for a custom site column including the *JSLink* property

```
<?xml version="1.0" encoding="utf-8"?>
<Elements xmlns="http://schemas.microsoft.com/sharepoint/">
  <Field
      ID="{d0a018ff-e6f8-4484-a8e3-c0dd6e11b65b}"
      Name="CustomerPhoneNumber2"
      DisplayName="Phone Number (JSLink)"
      Type="Text"
      Required="FALSE"
      JSLink="~sitecollection/_catalogs/masterpage/scripts/PhoneNumberValidator.js"
      Group="WingtipToys Columns">
  </Field>
</Elements>
```

You will deploy the JavaScript file to the MasterPage gallery, to a folder that you will create called *scripts*. This is arbitrary; you can also choose to deploy the JavaScript file to a folder in the site, to a different library, or even to a location in the SharePoint root folder. Note that you can only deploy the JavaScript file to a location in the SharePoint root folder if you are creating a farm solution. You can't deploy to the SharePoint root folder from a sandboxed solution or from a SharePoint app.

Both the CustomerPhoneNumber2 column and the module are deployed to a site collection by using a site collection–scoped feature called *Site-WingtipToysCustomerColumns*. Figure 10-5 shows the structure of the WingtipToysJSLink project.

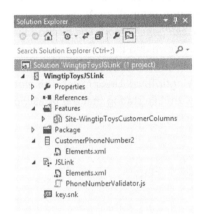

FIGURE 10-5 The WingtipToysJSLink project demonstrates creating a custom site column and modifying its behavior by using the *JSLink* property and a JavaScript file.

Next you start by overriding the behavior of the *EditForm* and *NewForm* of the column. You do this by specifying a custom function that will be executed when the form is loaded, which you can use to apply your custom rendering and validation. You can also choose to override the behavior of the *DisplayForm* and the *View* of the list, but you don't need this for the Customer Phone Number functionality, because the only customization is a custom validator. Note that the same method (*SPFieldPhoneNumber_Edit*) is used to override the behavior of the new form and the edit form; there is no need to create separate methods for both forms, because the intended behavior for both forms is the same. Also note that we explicitly state that the custom behavior should be applied to the CustomerPhoneNumber2 column. You can theoretically override the behavior of any column, as long as you know the internal name of the column:

```
function _registerCustomPhoneNumberFieldTemplate() {

    var phoneNrFieldContext = {};
    phoneNrFieldContext.Templates = {};
    phoneNrFieldContext.Templates.Fields = {
```

```
                'CustomerPhoneNumber2': {
                    'EditForm': CustomPhoneNumberFieldTemplate.SPFieldPhoneNumber_Edit,
                    'NewForm': CustomPhoneNumberFieldTemplate.SPFieldPhoneNumber_Edit
                }
        };
        SPClientTemplates.TemplateManager.RegisterTemplateOverrides(phoneNrFieldContext);
}
```

In the elements.xml file of the site column, you only specify a JavaScript file name and not the name of the function that should be called. In order to make sure that your code is executed when the column is loaded, you will use an Immediately Invoked Function Expression (IIFE). This is a function that is executed immediately when the file is loaded. The _registerCustomPhoneNumberFieldTemplate method will actually be part of the IIFE as well, as will the SPFieldPhoneNumber_Edit method that will contain the actual adjusted behavior of the column on the new form and the edit form. Listing 10-5, shown a bit later in this section, contains the entire contents of the PhoneNumberValidator.js file. The file will be deployed by using a module that you add to the WingtipToysJSLink project. The module will be called *JSLink* and will contain nothing but the elements.xml file stating that the JavaScript file should be deployed to the scripts folder in the MasterPage gallery:

```xml
<?xml version="1.0" encoding="utf-8"?>
<Elements xmlns="http://schemas.microsoft.com/sharepoint/">
  <Module Name="JSLink" List="116" Url="_catalogs/masterpage/scripts">
    <File Path="JSLink\PhoneNumberValidator.js"
          Url="PhoneNumberValidator.js"
          Type="GhostableInLibrary"
          IgnoreIfAlreadyExists="FALSE" />
  </Module>
</Elements>
```

Listing 10-5 shows that the *SPClientTemplates.Utility.GetFormContextForCurrentField* method is used in the *SPFieldPhoneNumber_Edit* method to get the context for the field for which you want to override the behavior. When you have the context of the field, you can retrieve its value, add the standard SharePoint validator in case the field is required, and add some callbacks. There are four callbacks:

- *registerInitCallback*   Sets the initial value of the column. On the new form, there won't be an initial value, so the text box will be left empty.

- *registerFocusCallback*   Sets the focus back to the CustomerPhoneNumber2 column after a postback of the page.

- *registerValidationErrorCallback*   Ensures that out-of-the-box SharePoint validation errors are correctly displayed.

- *registerGetValueCallback*   Gets the value of the field when the form is submitted, to make sure that the value can be saved.

```javascript
var _validationLabel = null;
var _phoneNrBox = null;

(function () {
    if (typeof CustomPhoneNumberFieldTemplate == "object") {
        return;
    }
    window.CustomPhoneNumberFieldTemplate = (function () {
        return {
            SPFieldPhoneNumber_Edit: function (rCtx) {
                if (rCtx == null)
                    return '';
                var _myData =
                  SPClientTemplates.Utility.GetFormContextForCurrentField(rCtx);

                if (_myData == null || _myData.fieldSchema == null) {
                    return '';
                }
                var _inputId_PhoneNr =
                  _myData.fieldName + '_' + _myData.fieldSchema.Id + '_$phoneNrField_
                    PhoneNr';
                var _inputId_Div =
                  _myData.fieldName + '_' + _myData.fieldSchema.Id + '_$phoneNrField_Div';
                var _inputId_ValidationLabel = _myData.fieldName + '_' +
                  _myData.fieldSchema.Id + '_$phoneNrField_ValidationError';

                var _value = _myData.fieldValue != null ? _myData.fieldValue : '';
                var listItem = rCtx['CurrentItem'];

                var validators = new SPClientForms.ClientValidation.ValidatorSet();
                if (_myData.fieldSchema.Required) {
                    validators.RegisterValidator
                        (new SPClientForms.ClientValidation.RequiredValidator());
                }
                _myData.registerClientValidator(_myData.fieldName, validators);

                // Post DOM initialization callback.
                _myData.registerInitCallback(_myData.fieldName, function () {

                    // Initialize the input control references.
                    _phoneNrBox = document.getElementById(_inputId_PhoneNr);
                    _validationLabel =
                        document.getElementById(_inputId_ValidationLabel);

                    // Set the initial values.
                    if (_phoneNrBox != null && _value != null) {
                        _phoneNrBox.value = _value;
                    }
```

```
        });
        // On focus call back
        _myData.registerFocusCallback(_myData.fieldName, function () {
            if (_phoneNrBox != null)
                _phoneNrBox.focus();
        });

        // Validation failure handler
        _myData.registerValidationErrorCallback
            (_myData.fieldName, function (errorResult)
        {
            SPFormControl_AppendValidationErrorMessage(_inputId_Div, errorResult);
        });


        // Register a callback just before submit.
        _myData.registerGetValueCallback(_myData.fieldName, function () {
            if (_phoneNrBox == null)
                return '';
            else {
                return _phoneNrBox.value;
            }
        });

        _myData.updateControlValue(_myData.fieldName, _value);
        var result = '<div width="100%" id=' + STSHtmlEncode(_inputId_Div) + '>';
        result += '<div><input id=' + STSHtmlEncode(_inputId_PhoneNr) +
                'type="text" name="PhoneNr" class="ms-long"
                onchange="validatePhoneNumber()" /></div>';
        result += '<span class="ms-formvalidation ms-csrformvalidation" '
                'id=' + STSHtmlEncode(_inputId_ValidationLabel) + ' '
                'style="display: none;" ></span>'
        result += '</div>';
        return result;


    },
    };
})();


function _registerCustomPhoneNumberFieldTemplate() {

    var phoneNrFieldContext = {};
    phoneNrFieldContext.Templates = {};
    phoneNrFieldContext.Templates.Fields = {

        'CustomerPhoneNumber2': {
            'EditForm': CustomPhoneNumberFieldTemplate.SPFieldPhoneNumber_Edit,
            'NewForm': CustomPhoneNumberFieldTemplate.SPFieldPhoneNumber_Edit
        }
    };
```

```
            SPClientTemplates.TemplateManager.RegisterTemplateOverrides(phoneNrFieldContext);
        }
    ExecuteOrDelayUntilScriptLoaded
        (_registerCustomPhoneNumberFieldTemplate, 'clienttemplates.js');
})();

function validatePhoneNumber() {
    var PN_RegularExpression = /^\+\d{1,2}\-\(0\)/i;
    var result = PN_RegularExpression.exec(_phoneNrBox.value);

    if (result == null) {
        _validationLabel.style.display = "";
        _validationLabel.innerText =
            "Phone Number must be formatted like +[CountryCode]-(0)...";
    }
    else {
        _validationLabel.style.display = "none";
        _validationLabel.innerText = "";
    }

}
```

The next step is to create the actual rendering of the text box. In this case, you use a simple HTML input control of type *text*, displaying a text box. You add the SharePoint CSS class *ms-long* to the text box so that it gets rendered just like the other text boxes on the form. You will also add an *onchange* attribute that will provide you with client-side validation similar to the validation that you created earlier in this chapter for the custom field type created for *CustomerPhoneNumber*. You will also add an HTML *span* element that can be used to display a message if validation fails. You will make sure that the message is rendered just like the out-of-the-box validation errors by adding more out-of-the-box CSS classes.

The final part of the JavaScript file is the custom validation method that will fire when the contents of the text box are changed. The method uses the same regular expression that was used for the custom field type, making sure that the value starts with +[CountryCode]-(0). If it doesn't, a message is displayed warning the user. If a user clicks the Save button directly after changing the field, the save action will be cancelled. This isn't a completely foolproof method, though, because the user can click the Save button again, which will submit the form and save the value for CustomerPhoneNumber2, even if it is not formatted correctly. You can add more logic to the JavaScript file to prevent this if you need to.

Figure 10-6 shows the end result of the Phone Number (JSLink) site column with the JavaScript linked to it using the JSLink property.

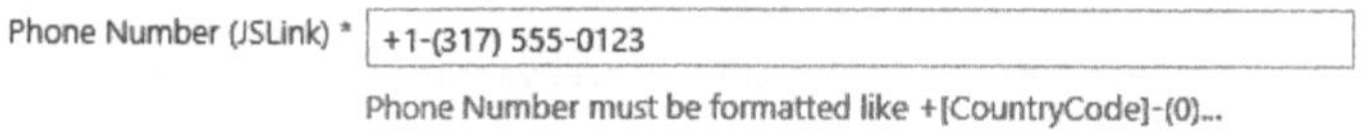

| Phone Number (JSLink) * | +1-(317) 555-0123 |

Phone Number must be formatted like +[CountryCode]-(0)...

FIGURE 10-6 The JavaScript that has been linked to the new and edit forms using the JSLink property is throwing a validation error.

Custom site columns and content types

In this section, we will look at different ways in which you can create custom site columns and content types in your SharePoint solutions. Site columns and content types can be created either by using Collaborative Application Markup Language (CAML) or by using the server-side object model.

If you had to write all the CAML yourself, it would be more tedious to write and test the functionality than if you were using the server-side object model. However, the SharePoint developer tools do most of the work for you, and for some tasks they even provide designers. There are pros and cons to using CAML compared to using server-side code. Reading CAML is generally easier than reading code, which means that it is easier for other developers to view what you have created. A downside of CAML is that it can be harder to maintain. Though modifying the XML and redeploying the solution is easy, it is not always supported. You have to know which changes are supported and which aren't. If you use code, you have more flexibility and can make changes to the actual object—the column, content type, or list instance in the site—rather than to the template, as you would if you were using CAML.

Creating site columns and content types by using CAML

As you begin working with CAML, it can be very educational to dissect the CAML-based definitions for site columns, content types, and list types that ship with SharePoint 2013. For example, you can examine the standard site columns defined in the *fields* feature and the standard content types defined in the *ctypes* feature. When you examine the features and CAML definitions that ship with the product, be sure to look—but don't touch. Modifying any of the built-in features or CAML definitions is not supported and can cause serious damage to the SharePoint farm.

In Chapter 3, "Server-side solution development," in the "Developing sandboxed solutions" section, you used CAML to create two custom site columns called AgeGroup and ToysPrice, and a content type called Toys. The companion code for this book contains the WingtipToysSandbox project, which contains the AgeGroup and ToysPrice site columns and the Toys content type. Although this project is set to be deployed as a sandboxed solution, it can also be deployed as a full-trust solution by changing the value of the *Sandboxed Solution* project property from *True* to *False*.

In this section, we will go over the CAML used in the WingtipToysSandbox project, in the next section you will rebuild the same functionality by using the server-side object model.

A site column definition is created by using a *Field* element. For example, the elements.xml file of the ToysPrice site column includes the following CAML definition. The ToysPrice site column definition also shows some attributes that you have to specify when creating a custom site column, such as *ID*, *Name*, *DisplayName*, *Group*, *Required*, and *Type*. You will need a new GUID each time you create a new site column definition. If you create the site column by using the SharePoint Developer Tools, the GUID will be generated for you. Also note that because the *ToysPrice* field is a *Currency* field, it also includes the attribute *Decimals*, which is set to 2. If you want to ensure that users can't fill in a negative price, it would also be possible to use the *Min* attribute and set it to 0:

```
<Field>
        ID="{f75c27ba-e321-4bbe-a30b-be0e085a5517}"
        Name="ToysPrice"
        DisplayName="Price"
        Type="Currency"
        LCID="1033"
        Decimals="2"
        Required="TRUE"
        Group="WingtipToys Columns">
</Field>
```

The AgeGroup column is an example of a *Choice* field. By default, choice fields are formatted as drop-down menus. You can also specify that you want the field to be formatted as radio buttons or check boxes by adding the *Format* attribute and specifying its value as *RadioButtons* or *Checkboxes*. Check boxes should be used when the user should be able to select more than one value for the field:

```
<Field>
        ID="{742e3245-a013-4537-82d3-727ddbfb981a}"
        Name="AgeGroup"
        DisplayName="Age Group"
        Type="Choice"
        Required="TRUE"
        Group="WingtipToys Columns">
    <CHOICES>
        <CHOICE>0-1</CHOICE>
        <CHOICE>2-3</CHOICE>
        <CHOICE>4-6</CHOICE>
        <CHOICE>7-9</CHOICE>
        <CHOICE>10-12</CHOICE>
        <CHOICE>12+</CHOICE>
    </CHOICES>
  </Field>
```

The attributes used in the examples are only a small subset of the attributes that you can use when creating site column definitions. For more information, you can look at the MSDN documentation at *http://msdn.microsoft.com/en-us/library/ms437580.aspx*.

After you have created a couple of custom site columns, you can either add them to a list one at a time, or you can use a *content type* to group them together and add the content type to a list. A content type definition is created by using a *ContentType* element. The *ContentType* element must contain a set of required attributes and a collection of links to fields that are created by using *FieldRef* elements. Each *FieldRef* element references a specific site column definition, using both the identifying GUID and its string-based name. Each content type definition also requires an ID that begins with the content type ID of its parent. The content type in this example, *Toys*, inherits from the *Item* content type. The *Item* content type has an ID of 0x01. Note that the content type ID is not a GUID. If you use the SharePoint Developer Tools to create a content type, the ID will be generated for you. Depending on the exact definition of you content type, you don't even have to worry about the XML, because the new SharePoint Developer Tools for Visual Studio 2012 contain a designer that you can use to create custom content types:

```xml
<?xml version="1.0" encoding="utf-8"?>
<Elements xmlns="http://schemas.microsoft.com/sharepoint/">
  <!-- Parent ContentType: Item (0x01) -->
  <ContentType ID="0x01007E6057B85C8A465D9A695CC2E60AB705"
               Name="Toys"
               Group="WingTipToys Content Types"
               Description="Content type used to store information about toys"
               Inherits="TRUE">
    <FieldRefs>
      <FieldRef ID="{742e3245-a013-4537-82d3-727ddbfb981a}"
                DisplayName="Age Group" Required="TRUE" Name="AgeGroup" />
      <FieldRef ID="{f75c27ba-e321-4bbe-a30b-be0e085a5517}"
                DisplayName="Price" Required="TRUE" Name="ToysPrice" />
    </FieldRefs>
  </ContentType>
</Elements>
```

Before you can create a content type definition, you must decide which base content type to inherit from. For example, you can inherit from a standard list content type such as *Item, Contact*, or *Task*. You can also elect to create a content type that inherits from *Document*, making it possible to add support for a document template and use it in a document library. In this example, we kept it simple and inherited the *Toys* content type from *Item*. When you use the SharePoint Developer Tools to create the content type, the wizard will prompt you to select a base content type. You can pick the base content type from a drop-down list that includes previously created custom content types. Do make sure, if you inherit your content type from another custom content type, that the other content type is deployed to all environments in which you want to deploy your content type; otherwise your content type will throw an error when it is deployed, and you won't be able to use it.

For each field link that you want to add, you must create a *FieldRef* element that references a site column definition. You can include both out-of-the-box SharePoint site columns and custom site columns. If you are using the SharePoint Developer Tools and Visual Studio 2012, you can use the designer to add site columns to your content type.

Creating site columns and content types by using the server-side object model

We have looked at creating site columns and content types by using CAML, but you can achieve the same thing by using the server-side object model. There is even one type of site column that you should only create by using the server-side object model. Creating a managed metadata site column using CAML is not supported. In order to create a managed metadata site column, you must use the server-side object model.

To create the AgeGroup and ToysPrice site columns and the *Toys* content type by using the server-side object model, you first have to determine when or how you want to create the columns. You can add the code needed to create the site columns and content type to a Web Part, a custom application page, a custom action, or a feature receiver. In the example in this section, you will add the code to a feature receiver, so that the site columns and the content type are created when the feature is activated.

First create a SharePoint 2013 - Empty Project and call it **WingtipToysColumnsContentTypes**. You will deploy the project as a farm solution. Next, right-click the Features node in the Solution Explorer and click Add Feature. This will generate a feature called Feature1 that is web scoped. Call it **Site-ColumnsContentTypes** and change its scope to Site, because site columns and content types should be created at the rootweb of a site collection and not at every subsite. Now right-click the feature and select Add Event Receiver. Next, just uncomment the *FeatureActivated* event handler, and you are ready to add the code to create the actual site columns and content type.

Call the custom site columns that you create using the server-side object model **ToysPrice2** and **AgeGroup2**, and the content type **Toys2**, to avoid conflicts if the columns and content type from Chapter 3 are deployed to the same site collection. To create the ToysPrice2 column, you will use the *SPFieldCurrency* object. You could also use the *SPField* object, but that won't allow you to set values for attributes that are specific to the currency field, such as *Decimals*. When setting the number of decimals by using code, you use the *SPNumberFormatTypes* enumeration:

```
SPCurrencyField.DisplayFormat = SPNumberFormatTypes.TwoDecimals;
```

In order to make sure that you won't cause any exceptions from trying to create duplicate site columns, you will test whether the column already exists by using the *SPFieldCollection. ContainsField(SPField)* method. To create the AgeGroup2 column, you use the *SPFieldChoice* object, which allows you to add choices to the field.

Before creating the content type, you again test whether it already exists. There is no graceful way to do this, so simply try to retrieve the content type and test whether it's null. When you create the new content type, use *SPContentTypeCollection[SPBuiltInContentTypeId.Item]* to specify the parent content type. SharePoint will then generate the new content type ID for the content type that you are creating. The last step is to add the links to the *ToysPrice2* and the *AgeGroup2* fields to the content type. You do this by creating a *SPFieldLink* to both fields and adding those field links to the content type. Listing 10-6 contains the complete *FeatureActivated* event handler that creates the site columns and the content types. You could have chosen to use the *FeatureDeactivating* event handler to remove the site columns and content type from the site, but removing site columns and content types is not always possible and might cause data loss, so you won't remove the columns and the content types when the feature is deactivated.

LISTING 10-6 Using server-side code to create site columns and a content type

```
public override void FeatureActivated(SPFeatureReceiverProperties properties)
{
    SPSite currentSite = properties.Feature.Parent as SPSite;

    SPWeb currentWeb = currentSite.OpenWeb();

    SPFieldCollection siteColumns = currentWeb.Fields;
    currentWeb.AllowUnsafeUpdates = true;

    if (!siteColumns.ContainsField("ToysPrice2"))
    {
        SPFieldCurrency toysPrice =
          siteColumns.CreateNewField("Currency", "ToysPrice2") as SPFieldCurrency;
        toysPrice.StaticName = "ToysPrice2";
        toysPrice.Title = "Price2";
        toysPrice.Group = "WingtipToys Columns";
        toysPrice.Required = true;
        toysPrice.DisplayFormat = SPNumberFormatTypes.TwoDecimals;
        currentWeb.Fields.Add(toysPrice);
    }

    if (!siteColumns.ContainsField("AgeGroup2"))
    {
        SPFieldChoice ageGroup =
          siteColumns.CreateNewField("Choice", "AgeGroup2") as SPFieldChoice;
        ageGroup.StaticName = "AgeGroup2";
        ageGroup.Title = "Age Group2";
        ageGroup.Group = "WingtipToys Columns";
        ageGroup.Required = true;
        ageGroup.Choices.Add("0-1");
        ageGroup.Choices.Add("2-3");
        ageGroup.Choices.Add("4-6");
        ageGroup.Choices.Add("7-9");
        ageGroup.Choices.Add("10-12");
        ageGroup.Choices.Add("12+");
        currentWeb.Fields.Add(ageGroup);
    }

    SPContentTypeCollection contentTypes = currentWeb.ContentTypes;
    if (contentTypes["Toys2"] == null)
    {
      SPContentType toys =
      new SPContentType(contentTypes[SPBuiltInContentTypeId.Item], contentTypes,
        "Toys2");
      toys.Group = "WingtipToys Content Types";
      toys.Description = "Content type used to store information about toys";
```

```
            SPField toysPrice = currentWeb.Fields.GetFieldByInternalName("ToysPrice2");
            SPField ageGroup = currentWeb.Fields.GetFieldByInternalName("AgeGroup2");
            SPFieldLink toysPriceLink = new SPFieldLink(toysPrice);
            SPFieldLink ageGroupLink = new SPFieldLink(ageGroup);
            toys.FieldLinks.Add(toysPriceLink);
            toys.FieldLinks.Add(ageGroupLink);

            contentTypes.Add(toys);
        }
        currentWeb.AllowUnsafeUpdates = false;
    }
```

Custom list definitions

The SharePoint Developer Tools contain a project item template for creating custom lists. When the
List template is selected, you get to choose whether to create a customizable or a non-customizable
list. When you choose a customizable list, a list definition is created; choosing a non-customizable
list creates a list instance. If you create a new project item by using the List project item template,
the SharePoint Customization Wizard prompts you to choose the type of list that you want to create
by selecting one of the built-in list definitions. When you are creating a customizable list, only the
base types can be selected. When a list instance is created, any of the out-of-the-box list definitions
can be chosen as a starting point. Creating non-customizable lists and list instances was discussed in
more detail in Chapter 3, in the discussion about declarative elements. In this section, we will focus on
creating customizable lists or list definitions.

For the purposes of this section, the.zip archive of companion code for this book contains a
SharePoint project named WingtipToysLists. This project contains working samples of the custom
list that we are going to examine over the next few pages. After the project is created as a farm
solution, you can add the new list to it by clicking Add | New Item and choosing List. You will
create a customizable list called WingtipToysProductsList and base it on Default (Custom List). The
SharePoint Developer Tools will do a lot of the work for you by creating the list definition. To modify
the definition, you can use the designer. The designer offers three different views: List, Views, and
Columns views.

It is important to note that when you create a new list by using the SharePoint Developer Tools in
Visual Studio 2012, the designer tools don't just create a new list definition, they also create a new list
instance. This means that when you activate the feature, a new list template will be made available
in the site and a new list instance will be created based on that template. This can be a bit confusing,
because some of the changes that you make in the designer are applied to both the list definition
and the list instance, and others are only applied to the list instance. The list instance is generated as
a subelement of the list template. The list template consists of an element.xml file and a schema.xml
file. The list instance has its own elements.xml.

The List tab of the designer, shown in Figure 10-7, enables you to modify the metadata of the *list instance*, such as Title (Display Name), URL, and Description. You can also select whether the list instance should appear on the Quick Launch area on the left of the screen or whether it should be hidden from the browser completely.

FIGURE 10-7 The List tab of the list designer is part of the SharePoint Developer Tools for Visual Studio 2012.

By using the Columns view, shown in Figure 10-8, you can add existing site columns to the list definition or create new columns specifically for use in this particular list. You can also add a content type, which will then automatically add all the columns from the content type to the list definition.

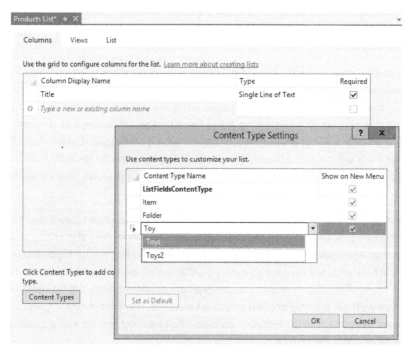

FIGURE 10-8 The Columns tab of the list designer is part of the SharePoint Developer Tools for Visual Studio 2012.

The Views tab of the designer is shown in Figure 10-9. This tab allows you to adjust an existing view or create a new one. By default, an All Items view is added that shows all items in the list and that pages the items to show only 30 at a time. You can add columns to, or remove columns from, the view. The views you create will be part of the list definition, which means that they will be available in all list instances that are created based on the new list template.

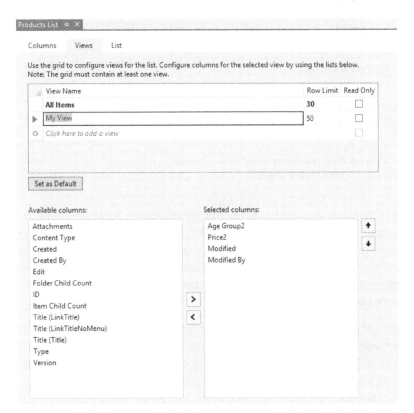

FIGURE 10-9 The Views tab of the list designer is part of the SharePoint Developer Tools for Visual Studio 2012.

In a lot of cases, when you create a custom list definition, you will want to offer users the opportunity to create lists of the custom type in their sites. When you add a list instance, a list will be created automatically with the title and description that you specified. If this is not the behavior that you want when the feature containing your list is activated, you can simply delete the list instance from the list definition. Users will then be able create their own list instances based on the custom list template.

The behavior of the SharePoint Developer Tools when a list instance is deployed using Visual Studio is also worth noting. If a list instance already exists when the solution is redeployed, the Developer Tools will detect a conflict. The Tools will offer to resolve the conflict, or you can stop the deployment. If you let the Developer Tools resolve the conflict, the list instance in the site will be deleted and a new one will be created. Sometimes that is how you want the conflict to be resolved, but if you had added data (such as test data) to the list instance in the site, having it deleted with every deployment might not be the behavior you are looking for.

You don't have to use the designer to work with lists in Visual Studio 2012. You can also open the generated XML files directly. When you create a new project item for a list definition, it contains two CAML-based files named elements.xml and schema.xml. Both of these files are required to create a list definition. We will begin by examining the elements.xml file that contains a *ListTemplate* element:

```
<Elements xmlns="http://schemas.microsoft.com/sharepoint/">
    <!-- Do not change the value of the Name attribute below.
        If it does not match the folder name of the List project item,
        an error will occur when the project is run. -->
    <ListTemplate
        Name="WingtipToysProductsList"
        Type="10000"
        BaseType="0"
        OnQuickLaunch="TRUE"
        SecurityBits="11"
        Sequence="410"
        DisplayName=" Products List"
        Description=" Wingtip Toys Products List"
        Image="/_layouts/15/images/itgen.png"/>
</Elements>
```

As you can tell, this *ListTemplate* element has a *Name* of *WingtipToysProductsList*. The value of the *Name* attribute is important within a *ListTemplate* element because SharePoint Foundation requires a child directory inside the root feature directory with the same name that will contain a file with the well-known name schema.xml. If you use the SharePoint Developer Tools to deploy or package your project, the required directory, named WingtipToysProductsList, will be created inside the root feature directory, and the schema.xml file will be placed inside.

The *ListTemplate* element defines a *Type* attribute with an integer value used to identify the creatable list type associated with the list definition. Microsoft uses lower-numbered identifiers for the built-in list types, such as *104* for *Announcements* and *105* for *Contacts*. When you use the SharePoint Developer Tools to create a list definition, a list type identifier of 10,000 or greater will be used. The tools will make sure that they don't generate a duplicate type identifier if multiple custom list definitions exist in the environment.

Now that you have learned what's required in the elements.xml file, let's move on to discuss what's inside the schema.xml file. The schema.xml file contains a top-level *List* element that contains several attributes and inner elements for content type, fields, views, and forms:

```
<List xmlns:ows="Microsoft SharePoint"
    Title="WingtipToysProductsList"
    FolderCreation="FALSE"
    Direction="$Resources:Direction;"
    Url="Lists/WingtipToysProductsList"
    BaseType="0"
    xmlns="http://schemas.microsoft.com/sharepoint/"
    EnableContentTypes="TRUE">
```

```
  <MetaData>
    <ContentTypes><!-- add content types here --></ContentTypes>
    <Fields><!-- add fields here --></Fields>
    <Views><!-- define views here --></Views>
    <Forms><!-- add support for forms here --></Forms>
  </MetaData>
</List>
```

Now we will take a little time to walk through the individual sections of the schema.xml file in more detail. We will begin with the *ContentTypes* element. The *ContentTypes* element can contain content type instances or content type references. The *ContentTypes* element in this example contains a *ContentType* element with an instance of the *ListFieldsContentType*. This content type was generated by the SharePoint Developer Tools. If you add your own content types to the list, you can choose to remove this one. The *ContentTypes* element also contains three content type references. The first one, with ID="0x01", references the out-of-the-box *Item* content type; the second, with ID="0x0120", references the out-of-the-box *Folder* content type; and the last one, with the long ID that is based on the *Item* ID, is a reference to the *Toys2* content type that was created in the previous section:

```
<ContentTypes>
  <ContentType ID="0x0100b5555c921f27445b8b00e0033f43e08c"
               Name="ListFieldsContentType">
    <FieldRefs>
      <FieldRef ID="{fa564e0f-0c70-4ab9-b863-0177e6ddd247}" Name="Title" />
      <FieldRef ID="{26863001-b37d-487e-8438-cec08fb6b205}" Name="ToysPrice2" />
      <FieldRef ID="{5d7e9e45-0798-4788-9b47-9934c7973e52}" Name="AgeGroup2" />
    </FieldRefs>
  </ContentType>
  <ContentTypeRef ID="0x01">
    <Folder TargetName="Item" />
  </ContentTypeRef>
  <ContentTypeRef ID="0x0120" />
  <ContentTypeRef ID="0x01009CC2D513D1E6E848B3A68900C289057D" />
</ContentTypes>
```

Now we will now examine the *Fields* section. Dealing with the fields of a content type in the schema.xml file is more complicated than the example shown in the previous chapter, when we added a content type to a list through the server-side object model. When you add a content type to a list by using the server-side object model, SharePoint automatically adds the fields of the content type to the *Fields* collection of the list. However, when you add a content type to the *ContentTypes* section of the schema.xml file, the fields aren't added automatically. If you modify the CAML of the schema.xml file directly, you have to add each field to the list's field collection explicitly. If you use the list designer, the Developer Tools will add the fields to the schema.xml for you, so you don't have to worry about adding them in properly. The requirement to add redundant field definitions into the schema.xml file doesn't seem very intuitive. After all, you've already defined the fields once in the *Toys2* content type, so why should you define them a second time in the schema.xml file? SharePoint, however, doesn't supply any mechanism to copy the fields from content types that are added or referenced in the schema.xml file to the list. The following shows the CAML for adding the fields to the list as it is generated by the list designer:

```
<Fields>
  <Field ID="{fa564e0f-0c70-4ab9-b863-0177e6ddd247}"
         Type="Text"
         Name="Title"
         DisplayName="$Resources:core,Title;"
         Required="TRUE"
         SourceID="http://schemas.microsoft.com/sharepoint/v3"
         StaticName="Title" MaxLength="255" />
  <Field Type="Currency"
         DisplayName="Price2"
         StaticName="ToysPrice2"
         Group="WingtipToys Columns"
         Decimals="2"
         ID="{26863001-b37d-487e-8438-cec08fb6b205}"
         SourceID="{6ecd59dd-c430-4a2c-a7c5-4c633d0b086e}"
         Name="ToysPrice2" />
  <Field Type="Choice"
         DisplayName="Age Group2"
         StaticName="AgeGroup2"
         Group="WingtipToys Columns"
         ID="{5d7e9e45-0798-4788-9b47-9934c7973e52}"
         SourceID="{6ecd59dd-c430-4a2c-a7c5-4c633d0b086e}"
         Name="AgeGroup2">
    <CHOICES />
  </Field>
</Fields>
```

After adding fields to the list, you also will want to specify which fields are to be added to the various views supported by the list, such as the standard All Items view, or the custom My View that was added in the example. In order to do this, the *Views* element of the schema.xml file has to be modified. The following *View* element demonstrates adding *FieldRef* elements to the *ViewFields* node of the My View view so that it displays the fields that were added in the *Fields* section earlier:

```
<Views>
  <View BaseViewID="2" Name="b4ac1dc2-9066-451c-87bd-517b1dfd3302"
        DisplayName="My View" Type="HTML" WebPartZoneID="Main"
        SetupPath="pages\viewpage.aspx" Url="My View.aspx">
    <ViewFields>
      <FieldRef Name="AgeGroup2" />
      <FieldRef Name="ToysPrice2" />
      <FieldRef Name="Modified" />
      <FieldRef Name="Editor" />
    </ViewFields>
    <Query />
    <Toolbar Type="Standard" />
    <XslLink Default="TRUE">main.xsl</XslLink>
    <JSLink>clienttemplates.js</JSLink>
    <RowLimit>50</RowLimit>
  </View>
</Views>
```

The *Forms* element at the bottom of the schema.xml file is used to define the default forms for displaying, editing, and adding items. A schema.xml file can be written to use custom forms for viewing and editing content. However, you can also rely on a generic form named form.aspx, which is installed along with SharePoint Foundation and deployed inside the SharePoint root directory at TEMPLATE\ Pages. When you create a new list definition by using the SharePoint Developer Tools, the schema.xml file is created to use the generic file form.aspx for each of its default forms:

```
<Forms>
  <Form Type="DisplayForm" Url="DispForm.aspx"
        SetupPath="pages\form.aspx" WebPartZoneID="Main" />
  <Form Type="EditForm" Url="EditForm.aspx"
        SetupPath="pages\form.aspx" WebPartZoneID="Main" />
  <Form Type="NewForm" Url="NewForm.aspx"
        SetupPath="pages\form.aspx" WebPartZoneID="Main" />
</Forms>
```

Summary

This chapter started by examining custom field types. We looked at several different types of fields that you can create, which showed how powerful and flexible custom field types can be. We also established that deploying custom field types has an impact on your entire SharePoint environment and can only be done by using farm solutions. The new *JSLink* property can be used to customize the behavior of fields with JavaScript. The JavaScript files can be deployed without using a farm solution and have a much smaller impact on the environment.

We also looked at creating custom site columns and content types. We compared creating columns and content types using CAML and using the server-side object model. Both are valid approaches, and in most cases it is possible to create the same result by using either approach. Using CAML means that it is easier to "read" what site columns and content types have been created. Using the server-side object model means that the site columns and content types will be easier to maintain.

In the final section of this chapter, we used CAML and the SharePoint Developer Tools designers to create list definitions and list instances. We studied the differences between list definitions and list instances and looked into when you might need one or the other.

## CHAPTER 11

SharePoint site provisioning

This chapter focuses on creating templates for sites. We will compare the different types of templates that can be created and discuss their strengths and weaknesses. You will learn about the underlying Microsoft SharePoint site provisioning architecture, in which every new site is created by using a specific site definition. We will examine the role of the GLOBAL site definition and discuss site definitions, web templates and site templates. We will also look at using server-side code to create sites by using site provisioning providers and web provisioning events. Finally, we'll look at templates for sites hosting SharePoint apps.

You can create a site in SharePoint through the user interface, by using Windows PowerShell, by using a farm or sandboxed solution, or by using the client-side object model from, for instance, a SharePoint app or an externally hosted application. Site collections can only be created through the user interface, by using Windows PowerShell, or by using a farm solution. From a sandboxed solution or the client-side object model it is not possible to create site collections.

Regardless of the approach you choose to create a site, and regardless of whether you create a site or a site collection, SharePoint will always use a template to fully provision your site. In the first section, we will discuss the different types of templates that you can use to provision sites. We will look into site definitions, site templates, and web templates, and the advantages and disadvantages of each of them when they are used to create your own templates.

Whenever a new site is created, the exact steps are that executed to provision the site differ depending on how the site is being created. The provisioning process always starts with the same steps, though. The first step of the site provisioning process is to reserve the URL. Before SharePoint 2010, you could tell that this was the case, because if site creation failed at some point after the URL had been reserved, you couldn't create a new site by using that same URL and you also couldn't browse to the site on that URL, because it wasn't completely provisioned. The URL was stored in the database, though, meaning that it couldn't be used again. Starting with SharePoint 2010, the site provisioning process was redesigned to be processed as a single transaction. If provisioning fails at some point during site creation, the whole site is removed again, and the URL can be reused to create another site.

The GLOBAL site definition

After the URL has been reserved, SharePoint begins the actual site provisioning process by executing the provisioning instructions defined in a special site definition called the GLOBAL site definition. The GLOBAL site definition contains a set of common provisioning instructions. It has an ONET.xml file that contains site provisioning instructions that are executed each time a new site is created. If you examine the ONET.xml file of the GLOBAL site definition, you will find a *Project* element that contains child elements named *NavBars*, *ListTemplates*, *BaseTypes*, *Configurations*, and *Modules*:

```
<Project>  <!-- can define navigation elements -->
  <NavBars/>  <!-- defines list definitions for system lists and galleries -->
  <ListTemplates/>   <!-- defines base types used by list and document libraries -->
  <BaseTypes/>  <!-- defines configuration with shared provisioning instructions -->
  <Configurations/>  <!-- provisions files for standard master pages and themes -->
  <Modules/>
</Project>
```

The *NavBars* element of the GLOBAL site definition is empty; no top-level or Quick Launch navigation elements are defined in it. The *ListTemplates* element contains *ListTemplate* elements that define list definitions for creating special system lists and galleries such as the Master Page Gallery, the Solution Gallery, and the Web Part Gallery. The *BaseTypes* section provides a definition for each of the supported base types. The base types are *Generic List*, *Document Library*, *Discussion Form*, *Vote or Survey*, and *Issues List*. All base type elements contain configurations that define which fields are added to every list and document library.

The *Configurations* element of the GLOBAL site definition is important because it is used to activate the built-in *fields* and *ctypes* features automatically whenever a new site collection is created. No other features are listed in the GLOBAL site definition; the only ones that are activated on all sites automatically are the *fields* and *ctypes* features. The *Configuration* element also contains a *Lists* element to create special system lists and galleries. There are six other *List* elements, which contain a *RootWebOnly* attribute with a value of *TRUE*. This attribute setting configures these *List* elements so that they create system lists and galleries in top-level sites only when a new site collection is being created. Examples of system lists that only exist in the root web of a site collection are the Master Page Gallery, the Solutions Gallery, the User Information List, and the Web Part Gallery.

The ONET.xml file in the GLOBAL site definition includes two *Module* elements, which are named *DefaultMasterPage* and *OOBThemesV15*. The *Module* element named *DefaultMasterPage* is used to add the standard SharePoint master pages to every new site. The *Module* element named *OOB-ThemesV15* has been written to add the .thmx files for the standard SharePoint themes into the Themes Gallery of each top-level site.

The next steps of the provisioning process depend on the way the site is being provisioned. There are three types of templates that can be used to provision a site in SharePoint:

- Site definitions

- Web templates

- Site templates

Site definitions

A site definition is a template that is used by SharePoint to create and provision new sites. Site definitions can provide information about the navigation, the lists and libraries that are available, features that are activated, and pages that are created when the site is provisioned. After a site has been created, the site definition that the site is based on will stay with the site forever. The *SPWeb.WebTemplate* property stores the name of the site definition that was used to create the site, and *SPWeb.WebTemplateId* stores the ID of the site definition that the site is based on. The *SPWeb.Configuration* property stores the ID of the configuration that was used. Even if other mechanisms, such as web templates or site templates, are used to create the site, the *WebTemplate*, *WebTemplateId*, and *Configuration* properties will still refer to a site definition and its configuration and not to the web template or site template. All the out-of-the-box templates that you can choose from when you create a site are site definitions. A site definition consists of a minimum of two different files, the webtemp*.xml file and the ONET.xml file. The metadata of the site definition, such as the name and ID and information about the configuration, is stored in the webtemp*.xml file.

Webtemp*.xml

The webtemp files are stored the SharePoint root directory at TEMPLATE/1033/XML. Note that the *1033* in this path refers to the English version of SharePoint, or the English language packs. If you are running a different version of SharePoint, such as a Spanish or a Chinese version, 1033 will be replaced by a different locale identifier. If you have multiple language packs installed on your SharePoint server and you want a site definition to be available for all of those languages, you will have to deploy your webtemp file to the XML folders for all those languages.

On a SharePoint server there are several webtemp files, all of which start with *webtemp* and end with *.xml*. The file name of the webtemp file can be made unique by adding something in between *webtemp* and *.xml*. The webtemp file that contains information about the eDiscovery site definitions, for instance, is called webtempediscc.xml. The webtemp of the basic SharePoint Foundation sites is simply called webtemp.xml. Figure 11-1 shows the contents of the TEMPLATE/1033/XML folder on a server that is running SharePoint Server 2013 Enterprise Edition.

Name	Date modified	Type	Size
DEADWEB.XML	10/1/2012 9:56 PM	XML File	2 KB
RGNLSTNG.XML	10/1/2012 9:56 PM	XML File	26 KB
WEBTEMP.XML	10/1/2012 9:56 PM	XML File	6 KB
webtempaccsrv.xml	10/1/2012 9:52 PM	XML File	1 KB
webtempaccsvc.xml	10/1/2012 9:52 PM	XML File	1 KB
webtempbdr.en-US.xml	10/1/2012 9:52 PM	XML File	1 KB
webtempdev.xml	10/1/2012 9:56 PM	XML File	1 KB
webtempdocmarketplace.xml	10/1/2012 9:52 PM	XML File	2 KB
webtempedisc.xml	10/1/2012 9:52 PM	XML File	2 KB
webtempoffile.xml	10/1/2012 9:52 PM	XML File	2 KB
webtemposrv.xml	10/1/2012 9:54 PM	XML File	1 KB
webtempppsma.xml	10/1/2012 9:54 PM	XML File	2 KB
webtempsps.xml	10/1/2012 9:55 PM	XML File	14 KB
webtempsrch.xml	10/1/2012 9:54 PM	XML File	2 KB
webtempvispr.xml	10/1/2012 9:55 PM	XML File	1 KB

FIGURE 11-1 The TEMPLATE\1033\XML folder containing the webtemp*.xml files

A single webtemp file can contain information about more than one site definition. The webtemp.xml file, for instance, contains information about 16 different site definitions. Some of them are hidden and should not be used by end users or by developers to create sites; others are visible and can be selected as templates when sites are created through the user interface. Site definitions can be made hidden for several reasons. In some cases, they are only for SharePoint internal usage, such as the GLOBAL site definition and the Central Administration site definitions. Other times, Microsoft might want to deprecate a site definition because it is no longer in line with how SharePoint can best be used, or because a better alternative exists. Because existing sites might break if a site definition is removed completely, Microsoft won't remove the site definition from SharePoint, but they will make it hidden so that existing sites in your environment will continue to work. The fact that the definitions can still be found in the file system of a SharePoint server does not mean that it is a good idea to use them to create sites. Changing the Hidden property of an out-of-the-box site definition so that end users can use the site definition to create sites is not supported and should not be attempted.

The webtemp file contains *Template* and *Configuration* elements. The template element is linked to an ONET.xml file. Multiple configurations can be defined in a single ONET.xml file, with a *Configuration* element for each one. In the *Configuration* element, the title as users will view it, whether a site definition is hidden, a description, and a display category are defined. The display category is the tab on which the site definition will appear in the site creation user interface in SharePoint. The image used to be visible when subsites were created from an existing site collection, but in SharePoint 2013 the image won't show up anywhere in the user interface:

```
<Template Name="STS" ID="1">
    <Configuration ID="0"
                Title="Team Site"
                Hidden="FALSE"
                ImageUrl="/_layouts/15/images/stts.png?rev=23"
                Description="A place to work together with a group of people."
                DisplayCategory="Collaboration" >
    </Configuration>
```

```
            <Configuration ID="1"
                           Title="Blank Site"
                           Hidden="TRUE"
                           ImageUrl="/_layouts/15/images/stbs.png?rev=23"
                           Description="A blank site for you to customize
                                        based on your requirements."
                           DisplayCategory="Collaboration"
                           AllowGlobalFeatureAssociations="False" >
            </Configuration>
            <Configuration ID="2"
                           Title="Document Workspace"
                           Hidden="TRUE"
                           ImageUrl="/_layouts/15/images/stdw.png?rev=23"
                           Description="A site for colleagues to work together on a document.
                           It provides a document library for storing the primary document
                           and supporting files, a tasks list for assigning to-do items,
                           and a links list for resources related to the document."
                           DisplayCategory="Collaboration" >
            </Configuration>
        </Template>
```

Figure 11-2 shows the template selection box that is displayed when a new subsite is created.

FIGURE 11-2 The template selection box as displayed when a new subsite is created

ONET.xml for site definitions

Now that we have discussed the webtemp file, we can move on to the ONET.xml file. The ONET.xml file serves as the top-level manifest for a site definition. This manifest file is used to define provisioning instructions that activate features and create site elements. ONET.xml files are deployed to a subfolder of the TEMPLATE\SiteTemplates folder. Each site definition has its own dedicated subfolder. The name of this subfolder matches the name of the site definition in the webtemp*.xml file. The ONET.xml file for the Team site and Blank site, for instance, is deployed to the TEMPLATE\SiteTemplates\STS folder.

Let's examine the contents of the ONET.xml file that serves as the manifest for the STS or Team Site site definition. The basic structure of the ONET.xml file includes a top-level *Project* element, which contains several child elements such as *NavBars*, *ListTemplates*, *DocumentTemplates*, *Configurations*, *Modules*, and *ServerEmailFooter*:

```
<Project
  Title="$Resources:onet_TeamWebSite;"
  Revision="2"
  ListDir="$Resources:core,lists_Folder;"
  xmlns:ows="Microsoft SharePoint"
  UIVersion="4">

  <NavBars />
  <ListTemplates />
  <DocumentTemplates />
  <Configurations/>
  <Modules />
  <ServerEmailFooter/>

</Project>
```

The *NavBars* node defines the set of navigation bars that are created when a new site is provisioned. The *NavBars* element inside the STS site definition has been written to create several navigation bars that are used by the top link bar and the Quick Launch bar:

```
<NavBars>
  <NavBar Name="$Resources:core,category_Top;" ID="1002" />
  <NavBar Name="$Resources:core,category_Documents;" ID="1004" />
  <NavBar Name="$Resources:core,category_Lists;" ID="1003" />
  <NavBar Name="$Resources:core,category_Discussions;" ID="1006" />
</NavBars>
```

Note that these *NavBar* elements are based on well-known ID values. The *NavBar* element with an *ID* of *1002* is used to create the navigation bar used by the top link bar. The *NavBar* elements with IDs of 1004, 1003, and 1006 are used to create dynamic collections of navigation nodes that are displayed in the Quick Launch bar. For example, the *NavBar* element with an ID of *1004* creates a dynamic collection of navigation nodes that link to document libraries that have been created, with the option to display them on the Quick Launch bar. If the *NavBar* elements are omitted, some navigation will still be displayed in the site, but it won't be possible to adjust the navigation by using the user interface.

The *Configurations* section of the ONET.xml file contains a child *Configuration* element for each supported configuration. This is what makes it possible for a single ONET.xml file to be used to provision several types of sites. The ONET.xml file in the STS site definition defines three separate *Configuration* elements for creating team sites, blank sites, and document workspace sites:

```
<Project>
  <Configurations>     <!-used to create team sites -->
    <Configuration ID="0" Name="Default" />     <!-used to create blank sites -->
    <Configuration ID="1" Name="Blank" />        <!-used to create document workspace sites -->
    <Configuration ID="2" Name="DWS" />
  </Configurations>
</Project>
```

A *Configuration* element contains attributes such as *ID, Name,* and *MasterUrl.* A *Configuration* element also contains child elements such as *Lists, Modules, SiteFeatures,* and *WebFeatures,* which are used to create site elements and activate features:

```
<Configuration ID="0" Name="Default"
               MasterUrl="_catalogs/masterpage/seattle.master">
  <Lists />
  <Modules />
  <SiteFeatures />
  <WebFeatures />
</Configuration>
```

The *Configuration* element for a team site contains a *Lists* element that creates the Documents document library:

```
<Lists>
  <List FeatureId="00BFEA71-E717-4E80-AA17-D0C71B360101"
        Type="101"
        Title="$Resources:core,shareddocuments_Title_15;"
        Url="$Resources:core,shareddocuments_Folder;"
        OnQuickLaunch="TRUE"
        QuickLaunchHeading="TRUE" />
</Lists>
```

The *Configurations* section contains a *Modules* element that is used to reference *Module* elements. For example, the *Configuration* element for a team site includes a *Modules* element that references a *Module* named *Default*:

```
<Modules>
  <Module Name="Default" />
</Modules>
```

Although *Module* elements are referenced inside the *Configurations* element, they are actually defined in a *Modules* element that is nested directly inside the top-level *Project* element. A *Module* element can contain a *File* element that creates a Web Part page and can optionally populate it with Web Part instances. The STS site definition contains a *Module* element named *Default*, which is referenced by the *Configuration* element for a team site. This *Module* element provisions a home page for a new team site named default.aspx and adds a link to the top link bar:

```
<Module Name="Default" Url="" Path="">
  <File Url="default.aspx" NavBarHome="True">
    <NavBarPage Name="~siteTitle" Url="~site" ID="1002" Position="Start" />
    <NavBarPage Name="~siteTitle" Url="" ID="0" Position="Start" />
  </File>
</Module>
```

The last two items in an ONET.xml file that are important to discuss are the two elements inside the *Configuration* element named *SiteFeatures* and *WebFeatures*. These two elements contain *Feature* elements whose purpose is to activate specific features during the site provisioning process. For example, the *SiteFeatures* element for the team site configuration activates two site collection–scoped features that add support for the standard SharePoint Foundation Web Parts and the Three-State Workflow template:

```
<SiteFeatures>
  <!-- BasicWebParts Feature -->
  <Feature ID="00BFEA71-1C5E-4A24-B310-BA51C3EB7A57" />
```

```
<!-- Three-State Workflow Feature -->
<Feature ID="FDE5D850-671E-4143-950A-87B473922DC7" />
</SiteFeatures>
```

The *WebFeatures* element for the team site configuration activates five site-scoped features that add support for the basic functionality of a team site, such as collaboration list types and a standard wiki library named *SitePages*:

```
<WebFeatures>
  <!-- TeamCollab Feature -->
  <Feature ID="00BFEA71-4EA5-48D4-A4AD-7EA5C011ABE5" />
  <!-- MobilityRedirect -->
  <Feature ID="F41CC668-37E5-4743-B4A8-74D1DB3FD8A4" />
  <!-- WikiPageHomePage Feature -->
  <Feature ID="00BFEA71-D8FE-4FEC-8DAD-01C19A6E4053" />
  <!-- SiteNotebook Feature -->
  <Feature ID="F151BB39-7C3B-414F-BB36-6BF18872052F" />
  <!-- Getting Started List instance -->
  <Feature ID="4AEC7207-0D02-4f4f-AA07-B370199CD0C7" />
  <!-- MDS -->
  <Feature ID="87294C72-F260-42f3-A41B-981A2FFCE37A" />
</WebFeatures>
```

Because of the link that will always exist between the site and the site definition, changing a site definition after it has been used to create sites is not supported. It is never supported to adjust out-of-the-box SharePoint files, so adjusting the out-of-the-box site definitions is not supported even if they haven't been used to create sites. If you need a new version of an existing site definition, you can either create a new site definition and hide the old one, or you can use *feature stapling* to add features and thus functionality to a site that is created based on the site definitions.

Feature stapling

A feature can be used to attach one or more features to a configuration of a site definition through a technique known as *feature stapling*. For example, instead of creating a custom site definition, you can elect to create a custom feature to extend configurations from a standard site definition. For example, you can create a feature to staple the *MainSite* feature to the Team Site configuration.

To staple a feature to a configuration such as Team Site, you must create a second feature to associate the feature to be stapled with one or more configurations. Feature stapling is achieved by adding a *FeatureSiteTemplateAssociation* element that contains an *Id* attribute specifying the feature that is being stapled and a *TemplateName* attribute specifying the target configuration. The following example demonstrates stapling the *MainSite* feature to the Team Site configuration by using the feature's ID and the name and configuration ID for Team Site:

```
<Elements xmlns="http://schemas.microsoft.com/sharepoint/">
  <FeatureSiteTemplateAssociation
    Id="edcdcd75-dff2-479d-ac32-b37f8fa9d459"
    TemplateName="STS#0" />
  </Elements>
```

The purpose of feature stapling is to activate features automatically when a new site is created. After a feature that staples other features has been activated, SharePoint automatically activates the stapled features when new sites are created. However, it is important that you know how the scope of a feature that staples other features affects the provisioning behavior of SharePoint.

The activation scope of the feature performing the stapling must be higher than the features being stapled. For example, a feature that is activated at the site collection scope can only staple features that activate at site-level scope. A feature that activates at the web application scope can staple features that activate at site-level scope or at the site collection scope. A feature that activates at the farm scope can staple features that activate at any of the other three scopes. If you define a feature that activates at the web application scope, it provides a quick and easy way to automate the activation of its stapled features within every new team site that is created in the target web application. Going one step further, you can associate stapling a feature to the main configuration of the GLOBAL site definition. This technique makes it possible to staple a feature to all new sites, as opposed to only sites created from a specific configuration:

```
<Elements xmlns="http://schemas.microsoft.com/sharepoint/">
  <FeatureSiteTemplateAssociation
    Id="edcdcd75-dff2-479d-ac32-b37f8fa9d459"
    TemplateName=" GLOBAL" />
</Elements>
```

This technique is powerful because it allows you to activate specific features on any type of site created within a farm. The one caveat here is that the configuration for blank sites is configured to ignore any features stapled to the GLOBAL site definition. This is done by setting the *AllowGlobalFeatureAssociations* attribute, that is added to the Configuration for the blank site in the webtemp.xml file, to *False*. Also, a feature stapled to a certain site definition will be stapled to that site definition in the entire farm. This might not always be appropriate.

Another downside of using stapled features is that it is not possible to define the order in which they are activated. When a site is provisioned, the features that are stapled to the site will be activated in a random order. This means that if one stapled feature requires another stapled feature to be activated first, you will have to use feature dependencies, or design your features in a different way.

Order of provisioning when using site definitions

When a site is provisioned by using a site definition, several steps are executed. We already discussed the first two. The full list is:

1. The URL of the site is reserved.

2. The configuration as stored in the GLOBAL site definition is provisioned.

3. If a site collection is being created, all site collection–scoped features that are listed in the *SiteFeatures* section of the relevant configuration in the ONET.xml file are activated in the order in which they are listed.

If a subsite is being created, SharePoint will check to make sure that all site collection–scoped features that are listed in the *SiteFeatures* section of the relevant configuration in the ONET.xml file are already activated on the site-collection level. If they are not, site provisioning will be aborted and steps that have already been executed will be rolled back.

4. If a site collection is being created, all site collection–scoped features that are stapled to the site definition are activated in a random order.

   If a subsite is being created, SharePoint will check to make sure that all site collection–scoped features that are stapled to the site definition are already activated on the site-collection level. If they are not, site provisioning will be aborted and steps that have already been executed will be rolled back.

5. All site-scoped features that are listed in the *WebFeatures* section of the relevant configuration in the ONET.xml file are activated in the order in which they are listed.

6. All site-scoped features that are stapled to the site definition are activated in a random order.

7. All list instances that are defined in the ONET.xml file will be created.

8. The contents of the modules that are defined in the ONET.xml file are created. These are usually pages.

From this list, you can note a couple of things that might cause problems. The fact that site collection–scoped features are always activated before site-scoped features and that features that are listed in the ONET.xml file are always activated before stapled features means that you have to take this into account when designing your features. The good news is that this behavior is predictable. So all it takes it some proper planning up front to avoid problems. Another common challenge is that all features are activated before the pages that are defined in the *Modules* element of the ONET.xml are created. This means that if you create a feature to modify one of these pages (for instance, if you add a Web Part to the home page), the feature will be activated before the page exists and you will be trying to add Web Parts to a nonexistent page. To avoid this, it is a best practice to create your pages by using a separate feature. That way you can make sure that the page gets created before it is modified.

Custom site definitions

Technically it is possible for you to create your own custom site definitions. However, you are advised not to create custom site definitions, because site definitions cannot be removed after they have been used—they will need to exist as long as those sites exist, even when the environment is updated to a new version of SharePoint, which adds significant extra complexity to upgrades. Custom site definitions will always have to be deployed by using farm solutions, because that is the only way to deploy files to the file system and thus the only way to deploy the webtemp*.xml and the ONET.xml file to the right file locations. This means that if you ever want to move to a cloud-hosted service such as Microsoft Office 365, you will not be able to deploy your own custom site definitions, and you won't be able to move your sites to that service. You will have to migrate the data from that site to new sites in the cloud-hosted environment.

So although the SharePoint Developer Tools have a predefined element called Site Definition, which you can use to create a custom site definition, you shouldn't use it. There is really only one scenario that might require you to create custom site definitions. In all other scenarios, it is better to create a custom web template or use custom code to adjust your sites after provisioning them based on an out-of-the-box site definition. Neither of these approaches will work if you are creating a *Variations Hierarchy*. A Variations Hierarchy is mainly used for creating multilingual web content management sites. If the same pages with the same content have to be published in multiple languages, you might want to use *Variations* for this. If you want to create custom templates for the sites used in the Variations Hierarchy, you will have to create custom site definitions. In all other cases, you should not create custom site definitions.

Web templates

Web templates were introduced in SharePoint 2010. They provide a more flexible way to create custom templates that can be used to create sites. Web templates use an ONET.xml just like site definitions, but they do not use a webtemp*.xml file. Instead, they use the *WebTemplate* element in an elements.xml file to define the metadata of the template. The ONET.xml file of a web template is not deployed to a subfolder of the SiteTemplates directory; instead, web templates are deployed by using features, and both the elements.xml file and the ONET.xml file are stored with the features.

Web templates are not deployed with a standard SharePoint installation. They are specifically designed so that developers can create custom templates for their sites without the templates themselves being persisted within the system like site definitions. From a customizations perspective, the ability to create web templates is one of most important changes of the SharePoint 2010 release. To start creating a new web template, first create a new Microsoft Visual Studio solution called **WingtipToysWebTemplates** by using the SharePoint 2013 - Empty Project template. This solution is included in the downloadable .zip archive of companion code for this book. Next add a new *Empty Element* item to it. Call the element **ProjectSite**. Rename the feature that was generated by the SharePoint Developer Tools when you added the empty element to **WingtipToysWebTemplates**.

elements.xml

Next open up the elements.xml file and add a *WebTemplate* element to it and fill in some of the attributes. When you add a *WebTemplate* element to an elements.xml file, you will notice that you can choose from a long list of properties. For this example, you will only use some of the basic and mandatory ones. The first one to fill in is the *Name* attribute. The name of the *WebTemplate* element has to be an exact match to the name of the *EmptyElement*. In this case, that is *ProjectSite*. The next properties are *Title* and *Description*. These are what users will see in the user interface when they are creating a site, so they should be something that a user can understand. The *DisplayCategory* is the tab of the template selection box that the template will show up in. You will choose *WingtipToys* and create your own tab, but you could have also used *Collaboration* to add it to the existing Collaboration tab.

The next three attributes are linked together: *BaseTemplateID*, *BaseTemplateName*, and *Base-ConfigurationID*. These properties are used to link the web template to a site definition. You saw earlier that the *SPWeb* has three properties—the *WebTemplateName* and the *WebTemplateId* that store the site definition that was used to create the site, and *Configuration*, which stores the ID of the configuration that was used. Even when a web template is used to create a site, SharePoint still requires a value for each of these properties. You will specify these values through the values that you assign to the *BaseTemplateID*, *BaseTemplateName*, and *BaseConfigurationID* attributes. The values are just for reference; the site definition and configuration that you select aren't actually used when a site is created. Only the information from your web template is used. You should still select a site definition and a configuration that are relatively similar to the template you are creating. After the site has been created for SharePoint, it will seem like the site was created by using the specified site definition, and the changes between the site definition and what the site actually looks like are made afterward. Though there is no requirement for the site definition and the configuration to be similar to what you're creating, it is less likely to cause problems in the future if the selected site definition doesn't deviate too much from what's specified in the web template. In this example, you will use the Team Site template as the base. The elements.xml contents are show in Listing 11-1. After the site has been created, it has no reference to the web template that was used to create it. The only reference the site has is to the site definition and configuration that you specified. This means that you can safely change or even remove a web template after it has been used to create sites, making it a lot easier to maintain and a lot more flexible than site definitions.

LISTING 11-1 The elements.xml contents, including the WebTemplate element.

```
<Elements xmlns="http://schemas.microsoft.com/sharepoint/">
  <WebTemplate BaseTemplateID="1"
               BaseTemplateName="STS"
               BaseConfigurationID="0"
               Name="ProjectSite"
               Title="WingtipToys Project Site"
               Description="Use this template to create
                            a Wingtip Toys project site"
               DisplayCategory="WingtipToys">
  </WebTemplate>
</Elements>
```

ONET.xml for web templates

The next file to create is an ONET.xml file. The ONET.xml file of a web template is very similar to that of a site definition, and because of that, the easiest way to start is by copying the ONET.xml file of a site definition into your empty element. Copy the ONET.xml of the standard Team Site definition from the TEMPLATE\SiteTemplates\sts\xml folder in the SharePoint root directory. If you copy files into your project this way, you always have to check the deployment type of the file by selecting the file in Solution Explorer and scrolling to the bottom of the properties pane. If the deployment type is set to No Deployment, you have to adjust it so that it is set to *ElementFile*, as shown in Figure 11-3.

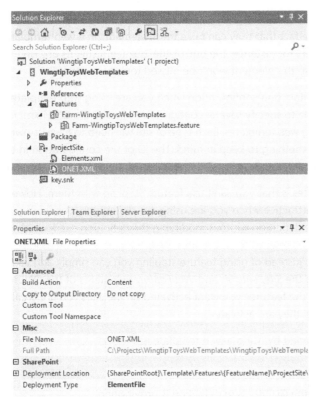

FIGURE 11-3 Solution Explorer and the properties pane showing the web templates solution and ONET.xml properties

Though the ONET.xml file of a web template is similar to that of a site definition, they are not the same. Some elements that are used in a site definition's ONET.xml file are not supported in the ONET.xml of a web template. Elements that are not supported are:

- **Modules**   A collection of Module elements that specify files and "all user" Web Parts with which to provision a website.

- **FileDialogPostProcessor**   A class used to modify the File Open and Save dialog boxes' interfaces in a document library.

- **ExternalSecurityProvider**   An interface that returns custom information about the security used in SharePoint Foundation for indexing by a search crawler on a portal.

- **ServerEmailFooter**   The footer section for server email, which includes both HTML and the text that is displayed.

Modules are used to add pages to your site. We already discussed earlier that it is a best practice not to use the *Modules* element, but to use a feature instead, so this limitation won't have much of an impact.

The *FileDialogPostProcessor* and *ExternalSecurityProvider* elements are hardly ever used, so there will be very few people affected by the fact that they can't use these elements in a web template. Although the *ServerEmailFooter* is used in, for instance, the out-of-the-box team site, its use isn't critical to the workings of the site definition, so this element won't be missed too much either.

The ONET.xml file can also only contain one configuration when you are using web templates. You saw that for site definitions it is possible to specify several configurations in a single ONET.xml file, but you can't use this technique when using web templates. Each type of site will need to have its own web template. This is not a problem, but something to keep in mind. The ID of the configuration in the ONET.xml file must match that specified in the *BaseConfigurationID* attribute in the elements.xml file.

Another "limitation" of web templates is that you can't use feature stapling with them. However, the reason that feature stapling is so attractive when you are using site definitions is because you can use it to adjust the behavior of the site definition without modifying the definition itself, which is not supported after the site definition has been used to create sites. Web templates can be modified after they have been used to create sites, so instead of using feature stapling you can simply add all features you want activated on the site to the *SiteFeatures* and *WebFeatures* elements of the ONET.xml file. This way you can not only modify the features you want activated on the sites you are creating, you can also specify the order in which they are activated.

The order in which sites are provisioned by using a web template is:

1. The URL of the site is reserved.

2. The configuration as stored in the GLOBAL site definition is provisioned.

3. If a site collection is being created, all site collection–scoped features that are listed in the *SiteFeatures* section of the relevant configuration in the ONET.xml file are activated in the order in which they are listed.

    If a subsite is being created, SharePoint will check to make sure that all site collection–scoped features that are listed in the *SiteFeatures* section of the relevant configuration in the ONET.xml file are already activated on the site-collection level. If they are not, site provisioning will be aborted and steps that have already been executed will be rolled back.

4. All site-scoped features that are listed in the *WebFeatures* section of the relevant configuration in the ONET.xml file are activated in the order in which they are listed.

5. All list instances that are defined in the ONET.xml are created.

If you add a lot of features to the *SiteFeatures* element of the ONET.xml file, it is worth paying attention to step 3 of the site provisioning process. If users are trying to create a subsite and the features specified in the *SiteFeatures* element aren't activated on the site collection site, creation will fail with an error. In some cases, this can be expected behavior and no problem at all. But if you are creating a new version of an existing web template, and after you have deployed the new template users can't create subsites anymore by using the same template they used to create the site collection, they might get annoyed. And they'd have a point. You can avoid this, especially when updating existing web templates, by not adding features to the *SiteFeatures* element. If you still have to add new site collection–scoped features to the web template, you can use a trick. You can create a web-scoped feature, and in the *FeatureActivated* event receiver of that feature run a little bit of code to activate the site collection–scoped feature. Before you write code like this, make sure that activating the site collection–scoped feature won't cause a problem on any existing sites, because you will no longer have control over exactly where the feature is activated.

After you have added the *WebTemplate* element and its attributes to the elements.xml file and have stripped the ONET.xml file of the elements that you cannot use in web templates, you have the absolute necessities for your web template. The only thing left to do before you can deploy is to determine the scope of the feature. You can choose whether to set the scope of the feature to farm or site. You cannot use web application–scoped or web–scoped features to deploy web templates.

Deploying web templates

If you use a farm-scoped feature to deploy a web template, the web template can be used to create sites throughout the SharePoint farm. If you deploy a web template this way, it will behave exactly like a site definition would. From the user interface it will be impossible to tell the difference between the web template and a site definition. You can use the template to create a site collection from Central Administration, and you can use the template to create subsites from every site in the environment.

If you use a site collection–scoped feature, the template will only be available on sites where you activate the feature. If you want to create subsites based on the web template, you have to browse to the site settings page and click the Site Collection Features link in the Site Collection Administration area of the page. You should find your feature on this page. If you activate it, you will make the template available for users to create subsites based on it. If you want to use the web template to create a site collection, but you deploy the template by using a site collection–scoped feature, you can still do this—it will just take a couple more steps. To do this, first go to Central Administration and browse to the Application Management page. From there, click Create Site Collections. As shown in Figure 11-4, you can fill in a title and URL and optionally a description. In the template selection box, select the Custom tab and < Select Template Later >. Next, select a site collection administrator, and click OK to create the site.

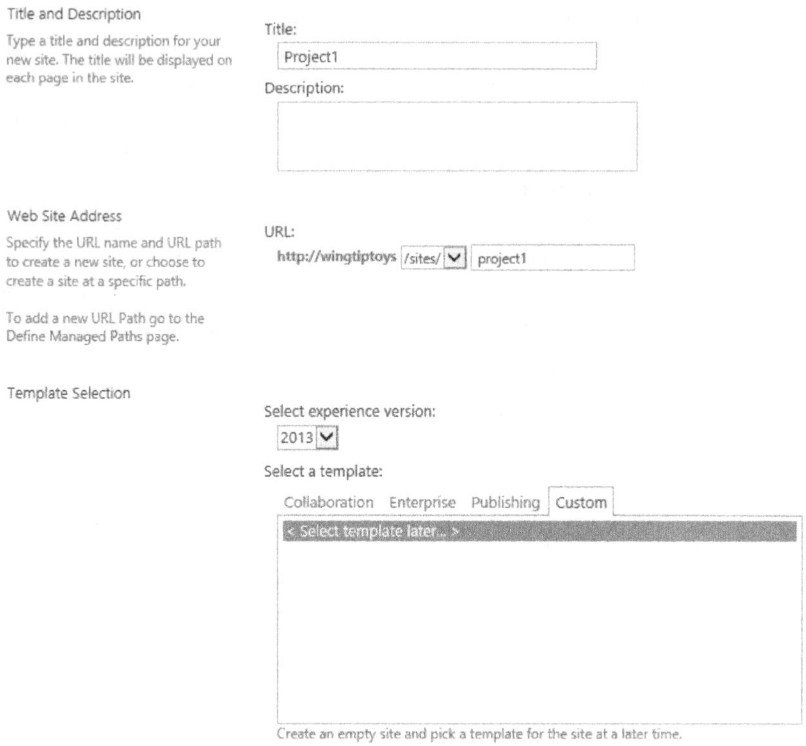

Title:

Project1

Description:

URL:

http://wingtiptoys /sites/ [V] project1

Select experience version:

2013 [V]

Select a template:

Collaboration   Enterprise   Publishing   Custom

< Select template later... >

Create an empty site and pick a template for the site at a later time.

FIGURE 11-4 Creating a site collection without selecting a template

Creating a site collection without selecting a template is relatively quick because the site won't be fully provisioned yet. When the site is ready, you can click the link to browse to it. This will take you directly to the template selection page of the site. However, because the feature isn't enabled yet, you can't select your template. From the template selection page, you can browse to the site settings and site collection features pages and activate your feature. If you now try to browse to the home page of the site, SharePoint will take you back to the template selection page on which you can now select your web template. You can click OK to complete the provisioning of the site. SharePoint will come back to ask you whether to use existing SharePoint groups for the Visitors, Members, and Owners groups, or whether to create new ones. Because the existing ones were just created when you provisioned the first part of the site, it makes sense to stick to these and create a new site of groups.

If you use a farm-scoped feature to make the web template available in your SharePoint farm, you will have to use a farm solution to deploy the web template and the feature. However if you use a site collection–scoped feature, you can use a sandboxed solution to deploy the web template. Using a sandboxed solution to deploy a web template is particularly appealing if you are using a cloud-hosted environment such as Office 365, or if you only want to make the template available to certain people or even just to yourself. You could simply upload the sandboxed solution to the site collection Solution Gallery and activate the feature to make the template available on a particular site. If you want to create a site collection by using the template, you can follow the steps described previously and click the Solution Gallery link, as shown in Figure 11-5, to upload your solution before activating the site collection–scoped feature.

Template Selection

2013 experience version will be used

Select a template:

Collaboration   Enterprise   Publishing   **WingtipToys**

WingtipToys Project Site

Use this template to create a Wingtip Toys project site

Solution Gallery

You can apply a custom Site Template to this site. To do this, upload a solution file that contains a custom site template to the solution gallery, activate the solution, and select the template in the Template Selection section.

Solution Gallery

OK

FIGURE 11-5 Selecting a web template on the template selection page in the site collection

Because there is no link between a site after it has been created and the web template that was used to create the site, it is a best practice to store this information about the web template when the site is created. This can easily be done by creating a web-scoped feature that will be activated as the last feature in the *WebFeatures* element in the ONET.xml file. The feature can contain an empty element that adds a couple of properties to the property bag of the site. You can add the properties by adding the *PropertyBag* and *Property* elements in the elements.xml file of the empty element. Storing information about the web template that was used to create the site makes it possible to identify sites and versions of sites later on, perhaps for grouping sites together, upgrading specific sites to new a new version of SharePoint, or maybe writing custom code to make the same changes to all sites of the same type or version:

```
<Elements xmlns="http://schemas.microsoft.com/sharepoint/">
  <PropertyBag ParentType="Web">
    <Property Name="WingtipToys.WebTemplate" Type="string" Value="ProjectSite" />
    <Property Name="WingtipToys.WebTemplateVersion" Type="string" Value="1.0.0.0"/>
    <Property Name="WingtipToys.WebTemplateFeature" Type="string" Value="c1dd0ae6-e166-4dec-
91eb-3eeacfc38257"/>
  </PropertyBag>
</Elements>
```

Using custom code to create sites

In some scenarios, you might not want to let your users create sites from the SharePoint user interface, but from a piece of custom code. In order to completely provision a site by using code, you will still have to specify either a site definition or a web template. You create a site by using *SPWebCollection.Add*; to create a site collection, you would use *SPSiteCollection.Add*. Both methods have several overloads. If you choose to use an overload that doesn't specify the template that should be used to provision the site, you can specify this later by using *SPWeb.ApplyWebTemplate*.

If you want to specify a site definition, you can do so by using the name of the site definition followed by a # and the configuration ID. For instance, to specify a team site, you would use STS#0, and to specify a blog site, you would use BLOG#0.

If you want to specify a web template, you will use the same format, but instead of the site definition name you will specify the feature ID of the feature that is used to deploy the template, and instead of the configuration ID you specify the web template name. So the format for specifying a web template is [*Feature Id*]#[*Web Template Name*]. To specify the Project Site web template from the example solution, you would use *c1dd0ae6-e166-4dec-91eb-3eeacfc38257#ProjectSite*.

Site templates

If you don't want to use Visual Studio to create a web template, but you still want to create custom templates for creating sites, you can create *site templates*. A site template can be created by browsing to the site settings page of a site and clicking Save Site As Template in the Site Actions area. Saving a site as a template will generate a .wsp file, just as deploying a Visual Studio project will, and will store it in the site collection's Solution Gallery. As soon as the template is saved to the Solutions Gallery, it can be used to create subsites within that same site collection. If you want to use the site template to create sites in a different site collection, you can browse to the Solution Gallery and download the solution. You can then upload the solution in a different site to make the site template available there.

The Save Site As Template functionality uses the web template technique behind the scenes. It generates an ONET.xml file and an elements.xml file containing a *WebTemplate* element. When a site is saved as a template, SharePoint has to make sure that everything that was available in the original site is also available in a new site that is created by using the site template. To ensure this, SharePoint packages all the features, site columns, content types, property bag values, and much more from the original site into the site template. This means that the site template doesn't just contain the few lists and some navigation settings that you might have created; it also contains a lot of things that someone might one day want to use, but that you never used in the original site. All these things in the site template won't cause a problem, and in fact, you won't even notice them except when you use the option to import the site template into Visual Studio.

When you create a new project in Visual Studio, one of the options that the SharePoint Developer Tools adds is SharePoint 2013 - Import Solution Package. This option allows you to select a site template and import it into Visual Studio. In theory this sounds really powerful, because you can have business users create the site they want or need, save the site as a template, and then import it into Visual Studio. In Visual Studio you can then make some slight adjustments and repackage it. However, because of all the properties, features, site columns, and content types that are added to the package, it quickly becomes very messy and unstable. Even if you don't import the solution into Visual Studio, all the information that is saved in the template can cause problems, because it's just too much to oversee and keep track of.

Site templates can be fairly powerful, but they aren't quite ready to be used as an enterprise solution to create templates for sites. It is better to just use a site template as is, to create sites on a small scale based on templates that were configured through the user interface, and to use web templates if sites have to be created on a large scale, or if modifications have to be made to the template that can't be created through the user interface.

There is one tangible limitation to using site templates. They can only be used on sites that don't have the publishing features enabled. Activating the publishing features on a site will make the Save Site As Template link disappear from the site settings page. Some clever users might figure out that if they know the URL they can still browse to the page and save a site as a template even if the publishing features are enabled on it. This is, however, not supported and will cause major issues. The advice is easy: don't save sites as templates that have the publishing features enabled on them, not even if you think you know how to trick SharePoint. The same is true for deactivating the feature just so you can save the site and then activating it again after the new site has been created. If you want to work with publishing features, you will have to use web templates to create custom templates for your sites.

Site provisioning providers

Yet another way to create sites is by using *site provisioning providers*. Using site provisioning providers is particularly useful if you want to create several sites at the same time according to a predefined structure. It is not recommended to create custom site provisioning providers, because you need a farm solution to deploy them. We will still demonstrate how they work, though, in case you run across one or feel that they are still the best way for you to create the behavior you need.

The purpose of a site provisioning provider is to create and initialize new sites. A site provisioning provider can be used with standard SharePoint site definitions or web templates. You create a site provisioning provider with a class that inherits from the *SPWebProvisioningProvider* base class and that overrides a single method named *Provision*:

```
using System;
using Microsoft.SharePoint;

namespace WingtipToysProvisioning {
  public class WingtipToysProvisioningProvider : SPWebProvisioningProvider {
    public override void Provision(SPWebProvisioningProperties properties) {
      // add code to provision new site
    }
  }
}
```

When you implement the *Provision* method, you get to specify the configuration that is used to provision the new site by calling the *ApplyWebTemplate* method. This makes it possible to create customized provisioning instructions while using standard configurations such as Team Site:

```
public override void Provision(SPWebProvisioningProperties properties) {

    // provision new site using Blank site configuration
    properties.Web.ApplyWebTemplate("STS#0");

    // TODO: add extra code here to initialize new site.
}
```

When the *ApplyWebTemplate* method completes, SharePoint has finished provisioning the new site by using the Team Site configuration. Now you can add whatever logic you would like to activate features, initialize site properties, and create any required site elements, such as lists and child sites. Note that due to security issues, you must call a method named *RunWithElevatedPrivileges* on the *SPSecurity* class to run your code with the privileges required to initialize a new site:

```
public override void Provision(SPWebProvisioningProperties properties) {
    // apply template using a configuration
    properties.Web.ApplyWebTemplate("STS#0");

    // elevate privileges before programming against site
    SPSecurity.RunWithElevatedPrivileges(delegate() {
        using (SPSite siteCollection = new SPSite(properties.Web.Site.ID)) {
            using (SPWeb site = siteCollection.OpenWeb(properties.Web.ID)) {
                // activate features and initialize site properties
                site.Features.Add(new Guid("00BFEA71-D8FE-4FEC-8DAD-01C19A6E4053"));
                site.Title = "My Custom Site Title";
                site.Update();
            }
        }
    });
}
```

The final step to deploying a site provisioning provider involves creating a webtemp file that references the site provisioning provider class. In this case, we have created a webtemp file named webtemp_WingtipSiteTemplates.xml, which is deployed to the TEMPLATE/1033/XML directory:

```
<Template Name=" WingtipToysProvisioning" ID="11001">

    <Configuration ID="0"
        Title="Wingtip Toys Standard Team Site"
        Hidden="FALSE"
        Description="Use this site template to create a Wingtip Toys team site."
        DisplayCategory="WingtipToys"
        ProvisionAssembly="$SharePoint.Project.AssemblyFullName$"
        ProvisionClass="WingtipToysProvisioning.WingtipProvisioningProvider"
        ProvisionData="StandardTeamSite" />

    <Configuration ID="1"
        Title="Wingtip Toys Sales Site"
        Hidden="FALSE"
        Description="Use this site template to create a Wingtip Toys team site."
```

```
        DisplayCategory="WingtipToys"
        ProvisionAssembly="$SharePoint.Project.AssemblyFullName$"
        ProvisionClass="WingtipToysProvisioning.WingtipProvisioningProvider"
        ProvisionData="SalesSite" />

  </Template>

</Templates>
```

As you can tell, this web template file defines two configurations called Wingtip Toys Standard Team Site and Wingtip Toys Sales Site. Both of these configurations are set to be displayed in the standard SharePoint template selection box on the WingtipToys custom tab. Both *Configuration* elements are configured to use the same provisioning provider class, but they have different values for the *ProvisionData* attribute. This makes it possible for the *WingtipProvisioningProvider* class to provide the *Provision* method that inspects the *ProvisionData* attribute to determine what type of new site to create and initialize:

```
public override void Provision(SPWebProvisioningProperties properties) {
  if (properties.Data.Equals("StandardTeamSite")) {
    // add code to provision standard team site
  }
  if (properties.Data.Equals("SalesSite")) {
    // add code to provision sales site
  }
}
```

Web provisioning events

Regardless of whether your site is provisioned by using a site definition, a web template, or custom code, you can hook into the events related to managing your site. These events are called *web provisioning events* and are part of the *SPWebEventReceiver* class. There are eight events that you can catch:

- **SiteDeleted**   An asynchronous event that occurs after a site collection has been deleted

- **SiteDeleting**   A synchronous event that occurs while a site collection is being deleted

- **WebAdding**   A synchronous event that occurs while a new subsite is being created, but that doesn't fire when the rootweb of a site collection is being created

- **WebDeleted**   An asynchronous event that occurs after a site has been deleted

- **WebDeleting**   A synchronous event that occurs when a site is being deleted

- **WebMoved**   An asynchronous event that occurs after an existing site has been moved

- **WebMoving**   A synchronous event that occurs while an existing site is being moved

- **WebProvisioned**   An asynchronous event that occurs after a subsite has been fully provisioned, but that doesn't fire when the rootweb of a site collection has been created

As you can tell, there are two event receivers that you can use to execute code after a subsite has been created: *WebAdding* to execute code during the provisioning process, and *WebProvisioned* to execute code after the subsite has been completely provisioned. It is important to note that neither of these will fire when the rootweb of a new site collection is created. These event receivers can only be used when subsites are created.

To view what this looks like in Visual Studio, you will add an *EventReceiver* to the WingtipToysWeb-Templates solution. Start by right-clicking the project and selecting Add New Item. Next choose the *EventReceiver* project item and name it **SetSubSiteNavigation**. The SharePoint Developer Tools will start the wizard in Figure 11-6, in which you can select the type of event receiver to create. Select Web Events as the type of event receiver and A Site Was Provisioned as the event to handle.

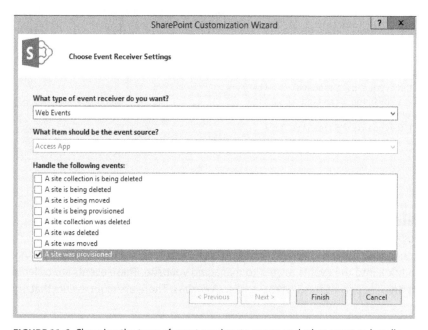

FIGURE 11-6 Choosing the type of event receiver to create and what event to handle

The SharePoint Developer Tools will create an event receiver that consists of an elements.xml file and a class file. The elements.xml file is used to link the class file to the *WebProvisioned* event:

```
<Elements xmlns="http://schemas.microsoft.com/sharepoint/">
  <Receivers >
    <Receiver>
      <Name>SetSubSiteNavigationWebProvisioned</Name>
      <Type>WebProvisioned</Type>
      <Assembly>$SharePoint.Project.AssemblyFullName$</Assembly>
      <Class>WingtipToysWebTemplates.SetSubSiteNavigation.SetSubSiteNavigation</Class>
      <SequenceNumber>10000</SequenceNumber>
    </Receiver>
  </Receivers>
</Elements>
```

The class inherits from *SPWebEventReceiver* and contains a method to which you can add the code that you want to execute when a subsite is created. In this example you will adjust the navigation of the subsite to let it inherit the navigation from the parent site. You will create a new web-scoped feature that will be used to deploy the event receiver, and you will add the feature to the WebFeatures section of the Project Site web template, as shown in Listing 11-2.

LISTING 11-2 A *WebProvisioned* event receiver that adjusts the navigation of a subsite

```
using System;
using Microsoft.SharePoint;

namespace WingtipToysWebTemplates.SetSubSiteNavigation
{
    /// <summary>
    /// Web Events
    /// </summary>
    public class SetSubSiteNavigation : SPWebEventReceiver
    {
        /// <summary>
        /// A site was provisioned.
        /// </summary>
        public override void WebProvisioned(SPWebEventProperties properties)
        {
            base.WebProvisioned(properties);

            SPWeb web = properties.Web;

            // Let sub-site navigation inherit from the parent site
            web.Navigation.UseShared = true;

            web.Update();
        }
    }
}
```

Web templates and SharePoint apps

In Chapter 4, "SharePoint apps," SharePoint apps and the app web were discussed in depth. We talked about how adding a SharePoint-hosted app to a host site will create an app web as a subsite of the host site. When an app web is created, normally the standard App Template site definition is used to provision it. This template is defined in the webtemp.xml file. The name of the template is APP, and it has one configuration, which is titled App Template and has an ID of 0. The ONET.xml for the app template can be found in the TEMPLATE\SiteTemplates\App folder in the SharePoint Root folder:

```
<Template Name="APP" SetupPath="SiteTemplates\app" ID="17">
  <Configuration ID="0"
                 Title="App Template"
                 Hidden="TRUE"
                 ImageUrl=""
                 Description="A base template for app development.
                   It provides the minimal set of features
                   needed for an app." >
  </Configuration>
</Template>
```

If you want to use your own template to create an app web, you can do this by using web templates. You can create a custom web template and use the appmanifest.xml file to make sure that your template is used when the app web is created. A web template that will be used to create an app web is deployed in the app itself by using a web-scoped feature. This is different from when you are creating a normal web template, because for those the scope of the feature can only be farm or site.

Unfortunately, it is not possible to deploy normal web templates by using a SharePoint app. Normal web templates can only be deployed by using farm or sandboxed solutions. This is one of the limitations of SharePoint apps; at least for now, it is not possible to use apps to create a template that can be used to provision sites. Apps can be added manually to any site after it has been created, but they cannot provision the site itself, and they can't automatically be added during site provisioning, either.

The app manifest file of an app has a *WebTemplate* element that can be used to define your own web template. In the *Id* attribute, you use the same format you would when using code to call you web template, [*Feature Id*]#[*Web Template Name*]. Microsoft IntelliSense in Visual Studio will tell you that the *WebTemplate* element also has a *FeatureId* attribute, but you don't need this; it is obsolete:

```
<App xmlns="http://schemas.microsoft.com/sharepoint/2012/app/manifest"
     Name="WingTipApp"
     ProductID="{5399d258-e7af-4b70-8b53-74ff3c9979f8}"
     Version="1.0.0.0"
     SharePointMinVersion="15.0.0.0">

  <Properties>
    <Title>WingTipApp</Title>
    <StartPage>~appWebUrl/Pages/Default.aspx?{StandardTokens}</StartPage>
    <WebTemplate Id="{1A74A5BD-BD62-4470-A0DB-C9421BC53F73}#WingtipToysAppWeb"/>
  </Properties>

  <AppPrincipal>
    <Internal />
  </AppPrincipal>
</App>
```

Be aware that if you do use your own web template to create the app web, you have to make sure that all the necessary app-related plumbing that is part of the standard app template is in your web template as well. Also be aware that most users will be browsing to the host site and not to the app web. If you are creating your own template, it will mostly be because of some extra plumbing that you need in the app web in order for your app to work properly, not because you want the user to view your spiffy template. In most cases, the standard app template will do just fine, and you won't need a custom web template to create your app web.

Summary

This chapter explained that site definitions play a key role in the provisioning process of SharePoint site collections and sites. You shouldn't create custom site definitions anymore though, because they cannot be updated or removed from your farm after they have been used. This makes them hard to maintain and means that you will have to upgrade them whenever you want to update your farm to a new version of SharePoint.

If you want to create a custom template to provision sites, you should use web templates. Web templates are just as powerful as site definitions but are a lot more flexible. They can be updated or even removed after they have been used, because there is no link between the web template and the site that has been created with it. To make sure that you can still identify what template and what version of the template has been used to create a site, you should create a custom hidden web-scoped feature that stores this information in the site—for instance, in the property bag.

If you need more flexibility, or if you want to create sites by using an automated process, you can use custom code to create sites. When using custom code, you will still have to select a template for the site. This can be either a site definition or a web template. You can also use the web provisioning events to run custom code during or after the site provisioning process. This approach only works for subsites, though; it doesn't work for the rootweb of a site collection.

## CHAPTER 12

SharePoint workflows

Starting with Microsoft SharePoint 2007 and continuing with SharePoint 2010, the core SharePoint engine hosted the Windows Workflow Foundation runtime and stored all workflow-related data within the SharePoint content databases. This approach was convenient because customers did not have anything to configure: workflow functioned right out of the box in even the most basic installations. However, there were downsides to this approach: it was hard to get telemetry data on the deployed and running workflows because developers and administrators were limited to the exposure provided by the SharePoint application programming interfaces (APIs).

Microsoft has taken a very different approach to workflow in SharePoint Server 2013 from previous versions of SharePoint. The workflow team worked with the Windows Azure team to create a new product called *Workflow Manager*. Workflow Manager serves the role of hosting the latest version of the Workflow Foundation runtime and all the necessary services in a highly available and scalable way. It takes advantage of Service Bus for performance and scalability and, when deployed, runs in exactly the same way in an on-premises deployment and in Office 365. SharePoint is then connected and configured to hand off all workflow execution and related tasks to the Workflow Manager farm.

This chapter explains the architecture of how workflow and SharePoint work together from a high level. With this solid foundation established, the chapter then goes into the details of how to create custom workflows by using both Microsoft SharePoint Designer 2013 and Microsoft Visual Studio 2012 to take advantage of this new more scalable, powerful, and feature-rich platform.

Workflow architecture in SharePoint 2013

At first, the way in which SharePoint Server 2013 and Workflow Manager work together might sound complicated, but Microsoft has made installing, configuring, setting up, and maintaining both products very easy. All the complexity is handled within the products. After installing and configuring SharePoint Server 2013, customers are left with the same workflow execution engine that was included with prior versions of SharePoint. This means that customers can build workflows based on the former model of Workflow Foundation included in the Microsoft .NET Framework 3.5 Service Pack 1, but they cannot take advantage of any of the new features outlined in the remainder of this chapter. To take advantage of the new features, you need to perform two tasks:

- Install and configure a Workflow Manager 1.0 farm.

- Connect the SharePoint Server 2013 and Workflow Manager 1.0 farms together.

Installing and configuring a Workflow Manager 1.0 farm

The installation and configuration of a Workflow Manager farm is very similar to the installation and configuration of a SharePoint farm. Just like with SharePoint, the entire product and dependencies are installed on the server; the installer does not enable the user to pick what is and is not installed. Workflow Manager is best installed by using the Web Platform Installer tool (available at *http://www.microsoft.com/web/downloads/platform.aspx*) from Microsoft, because the tool will also download and install all dependencies such as Service Bus 1.0, which Workflow Manager uses. After Workflow Manager is installed, the next step is to configure the farm, which includes creating the required databases and provisioning the core services. This is all handled by the Workflow Manager Configuration Wizard, which should sound familiar to you if you have installed and configured SharePoint in the past.

With a SharePoint 2013 farm and Workflow Manager farm, the next step is to configure both environments to communicate with each other. This is done by going to a server in the SharePoint 2013 farm and running a specific Windows PowerShell cmdlet: **Register-SPWorkflowServices**. This cmdlet does two important things. First, it configures the SharePoint farm to send all workflow requests and tasks to the Workflow Manager's front-end component endpoint. The cmdlet also configures the Workflow Manager farm with the endpoint of the SharePoint farm so that Workflow Manager knows where to send Representational State Transfer (REST) requests, which is how Workflow Manager communicates with SharePoint, in order to retrieve and submit data.

Internally, the Workflow Manager farm logs to a Service Bus topic the requests that SharePoint submits to it. Service Bus utilizes the Pub/Sub model to maintain a list of all things that want to be notified when specific messages that meet specific criteria are received by Workflow Manager. If the criteria are met, Service Bus sends the message (which is stored in a topic) to the registered subscriber of that topic. Frequently this is the workflow back-end service, which is a Windows service that is responsible for processing the workflow episodes. An *episode* is the short burst of workflow processing; that is, events that happen when the workflow is not waiting for an external action. When the workflow needs to communicate with SharePoint—for example, about details regarding the user who initiated the workflow, or to create and assign a task to a user—the workflow calls back to SharePoint by using the SharePoint REST services. When installing and configuring the Workflow Manager farm with SharePoint, SharePoint configures the Workflow Manager farm as an app by using the new SharePoint app model. This is also facilitated by a new service application proxy that connects SharePoint to the Workflow Manager farm. Then, Workflow Manager, in turn when connecting to SharePoint, takes advantage of the server-to-server high-trust authentication. This way, SharePoint can identify that these calls are coming from Workflow Manager, which has been granted specific permissions within SharePoint and can act on the behalf of some users.

One requirement of Workflow Manager is that the SharePoint 2013 farm must have a User Profile Service Application provisioned and running. This is because Workflow Manager uses OAuth to establish its identity with SharePoint. This is also why SharePoint Server 2013 is required to use Workflow Manager; SharePoint Foundation 2013 does not have a User Profile Service Application.

Understanding workflow in SharePoint 2013

Before diving into creating custom workflows, it helps to have a good understanding of the different components that make up the entire workflow story in SharePoint 2013. The workflow artifact that is developed by using Visual Studio deployed to SharePoint is called the *workflow definition*. This is simply the business logic and series of activities within the workflow that define the business process. Users cannot start a workflow from a definition. The workflow definition must first be linked with a site, list, or library that contains core parameters about this link, such as the friendly name of the workflow for users, the task and history list where all tasks and logging messages generated by the workflow definition will be stored, how the workflow can be started (manually or automatically when something is created or updated), and any additional parameters specified in the workflow definition. This link is called the *workflow association*. When workflows are created by using SharePoint Designer 2013, a template is not created but rather the workflow is created directly as an association, which is why SharePoint Designer 2013 workflows are not nearly as portable as workflows developed by using Visual Studio 2012. Finally, when a workflow is started and based on an existing association, it is referred to as an *instance*. One site or item in a list could have multiple instances of the same association running at any particular time. When an instance is running, a workflow can either be actively running (in which case it is also referred to as an *episode*) or paused and persisted while it waits for something to occur that triggers another episode.

For each instance of the workflow, SharePoint maintains a status page where users can view the status of the workflow, what item and user started the instance, and all tasks and history log entries created by the workflow.

Developers creating workflows with Visual Studio 2012 have access to a large number of activities. Workflow Manager 1.0 a nd SharePoint 2013 support activities included in the Microsoft .NET Framework 4.5 Workflow Foundation (anything in the *System.Activities* namespace), activities specific to Workflow Manager (found in the *Microsoft.Activities* namespace), SharePoint 2013 activities (found in the *Microsoft.SharePoint.WorkflowServices.Activities* namespace), and those specific to Microsoft Project server (found in the *Microsoft.Office.Project.Server.WorkflowActivites* namespace). SharePoint Designer 2013 workflows are limited to the activities exposed by *.action4 files. Action files are covered later in this chapter, in the "Creating custom activities" section.

Creating custom workflows for SharePoint 2013

SharePoint 2013 does include a workflow or two out of the box, but the real value in a workflow engine is in providing customers with the ability to create custom workflows that satisfy their business processes. This new architectural model for workflow in the SharePoint 2013 ecosystem does bring some changes to the process of creating custom workflows. One of the biggest changes is the fact that all custom workflows in SharePoint 2013 and Workflow Manager are completely declarative, including those built by using Visual Studio 2012. This differs from previous versions of SharePoint in that workflows developed with Visual Studio 2012 are not exclusively declarative; rather, they are a mix of declarative XAML and an assembly that contains the business logic.

This might come as a shock to seasoned SharePoint developers, who are now asking, "So how do I implement my custom business logic?" Microsoft's recommendation is to create a custom web service, ideally a Windows Communication Service (WCF) service that returns data in the JavaScript Object Notation (JSON) format, and use some new activities and objects in this new version. The new *HTTPSend* activity enables calls to the simplest web services or allows you to create more complex calls with specific HTTP verbs and to provide specific HTTP headers. The web service responses that are returned as JSON are assigned to a variable that uses a new data type that understands the hierarchical structure of JSON data: *DynamicValue*. Microsoft has also provided a series of other activities that enable developers to extract specific values from the JSON response. The *DynamicValue* activity is available only to Visual Studio 2012, so the *Dictionary* data type is used to wrap objects of type *DynamicValue* so that those objects will have the same support within workflows authored in SharePoint Designer 2013.

Building custom workflows

Just like previous versions of SharePoint, SharePoint 2013 offers customers a few different options for creating custom workflows that are typically targeted at different audiences. In SharePoint 2010, Microsoft introduced the use of Microsoft Visio 2010 to model workflows. This made it easy for consultants and users to model workflows without having to have a live SharePoint site. The Visio 2010 workflow model would then be imported into SharePoint Designer 2010 so that business logic and additional functionality could be added to the workflow. By combining Visio 2010 and SharePoint Designer 2010, customers could easily create and share workflows with their clients without involving a developer. However, when more advanced customizations were required, developers could get involved by creating custom workflows with Visual Studio 2010. The significant downside to workflows developed in Visual Studio is that they have a programmatic component to them. This means they can be deployed only by using fully trusted solutions, and thus they can be used only in on-premises deployments, not to hosted deployments, which are limited to sandboxed solutions.

SharePoint 2013 has made great strides in the development and deployment of custom workflows. The following two sections outline the major changes between the two main options: Visio with SharePoint Designer, and Visual Studio.

Custom workflows with Visio 2013 and SharePoint Designer 2013

Those who have created workflows with Visio 2010 and SharePoint Designer 2010 in SharePoint 2010 will be very comfortable with the latest releases, because both tools have been improved to support the new workflow capabilities. One of the biggest customer feedback points in SharePoint Designer 2010 was the lack of support for any type of looping. Two new activities have been added to SharePoint

Designer 2013 to support looping: *Loop [n] Times* and *Loop with Condition*. These two activities should satisfy many looping scenarios; however, a more significant improvement that supports more complex loops is the addition of stages. Stages are founded on the concept of Workflow Foundation flowchart activities. Workflow authors can put any number of activities within a stage and then specify one or more conditions at the end of the stage that dictate how the workflow should proceed. In this Transition To Stage section, as shown in Figure 12-1, authors can choose to transition directly to another stage (including the default *End of Workflow*, which terminates the workflow) or add a conditional statement by using an *If* activity to route to a desired stage. Revising the previous point about looping, a stage could be configured to transition back to itself, effectively creating a conditional loop.

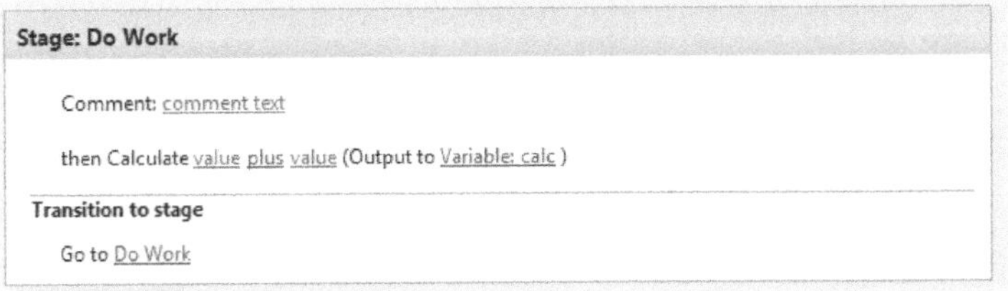

Stage: Do Work

    Comment: comment text

    then Calculate value plus value (Output to Variable: calc)

Transition to stage

    Go to Do Work

FIGURE 12-1 In this text-based designer of a stage in SharePoint Designer 2013, a conditional loop is created.

Another improvement to SharePoint Designer 2013 is the addition of common semantics found in other Microsoft Office products such as Microsoft Word, Excel and PowerPoint; these include cut, copy, paste, move up, and move down. These additions make it easier to customize an existing workflow; in previous versions of SharePoint Designer, the workflow author had to delete and recreate the steps where they were intended to be.

Although SharePoint Designer's workflow authoring experience has traditionally been text based, Visio 2010 introduced a new visual designer, which made it easier for customers to view the workflow in a more familiar flowchart diagram. This visual designer has been improved in Visio 2013 in that it supports all the new activities for looping and stages that were added in SharePoint 2013 but also adds two more significant additions. First, unlike the visual designer in Visio 2010, which was limited to simply adding and linking activities, in Visio 2013 you can now modify the properties of an activity. Therefore, workflow authors can express business rules, such as the parameters of an *If* statement activity. The other major improvement associated with the visual designer is that now SharePoint Designer 2013 users who have Visio 2013 installed will also get the visual designer. This means that within SharePoint Designer, users can author workflows either by using the traditional text-based designer or by using the Visio visual designer, as shown in Figure 12-2.

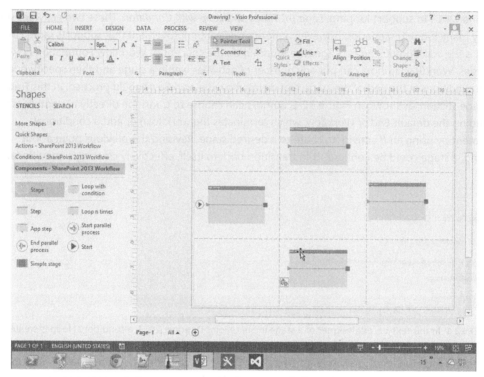

FIGURE 12-2 The Visio 2013 visual workflow designer is a new alternative to text-based design.

Creating a workflow with Visio 2013 and SharePoint Designer 2013

This walkthrough will demonstrate how to create a simple workflow that uses stages with Visio 2013 and SharePoint Designer 2013. Open Visio 2013 and create a new drawing based on the Microsoft SharePoint 2013 Workflow template, found in the Flowchart category. By using the Shapes task pane, look in the Components - SharePoint 2013 Workflow section and drag three more stages onto the design surface, as shown earlier in Figure 12-2. To make things easier to follow, rename each of the stages to the following names:

- Leftmost stage: **Initial Stage**

- Top stage: **Item Needs Updating**

- Bottom stage: **Item Does Not Need Updating**

- Rightmost stage: **Workflow Finishing**

Now do the following to model the workflow stages:

1. Look in the Actions - SharePoint 2013 Workflow section of the Shapes task pane, add two Log To History List actions to the Initial Stage, and rename them **Log entry into stage** and **Log value from form**, respectively.

2. With the first stage model complete, look in the Conditions - SharePoint 2013 Workflow section of the Stage task pane, add If Any Value Equals Value immediately to the right of the Initial Stage, and rename it **If user entered something**.

3. Use the Connector tool on the Home tab of the Visio 2013 ribbon to connect the red stage finished box to the decision action.

4. Use the Connector tool to connect the decision to the start of the Item Needs Updating and Item Does Not Need Updating stages. Right-click each connector and set the one going to Item Needs Updating to Yes and the other connector to No.

5. Add two Log To History List actions to the three remaining stages (Item Needs Updating, Item Does Not Need Updating, and Workflow Finishing).

6. Add the Set Field In Current Item action, found in the Actions - SharePoint 2013 Workflow category of the Shapes task pane, as the second action in the Item Needs Updating stage, and rename it **Update Announcement Body with Value**.

7. Connect the Item Needs Updating and Item Does Not Need Updating stages to the Workflow Finishing stage.

8. Save the Visio 2013 drawing, which should look like Figure 12-3, and then close Visio 2013.

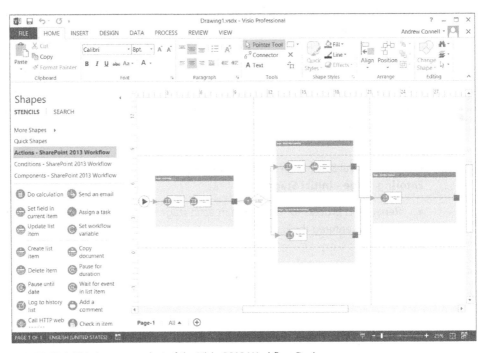

FIGURE 12-3 This is a screen shot of the Visio 2013 Workflow Designer.

The next task is importing the workflow into SharePoint Designer, so open SharePoint Designer 2013 and do the following:

1. Within SharePoint Designer 2013, click the Open button and enter the URL of a SharePoint site to connect to, logging on if necessary.

2. In the Navigation pane on the left, click Lists And Libraries to check if there is an existing Announcements list. If not, create one:

   a. Click the SharePoint List button on the ribbon and select Announcements.

   b. When prompted for a name, enter **Announcements** and click OK.

3. Import the Visio drawing to create the workflow:

   a. Click Workflows in the Navigation pane on the left.

   b. Click the Import From Visio button on the ribbon and select Import Visio 2013 Diagram.

   c. Find the drawing saved from Visio and click Open.

   d. In the Create Workflow dialog box, set the name to **Update Announcement Item**, Workflow Type to **List Workflow**, and SharePoint List to **Announcements**, and click OK.

4. SharePoint Designer will create the workflow and present the visual designer view of the model. Although it is possible to edit the workflow in the visual designer, switch to the text designer by clicking Views on the ribbon and then selecting Text-Based Designer.

5. In the text-based designer, SharePoint Designer will display the stages in a top-down list. The order does not really matter; however, it may make sense to ensure that they are in the correct order. This can be done by selecting a stage and then right-clicking to use either the Move Up or Move Down option. Also notice how the Transition To Stage section of each stage has been wired up to route the workflow to the next stage.

6. Within the Initial Stage stage, click the Message link on the first action and set the message to **Entering Stage - Initial Stage**.

   a. Repeat this process for the action in each stage to write a message to the log that the workflow entered the name of the current stage.

7. When the workflow has been initiated, this workflow will prompt the user to enter a value to write to the body of the announcement. To add this field to the initiation form, follow these steps:

   a. On the ribbon, click Initiation Form Parameters.

   b. Click the Add button to create a new form parameter.

   c. Set the Name of the parameter to **Body Value** and click Next, then click Finish and OK.

8. Use the second Log action in the Initial Stage to write the value the user entered to the log:

   a. Click the Message link and then click the ellipsis (...) button to the right to bring up the builder.

   b. In the text area, enter **Value entered by user:**.

   c. Click the Add Or Change Lookup button.

   d. In the Lookup For String dialog box, set the Data Source to Workflow Variables And Parameters and the Field From Source to Parameter: Body Value, and click OK twice to close the two dialog boxes.

9. Update the condition to route to the correct stage from the Initial Stage:

   a. In the Transition To Stage section of the Initial Stage, click the first Value link and then click the Fx button.

   b. In the Define Workflow Lookup dialog box, set the Data Source to Workflow Variables And Parameters and the Field From Source to Parameter: Body Value, and then click OK.

   c. Click the Equals link in the If statement and select the Is Not Empty condition, and then click OK.

10. Update the list item within the Item Needs Updating stage:

    a. In the Item Needs Updating stage, select the Field link on the Set Field To Value action and select Body.

    b. Click the Value link and click the Fx button.

    c. In the Define Workflow Lookup dialog box, set the Data Source to Workflow Variables And Parameters and the Field From Source to Parameter: Body Value, and then click OK.

11. The workflow is now finished and can be tested. Click the Save button on the ribbon to save the workflow. Then click Publish to publish the workflow to Workflow Manager.

Open a browser and go to the Announcements list. Create a new item with no value in the body field and click Save. Now select the item and, by using the Items tab on the ribbon, select Workflows. On the Workflows page, select Update Announcement Item to start the workflow. When the workflow starts, you will be taken to the initiation form. Enter a value in the Body Value text box and click Start. The browser will redirect back to the list. Click the Workflows button again. This time, further down the page, notice that there is a workflow under Running Workflows or Completed Workflows (depending on whether it has already finished). Click the value of the Internal Status field to view the status page that shows all history log information. Go back to the actual list item and notice that the body value has also been updated.

Custom workflows with Visual Studio 2012

The previous section discussed some of the changes in custom workflow development found in both Visio 2013 and SharePoint Designer 2013. Many of these changes, though important, are iterative and are improvements upon the previous versions of the tools. The story with Visual Studio 2012 workflow development for SharePoint, in contrast, is quite different. The biggest change developers will quickly notice, as mentioned previously in this chapter, is the fact that there is no code view for the workflow because it is entirely declarative. All custom business logic, if it cannot be expressed by using the provided activities, should be refactored to external web services that the workflow can call.

Developers can create workflows in either a traditional SharePoint full trust farm solution or within a new SharePoint app and use either of the new project item templates added by the Microsoft Office Developer Tools for Visual Studio 2012 for SharePoint projects: Workflow and Workflow Custom Activity. Both of these project item templates are available in full trust solutions as well as in apps, but the real-world usefulness of custom activities will be dependent on the type of project selected. Custom activities are covered in the "Creating custom activities" section later in this chapter.

Though SharePoint Designer 2013 is limited to creating workflows made up of stages, which are effectively flowcharts, Visual Studio supports another powerful type of workflow: state machine. This means that workflows developed in Visual Studio 2012 effectively support three different types of workflow authoring:

- **Sequential** A *sequential* workflow follows a specific path, as shown in Figure 12-4. There might be decision branches and loops, and the workflow might not have a termination point, but it is easy to follow the predictable path in the designed process.

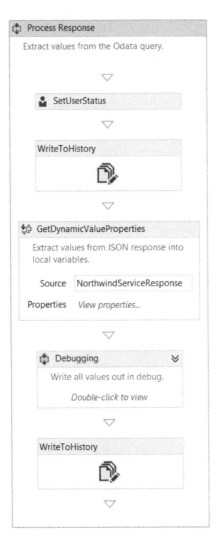

FIGURE 12-4 This screen shot shows the creation of a simple sequential workflow in Visual Studio 2012.

- **Flowchart**   A *flowchart* workflow is one in which the workflow can transition into different sections depending on specific conditions, as shown in Figure 12-5. The flowchart activity, along with the associated FlowDescision and FlowSwitch activities, are typically placed within a sequence activity and act like either traditional if or switch statements in common programming languages such as C#, Microsoft Visual Basic .NET, or JavaScript. The stage construct within a workflow based on SharePoint Designer 2013 is based on the principles of a flowchart. This type of workflow, unlike a sequential workflow, does not have a prescribed path that it follows. Instead, the things that happen during the workflow dictate the path the workflow follows.

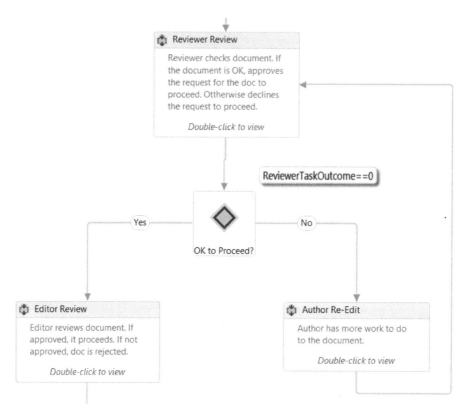

Reviewer Review

Reviewer checks document. If
the document is OK, approves
the request for the doc to
proceed. Ottherwise declines
the request to proceed.

Double-click to view

ReviewerTaskOutcome==0

Yes

No

OK to Proceed?

Editor Review

Editor reviews document. If
approved, it proceeds. If not
approved, doc is rejected.

Double-click to view

Author Re-Edit

Author has more work to do
to the document.

Double-click to view

FIGURE 12-5 This screen shot shows the creation of a flowchart workflow in Visual Studio 2012.

- **State machine** A *state machine* workflow, like a flowchart workflow, does not typically follow a specific path of execution. These types of workflows consist of two or more states, as shown in Figure 12-6. Think of each state as a smaller workflow that contains multiple activities. Developers can set specific activities to happen when the workflow enters or exits the state. What really makes state machines interesting is the transitions developers define. Each state can have one or more transitions that tell the workflow engine how to move from one state to another state. The workflow is always going to be in one of the states in a state machine workflow. A transition dictates the trigger for the workflow to move from one state to another. Many people favor state machine workflows over the other types of workflows because they can be made to more closely mirror real-world business processes. However, these types of workflows can quickly get very complicated.

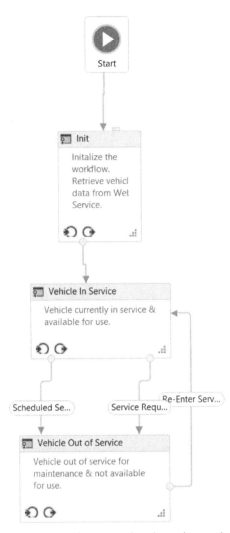

FIGURE 12-6 This screen shot shows the creation of a state machine workflow in Visual Studio 2012.

When adding a new workflow to a SharePoint project, the template adds a single *Sequence* activity, which serves as the main container. If you want to create a flowchart or state machine workflow, simply delete this default activity and drag either a *StateMachine* or *Flowchart* activity onto the design surface.

Before building a custom workflow, developers should have a good understanding of the tool windows and design surface that Visual Studio 2012 provides. Many of the elements, as shown in Figure 12-7, are quite common:

1. The Solution Explorer tool window, which contains your project

2. The toolbox, which contains all the activities used in assembling the workflow

3. The design surface, where the activities will be placed and linked together

4. The Properties pane, where most aspects of the selected activity or selected item in the Solution Explorer are managed

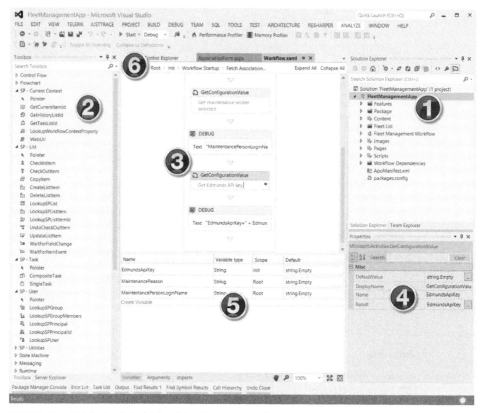

FIGURE 12-7 This is the default Visual Studio 2012 workflow authoring interface.

There are two additional components within the design surface that might not be familiar to you and might need additional explanation:

5. At the bottom of the designer, notice three tabs: Variables, Arguments, and Import. Click Variables to view a list of all the variables used within the workflow that are available at the current scope. Scoping works the same way as it does in standard object-oriented programming design: a variable scoped at the root is accessible to all lower scopes (such as methods within a class), but a variable within a lower scope (such as a method in a class) is accessible only within that scope and its children, not in parallel or parent scopes. Click Arguments to view a list of the arguments that are used to pass values into the workflow, such as those passed in from an initiation form, as covered later in this chapter in the "Adding custom forms to workflows" section, or as properties within a custom activity.

6. Near the top of the designer is a breadcrumb navigation area. As workflows acquire more and more nested activities, it sometimes is easier to manipulate them by zooming into a specific area. This breadcrumb navigation area can make it easier to back out to a higher level within the workflow. It is for this reason that one approach is to rename composite activities, or those activities that contain child activities, such as *Sequence*, to something more appropriate. For example, the topmost *Sequence* activity could be renamed "Root" instead of the default "Sequence" name.

Creating a workflow with Visual Studio 2012

The following walkthrough demonstrates how to create a custom workflow that calls the OData web service of the well-known Northwind database publically hosted at the *http://www.odata.org* site. The user enters a customer ID and then starts the workflow, which will retrieve additional customer information and update the list item with this data. First, start Visual Studio 2012 and create a new SharePoint-hosted app project, a task that has been shown repeatedly throughout this book. Next, create a new custom list named **Customers** in the project. Include the following fields, leaving their default data type of *String*:

- **CustomerId** (renamed from the default Title field)

- **Customer Name**

- **Job Title**

- **Address**

- **Country/Region**

- **Business Phone**

- **Fax Number**

After creating the list, add a workflow to the project by following these steps:

1. Repeat the process of adding a new item to the app, but select the Workflow template.

2. In the SharePoint Customization Wizard, give the workflow a friendly name and specify it as a List Workflow.

3. The next step in the wizard asks whether Visual Studio should automatically create an association. Select the check box to create the association, and select the only option for all drop-down list boxes.

4. Set the different ways in which the workflow can be started. For development, select only the A User Manually Starts The Workflow check box and leave the other automatic start options cleared. Then click the Finish button.

Visual Studio will then display the basic workflow design surface with a single *Sequence* activity. To keep things organized and easier to manage, rename this activity **Root** and add four more *Sequence* activities within the Root sequence, using the following names:

- **Init**

- **Get Customer Data from Service**

- **Process Service Response**

- **Update List Item**

The first step in this workflow is to retrieve the customer ID entered by the user. For this, two variables are needed, so click the Variables tab at the bottom of the designer and create the following two variables:

- ***CustomerItemProperties* (Variable Type = *DynamicValue*; Scope= *Init*)** This will be used to store the results from the activity that will get all properties from the list item. The *DynamicValue* data type is not shown by default. To find it, select the Browse For Types option in the Variable Type column. In the search box at the top of the dialog box, enter **DynamicValue** and select the *Microsoft.Activities.DynamicValue*.

- ***CustomerId* (Variable Type = *String*; Scope = *Root*)** This will be used to store the actual customer ID entered by the user in the list item.

Next, drop the *LookupSpListItem* activity in the *Init* sequence, found in the SP - List section of the toolbox, and use the values shown in Figure 12-8 to set the values in the Properties pane when this activity is selected. This activity tells Workflow Manager to use the SharePoint REST API to retrieve the properties of the current list item and store the JSON response in the *DynamicValue* variable previously created.

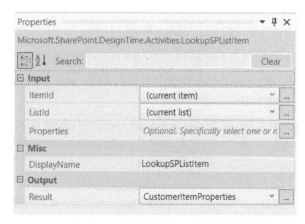

FIGURE 12-8 Use the Properties pane for the *LookupSPListItem* activity to modify settings.

To retrieve the customer ID from the item, click the Get Properties link within the *LookupSpListItem* activity, which will add a *GetDynamicValueProperties* activity to the design surface. In the Properties pane, click the ellipsis (...) button to bring up the Property selector wizard. In the wizard, set the Entity Type to List Item Of Customers and add a single property with *Path = CustomerId* and *Assign To = CustomerId* (the variable previously created).

The workflow now has a reference to the customer ID, so the next step is to call the web service. Select the sequence *Get Customer Data from Service* to set the current context, and create two new variables:

- **NorthwindServiceUri (Variable Type = *String*; Scope= *Get Customer Data from Service*)** This will contain the URI that will be used to query the web service.

- **NorthwindServiceResponse (Variable Type = *DynamicValue*; Scope = *Root*)** This will be used to store the web service response.

Create the URL that will be used to query the web service by dropping an *Assign* activity in the *Get Customer Data from Service* sequence. Set the left part of the *Assign* activity to **NorthwindServiceUri** and the right part to **"http://services.odata.org/Northwind/Northwind.svc/Customers('"** + **CustomerId + "')?$format=json"**. Now add an *HttpSend* activity to the *Get Customer Data from Service* sequence immediately after the *Assign* activity, and use the values shown in Figure 12-9 to set the properties on this activity.

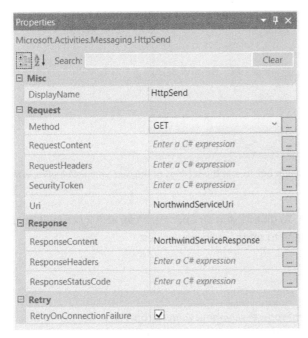

FIGURE 12-9 Use the Properties pane to edit the settings on the *HttpSend* activity.

After the web service request has been made and the results are stored in the local variable, the next step is to process the response. Each value in the response will need to be added to a different variable, so create string variables, scoped to the *Root* sequence, for each of the fields except *customer ID* in the list created at the start of this walkthrough. Next, add a *GetDynamicValueProperties* activity to the *Process Service Request* sequence. In the Properties pane, set the Source value to **NorthwindServiceResponse**. Now click the ellipsis button for the Properties property to map paths in the response to the local variables by using the settings shown in Figure 12-10. (Note that the Assign To column contains the variables created for each field in the Customers list.)

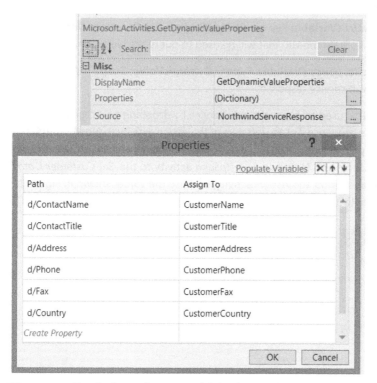

FIGURE 12-10 Use the Properties pane and dialog box to edit the settings of the *GetDynamicValueProperties* activity.

The last step is to update the list item. To do this, add an *UpdateListItem* activity to the *Update List Item* sequence, and use the Properties pane to set the following values:

- **ListId**   (current list)
- **ItemId**   (current item)

Click the ellipsis button for the *ListItemPropertiesDynamicValues* property. In the dialog box, set the Entity Type to List Item Of Customers and, for each of the values extracted from the web service, set the value of the list item to the variable within the workflow, as shown in Figure 12-11.

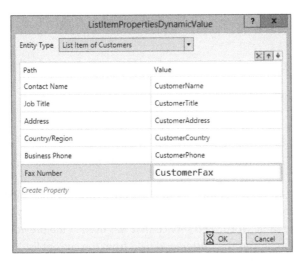

FIGURE 12-11 Use the Properties dialog box to edit the settings on the *ListItemPropertiesDynamicValue* activity.

At this point, the workflow is complete, so press F5 to start debugging. Visual Studio will build and deploy the SharePoint-hosted app.

> **Note** Notice that a console box also appears in the deployment process. This is a debugging tool for testing workflows in an on-premises deployment. It will display the contents of *WriteLine* activities.

When the browser opens, find the Customers list, create a single customer with an ID of **ALFKI**, and save the item. Next, manually start the workflow by using the same process outlined in the previously created SharePoint Designer 2013 workflow, and then go back to the list item and keep refreshing the page to observe the workflow update the list item.

SharePoint Designer 2013 and web services

As previously mentioned in this chapter, Microsoft has added support for workflows deployed to Workflow Manager 1.0 to call external web services. With this capability, workflow authors can add custom business logic to their workflows and take advantage of existing services. Unlike workflows based on Visual Studio 2012, which use the *DynamicValue* type, SharePoint Designer 2013 uses the *Dictionary* data type with variables to send data to the workflow and to process the results from a web service call.

Working with web services in workflows authored in SharePoint Designer 2013 is very similar to working with them in workflows authored in Visual Studio 2012. To call a web service, use the Call HTTP Web Service action in SharePoint Designer 2013. The first step is to set the address of the web service to call. Do this by clicking the *this* hyperlink in the action, as shown in Figure 12-12.

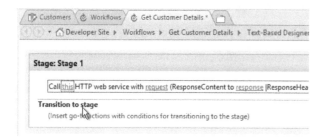

FIGURE 12-12 Developers can now use the Call HTTP Web Service action in SharePoint Designer 2013.

When the String Builder dialog box opens, construct the URL to the service by using values in the current list item and the Add Or Change Lookup button in the footer of the dialog box, as shown in Figure 12-13. This figure shows a call to the same Northwind service that was used in the previous workflow authored in Visual Studio 2012, but it uses the *CustomerId* field from the current list item and selects only the *ContactName* and *CompanyName* fields.

FIGURE 12-13 Use the String Builder to construct the web service URL in SharePoint Designer 2013.

The next step is to extract the value from the web service response. First, the web service response must be stored in a new variable. Click the *response* link in the Call HTTP Web Service action and either select an existing variable or create a new variable of type *Dictionary*. To extract the values from the service response, add a *Get Item from Dictionary* action to the workflow. This activity has three things to set:

- **Item by name or path**   This is the path to the item within the dictionary variable or the web service response. For instance, to get the results from the service used in Figure 12-14, the path would be *d/ContactName*.

- **Dictionary** This is the name of the variable that contains the web service response.

- **Item** This is the name of the variable where the result should be stored for later use in the workflow.

FIGURE 12-14 This demonstrates a workflow in SharePoint Designer 2013 that calls and processes a web service response.

That is all there is to working with services in SharePoint Designer 2013. From this point, the variable can be used to update a list item or inclusion within an email message or any other task that can be performed with a workflow.

Creating custom activities

Another workflow customization supported by both SharePoint 2013 and Workflow Manager is creating custom activities. With a custom activity, a developer can create a subprocess that achieves a specific task. A custom activity can be thought of as a small workflow, which is ideal for a process that could be reused multiple times in various workflows. Before creating a custom activity, the developer needs to consider where and how it will be used. If the goal is to simply refactor a complex workflow into smaller or reusable components that are stored in files separately from the main workflow, the development approach is quite simple. Only Visual Studio 2012 supports creating custom activities; SharePoint Designer 2013 contains no support for creating custom activities. To create a custom activity in Visual Studio, add a new project item to a SharePoint project (either a traditional SharePoint solution or SharePoint app) by using the Workflow Custom Activity template; add the business logic; and finally, add the activity to the workflow as demonstrated in the next section.

Creating a custom workflow activity in a SharePoint app

The following walkthrough demonstrates how to create a custom activity for use within a workflow hosted in a SharePoint app. It will use the workflow project previously created in this chapter that calls the Northwind OData service as a starting point to retrieve additional customer data. The custom activity will refactor the process of querying the web service and processing the response so that the workflow can call this activity by passing in a customer ID and get back the additional customer details without having to deal with the web service.

First, add a new item to the project by using the Workflow Custom Activity template and name it **GetCustomerDetailsActivity**. Next, cut and paste the sequences *Get Customer Data from Service* and *Process Service Response* from the previously created workflow into the sequence in the custom activity. Rename the default *Sequence* activity to **Root**. Now create two variables by clicking the Variables tab at the bottom of the designer. These variables will be used in the workflow to store the URL of the service and the response:

- *NorthwindServiceUri* **(Variable Type = *String*; Scope= *Get Customer Data from Service*)**   This will contain the URI that will be used to query the web service.

- *NorthwindServiceResponse* **(Variable Type = *DynamicValue*; Scope = *Root*)**   This will be used to store the web service response.

The next step involves modifying the arguments used to pass data to and from the activity. Within the activity, click the Arguments tab at the bottom of the designer, as shown in Figure 12-15. Create one input argument for the customer ID that the calling workflow will supply, and output parameters for all the values extracted from the web service response, as shown in Figure 12-15. As long as the argument names are the same as the variable names in the previous workflow, the activities will not need to be updated.

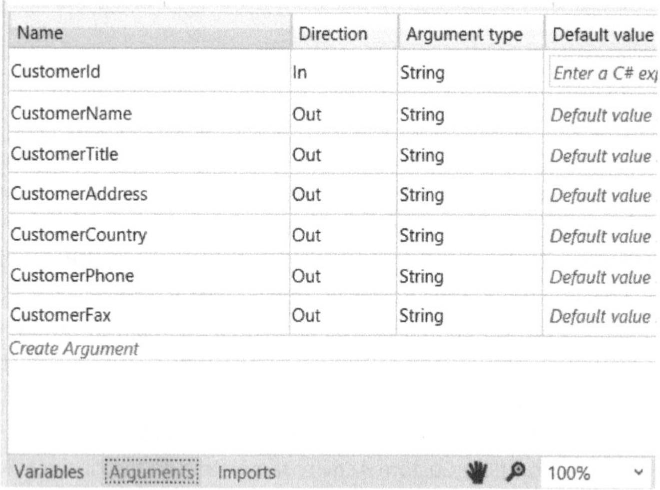

Name	Direction	Argument type	Default value
CustomerId	In	String	*Enter a C# ex*
CustomerName	Out	String	*Default value*
CustomerTitle	Out	String	*Default value*
CustomerAddress	Out	String	*Default value*
CustomerCountry	Out	String	*Default value*
CustomerPhone	Out	String	*Default value*
CustomerFax	Out	String	*Default value*
Create Argument			

| Variables | Arguments | Imports | | | 100% | ∨ |

FIGURE 12-15 Add arguments to the activity to pass values in and out.

The custom activity is now finished, and the next step is to update the workflow. With the workflow open in the designer, remove the two variables *NorthwindServiceUri* and *NorthwindService-Reponse*; they are no longer needed, because the activity handles them. To add the activity to the workflow, you must compile the project so that the toolbox will show the activity as one to use in the workflow. Build the project, and then drag the custom activity into the designer between the *Init* and *Update List Item* sequences, as shown in Figure 12-16.

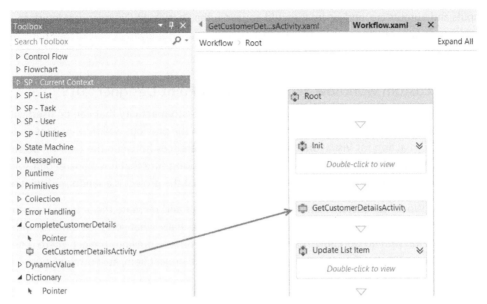

FIGURE 12-16 Add the custom activity, *GetCustomerDetailsActivity*, to the workflow.

The last step is to select the custom activity in the designer and associate all the input and output parameters with the variables in the workflow.

This example showed how to use a custom activity within a workflow deployed as a SharePoint app. This is great for many solutions, but many business requirements demand that the activity be used in multiple workflows. Sharing a single activity XAML file between projects and limiting it to workflows built with Visual Studio 2012 is cumbersome. Another option is to deploy the activity to Workflow Manager and advertise the existence of it to SharePoint so that workflows authored by using SharePoint Designer 2013 can use it. There are two extra requirements to creating a custom activity for use in SharePoint Designer 2013 workflows.

First, the activity must be deployed by using a solution, not in an app. Deploying it in an app would make the activity available only within the AppWeb, which is quite limiting. The solution used for deployment can be a sandboxed or fully trusted farm solution, but it probably makes the most sense to do it as a sandboxed solution. Because the custom activity will be fully declarative like workflows authored in Visual Studio 2012, there is no custom code, and thus it can be deployed by using a sandboxed solution. Further, because fully trusted farm solutions are supported only in on-premises deployments, the sandbox makes more sense because it can be used in either on-premises or hosted deployments such as Office 365.

The other requirement in creating a custom activity that will be used in SharePoint Designer 2013 workflows is that the activity must be advertised to SharePoint Designer. This is achieved by using an actions file. When you are creating a new workflow with SharePoint Designer 2013, the site collection interrogates the target site collection for all available actions supported by the site collection. These actions map to activities and tell SharePoint Designer how the user-friendly designer should work, what the inputs and outputs are, and where it should appear in the SharePoint Designer user interface—for example, which category it should be present in. Actions files are deployed as part of the SharePoint solution package that includes the custom activity.

Creating a custom workflow activity for SharePoint Designer 2013

The following walkthrough demonstrates how to create a custom activity that can be used within SharePoint Designer 2013. It is a variant of the one included in the previous walkthrough that addressed creating a custom action for Visual Studio 2012, so the differences between the two will be easily noticeable. First, create a SharePoint 2013 empty project, making sure that it is a SharePoint solution and not a SharePoint app project. When prompted, specify that the project is a sandboxed solution.

Next, add a Workflow Custom Activity item to the project and recreate the activity from the previous example, including the variables and arguments. Essentially, what you should be left with is a sandboxed solution with no workflow, but the same activity from the previous project. There is one very important difference in that there is now a *.actions4 file in the project item, as shown in Figure 12-17.

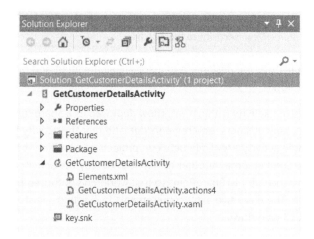

FIGURE 12-17 This project's Solution Explorer pane shows the activity and associated *.actions4 file.

After the activity has been created, it must be exposed as an action for it to be accessible in SharePoint Designer 2013 workflows. This is done by using the *.actions4 file. Open this file and add the contents shown in the following code. This file dictates how the activity will appear in SharePoint Designer 2013 and how the values entered by the workflow author will be passed to and from the activity:

```
<Action Name="GetCustomerDetailsActivity"
        ClassName="GetCustomerDetailsActivity.GetCustomerDetailsActivity"
        Category="Custom Activities"
        AppliesTo="all">
 <RuleDesigner Sentence="Fetch customer details for
                         customer %1 from Northwind as %2, %3, %4, %5, %6 and %7">
   <FieldBind Field="CustomerId" Id="1"
              DesignerType="TextBox" Text="id" DisplayName="Customer Id" />
```

```
     <FieldBind Field="CustomerName" Id="2"
                DesignerType="TextBox" Text="fullName" DisplayName="Customer Name" />
     <FieldBind Field="CustomerTitle" Id="3"
                DesignerType="TextBox" Text="jobTitle" DisplayName="Customer Job Title" />
     <FieldBind Field="CustomerAddress" Id="4"
                DesignerType="TextBox" Text="address" DisplayName="Customer Address" />
     <FieldBind Field="CustomerCountry" Id="5"
                DesignerType="TextBox" Text="country" DisplayName="Customer Country" />
     <FieldBind Field="CustomerPhone" Id="6"
                DesignerType="TextBox" Text="phone" DisplayName="Customer Phone" />
     <FieldBind Field="CustomerFax" Id="7"
                DesignerType="TextBox" Text="fax" DisplayName="Customer Fax" />
  </RuleDesigner>
  <Parameters>
    <Parameter Name="CustomerId" Type="System.String, mscorlib"
               Direction="In" DesignerType="Hide" />
    <Parameter Name="CustomerName" Type="System.String, mscorlib"
               Direction="Out" DesignerType="Hide" />
    <Parameter Name="CustomerTitle" Type="System.String, mscorlib"
               Direction="Out" DesignerType="Hide" />
    <Parameter Name="CustomerAddress" Type="System.String, mscorlib"
               Direction="Out" DesignerType="Hide" />
    <Parameter Name="CustomerCountry" Type="System.String, mscorlib"
               Direction="Out" DesignerType="Hide" />
    <Parameter Name="CustomerPhone" Type="System.String, mscorlib"
               Direction="Out" DesignerType="Hide" />
    <Parameter Name="CustomerFax" Type="System.String, mscorlib"
               Direction="Out" DesignerType="Hide" />
  </Parameters>
</Action>
```

In this markup, notice the *<RuleDesigner>* element, specifically the *Sentence* attribute. It contains a string that is shown in the SharePoint Designer experience. Each of the pieces of the sentence that start with the % character are treated as linked placeholders. They map to the *<FieldBind>* elements in the markup. For instance, *%2* maps to the *fullName* field. What is shown in the design experience is a hyperlinked string *fullName*, which the workflow author can click. The *<Parameters>* section tells the designer how each field should be treated; for instance, whether it is an email address, string, number, or datetime field. Based on the type specified, the designer shows different designers and applies different validation rules.

When you are finished, deploy the sandboxed solution to a SharePoint 2013 site and create a new workflow. The activity will appear in the category that the *.actions4 file specified and will appear in the designer, as shown in Figure 12-18.

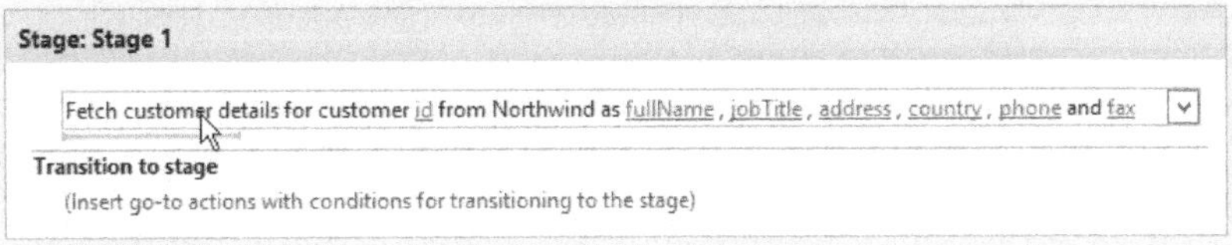

Stage: Stage 1

Fetch customer details for customer id from Northwind as fullName, jobTitle, address, country, phone and fax

Transition to stage
(Insert go-to actions with conditions for transitioning to the stage)

FIGURE 12-18 This shows using the custom activity, as shown in the text-based designer in SharePoint Designer 2013.

Using tasks in workflows

One of the biggest value propositions that SharePoint brings to Workflow Foundation is the incorporation of tasks and task management. When you are associating a workflow with a site or list, one of the requirements is to specify the list that will contain any of the tasks that are created within the workflow. Both SharePoint Designer 2013 and Visual Studio 2012 support creating tasks and assigning them to users. Handing the outcome of the tasks is much simpler than it was in prior versions of SharePoint.

Developers using Visual Studio 2012 can create tasks by using one of two activities: *SingleTask* or *CompositeTask*. The first one creates and assigns a task to a specified user or group. With the latter, a developer can create multiple tasks and assign them to multiple people, such as everyone within a group. A task can be configured to stop the workflow until everyone or a percentage of people have addressed the assigned task. Both activities have properties that allow the workflow author to specify the subject and body of the different email messages that are sent out when the task is assigned to someone, when it is overdue, or when it has been canceled. Unlike in previous versions of SharePoint, developers do not have to keep track of correlation tokens if they don't want to, because the tasks can be flagged to wait until the task has been completed by the person it was assigned to.

Microsoft has created a new task list definition in SharePoint 2013 (list template ID = 171) that provides a timeline view and uses the new *Workflow Task (SharePoint 2013)* content type. This content type is derived from the base *Task* content type (ID = 0x0108), but it adds two columns. The first column, *WorkflowInstanceId*, is used to track which instance the task is associated with. The other column is *TaskOutcome*, which is used to provide the two default outcomes available for a task: *Approved* and *Rejected*.

Adding tasks to a workflow

The following walkthrough demonstrates how to use the *SingleTask* activity to add a task to a workflow by using the out-of-the-box workflow task and task outcomes. Create a new SharePoint-hosted app by using Visual Studio 2012, add an Announcements list to the app project, and then add a workflow that is associated with the Announcements list and starts only manually, not automatically. Because the task needs to be assigned to someone, for the sake of simplicity, use the creator of the list item that will trigger the workflow. Therefore, use the same techniques that were demonstrated in the previous workflows to get the list item's properties, but this time put the *Created By* field value from the list item in a local string variable called *AnnouncementItemAuthorId*.

Next, by using the toolbox, add a *SingleTask* activity to the end of the workflow and click the Properties link within the activities to open the Task Options dialog box. Set the Assigned To property to the *AnnouncementItemAuthorId* variable, and update the other fields such as the Task Title and Body to something descriptive. Notice that there are additional sections for Due Date, Task Options, Email Options, and Outcome Options that can be set, as shown in Figure 12-19.

FIGURE 12-19 Use the Task Options dialog box to customize the *SingleTask* activity Task Options.

Although the Task Options dialog box has quite a few options that the workflow author can set, selecting the *SingleTask* activity in the designer will expose a significant number of additional properties in the Properties pane, as shown in Figure 12-20. These include custom email subjects and bodies for the three types of email messages that can be sent, and configuration of the variable where the task outcome should be saved for evaluation later in the workflow.

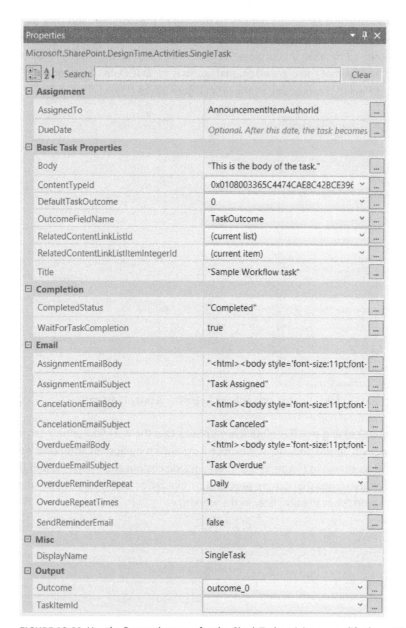

Properties	▾ ⯆ ✕
Microsoft.SharePoint.DesignTime.Activities.SingleTask	

Search:		Clear
Assignment		
AssignedTo	AnnouncementItemAuthorId	...
DueDate	*Optional. After this date, the task becomes*	...
Basic Task Properties		
Body	"This is the body of the task."	...
ContentTypeId	0x0108003365C4474CAE8C42BCE39E ⌄	...
DefaultTaskOutcome	0 ⌄	...
OutcomeFieldName	TaskOutcome ⌄	...
RelatedContentLinkListId	(current list) ⌄	...
RelatedContentLinkListItemIntegerId	(current item) ⌄	...
Title	"Sample Workflow task"	...
Completion		
CompletedStatus	"Completed"	...
WaitForTaskCompletion	true	...
Email		
AssignmentEmailBody	"<html><body style='font-size:11pt;font·	...
AssignmentEmailSubject	"Task Assigned"	...
CancelationEmailBody	"<html><body style='font-size:11pt;font·	...
CancelationEmailSubject	"Task Canceled"	...
OverdueEmailBody	"<html><body style='font-size:11pt;font·	...
OverdueEmailSubject	"Task Overdue"	...
OverdueReminderRepeat	Daily ⌄	...
OverdueRepeatTimes	1	...
SendReminderEmail	false	...
Misc		
DisplayName	SingleTask	
Output		
Outcome	outcome_0 ⌄	...
TaskItemId	⌄	...

FIGURE 12-20 Use the Properties pane for the *SingleTask* activity to modify the settings.

Custom task outcomes

Workflow task outcomes are presented on the task edit form as buttons at the bottom of the form, alongside the Save and Cancel buttons. Workflows in SharePoint 2013 are not limited to just the two options *Approved* and *Rejected*. Many times the out-of-the-box options do not meet a company's business requirements. For instance, consider a task that is assigned to a reviewer of a draft document for a manuscript. When the reviewer surveys the submitted draft document, the two options should be to either send the draft document back to the author for more edits or pass it along to the editor. In this case, *Approved* and *Rejected* do not really fit; more appropriate options could be "Return to Author" and "Proceed to Editor."

Workflow authors using either SharePoint Designer 2013 or Visual Studio 2012 can create custom workflow tasks that include custom task outcomes. This is achieved by creating a custom task as a special content type and adding a custom site column that defines all the possible outcomes. The custom column should be derived from the field type called *OutcomeChoice*, which is a choice field. This can pose a challenge in that the content type the custom task is derived from is the *Workflow Task (SharePoint 2013)* content type, which includes the default *TaskOutcome* site column, which contains the *Approved* and *Rejected* options. Therefore, what Microsoft recommends is to remove the *TaskOutcome* column from the custom task content type and ensure that it is not present in the workflow task list; otherwise, the result would show multiple options. For instance, consider a custom outcome that has two options, *Red Pill* and *Blue Pill*. If the default outcome is not removed, the users completing the task will be presented, in the browser, with the options shown in Figure 12-21. Not only is this confusing, it simply makes no sense in this context.

FIGURE 12-21 Notice all the buttons for the custom task content type rendering with the default and custom outcome columns.

Microsoft recommends creating different workflow task lists for each type of task being created in a workflow. Depending on the tool used to create the workflow, the steps could be a bit different.

Creating custom task outcomes for a SharePoint Designer 2013 workflow

When creating custom tasks and custom task outcomes in workflows authored by using SharePoint Designer 2013, workflow authors needs to keep in mind that they are going to be responsible for creating the workflow task list. The basic steps for creating the custom outcome are as follows:

1. Create a custom site column by using the field type *Task Outcome* with custom choices.

2. Create a custom content type that is derived from *Workflow Task (SharePoint 2013)*, found in the List Content Types group.

   a. To this content type, add a reference to the custom site column previously created.

   b. Remove the default *TaskOutcome* site column that comes from the *Workflow Task (SharePoint 2013)* content type.

3. Create a new list and add the custom content type to it.

4. Verify that the *TaskOutcome* site column is not in the task list. If it is, remove it.

Following these steps will render a single set of outcome buttons, as shown in Figure 12-22.

FIGURE 12-22 Notice the corrected buttons for the custom task content type rendering only the custom outcome columns.

When you are adding the task action in the workflow by using SharePoint Designer 2013, simply select the correct task content type and outcome column to ensure that the workflow uses the correct settings. Notice that the dialog box warns the author to ensure that the content type has been added to the associated workflow task list. This is not checked in the publication process of the workflow, nor at runtime. Instead, the workflow will produce an error during the process of creating a task, with a message about an *ArgumentException* on the *ContentTypeId*, as shown in Figure 12-23. This is something that might not be intuitive to the experienced user or end user, so make sure that this is set ahead of time.

FIGURE 12-23 Use the SharePoint Designer 2013 Assign A Task dialog box to modify the task settings.

Creating custom task outcomes for a Visual Studio 2012 workflow

The process of creating custom task outcomes for custom tasks with workflows built by using Visual Studio 2012 is similar to that of SharePoint Designer 2013. The most important difference is to keep in mind that the workflow author is responsible for binding the custom content type to the workflow task list. This can be done by opening the Elements.xml file for the WorkflowTaskList project item and adding a second *<ContentTypeBinding />* element referencing the content type ID of the custom content type, as shown in the following code snippet:

```xml
<?xml version="1.0" encoding="utf-8" ?>
<Elements xmlns="http://schemas.microsoft.com/sharepoint/">
  <ListInstance FeatureId="{f9ce21f8-f437-4f7e-8bc6-946378c850f0}"
                TemplateType="171"
                Title="WorkflowTaskList"
                Description="This list instance is used for workflow Task items."
                Url="Lists/WorkflowTaskList"
                RootWebOnly="FALSE" />
    <ContentTypeBinding ListUrl="Lists/WorkflowTaskList"
                        RootWebOnly="FALSE"
                        ContentTypeId="0x0108003365C4474CAE8C42BCE396314E88E51F"/>
  <ContentTypeBinding ListUrl="Lists/WorkflowTaskList"
                      RootWebOnly="FALSE"
                      ContentTypeId="0x010800C5462A9EBAE14BFC8DA48A659BFC2C80"/>
</Elements>
```

Workflow services CSOM and JSOM

In SharePoint 2013, Microsoft also invested in bolstering the client-side object model (CSOM), both the managed implementations and the JavaScript object model (JSOM), for the workflow services. The way it works is that everything is routed through the Workflow Service Manager. This is the client component that is hosted in SharePoint and knows how to communicate through a client proxy with the SharePoint farm's configured Workflow Manager farm. The Workflow Service Manager provides interfaces to a few specialized workflow services:

- **Deployment service**   This service provides a vehicle for interrogating and exploring all deployed workflow definitions. In addition, developers can validate and submit workflow definitions to SharePoint and Workflow Manager through this service.

- **Subscription service**   This service provides a vehicle for interrogating, exploring, modifying, and creating new or existing workflow associations of a workflow definition with a specified site, list, or library.

- **Instance service**   This service, like the two other services previously mention, provides a vehicle for interrogating, exploring, creating, and interacting with new and existing workflow instances on a specific SharePoint site, list item, or document.

By using these new services, developers can create some really interesting solutions. However, from a practical standpoint, the Workflow Services JSOM will be most used within workflow forms, as covered in the next section of this chapter. To use the workflow CSOM or JSOM, add the necessary references to your project (*Microsoft.SharePoint.Client.WorkflowServices.dll* in the case of the CSOM; *sp.workflowservices.js* in the case of JSOM). Next, pass a SharePoint client context and the target site to connect to. The following sample demonstrates how to do this by using JSOM:

```javascript
var context = SP.ClientContext.get_current();
var wfManager = SP.WorkflowServices.WorkflowServicesManager.newObject(context,
  context.get_web());
```

For a practical implementation and demonstration of how to use the Workflow Services JSOM, refer to the next section on working with forms in SharePoint 2013 workflows.

Adding custom forms to workflows

Workflows in prior versions of SharePoint supported three different types of custom forms. The first type, custom task forms, has already been covered in this chapter and is handled by custom content types and outcome columns. The other two types of forms are *association* and *initiation* forms. In previous versions of SharePoint, creating these custom forms was challenging because they had special undocumented and confusing logic that was not exposed to customers and was used to implement them by using either InfoPath or ASP.NET pages. SharePoint 2013 has made this task much easier. First, all forms should be created as ASP.NET pages, and there are templates for the available forms within the Office Developer Tools for Visual Studio 2012. Just like traditional SharePoint apps, the ASP.NET forms should not have any server-side code and instead only utilize client-side code such as JavaScript. The form templates in Visual Studio 2012 already contain the base Workflow Services JSOM code needed by the forms. For the most part, all the developer needs to do is modify a little section that collects values from the form controls specific to the workflow, and then pass them along in the Workflow Services JSOM call to SharePoint.

Association forms in SharePoint 2013

An association form is presented after the user creates a new association for a workflow definition and SharePoint site, list, or library. The first part of the association is selecting the workflow definition and giving it a friendly name, followed by selecting the workflow task and history list the workflow will be associated with, and finally, selecting how it can start. If there is a linked association form with the workflow, it is presented when the user clicks Next on the default association form. These types of forms are very useful when the workflow needs some configuration information, such as an API key that needs to be submitted to a workflow that the workflow is calling, or when the workflow needs some default data.

Creating association forms

This walkthrough demonstrates creating a custom association form and using it to collect some information that is then passed along to the workflow. Following the same setup process you used with the other workflows you built in Visual Studio 2012 in this chapter, create a new SharePoint-hosted app project with an Announcement list, and add a workflow, but this time do not associate the workflow with the list. Instead, the workflow will be manually associated after it is deployed.

To demonstrate how association forms work, the workflow will simply show the value of one field submitted from the custom association form. Right-click the workflow and add a new project item by using the Workflow Association Form template. Visual Studio will add the form to the *Pages* module in the project and update the workflow's properties to point to the URL of the item. The ASPX page that is created for the association form is nearly complete because it will use the Workflow Services

JSOM to create the workflow history list and task list (if necessary), as well as the association. First, notice that within the *PlaceHolderMain* section there is a server control that's worth mentioning:

```
<WorkflowServices:WorkflowAssociationFormContextControl />
```

This control collects the input form controls from the HTTP POST submitted on the previous page, the one in which the user selects the workflow definition, task list, history list, and workflow start configuration. Without this, the association could not be created. The control simply adds a handful of hidden form controls on the page that are accessed by the JavaScript generated in this template. Scroll a little further down to find the core form within a table. By default, it includes a handful of form controls, but to simplify things, delete the two form controls and just leave the single *textarea* field control.

The form also includes a button that will call a JavaScript function on the page to trigger the association creation process. Scroll through the JavaScript to a section that creates a new variable called *metadata*. When you find it, change the key of the array item to **AssociationFormValue**:

```
var metadata = new Object();
// Get form input values and set workflow in-argument values
var strInputValue = document.getElementById("strInput").value;
if (strInputValue) {
    metadata['AssociationFormValue'] = strInputValue;
}
```

This block is collecting three form values and placing them in the *metadata* array. Remove the code block that creates *intInputValue* and *dateTimeInputValue* variables, because those were previously removed in an earlier step. Now scroll down to the comment *"Add new workflow association"*, past the code that creates a history list and task list if mandated on the previous form:

```
// Add new workflow association
var newSubscription = SP.WorkflowServices.WorkflowSubscription.newObject(context);
newSubscription.set_definitionId(definitionId);
newSubscription.set_eventSourceId(eventSourceId);
newSubscription.set_eventTypes(eventTypes);
newSubscription.set_name(workflowName);
for (var key in metadata) {
    newSubscription.setProperty(key, metadata[key]);
}
// Publish
wfManager.getWorkflowSubscriptionService().publishSubscriptionForList(newSubscription, listId);
```

This section uses the Workflow Service JSOM to do the following things:

1. Create a new workflow association, referred to in the API as a *subscription*.

2. Set the workflow definition ID of the association, which is the ID of the workflow developed in Visual Studio 2012.

3. Set the ID of the list or library the workflow is being associated with.

4. Set the start type or types for the workflow, such as *manual* or *automatic* when something is created or updated.

5. Set the name of the workflow to that specified by the user creating the association.

6. Walk through the contents of the metadata collection and set each property on the workflow.

7. Create the workflow subscription.

Notice that the only things that need to be modified are the form and form controls, and the section in which those values are collected and saved into the metadata array. The next step is to add an activity to the workflow itself to collect these properties being passed in.

Within the workflow, create a new variable named *AssociationFormValue* of type *string*. Next, add a *GetConfigurationValue* to the workflow and set the *Name* property equal to the name of the property being passed in from the form via the Workflow Services JSOM, and set the *Result* property to the local variable: *AssociationFormValue*. Now the workflow has access to the values passed in from the association form!

To test it, deploy the SharePoint-hosted app and, when the browser opens, navigate to the Announcement list. On the List tab on the ribbon, click the Workflow button. Click the Add A Workflow link. Select the custom workflow, give it a friendly name, and select the history and task lists. When the Next button is clicked, the custom form is displayed.

Initiation forms in SharePoint 2013

Initiation forms are used to collect some information from the user when a workflow is manually started. All the characteristics of an association form apply to initiation forms, including the fact that developers should use JavaScript only to implement business logic. The project item template in Visual Studio 2012 contains most of this script by default. One thing is important to keep in mind with respect to initiation forms: these forms are displayed only when a workflow is started manually. Workflows that start automatically when items are created or updated in a list, or that start programmatically, do not show the initiation form to the user. Your workflow should account for this, and if some information is required from the user, it is a good idea to also create an association form that enables the person creating the association to supply default values for the workflow.

Creating initiation forms

This walkthrough demonstrates creating a custom initiation form and using it to collect some information from the user when the workflow is started manually. Following the same setup process you used for the other workflows you built in Visual Studio 2012 in this chapter, create a new SharePoint-hosted app project with an Announcement list, and add a workflow that is associated with the Announcement list and starts manually.

Right-click the workflow and add a new project item by using the Workflow Initiation Form template. Visual Studio will add the form to the *Pages* module in the project and update the workflow's properties to point to the URL of the item. The .aspx page that is created for the initiation form, just like with the association form, is nearly complete because it will use the Workflow Services JSOM to start the workflow and pass in specific values.

Following the same process as the association form, find the form controls and remove the second *textarea* and datetime controls. Next, change the *strInput textarea* control to an input control. To make things a little interesting, add another control, the SharePoint server-side people picker:

```
<SharePoint:PeopleEditor runat="server" AllowEmpty="False"
                         ValidatorEnabled="False" MultiSelect="False" ID="peoplePicker" />
```

To make development a bit easier, add a reference to the included jQuery library to the head portion of the page, within the *PlaceHolderAdditionalPageHead* section, just after the *sp.workflowservices.js* reference.

Now, scroll down into the JavaScript code to the comment *"Set workflow in-arguments/initiation parameters"* section, which is where another array is created with all the things to send to the workflow. First, remove the two sections that are collecting the second *textarea* and datetime controls previously removed. Rename the parameter that is being passed in to **SomeRandomString**, and add some additional JavaScript that will get a reference to the people picker client-side control and extract the logon name of the selected user, as shown in the following code:

```
// get people picker value
var html = $("#ctl00_PlaceHolderMain_peoplePicker_upLevelDiv");
wfParams['UserLoginName'] = $("#divEntityData", html).attr("key");
// get string input
var strInputValue = document.getElementById("strInput").value;
if (strInputValue) {
 wfParams['SomeRandomString'] = strInputValue;
}
```

With the parameters selected, find the comment *"Get workflow subscription and then start the workflow"* further along in the JavaScript. This section obtains a reference to the Workflow Services Manager, the core component of the Workflow Services JSOM, in addition to references to the deployment and subscription services, which were covered earlier in this chapter, in the section "Workflow services CSOM and JSOM." This code then obtains a subscription (association) by using the *subscriptionID* that was passed, by SharePoint 2013, into the page via a value on the query string.

The code then, by using an instance of the workflow instance service, starts a workflow on a specific list item by passing in the workflow subscription, the ID of the item the workflow should be associated with, and a collection of the parameters from the form:

```
// Get workflow subscription and then start the workflow
var context = SP.ClientContext.get_current();
var wfManager = SP.WorkflowServices.WorkflowServicesManager.newObject(context,
  context.get_web());
var wfDeployService = wfManager.getWorkflowDeploymentService();
var subscriptionService = wfManager.getWorkflowSubscriptionService();

context.load(subscriptionService);
context.executeQueryAsync( function (sender, args) {
// Success
 var subscription = null;
 // Load the workflow subscription
 subscription = subscriptionService.getSubscription(subscriptionId);
```

```
    if (itemId != null && itemId != "") {
        // Start list workflow
        wfManager.getWorkflowInstanceService().startWorkflowOnListItem(subscription, itemId,
wfParams);
    } else {
        // Start site workflow
        wfManager.getWorkflowInstanceService().startWorkflow(subscription, wfParams);
    }
    context.executeQueryAsync(
        function (sender, args) { window.location = redirectUrl; },
        function (sender, args) { ... }
    )
});
```

The last step is to configure the workflow to collect these values being passed in. Within the workflow, add two input arguments for *SomeRandomString* and *UserLoginName*, both strings. The workflow engine and SharePoint will handle sending the form values into the workflow and linking them up with these arguments, which can then be used within the workflow for various use cases.

Summary

This chapter covered the new workflow platform in SharePoint 2013. It first explained how the architecture is very different in SharePoint with the addition of Workflow Manager and how this change benefits customers greatly. The chapter then explained the process for creating custom workflows both with SharePoint Designer 2013 and Visual Studio 2012. Next, the topics of custom tasks, custom outcomes, and how to add custom forms to custom workflows was covered. At this point, developers and experienced users alike should have a solid understanding of how things work and how to model simple or complex business processes by using the new workflow engine in SharePoint 2013.

CHAPTER 13

SharePoint search

Of all the components available in Microsoft SharePoint Server 2013, Enterprise Search has the highest profile and the greatest impact on users. Searching has become a normal part of everyday life. Users utilize web-based search engines such as Bing and Google for both personal and professional needs. Concepts such as keyword searching, advanced searching, and search links are familiar to everyone. In fact, Enterprise Search has become a primary entry point into SharePoint—the first place someone goes when trying to find information. If the search engine returns strong results, then users will be satisfied with SharePoint. On the other hand, poor search results can lead to negative opinions of SharePoint overall. Because Enterprise Search plays such a significant role in the success of SharePoint Server 2013, it is important to deploy, configure, and customize it correctly.

Fortunately, the search story in SharePoint 2013 is cleaner and more powerful than it was in previous versions. The story is cleaner because both FAST and Search Server have been eliminated from the products, leaving only SharePoint 2013 Foundation, SharePoint Server 2013 Standard, SharePoint Server 2013 Enterprise, and SharePoint Online as the available products. The search story is more powerful because FAST and SharePoint Search have been unified into a single platform with many new capabilities. Table 13-1 summarizes the functionality available in each version. Although this chapter will cover many of the capabilities listed in Table 13-1, keep in mind that the focus will be on extensibility points for developers. Furthermore, all of the material presented in this chapter assumes that you are working with SharePoint 2013 Enterprise.

TABLE 13-1 Search capabilities by version

Capability	Foundation	Standard	Enterprise	Online
Advanced content processing	Yes	Yes	Yes	No
Content Processing Enrichment	No	No	Yes	No
Content Search Web Part	No	No	Yes	No
Continuous crawl	Yes	Yes	Yes	No
Custom entity extraction	No	No	Yes	No
Deep links	No	Yes	Yes	Yes
Event-based relevancy	No	Yes	Yes	Yes
Expertise Search	Yes	Yes	Yes	Yes
Graphical refiners	No	Yes	Yes	Yes
Hybrid search	Yes	Yes	Yes	Yes

Capability	Foundation	Standard	Enterprise	Online
Managed navigation	No	Yes	Yes	Yes
Phonetic name matching	Yes	Yes	Yes	Yes
Query rules—add promoted results	No	Yes	Yes	Yes
Query rules—advanced actions	No	No	Yes	Yes
Query spelling correction	Yes	Yes	Yes	Yes
Query suggestions	No	Yes	Yes	Yes
Query throttling	No	Yes	Yes	Yes
Quick preview	Yes	Yes	Yes	Yes
Recommendations	No	Yes	Yes	Yes
Refiners	Yes	Yes	Yes	No
RESTful query API	Yes	Yes	Yes	Yes
Result sources	Yes	Yes	Yes	Yes
Search connector framework	No	No	Yes	No
Search results sorting	Yes	Yes	Yes	Yes
Search vertical: "Conversations"	No	Yes	Yes	Yes
Search vertical: "People"	No	Yes	Yes	Yes
Search vertical: "Video"	No	No	Yes	Yes
Tunable relevancy	No	No	Yes	No

Introducing search-based applications

Traditionally, search engines have been used to return results for a specific user request as a list ranked by relevance. The results might provide some basic information, such as the title of a document or the date of a webpage, along with a description, but users typically have had to follow links to determine whether the item was of interest. More recently, however, this paradigm is being replaced with the concept of a search-based application. A search-based application is a custom application that is written around a search engine.

The value of a search-based application is that it presents search results in an appropriate form and allows the user to operate on the results directly. A good example of a search-based application is the Bing video search. Figure 13-1 shows the results of searching for the term *SharePoint 2013 Development*. You can tell that the search results are returned as videos that can be played directly from the page, thus making it significantly easier to locate items of interest.

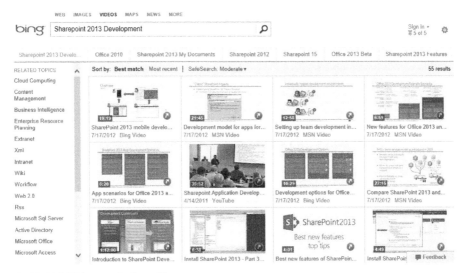

FIGURE 13-1 Video results from Bing

Although the default search results page in SharePoint still displays items in a simple list, you will find that the customization opportunities tend to support the creation of search-based applications. These customizations include the ability to modify the sorting and ranking, changing the way search results appear on the page, and creating completely custom solutions against the search object model. The concept of search-based applications is important to keep in mind as you work through this chapter. Instead of simply returning items from a search, give consideration to how the results appear and what operations can be performed. Then think about how the customizations presented in this chapter come into play.

As a quick example of a search-based application in SharePoint, consider the management of tasks for users. Task lists can be created in any site within SharePoint, so it is often the case that an individual is assigned tasks in multiple sites. In many cases, a users might not even know that he has been assigned a particular task. Setting alerts on all the lists is unmanageable because the notifications become a form of internal spam. Thus, users are sometimes left unable to effectively manage their tasks.

In the past, developers have often created "rollups" to solve this problem. Rollup solutions go out to all sites looking for tasks and then display them in a single master list to the user. The problem with this, however, is that it can be very CPU-intensive if done incorrectly. A search-based solution is a better idea.

Instead of a single master list of tasks, imagine that a user goes to a specialized Search Center that runs a query to return all the task items for the current user sorted by due date. In addition, the user can view the key information for each task. The user could also operate on the task directly in the search results by changing its status or editing the description. This is a search-based solution that is truly useful to a user. Figure 13-2 shows such a solution created in SharePoint 2013. This solution is discussed in more detail in the section "Extending the Search Center" later in this chapter.

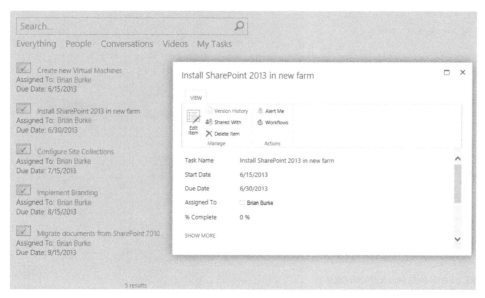

FIGURE 13-2 A search-based application for managing tasks

Understanding search architecture

The search architecture for SharePoint Server 2013 is complex. It includes components for crawling, indexing content, administration, and executing search queries. Figure 13-3 shows a block diagram of the search architecture. Components in the diagram represented in darker shades are not extensible by developers. Components represented in lighter shades represent extensibility points covered in this chapter.

In the center of the search architecture is the Search Service Application (SSA). The SSA is the primary administrative interface for search and is one of the many shared services available in SharePoint Server 2013. You can create and share multiple instances of the SSA across farms just like any other service application. From the Central Administration website, you can access the SSA by selecting Manage Service Applications. From the list of service applications, you can select the SSA, set its properties, designate administrators, and perform search administration.

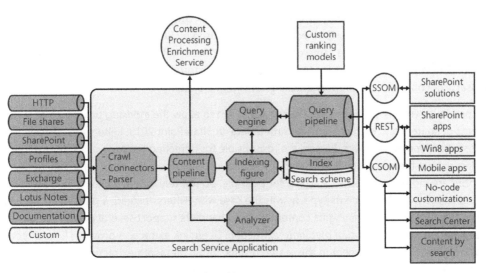

FIGURE 13-3 SharePoint Server 2013 search architecture

Understanding the indexing process

The indexing process is responsible for building the index file. The index file contains *crawled properties* from content sources, along with access control lists (ACL) that ensure that search results display only content for which the user has rights. The process of building the index file involves crawling designated content sources. A content source is a repository that can be searched. Content sources can be SharePoint sites, websites, external file systems, Microsoft Exchange Server public folders, Business Connectivity Services (BCS) External Systems, or other custom repositories. New content sources are defined within the SSA.

SharePoint 2013 supports three different kinds of crawls: full, incremental, and continuous. A full crawl indexes the entire content source whether or not specific items have changed since the last crawl. An incremental crawl indexes only those items that have changed based on either a time stamp or a change log. A continuous crawl is an option that can be used instead of an incremental crawl for any specified content source.

A continuous crawl, as the name implies, indexes a content source continuously. The purpose of the continuous crawl is to achieve maximum freshness. Incremental crawls cannot run in parallel, but continuous crawls can. Parallel indexing allows continuous crawling to achieve a level of freshness not possible with incremental crawls.

Connecting and parsing

The crawler gains access to content sources through *connectors*. SharePoint 2013 ships with several out-of-the-box connectors, which allow search to index many common repositories, as shown earlier in Figure 13-3. If you have a custom repository, however, you will need to build a Microsoft .NET

Assembly Connector to index that repository. Chapter 12, "SharePoint workflows," presented the fundamentals of .NET Assembly Connectors, which are used by BCS to connect with External Systems. The indexing process uses these same components to connect with content sources. The section "Creating .NET Assembly Connectors for search" later in this chapter covers the additional development necessary for connectors to support indexing an External System.

In previous versions of SharePoint, IFilters were used to allow the indexing process to access the contents of an item and extract associated metadata. In SharePoint 2013, IFilters are partially replaced by *parsers* and *format handlers*. Parsers are responsible for detecting the type of an item, and format handlers extract the metadata. Parsers and format handlers perform the same basic function as an IFilter but are more sophisticated. Parsers, for example, do not rely on the file extension associated with a document to determine its type, as was the case with IFilters. Instead, a parser can identify the type of a document by examining its content. Format handlers support several powerful features such as *deep link extraction* and *visual metadata extraction*. Deep link extraction provides links directly to major subsections of a document in the search results. Visual metadata extraction extracts key metadata such as titles, authors, and dates directly from the document content in case those values are incorrectly set in the document metadata.

Enhancing metadata

The processing of crawled items is represented in Figure 13-3 by the content pipeline component. In SharePoint 2013, developers are able to extend the content pipeline with a custom Content Processing Enrichment Service (CPES). The CPES is a custom web service that accepts a collection of document metadata properties. Within the CPES, this collection can be modified in order to enhance the metadata associated with an item. Such enhancement supports data cleansing, entity extraction, classification, and tagging.

Data cleansing allows for the normalization of data across crawled items. As an example, consider a *company* property, which is set manually by users. If the company in question were Microsoft, it would not be uncommon for various users to set the metadata value to be *Microsoft, Microsoft Corporation*, or even the ticker symbol *MSFT*. In this case, the CPES could normalize all of these values to be *Microsoft Corporation*.

Entity extraction allows new properties to be added to an item. In the case in the previous paragraph, a new property, *ticker*, could be added to the item through the CPES. That property could then be set to *MSFT*, allowing people to search for documents by ticker symbol as well as company name.

Classification and tagging also relies on the ability to add new properties, but for the purpose of classifying a document based on a set of rules. Additional tags could also be added based on a taxonomy. All of this makes the documents easier to find in search.

Analyzing searches

The analyzer component is used to improve the quality of search results. The analyzer performs click analysis on search results to determine the most relevant results from a specific query. The click analysis is fed back into the content pipeline to enhance the information associated with a crawled item.

Understanding the query process

After the index file is created, it can be used to support query execution. Query execution typically begins when a user navigates to the Search Center and enters a query, but a query can also be issued from an app or other customization. Regardless of whether the query comes from an out-of-the-box component or a custom component, it interfaces with the query pipeline through one of the available application programming interfaces (APIs): the server-side object model (SSOM), the client-side object model (CSOM), or the Representational State Transfer (REST) interface.

Creating managed properties

The issued search query can be a simple text keyword or a search against *managed properties*. Managed properties simplify the search schema and provide more control over how metadata is used in search. Managed properties are defined at the tenant, SSA, or site. To use managed properties in SharePoint Online, start in the SharePoint Admin Center and click Search | Manage Search Schema. For SSA, in Central Administration, you would start in the Search Service Application and click Search Schema. In a site, you would start on the Site Settings page and click Schema.

Managed properties are mapped to one or more crawled properties. Mapping a managed property to multiple crawled properties is important because different repositories use different field names to represent the same data. For example, imagine that you have three different document repositories. The first repository uses the field name *Title* for the document title. The second repository uses a *Name* field, but that field actually contains a document title. The third repository uses a field called *DOCTTL* for the title. When performing a search, end users cannot be expected to know about these fields. So a single managed property named *Title* is created and mapped to all three of the crawled properties. Now users can simply ask for any document containing the word *Training* in its title, and search will query all three underlying crawled properties.

Managed properties also have attributes that control the way they are used in search. These attributes allow for the managed property to be used for such things as querying, refining, sorting, or other purposes. Table 13-2 lists the various attributes of managed properties and their purpose.

TABLE 13-2 Managed property attributes

Attribute	Purpose
Searchable	Allows the managed property to be searched by using a simple keyword (for example, *Training*)
Queryable	Allows the managed property to be used in a Keyword Query Language (KQL) query (for example, *Title:Training*)
Retrievable	Allows the managed property to be returned as a field to the search results page
Refinable	Allows the managed property to be used as a refiner in search results
Sortable	Allows the managed property to be used for sorting search results

Introduction to ranking models

When the user issues a search, the query is sent to the query engine through the query pipeline. Within the query pipeline, ranking models are applied to order the returned results. Although SharePoint has several out-of-the-box ranking models, developers can affect the query results by creating a custom ranking model. Custom ranking models are used to give additional weight to certain managed properties. This can be useful when the standard ranking models are not pushing important items far enough to the top. However, custom ranking models should be used sparingly, because they tend to be created in such a way as to force certain items to the top of the results while burying other potentially important items much deeper.

Executing queries

The search query is executed by the query engine against the managed properties and index. However, SharePoint does not run the query against the entire index. Instead, it uses a *result source* to specify the scope of the query. Result sources are new to SharePoint 2013 and are a new way to define a scope by using query language. Result sources are covered in more detail in the section "Creating result sources" later in this chapter.

Understanding Keyword Query Language

SharePoint 2013 supports two different languages for issuing queries: FAST Query Language (FQL) and Keyword Query Language (KQL). Previous versions of SharePoint also supported a third query language known as SQL query. FQL is the language used with the FAST search product. Though FQL has been carried over to SharePoint 2013, Microsoft does not recommend teaching it to end users or using it in development. The SQL query language has been completely removed from SharePoint 2013, and any solutions that relied on this query language must be rewritten. This leaves KQL as the query language of choice for both end users and developers.

KQL queries can be entered directly in the Search Center by an end user, appended to a Search Center URL, used in the definition of result sources, or issued programmatically to any of the search APIs. In all cases, the query is formed in exactly the same way: a KQL query consists of one or more free-text terms and managed property restrictions.

Issuing free-text queries in KQL causes the search engine to look in the index for matching terms. These terms include text from the body of documents as well as the value   for any managed property whose *Searchable* attribute is *true*. Free-text queries are case-insensitive and limited to 2,048 characters. Free-text queries support wildcarding the end of a term by using the asterisk (*) as well as complete phrases by surrounding terms with double quotes ("). Table 13-3 shows some examples of free-text queries.

TABLE 13-3 Free-text queries

Query	Description
Microsoft	Searches for items containing the term Microsoft in the index and managed properties marked as *Searchable*
Microsoft Training	Searches for items containing both the words Microsoft AND Training, but not in any particular order
"Microsoft Training"	Searches for items containing the exact phrase Microsoft Training
Micro*	Searches for items containing terms that begin with Micro

Managed properties can be used in conjunction with free-text or alone to form a query. When managed properties are used, the query is formed by specifying the name of a managed property, followed by an operator, followed by a value (for example, *Title=SharePoint*). A managed property must have its *Queryable* attribute set to *true* before it can be used in a KQL query. Table 13-4 lists the operators that can be used with managed properties.

TABLE 13-4 Managed property operators

Operator	Description	Example
property:value	Searches for items whose property contains the specified value	*Title:SharePoint*
property=value	Searches for items whose property equals the specified value	*FileExtension=docx*
property<>value	Searches for items whose property does not equal the specified value	*FileExtension<>pdf*
property>value	Searches for items whose property is greater than the specified value	*Created>1/1/2013*
property>=value	Searches for items whose property is greater than or equal to the specified value	*LastModifiedTime>=1/1/2013*
property<value	Searches for items whose property is less than the specified value	*Created<1/1/2013*
property<=value	Searches for items whose property is less than or equal to the specified value	*LastModifiedTime<=1/1/2013*
property=value1..value2	Searches for items whose property falls in the specified range	*LastModifiedTime=1/1/2012..1/1/2013*

Multiple sets of free text and managed property elements can be combined when forming a query. KQL supports several operators, including Boolean operators, proximity operators, synonym operators, and ranking operators. Additionally, parentheses can be used in the query to group the operations. Table 13-5 lists the various operators for use with multiple sets of query elements.

TABLE 13-5 Multiple managed property operators

Operator	Description	Example
element AND element *element + element*	Searches for items where both elements are true.	*Title:Training AND Created>1/1/2012* *Title:Training + Created>1/1/2012*
element OR element	Searches for items where either element is true.	*Title:Training OR Title:SharePoint*
NOT element *-element*	Searches for items where the element is false.	*NOT FileExtension=docx* *-FileExtension=docx*
element NEAR(x) element	Searches for items where the elements are in close proximity without regard for the order. The *x* parameter specifies the maximum distance between the elements.	*App NEAR(5) JavaScript*
element ONEAR(x) element	Searches for items where the elements are in close proximity while preserving the order. The *x* parameter specifies the maximum distance between the elements.	*App ONEAR(5) JavaScript*
WORDS(element, element))	Searches in the same way as the OR operator, but ranks the results as if the elements specified were exactly the same term. This raises the relevancy of items containing both terms.	*WORDS(Microsoft, MSFT)*
element1 XRANK element2	Searches for items matching *element1*, then boosts the items matching *element2* to the top of the results. There are several complex factors involved in the rank boost, which can be explored further at the following URL: *http://msdn.microsoft.com/en-us/library/ ee558911.aspx*.	*"Training" XRANK(cb=100, rb=0.4, pb=0.4, avgb=0.4, stdb=0.4, nb=0.4, n=200) FileExtension=docx*

Although any managed property whose *Searchable* or *Queryable* attribute is *true* can be used in KQL, there are a few critical managed properties that stand out as particularly useful. Both end users and developers will benefit from knowing these managed properties. Table 13-6 lists the key managed properties, describes them, and shows some examples.

TABLE 13-6 Key managed properties

Property	Description	Example
Title	Searches for items with a specified title	*Title:SharePoint*
Author	Searches for the author of an item	*Author:Cox*
Created	Searches for the date an item was created	*Created=1/1/2012..1/1/2013*
LastModifiedTime	Searches for the date an item was modified	*LastModifiedTime>1/1/2012*
IsDocument	Specifies whether search results should include only documents	*"SharePoint" IsDocument:1*
FileExtension	Specifies the file extension to search for	*FileExtension=docx*
LastName	Searches for a person by last name	*LastName:C**
ContentClass	Searches for items based on their type	ContentClass:STS_Site Content_Class:STS_Web ContentClass:STS_ListItem_Tasks ContentClass:STS_ListItem_Events
Path	Searches for items based on a URL location	Path:"http://dev.wingtiptoys.com/ lists/contacts"

Creating no-code customizations

Although SharePoint 2013 provides complete support for developing apps and solutions, many common customizations simply don't require writing code anymore. Furthermore, most search customizations do not even require the use of the SharePoint Designer. Microsoft has done a particularly good job in this release of supporting search customizations directly in the browser. Therefore, developers should thoroughly understand the possibilities for no-code customizations before proceeding with code-based development.

Creating simple link queries

Developers often overlook the fact that the out-of-the-box Search Center is URL accessible. This means that you can issue queries to the Search Center by constructing a URL containing KQL. When this idea is coupled with an out-of-the-box links list, powerfully simple search customizations can be created. As an example, consider the A though Z employee directory shown in Figure 13-4.

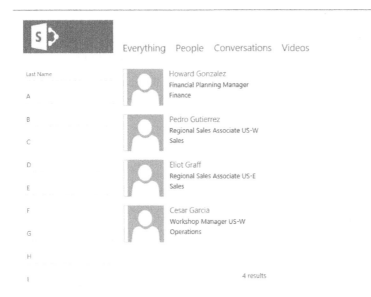

FIGURE 13-4 An employee directory made from a simple list of links

The directory solution was created by first filling a links list with links to the people search in the Search Center. Each link in the list carries a KQL query for the last name (such as *LastName:C**). For example, the link for people whose last name starts with *C* looks like the following, where the KQL is encoded into the *k* parameter:

http://intranet.wingtiptoys.com/SearchCenter/Pages/PeopleResults.aspx?k=LastName%3AC%2A

After creating the list of links for each letter in the alphabet, the list view was altered to hide every field except the URL. The URL field was then renamed to *Last Name*. Finally, the list was added as a Web Part to the people search page. This is an incredibly simple solution that satisfies a very common request quite elegantly. Many other similar solutions can be created by using this approach.

Extending the Search Center

The Search Center in SharePoint 2013 is the hub for search-based applications. Thus you will find that extending the Search Center to include your custom search-based applications makes good sense. You will also find that these solutions can be created almost entirely within the browser. Though this section explains the components and techniques necessary to extend the Search Center, it is important to point out that the concepts presented are used in more advanced solutions as well. To support the explanation of these concepts, this section will explain how to create the task-management solution shown earlier in Figure 13-2.

Adding pages to search navigation

The out-of-the-box Search Center consists of several pages that allow searching against different results sources: Everything, People, Conversations, and Video. Each source in the Search Center has a dedicated page for displaying search results. In order to extend the Search Center, you will need to add a new page to the Search Center navigation.

New pages are created and added directly in the Search Center site. To create a new page, on the Site Contents page, locate the Pages document library. From this library, you can create new search results pages to extend the Search Center. Figure 13-5 shows the Create Page form.

After the new search results page is created, it can be added to the Search Center navigation. To do so, starting on the Site Settings page, click Search Settings in the Search area. From here, you can add new nodes to the Search Center, as shown in Figure 13-6.

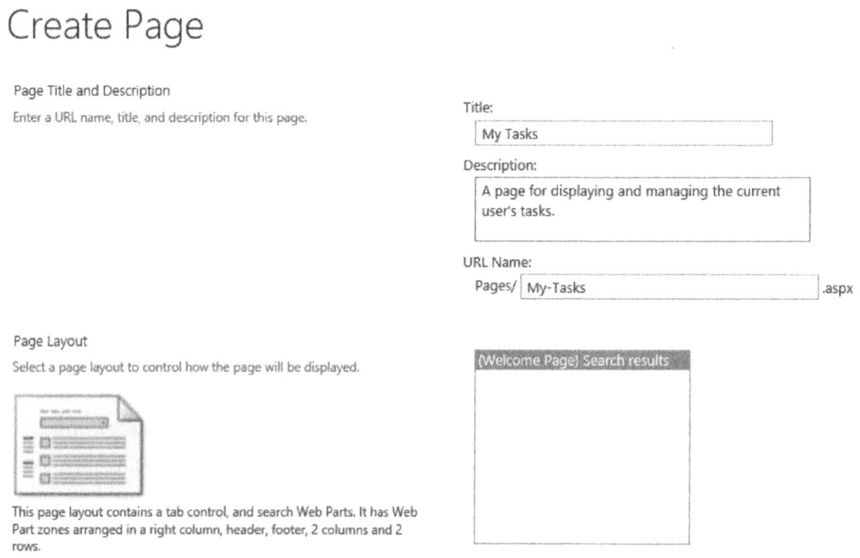

Create Page

Page Title and Description
Enter a URL name, title, and description for this page.

Title:

My Tasks

Description:

A page for displaying and managing the current user's tasks.

URL Name:

Pages/ My-Tasks .aspx

Page Layout
Select a page layout to control how the page will be displayed.

(Welcome Page) Search results

This page layout contains a tab control, and search Web Parts. It has Web Part zones arranged in a right column, header, footer, 2 columns and 2 rows.

FIGURE 13-5 Creating new search results pages

Search Navigation allows users to move quickly between search experiences listed in the Navigation. Navigation is displayed in the Quick Launch control on search pages, and can also be shown as a drop-down menu from the search box.

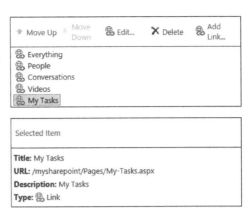

FIGURE 13-6 Adding pages to the Search Center navigation

Creating result sources

After you have added a page to the Search Center navigation, you will find that the new search page works, but that it yields the same results as the Everything page. In order to display custom results, you must create a new result source. Result sources can be defined in the tenant, SSA, site collection, or site. In SharePoint Online, you would start in the SharePoint Admin Center and click Search | Manage Result Sources. In Central Administration, you would start in the Search Service Application and click Result Sources. In a site collection or site, you would start on the Site Settings page and click Result Sources. The result source should be created at the level appropriate for the scope of its intended use.

When a new result source is created, you must first select one of four indexes as a starting point: Local SharePoint, Remote SharePoint, OpenSearch, or Exchange. Local SharePoint refers to the index associated with the current SharePoint farm. Remote SharePoint refers to the index associated with a different SharePoint farm. OpenSearch refers to the index associated with a non-SharePoint search engine that supports OpenSearch. Exchange refers to a Microsoft Exchange server.

When the index is selected, you can define a *query transform* to define the new result source. A query transform uses KQL to define a subset of the index to include in the result source. Clicking the Launch Query Builder button opens a dialog box for defining the query transform. This dialog has three tabs: Basics, Sorting, and Test. The Basics tab allows you to define KQL by using a combination of placeholder tokens and managed properties. The Sorting tab allows you to specify the sort order of the results by using managed properties. The Test tab allows you to test the result source definition. Figure 13-7 shows the Basics tab defining the result source to return tasks for the current user.

BASICS   SORTING   TEST

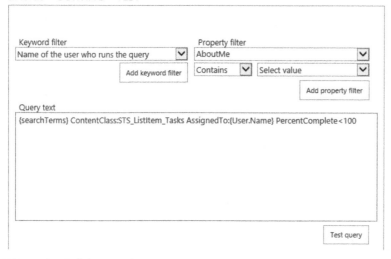

FIGURE 13-7 Defining a result source

The Keyword Filter list contains all of the possible tokens for use in the result source definition. Table 13-7 lists the available tokens and provides a description of each. The Property Filter list contains the names of all the managed properties marked as *Searchable* or *Queryable*. Note that you may have to create several managed properties before you can properly define a result source. In the example, the *PercentComplete* and *DueDate* managed properties had to be created to define the result source membership and sort order, respectively.

TABLE 13-7 Query tokens

Token	Description
{CurrentDisplayLanguage}	The current display language based on MUI in ll-cc format
{CurrentDisplayLCID}	The numeric value of the current display language based on MUI in ll-cc format
{List}	The URL of the current list
{List.<property>}	Any property of the current list
{ListItem}	The URL of the current list item
{ListItem.<property>}	Any property of the current list item
{Page.<FieldName>}	The value of a field on the page from which the query was issued
{Page.URL}	The URL of the page from which the query was issued
{Page.UsageAnalyticsId}	The item ID for Usage Analytics
{QueryString.<ParameterName>}	A query string parameter from the URL of a page specified by name
{Request.<PropertyName}	A value from the current HTTP request—for example, {Request.RawUrl}
{SearchBoxQuery}	The query value entered into a search box on a page

Token	Description
{SearchTerms}	The query value entered into the search box on a page with all query transformations applied
{Site.ID}	The GUID of the site from which the query was issued
{Site.LCID}	The numeric value of the locale in the site from which the query was issued
{Site.Locale}	The language of the site from which the query was issued in ll-cc format—for example, en-us
{Site.<property>}	Any property from the property bag of the SPWeb from which the query was issued
{Site.URL}	The URL of the site from which the query was issued
{SiteCollection.ID}	The GUID of the root web from the site collection from which the query was issued
{SiteCollection.LCID}	The numeric value of the locale in the site collection from which the query was issued
{SiteCollection.Locale}	The language of the site collection from which the query was issued
{SiteCollection.<property>}	Any property from the property bag of the root SPWeb
{SiteCollection.URL}	The URL of site collection from which the query was issued
{Term.ID}	The GUID of the current site navigation node with a prefix of #0
{Term.IDWithChildren}	The GUID of the current site navigation node with a prefix of #
{Term.Name}	The label of the site navigation node
{Term.<property>}	Any property from the property bag of the term
{TermSet.ID}	The GUID of the term set used for current site navigation
{TermSet.Name}	The label of the term set used for current site navigation
{Today+/- <integer>}	A date calculated from the date when the query is issued
{URLToken.<integer>}	A portion of the URL of a page specified in sequential order
{User.Email}	The email address of the user who issued the query
{User.LCID}	The numeric value of the locale as defined in the profile of the user who issued the query
{User.Name}	The display name of the user who issued the query
{User.PreferredContentLanguage}	The Preferred Content Language specified in the profile of the user who issued the query
{User.PreferredDisplayLanguage}	The Display Content Language as specified in the profile of the user who issued the query
{User.<property>}	Any property from the user profile of the user who issued the query
{User.SID}	The SID of the user who issued the query

When the new result source is created, it can be used with the new page that was added to the Search Center. Each search results page in the Search Center hosts four Web Parts: Refinement, Search Box, Search Navigation, and Search Results. In order to use the new result source, you must edit the properties for the Search Results Web Part. Clicking the Change Query button in the Web Part properties opens a dialog box that is similar to the one used in creating the result source, but with more functionality.

The Basics tab allows you to select the result source to be used by the Web Part. On this tab, you would select the new result source you just created. Note that you can narrow the results further in this tab by using additional tokens and managed properties. This allows you to create result sources that are more generalized and rely on each consuming Web Part to further define them for a specific purpose. After the new result source is set, the associated search result page will only return items from that source.

Displaying search results

When extending the Search Center, you will undoubtedly want to change the way search results are displayed based on the type of data. In the example of a user's tasks shown earlier in Figure 13-2, the task tile, responsible person, and due date are shown, with a nice icon next to each item. Furthermore, clicking any item opens a dialog box that allows the user to edit the task item. This type of functionality is accomplished by using *result types* and *display templates*.

Result types can be defined in a site collection or site by clicking Result Types on the Site Settings page. When creating a new result type, you must associate it with a particular result source. You can also choose to associate it with a specific type of content so that a single result source can be associated with several different result types. Finally, you select the display template to be used with the result type. In this way, you can change the way an item appears in search results based on the rules defined for the result types.

SharePoint 2013 has several out-of-the-box display templates defined, but you will likely want to create your own. Display templates are created as HTML files that use special markup syntax to define placeholders for managed properties. These HTML files are saved into the Master Page Gallery for use by the Search Results Web Part. The Master Page Gallery has different folders for organizing the display templates, but you can locate all of the display templates for search by starting at the Site Settings page and clicking Master Pages and Page Layouts | Display Templates | Search.

When creating a custom display template, you should always start with an existing template. The Item_Default.html file represents the default display template for search results. To create a custom display template, download this file from the Master Page Gallery and rename it to something appropriate. In the case of the example, it was renamed to Task_Default.html. After renaming it, you can open it in Microsoft Visual Studio for editing.

The first task in creating a custom display template is to add the managed properties that the template will need to successfully render. Defining the managed properties is done in the *mso:ManagedPropertyMapping* element by using a format that maps a markup name to the property name. The simplest way to approach this is to use the same name for both parts, as shown in the following code:

```
<mso:ManagedPropertyMapping msdt:dt="string">
'Title':'Title','Path':'Path','Description':'Description',
'AssignedTo':'AssignedTo','DueDate':'DueDate'
</mso:ManagedPropertyMapping>
```

After the managed properties are defined, you can use them in the markup associated with the display template. The basic approach is to include them in the generated HTML by surrounding them with the delimiting strings _# and =#_. This allows you to build up an HTML template that will substitute in the values of the managed property for each item in the results. The following code shows how this is done for the example solution:

```
<h3>
  <img src="/_layouts/images/icon_tasklist.gif" alt="Task"/>
  <a title="Open task" style="cursor:pointer" href="#">_#=ctx.CurrentItem.Title=#_</a><br />
  <span>Assigned To: _#=ctx.CurrentItem.AssignedTo=#_</span><br />
</h3>
<div id="_#= $htmlEncode(hoverId) =#_" class="ms-srch-hover-outerContainer"></div>
```

In addition to using the managed properties in the HTML, you can also call to custom JavaScript functions defined in the markup. These custom functions must be defined between the delimiting strings <!--#_ and _#-->. The following code shows a date formatting and style function used in the example:

```
<!--#_
  getFormattedDate = function() {
    var d = new Date(ctx.CurrentItem.DueDate);
    return (d.getMonth() + 1) + "/" + d.getDate() + "/" + d.getFullYear();
  };

  getDueDateStyle = function() {
    var d1 = new Date(ctx.CurrentItem.DueDate);
    var d2 = new Date();
    if(d2>d1)
    return 'color:red';
    else
      return 'color:black';
    };
_#-->
```

Notice how the *getFormattedDate* and *getDueDateStyle* functions refer to the *ctx.CurrentItem* object. This object represents the current item in the search results. The function is called once for each item in the search results, and the call must be included in the markup surrounded by the delimiting strings _#= and =#_ as shown in the following code:

```
<span style="_#=getDueDateStyle()=#_">Due Date: _#=getFormattedDate()=#_</span>
```

The JavaScript functions included in the display template markup should not be confused with JavaScript you want to inject into the search results page. You can include references to JavaScript in the template you create by using the *$includeScript* function to register an external library. The following code shows an example:

```
$includeScript(this.url, "~sitecollection/SiteAssets/custom.js");
```

Note that it is also possible to inject JavaScript by writing it directly in the action element attributes, such as *onclick*. Though this approach can quickly become unwieldy, it does offer the powerful ability to substitute managed property values into the JavaScript code. In the example, the following JavaScript is used to open a task item for editing when it is clicked in the search results page:

```
<a title="Open task" style="cursor:pointer" href="#" onclick="
var title='_#=ctx.CurrentItem.Title=#_';
var path='_#=ctx.CurrentItem.Path=#_';
SP.SOD.executeFunc('sp.ui.dialog.js', null, function () {
  SP.UI.ModalDialog.showModalDialog({
    width: 600, height: 338, allowMaximize: true, title: title, url: path,
    dialogReturnValueCallback: function (dialogResult, returnValue) {
      SP.UI.ModalDialog.RefreshPage(SP.UI.DialogResult.OK); }
  });
});
">_#=ctx.CurrentItem.Title=#_</a>
```

Finally, if you would like to run some JavaScript after all of the display template processing is complete, you can use the *OnPostRender* method. This method can invoke a function contained in the custom JavaScript library you registered earlier. Just ensure that the following code appears first in the display template before any other code:

```
<!--#_
  ctx.OnPostRender = [];
  ctx.OnPostRender.push(function(){ CustomMethodCall() });
_#-->
```

When the display template is complete, it must be uploaded to the Master Page Gallery before it can be used. Simply upload the HTML file to the same folder where the other search display templates are located. Upon uploading, SharePoint will automatically generate a JavaScript file with the same name as the template. This JavaScript file is the one that is actually used by SharePoint, but the developer simply focuses on the HTML file, which provides a reasonable experience for customizing templates. After the display template is uploaded, it can be associated with a result type. Finally, you can edit the Search Results Web Part to use the defined result type, which will in turn use the associated display template for rendering.

Defining query rules

Query rules allow you to add *promoted results*, add a *result block*, or change the user's issued query based on a condition such as the terms contained in a search query. A promoted result allows you to add a new link that will show up at the top of the search results just like a best bet in previous versions of SharePoint. Result blocks execute a secondary search query but display the results in a block along with the original query results. This allows you to call out related or special items for attention. Changing the user's query allows you to modify or completely change the issued query.

Query rules can be defined in the tenant, SSA, site collection, or site. To define a query rule, in SharePoint Online, start in the SharePoint Admin Center and click Search | Manage Query Rules. In Central Administration, start in the Search Service Application and click Result Rules. In a site collection or site, start on the Site Settings page and click Query Rules. When you create a query rule, you specify the triggering condition and the responding action. You can also specify the dates during which the rule is active. Setting dates for a rule to be active makes sense when you want to promote results for a period of time, such as when items go on sale.

For the example task management solution, three query rules were created named *past, present,* and *future.* The idea behind these query rules was to allow the end user to enter one of the terms and easily search for overdue tasks, tasks due in the next 30 days, or tasks due more than 30 days from now, respectively. Each query rule uses the condition *Query Matches Keyword Exactly.* The associated action is *Change ranked results by changing the query.* If the term *past* is entered, the query is changed to *DueDate<{Today}.* If the term *present* is entered, the query is changed to *DueDate>{Today} AND DueDate<{Today+30}.* If the term *future* is entered, the query is changed to *DueDate>{Today+30}.*

Adding refiners

Managed properties whose *Refinable* attribute is set to *true* can be used as the basis for a refiner in the Search Center. The Refinement Web Part provides a configuration dialog box that lets you choose the refiners to be used with the search results. Like result types, refiners also use display templates to control how the refinement information is presented. SharePoint 2013 provides several display templates for refiners, which are located in the Master Page Gallery | Display Templates | Filters folder. These display templates can be selected when you are configuring the Refinement Web Part, as shown in Figure 13-8.

FIGURE 13-8 Configuring refiners in the Refinement Web Part

Along with managed properties, refiners can also be defined by using Managed Metadata. Managed Metadata refiners are primarily used in the Web Content Management system when you are using a list as a catalog to drive site content. Web Content Management is covered in Chapter 14, "SharePoint Enterprise Content Management."

Exporting search customizations

Although creating search-based applications directly in the browser is powerful and convenient, the production environment is not the place to develop these applications. As with all development, these applications should be created in a development environment and verified in a staging environment before being moved to production. To support migrating the applications, SharePoint 2013 provides the ability to export and import search settings.

Exporting and importing can be done through the Site Settings page by clicking Configuration Import or Configuration Export under the Search heading. Exporting search configurations produces an XML file with information about result sources, result types, query rules, and managed properties. Unfortunately, the export file does not contain information about master pages, display templates, and Web Parts, which must be migrated separately.

In addition to using the export capability to migrate between environments, you can also use the exported search settings within a search-based app. In Visual Studio 2012, you can add a new Search Configuration item, which will allow you to import the search settings XML file into an app project. The purpose of importing the search settings XML file is to allow your app to use those settings when it is installed in a different farm. Suppose your app, for example, needs a certain result source defined in order to function. Including a search settings XML file will allow that to happen.

Apps that include search settings XML files can choose to import the settings only into the app web or the hosting site collection. Importing into the app web is a simple matter of including the search settings XML file in the app. Importing into the site collection, however, requires two modifications. First, the app must request full control over the site collection in the app manifest. Second, the search settings XML file must be edited so that the *<DeployToParent>* element has a value of *true*. Now, when the app is installed, the search settings will be imported into the hosting site collection.

One thing to note about this capability—it does not support importing any managed properties. Even though the managed properties will be included in the search settings XML file, they will not be imported; the tools simply don't support managed properties in this release.

Using the Content Search Web Part

The Content Search Web Part (CSWP) is new to SharePoint 2013 and allows search results to be displayed on any page in a site. The CSWP works a lot like the Search Results Web Part in that it uses result sources, result types, and display templates to generate search results. The CSWP keeps its templates in the Master Page Gallery in the Content Web Parts folder. Here you'll find two types of templates: control and item. Control templates are run once and generate the beginning and end of the display. Item templates are run once for each item in the search results and are similar to the display templates used by the Search Results Web Part.

The difference between the CSWP and the standard Search Results Web Part is that the CSWP provides a few more out-of-the-box configurations so that it is easier for an end user to set up without having to create custom display templates. Both control and item templates are selectable within the properties pane for the CSWP. Additionally, managed properties can be mapped to placeholders in the template directly in the property pane.

Finally, the CSWP plays a big role in creating search-driven sites in the Web Content Management workload. This capability is covered in detail in Chapter 14.

Using the client-side API

When creating search-based apps, you can use either the REST or CSOM API to execute searches. These interfaces can be used from either JavaScript or C# just like any of the other client-side endpoints. As discussed in Chapter 5, "Client-side programming," the choice is really based on the architecture of your app.

Using the REST API

SharePoint 2013 provides three RESTful endpoints to execute queries and return suggestions. By using these endpoints, you can create sophisticated search-based apps. Table 13-8 describes the available search endpoints.

TABLE 13-8 Search REST endpoints

Endpoint	Description
http://[host]/[site]/_api/search/query	Used to run search queries by using HTTP GET
http://[host]/[site]/_api/search/postquery	Used to run search queries by using HTTP POST to overcome URL length limitations
http://[host]/[site]/_api/search/suggest	Used to retrieve query suggestions by using HTTP GET

To use the search REST API, an app must make a permission request, and that request must be granted during app installation. The required permission request is formatted similar to any other permission request, and you can access it in Visual Studio by using the designer associated with the app manifest. The following code shows the underlying XML that forms the requested permission:

```
<AppPermissionRequests>
  <AppPermissionRequest Scope="http://sharepoint/search" Right="QueryAsUserIgnoreAppPrincipal" />
</AppPermissionRequests>
```

The simplest way to run a query against the REST API is to pass a keyword query. You do this by setting the value of the *querytext* parameter in the RESTful Uniform Resource Identifier (URI). You can use this approach for either the *query* or *suggest* endpoints. The *querytext* value can be any legal Keyword Query Language (KQL) construction, including managed properties and operators. The following code shows two examples of returning search results with keyword queries:

```
http://wingtiptoys.com/_api/search/query?querytext='SharePoint'
http://wingtiptoys.com/_api/search/query?querytext='Title:SharePoint'
```

The real power of the REST API lies in all of the available query parameters that can be used. These parameters reflect many of the properties historically available through the *KeywordQuery* class. By using these parameters, you can control the columns returned, sorting, paging, and relevance model, to name just a few. Table 13-9 lists some of the key query parameters.

TABLE 13-9 Query parameters

Parameter	Description	Example

selectproperties	Specifies the managed properties to return	`http://wingtiptoys.com/_api/search/`
		`query?`
		`querytext='SharePoint'`
		`&selectproperties='Title,Path'`

sortlist	Specifies the managed properties by which to sort the results	`http://wingtiptoys.com/_api/search/`
		`query?`
		`querytext='SharePoint'`
		`&sortlist='Title:ascending'`

startrow	The zero-based index of the first result to return	`http://wingtip.com/_api/search/query?`
		`querytext='SharePoint'`
		`&startrow=10`

rowsperpage	Specifies the number of results per page	`http://wingtiptoys.com/_api/search/`
		`query?`
		`querytext='SharePoint'`
		`&startrow=10&rowsperpage=10`

rowlimit	Specifies the maximum number of records to return	`http://wingtiptoys.com/_api/search/`
		`query?`
		`querytext='SharePoint'`
		`&rowlimit=100`

sourceid	Specifies the ID of the result source against which the query should run	`http://wingtiptoys.com/_api/search/`
		`query?`
		`querytext= 'LastName:B*'`
		`&sourceid='B09A7990-05EA-4AF9-81EF-`
		`EDFAB16C4E31'`

Because access to the search engine is available through the REST API, building search-based apps is just a matter of creating a library that forms the appropriate URI and parses out the results. Listing 13-1 shows how to execute a keyword query by using REST, JavaScript, and jQuery.

LISTING 13-1 Executing a query from JavaScript by using REST

```
$(document).ready(function () {
    (function () {
        $.ajax(
            {
                url: _spPageContextInfo.webAbsoluteUrl +
                    "/_api/search/query?querytext='Title:SharePoint'" +
                    "&selectproperties='Title,Path'",
                method: "GET",
                headers: { accept: "application/json;odata=verbose" },
                success: function (data) {
                    var results =
                        data.d.query.PrimaryQueryResult.RelevantResults.Table.Rows.results
                    var count = results.length;
                    alert("Found " + count + " results. Showing first 5.");
                    for (var r = 0; r < 5; r++) {
                        alert(results[r].Cells.results[2].Value);
                    }
                },
                error: function (err) {
                    alert(JSON.stringify(err));
                }
            }
        );
    })();
});
```

Although executing JavaScript calls against the RESTful endpoints is certainly useful in app development, nothing prevents the use of RESTful calls from C#. This approach can be useful when you are trying to create more traditional solutions, such as console applications. Listing 13-2 shows how to make a RESTful search query by using C#.

LISTING 13-2 Executing a query from C# by using REST

```
static void Main(string[] args)
{
    string url = "http://intranet.wingtiptoys.com/" +
                 "_api/search/query?querytext='Title:SharePoint'" +
                 "&selectproperties='Title,Path'";
    HttpWebRequest request = (HttpWebRequest)WebRequest.Create(url);
    request.Method = "GET";
    request.Credentials = System.Net.CredentialCache.DefaultNetworkCredentials;

    WebResponse response = request.GetResponse();
    using (XmlReader reader = XmlReader.Create(
        new StreamReader(response.GetResponseStream())))
    {
        bool titleFlag = false;
        while (reader.Read())
        {
            if (reader.NodeType == XmlNodeType.Text && titleFlag == true)
            {
                Console.WriteLine(reader.Value);
                titleFlag = false;
            }
            if (reader.NodeType == XmlNodeType.Text && reader.Value == "Title")
            {
                titleFlag = true;
            }
        }
    }
}
```

Using the CSOM API

The CSOM API for search is centered on two key objects: *KeywordQuery* and *SearchExecutor*. The *KeywordQuery* object supports the construction of the query, and the *SearchExecutor* object executes the query against SharePoint. Both JavaScript and C# have versions of these objects.

In JavaScript, the objects are found in the *Microsoft.SharePoint.Client.Search.Query* namespace. This namespace is part of the *sp.search.js* library, so you must add a reference to this library in your app. After the reference is added, the usage is fairly straightforward, as shown in Listing 13-3.

LISTING 13-3 Executing a query from JavaScript by using CSOM

```
"use strict";

var WingtipToys = window.WingtipToys || {};
WingtipToys.Results = {};

WingtipToys.Search = function () {

    var execute = function (kql) {
        var context = SP.ClientContext.get_current();
        var keywordQuery = new Microsoft.SharePoint.Client.Search.Query.
        KeywordQuery(context);
        keywordQuery.set_queryText(kql);
        var searchExecutor =
        new Microsoft.SharePoint.Client.Search.Query.SearchExecutor(context);
        WingtipToys.Results = searchExecutor.executeQuery(keywordQuery);
        context.executeQueryAsync(onGetEventsSuccess, onGetEventsFail);
    },

    onGetEventsSuccess = function() {
        var relevantResults = WingtipToys.Results.m_value.ResultTables[0];
        $('#message').text(relevantResults.RowCount +
        " events were found in farm calendars.");
    },

    onGetEventsFail = function (sender, args) {
        alert('Failed. Error:' + args.get_message());
    }

    return {
        execute: execute
    }
}();

$(document).ready(function () {
    WingtipToys.Search.execute("ContentClass=STS_ListItem_Events");
});
```

In order to query with CSOM from C#, you must add a reference to the *Microsoft.SharePoint.Client*, *Microsoft.SharePoint.ClientRuntime*, and *Microsoft.SharePoint.Client.Search* assemblies. Using the *KeywordQuery* and *SearchExecutor* classes in code then follows the same basic pattern as the JavaScript approach. The biggest difference is that the C# code can execute synchronously, as shown in Listing 13-4.

LISTING 13-4 Executing a query from C# by using CSOM

```
using (ClientContext ctx = new ClientContext("http://intranet.wingtip.com/"))
{
    KeywordQuery query = new KeywordQuery(ctx);
    query.QueryText = "Title:SharePoint";
    query.SelectProperties.Add("Title");
    query.SelectProperties.Add("Path");

    SearchExecutor executor = new SearchExecutor(ctx);
    ClientResult<ResultTableCollection> results = executor.ExecuteQuery(query);
    ctx.ExecuteQuery();

    foreach (var row in results.Value[0].ResultRows)
    {
        Console.WriteLine(row["Title"]);
    }
}
```

Using the script Web Parts

When building search-based apps, you can certainly create your own user interface to display search results. However, you can also use a simple set of script-based Web Parts found in the *Microsoft. Office.Server.Search.WebControls* namespace located in the *Microsoft.Office.Server.Search.dll* assembly. The Web Parts *ResultScriptWebPart*, *SearchBoxScriptWebPart*, and *RefinementScriptWebPart* allow you to easily surface search results, a query box, and a refinement panel, respectively. You can include these script Web Parts in an ASP.NET page by adding the following reference:

```
<%@ Register Tagprefix="SearchWC" Namespace="Microsoft.Office.Server.Search.WebControls"
    Assembly="Microsoft.Office.Server.Search, Version=15.0.0.0, Culture=neutral,
    PublicKeyToken=71e9bce111e9429c" %>
```

The *ResultScriptWebPart* is the only one of the three Web Parts that requires any serious configuration. Typically, you will configure the data source to search by setting the *UseSharedDataProvider* and the *DataProviderJSON* properties. *UseSharedDataProvider* indicates whether the Web Part receives data from another part on the page and should be set to *false*. The *DataProviderJSON* property is a JSON object that defines the name of the result source to use and the level where it can be found (*Tenant*, *SSA*, *SPSite*, or *SPWeb*). The following code shows an example JSON object:

```
{ "SourceName":"MyResultSource","SourceLevel":"SPSite" }
```

Along with specifying the result source, you can also specify the result template to use. This is done by setting the *ItemTemplateId* property to the URL of the desired template. The following code shows a typical *ResultScriptWebPart* configured to use a result source and template in the host site collection:

```
<SearchWC:ResultScriptWebPart ID="ResultScriptWebPart1"
        runat="server" ChromeType="None" UseSharedDataProvider="false"
        DataProviderJSON="{ &quot;SourceName&quot;:&quot;Documents&quot;,
                        &quot;SourceLevel&quot;:&quot;SPSite&quot; }"
        ShowAdvancedLink="false"
        ScrollToTopOnRedraw="true"
        ShowUpScopeMessage="true"
        UseSimplifiedQueryBuilder="false"
        ItemTemplateId=
"~sitecollection/_catalogs/masterpage/Display Templates/Search/Item_Default.js" />
```

The *SearchBoxScriptWebPart* must be configured with the address of the results page where it will redirect when searching. The *RefinementScriptWebPart* requires no real configuration—just place it on the same page as the *ResultScriptWebPart*. The following code shows an example configuration for the *SearchBoxScriptWebPart* and the *RefinementScriptWebPart*:

```
<SearchWC:SearchBoxScriptWebPart
        ID="SearchBoxScriptWebPart1"
        ChromeType="None" runat="server"
        ResultsPageAddress="../pages/Default.aspx"/>
<SearchWC:RefinementScriptWebPart
        ID="RefinementScriptWebPart1"
        runat="server" ChromeType="None"/>
```

Improving relevancy

When end users execute a query, they have a strong expectation that the content they have in mind will be near the top of the search results. When this doesn't happen, end users may abandon the search and complain that it just doesn't work. The challenge, of course, is that there are many factors that determine the quality of search results, not the least of which is the query entered by the user. Still, improving the relevancy of search results is critical to the success of any search-based solution. In SharePoint 2013, you can affect relevancy through the use of authoritative pages, dynamic reordering rules, and ranking models.

When looking to improve relevancy, the first place to start is with *authoritative pages*. Authoritative pages are pages that link to critical information within the SharePoint farm. When authoritative pages are defined, it affects the ranking of every page that is connected by links to that page by *click distance*. Click distance is the number of clicks required to get from the authoritative page to the content in question. Authoritative pages are defined in the SSA. For on-premises deployments, no authoritative pages are defined by default. For SharePoint Online, the home page of the main site collection is defined as authoritative. In the SSA, you can define three levels of authoritative pages as well as pages that are not authoritative, which helps eliminate irrelevant information from the relevancy calculation.

Dynamic reordering rules let you reorder the results of a query based on a set of conditions. Dynamic reordering rules are like query rules except that they are applied after the query is run instead of before. Although SharePoint 2013 provides a graphic interface for setting up dynamic reordering rules, they are implemented by using the XRANK keyword behind the scenes.

Dynamic reordering rules are defined within the Query Builder on the Sorting tab. On the Sorting tab, the primary sort key must be set to Rank in order to define dynamic reordering rules. You can then add one or more rules, which allows for the definition of the condition and the resulting rank change to promote or demote an item. Figure 13-9 shows the settings in the Query Builder.

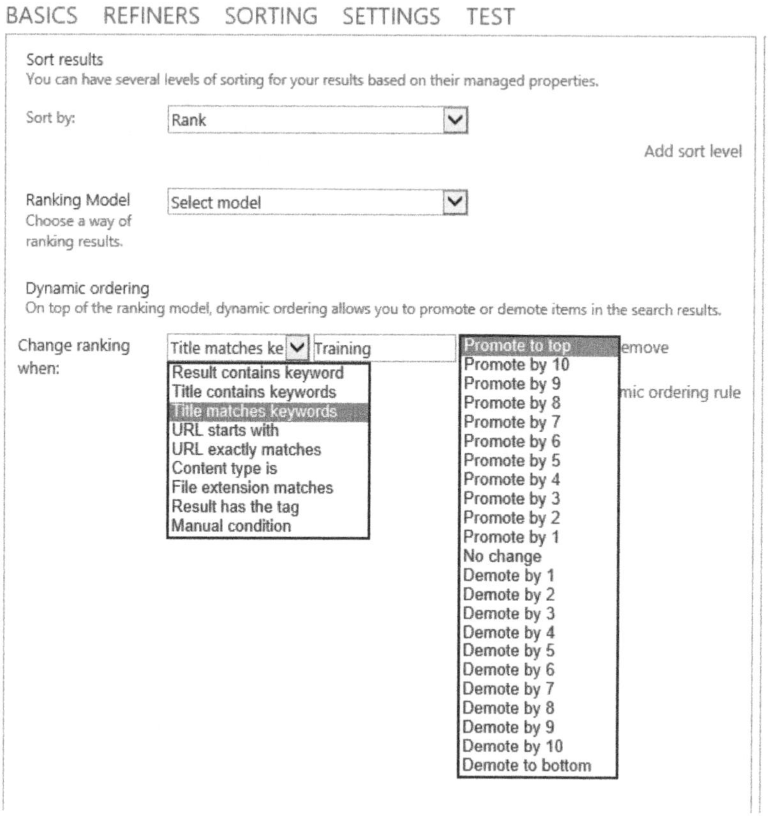

FIGURE 13-9 Adding a dynamic reordering rule

The query engine is responsible for assigning a ranking score to each returned item based upon a number of factors defined in a *ranking model*. The ranking model contains the rules that will be applied to the search results to determine ranking. SharePoint Server 2013 ships with several ranking models that are applied when you search different contexts such as documents or people. You can list all of the ranking models available in your environment with the following Windows PowerShell commands:

```
$ssa = Get-SPEnterpriseSearchServiceApplication -Identity "Search Service Application"
$owner = Get-SPEnterpriseSearchOwner -Level Ssa
Get-SPEnterpriseSearchRankingModel -SearchApplication $ssa -Owner $owner
```

When you list the ranking models, you will notice that each one uses a GUID as an identifier. These GUIDS can be used in your custom search solutions to set the ranking model that should be used with a particular query. The REST, CSOM, and SSOM objects all support properties for setting this value.

Additionally, you can select the ranking model to use directly in the Query Builder, as shown in Figure 13-10.

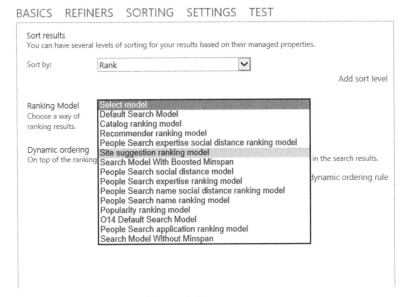

FIGURE 13-10 Selecting a ranking model

Ranking models are created as XML files and registered with the search engine for use. These are complex files for which there is very little documentation. You can, however, view the XML associated with any ranking model by using the following Windows PowerShell commands:

```
$ssa = Get-SPEnterpriseSearchServiceApplication -Identity "Search Service Application"
$owner = Get-SPEnterpriseSearchOwner -Level Ssa
$model = Get-SPEnterpriseSearchRankingModel -SearchApplication $ssa
        -Owner $owner -Identity {RankingModelID}
$model.RankingModelXml
```

In SharePoint 2013, it is possible to modify or create new ranking models. However, Microsoft strongly recommends against this. The recommendation from the search team at Microsoft is to make use of dynamic reordering rules rather than creating a custom ranking model. This is likely the reason why there is little documentation available concerning the structure of these models.

Enhancing content processing

During the crawl process, SharePoint 2013 allows you to inspect and modify the values of managed properties for selected items through the creation of a custom Content Processing Enrichment Service (CPES). As mentioned in the section "Understanding the indexing process" earlier in this chapter, content enhancement supports data cleansing, entity extraction, classification, and tagging, all of which can significantly enhance the quality of search results.

A custom CPES is a SOAP web service that implements the *IContentProcessingEnrichmentService* interface. This interface implements a *ProcessItem* method that passes in a collection of managed properties associated with a particular item being crawled. The custom CPES can then modify the values of the managed properties in the set, add new managed properties, or delete managed properties from the set.

As an example, consider a custom CPES that will look for items that have a company name associated with them and will add a new managed property containing the ticker symbol for the company. This will allow users to search for a company by either its proper name or ticker symbol. Before the custom CPES can be created, however, all of the managed properties that will be used for both input and output must be created.

In this example, the managed property *FictitiousCompany* is used as the input and *FictitiousTickerSymbol* is the new managed property that gets added during the crawl process. The input managed property should be set up in the SSA and associated with any crawled properties that represent a company name. The output managed property, however, does not need to be associated with any crawled properties because its value will be set by the custom CPES. Figure 13-11 shows the managed properties defined in the SSA.

Property Name	Type	Multi	Query	Search	Retrieve	Refine	Sort	Safe	Mapped Crawled Properties	Aliases
FictitiousCompany	Text	-	Query	Search	Retrieve	Refine	Sort	-	Company, ows_Company, ows_q_TEXT_Company	
FictitiousTickerSymbol	Text	-	Query	Search	Retrieve	Refine	Sort	-		

FIGURE 13-11 Defining managed properties for use with a custom CPES

After the managed properties are defined, you can create a web service in Visual Studio 2012. You must then add a reference to the *Microsoft.Office.Server.Search.ContentProcessingEnrichment.dll* assembly located at C:\Program Files\Microsoft Office Servers\15.0\Search\Applications\External. After the reference is set, the following statements will allow you to use the assembly in your service:

```
using Microsoft.Office.Server.Search.ContentProcessingEnrichment;
using Microsoft.Office.Server.Search.ContentProcessingEnrichment.PropertyTypes;
```

Creating the custom CPES is a simple matter of implementing the *ProcessItem* method. This method receives an *Item* and returns a *ProcessedItem*. The typical process is to examine the *ItemProperties* collection associated with the input *Item* for managed properties of interest. You can then add, modify, or delete properties as required. Listing 13-5 shows the code to identify the presence of the *FictitiousCompany* property and then add a new *FictitiousTickerSymbol* property.

LISTING 13-5 Implementing a custom CPES

```
//The new managed property to add
private Property<string> tickerSymbol =
    new Property<string> { Name = "FictitiousTickerSymbol" };

//A temporary holder for the item being processed
private readonly ProcessedItem processedItemHolder =
        new ProcessedItem { ItemProperties = new List<AbstractProperty>() };

//The dictionary of ticker symbols
private readonly Dictionary<string, string> tickerSymbolsDictionary =
        new Dictionary<string, string> {...}

public ProcessedItem ProcessItem(Item item)
{
    foreach (AbstractProperty property in item.ItemProperties)
    {
        //Determine if this managed property is the company property
        if (property.Name.Equals("FictitiousCompany",
            StringComparison.InvariantCultureIgnoreCase))
    {
    //Get the managed property
    Property<string> companyProperty = property as Property<string>;

    if (tickerSymbolsDictionary.ContainsKey(property.ObjectValue.ToString()))
    {
        //Add the ticker symbol managed property
        tickerSymbol.Value = tickerSymbolsDictionary[property.ObjectValue.ToString()];
        processedItemHolder.ItemProperties.Add(tickerSymbol);
    }

    return processedItemHolder;
}
```

After the web service is created, it must be deployed and then registered with the search service. When the service is registered, the input and output managed properties are defined as well as the service endpoint. This registration process ensures that only items meeting the specified criteria get sent to the custom CPES for processing, ensuring that the additional processing does not unnecessarily slow down the overall crawl process. The following code shows how to register the service by using Windows PowerShell:

```
$ssa = Get-SPEnterpriseSearchServiceApplication
$config = New-SPEnterpriseSearchContentEnrichmentConfiguration
$config.Endpoint = "http://webs.wingtiptoys.com/ContentProcessingEnrichment/CPE.svc"
$config.InputProperties = "FictitiousCompany"
$config.OutputProperties = "FictitiousTickerSymbol"
Set-SPEnterpriseSearchContentEnrichmentConfiguration
   -SearchApplication $ssa -ContentEnrichmentConfiguration $config
```

If you no longer want to use the custom CPES for processing, then it can be removed from the pipeline. The following Windows PowerShell command will remove the service:

```
Remove-SPEnterpriseSearchContentEnrichmentConfiguration -SearchApplication $ssa
```

Creating .NET Assembly Connectors for search

Chapter 12 showed in detail how to create a .NET Assembly Connector to allow Business Connectivity Services access to any external system. You can also use a .NET Assembly Connector to index any external system by search-enabling the connector. Because .NET Assembly Connector fundamentals were covered in Chapter 12, this chapter will focus only on the requirements for enabling search.

Search-enabling a model

Whenever any External Content Type (ECT) is created in BCS, there is an XML model that gets created behind the scenes. This model defines the external system, entities, relationships, methods, and user access rights for the ECT. The same is true when a .NET Assembly Connector is created. The primary difference is that the external system is defined as an association between a .NET assembly and the ECT.

When you use SharePoint Developer to create ECTs, the model is generated for you so that you never have to deal with XML directly. When you use Visual Studio 2012 to create a .NET Assembly Connector, you also have design tools that hide the XML, but you often have to edit the XML model manually to get the exact capabilities you need. In Visual Studio, the XML model is contained in a file with a .bdcm extension. When this file is opened, it appears in three windows. First, a design surface is available for creating entities. Second, a detail section is available for method definitions. Third, the Business Data Connectivity (BDC) Explorer is available for browsing the model. Figure 13-12 shows the three windows of information for the model described in Chapter 12. This model used a .NET Assembly Connector to connect with product information.

You can view the XML for the model directly by right-clicking the .bdcm file in the Solution Explorer and selecting Open With from the shortcut menu. When the Open With dialog box appears, select the option to open the file with the XML Editor. If you study the XML model alongside the BDC Explorer, you will begin to notice that the BDC Explorer contains a node for each key element in the model. This concept is important because you typically will be adding information to model elements when you prepare a .NET Assembly Connector to support search.

To search-enable an existing model, you must make two changes. The first change is to designate which method to call during the indexing process. The second change allows the model to appear as a content source in search. Both changes are simple edits to the XML.

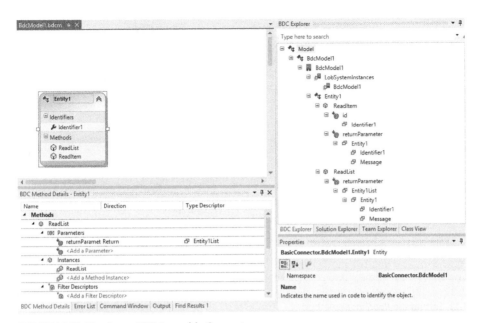

FIGURE 13-12 Viewing a .NET Assembly Connector

Chapter 12 discussed BCS operations in detail. In particular, *Finder* methods were defined as methods that return many records from an external system. Essentially, a *Finder* method defines a view of an external system. When search crawls an external system, it needs to know which of the available *Finder* methods represents the entire population of records to index. This finder method is known as the *RootFinder* method.

In your .NET Assembly Connector, you designate the *RootFinder* by first selecting the method instance in the Method Details pane. When you select it, the Properties window in Visual Studio 2012 will show details for the method. From this window, you can open the Custom Properties collection. In the Property Editor window, you can enter the *RootFinder* designation with a Type of *System.String*. Optionally, you can include the *UseClientCachingForSearch* property, which instructs the crawler to manage data directly in memory for more efficiency. This setting is appropriate for situations in which the width of the record is less than 32K. If records are larger, they might be dropped during the crawl process. Figure 13-13 shows the modifications being made to an existing .NET Assembly Connector.

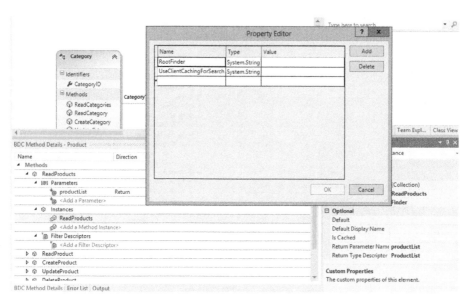

FIGURE 13-13 Setting the *RootFinder* method

After setting *RootFinder*, you can open the model XML in Visual Studio and view how the new in-formation was added to the model. In fact, it's often easier to simply add the properties directly in the XML rather than using the Visual Studio dialog boxes. The following code shows the resulting XML:

```
<MethodInstances>
  <MethodInstance Type="Finder"
     ReturnParameterName="returnParameter"
     Default="true" Name="ReadList"
     DefaultDisplayName="Entity1 List">
    <Properties>
        <Property Name="RootFinder" Type="System.String">x</Property>
    </Properties>
  </MethodInstance>
</MethodInstances>
```

After *RootFinder* is defined, you must make an additional change to allow the .NET Assembly Con-nector to appear as a content source in search. This is accomplished by applying the *ShowInSearchUI* property to the model. This property is applied by selecting the *LobSystemInstance* for your project under the *LobSystemInstances* folder in the model explorer. You can then create the property by using the same technique as for *RootFinder*. Optionally, you can make the change directly in the XML. The following code shows the modified model:

```
<LobSystemInstances>
  <LobSystemInstance Name="BdcModel1" >
    <Properties>
      <Property Name="ShowInSearchUI" Type="System.String"></Property>
    </Properties>
  </LobSystemInstance>
</LobSystemInstances>
```

After you have completed the two modifications, the model is search-enabled. You can deploy the feature and immediately select it as a search content source. It is worth noting that when you create models using SharePoint Designer, the *RootFinder* and *ShowInSearchUI* properties are added automatically.

Implementing security in search results

Though search-enabling a BCS model is fairly simple, this process provides no security checking against search queries. This means that when a search is run against the external system, all matching results will be returned regardless of whether the current user is supposed to see them. In most production applications, you will want to implement an access control list (ACL) that specifies rights for the records returned when you are searching with a .NET Assembly Connector. This is accomplished by adding a special method to the model called a *BinarySecurityDescriptorAccessor* method.

The process to implement security begins by adding a new method to the model. In Visual Studio, you can right-click the entity in the design surface and select Add New Method from the context menu. You can then give it a name such as *ReadSecurityDescriptor*. After it is created, the method will appear in the Method Details pane. Next, in the Method Details pane, you must create a new method instance beneath the new method. After the new method instance is created, you can change its type in the Properties window to *BinarySecurityDescriptorAccessor*.

The new method instance will require input and output parameters. Typically, the input parameters are the identifier for an item and the user name of the current user. The output parameter must be a byte array that holds the security descriptor. The following code shows the XML for the new method:

```
<Method Name="ReadSecurityDescriptor">
  <Parameters>
    <Parameter Name="id" Direction="In">
      <TypeDescriptor Name="ID" TypeName="System.String" IdentifierName="ID" />
    </Parameter>
    <Parameter Name="acl" Direction="Return">
      <TypeDescriptor Name="SecurityDescriptor"
        TypeName="System.Byte[]" IsCollection="true" >
        <TypeDescriptors>
          <TypeDescriptor Name="SecurityDescriptorByte" TypeName="System.Byte"/>
        </TypeDescriptors>
      </TypeDescriptor>
    </Parameter>
  </Parameters>
  <MethodInstances>
    <MethodInstance Name="ReadSecurityDescriptorInstance"
      Type="BinarySecurityDescriptorAccessor" ReturnParameterName="acl"/>
  </MethodInstances>
</Method>
```

When you create the new method definition, Visual Studio will automatically generate a method stub in code that accepts the input parameters and returns a byte array. Your job is to write code for this method that creates an ACL for the item. When the *BinarySecurityDescriptorAccessor* method is called during the indexing process, the crawl account will be the account accessing the system. This account should be designated as the owner account for the ACL. In the implementation, you can add other permissions for users based on whatever criteria you need. For example, the code in Listing 13-6 grants access to all users.

LISTING 13-6 Creating a security ACL

```
public static byte[] ReadSecurityDescriptor(string id, string username) {
  try {
    //Grant everyone access
    NTAccount workerAcc = new NTAccount(
    username.Split('\\')[0], username.Split('\\')[1]);
    SecurityIdentifier workerSid =
        (SecurityIdentifier)workerAcc.Translate(typeof(SecurityIdentifier));
    SecurityIdentifier everyone =
        new SecurityIdentifier(WellKnownSidType.WorldSid, null);
    CommonSecurityDescriptor csd = new CommonSecurityDescriptor(
        false, false, ControlFlags.None, workerSid, null, null, null);
    csd.SetDiscretionaryAclProtection(true, false);
    csd.DiscretionaryAcl.AddAccess(
    AccessControlType.Allow, everyone, unchecked((int)0xffffffffL),
    InheritanceFlags.None, PropagationFlags.None);
    byte[] secDes = new byte[csd.BinaryLength];
    csd.GetBinaryForm(secDes, 0);
    return secDes;
  }
  catch (Exception x) {
    PortalLog.LogString("Product Model (ReadSecurityDescriptor): {0}", x.Message);
    return null;
  }
}
```

After you have created the *BinarySecurityDescriptorAccessor* method, you must add a property to the ECT entity to hold the ACL. This property is named *SecurityDescriptor*. The model must then be updated to relate the *BinarySecurityDescriptorAccessor* method to the *SecurityDescriptor* property. The following code shows how to relate the entity and the method instance:

```
<MethodInstances>

  <MethodInstance Name="ReadSecurityDescriptorInstance"
                  Type="BinarySecurityDescriptorAccessor"
                  ReturnParameterName="acl">
    <Properties>
      <Property Name="WindowsSecurityDescriptorField" Type="System.String">
        SecurityDescriptor
      </Property>
    </Properties>
  </MethodInstance>

<MethodInstances>
```

Crawling the .NET Assembly Connector

When your .NET Assembly Connector is complete, you should be able to select it as a content source and initiate a full crawl. When you crawl the solution for the first time, it's a good idea to attach Visual Studio to the crawl process (mssdmn.exe) and watch how the crawl progresses. Set breakpoints in the *Finder*, *SpecificFinder*, and *BinarySecurityDescriptorAccessor* methods. Also, be sure that you have granted access in the BCS service to the account that will perform the crawling.

When the crawl is initiated, you should notice the *Finder* method called first. You'll then notice the *SpecificFinder* called for each individual item returned from the *Finder* method. Along the way, the security descriptor should be built for each item. After the crawl completes, check the crawl log for errors. Now you can run a search against the crawled data. SharePoint should use the security descriptors that you constructed to limit access to items as appropriate.

Summary

This chapter focused on all the components necessary to create search-based solutions in SharePoint 2013. When designing your solutions, you should give consideration to creating solutions that use search, either through apps, keyword queries, or .NET Assembly Connectors, and present results to users so that they can be understood and acted upon. In this way, you can create search-based solutions that provide value to end users.

## CHAPTER 14

SharePoint Enterprise Content Management

I n Microsoft SharePoint 2013, Microsoft has again improved and extended SharePoint's Enterprise Content Management (ECM) capabilities. This chapter explains the different components that can be used with document management and records management in SharePoint and how they can be extended. There are many different features and components that can be used to create document management and records management solutions in SharePoint. If you are designing one of these solutions, you will have to decide which features and components are useful in your scenario. Just having a lot of document and records management–related capabilities available to you in SharePoint doesn't mean you should use them in every document or records management solution. For every solution that you are creating, you should carefully evaluate the options that SharePoint offers out of the box and use the ones that will offer the most value. Don't only use the options that look shiny and new.

Understanding the Managed Metadata Service Application

The first thing we examine in this chapter is the *Managed Metadata Service Application*. This is a service application that was introduced in SharePoint 2010 and that has enabled users to create more serious document and records management solutions in SharePoint. The Managed Metadata Service Application introduces several capabilities that allow you to scale your ECM solutions across site collections, web applications, or even farms in a consistent way. The two most important features of the Managed Metadata Service Application are the *term store* that contains the managed metadata terms, and the *content type syndication* capabilities that allow users to distribute content types across the site collection boundary.

Managed metadata in SharePoint allows you to do exactly what the name suggests: to manage the metadata in your environment. The managed metadata is stored in the term store, which is part of the Managed Metadata Service Application. Every site collection in every web application that is connected to the Managed Metadata Service Application can use the metadata stored in the term store. If the service application is published and used in multiple farms, site collections in the farms that consume the services from the published service application can also use the same metadata.

Understanding managed metadata

There is only one term store per Managed Metadata Service Application. The term store can be accessed from Central Administration by clicking the Managed Metadata Service Application or Service Application Proxy link on the Manage Service Applications page, and also by clicking the Term Store Management link on the Site Settings page in a site collection. Whether a user accessing the term store can manage the contents of the term store depends on whether the user is a term store administrator.

A term store contains *term groups*, which contain *term sets*, which contain *terms*. A term store will generally contain a limited number of term groups. Usually there are between 4 and about 20 term groups. By default, there are three term groups in the term store that are all used by SharePoint itself:

- The *People* term group, which contains term sets and terms used in user profile properties.

- The *Search Directories* term group, which contains information and settings related to the Search Service Application.

- The *System* term group, which contains the *Hashtags*, *Keywords*, and *Orphaned Terms* term sets. The *Keywords* term set is also called a *folksonomy*; it is open and users can add terms to it at all times. This will happen automatically when a user fills in a value that is not in the term set yet in the Keywords column in a library or list.

In most environments, you will add at least one term group yourself. At the term group level, a description, administrators, and contributors can be selected. This means that a term group can be used as a security boundary in the term store. You can add more than just one enterprise-wide term group if different people or departments will have to manage different parts of the managed metadata. You could, for instance, create a separate term group for Human Resources, one for Legal, and one for Finance.

When term groups are created by term store or term group administrators or contributors, the terms in the term group are available in site collections that are connected to the managed metadata service application that the term store is part of. Term sets that are created in this way are called *global term sets*.

A site collection administrator, without specific access to the term store, can also add term sets to the term store, either directly or by creating a term set to bind to a site column in the site. These term sets will be added to a new term group, the name of which is the URL of the site collection. Term sets that are created by site collection administrators are available only within the site collection and are called *local term sets*. Local term sets cannot be seen or managed from the term store when it's accessed from outside the site collection, not even by term store administrators.

Within a term group you can create many different term sets. Term sets are logical collections of terms. Examples of term sets are *Country, Language, Department, Document Status* and *Document Type*. You can have up to 1,000 term sets in a term store. At the term set level it is possible to set:

- **Description**

- **Owner**

- **Contact**   This is an email address to which suggestions and feedback about the term set can be sent. If no contact is filled in, the suggestion feature is disabled for that term set.

- **Stakeholders**   This is a list of users and groups that should be notified when changes to the term set are made.

- **Submission Policy**   This policy setting determines whether users can add terms to this term set, or whether only users with specific permissions on the term store or term group can add terms. If the term set is *Open*, it will behave like a folksonomy; if it is *Closed*, it is called a *taxonomy*.

- **Available for Tagging**   If this is set to *True*, users can use terms from this term set in their sites and libraries.

- **Use This Term Set for Site Navigation**   This setting enables this term set for usage in the new Managed Navigation features such as friendly URLs, target page settings, and catalog item page settings. This is not related to the Managed Metadata Navigation that is available in lists and libraries.

- **Custom Sort Order**   A term set can either be ordered alphabetically or manually. If *Use custom sort order* is selected, an administrator will have to go in to manually select the position of each term in the term set. Depending on the number of terms in a term set and on how often the terms in the term set change, this can be a very labor-intensive task. This option is new in SharePoint 2013.

- **Custom Properties**   Another new feature in SharePoint 2013 is the ability to add custom properties to a term set. This can be very useful if additional information has to be stored with a term or, for instance, if the terms are used in a custom application. Instead of having to use (or possibly misuse) the description to store this information, it is now possible to create your own custom properties.

A term set can contain up to 30,000 individual terms. Each term can have several properties added to it, which don't count toward the number of terms:

- **Available for Tagging**

- **Language**   This setting is relevant only if more than one language pack is installed in the environment.

- **Description**

- **Default Label**   This is the actual label of the term.

- **Other Labels**   These are synonyms.

- **Member Of**   This specifies the term sets that the term is part of. There can be more than one term set in this collection if the term is reused.

- **Shared Properties**   These are custom properties that are available on each instance of this term in the term store, and thus they are available in the original term and also in the reused terms.

- **Local Properties**   These are custom properties available only on this instance of the term.

A term store can contain a total of 1 million term sets and terms. If your environment needs more than a million term sets and terms, you will have to create a second Managed Metadata Service Application.

One thing that you might have noticed when reading this chapter, or when looking at the term store in your SharePoint environment, is that there is no recycle bin and that there are no versioning options. This means that there is no history of changes made to the term store, there is no audit trail, and it is also not possible to reverse or undo a change made to the term store. This can be a real problem, especially in a large environment, because changes made to term sets and terms in the term store can affect users when they are editing documents or items in their sites.

If a managed metadata site column is a mandatory column in a list or library, users have to select a valid term from the term set that the column is linked to before they can check in a document or list item. Suppose a user has done this; imagine the following scenario:

1. After the user selected a term from the term store and checked in the document, a term group administrator removes the term that the user selected from the term store, because it is no longer seen as a valid value.

2. The user comes back to the document and makes a small change—let's say the table of contents was updated.

3. The user now wants to save the document and check it back in.

4. Because the previously selected term is no longer a valid term and the managed metadata site column is a mandatory column in the library, the user won't be able to check the document back in until a different term (one that is still valid) has been selected from the term set.

This kind of behavior can be very frustrating for an end user and very hard to explain. The same behavior will occur when a term is deprecated or moved to a different term set, but it is easier to undo these changes because the term is still in the term store. If the term set were deleted completely it would have been worse, because that would have meant that the user wouldn't be able to select a valid term and thus would not be able to check the document back in.

Besides the lack of history and auditing options, there is another challenge with the user interface of the term store: it doesn't scale very well. If you have many terms in a term set, administrators will have to scroll through a lot of them to get to the terms that they want to adjust. To overcome the challenges of the term store user interface, you will have to create both a process and a technical solution for managing terms in the term store. Because this is a development book, we will not go into detail about the process around managing metadata, but we will look at some examples around a possible technical solution for managing the contents of the term store.

Using managed metadata in a custom solution

SharePoint offers the option of importing term sets and terms by using a .csv file. This allows administrators to import large numbers of term sets and terms without having to use the user interface of the term store. This doesn't provide a solution for most of the problems described in the previous section, though, because you can use only the .csv file for importing terms and not for managing and deleting terms. You also can't use all properties that are available for term sets and terms when you import them by using a .csv file. The properties in the .csv file are:

- Term Set Name
- Term Set Description
- LCID
- Available for Tagging
- Term Description
- Level 1 Term
- Level 2 Term
- Level 3 Term
- Level 4 Term
- Level 5 Term
- Level 6 Term
- Level 7 Term

As the preceding list shows, the .csv file also reflects the maximum depth of the term store. The term store has a supported depth limit of seven levels of terms. Technically you could create more by using the term store user interface, but Microsoft doesn't support this, so you should stick to a maximum of seven, which is more than you will want to make users traverse anyway.

The only way to allow an organization to properly manage the contents of the term store is by creating a custom solution. For a real solution, you would have to include business users and set up a change process that allows users to request changes to the metadata. You would also need a user interface that allows a term store manager to make changes, preferably both for large sets of changes and for individual changes. You would need a proper sign-off before changes could be processed, and a good auditing system to be able to track who changed what. You would also have to be able to at least make changes to all or most properties of term sets and terms. In the following example, a

SharePoint list will be used to add, update, delete, deprecate, and restore terms. This is not a complete and production-ready solution, but it should give you enough inspiration to get started.

Managing the contents of the term store

The downloadable .zip archive of companion code for this book contains a sample SharePoint project named *WingtipToysTermStoreManager*. This project contains working samples of the solution that you are going to examine over the next few pages. The solution uses a SharePoint list that can be used to add, update, delete, deprecate, and restore terms in the term store. The list has an event handler attached to it that will fire when items are added or updated. Figure 14-1 shows the list designer that is part of the SharePoint Developer Tools, showing the columns that were added to the *TermStore-ManagerList*.

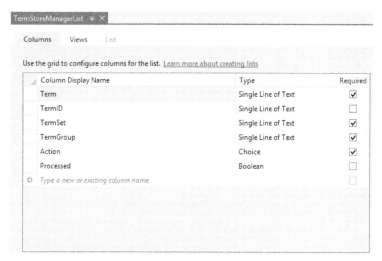

FIGURE 14-1 This screen shot shows the Columns view of the list designer that is part of the SharePoint Developer Tools.

Because not all properties are available in the designer, you will also have to open up the list's Schema.xml file to add the missing properties. The *DisplayName* and *Type* of a column and whether it's required can be set in the list designer. However, to specify a *Description*, a *MaxLength*, and whether the column should show up in the Edit and New forms through *ShowInEditForm* or *ShowIn-NewForm*, you will need to edit Schema.xml. The fields are defined in the *Fields* element. Listing 14-1 shows the fields as they are defined in the Elements.xml file, including the *Description* of the *Term* element and the *ShowInNewForm* and *ShowInEditForm* attributes for the *Processed* field. It also shows the choices for the *Action* column added through the *Choice* element.

LISTING 14-1 Snippet from the Elements.xml file of the *TermStoreManager* list showing the fields added to the list and their attributes

```xml
<Fields>
 <Field ID="{fa564e0f-0c70-4ab9-b863-0177e6ddd247}" Type="Text"
   Name="Title" DisplayName="Term" Required="TRUE"
 SourceID="http://schemas.microsoft.com/sharepoint/v3"
 StaticName="Title" MaxLength="255" />
 <Field Name="TermID" ID="{6be4f6cb-fa19-464a-ad07-0cbeebb8b6ed}"
   DisplayName="TermID" Type="Text"
   Description="You can leave this empty if you are creating a new term.
   To update, delete, deprecate, restore, or recreate an existing term,
   please use the existing TermID" />
 <Field Name="TermSet" ID="{0a05f0ce-1159-4a6f-ae23-88778afdb6f5}"
 DisplayName="TermSet" Type="Text" Required="TRUE" />
 <Field Name="TermGroup" ID="{9bc3fa00-60e0-40de-a05d-fec8fa5755fc}"
 DisplayName="TermGroup" Type="Text" Required="TRUE" />
 <Field Name="Action" ID="{0c0d3817-1415-44eb-b5ae-4718855b72d6}"
 DisplayName="Action" Type="Choice" Required="TRUE">
   <CHOICES>
     <CHOICE>Create</CHOICE>
     <CHOICE>Update</CHOICE>
     <CHOICE>Deprecate</CHOICE>
     <CHOICE>Restore</CHOICE>
     <CHOICE>Delete</CHOICE>
   </CHOICES>
 </Field>
 <Field Name="Processed" ID="{45a7e18b-b5dc-400a-a7f0-f1177776d50a}"
 DisplayName="Processed" Type="Boolean" ShowInEditForm="FALSE"
 ShowInNewForm="FALSE" />
</Fields>
```

Figure 14-2 shows the edit form of the list.

Term *

TermID

You can leave this empty if you are creating a new term. To update, delete, deprecate, restore, or recreate an existing term, please use the existing TermID

TermSet *

TermGroup *

Action *

Save   Cancel

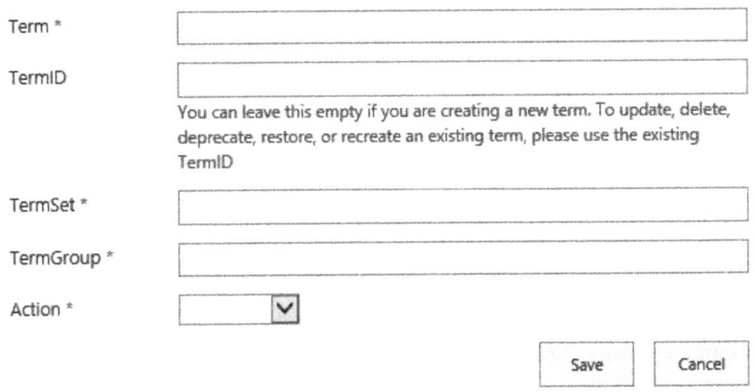

FIGURE 14-2 This screen shot shows the edit form of the list used to manage terms in the term store.

Next you can add the event handler to the list. The event handler will be configured to fire on the *ItemAdded* and the *ItemUpdated* events. The code makes sure that an item isn't processed yet (the *Processed* field should be *False*). Then it makes sure that the term store is available. If there is more than one term store—because you might be using more than one managed metadata service application—you should also make sure you are making the changes to the correct term store. Make sure to add a reference to the *Microsoft.SharePoint.Taxonomy* assembly, because the classes that allow you to work with the term store and its terms are in it. Next, it's time to determine what action is required by checking the value selected in the Action column. For all actions, the code tests whether a *TermID* is already specified. If the action is *Create* and the *TermID* is not specified, a new *TermID* will be generated. For all other actions, no changes will be processed when the *TermID* isn't specified. When a new *TermID* is generated for a new term, the ID will be written back to the *TermID* column in the list. The methods that can be used to update the terms in the term store, including sample values for the parameters, are listed here:

- To create a new term, you have to add it to the term set: *TermSet.CreateTerm(termValue, 1033, termGuid).*

- To update a term, you have to first retrieve the label of a term: *Label updatedLabel = TermSet. GetTerm(termGuid).Labels[0].* Then you must update the label of that term: *updatedLabel.Value = termValue.*

- To deprecate a term, you can simply set the *Deprecate* property of a term to *true*: *TermSet. GetTerm(termGuid).Deprecate(true).*

- To restore a term, you can simply set the *Deprecate* property of a term to *false TermSet. GetTerm(termGuid).Deprecate(false).*

- To delete a term, you call the *Delete* method of that term: *TermSet.GetTerm(termGuid).Delete().*

Listing 14-2 shows the code used in the event handler. Make sure to commit any changes that you have made to the term store. If you are making a lot of changes in a batch, make sure you commit changes in batches of reasonable size.

LISTING 14-2 The event handler that processes list items to update the term store

```
/// <summary>
/// An item was added.
/// </summary>
public override void ItemAdded(SPItemEventProperties properties)
{
    if (properties.List.Title.Contains("Term Store Updates"))
    {
        SPListItem itemToProcess = properties.ListItem;
        Guid siteId = properties.SiteId;

        ProcessChanges(itemToProcess, siteId);

        base.ItemAdded(properties);
```

```
        }
    }

    /// <summary>
    /// An item was updated.
    /// </summary>
    public override void ItemUpdated(SPItemEventProperties properties)
    {
        if (properties.List.Title.Contains("Term Store Updates"))
        {
            SPListItem itemToProcess = properties.ListItem;
            Guid siteId = properties.SiteId;

            ProcessChanges(itemToProcess, siteId);

            base.ItemUpdated(properties);
        }
    }

    /// <summary>
    /// Process list item changes in the term store
    /// </summary>
    /// <param name="itemToProcess"></param>
    /// <param name="siteId"></param>
    public void ProcessChanges(SPListItem itemToProcess, Guid siteId)
    {
        if (!Convert.ToBoolean(itemToProcess["Processed"]))
        {
            using (SPSite site = new SPSite(siteId))
            {
                TaxonomySession taxonomySession = new TaxonomySession(site);
                if (taxonomySession.TermStores.Count > 0)
                {
                    TermStore termStore = taxonomySession.TermStores[0];

                    // Check to make sure that the termstore is online
                    if (termStore.IsOnline)
                    {
                        Group termGroup;
                        TermSet termSet;
                        string action = itemToProcess["Action"].ToString().ToLower();
                        bool itemUpdated = false;

                        // TermGroup
                        try
                        {
                            // Get the term group
                            termGroup =
                            termStore.Groups[itemToProcess["TermGroup"].ToString()];
                        }
                        catch (ArgumentOutOfRangeException ex)
                        {
                            termGroup =
                            termStore.CreateGroup(itemToProcess["TermGroup"].ToString());
```

```csharp
        }

        // TermSet
        try
        {
            termSet = termGroup.TermSets[itemToProcess["TermSet"].ToString()];
        }
        catch (ArgumentOutOfRangeException ex)
        {
            termSet =
            termGroup.CreateTermSet(itemToProcess["TermSet"].ToString());
        }

        string termValue = itemToProcess["Term"].ToString();
        Guid termGuid;

        switch (action)
        {
            case "create":
                if (itemToProcess["TermID"] != null)
                {
                    termGuid = new Guid(itemToProcess["TermID"].ToString());
                }
                else
                {
                    termGuid = Guid.NewGuid();
                }

                Term newTerm = termSet.CreateTerm(termValue, 1033, termGuid);
                itemToProcess["TermID"] = termGuid;
                itemUpdated = true;

                break;
            case "update":
                if (itemToProcess["TermID"] != null)
                {
                    termGuid = new Guid(itemToProcess["TermID"].ToString());
                    Term updatedTerm = termSet.GetTerm(termGuid);
                    Label updatedLabel = updatedTerm.Labels[0];
                    updatedLabel.Value = termValue;
                    itemUpdated = true;
                }
                break;
            case "deprecate":
                if (itemToProcess["TermID"] != null)
                {
                    termGuid = new Guid(itemToProcess["TermID"].ToString());
                    Term deprecatedTerm = termSet.GetTerm(termGuid);
                    deprecatedTerm.Deprecate(true);
```

```
                        itemUpdated = true;
                    }
                    break;
                case "restore":
                    if (itemToProcess["TermID"] != null)
                    {
                        termGuid = new Guid(itemToProcess["TermID"].ToString());
                        Term deprecatedTerm = termSet.GetTerm(termGuid);
                        deprecatedTerm.Deprecate(false);
                        itemUpdated = true;
                    }
                    break;
                case "delete":
                    if (itemToProcess["TermID"] != null)
                    {
                        termGuid = new Guid(itemToProcess["TermID"].ToString());
                        Term deletedTerm = termSet.GetTerm(termGuid);
                        deletedTerm.Delete();
                        itemUpdated = true;
                    }
                    break;
                default:
                    break;
                }

                termStore.CommitAll();
                if (itemUpdated)
                {
                    itemToProcess["Processed"] = true;

                    itemToProcess.Update();
                }
            }
        }
    }
}
```

Now that you can manage the term store in a custom solution, it is time to look at how you can use the term store's contents in a site or list.

Creating managed metadata site columns

The most common way to use managed metadata in sites and lists is to add managed metadata site columns to them. Adding a managed metadata column though the SharePoint user interface is exactly the same as adding any other column. When you are using custom code, there a few things that are worth noting, though. Creating a managed metadata site column by using a declarative approach with Collaborative Application Markup Language (CAML) is not supported. To create a managed metadata site column from a custom solution, you will have to use code-behind. To do this, you can use the *TaxonomyField* class. This class inherits from *SPFieldLookup*, which inherits from the generic *SPField* class. The fact that the *TaxonomyField* class inherits from the *SPFieldLookup* class also means that it counts toward the *List view lookup threshold*. The List view lookup threshold is part of the List Throttling functionality. The threshold has been established to prevent users from creating list views that create database queries behind the scenes with more than eight joins. By creating views that add many joins to a single query, users could severely hamper the performance of the SharePoint environment, without being aware of doing so. The default value of the List view lookup threshold is 8, which means that eight columns that cause joins can be returned in a single query. Apart from lookup and managed metadata columns, field types that count toward the List view lookup threshold are person/group fields and workflow status fields.

A *TaxonomyField* has several properties that are specific to a managed metadata field:

- **SspId** The ID of the term store that this managed metadata column is linked to.

- **TermSetId** The ID of the term set from which a value should be selected.

- **AnchorId** The ID of the only term from which descendants can be selected. This is relevant if the selected term set has multiple levels and if only subterms of a specific term should be selectable.

- **CreateValuesInEditForm** If this property is set to *True*, values that are filled in that aren't in the term set will be added to the term set, providing the term set itself is open.

- **Open** If this property is set to *True*, the user will be given the option to add new terms to the term set, providing that the term set itself is open.

Listing 14-3 shows the code that can be used to create a managed metadata site column.

LISTING 14-3 Creating a managed metadata column

```
using (SPSite site = new SPSite("http://teamsite.wingtiptoys.com/"))
{
    TaxonomySession taxonomySession = new TaxonomySession(site);
    TermStore termStore = taxonomySession.TermStores[0];
    Group termGroup = termStore.Groups["Enterprise"];
    TermSet termSet = termGroup.TermSets["ToyTypes"];

    using (SPWeb web = site.OpenWeb())
    {
        web.AllowUnsafeUpdates = true;

        TaxonomyField taxonomyField = null;

        taxonomyField =
            web.Fields.CreateNewField("TaxonomyFieldType", "Type of Toys")
                as TaxonomyField;
        taxonomyField.StaticName = "ToyType";
        // Sets whether the field accepts multiple values or not
        taxonomyField.AllowMultipleValues = false;
```

```
            // The GUID of the term of which only descendants of the term can be picked
            taxonomyField.AnchorId = termSet.Id;
            // If this is set to true terms that are not validated will be created
            taxonomyField.CreateValuesInEditForm = false;
            // If this is set to true the user will be given the option
            // to add new terms
            taxonomyField.Open = false;
            // Id of the term store
            taxonomyField.SspId = termStore.Id;
            // Id of the term set from which a value can be selected
            taxonomyField.TermSetId = termSet.Id;
            taxonomyField.Required = false;
            taxonomyField.ShowInDisplayForm = true;
            taxonomyField.ShowInEditForm = true;
            taxonomyField.ShowInNewForm = true;
            taxonomyField.Group = "Wingtip Toys Columns";

            // After creating the taxonomy field you have to add it to the list
            web.Fields.Add(taxonomyField);

            taxonomyField.Update();

            web.AllowUnsafeUpdates = false;
    }
}
```

Using a *TaxonomyWebTaggingControl*

If you want to use managed metadata fields on a custom Web Part or a custom page, you will need to use a specific control. This control is the *TaxonomyWebTaggingControl*. When a *TaxonomyWebTaggingControl* is added to a page, the control will look like a managed metadata column on the page. The properties that have to be set on a *TaxonomyWebTaggingControl* are very similar to those that are set on the *TaxonomyField*:

- **SSPList**   A string of term store GUIDs, delimited by semicolons (;), that the control should validate against.

- **GroupId**   A GUID that represents the ID of the group that the control will validate against. The documentation states that this is IDs, plural, but because the data type of the property is *GUID*, it will have to be a single ID. This property is optional, though, because you could get by with using *SSPList* and *TermSetList*.

- **TermSetList**   A string of term set GUIDs, delimited by semicolons (;), that the control should validate against.

- **AnchorId**   A GUID that represents the ID of the only term from which descendants can be selected. This is relevant if the selected term set has multiple levels and if only subterms of a specific term should be selectable.

- **AllowFillIn**   A Boolean that, if set to *True*, gives the user the option to add new terms to the term set, providing that the term set itself is open.

- **IsAddTerms**   A Boolean that, if set to *True*, allows unvalidated values to be added to the term set, providing the term set itself is open and only one term set is listed in the *TermSetList*.

Listing 14-4 shows the code that can be used to set the properties of a *TaxonomyWebTagging-Control*. The code also sets the value of the control to the default value of the *ToyType* field that was created in Listing 14-3. If you want to use the code in Listing 14-4, you will have to add the *TaxonomyWebTaggingControl* to a page by using *<Taxonomy:TaxonomyWebTaggingControl runat= "server" ID="WebTaggingControl" />*. An in-depth description of all *TaxonomyWebTaggingControl* properties can be found on MSDN at *http://msdn.microsoft.com/en-us/library/microsoft.sharepoint. taxonomy.taxonomywebtaggingcontrol.aspx*.

LISTING 14-4 Adding a *TaxonomyWebTaggingControl* to a page or Web Part to display a managed metadata field

```
using (SPSite site = new SPSite("http://teamsite.wingtiptoys.com/"))
{
    TaxonomySession taxonomySession = new TaxonomySession(site);
    TermStore termStore = taxonomySession.TermStores[0];
    Group termGroup = termStore.Groups["Enterprise"];
    TermSet termSet = termGroup.TermSets["ToyTypes"];

    WebTaggingControl.SSPList = termStore.Id.ToString();
    WebTaggingControl.TermSetList = termSet.Id.ToString();
    // This controls whether you can add new terms to the term set
    WebTaggingControl.AllowFillIn = false;
    // This controls whether we use an anchor term
    WebTaggingControl.AnchorId = termSet.Id;
    // This controls whether unresolved terms will be added to the term set
    WebTaggingControl.IsAddTerms = false;
    // This setting allows you to use the picker to browse the term set
    WebTaggingControl.IsDisplayPickerButton = true;
    // This setting enables/disables validation highlighting
    WebTaggingControl.IsIgnoreFormatting = false;
    WebTaggingControl.IsIncludeDeprecated = false;
    WebTaggingControl.IsIncludeUnavailable = false;
    // This setting modifies what is shown in/returned by the control,
    // if you want the GUIDS of parent terms then set this to true
    WebTaggingControl.IsIncludePathData = true;
    // This setting will include term set name resolution as well
    WebTaggingControl.IsIncludeTermSetName = false;
    WebTaggingControl.ID = termSet.Id.ToString();

    TaxonomyField taxonomyField =
      (TaxonomyField)site.RootWeb.Fields.GetFieldByInternalName("ToyType");
    WebTaggingControl.Text = taxonomyField.DefaultValue;
}
```

Putting a control that allows users to select values from the term store on a page is not much good if you can't process the value that is selected. To work with the values selected in a *TaxonomyWebTaggingControl* or a *TaxonomyField*, you should use the *TaxonomyFieldValue* class. This class has four properties and one method that you should use when saving a taxonomy value:

- **Label**   A string representing the actual label of the selected term.

- **TermGuid**   A string representing the GUID of the selected term. This GUID must be lower-cased. If the GUID is uppercased, it will work fine within SharePoint, but it might cause the Document Information Panel in programs in the Microsoft Office suite, such as Microsoft Word or Excel, to not recognize your term as a valid term in the term store. The term will be marked as if it doesn't exist in the term store and will be displayed in red. This will mean that the document can't be saved or checked in until the term is selected again from the term store.

- **ValidatedString**   A read-only, validated, serialized string representation of the *Taxonomy-FieldValue* object.

- **WssId**   An integer that uniquely identifies the list item containing the taxonomy field in a list.

- **PopulateFromLabelGuidPair(text)**   A method to update the value of the *TaxonomyField-Value* object with the value specified as the text parameter. The text parameter is a formatted string that contains the label, path GUIDs, and term GUID.

Listing 14-5 shows an example in which the value selected in the *TaxonomyWebTaggingControl* from Listing 14-4 is stored as the default value of the *TaxonomyField* from Listing 14-3. You first get the value that was selected in the *TaxonomyWebTaggingControl* and use that as input for the *PopulateFromLabelGuidPair* method. Then you select a *WssId*, which is the ID of the list item that the value has to be saved to. In this example, no list item is involved, because you are storing the value as the default value of a site column. In this case, you select –1 as the *WssId*. Even if you are saving a value to a list item, you can use –1 instead of the real list item ID, as long as you make sure that you store the value with the correct *SPListItem*. The next thing to do is define the GUID of the selected term and use this as input for the *TermGuid* property of the *TaxonomyFieldValue* object. Note that you convert the GUID to lowercase to make sure the value is recognized by the Office Document Information Panels. After you have properly set the value of the *TaxonomyFieldValue* object, you can use the *Validated-String* property to save the value to the default value of the *TaxonomyField*.

```
using (SPSite site = new SPSite("http://teamsite.wingtiptoys.com/"))
{
    TaxonomySession taxonomySession = new TaxonomySession(site);

    using (SPWeb web = site.OpenWeb())
    {
        TaxonomyField taxonomyField =
            site.RootWeb.Fields.GetFieldByInternalName("ToyType")
            as TaxonomyField;
        TaxonomyFieldValue defaultValue =
            new TaxonomyFieldValue(taxonomyField);

        try
        {
            defaultValue.PopulateFromLabelGuidPair(WebTaggingControl.Text);
            defaultValue.WssId = -1;
            // GUID should be stored lowercase, otherwise it will
            // not work in Office DIPs
            defaultValue.TermGuid = defaultValue.TermGuid.ToLower();
            // Set the selected default value for the site column
            taxonomyField.DefaultValue = defaultValue.ValidatedString;
        }
        catch (ArgumentNullException ex)
        {
            ErrorMessage.Text = "Creating a new value is not allowed ";
            ErrorMessage.Text += "in this term set, please select from ";
            ErrorMessage.Text += "the existing terms.";
            taxonomyField.DefaultValue = String.Empty;
        }

        taxonomyField.Update(true);
    }
}
```

Understanding content type syndication

In the previous sections you have looked at the Managed Metadata Service Application term store and how its contents can be used in custom solutions. The Managed Metadata Service Application is more than just the term store, though. One of its other important features is the *content type syndication* feature. Content type syndication can be used to synchronize content types across site collections.

The content type syndication feature uses one site collection as the central storage point for content types. This site is called the *Content Type Hub*. A site collection can be promoted to a Content Type Hub by activating the site collection–scoped Content Type Syndication Hub feature. The hub will then have to be registered as the hub in the properties of the Managed Metadata Service Application. This will enable the service application to publish the content types to all site collections that are set as consumers (see Figure 14-3).

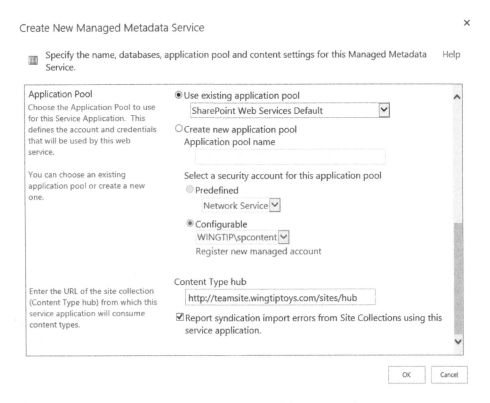

FIGURE 14-3 The Content Type Hub is defined in the properties of the Managed Metadata Service Application.

In the properties of the Managed Metadata Service Application Proxy, the hub can be selected so that site collections in web applications that are using the service application will consume the published content types (see Figure 14-4).

FIGURE 14-4 The properties of the Managed Metadata Service Application Proxy show that site collections that use this service application will also consume content types from the Content Type Hub.

After syndication has been set up, content types can be created in the site collection that has been defined as the Content Type Hub. Content types can be created either manually or by using CAML or code-behind. Because content types have to be created only once and are distributed to other site collections by using the syndication functionality, they will usually be created manually in the Content Type Hub. If you wanted to use the same content types in multiple site collections without using content type syndication, you would have to create a custom solution and activate the feature that creates the content types on all sites where the content types should be used.

When a content type has been created in the Content Type Hub, the content type can be published. Figure 14-5 shows the content type publishing user interface. When a published content type is changed, it can be republished, and if a published content type should no longer be used, it can be unpublished. A published content type doesn't become available in the site collections that are consuming content types from the Content Type Hub immediately. Before content types are available to the site collections, there are two timer jobs that have to run. The first one is the Content Type Hub timer job. This job only has to run once after a Content Type Hub has been registered with the Managed Metadata Service Application. By default, it runs once per day at 1:00 A.M. If you have access to the SharePoint server and to Central Administration, it will be worth it to start this job manually so that you can use the Content Type Hub on the day that you create it, instead of having to wait until the next day. The second timer job is the Content Type Subscriber job. This job is responsible for picking up the published content types from the Content Type Hub and pushing them to the consuming site collections. The Content Type Subscriber job runs once per hour by default.

Content Type Publishing: Customers

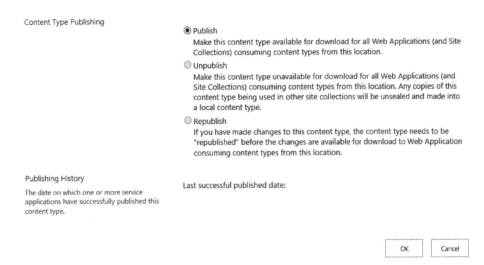

Content Type Publishing

◉ Publish
  Make this content type available for download for all Web Applications (and Site Collections) consuming content types from this location.

◯ Unpublish
  Make this content type unavailable for download for all Web Applications (and Site Collections) consuming content types from this location. Any copies of this content type being used in other site collections will be unsealed and made into a local content type.

◯ Republish
  If you have made changes to this content type, the content type needs to be "republished" before the changes are available for download to Web Application consuming content types from this location.

Publishing History

The date on which one or more service applications have successfully published this content type.

Last successful published date:

[OK]   [Cancel]

FIGURE 14-5 This screen shot shows the content type publishing page that is available for content types in the Content Type Hub.

In summary, to use published content types in a site collection, you have to register the Content Type Hub with the Managed Metadata Service Application and the Managed Metadata Service Application Proxy. If this didn't happen automatically (in which case SharePoint will warn you), you have to activate the Content Type Syndication Hub. Then you will have to create and publish the content type you want to use and, as a last step, both the Content Type Hub timer job and the Content Type Subscriber timer job have to run.

Using document services

SharePoint has a long list of simple and complex features that are related to document and records management. In this section, a couple of them will be discussed, either because they have changed in SharePoint 2013 or because they are the more complex features.

Understanding versioning

When versioning is enabled on a library or list, it enables users to keep track of changes that were made to a document or list item, and it allows users to look at previous versions of the document or item. You can choose whether you want to keep major or minor versions and how many major and minor versions you want to keep. Generally speaking, a major version is a published version (1.0, 2.0, 3.0), and a minor version is a work in progress (1.3, 2.1, 3.4). If you do enable versioning, it is a best practice to set a maximum number of major and minor versions that should be kept. If you don't explicitly set this, all versions of all documents or items in the list will be stored, which, especially for documents, could add up to quite a lot of storage. Former versions do count toward the storage quota of a site.

You can use the versioning–specific security settings to determine who can view draft items or documents. You can choose between Readers and Contributors. You can also select to require content approval. If content approval is required, items have to be approved before they can be published and made visible to all users. If content approval is required, an extra versioning security option is enabled that allows you to make draft items visible to only Approvers and the author. Figure 14-6 shows the versioning settings page of a document library. The page for a list looks almost the same, except for the fact that it doesn't have the Require Check Out option on it. Setting Require Check Out to Yes is a good idea in many cases. Though it might be a little annoying for users to have to check documents in and out, it is nowhere near as annoying as running into saving conflicts when two people are working on the same document without realizing they are working on the same document. When check out is not required, users can check out a document manually, but most users will not remember to do so.

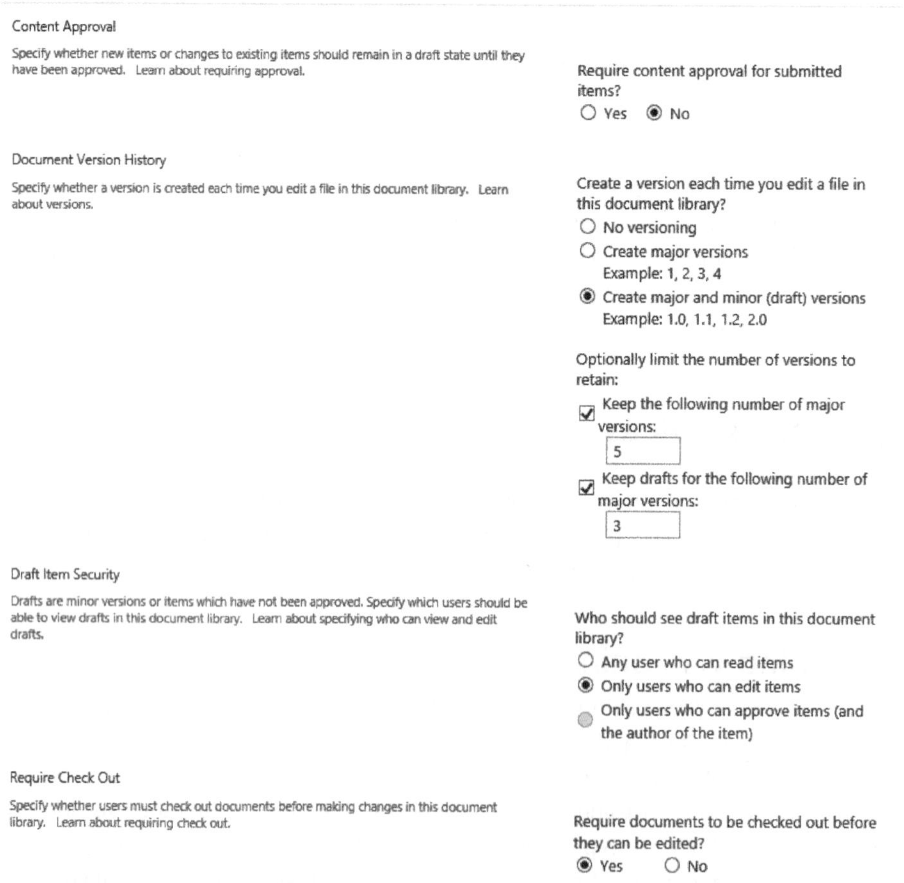

Content Approval

Specify whether new items or changes to existing items should remain in a draft state until they have been approved. Learn about requiring approval.

Require content approval for submitted items?
○ Yes   ◉ No

Document Version History

Specify whether a version is created each time you edit a file in this document library. Learn about versions.

Create a version each time you edit a file in this document library?
○ No versioning
○ Create major versions
 Example: 1, 2, 3, 4
◉ Create major and minor (draft) versions
 Example: 1.0, 1.1, 1.2, 2.0

Optionally limit the number of versions to retain:
☑ Keep the following number of major versions:
[5]
☑ Keep drafts for the following number of major versions:
[3]

Draft Item Security

Drafts are minor versions or items which have not been approved. Specify which users should be able to view drafts in this document library. Learn about specifying who can view and edit drafts.

Who should see draft items in this document library?
○ Any user who can read items
◉ Only users who can edit items
○ Only users who can approve items (and the author of the item)

Require Check Out

Specify whether users must check out documents before making changes in this document library. Learn about requiring check out.

Require documents to be checked out before they can be edited?
◉ Yes   ○ No

FIGURE 14-6 This screen shot shows the versioning settings page of a document library.

When using CAML to create a list, as shown in the following code, you can enable versioning by setting the *VersioningEnabled* attribute to *true*. With CAML it is not possible to add the nuances such as the number of major and minor versions and who can view draft items, though:

```
<ListInstance Title="Products List"
              OnQuickLaunch="TRUE"
              TemplateType="10000"
              Url="Lists/WingtipToysProductsList"
              Description="Wingtip products list"
              VersioningEnabled="TRUE"
              Hidden="FALSE">
</ListInstance>
```

With code-behind you have a lot more flexibility than when you are using CAML. The following properties would cause the same behavior as the settings from Figure 14-6:

```
SPList.EnableModeration = false;
SPList.EnableVersioning = true;
SPList.EnableMinorVersions = true;
SPList.MajorVersionLimit = 5;
SPList.MajorWithMinorVersionsLimit = 5;
SPList.DraftVersionVisibility = DraftVisibilityType.Author;
SPList.ForceCheckout = true;
```

The settings are further described in the following list:

- **EnableModeration**   Enables or disables content approval

- **EnableVersioning**   Enables versioning using only major versions

- **EnableMinorVersions**   Also enables the use of minor versions

- **MajorVersionLimit**   Limits the number of major versions that are stored to the number that is assigned to it, for lists and libraries on which minor versioning is not enabled

- **MajorWithMinorVersionsLimit**   Limits the number of major versions that are stored to the number that is assigned to it, for lists and libraries on which minor versioning is enabled

- **DraftVersionVisibility**   Allows you to use the *DraftVisibilityType* enumeration to select who can view draft versions of documents and items

- **ForceCheckOut**   Can be used to force users to check out a document before they can edit the document

In Figure 14-6, the obvious property that is missing is the one to limit the number of minor versions. You can't set a maximum number of minor versions that should be stored by using the object model. This is one of the few places where the SharePoint user interface can do more than what you can achieve by using the object model.

If versioning is enabled on a library or list, updating items by using the object model can have an impact on versions that are created. If a maximum number of major and minor versions is set, creating a new version might cause a user's version to be deleted. The following list describes how the different methods in the object model that allow you to update items influence the creation of new versions and version numbers.

- **SPListItem.Update()** Updates the item, creates a new version, and increases the version number.

- **SPListItem.UpdateOverwriteVersion()** Does the same as *Update()*, but without creating a new version and version number.

- **SPListItem.SystemUpdate(true)** Updates the item, but doesn't change the *Modified* or *Modified By* field. It does create a new version and will increment the version number.

- **SPListItem.SystemUpdate(false)** Updates the item, but doesn't change the *Modified* or *Modified By* field. It also doesn't create a new version and will not increment the version number.

- **SPListItem.SystemUpdate()** Calling *SystemUpdate()* is the same as calling *SystemUpdate(false)*.

When working with SharePoint sites, users can use the shortcut menu and the Version History button to get to previous versions of the item or document. The equivalent is also available through the object model by using the *SPListItemVersion* class, as shown in Listing 14-6.

LISTING 14-6 Using the *SPListItemVersion* class

```
using (SPSite site = new SPSite("http://teamsite.wingtiptoys.com/"))
{
  SPWeb web = site.OpenWeb();
  SPListItemCollection listitems =
    web.GetList("http://teamsite.wingtiptoys.com/Shared Documents").Items;
  string versionNr;
  bool isCurrentVersion;
  SPListItem versionItem;
  string createdBy;

  foreach (SPListItem listitem in listitems)
  {
    foreach (SPListItemVersion itemVersion in listitem.Versions)
    {
      versionNr = itemVersion.VersionLabel;
      isCurrentVersion = itemVersion.IsCurrentVersion;
      versionItem = itemVersion.ListItem;
      createdBy = itemVersion.CreatedBy.User.Name;
    }
  }
}
```

Understanding Document IDs

When users create a document in a document library, or add a document to a document library, they can share it with their colleagues by sending them a URL that points to the document. This is a great way to find the document at a later date. If the document is moved or renamed, though, its URL will change. The URL that users were using to access the document will no longer work and will become useless.

In SharePoint 2010, Document IDs were introduced to address this challenge. When the Document ID Service feature is activated on a site collection, the *Document* and *Document Set* content types in that site collection get three new columns added to them:

- **DocID**   Contains the Document ID

- **Static URL**   Contains a URL that includes the Document ID that can be used to access the document

- **PersistID**   Used to determine whether a Document ID should be kept, or whether it should be reassigned

After the columns have been added to the content types, all documents and Document Sets that are added to the site collection are automatically assigned a unique Document ID that is stored in the DocID column. A Static URL is generated and stored as well. The Static URL stays with the document, even if it is renamed or moved, provided that the Move or Send To functionality from SharePoint is used. When a document is saved to a local hard disk and then uploaded again to a different site, it will effectively have been moved, but SharePoint will not be aware that this was a move and not a Delete and Add, so SharePoint will assign the document a new Document ID and Static URL. Propagating the DocID, Static URL, and PersistID columns to all content types in all subsites of the site collection is done by the Document ID Enable/Disable timer job. This job runs once per day at 9:00 P.M. by default.

Any existing documents already in the site collection when the Document ID Service feature is activated will be assigned Document IDs and Static URLs in a deferred batch process implemented by the Document ID Assignment Job timer job. By default, this job runs once per day at 10:00 P.M. If you do activate the Document ID Service feature and you have access to Central Administration, you can start the timer job manually. Don't increase the frequency of the timer job, though, because you need it to run only after you have activated the Document ID Service feature on a site; if you increase the frequency, you will waste valuable resources on your server.

To enable users to use the Document ID to access documents, SharePoint contains a special application page, DocIdRedir.aspx, which accepts the Document ID as a query string value and redirects the requester to the document. The URL will look similar to this: *http://teamsite.wingtiptoys.com/ sites/hr/_layouts/15/DocIdRedir.aspx?ID=ZTWDNX7TXESH-3-1*. Translated, this URL tells you that the document was originally stored in the */sites/hr* site collection, of which the Document ID prefix is *ZTWDNX7TXESH*. The document is stored in a library with an ID of 3, and this document is the first document in this library. When this URL is requested, the DocIdRedir.aspx page first tries to use the SharePoint out-of-the-box search functionality to find the document by searching for the Static URL.

The search functionality won't be able to find the document unless it is indexed, though, meaning that depending on your crawl schedule, it might take a while before the document can be found by using search. If the document can't be found by using search, SharePoint will use the Document ID provider lookup logic to try to find the document. This will work only if the document is still stored in the site collection that is part of the Static URL.

A Document ID consists of three parts:

- **A Document ID prefix**   A site collection–scoped unique string value. When the Document ID Services feature is activated, this prefix is automatically generated by SharePoint, but it can be changed by the site collection administrator to something more meaningful. When changing the Document ID prefix manually, the site collection administrator will have to make sure that the prefix is still unique across all site collections that use the same Search Service Application (usually this means all site collections in the farm), otherwise the Document ID functionality will not function properly.

- **A list ID**   An ID that is automatically assigned to every list. Within each site collection, lists are numbered 1 to *x*, with *x* being the number of lists in the site collection.

- **A Document ID**   An ID that is automatically assigned to every document and Document Set in the site collection. Within each list, documents are numbered 1 to *x*, *x* being the number of documents in the list.

A Document ID is formatted as *[Document ID prefix]-[List ID]-[Document ID]*. Because the list ID is unique only within a site collection and the document ID is unique only within a list, it is very important that the Document ID prefix is unique across all site collections, because otherwise you'll end up with duplicate Document IDs.

Creating custom Document ID providers

Developers can create custom Document ID providers when they want to override either the default Document ID string pattern or how documents are found. This is done by first creating a provider and then registering it with a site collection.

To create a new Document ID provider, create a new class that inherits from the *Microsoft.Office. DocumentManagement.DocumentIdProvider* class. This class has four members that should be overridden:

- *GenerateDocumentId()*   This method is responsible for creating the unique Document ID string. Overriding this allows the developer to change how new Document IDs are generated. It is the responsibility of the developer to ensure that the generated ID is unique across the site collection. Also note that, if desired, this method could be used to generate an ID that is unique at a scope higher than site collection, such as web applications or even the whole farm.

- *GetDocumentUrlsById()*   This method accepts a Document ID string and returns a list of URLs for the corresponding document. It can return multiple values, because developers can copy documents programmatically from one location to another and specify that the Document ID be retained on the copied instance.

- **GetSampleDocumentIdText()** This method generates a sample Document ID string that is displayed in the Find By Document ID Web Part, giving users a hint as to what the ID looks like.

- **DoCustomSearchBeforeDefaultSearch** This Boolean property tells SharePoint whether it should default to using the SharePoint search feature or the Document ID provider to find the URL of the Document ID string.

The code shown in Listing 14-7 demonstrates a custom Document ID provider that uses the first part of the hosting web application, site collection, site, list, and list item's ID as the Document ID string.

LISTING 14-7 A custom Document ID provider

```
public class MoreUniqueDocumentIDProvider : DocumentIdProvider
{
  private const string DOCID_FORMAT = "{0}-{1}-{2}-{3}-{4}";

  public override bool DoCustomSearchBeforeDefaultSearch
  {
    get { return false; }
  }

  public override string GenerateDocumentId(SPListItem listItem)
  {
    string listItemID = listItem.ID.ToString();
    string listID = listItem.ParentList.ID.ToString().Substring(0, 4);
    string webID = listItem.Web.ID.ToString().Substring(0, 4);
    string siteID = listItem.Web.Site.ID.ToString().Substring(0, 4);
    string webAppID =
          listItem.Web.Site.WebApplication.Id.ToString().Substring(0, 4);
    return string.Format(DOCID_FORMAT, webAppID, siteID,
                    webID, listID, listItemID);
  }

  public override string[] GetDocumentUrlsById(SPSite hostingSiteCollection,
                                      string documentId)
  {
    List<string> possibleURLs = new List<string>();
    string[] brokenDownDocID = documentId.Split("-".ToCharArray()[0]);

    // find the Web application
    SPWebService webService = hostingSiteCollection.WebApplication.WebService;

    foreach (SPWebApplication webAppplication in webService.WebApplications)
    {
      if (webAppplication.Id.ToString().StartsWith(brokenDownDocID[0]))
      {
        // find the SPSite (if multiple, won't matter as it will go to next one...)
        foreach (SPSite site in webAppplication.Sites)
```

```
              {
        if (site.ID.ToString().StartsWith(brokenDownDocID[1]))
        {
          // find the SPWeb
          // (if multiple, won't matter as it will go to next one...)
          foreach (SPWeb web in site.AllWebs)
          {
            if (web.ID.ToString().StartsWith(brokenDownDocID[2]))
            {
              foreach (SPList list in web.Lists)
              {
                if (list.ID.ToString().StartsWith(brokenDownDocID[3]))
                {
                  // find the item in the list
                  SPListItem targetItem = list.GetItemById(
                                          Int32.Parse(brokenDownDocID[4]));

                  if (targetItem != null)
                  {
                    possibleURLs.Add(String.Format("{0}//{1}", web.Url, targetItem.Url));
                  }
                }
              }
            }
            web.Dispose();
          }
        }
        site.Dispose();
      }
    }
  }
  return possibleURLs.ToArray();
}

public override string GetSampleDocumentIdText(Microsoft.SharePoint.SPSite site)
{
  return string.Format(DOCID_FORMAT, "55DA526F",
  "FD9D4836", "FD0910DC", "15B4AD8A", "ABDC1A45");
}
}
```

After the Document ID provider has been created, it needs to be registered with a site collection. This can be done by using the Feature receiver of a site collection–scoped feature. Use the *Microsoft. Office.DocumentManagement.DocumentId* class to set the provider for a specified site collection, as shown in Listing 14-8.

LISTING 14-8 Registering a custom Document ID provider

```
public override void FeatureActivated(SPFeatureReceiverProperties properties)
{
  SPSite site = properties.Feature.Parent as SPSite;
  MoreUniqueDocumentIDProvider docIDProvider = new MoreUniqueDocumentIDProvider();
  DocumentId.SetProvider(site, docIDProvider);
}

public override void FeatureDeactivating(SPFeatureReceiverProperties properties)
{
  SPSite site = properties.Feature.Parent as SPSite;
  DocumentId.SetDefaultProvider(site);
}
```

Understanding Document Sets

SharePoint document libraries allow users to create and interact with individual files. These individual files can be the targets of workflows and event receivers, support versioning, or have unique permissions applied to them. A single document, however, does not always represent a complete work product. A work product might consist of multiple documents, such as a proposal with an invoice with supporting timesheets, travel receipts, a statement of work, and other resources. SharePoint includes a capability that supports creating and managing sets of documents as a single work product: the Document Set.

A *Document Set* is a specific content type that inherits from the *Folder* content type. It allows users to group documents in the same way that folders do; however, it also adds the following characteristics:

- **Allowed content types** The types of content that are permitted within the *Document Set*. Documents within the *Document Set* can use these content types.

- **Shared fields** Common columns that exist on the *Document Set* and child content types. Values for these columns can be set on the Document Set level and are propagated to all documents within the *Document Set*.

- **Welcome page** SharePoint implements a *Document Set* as a Web Part page when users view it with a browser. The Welcome page displays specified fields from the *Document Set* content type, in addition to the individual documents that are part of the *Document Set*.

- **Default content** When users create a new instance of the *Document Set*, the default content can provision new content that is associated with one of the allowed content types automatically.

To make the *Document Set* content type available in a site collection, you have to activate the Document Sets site collection–scoped feature. After the feature has been activated, you can add the *Document Set* content type to libraries in the site collection, or you can create your own content type that inherits from the *Document Set* content type. When interacting with a *Document Set*, the

SharePoint interface adds a new tool tab group called *Manage* that provides additional buttons that allow you to manage the *Document Set* as a whole. The buttons are mostly the same as the some of the ones that are available for items and files, such as Edit Properties, Delete, Version History, and Workflows, except for the fact that they all apply to the *Document Set* as a whole and not to a single document. Figure 14-7 shows a *Document Set* Welcome page and the Manage tab and its buttons.

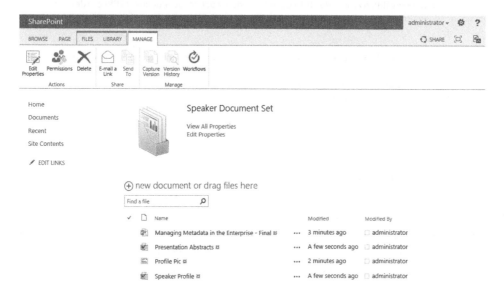

FIGURE 14-7 A screen shot showing a *Document Set* Welcome page and Manage tab.

Creating a new Document Set by using the browser is straightforward. After making sure that the Document Sets feature is activated, you can create a new content type that derives from the *Document Set* content type and configure its settings. As with any content type, you can add site columns to it; however, for a *Document Set*, you can also determine what columns should be displayed on the Welcome page and what columns should be shared columns. *Shared columns* and their values are automatically synchronized to all files in the *Document Set*.

The new content type can be added to a document library in the same way that regular content types are added. Creating a new *Document Set* based on the new content type can be done by clicking the arrow below the New Document button on the Files tab and selecting the new *Document Set* content type. After a *Document Set* has been created, documents can be added to it, in addition to metadata.

Creating Document Sets declaratively

Creating *Document Set* content types by using the browser is simple, but it is not a very reusable approach. If you want to use a *Document Set* content type in multiple sites and you don't want to use content type syndication, the best approach is to create them declaratively in Microsoft Visual Studio and package them in a .wsp file. The first step in creating a *Document Set* content type in Visual Studio is the same as the first step in creating any other content type. You create a new project, based on the SharePoint 2013 - Empty Project template. Then you add a new content type to it. In the SharePoint Customization Wizard, you can select the content type that your content type should inherit from. Here you can select the *Document Set* content type. The *Document Set* content type will be created in exactly the same way that other content types are created in Visual Studio. The only thing that might reveal that you just created a content type that inherits from the *Document Set* content type is the *ContentType* ID. The *Document Set ContentType* ID is *0x0120D520*, which means that the *ContentType* ID of all content types inheriting from *Document Set* will start with *0x0120D520*.

Because Visual Studio creates all content types as equal, you will have to add the extra plumbing and features that are specific to a *Document Set* yourself. If you want to add allowed content types and custom site columns to the *Document Set*, you will have to create those first. You can do this in the same solution, or in a different one. It is easier to create all the parts of the *Document Set* content type in the same solution, so that you don't create two solutions that are dependent on one another. The allowed content types can only be the *Document* content type, or any content types that inherit from the Document or Folder content type.

Either you can set the Name, Description, and Group on the Content Type tab in Visual Studio, or you can adjust the CAML in the Elements.xml file. The same is true for the site columns, but for site columns it is a lot quicker to use the Columns tab, so that you can simply select the columns instead of having to write a lot of CAML and look up the IDs and internal names of the columns that have to be added to the new *Document Set* content type. Adding columns by using the form will automatically update the Elements.xml file. Listing 14-9 shows the CAML in the Elements.xml file after the Keywords and Categories columns have been added to the content type.

LISTING 14-9 *Document Set* content type fields and configuration information

```xml
<Elements xmlns="http://schemas.microsoft.com/sharepoint/">
  <!-- Parent ContentType: Document Set (0x0120D520) -->
  <ContentType ID="0x0120D52000A0DD237060674E6D803E68B19DB425A2"
    Name="Toy Specification Doc Set"
    Group="Wingtip Toys Content Types"
    Description="Document Set used to store all information that specifies a toy."
    Inherits="FALSE">
    <FieldRefs>
      <FieldRef ID="{b66e9b50-a28e-469b-b1a0-af0e45486874}"
                Name="Keywords"
                DisplayName="Keywords" />
      <FieldRef ID="{9ebcd900-9d05-46c8-8f4d-e46e87328844}"
                Name="Categories"
                DisplayName="Categories" />
  </ContentType>
</Elements>
```

The rest of the content type definition is specific to creating a Document Set. SharePoint sets the Document Set–specific characteristics via the *<XmlDocuments />* section of the content type. First, add all the content types that are allowed in the Document Set, referencing them by their *ContentTypeId*, as shown in Listing 14-10.

LISTING 14-10 Specifying the allowed content types in the toy specification *Document Set* content type

```
<XmlDocument NamespaceURI=
"http://schemas.microsoft.com/office/documentsets/allowedcontenttypes">
<act:AllowedContentTypes xmlns:act=
"http://schemas.microsoft.com/office/documentsets/allowedcontenttypes"
LastModified="1/1/1 0:00:01 AM">
  <!-- Document -->
  <AllowedContentType id="0x0101" />
  <!-- Picture -->
  <AllowedContentType id="0x010102" />
  <!-- Summary Tasks-->
  <AllowedContentType id="0x012004" />
</act:AllowedContentTypes>
</XmlDocument>
```

There are three columns in the toy specification *Document Set* that should be kept in sync with all other content types in the collection:

- Description

- Keywords

- Categories

These fields are defined as shared fields, referencing the ID of the Site Column definition, as shown in Listing 14-11.

LISTING 14-11 Specifying the shared fields in the toy specification *Document Set* content type

```
<XmlDocument
NamespaceURI="http://schemas.microsoft.com/office/documentsets/sharedfields">
<sf:SharedFields
  xmlns:sf="http://schemas.microsoft.com/office/documentsets/sharedfields"
  LastModified="1/1/1 0:00:01 AM">
  <!-- Categories -->
  <SharedField id="9ebcd900-9d05-46c8-8f4d-e46e87328844" />
  <!-- Description -->
  <SharedField id="cbb92da4-fd46-4c7d-af6c-3128c2a5576e" />
  <!-- Keywords -->
  <SharedField id="b66e9b50-a28e-469b-b1a0-af0e45486874" />
</sf:SharedFields>
</XmlDocument>
```

Next, specify the fields in the *Document Set* content type that should be displayed on the Welcome page when users view an instance of the toy specification *Document Set*, again referencing the ID of the Site Column definition, as shown in Listing 14-12.

LISTING 14-12 Specifying the Welcome page fields in the toy specification *Document Set* content type

```
<XmlDocument
 NamespaceURI=
   "http://schemas.microsoft.com/office/documentsets/welcomepagefields">
 <wpf:WelcomePageFields xmlns:wpf=
    "http://schemas.microsoft.com/office/documentsets/welcomepagefields"
   LastModified="1/1/1 0:00:01 AM">
  <!-- Categories -->
  <WelcomePageField id="9ebcd900-9d05-46c8-8f4d-e46e87328844" />
 </wpf:WelcomePageFields>
</XmlDocument>
```

When users create new instances of the *Document Set*, those instances should contain a toy specification sheet and a toy specification guidelines PDF file. Both files are attached to the Document content type. Before you can add these files, you should define where they can be found. You can do this by defining the toy specification *Document Set* content type's folder directly underneath the *<ContentType>* element, as shown here:

```
<Folder TargetName="_cts/Toy Specification Doc Set" />
```

Listing 14-13 shows how to provision the default content for the *Document Set*.

LISTING 14-13 Specifying default content for the toy specification *Document Set* content type

```
<XmlDocument
 NamespaceURI=
   "http://schemas.microsoft.com/office/documentsets/defaultdocuments">
 <dd:DefaultDocuments xmlns:dd=
    "http://schemas.microsoft.com/office/documentsets/defaultdocuments"
   LastModified="1/1/1 0:00:01 AM"
   AddSetName="True">
  <DefaultDocument name"Toy Specification Guidelines.pdf"
    idContentType="0x0101" />
  <DefaultDocument name="Toy Specification Sheet.xlsx"
    idContentType="0x0101" />
 </dd:DefaultDocuments>
</XmlDocument>
```

Because SharePoint won't be able to make up the default content out of nothing, you have to make sure that the specification sheet and guideline documents are provisioned in the SharePoint site. The best way to do this is by using a Module. Add a new Module project item in the Visual Studio 2012 project that contains an Excel file and a PDF file, and provision them to the folder referenced in Listing 14-13. Listing 14-14 shows how to add the default content.

LISTING 14-14 Provisioning the default content of the *Document Set*

```xml
<Elements xmlns="http://schemas.microsoft.com/sharepoint/">
  <Module Name="ToySpecificationDefaultContent">
    <File Path="ToySpecificationDefaultContent\Toy Specification Sheet.xlsx"
          Url="_cts/Toy Specification Doc Set/Toy Specification Sheet.xlsx" />
    <File Path=
          "ToySpecificationDefaultContent\Toy Specification Guidelines.pdf"
          Url="_cts/Toy Specification Doc Set/Toy Specification Guidelines.pdf" />
  </Module>
</Elements>
```

At this point, the *Document Set* is complete. An optional step is to create a custom Welcome page that users will be taken to when they view the Document Set. When showing the Document Set, SharePoint looks for a file named DocSetHomePage.aspx in the Document Set's folder. If it exists, it will be used as the Welcome page for that Document Set. If it doesn't exist, a generic Welcome page will be shown instead.

In the case of the toy specification Document Set, the Welcome page could display Wingtip Toy's tagline: *More fun with Wingtip Toys!* To create a custom Welcome page, create a copy of the default Welcome page that is provisioned by the Document Set Feature found in *{SharePoint Root}\TEMPLATE\ FEATURES\DocumentSet* and provision it by using a Module SharePoint project item, as shown in Listing 14-15.

LISTING 14-15 Provisioning the Document Set Welcome page

```xml
<Module Name="ToySpecificationWelcomePage" RootWebOnly="TRUE">
  <File Path="ToySpecificationWelcomePage\DocSetHomePage.aspx"
        Url="_cts/Toy Specification Doc Set/DocSetHomePage.aspx">

    <AllUsersWebPart WebPartOrder="0" WebPartZoneID="WebPartZone_TopLeft">
      <!-- WebPart element omitted for clarity -->
    </AllUsersWebPart>

    <AllUsersWebPart WebPartOrder="0" WebPartZoneID="WebPartZone_CenterMain">
      <!-- WebPart element omitted for clarity -->
    </AllUsersWebPart>

    <AllUsersWebPart WebPartOrder="0" WebPartZoneID="WebPartZone_Top">
      <!-- WebPart element omitted for clarity -->
    </AllUsersWebPart>

  </File>
</Module>
```

The three *<AllUsersWebPart />* elements provision an Image Web Part with the default Document Set image, a Document Set Contents Web Part that shows the contents of the Web Part, and the Document Set Properties Web Part that shows all the Welcome page properties. The easiest way to get these values is to copy them from the element manifest in the out-of-the-box *Document Set* Feature.

The final step is to make sure that there is one feature in the project that is set to site scope and that is named appropriately. The content type and modules should all be added to this one feature. At this point, the Visual Studio 2012 project should look similar to the one shown in Figure 14-8.

FIGURE 14-8 This screen shot shows the Toy Specification Document Set project in Visual Studio 2012.

Now that the solution is ready, you can package and deploy it. This will activate the feature that provisions the Toy Specification Document Set on your target site. To start using it, you just have to add the Toy Specification Document Set content type to a library, and you will be able to create a new instance of the Document Set to view the result. Figure 14-9 shows the result, a Toy Specification Document Set for a doll called Aglaia.

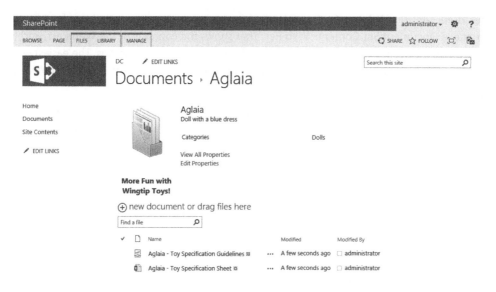

FIGURE 14-9 This screen shot shows the Toy Specification Document Set.

Using the Content Organizer

Designing a large document repository in SharePoint requires proper planning to make sure that the repository is set up in a way that is scalable. Content in large repositories is often organized based on its metadata. In a repository with millions of documents, users will need help to store their documents in the right place. Help could be provided by document librarians or content stewards, but it would be easier if the support for users were automated. To help manage the contents of large document repositories in SharePoint, the Content Organizer can be used. The Content Organizer assists by checking the metadata of a new document against some predefined and prioritized rules and, if a matching rule is found, routing or moving the content to the document library and folder specified in the rule. The Content Organizer can even manage large libraries by automatically creating new folders if the content in the target folder grows beyond a specified threshold.

The Content Organizer functionality can be enabled on a site by activating the site-scoped Content Organizer feature. This adds a library to the site called the *Drop Off* library, and it adds two new links to the Site Administration section in the Site Settings page: the Content Organizer Settings and Content Organizer Rules links. The Content Organizer Settings page allows the site owner to determine how the Content Organizer feature should be used, for instance, whether users should be redirected to the Drop Off library when they try to upload a document to libraries that have Content Organizer rules pointed at them, whether a Content Organizer rule can route documents to a different site collection, and whether a folder's size should be managed automatically. The Content Organizer Rules page shows a special type of list that stores all the Content Organizer rules that are created for the site. The list is called the *RoutingRules* list, and items that are added to it are based on the *Rule* content type.

The site used for this example is based on the Document Center template (the template is BDR#0, in case you want to create the site by using code or Windows PowerShell). A document library called *Spreadsheets* has been added to the site, in addition to a picture library called *Pictures*. A new Choice site column called *Document Type* has been created with two possible values: *Document* and *Spreadsheet*. The column has been added to the *Document* content type. For most Content Organizer settings, the defaults are used, except for the Rule Managers, for which the Owner group of the site is used, as shown in Figure 14-10.

FIGURE 14-10 The Content Organizer Settings page shows mostly default values and adjusted Rule Managers.

The next step is to create the Content Organizer rules. The first rule (shown in Figure 14-11) will pick up all documents that are linked to the *Document* content type and that have the *Document Type* property set to *Document*, to move the documents to the Document library.

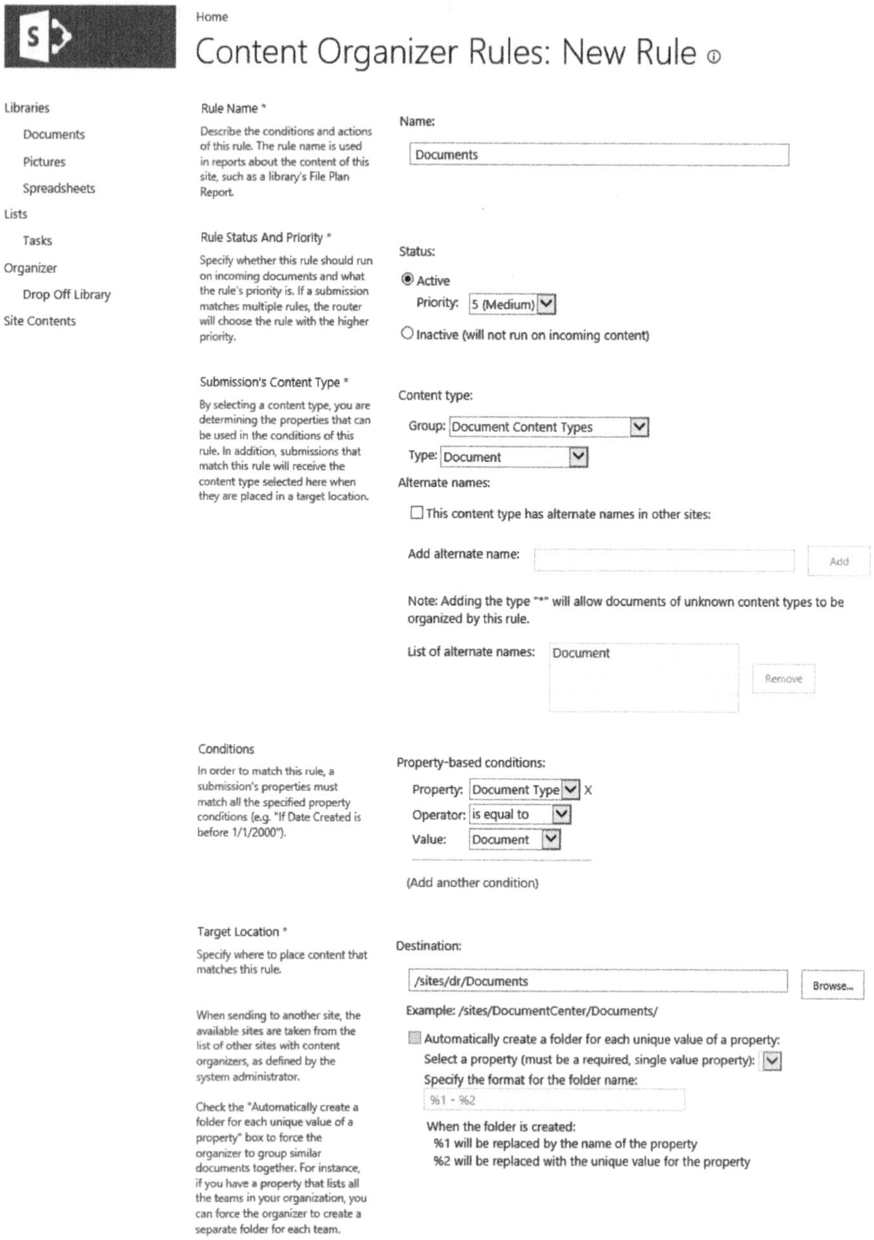

S

Home

Content Organizer Rules: New Rule ⓘ

Libraries

Documents

Pictures

Spreadsheets

Lists

Tasks

Organizer

Drop Off Library

Site Contents

Rule Name *

Describe the conditions and actions of this rule. The rule name is used in reports about the content of this site, such as a library's File Plan Report.

Name:

Documents

Rule Status And Priority *

Specify whether this rule should run on incoming documents and what the rule's priority is. If a submission matches multiple rules, the router will choose the rule with the higher priority.

Status:

◉ Active

Priority: 5 (Medium) ▾

○ Inactive (will not run on incoming content)

Submission's Content Type *

By selecting a content type, you are determining the properties that can be used in the conditions of this rule. In addition, submissions that match this rule will receive the content type selected here when they are placed in a target location.

Content type:

Group: Document Content Types ▾

Type: Document ▾

Alternate names:

☐ This content type has alternate names in other sites:

Add alternate name: Add

Note: Adding the type "*" will allow documents of unknown content types to be organized by this rule.

List of alternate names: Document

Remove

Conditions

In order to match this rule, a submission's properties must match all the specified property conditions (e.g. "If Date Created is before 1/1/2000").

Property-based conditions:

Property: Document Type ▾ X

Operator: is equal to ▾

Value: Document ▾

(Add another condition)

Target Location *

Specify where to place content that matches this rule.

When sending to another site, the available sites are taken from the list of other sites with content organizers, as defined by the system administrator.

Check the "Automatically create a folder for each unique value of a property" box to force the organizer to group similar documents together. For instance, if you have a property that lists all the teams in your organization, you can force the organizer to create a separate folder for each team.

Destination:

/sites/dr/Documents   Browse...

Example: /sites/DocumentCenter/Documents/

☐ Automatically create a folder for each unique value of a property:
  Select a property (must be a required, single value property): ▾
  Specify the format for the folder name:
  %1 - %2

  When the folder is created:
  %1 will be replaced by the name of the property
  %2 will be replaced with the unique value for the property

FIGURE 14-11 The Content Organizer Rules page shows the settings for a specific rule.

Not only can Content Organizer rules be created through the user interface, they can also be created programmatically by using the classes from the *Microsoft.Office.RecordsManagement. RecordsRepository* namespace. Listing 14-16 shows the code that creates a rule to route documents, where *Document Type* is set to *Spreadsheet*.

LISTING 14-16 Creating a Content Organizer rule

```
SPSite currentSite = new SPSite("http://teamsite.wingtiptoys.com/");
SPWeb currentWeb = currentSite.OpenWeb();
currentWeb.AllowUnsafeUpdates = true;

EcmDocumentRoutingWeb contentOrganizerWeb = new EcmDocumentRoutingWeb(currentWeb);

EcmDocumentRouterRule newRule = new EcmDocumentRouterRule(currentWeb);
newRule.Name = "Spreadsheets";
newRule.Priority = "5";

SPContentType documentContentType = currentWeb.ContentTypes["Document"];
newRule.ContentTypeString = documentContentType.Name;

SPField documentTypeField = currentWeb.Fields.GetField("Document Type");
string ruleOperator = "IsEqual";
string ruleValue = "Spreadsheet";
string conditionString = String.Format(@"<Condition Column=""{0}|{1}|{2}""
                                          Operator=""{3}""
                                          Value=""{4}"" />",
                    documentTypeField.Id,
                    documentTypeField.InternalName,
                    documentTypeField.Title,
                    ruleOperator,
                    ruleValue);

string conditionsXml = String.Format("<Conditions>{0}</Conditions>", conditionString);

newRule.ConditionsString = conditionsXml;

SPList spreadSheetLibrary = currentWeb.Lists["Spreadsheets"];
newRule.TargetPath = spreadSheetLibrary.RootFolder.ServerRelativeUrl;

newRule.Enabled = true;

contentOrganizerWeb.RoutingRuleCollection.Add(newRule);
currentWeb.AllowUnsafeUpdates = false;

currentWeb.Dispose();
currentSite.Dispose();
```

If you look at the code in Listing 14-16, you might notice that all properties are strings that you have to compose yourself. There are no enumerators to help you by letting you choose a rule operator, for instance, or by letting the type of the *ContentTypeString* be an *SPContentType* instead of a string. This means that you will have to pay close attention to make sure that you format all properties correctly yourself.

When a user now uploads a new document to the Drop Off library, or to one of the libraries that has rules pointed at it, the Submit Document dialog box displays a message stating that the content will be moved according to the defined rules, as shown in Figure 14-12.

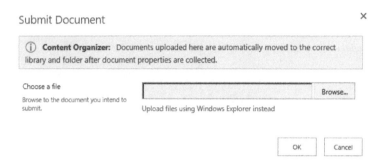

Submit Document   ×

ⓘ **Content Organizer:** Documents uploaded here are automatically moved to the correct library and folder after document properties are collected.

Choose a file
Browse to the document you intend to submit.

Upload files using Windows Explorer instead

Browse...

OK   Cancel

FIGURE 14-12 This screen shot shows the uploading of documents when the Content Organizer is activated.

When the uploaded document is linked to the *Document* content type and a Document Type is selected, the document will be redirected to the appropriate library based on the Content Organizer rules. When a document is uploaded for which a different content type is selected, or for which no document type is selected, the document will be stored in the Drop Off library. The owners of the site will get an email message warning them that there is content in the Drop Off library that cannot be routed to a location based on the currently existing rules. At 11:30 P.M. each night, the Content Organizer Processing timer job will run to reevaluate the documents in the Drop Off library. If during the day a new rule has been added that matches the document in the Drop Off library, the document will be sent to the appropriate location by the timer job. Documents that still don't match a rule will stay in the Drop Off library. If the metadata of a document in the Drop Off library is adjusted, the document will be reevaluated against all existing rules right away.

A typical usage of the Content Organizer is to create large, distributed records centers. The content organizer can help to keep the size of individual records centers manageable by allowing you to spread the documents over multiple records centers in different site collections or even different web applications.

Understanding Word Automation Services

Word Automation Services, introduced in SharePoint 2010, is primarily intended to provide format conversion services. Indeed, in numerous places you will notice that the service application is referred to as *Word Conversion*—for example, in its API and Windows PowerShell cmdlets. Although conversion is the primary use case of Word Automation Services, it can also be combined with Open XML APIs to build powerful document assembly solutions.

Word Automation Services is a service application that can be created by using the Manage Service Applications page in Central Administration, or by using Windows PowerShell. There is also a Word Automation Services service that can be started through the Services On Server page and Windows PowerShell. Creating the service application and starting the service doesn't add any functionality to a SharePoint farm, though; it allows a developer only to create a custom farm solution that can initiate a conversion.

Word Automation Services supports conversions from and to the most common file formats. The service can read the following types of files:

- Office Open XML (.docx, .docm, .dotx, .dotm)
- Word 97-2003 document (.doc) and Word 97-2003 template (.dot)
- Older versions of Word (as far back as Word 2.0 for Windows)
- Rich Text Format (.rtf)
- Single File Web Page (.mhtml)
- HTML
- Word 2003 XML
- Word 2007/2010 XML

The services can convert files of the file formats just listed into files of the following file formats:

- PDF
- XPS
- Office Open XML (.docx, .docm)
- Word 97-2003 document (.doc)
- Rich Text Format (.rtf)
- Single File Web Page (.mhtml)
- Word 2007/2010 XML

File formats that expose extended options (for example, Accessible PDF) can also be saved by Word Automation Services.

When Word Automation Services was introduced in SharePoint 2010, it was built to asynchronously convert documents in bulk, by using a timer job. Only documents that were stored in SharePoint could be converted. This functionality still exists in SharePoint 2013, but because of feedback from users and developers, the SharePoint 2013 version of Word Automation Services now also allows you to convert document streams, which don't have to be stored in SharePoint. These streams can be converted synchronously, or on demand, and thus without having to wait for a timer job to run. Only one document can be converted at a time with this approach. Asynchronous bulk conversions can still only be done on documents that are stored in SharePoint.

Synchronous and asynchronous conversion can be used at the same time. To manage this, Word Automation Services creates and manages two separate queues, one for the synchronous or on-demand conversions and one for asynchronous conversions. When a document enters the on-demand queue, conversions in the asynchronous queue will be paused. In principle, Word Automation Services will keep processing on-demand conversions until that queue is empty. Then it will continue to process asynchronous conversions. If there is an endless stream of on-demand conversions coming in, eventually SharePoint will allow some documents from the asynchronous queue to be processed. Exact numbers in terms of when this override behavior will kick in and how many documents it will allow to get processed are not documented.

The queues are "first in, first out" queues that are managed by the *document queue manager*, which resides on the servers running the Word Automation Launcher service instances. The manager moves incoming requests into the document queue and sends requests to the Word Automation Services engine for processing. On a database server, in the Word Automation database, the Word Automation Services engine stores a persistent queue of requested, current, and completed conversions. Storing the history of the queue in a database gives the queue improved scalability, reliability, and availability for tracking large sets of conversions for long periods of time.

Word Automation Services doesn't just allow developers to convert documents from one type to another, it can also make some other changes to documents, such as:

- Updating the table of contents and index fields.

- Recalculating all field types.

- Importing "alternate format chunks."

- Changing the compatibility mode version.

To allow you to use Word Automation Services and to build on top of it, the services expose two APIs. There is an API for synchronous conversions and an API for asynchronous conversions. The Word Automation Services functionality for synchronous services can be found in the *Microsoft.Office. ConversionServices.Conversions* namespace (see Table 14-1). The functionality for the asynchronous services can be found in the *Microsoft.Office.Word.Server.Conversions* namespace (see Table 14-2).

TABLE 14-1 An overview of the classes that are available in the *Microsoft.Office.ConversionServices.Conversions* namespace

Class	Description
ConversionItemInfo	Contains information about a conversion
ConversionJob	Is a conversion job
ConversionJobInfo	Contains information about a conversion job
ConversionJobStatus	Provides information about the status of the conversion job
SyncConverter	Is a synchronous conversion

TABLE 14-2 An overview of the classes that are available in the *Microsoft.Office.Word.Server.Conversions* namespace

Class	Description
ConversionInfo	Contains information about a single conversion within a conversion job
ConversionJob	Is a collection of file conversions that are tracked together as one
ConversionJobInfo	Contains information about a single conversion job
ConversionJobSettings	Defines the settings for all conversions in a single conversion job
ConversionJobStatus	Provides information about the status of all conversion items in a single conversion job
FixedFormatSettings	Defines the settings for all fixed-format output in a single job

For doing on-demand conversions, the *SyncConverter* class is the most important class, because you can do a complete conversion just by using *SyncConverter*. The most important class when creating asynchronous conversions is the *ConversionJob* class, because that is responsible for doing the actual conversions.

The following example shows how to add a Convert To PDF link to the shortcut menu of Word documents with a .docx extension and how to convert the Word document to a PDF file. The link to the shortcut menu is added by a custom action. Listing 14-17 shows the XML that creates the custom action.

LISTING 14-17 Creating a custom action

```xml
<?xml version="1.0" encoding="utf-8"?>
<Elements xmlns="http://schemas.microsoft.com/sharepoint/">
 <CustomAction Id="WingtipToys.ConversionMenuItem"
               RegistrationType="FileType"
               RegistrationId="docx"
               Location="EditControlBlock"
               ImageUrl="/_layouts/IMAGES/DOCLINK.GIF"
               Sequence="20000"
               Title="Convert to PDF"
               Description="Converts this document to a PDF." >
    <UrlAction
      Url="~site/_layouts/wingtiptoyswordconversion/convertmetopdf.aspx?ItemUrl={ItemUrl}"
/>
 </CustomAction>
</Elements>
```

Figure 14-13 shows the Convert To PDF link on the shortcut menu of a .docx file.

Documents

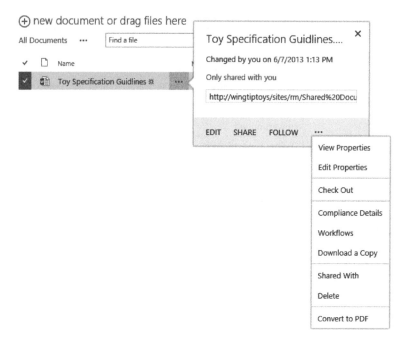

⊕ new document or drag files here

All Documents   ··· | Find a file |

✓ ☐ Name

✓ 📄 Toy Specification Guidlines ✳   ···

Toy Specification Guidlines.... ✕
Changed by you on 6/7/2013 1:13 PM
Only shared with you
http://wingtiptoys/sites/rm/Shared%20Docu
EDIT   SHARE   FOLLOW   ···

View Properties
Edit Properties
Check Out
Compliance Details
Workflows
Download a Copy
Shared With
Delete
Convert to PDF

FIGURE 14-13 This document's shortcut menu shows the Convert To PDF link.

The custom action from Listing 14-17 links to a custom .aspx page. The code-behind of the .aspx page converts the .docx file into a PDF file by using the *SyncConverter* class. Listing 14-18 shows the code-behind that converts the document.

LISTING 14-18 Converting a document to a PDF file by using the *SyncConverter* class

```
using System;
using Microsoft.SharePoint;
using Microsoft.SharePoint.WebControls;
using Microsoft.Office.Word.Server.Conversions;
using Microsoft.Office.Word.Server.Service;

namespace WingtipToysWordConversion.Layouts.WingtipToysWordConversion
{
  public partial class ConvertMeToPDF : LayoutsPageBase
  {
    protected void Page_Load(object sender, EventArgs e)
    {
      // Only run the conversion when the page is first loaded
      if (!IsPostBack)
      {
        SPSite currentSite = SPContext.Current.Site;
```

```
SPServiceContext serviceContext = SPServiceContext.Current;

string itemUrl = Request.QueryString["ItemUrl"];
string siteUrl =
  currentSite.Url.Replace(currentSite.ServerRelativeUrl, "");
string sourceFile = siteUrl + itemUrl;
string targetFile = sourceFile.ToLower().Replace("docx", "pdf");
string libraryUrl = sourceFile.Remove(sourceFile.LastIndexOf('/'));

//Get default Word Automation Service Application Proxy
//for the site collection
WordServiceApplicationProxy wordProxy =
  serviceContext.GetDefaultProxy(typeof(WordServiceApplicationProxy))
  as WordServiceApplicationProxy;

ConversionJobSettings jobSettings = new ConversionJobSettings();
//SaveFormat.Automatic will try to select the format
//based on the extension of outPuthPath
 jobSettings.OutputFormat = SaveFormat.Automatic;

SyncConverter converter = new SyncConverter(wordProxy, jobSettings);
converter.UserToken = currentSite.RootWeb.CurrentUser.UserToken;

ConversionItemInfo result = converter.Convert(sourceFile, targetFile);

Response.Redirect(libraryUrl);
        }
      }
    }
  }
```

Figure 14-14 shows the converted document and the original document.

Documents

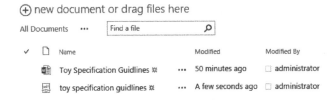

FIGURE 14-14 This document library shows both the original and the converted document.

Records management

Records management is all about maintaining and eventually disposing of formal information (records) within an organization. It might include identifying, classifying, archiving, and disposing of records. In most cases, when information is identified as a record, the information can't change anymore. One of the roles of a records management system is to ensure and to be able to prove that the record hasn't been tampered with. Records also can't be deleted, unless they are disposed of as part of a retention policy.

The most important part of records management is about policies and organization. The role of systems such as SharePoint is just to support the organization's policies. Many of the features described earlier in this chapter can be used to support records management in SharePoint. Two SharePoint features that are specifically created for records management are in-place records and records centers. Records can either be stored in their original location—for instance, in a project or department site—or they can be stored in a central archive called a *records center*. When a document is declared as a record, it is then either moved or copied to the records center.

In-place records management

With in-place records management, records are stored in their original location. When a document is identified and declared as a record, it will be protected. Users can no longer modify or delete the document. To indicate to users that the document is now a record, the icon of the document changes when the document is declared.

The advantage of in-place records management is that it is easier for users to find the records. It will be more difficult for the person who is in charge of managing all records, though, because he or she will have to keep track of records that are scattered throughout the SharePoint environment. Another downside is that if the original project site has records stored in it, the site cannot be disposed of after the project has finished.

The SharePoint In-Place Records Management Feature enables users to declare records in a document library alongside other collaborative content. Though this Feature can be configured to allow users to declare (and undeclare) records manually, it is better to automatically declare records as part of the business process. This way, the important act of protecting the information as a record doesn't depend on a user remembering to declare it. A workflow could, for instance, declare a document as a record when a document is approved as part of an approval workflow. Documents can also be declared as records by using an event receiver that runs when a document is updated and that declares the document to be a record when certain metadata properties are found—for instance, when the status of the document changes to Final. To programmatically work with SharePoint's records management features, you can use the *Microsoft.Office.RecordsManagement.RecordsRepository* namespace. Declaring a record programmatically involves only a single line of code. Listing 14-19 shows the code of a highly simplified event receiver that declares a document as a record when the status is set to Final.

LISTING 14-19 Declaring files as records programmatically

```
using System;
using Microsoft.SharePoint;
using Microsoft.Office.RecordsManagement.RecordsRepository;

namespace WingtipToysRecordsManagement.CheckDeclareItemAsRecord
{
 /// <summary>
 /// List Item Events
 /// </summary>
 public class CheckDeclareItemAsRecord : SPItemEventReceiver
 {
   /// <summary>
   /// An item was updated.
   /// </summary>
   public override void ItemUpdated(SPItemEventProperties properties)
   {
     base.ItemUpdated(properties);

     SPListItem updatedItem = properties.ListItem;
     if (updatedItem["Status"] == "Final")
     {
       Records.DeclareItemAsRecord(updatedItem);
     }
   }
 }
}
```

Figure 14-15 displays a document library that contains a document that has been declared as a record in place. The ribbon shows that the buttons that are related to modifying a document are all unavailable. The document is now protected from users making changes to it, even if those users have contributor permissions on the document.

FIGURE 14-15 This document library shows a record that is declared in place.

Records archives

If an organization decides that it wants to store all records in a central location dedicated to records, a site collection can be created in SharePoint based on the Records Center site definition. Records can be added to the records center manually or automatically, for instance, by using the Content Organizer. If a very large number of records need to be stored in the records center and you feel that it would be better to spread out the records across multiple site collections, multiple records centers can be created. The Content Organizer can be used to submit records to a central records center site and to then distribute records across records centers based on metadata values. Document libraries in records centers can be configured to declare files as records automatically when they are added.

eDiscovery

eDiscovery is the process that allows records managers and people performing an audit to discover and preserve electronic information, usually related to a legal case. eDiscovery can encompass every type of electronic information, such as email messages stored on laptops and servers,; and documents stored in SharePoint, on laptops, and on file shares. But also blogs and audio and instant messaging chats can be relevant. There is an eDiscovery standard that is called the *Electronic Discovery Reference Model (EDRM)* (*http://www.edrm.net/*). This standard includes models and guides in addition to XML schemas. The SharePoint 2013 eDiscovery features are implemented according to the EDRM model and XML schemas.

In large organizations that have a lot of data that is stored in a lot of different systems, it is often very difficult and labor-intensive to discover and preserve all relevant information across possibly thousands of laptops and personal computers and hundreds of other systems. An additional challenge is that when the information has to be put on hold, it often has to be put on hold quickly.

The eDiscovery features in SharePoint 2013 can be used to discover and preserve all content in SharePoint and content in Microsoft Exchange mailboxes. New additions to SharePoint 2013 are the eDiscovery Center and eDiscovery Case site definitions. The eDiscovery Center is a central site collection that can be used to manage eDiscovery holds. You will need one eDiscovery Center per Search Service Application. Under an eDiscovery Center, several eDiscovery Cases can be created as subsites. Figure 14-16 shows the home page of a specific eDiscovery Case called *Case 1*.

FIGURE 14-16 This screen shot shows an empty eDiscovery Case subsite.

On an eDiscovery Case subsite, eDiscovery sets can be created. A set can be named and sources can be selected for it. Sources can be Exchange mailboxes, SharePoint site collections, subsites, or folder and file shares. SharePoint content will have to be selected per site collection, which can be a bit inconvenient in large organizations, because it might mean that a lot of site collections will have to be added to the set. It is also possible to select a subsite, library, or folder as a source location in SharePoint. The container that is selected in SharePoint will have to be indexed by the Search Service Application. When you try to save the eDiscovery set, SharePoint checks to make sure that the SharePoint sources are present in the search index. Figure 14-17 shows the eDiscovery set after it has been created. To view what information is put on hold as part of the eDiscovery set, you can click the Preview Results button. The content that is put on hold can be limited by using a query filter. If no filter is applied, all content in the source will be put on hold.

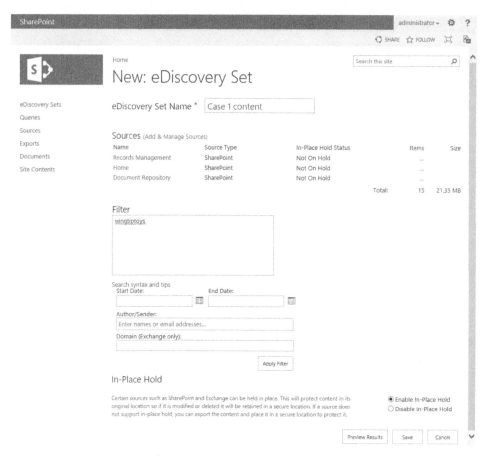

FIGURE 14-17 This screen shot shows the creation of an eDiscovery set.

When creating an eDiscovery set, you also have to decide whether the hold should be in place. If the hold is created in place, the content will be preserved in its original location, for instance, in a SharePoint site or an Exchange mailbox. Content that is placed on hold in a SharePoint site can still be modified or deleted by users. When content that is placed on hold is modified, a new library is created, called the *Preservation Hold library*, on the SharePoint site where the content was modified. The original content (as it was put on hold) is copied to this library automatically before the original copy is modified. Content that is not modified or deleted stays in its original location and is not copied to the Preservation Hold library. This approach reduces the amount of storage that is needed to put a source on hold.

Instead of being put on hold, the results of an eDiscovery set can also be exported. The results can then be imported into a review tool. You can export all of the content that is associated with an eDiscovery case. This includes:

- **Documents** Both documents and their versions can be exported from SharePoint 2013.

- **Lists** When a list item is included in an eDiscovery set, the entire list is exported as a .csv file.

- **Pages**   SharePoint 2013 pages are exported as .mht (MIME HTML) files.

- **Exchange objects**   Exchange objects are exported as .pst files.

An XML manifest that complies with the EDRM specification provides an overview of the exported information.

In most cases, eDiscovery settings will be configured by using the SharePoint user interface, but there is also an API that can be used to build custom solutions using the SharePoint eDiscovery functionality. The namespace where the eDiscovery classes can be found is *Microsoft.Office.Server. Discovery*, which in turn can be found in the Microsoft.Office.Policy.dll file.

Summary

In this chapter, a mix of several different features related to document and records management were explored. The first one was the Managed Metadata Service Application and managed metadata itself. The features that come with SharePoint out of the box were discussed, in addition to how to use managed metadata in custom solutions. Both the features and the extensibility options are very powerful, but both have a few quirks in them as well, and understanding what those quirks are can save you a lot of time and frustration.

Several document services that aren't new in SharePoint 2013, but that can still provide great value in your solutions, were discussed, such as versioning, Document IDs, Document Sets, and the Content Organizer. The Content Organizer can help you to distribute documents across folders, libraries, sites, site collections, web applications, or even farms. It is a feature that enables creating large-scale records repositories using out-of-the-box SharePoint features.

A feature that improved significantly in SharePoint 2013 is Word Automation Services. In particular, the ability to synchronously convert documents and the ability to convert documents that aren't stored in SharePoint means that Word Automation Services can be used in more scenarios.

The records management features didn't change significantly between SharePoint 2010 and SharePoint 2013. Documents can still be declared as records in place in their original location, and also be sent to a central records center. Both approaches have pros and cons, and the best one depends on aspects such as the amount of data, what will happen to the sites in which documents are created, who manages the records, and who needs to be able to access the records.

The eDiscovery features, though, got a good redesign in SharePoint 2013. The new eDiscovery Center and eDiscovery Case site definitions can be used to manage cases and holds. eDiscovery sets can be created to select locations in SharePoint or Exchange, or on file shares. You can choose to put all information in the selected location on hold, or use a query to determine what information should be put on hold. Holds can be created in place in the original location, or information that is part of a hold can be exported so that it can be reviewed outside of SharePoint.

CHAPTER 15

Web content management

The Web Content Management (WCM) features within Microsoft SharePoint are basically a vast network of capabilities that are centered on content rather than collaboration, in the benefits that they provide both to users and to content creators of sites or systems that take advantage of these features.

A SharePoint site is considered to be a publishing site if the SharePoint Server Publishing feature that is scoped at the site level is active. When you activate this feature manually or by choosing a site template that automatically activates the feature, many changes take place from a site infrastructure perspective. For example, additional libraries and layout templates that are focused heavily on the presentation of content instead of a more collaborative interaction are made available.

Other capabilities that are presentation-focused are device channels that allow a site to be presented differently depending on the type of device that is accessing it, and managed navigation, in which terms are used both to tag content and also to provide users with a way to navigate through menus and URLs by providing friendly URLs that contain these terms. Another very important feature is content aggregation. On collaboration sites, content might not have to be accessed beyond the site itself, but on a publishing site, many sites might need to have their content aggregated into a single view or list so that users can have a menu of items from which to select.

Many of the features and capabilities within the WCM space will be discussed throughout this chapter.

Understanding the WCM features

The WCM features found in SharePoint are designed to provide organizations and individual users with a mechanism to publish content for a group of consumers or readers that is much larger than the group of content creators.

The types of portals or sites that would take advantage of these WCM features are messaging portals such as those used in a corporate intranet, or public-facing sites that serve as a company's primary Internet presence. Another way to refer to these sites is to call them *authoritative* or *publishing sites*, and anything authoritative should include company branding and approval along with the content to ensure that the corporate identity is well represented and accurate. This is much different from other sites found in a SharePoint implementation, which might be more collaborative in nature.

Therefore, the features, templates, and processes that a publishing site should have are not appropriate on a collaboration site, and vice versa.

Publishing site templates

As stated earlier in this chapter, a publishing site in SharePoint is simply a site that has the SharePoint Publishing Server feature active. This feature introduces a Pages library that can be viewed as a special document library that stores publishing pages within it. You can use these pages to embed text, images, and other content and then make them accessible to end users. The Pages library is similar to the Wiki Pages library, but with a lot more functionality. Publishing pages use page layouts to present their content in a rich and consistent manner. Other added features include additional Web Parts, found within the Web Part Gallery, that can be used to perform activities such as content rollups.

Additional changes beyond those that the SharePoint Publishing Server feature implements when it is active can be automatically configured. When you use a publishing site template, the template implements additional features and configuration. For example, if you choose the Publishing Site With Workflow site template, approval workflows are configured on libraries within the site during the site provisioning process. This template also restricts all subsites to using the same site template.

The publishing site templates available within the web user interface of SharePoint 2013 on an existing site are:

- Publishing Site
- Publishing Site With Workflow

You can view this list when you go to Site Content and then choose to create a new subsite. Figure 15-1 shows the Publishing tab displaying the two publishing sites, in addition to the enterprise wiki.

FIGURE 15-1 The Publishing tab of the New SharePoint Site page shows the publishing sites and the enterprise wiki.

If you wanted to view these same templates by using Windows PowerShell, one way you could do so is to filter the results returned by the *Get-SPWebTemplate* cmdlet to only return those templates with the word "Publishing" within their titles. This could be accomplished by executing the following code:

```
Get-SPWebTemplate | Where-Object {$_.Title -like "*Publishing*"} '
| select Name, Title, Description, CompatibilityLevel | Format-List
```

This code actually returns more than the two publishing sites shown in Figure 15-1; in fact, eight templates are returned. The complete list is shown Table 15-1.

TABLE 15-1 Publishing Site templates returned by the *Get-SPWebTemplate* cmdlet

Name	Title	Description	Compatibility level
CMSPUBLISHING#0	Publishing Site	A blank site for expanding your website and quickly publishing webpages. Contributors can work on draft versions of pages and publish them to make them visible to readers. The site includes document and image libraries for storing web publishing assets.	15
BLANKINTERNET#0	Publishing Site	A template that creates a site for publishing webpages on a schedule, with workflow features enabled. By default, only publishing subsites can be created under this site. A document and picture library are included for storing web publishing assets.	15
BLANKINTERNET#2	Publishing Site with Workflow	A site for publishing webpages on a schedule by using approval workflows. It includes document and image libraries for storing web publishing assets. By default, only sites with this template can be created under this site.	15
BLANKINTERNETCONTAINER#0	Publishing Portal	A starter site hierarchy for an Internet-facing site or a large intranet portal. This site can be customized easily with distinctive branding. It includes a home page, a sample press releases subsite, a Search Center, and a logon page. Typically, this site has many more readers than contributors, and it is used to publish webpages with approval workflows.	15
CMSPUBLISHING#0	Publishing Site	A blank site for expanding your website and quickly publishing webpages. Contributors can work on draft versions of pages and publish them to make them visible to readers. The site includes document and image libraries for storing web publishing assets.	14
BLANKINTERNET#0	Publishing Site	A template that creates a site for publishing webpages on a schedule, with workflow features enabled. By default, only publishing subsites can be created under this site. A document and picture library are included for storing web publishing assets.	14

Name	Title	Description	Compatibility level
BLANKINTERNET#2	Publishing Site with Workflow	A site for publishing webpages on a schedule by using approval workflows. It includes document and image libraries for storing web publishing assets. By default, only sites with this template can be created under this site.	14
BLANKINTERNETCONTAINER#0	Publishing Portal	A starter site hierarchy for an Internet-facing site or a large intranet portal. This site can be customized easily with distinctive branding. It includes a home page, a sample press releases subsite, a Search Center, and a logon page. Typically, this site has many more readers than contributors, and it is used to publish webpages with approval workflows.	14

The first thing you should notice about the site templates is that they can be grouped into two sets of four templates based on Compatibility Level. If you are not already familiar with levels 14 and 15, they equate to the 2010 and 2013 versions of SharePoint, respectively. The description of each site template can give you a good idea of the degree of extra functionality introduced by selecting one template over another. One additional note about Compatibility Level, as it pertains to sites, is that when you choose to create a new site through the web UI or by using *New-SPSite*, the default Compatibility Level is 15, which is the 2013 version. By default, you only have the option to create 2010 versions of a site if you elect to use the *New-SPSite* cmdlet and specify 14 for the Compatibility Level parameter.

Accessing SharePoint publishing files

Because most publishing sites have some level of branding at the site, page, and Web Part level, a lot of files (such as CSS, images, and scripts) can start to accumulate. As a result, it's important to be able to access these files in a timely fashion. In addition to the already identified branding files that can be found in previous versions of SharePoint, additional files have been introduced in SharePoint 2013. To reduce the amount of time it takes to access the files stored within the Master Page Gallery, you can now access the gallery via a network path.

Mapping to the SharePoint Master Page Gallery

The method you use to map the Master Page Gallery as a network drive on your local machine depends on whether your machine has Windows XP, Windows 8, another Windows-based operating system, or another operating system altogether. If you are using a Windows operating system that is later than Windows XP and up to Windows 8.1, as of this writing, you can use the article at the following URL to learn how you map the Master Page Gallery as a network drive: *http://msdn.microsoft.com/en-us/library/jj733519.aspx*. If you are on another operating system or are comfortable with how you map paths, then the only important thing to remember is the URL structure to follow. The URL structure is http://<siteURL>/_catalogs/masterpage/. There is really just one prerequisite to being able to successfully create the mapping, and it is security based. You must have at least Designer permission, which is the same permission you need to be able to access the Master Page Gallery through the web UI.

Page layouts

Page layouts in SharePoint are essentially presentation templates that control how the metadata or content stored in a Pages library for a page is presented to a user. In addition to displaying the content stored within the Pages library, a page layout can also include Web Part zones, which allow supplemental content to be exposed through Web Parts.

Understanding the page model

To really grasp the role that master pages, page layouts, and pages play within a publishing site, as well as how they interact with each other, you need to understand what the page model is.

At its lowest level, the page model starts with a master page. A master page contains the common elements that should be displayed on every page for a site. Some of the typical common elements are:

- Site logo
- Search box
- Global navigation
- Footer
- Content placeholders for page layouts

The next level up is the page layout, which we have already discussed in some detail; however, more detail is needed to help clarify its role in the page model. Page layouts are able to identify what to correctly render where, along with how to render it, through the use of page field controls and their mapping to site columns. A sample code extraction of a page field control found in a page layout is shown in Listing 15-1. The mapping is accomplished by using the *FieldName* parameter of the field control, which needs to have its value set to the internal name of the site column whose content the page field control should display.

LISTING 15-1 Sample page field control

```
<PublishingWebControls:RichHtmlField FieldName="PublishingPageContent"
HasInitialFocus="True" MinimumEditHeight="400px" runat="server"/>
```

The field control shown in the listing is of type *RichHtmlField*, which is available under the namespace *Microsoft.SharePoint.Publishing.WebControls*. There are many other control types found within this namespace, in addition to other control types found in other namespaces. For example, the *TaxonomyFieldControl*, which is used to expose the value of a managed metadata field or site column, is found in the *Microsoft.SharePoint.Taxonomy* namespace.

The final layer is the page, which is the content. As mentioned earlier, page field controls on a page layout map to site columns. These site columns are grouped into a content type and made available in a Pages library that it is associated with the page. It is important to note that not all site columns for a page need to be mapped to field controls within a page layout. Because of this, it is best to categorize the site columns for a particular page into one of two groups: those that are used for presentation and metadata and those that are used strictly for metadata. An example of one that is used for presentation would be a site column that is used for storing a news article image or the body for a news article. An example of one that is used strictly for metadata could be one that is used for metadata keywords or audience targeting.

When you add the layers together you get the final rendered page that a user would get. Figure 15-2 shows a rendered SharePoint publishing page broken down by using the page model.

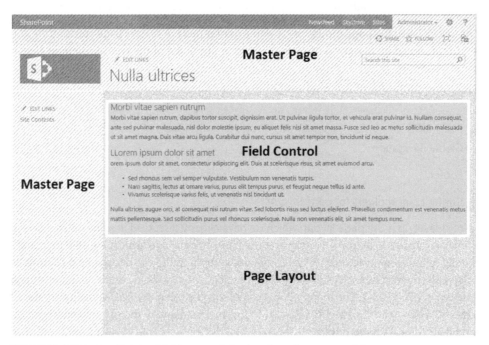

FIGURE 15-2 This SharePoint publishing page is broken down by page model.

To learn more about SharePoint master pages, pages, and the deployment of each of these, see the section "Using pages in SharePoint" in Chapter 7, "SharePoint pages."

Creating a new page layout

We have already discussed why a page layout is important for publishing in SharePoint and how it is involved in the page model. This section discusses the options for creating a page layout and then goes into detail on how to control the presentation and editing of a page by using a page layout.

There are more ways to create page layouts in SharePoint 2013 than there were in SharePoint 2010, thanks to the new Design Manager. When you choose to use the Design Manager approach, you will interact with an HTML page when you want to make changes to a page layout, and that HTML page in turn is associated with an .aspx file that SharePoint uses in the page model. When you make a change to the HTML page, this change is then propagated to the associated .aspx file. It is important to remember that this propagation is in one direction only, going from the HTML page to the .aspx file. Because of this, any changes made to the .aspx file that did not first occur in the HTML page will get overwritten when the next change to the HTML page occurs. To learn more about how to create a page layout, see the article "How to: Create a page layout in SharePoint 2013" at *http://msdn.microsoft.com/en-us/library/jj822368.aspx*.

The approach taken in previous versions of SharePoint, in which only an .aspx file is created and then deployed to a SharePoint site, is still supported. Some developers might be more familiar with this and might prefer it in place of using the Design Manager.

Managing the presentation of page fields

Page fields, as described in the "Understanding the page model" section earlier in this chapter, are visible through a page layout when you are creating a new publishing page. These fields are associated with a content type, and each page field on a page layout should reference a field within the associated content type. Page fields are able to read and write to a content type field because they too have an assortment of available types. For example, if you needed to expose the *Title* field for a content type that had a column type of *Single Line of Text*, you would use a page field with a field type of *TextField* to support read and write operations on the *Title* field, as shown in the following code:

```
<SharePointWebControls:TextField ID="tfTitle" runat="server" FieldName="Title"/>
```

The *TextField* uses a *SharePointWebControls* prefix, which requires a reference as shown in the following code:

```
<%@ Register Tagprefix="SharePointWebControls" Namespace="Microsoft.SharePoint.WebControls"
Assembly="Microsoft.SharePoint, Version=15.0.0.0, Culture=neutral, PublicKeyToken=71e9bce111e94
29c" %>
```

A *TextField* field type is considered a simple field type and can be styled by simply wrapping the page field with a *div* that has an ID that you can reference by using cascading style sheets (CSS). This allows developers and designers to control the presentation of the content rendered through the controls.

Most field types are considered simple; however, the *RichHtmlField* is an exception. As its name implies, this field type allows the author to have an experience similar to using a word processor when authoring content within it. A ribbon with a multitude of options is available for managing fonts, paragraphs, and other text-centric functions, as shown in Figure 15-3.

FIGURE 15-3 The SharePoint ribbon is used for editing a *RichHtmlField*.

Because of the many options available to the author during the editing experience, the brand or presentation consistency of the content might be at risk if too many liberties are taken with the available options. Because of this, the *RichHtmlField* field type has properties that can be used to control which of the editing or formatting options should be available to the author. Table 15-2 shows a breakdown of the primary Allow properties that can be used to control the editing and formatting experience.

TABLE 15-2 *RichHtmlField* field type properties

Name	Type	Description
AllowDragDrop	Boolean	Retrieve or set whether or not the dragging and dropping of elements is allowed
AllowEmbedding	Boolean	Retrieve or set whether or not iFrames are allowed
AllowFontColorsMenu	Boolean	Retrieve or set whether or not a font colors menu is shown
AllowFontCustomColors	Boolean	Retrieve or set whether or not font custom colors are allowed
AllowFonts	Boolean	Retrieve or set whether or not inline fonts are allowed
AllowFontSizesMenu	Boolean	Retrieve or set whether or not the font size menu is available on the ribbon
AllowFontsMenu	Boolean	Retrieve or set whether or not the font menu is available on the ribbon
AllowHeadings	Boolean	Retrieve or set whether or not header tags are allowed
AllowHtmlSourceEditing	Boolean	Retrieve or set whether or not you can switch the Source Editor mode of the field
AllowHyperlinks	Boolean	Retrieve or set whether or not hyperlinks are allowed
AllowImageFormatting	Boolean	Retrieve or set whether or not image formatting is available
AllowImagePositioning	Boolean	Retrieve or set whether or not image positioning is available on the ribbon
AllowImages	Boolean	Retrieve or set whether or not images are allowed
AllowLists	Boolean	Retrieve or set whether or not list tags such as <li> are allowed
AllowParagraphFormatting	Boolean	Retrieve or set whether or not paragraph formatting is allowed

Name	Type	Description
AllowStyles	Boolean	Retrieve or set whether or not the style menu is enabled
AllowTables	Boolean	Retrieve or set whether or not tables are allowed
AllowTextMarkup	Boolean	Retrieve or set whether or not explicit text tags such as bold <b> and italic <i> are allowed

There are many more properties than those listed in this table, but these are the most common properties needed for content authoring and the editing experience. To view the complete set of properties, see *http://msdn.microsoft.com/en-us/library/microsoft.sharepoint.publishing.webcontrols. richhtmlfield_properties.aspx*. The following code snippet shows an example of some of these properties being configured for use within a page layout:

```
<PublishingWebControls:RichHtmlField ID="rhfPageContent" FieldName="PageContent"
HasInitialFocus="True" AllowFonts="True" AllowTextMarkup="False" runat="server"/>
```

If you compare this code snippet to the previous example for a *TextField*, you will notice that both controls come from the same namespace. The two Allow properties in this example affect the way the ribbon renders for an author, as shown in Figure 15-4.

FIGURE 15-4 This Format Text ribbon tab has some of the Font group options unavailable.

In Figure 15-4 you can tell that the ability to choose fonts and pretty much everything else is still there, but the ability to use bold or other text styles is not available.

Working with edit mode panels

An edit mode panel primarily allows a designer or a developer to wrap fields and content within it to control what is visible while an author is editing a page, hence the naming of the control. There are in fact two different modes that a page can be in: display mode and edit mode. Display mode is the only mode that visitors to a site will ever experience, whereas an author will also view the edit mode when creating or modifying a page. The interesting thing about an edit mode panel is that it can be used to control the visibility of content and controls in either display mode or edit mode, even though its name would suggest that its scope is limited to the edit mode. To help explain this, the following code snippet is used to render the text *Contoso* on the page, but only while the page is in display mode:

```
<PublishingWebControls:EditModePanel ID="MyEditModePanel" runat="server" PageDisplayMode="Displa
y">Contoso</PublishingWebControls:EditModePanel>
```

Notice that this is controlled by means of the *PageDisplayMode* property of the *EditModelPanel* control. Furthermore, the two available choices are in fact *Display* and *Edit*.

Working with Web Part zones

Page fields, as this chapter has just covered, are crucial to authoring content-driven pages. There are, however, many times that the content being authored directly on the page is not the only content that the author would like to use. You might discover a list or a library of documents that you would like to reuse or surface as links on a page. The obvious solution is to use a Web Part to surface the content; other than the *RichHtmlField* that was discussed earlier, there are no other page fields that support embedding a Web Part. And even then, the author is burdened with how to use HTML mark-up within a *RichHtmlField* to control the presentation of multiple Web Parts. Because of this need, requirements should be gathered and Web Parts zones should be identified as part of the solution.

Simply put, a Web Part zone is an area on a page that is dedicated to Web Parts and the ability to add, modify, or remove them. Further, Web Parts have the ability to control such things as the default chrome setting for added Web Parts and also the orientation of added Web Parts, whether they should be stacked vertically or horizontally. The following code snippet shows a simple Web Part zone that sets the orientation of the Web Parts placed inside of it in a horizontal format and sets the default chrome to be *BorderOnly*:

```
<WebPartPages:WebPartZone runat="server" Title="First Row" ID="FirstRow"
PartChromeType="BorderOnly" Orientation="Horizontal"><ZoneTemplate></ZoneTemplate></
WebPartPages:WebPartZone>
```

The namespace used to add a Web Part zone is *Microsoft.SharePoint.WebPartPages*. The horizontal format is set by using the *Orientation* property, and the default chrome is set to only show the border for Web Parts that are within the zone by using the *PartChromeType* property. Figure 15-5 shows how this would look when a page is in edit mode.

FIGURE 15-5 Web Part zones are visible when the page is in edit mode.

Understanding device channels

The number and types of devices that access digital information are forever increasing. This also holds true for accessing information stored inside of SharePoint, whether on a corporate intranet or an Internet site. The device that has been most commonly used for digital information access has been the desktop or laptop computer, but now mobile devices such as phones and tablets are starting to assume almost an equal share. As a result, the way in which information is presented to a user is expected to accommodate whichever device the user chooses. This can be a costly requirement, which might translate to building and maintaining multiple websites; however, this can be greatly alleviated if you have chosen to include SharePoint 2013 in your solution. Device channels, which are a part of the publishing infrastructure, allow you to have a single publishing page that is accessed from the same URL, but that renders differently depending on the type of device that is accessing it. The differences might include optimizations for mobile devices, such as exclusion of larger content or images, simpler navigation, and a touch-centric style. The differences for a high-resolution desktop computer might include multiple navigation menus, rich image rotators, and attractive animations. This is a huge benefit, not only in the initial cost savings, but also for future maintenance and enhancements.

The way this solution is accomplished is by taking advantage of the user agent string that is passed by every browser, regardless of the device, to a page that is being requested and then redirecting the user to the appropriate master page for the device. The information that is passed in this string can be used to determine the browser and its version along with the operating system of the device making the request. If a Windows Phone 8 were to access a page and you viewed the user agent string, you could find the following:

```
Mozilla/5.0 (compatible; MSIE 10.0; Windows Phone 8.0; Trident/6.0; IEMobile/10.0; ARM; Touch; NOKIA; Lumia 920)
```

If you were to view the user agent string for a server running Windows Server 2012, it would look like the following:

```
Mozilla/5.0 (compatible; MSIE 10.0; Windows NT 6.2; WOW64; Trident/6.0; .NET4.0E; .NET4.0C; .NET CLR 3.5.30729; .NET CLR 2.0.50727; .NET CLR 3.0.30729; InfoPath.3)
```

The important thing to note from all of this is that the user agent string is used by device channels to determine what to render for what device. It is not reasonable or cost-friendly to expect website developers to account for all the variances that occur simply due to the device maker, browsers, or even the operating system version. Because of this, device channels can work off of a substring of the user agent string. An important limitation to remember is that a maximum of 10 device channels can exist for a site, so you should plan ahead how to choose to group devices by device channels.

Device channels are accessible through the Device Manager, on the Manage Device Channels page. A device channel is very simple to provision, even though it accomplishes great things. There are only five properties for a device channel; these are shown in Table 15-3.

TABLE 15-3 Device channel properties

Field	Required	Description
Name	True	A friendly or display name of the device channel.
Alias	True	An internal name of the device channel used when referencing a device channel in code or a device channel panel.
Description	False	A description or summary of the device channel's purpose.
Device Inclusion Rules	True	A value that contains the user agent substring(s); for example, Windows Phone, Chrome, Windows NT, or iPhone. At least one of these values must exist for the device channel to be used.
Active	False	If this is set to True, the site will begin to use the device channel.

There is a possibility that a match to more than one device channel could occur. If this happens, the device channel that has the highest order number will be the one used.

After you have at least two device channels, as shown in the example in Figure 15-6, you can configure the redirections to the correct master page.

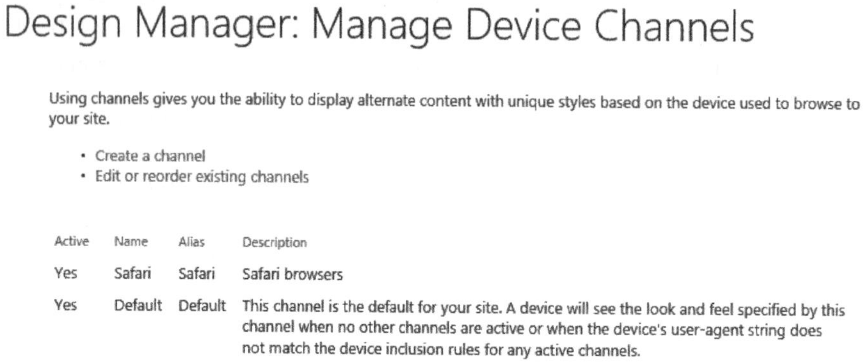

Design Manager: Manage Device Channels

Using channels gives you the ability to display alternate content with unique styles based on the device used to browse to your site.

- Create a channel
- Edit or reorder existing channels

Active	Name	Alias	Description
Yes	Safari	Safari	Safari browsers
Yes	Default	Default	This channel is the default for your site. A device will see the look and feel specified by this channel when no other channels are active or when the device's user-agent string does not match the device inclusion rules for any active channels.

FIGURE 15-6 This page shows the listing of the device channels for a site.

To configure the master page that each device channel should redirect to, go to the Site Master Page Settings page, found at Site Settings | Master Page, as shown in Figure 15-7, and then simply choose an available master page from the drop-down menu for each of the device channels.

Site Settings ‣ Site Master Page Settings ⓘ

Site Master Page

The site master page will be used by all publishing pages - the pages that visitors to your website will see. You can have a different master page for each Device Channel. If you don't see the master page you're looking for, go to the Master Page Gallery in Site Settings and make sure it has an approved version.

You may inherit these settings from the parent site or select unique settings for this site only.

○ Inherit site master page from parent of this site
● Specify a master page to be used by this site and all sites that inherit from it:

| Safari | oslo ▼ |
| Default | seattle ▼ |

☐ Reset all subsites to inherit this site master page setting

FIGURE 15-7 The Site Master Page Settings page is used to choose the master page for each device.

To test whether or not a device channel is redirecting correctly, or to just preview its behavior, you can simply include a query string parameter called *DeviceChannel* and pass the alias for the device channel you would like to test as its value. Figure 15-8 shows a page being tested with the Safari device channel that was configured in the previous figure. Notice that in place of the *seattle* master page the *oslo* master page is being used.

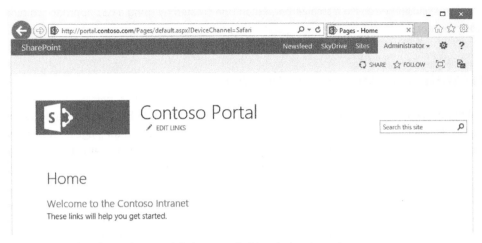

FIGURE 15-8 This SharePoint page is being tested with a device channel.

Working with device channel panels

By using device channels, you can redirect users to the correct master page that is targeted for their type of device. This concept alone is powerful, but being able to take it to the next level is where device channel panels come in. A device channel panel is used within a master page or a page layout to wrap content or functionality and target specific device channels. The following code shows a sample device channel panel:

```
<Publishing:DeviceChannelPanel runat="server" IncludedChannels="Safari">
    <div>Only visible to those devices included in the Safari device channel.</div>
</Publishing:DeviceChannelPanel>
```

The code is self-explanatory, but it is important to note that the *DeviceChannelPanel* object is found in the *Microsoft.SharePoint.Publishing.WebControls* namespace. Also, the *IncludedChannels* is where you identify which device channels, by their alias, will be able to see what is contained within the *DeviceChannelPanel*. If you would like to include more than one device channel, the aliases should be comma delimited and passed to the same property.

There are a few different strategies or approaches that you can use device channel panels in. The first is to help lower the number of one-to-one relationships between master pages and device channels. You can use device channel panels to limit the number of master pages by pairing up more device channels to a single master page and then use device channel panels to fine-tune the experience by hiding or showing sections of the master page that each device channel should see. A limitation that needs to be accounted for during the planning phase of device channel panels is that they cannot be used to wrap Web Part zones; however, if a Web Part is embedded within a page layout or master page, it could be wrapped by a device channel panel.

Another strategy is to reduce the size of pages being sent to a mobile device. This is accomplished by directing the server to not render the content found within a device channel panel whose *IncludedChannels* property does not contain a match to the device channel being used by the current device. This exclusion results in a smaller page than one created by using a CSS approach to hide non-relevant content, which still results in the page being too large and slow for a mobile device.

Understanding managed navigation

Publishing sites built on SharePoint have typically been easy to identify by certain always-present URL indicators. For example /pages is usually found in the URL, indicating that the page being viewed is stored in the Pages library of the site. Some developers might go through the effort of performing URL rewrites to remove the unwanted characters in the URL, but this can be an added effort that most do not want to exert, or that they expect to already be available in a WCM platform. Another point is that the presence of the library's name in the URL indicates that the physical structure of the site is directly tied to the navigational structure of the site. Forcing the navigational structure and physical site structure to be aligned with one another can cause a lot more work than what was initially planned, because the two do not always line up with one another. Additionally, this will likely cause the same amount of effort when maintenance or structural changes to the site need to be performed.

The good news is that with the advent of SharePoint 2013 we now have the ability to separate the physical and navigational structures of a SharePoint site by using a new type of navigation called managed navigation. The ability to use managed navigation is dependent upon taxonomy, which is found in a Managed Metadata Service (MMS) Application. From this dependency comes two advantages. The first is that we can now have a term set be the global and/or current navigational structure for a site, and the second is that we can now have friendly URLs (FURLs) in place of URLs that have the SharePoint structure injected into them.

Because of the overwhelming advantages of managed navigation over structured navigation for publishing sites, there arises the need to ensure that this capability can be extended and also deployable in a consistent method across environments. To meet these needs there are APIs that Microsoft has made available for managed navigation.

Working with managed navigation APIs

To begin working with the managed navigation APIs, you first need to choose which API you want to use. There are APIs for the following:

- Microsoft .NET client-side object model (CSOM)

- Microsoft .NET server-side object model (SSOM)

- Microsoft Silverlight

- JavaScript

Not only can you take advantage of any of these four APIs , but each has been extended and enhanced from the SharePoint 2010 APIs. Some of the common uses for the APIs are to manage the creation and customizations of terms, term sets, and other properties found in an MMS Application that are related to managed navigation.

Later in this chapter we will work through an example of creating a new term set that can be used as a site's managed navigation. The example will use CSOM using C#. Before we get started, though, we will identify the reference and namespace that are required. The following are the required reference for using the CSOM approach:

- *Microsoft.SharePoint.Client*

- *Microsoft.SharePoint.Client.Runtime*

- *Microsoft.SharePoint.Client.Publishing*

- *Microsoft.SharePoint.Client.Taxononmy*

The first two are standard requirements for any CSOM interactions to even occur. The remaining two, however, are needed to create the new term set through a site. The namespaces needed after the references are included are:

- *Microsoft.SharePoint.Client*

- *Microsoft.SharePoint.Client.Taxonomy*

- *Microsoft.SharePoint.Client.Publishing.Navigation*

Creating a navigational term set

To begin creating a navigational term set by using CSOM, you must begin by gaining context of the site collection that you want to create the term set under and instantiating a *TaxonomySession* object, as shown in the following code:

```
//Gain context
ClientContext clientContext = new ClientContext("http://portal.contoso.com");
//Instantiate TaxonomySession
TaxonomySession taxonomySession = TaxonomySession.GetTaxonomySession(clientContext);
taxonomySession.UpdateCache();
//Request TaxonomySession TermStores property
clientContext.Load(taxonomySession, ts => ts.TermStores);
clientContext.ExecuteQuery();
```

After you have gained access to the *TermStores* property for the *TaxonomySession* object, you can select the term store that you will create the term set in. The following code simulates this by using the first term store within the *TermStores* property:

```
//Throw error if no Term Stores are found
if (taxonomySession.TermStores.Count == 0)
throw new InvalidOperationException("MMS not found");
//Request first Term Store Name and Working Language Properties
TermStore termStore = taxonomySession.TermStores[0];
clientContext.Load(termStore, ts => ts.Name, ts => ts.WorkingLanguage);
```

After you have access to the term store, you need to create a new term group for the site collection, and then you can create a term set underneath it, as shown here:

```
// Create a new Term Group for the Site Collection
TermGroup scTermGroup = termStore.GetSiteCollectionGroup(clientContext.Site, createIfMissing:
true);
//Create a new Term Set within the Term Group called "Contoso Site Navigation"
TermSet termSet = scTermGroup.CreateTermSet("Contoso Site Navigation", Guid.NewGuid(),
termStore.WorkingLanguage);
//Commit all changes
termStore.CommitAll();
clientContext.ExecuteQuery();
```

At this point, you have a term group that has been created within the scope of the site collection at *http://portal.contoso.com.* You have populated this term group with a new term set called *Contoso Site Navigation.* The next step is to identify the newly created term set as a navigational term set and fill it with a few sample terms:

```
//Access and edit the term set as if it were associated with the web at "http://portal.contoso.
com"
NavigationTermSet navTermSet = NavigationTermSet.GetAsResolvedByWeb(clientContext, termSet,
clientContext.Web, "GlobalNavigationTaxonomyProvider");
//Set the term set as a navigational term set
navTermSet.IsNavigationTermSet = true;

//Commit changes so far
termStore.CommitAll();
clientContext.ExecuteQuery();

//Create a term for the homepage
NavigationTerm term1 = navTermSet.CreateTerm("Home", NavigationLinkType.SimpleLink, Guid.
NewGuid());
term1.SimpleLinkUrl = "http://portal.contoso.com/";

//Create a term for the default page of the news subsite
NavigationTerm term2 = navTermSet.CreateTerm("News", NavigationLinkType.FriendlyUrl, Guid.
NewGuid());
term2.FriendlyUrlSegment.Value = "news";
term2.TargetUrl.Value = "~site/news/pages/default.aspx";

//Commit all changes
termStore.CommitAll();

//Request the term set's ID property
clientContext.Load(navTermSet, nts => nts.Id);
clientContext.ExecuteQuery();
```

The final step is to configure the web object for *http://portal.contoso.com* to start using the navigational term set that has just been created. This is done by the use of the *WebNavigationSettings* object. This object contains the means to specify the navigation model for a web object, including the ability to switch between structured navigation, which uses the *PortalSiteMapProvider,* and managed navigation, which uses the *TaxonomySiteMapProvider.* If managed navigation is used, then you also can dictate the term store and term set that should be used to drive the managed navigation. The following code shows how this can be accomplished:

```
//Reset the web object to the default settings
WebNavigationSettings webNavSettings = new WebNavigationSettings(clientContext, clientContext.
Web);
webNavSettings.ResetToDefaults();
//Configure the web object to use managed navigation
webNavSettings.GlobalNavigation.Source = StandardNavigationSource.TaxonomyProvider;
//Set the term store and term set to use for managed navigation
webNavSettings.GlobalNavigation.TermStoreId = termStore.Id;
webNavSettings.GlobalNavigation.TermSetId = navTermSet.Id;
webNavSettings.Update(taxonomySession);
//flush the cache
TaxonomyNavigation.FlushSiteFromCache(clientContext, clientContext.Site);

clientContext.ExecuteQuery();
```

After executing all the code blocks shown within the section, you should have a site that has two navigation nodes visible within the global navigation of the site, as shown in Figure 15-9.

FIGURE 15-9 The site's global navigation displays the navigational term set's terms.

The example shown within this section demonstrates just one of the many possibilities available with the managed navigation APIs. Following this approach to code the creation of a site's navigation settings along with the initial values allows for a consistent and efficient way to provision sites.

Content aggregation

Content aggregation is a very powerful capability found within the Web Content Management (WCM) features of SharePoint 2013. Its ability to roll up content from across different sites and lists, and now to roll up content from across site collections, web applications, and even other SharePoint farms cannot be underestimated. Of the features available in SharePoint 2010, the most popular Web Part used for aggregation is quite possibly the Content Query Web Part (CQWP). Its popularity stems from its ease of use, the ability that it gives to a power user to surface content queried by its properties, and last but not least, its ability to be branded at the presentation layer. It is not without its shortcomings, mainly its inability to query beyond a single site collection. However, you could say that it is because of this inability that SharePoint 2013 is now equipped with a search-driven Web Part that provides similar ease of use, user empowerment, and the ability to be branded at the presentation layer. This new Web Part is called the Content Search Web Part (CSWP). Both Web Parts can be found in the Web Part Gallery under the Content Rollup category when the correct features have been activated at the site collection and web levels, as shown in Figure 15-10.

FIGURE 15-10 The Web Part Gallery is shown with the Content Rollup category selected.

For a visual depiction of the boundaries and rollup capabilities of each of these Web Parts, see Figure 15-11.

Content Search

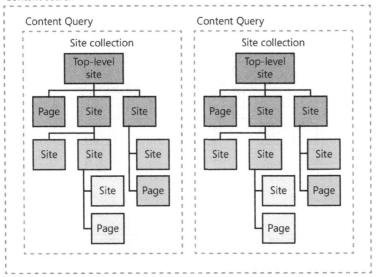

FIGURE 15-11 The scope of the Content Search Web Part can go beyond that of the Content Query.

Deciding between the Content Query and Content Search Web Parts

Simply because the Content Search Web Part (CSWP) can do more does not always mean that it should be used over the Content Query Web Part (CQWP). Careful consideration should be given to requirements and the available infrastructure that supports the SharePoint implementation before making a solution decision.

When considering the requirements, if content must be available only moments after it is authored or approved, the site would not lend itself to the CSWP. In this situation, the CQWP would be the best fit because it can access the content instantly without needing to be crawled and indexed by the Search service. Another situation that would support the CQWP over the CSWP is when the SharePoint implementation is on a small two-server farm topology that needs to support several user requests and other services. This type of topology would not be able to support the constant demand of a search application's crawl and index component on a highly demanding schedule. However, a situation in which the CSWP is the prime candidate and best choice is when you need to roll up content across site collection, web application, or farm boundaries, as shown in Figure 15-12.

Content Search

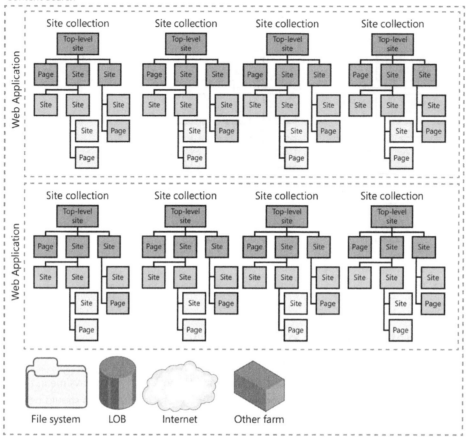

FIGURE 15-12 The rollup abilities of the Content Search Web Part are extensive.

More than what this chapter has covered so far should be considered when choosing the correct rollup Web Part. Figure 15-13 shows a rollup comparison of both the Content Query and Content Search Web Parts broken down by key areas.

	Content Query (CQWP)	Content Search (CSWP)
Filter Scope	Limited by site collection	Limited by indexed content
	Three max	No reasonable limit = endless refiners
Style	- Requires exporting .webpart file to change item XSL path (not very clean) - Requires SP XSL knowledge	- Simplified using HTML and JS - Content is inserted into page in JSON format
Other	- Optimized for caching - Resource friendly	Requries constant crawls to keep content fresh and available

- Search crawls only the major versions of content, never the minor versions. If you want to display the minor versions of your content, do that by using a CQWP.
- Some site collection administrators mark sites to not be indexed. Content marked in this way is not available in a CSWP. If you want to return results from a site that is marked to not index, use the CQWP instead.

FIGURE 15-13 A rollup comparison between the Content Query and Content Search Web Parts highlights their differences.

As the comparisons play out you can tell that both the Content Query and Content Search Web Parts have an important role in SharePoint 2013 and each has a vital role to play in the success of Web Content Management solutions that involve content rollup.

Working with display templates

If you have spent time branding the results of a Content Query Web Part or a Core Search Result Web Part in SharePoint 2010, you have had the opportunity to experience the benefits and pains of working with Extensible Stylesheet Language for Transformations (XSLT) within SharePoint. The understanding needed to complete even simple branding techniques by using XSLT with these Web Parts requires more than just typical XSL knowledge. XSL is still used within SharePoint 2013 for the Content Query Web Part, but display templates have become the de facto solution for the all search-driven Web Parts. A display template is one of two types:

- **Control template**   Called once per Web Part, this type of display template is responsible for the framing of the results being returned (for example, List or Content Rotator).

- **Item template**   Called once per item, this type of display template is responsible for rendering item properties (for example, title, description, image, or other properties).

Figure 15-14 shows how a control template and item template would be used to present results as a content rotator.

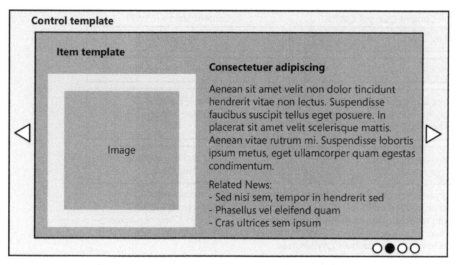

FIGURE 15-14 This display template is broken down by control and item template.

Display templates have the following primary categories:

- Content Web Parts (Content Search Web Part)

- Search (Search Core Result Web Part, search box, and so on)

- Filters (search refiners)

Display templates are stored at the site collection level within a root folder aptly named Display Templates, which is inside the Master Page Gallery. Each of the categories just listed is a folder within the Display Templates folder, as shown in Figure 15-15.

Content Web Parts	8/13/2013 5:30 PM	File folder
Filters	8/1/2013 10:07 AM	File folder
Language Files	8/1/2013 10:07 AM	File folder
Search	8/13/2013 1:41 PM	File folder
Server Style Sheets	8/1/2013 10:07 AM	File folder
System	8/1/2013 10:07 AM	File folder

FIGURE 15-15 Display template categories are stored in this folder structure.

Display templates are made up of two associated files, much like the new HTML page layouts are in the Designer Manager. The files are an HTML file with which developers and designers interact, and an associated JavaScript file that SharePoint uses when the display template is being called. It is important to remember that, as with all other associated files in SharePoint 2013, you should modify the HTML file only. This is because SharePoint updates the JavaScript file whenever there is a change that has been made to the HTML file. So if you make a change directly to the JavaScript file it would work as intended, but you run the risk of having that change be overwritten the next time someone decides to update the HTML file instead.

The code markup within a control template and an item template have some similarities, but there are also some key differences. We will start by looking at a simple control template and then will progress to looking at an item template.

A control template named *Control_List.html*, which is available out of the box, is shown here:

```html
<html xmlns:mso="urn:schemas-microsoft-com:office:office" xmlns:msdt="uuid:C2F41010-65B3-11d1-
A29F-00AA00C14882">
<head>
<title>List</title>
<!--[if gte mso 9]><xml>
<mso:CustomDocumentProperties>
<mso:TemplateHidden msdt:dt="string">0</mso:TemplateHidden>
<mso:MasterPageDescription msdt:dt="string">This is the default Control Display
Template that will list the items. It does not allow the user to page through items.</
mso:MasterPageDescription>
<mso:ContentTypeId msdt:dt="string">0x0101002039C03B61C64EC4A04F5361F385106601</
mso:ContentTypeId>
<mso:TargetControlType msdt:dt="string">;#Content Web Parts;#</mso:TargetControlType>
<mso:HtmlDesignAssociated msdt:dt="string">1</mso:HtmlDesignAssociated>
</mso:CustomDocumentProperties>
</xml><![endif]-->
</head>

<body>

    <!--
        Warning: Do not try to add HTML to this section. Only the contents of the first
        <div> inside the <body> tag will be used while executing Display Template code. Any
        HTML that you add to this section will NOT become part of your Display Template.
    -->
    <script>
        $includeLanguageScript(this.url, "~sitecollection/_catalogs/masterpage/Display
        Templates/Language Files/{Locale}/CustomStrings.js");
    </script>

    <!--
        Use the div below to author your Display Template. Here are some things to keep in mind:
        * Surround any JavaScript logic as shown below using a "pound underscore" (#_ ... _#)
        token inside a comment.

        * Use the values assigned to your variables using an "underscore pound equals"
        (_#= ... =#_) token.
    -->

    <div id="Control_List">

<!--#_
if (!$isNull(ctx.ClientControl) &&
    !$isNull(ctx.ClientControl.shouldRenderControl) &&
    !ctx.ClientControl.shouldRenderControl())
{
    return "";
```

```
}
ctx.ListDataJSONGroupsKey = "ResultTables";
var $noResults = Srch.ContentBySearch.getControlTemplateEncodedNoResultsMessage(ctx.
ClientControl);

var noResultsClassName = "ms-srch-result-noResults";

var ListRenderRenderWrapper = function(itemRenderResult, inCtx, tpl)
{
    var iStr = [];
    iStr.push('<li>');
    iStr.push(itemRenderResult);
    iStr.push('</li>');
    return iStr.join('');
}
ctx['ItemRenderWrapper'] = ListRenderRenderWrapper;
_#-->
    <ul class="cbs-List">

            _#= ctx.RenderGroups(ctx) =#_
        </ul>
<!--#_
if (ctx.ClientControl.get_shouldShowNoResultMessage())
{
_#-->
        <div class="_#= noResultsClassName =#_">_#= $noResults =#_</div>
<!--#_
}

_#-->

    </div>
</body>
</html>
```

When you work through this code, you can tell that it follows the typical HTML markup using HTML, HEAD, BODY, and DIV tags. Let's start with the code found in the HEAD section. The TITLE element value is important because it is the text that shows up in the control template drop-down box when you are using a search-driven Web Part. The next section is the *CustomDocumentProperties* section. It has five properties that need to be filled out. Table 15-4 lists each of these properties with descriptions.

TABLE 15-4 Control Template *CustomDocumentProperties*

Name	Description
TemplateHidden	Supported value is 0 or 1. Used to classify the template as hidden.
MasterPageDescription	Used to expose a description when the control template is viewed in the Master Page Gallery or when the ToolTip is exposed when the user is pointing to the control template within the drop-down box of a search-driven Web Part when choosing a control template.
ContentTypeId	This ID is the same for all control templates: 0x0101002039C03B61C64E-C4A04F5361F385106601

Name	Description
TargetControlType	Used to identify the target control type, which matches one of the available categories (for example, TaxonomyRefinement or Content Web Parts)
HtmlDesignAssociated	Supported value is 0 or 1. This bit is set by SharePoint and will be set to 1 after an HTML file has been added to the Master Page Gallery and SharePoint has created an associated JavaScript file.

The BODY is where you place your design markup. The first section you find should be a script element. This is where you can include external JavaScript by using the *$includeScript* method or external CSS references by using the *$includeCSS* method.

After the script element you can finally start to use HTML markup to interact with the results being returned. It is important to note that up until this point in the display template, HTML markup is not supported. A client context object is available by using the *ctx* object inside the display template. If you would like to use JavaScript within the display template, you must wrap these sections with a "pound underscore" token as shown in the following code:

```
<!--#_
var jsVariable = "Contoso"
_#-->
```

When you need to reference a variable declared within a "pound underscore" token, you do so by using an "underscore pound equals" token, as shown in the following code:

```
<div>_#= jsVariable =#_ </div>
```

By working through this example you can begin to tell that there are some particulars that you must account for when using display templates, but even accounting for these, the ease of use and the learning curve is far shorter than that of the XSL approach in SharePoint 2010.

The primary difference between an item template and a control template is an additional property called *ManagedPropertyMapping* found in the *CustomDocumentProperties* element. This property is only relevant inside an item template, because it is the only template that needs to interact with properties being returned. Furthermore, as the name implies, only managed properties can be used in this property and within a display template. The *ManagedPropertyMapping* property allows a developer or designer to create properties that are exposed through the tool pane for a search-driven Web Part and also to map default managed properties to them. The following code sample is from the SharePoint native item template named Item_TwoLines.html and shows the *ManagedProperty-Mapping* element:

```
<mso:ManagedPropertyMapping msdt:dt="string">'Link URL'{Link URL}:'Path','Line
1'{Line 1}:'Title','Line 2'{Line 2}:'','FileExtension','SecondaryFileExtension'</
mso:ManagedPropertyMapping>
```

We will focus on the section that is specific to Line 1. You first will find *'Line 1'*, which is used to set the display name of the field exposed within the Web Part tool pane, as shown in Figure 15-16.

FIGURE 15-16 The Content Search Web Part tool pane shows the Property Mappings exposed.

The next piece that follows is *{Line 1}*, which is a way to use a variable within the display template that is constant. This is because of the succeeding section after the variable *'Title'*. This sets the default value for the Line 1 property, but as you can see in Figure 15-16, a user can select the box to change the mappings. If this were to happen, you would not be able to support this type of dynamic function unless there was at least one constant, hence the *{Line 1}*.

You can also map multiple values as the default for a property to help alleviate the need to change the mappings. The following code snippet accounts for three of the managed properties that are image-based and applies them to the mapping:

```
'Picture URL'{Picture URL}:'PublishingImage;PictureURL;PictureThumbnailURL'
```

By using the variable *Picture URL*, you now have a constant reference that you can use for the remainder of the display template.

There is much more that can be discussed about display templates and how to take advantage of them; however, it is beyond the scope of this book to extend this discussion any further. If you would like to continue reading on this topic, you can visit the MSDN and TechNet sites for additional information.

Understanding cross-site publishing

Cross-site publishing has for the longest time been a want in the SharePoint community. Solutions have been affected because of the requirement to have the majority of the content found within them available for rollups using Web Parts. This resulted in oversized site collections that proved to be difficult when considering upgrades or recovery needs.

Cross-site publishing is really the act of making the content found in one SharePoint site collection reusable across any number of other site collections. This capability has been exposed in SharePoint 2013 through a feature scoped at the site collection level, as shown in Figure 15-17.

Cross-Site Collection Publishing
Enables site collection to designate lists and document libraries as catalog sources for Cross-Site Collection Publishing.

FIGURE 15-17 The Cross-Site Collection Publishing feature is new in SharePoint 2013.

From the surface, enabling this feature simply adds an additional link under the list or library settings page for configure catalog settings, as shown in Figure 15-18, though there is a lot more going on than this.

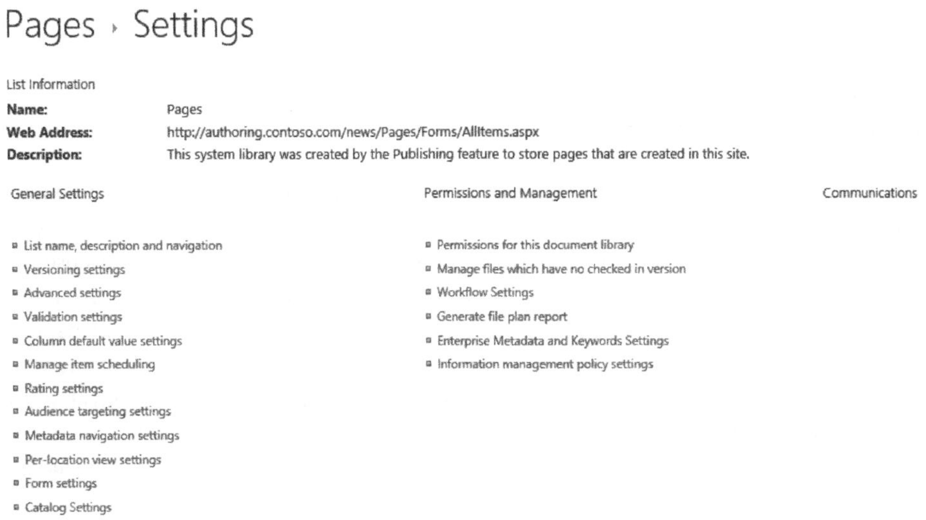

Pages › Settings

List Information

Name: Pages

Web Address: http://authoring.contoso.com/news/Pages/Forms/AllItems.aspx

Description: This system library was created by the Publishing feature to store pages that are created in this site.

General Settings	Permissions and Management	Communications
▫ List name, description and navigation	▫ Permissions for this document library	
▫ Versioning settings	▫ Manage files which have no checked in version	
▫ Advanced settings	▫ Workflow Settings	
▫ Validation settings	▫ Generate file plan report	
▫ Column default value settings	▫ Enterprise Metadata and Keywords Settings	
▫ Manage item scheduling	▫ Information management policy settings	
▫ Rating settings		
▫ Audience targeting settings		
▫ Metadata navigation settings		
▫ Per-location view settings		
▫ Form settings		
▫ Catalog Settings		

FIGURE 15-18 This library settings page shows a library in which the site collection has cross-site publishing enabled.

Working with catalogs

When you click the Catalog Settings link for a library or list from the settings page you are intending to make this list or library available as a catalog. There are a few important properties to configure to ensure that the content is exposed in the correct fashion. Figure 15-19 shows the Catalog Settings page.

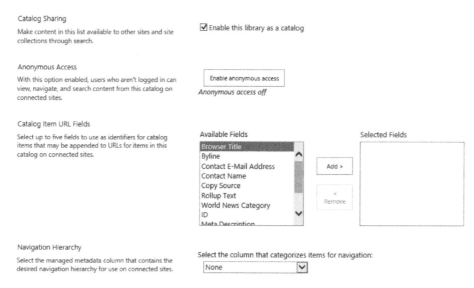

Catalog Sharing

Make content in this list available to other sites and site collections through search.

☑ Enable this library as a catalog

Anonymous Access

With this option enabled, users who aren't logged in can view, navigate, and search content from this catalog on connected sites.

Enable anonymous access

Anonymous access off

Catalog Item URL Fields

Select up to five fields to use as identifiers for catalog items that may be appended to URLs for items in this catalog on connected sites.

Available Fields

- Browser Title
- Byline
- Contact E-Mail Address
- Contact Name
- Copy Source
- Rollup Text
- World News Category
- ID
- Meta Description

Add >

< Remove

Selected Fields

Navigation Hierarchy

Select the managed metadata column that contains the desired navigation hierarchy for use on connected sites.

Select the column that categorizes items for navigation:

None

FIGURE 15-19 The catalog settings page for a library allows you to set catalog properties.

The first and most important setting is the Catalog Sharing property, which is used to enable the library as a catalog. The next property determines whether or not you enable anonymous access to the catalog. This setting is enabled more often for Internet sites than intranet sites, because that is typically where anonymous access is enabled for a web application and site. The Catalog Item URL Fields property allows you to choose which properties can be used as tokens within the page URL. This has a visual impact on what the user could view as part of the URL to access the content from a consuming site collection. The last property is the Navigation Hierarchy property, which is used to categorize the content via a term set. The important thing to remember is that this term set is exposed through a site column, which is what you actually pick from for the Navigation Hierarchy property, and it must only support single values.

After a catalog has been enabled, a full crawl must take place to surface the library as an option for consumption in other site collections. After this has taken place, you should be able to navigate to the site collection that you would like to consume your catalog from and select the Manage Catalog Connections link under the Site Administration section on the Site Settings page, as shown in Figure 15-20.

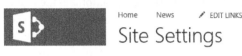

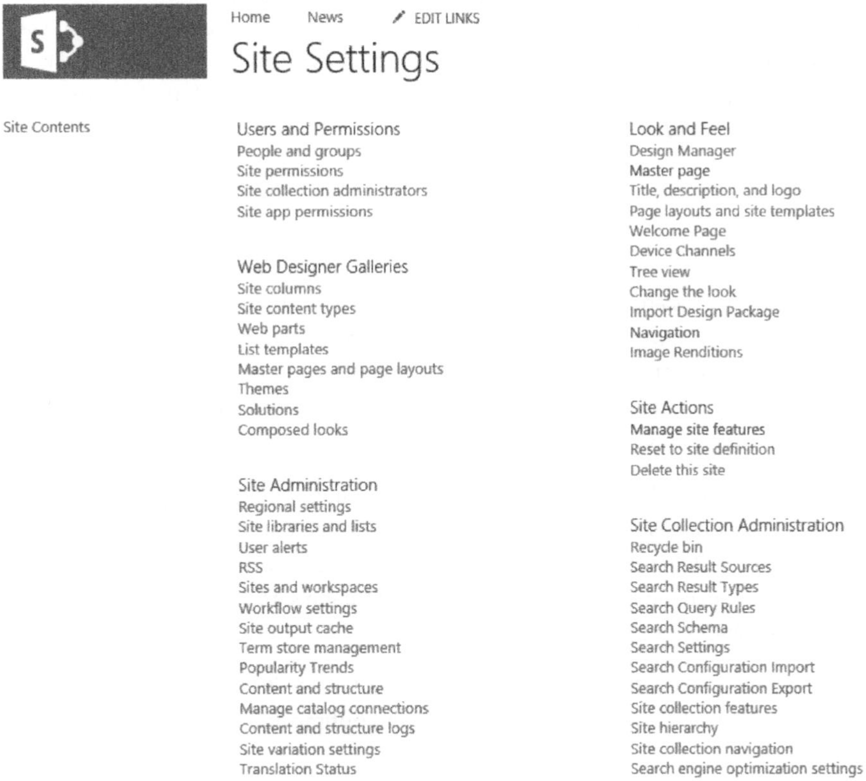

Home
News
EDIT LINKS
Site Settings
Site Contents
Users and Permissions
People and groups
Site permissions
Site collection administrators
Site app permissions
Web Designer Galleries
Site columns
Site content types
Web parts
List templates
Master pages and page layouts
Themes
Solutions
Composed looks
Site Administration
Regional settings
Site libraries and lists
User alerts
RSS
Sites and workspaces
Workflow settings
Site output cache
Term store management
Popularity Trends
Content and structure
Manage catalog connections
Content and structure logs
Site variation settings
Translation Status
Look and Feel
Design Manager
Master page
Title, description, and logo
Page layouts and site templates
Welcome Page
Device Channels
Tree view
Change the look
Import Design Package
Navigation
Image Renditions
Site Actions
Manage site features
Reset to site definition
Delete this site
Site Collection Administration
Recycle bin
Search Result Sources
Search Result Types
Search Query Rules
Search Schema
Search Settings
Search Configuration Import
Search Configuration Export
Site collection features
Site hierarchy
Site collection navigation
Search engine optimization settings

FIGURE 15-20 This site settings page has the Manage Catalog Connections link under the Site Administration section.

From this page you should be able to click Connect To A Catalog and view a list of catalogs that are available, as shown in Figure 15-21.

Home
News
EDIT LINKS
Search this site
Site Settings › Manage catalog connections › Connect to catalog
Note: Catalogs shared in the last few minutes will not appear in this list until the next scheduled search crawl.
Search
Available Catalogs:
Catalog Name
URL
Procedures - Pages
http://authoring.contoso.com/products/procedures/Pages
Connect
News - Pages
http://authoring.contoso.com/news/Pages
Connect

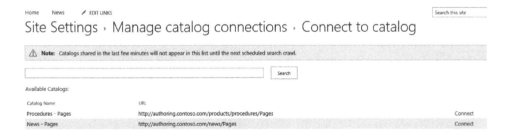

FIGURE 15-21 This Connect To Catalog page for a site shows two available catalogs.

SharePoint 2013 also has cross-site publishing APIs that can be used to automate the manual process of discovering and connecting to catalogs. By using the server-side approach you can expose a list or library or consume one that has already been enabled as a catalog. If you would like to learn more about this ability, you cam read the cross-site publishing APIs section found at *http://msdn. microsoft.com/en-us/library/jj163225.aspx.*

Summary

We have covered many topics and capabilities found within the Web Content Management (WCM) feature of SharePoint 2013; however, just as many if not more have escaped the scope of this chapter. The breadth of what SharePoint has to offer in WCM space should be a testament to its ongoing importance to the success of SharePoint and to organizations that take full advantage of its capabilities for their public and internal sites.

You have learned how SharePoint tales advantage of the page model for applying branding and presentation styles through master pages and page layouts to the content that authors create within a special library called the Pages library. You walked through the how developers and designers can lock down the authoring experience through the use of edit panels, managing the presentation of page fields, and using Web Part zones.

We covered the new device channel ability and how you can use it to limit the number of sites needed to handle different devices and the experience and optimizations that you would like each to have.

We discussed content aggregation within SharePoint and the new Content Search Web Part, along with how to style its results by using display templates.

Finally, we wrapped up by discussing the new cross-site publishing capabilities available through the Cross-Site Publishing feature.

Business Connectivity Services

Although Microsoft SharePoint Server 2013 provides a platform with significant capabilities, there will always be other systems in an organization that maintain critical business data. Systems such as customer relationship management (CRM) and enterprise resource planning (ERP) services have special roles that are not replaced easily by SharePoint. As a result, strategies must be adopted to provide interoperability between SharePoint and these systems.

In the absence of a strategy for integrating systems with SharePoint, many organizations duplicate information in SharePoint lists. Customer contact information, for example, may exist in a CRM system and also be entered into a contact list in SharePoint. Worse still, the data may be duplicated many times in different team sites by different groups. This kind of duplication leads to significant data maintenance issues because updates must be performed in many lists.

Along with these existing systems, custom applications, databases, and web services are common within organizations. When a separate database is required, developers have historically created Microsoft ASP.NET applications or custom Web Parts that act as front ends for the database to have the data appear in the SharePoint environment. However, these types of solutions generally offer little integration with SharePoint capabilities; they are largely limited to presenting data within a SharePoint page.

Business Connectivity Services (BCS) greatly enhances the ability to integrate systems, databases, and web services with SharePoint. Beyond simply bringing data into SharePoint for display, BCS allows for capabilities that simply can't exist in an ASP.NET application or custom Web Part without a significant investment. These capabilities include enterprise search, External Data Columns, user profile integration, app development, client synchronization, offline support, and Microsoft Word integration.

We should point out at the beginning of this chapter that BCS is a large subsystem within the SharePoint 2013 product; it is simply impossible to cover the entire depth of it in a single chapter. If you have been working with BCS in SharePoint 2010, then you will find that all of its functionality has been carried forward into SharePoint 2013, and several new capabilities have been added; these are summarized in Table 16-1. If you have never worked with BCS before, then this chapter will provide you with a good overview from which to get started.

TABLE 16-1 New capabilities and improvements in BCS

Capability/improvement	Description
App-level ECTs	External Content Types that are scoped to a single SharePoint app can be created.
Notification and event receivers	External Lists and External Content Types support "Alert Me" functionality and attaching custom event receivers.
OData sources	Microsoft Visual Studio 2012 provides tooling for creating ECTs that are based on OData sources.
REST and CSOM	Both Representational State Transfer (REST) and client-side object model (CSOM) programming APIs are available.
SharePoint Online	New and improved support for using External Content Types in SharePoint Online is provided.
Sorting and filtering	Sorting and filtering infrastructure is improved, making External Lists much more efficient when querying external systems.

Introduction to Business Connectivity Services

Business Connectivity Services is a term for a set of technologies that integrates external system data with SharePoint 2013 and Microsoft Office 2013. Figure 16-1 shows a block diagram of the major components in BCS. In our discussions of BCS, several new terms are introduced that will be used throughout the chapter. These terms all start with the word *External* to signify their association with BCS. The terms are listed here for reference:

- **External System**   Any data source with which BCS can connect

- **External Content Type (ECT)**   The definition of the fields and operations for connecting with an External System

- **External Data**   The data exchanged with an External System

- **External List**   A list in SharePoint based on External Data

- **External Data Column**   A column in a standard list or library whose source is External Data

- **External Data Web Part**   Any of several out-of-the-box Web Parts that can display External Data

BCS uses the term *External System* to refer to any application that is outside SharePoint. These External Systems can include third-party software, custom applications, databases, web services, and even cloud computing solutions. The Business Data Connectivity (BDC) layer contains the plumbing, BDC Runtime application programming interface (API), and connectivity functionality necessary to communicate with External Systems. Out of the box, the BDC layer provides connectors for databases, web services, and OData sources, but you can create your own connectors for any system.

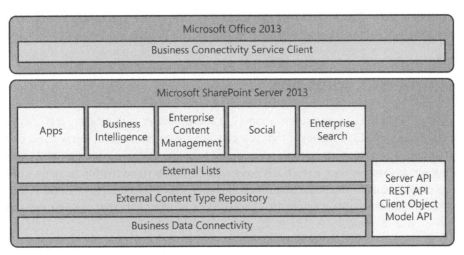

FIGURE 16-1 The major BCS components

The operations performed on the External Data and the schema for the returned data set are defined by an External Content Type (ECT). ECTs define fields, operations, and filters to be used with the External Data and are the heart of the BCS infrastructure. As an example, consider a manufacturing database that contains product information. An ECT named *Product* can be created that defines *ProductID, ProductName*, and *ProductDescription* fields. Furthermore, it might define operations for retrieving data based on a keyword query or exact product identifier. Defining ECTs is one of the primary activities involved in creating a BCS solution and can be performed in either Microsoft SharePoint Designer 2013 or Microsoft Visual Studio 2012. ECTs are stored in a metadata catalog, which is either part of the BDC Service application or created locally inside a SharePoint app.

Although you can create many custom solutions by using code, the easiest way to create a solution in BCS is through an External List. An External List is a list that is based on an ECT definition and displays External Data. Conceptually, External Lists use ECTs the same way that standard SharePoint lists use standard content types. You can create External Lists in a browser or through SharePoint Designer without writing any code; External Lists are accessible through the *SPList* object in the server object model or through the _api RESTful endpoint just like a standard SharePoint list.

Along with External Lists, ECTs can also be used in other ways through SharePoint. SharePoint ships with a set of Web Parts called *External Data Web Parts* that can display data from External Systems based on an ECT. ECTs can also be used to create lookup fields in standard SharePoint lists. ECTs can be used to enhance the information in a user's profile by drawing on human resource systems such as PeopleSoft. Finally, ECTs can be used to facilitate searching External Systems and displaying results in SharePoint.

In Office 2013, the BCS Client layer provides the ability to display External Data in Office clients. Microsoft Outlook can display data using standard forms, such as contact lists or calendar items. Microsoft Word can use External Data to support document creation. Microsoft InfoPath is also available to customize the display and edit forms for External Data. In addition, clients running Office 2013 support access to External Data in an offline mode using a cache system that updates the External System when the client reconnects.

Creating simple BCS solutions

The BCS infrastructure is complex and covers a variety of authentication, authorization, and operation scenarios. The beauty of BCS, however, is that you can also create simple solutions with no code. SharePoint Designer provides a set of tools you can use to create ECTs against External Systems and surface them as External Lists. In fact, the easiest way to understand the fundamentals of BCS is to create a simple solution. The classic solution is to create an ECT based on data found in the AdventureWorks sample database. Figure 16-2 shows some product data that can be used as a source for a no-code solution.

	ProductID	Name	Number	Color	Description
1	680	HL Road Frame - Black, 58	FR-R92B-58	Black	Our lightest and best quality aluminum frame mad...
2	706	HL Road Frame - Red, 58	FR-R92R-58	Red	Our lightest and best quality aluminum frame mad...
3	707	Sport-100 Helmet, Red	HL-U509-R	Red	Universal fit, well-vented, lightweight , snap-on vi...
4	708	Sport-100 Helmet, Black	HL-U509	Black	Universal fit, well-vented, lightweight , snap-on vi...
5	709	Mountain Bike Socks, M	SO-B909-M	White	Combination of natural and synthetic fibers stays ...
6	710	Mountain Bike Socks, L	SO-B909-L	White	Combination of natural and synthetic fibers stays ...
7	711	Sport-100 Helmet, Blue	HL-U509-B	Blue	Universal fit, well-vented, lightweight , snap-on vi...
8	712	AWC Logo Cap	CA-1098	Multi	Traditional style with a flip-up brim; one-size fits all.
9	713	Long-Sleeve Logo Jersey, S	LJ-0192-S	Multi	Unisex long-sleeve AWC logo microfiber cycling j...
10	714	Long-Sleeve Logo Jersey, M	LJ-0192-M	Multi	Unisex long-sleeve AWC logo microfiber cycling j...

FIGURE 16-2 Product data in AdventureWorks

Creating External Content Types

BCS solutions always begin by defining External Content Types for the schema and operations. These definitions are nearly always created by using SharePoint Designer. SharePoint Designer provides all the basic tooling necessary to create ECTs and External Lists. In addition, ECTs can be exported from SharePoint Designer so that they can be migrated from a development environment to a quality as-surance (QA) environment and then to a production environment. To begin creating an ECT, you open a SharePoint site in SharePoint Designer and click the External Content Types object in the list of Site Objects, as shown in Figure 16-3. This produces a list of all the existing ECTs in the farm.

After you have a view of the available ECTs, you can define a new one by clicking the New External Content Type button on the ribbon. The basic ECT information consists of a name, display name, namespace, and version. You can also select from a list of various Office types, which determine what form will be used to render the information when it is displayed in Outlook. Figure 16-4 shows the basic ECT information for the walkthrough with the *Post* type selected.

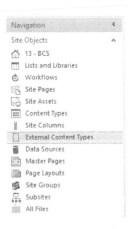

FIGURE 16-3 Displaying the available ECTs

External Content Type Information ⌃

Key information about this external content type.

Name	Product
Display Name	Product
Namespace	http://www.wingtip.com/aw
Version	1.1.0.0
Identifiers	ProductID(Int32)
Office Item Type	Post ⌄
Offline Sync for external list	Enabled ⌄
External System	AdventureworksBCS

FIGURE 16-4 Basic ECT information

After the basic ECT information is defined, you will define connection information for the External System. Clicking the Operations Design View button on the ribbon presents a form for defining the connection information. From this form, clicking Add Connection allows you to select from three types of connections: WCF, SQL, and .NET Type. Selecting WCF allows you to connect to a web service, SQL allows you to connect to a database, and .NET Type allows you to use a custom Microsoft .NET Assembly Connector (which is covered in the section "Creating .NET Assembly Connectors" later in this chapter).

BCS supports a number of authentication mechanisms for connecting to the External System. You can connect as the current user or the BDC service account, you can transform credentials to another account, or you can even use claims-based access. In this walkthrough, the connection is made by using the BDC service account. The details concerning authentication options are discussed in the section "Understanding authentication scenarios" later in this chapter. Figure 16-5 shows the connection information for the walkthrough.

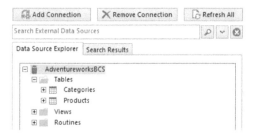

FIGURE 16-5 Connection information

After the data source connection is made, SharePoint Designer can create operations for the ECT. When a SQL connection is used, SharePoint Designer can infer a significant amount of information about the data source and the operations, so it is easy to create the entire set of create, read, update, and delete (CRUD) operations. In fact, all you have to do is right-click the table in the connection and select Create All Operations from the shortcut menu, which will start the Operation Wizard to collect the small amount of information required to complete the operation definitions. Figure 16-6 shows the shortcut menu in SharePoint Designer.

FIGURE 16-6 Creating ECT operations

The Operation Wizard starts whenever SharePoint Designer needs additional information to complete the operation definition. The information required typically includes a mapping of fields between the ECT and Outlook, identification of the primary key for the ECT, and the definition of filters to throttle the size of returned result sets. SharePoint Designer displays errors and warnings throughout the wizard to guide you in correctly defining the operations.

After the operations are defined, the ECT should be saved. Saving the ECT writes the definition to the metadata catalog, where it becomes available to the entire farm. After the ECT is saved, it will appear in the list of External Content Types in SharePoint Designer. From the list of External Content Types, you can also export the ECT definition as an XML file. This XML file can subsequently be imported through the Business Data Connectivity service interface in Central Administration.

Creating External Lists

After the ECT is created, it can be used as the basis for an External List. External Lists can be created directly in SharePoint Designer or in the browser by using the Add An App button in SharePoint. For this walkthrough, a new External List was created directly from the summary page in SharePoint Designer. Figure 16-7 shows the dialog box for defining the list name and associating operations.

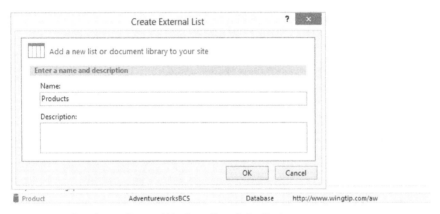

FIGURE 16-7 Creating an External List from SharePoint Designer

After the new External List is created, it can be viewed in the browser. Because all the CRUD operations were created, the resulting list supports editing, adding, and deleting items. Figure 16-8 shows the new list in SharePoint Server 2013. Note how the appearance of the External List closely resembles a standard SharePoint list. The ribbon is functional, as well as the edit-control block (ECB) associated with individual items. Any changes to items in the list will be reflected immediately in the External System.

Just like regular lists, External Lists can be taken offline through Outlook. For this walkthrough, the ECT was defined as a generic list in Outlook. If the Offline Synchronization For External Lists site feature is activated, Outlook will display the data when the Connect To Outlook button on the List tab of the ribbon is clicked. When an External List is synchronized with Outlook, BCS delivers a Visual Studio Tools for Office (VSTO) package to the client for accessing the External System. Figure 16-9 shows the VSTO solution installation dialog box.

Products

⊕ new item

ReadProducts •••

✓	ProductID		Name	Description
	680	•••	HL Road Frame - Black, 58	Our lightest and best quality aluminum frame made from the newest alloy; it is welded and he Our innovative design results in maximum comfort and performance.
	706	•••	HL Road Frame - Red, 58	Our lightest and best quality aluminum frame made from the newest alloy; it is welded and he Our innovative design results in maximum comfort and performance.
	707	•••	Sport-100 Helmet, Red	Universal fit, well-vented, lightweight , snap-on visor.
	708	•••	Sport-100 Helmet, Black	Universal fit, well-vented, lightweight , snap-on visor.
	709	•••	Mountain Bike Socks, M	Combination of natural and synthetic fibers stays dry and provides just the right cushioning.
	710	•••	Mountain Bike Socks, L	Combination of natural and synthetic fibers stays dry and provides just the right cushioning.
	711	•••	Sport-100 Helmet, Blue	Universal fit, well-vented, lightweight , snap-on visor.
	712	•••	AWC Logo Cap	Traditional style with a flip-up brim; one-size fits all.
	713	•••	Long-Sleeve Logo Jersey, S	Unisex long-sleeve AWC logo microfiber cycling jersey
	714	•••	Long-Sleeve Logo Jersey, M	Unisex long-sleeve AWC logo microfiber cycling jersey
	715	•••	Long-Sleeve Logo	Unisex long-sleeve AWC logo microfiber cycling jersey

FIGURE 16-8 The External List

FIGURE 16-9 Installing External Data in Outlook

Understanding External List limitations

Though an External List appear similar visually to a standard SharePoint list and is supported by a *SPList* object, External Lists do have significant limitations that must be considered in any design. These limitations include lack of workflow support and several standard list features. The following lists some of the major limitations of External Lists:

- **Approval**   Approval of items is not supported.

- **Attachments**   Attachments are not supported directly but must be implemented by using a *StreamAccessor* operation in a custom solution.

- **Checking in/checking out**   Checking in and checking-out of items are not supported.

- **Content types**   Using standard site content types in External Lists is not supported.

- **Drafts**   Drafts of items are not supported.

- **ECB**   Send-To operations are not supported.

- **Ribbon**   Datasheet View is not supported.

- **SPLINQ**   Querying through LINQ to SharePoint is not supported.

- **Templates**   Document templates are not supported.

- **Versioning**   Versioning of items is not supported.

- **Workflow**   Starting workflows from items is not supported, but workflows can read or write to External Lists through the *SPList* object.

- **Validation**   Validation formulas are not supported.

Despite these limitations, BCS solutions provide a powerful authentication and resource infrastructure that allows you to integrate External Data with SharePoint in a way that provides good performance and security. External Lists are not intended to be a substitute for an External System or a SharePoint list. Instead, you should think of External Lists as miniature versions of the External Systems that they represent. Through this perspective, you can tell that they are intended to bring commonly used data directly to information workers without requiring a separate logon to an External System. Also, don't forget the additional capabilities that External Lists provide, such as offline access and search support.

The standard *SPList* object can be used in code running against the *Microsoft.SharePoint* namespace to access the items in External Lists, but there are a few special requirements. When code accesses the items in an External List, the unique identifier for an item is found in the *BdcIdentity* field, not the standard ID of the item. In addition, to access the list items, you must enumerate the *SPListItem* collection. Other than those restrictions, accessing the items in the list is straightforward. The following code shows how to access the items in the Products list created in the walkthrough:

```
SPWeb site = SPContext.Current.Web;
SPList externalList = site.Lists["Products"];

foreach (SPListItem item in externalList.Items) {
  foreach (SPField field in item.Fields) {
    if (field.Title != null) {
      string title = item[field.Title].ToString();
    }
  }
}
```

External Lists can also be accessed from the client side by using both the RESTful endpoint and CSOM. The REST pattern is similar to the approach taken with standard lists, by making an asynchronous call to the RESTful endpoint using the jQuery *ajax* function. The following code shows how to make such a call against the Products list created in the walkthrough:

```
$.ajax({
    url: _spPageContextInfo.webServerRelativeUrl +
        "/_api/lists/getByTitle('Products')/items?$select=ProductID,CategoryName",
    headers: {
        "accept": "application/json;odata=verbose",
        "X-RequestDigest": $("#__REQUESTDIGEST").val()
    },
    success: onSuccess,
    error: onError
});
```

Accessing an External List by using CSOM is also similar to the approach used for standard lists. A Collaborative Application Markup Language (CAML)query must be created and then executed asynchronously. The following code shows how to execute a CAML query against the External List from the walkthrough using CSOM:

```
var products;
var ctx = SP.ClientContext.get_current();
var query = "<View><ViewFields><FieldRef Name='ProductID'/>" +
            "<FieldRef Name='CategoryName'/></ViewFields></View>";
var camlQuery = new SP.CamlQuery();
camlQuery.set_viewXml(query);
var list = ctx.get_web().get_lists().getByTitle("Products");
ctx.load(list);
products = list.getItems(camlQuery);
ctx.load(products, 'Include(ProductID,CategoryName)');
ctx.executeQueryAsync(onSuccess, onError);
```

Understanding BCS architecture

BCS architecture consists of components on both the server and client. These components support connectivity, ECT definition, operations, and data management. The design of BCS provides for a symmetry between client and server so that clients can have equivalent functionality when offline. Figure 16-10 shows a block diagram of the BCS architecture.

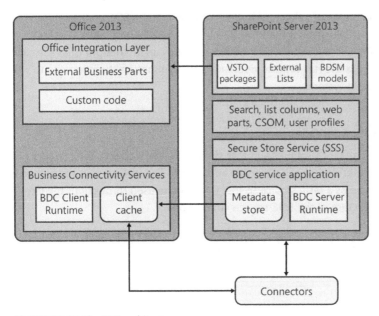

FIGURE 16-10 The BCS architecture

Understanding connectors

BCS communicates with External Systems by using connectors. Connectors contain the functionality necessary to communicate with databases, web services, and other systems. The walkthrough presented earlier used the SQL connector to access a Microsoft SQL Server database, but BCS also supports a WCF connector for accessing web services, and an OData connector for RESTful services. The SQL, WCF, and OData connectors provide a lot of the functionality you will need for basic BCS solutions, but in more advanced cases, you may need to create a connector. When you create your own connector, you can create a .NET Assembly Connector.

A .NET Assembly Connector is a project that you create in Visual Studio 2012 that contains the ECT definition and associated business logic for accessing a specific External System. The .NET Assembly Connector differs from the out-of-the-box connectors because it targets a specific system, as opposed to all instances of a specific system type.

Understanding Business Data Connectivity

The Business Data Connectivity (BDC) layer provides the plumbing and runtime components of BCS. In SharePoint 2013, both the server and the client have BDC components to support the symmetry of operations on the client and the server. You can use a similar approach to creating BCS solutions whether you are focused on the server, client, or both. On the server, the BDC components consist of the ECT catalog and the BDC Server Runtime. On the client, the BDC components consist of a metadata cache and the BDC Client Runtime. The metadata cache can be thought of as the client-side metadata catalog, whereas the run-time components have symmetrical functionality to support operations against the External Systems.

Managing the BDC service

When you create ECTs in SharePoint Designer and save them, they are stored in the metadata catalog, which is a database accessed through the BDC service application. The BDC service application wraps the BDC and makes it available as a farm service so that ECTs can be used throughout the farm. Figure 16-11 shows the basic architecture of the BDC service application.

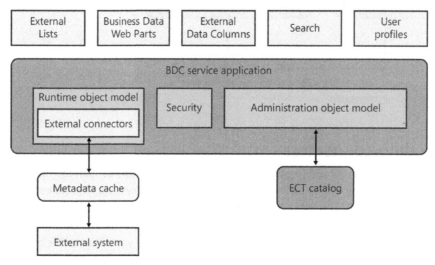

FIGURE 16-11 The BDC service application architecture

The BDC service application wraps the BDC plumbing and makes BDC functionality available as a service. When External Systems are accessed through connectors, the returned data is made available by the BDC service application to support External Lists, searching, Web Parts, and so on. The metadata cache is maintained in the BDC service so that ECT data is accessed easily without having to be read from the database. This metadata cache is updated every minute by a timer job so that the latest changes are available. Note that External Data itself is never cached by the server—only the ECT metadata.

Along with caching metadata to improve performance, BCS implements limits on the number of connections that can be made to an External System. In addition, the BDC service application also implements five different throttle settings to limit the connections made and data returned from External Systems. Table 16-2 lists the throttle settings for the BDC service application.

TABLE 16-2 BDC service application throttles

Type	Description	Scope	Default	Maximum
Connections	Total number of connections allowed to External Systems	Global	100	500
Items	Number of rows returned from a database query	Database	2000	25,000
Timeout	Database connection timeout	Database	60 seconds	600 seconds
Size	Size of returned data	WCF	3 MB	150 MB
Timeout	Web service connection timeout	WCF	60 seconds	600 seconds

You can view and change throttle values by using Windows PowerShell commands. Before you can change them, however, you must get a reference to the BDC service application. The following Windows PowerShell code shows how to return a reference to the BDC service application named Business Data Connectivity:

```
$bdc = Get-SPServiceApplicationProxy | Where {$_ -match "Business Data Connectivity"}
```

After you have a reference to the BDC service application, you can use the *Get-SPBusinessData-CatalogThrottleConfig* cmdlet and the *Set-SPBusinessDataCatalogThrottleConfig* cmdlet to view and change throttle settings. Each of these cmdlets requires you to specify the throttle that you are viewing or changing. The following code shows how to view the current throttle settings by using Windows PowerShell:

```
Get-SPBusinessDataCatalogThrottleConfig -ThrottleType Connections -Scope Global '
                                        -ServiceApplicationProxy $bdc
Get-SPBusinessDataCatalogThrottleConfig -ThrottleType Items -Scope Database '
                                        -ServiceApplicationProxy $bdc
Get-SPBusinessDataCatalogThrottleConfig -ThrottleType Timeout -Scope Database '
                                        -ServiceApplicationProxy $bdc
Get-SPBusinessDataCatalogThrottleConfig -ThrottleType Size -Scope Wcf '
                                        -ServiceApplicationProxy $bdc
Get-SPBusinessDataCatalogThrottleConfig -ThrottleType Timeout -Scope Wcf '
                                        -ServiceApplicationProxy $bdc
```

When changing throttle settings, you must specify the new value in the *Set-SPBusinessDataCatalog-ThrottleConfig* cmdlet. New throttle settings take effect immediately. As an example, the following code shows how to change the number of items that can be returned from a database:

```
$bdc = Get-SPServiceApplicationProxy | Where {$_ -match "Business Data Connectivity"}
$throttle = Get-SPBusinessDataCatalogThrottleConfig -ThrottleType Items -Scope Database
                                        -ServiceApplicationProxy $bdc
Set-SPBusinessDataCatalogThrottleConfig -Maximum 3000 -Default 1000 -Identity $throttle
```

Along with viewing or editing throttle values, you can disable them. However, disabling or changing throttles is not something that should be done lightly. Disabling throttles can result in poor BCS performance and can affect the performance of the SharePoint farm as a whole. The following code shows how to disable the connection limit throttle:

```
$bdc = Get-SPServiceApplicationProxy | Where {$_ -match "Business Data Connectivity"}
$throttle = Get-SPBusinessDataCatalogThrottleConfig -ThrottleType Connections
            -Scope Global -ServiceApplicationProxy $bdc
Set-SPBusinessDataCatalogThrottleConfig -Enforced:$false -Identity $throttle
```

The BDC service application is part of the service application framework in SharePoint. As such, it functions like any of the other shared services in SharePoint. You can access the management interface for the BDC service application through the Central Administration home page by selecting Application Management, Manage Service Applications. Figure 16-12 shows the BDC service application in Central Administration.

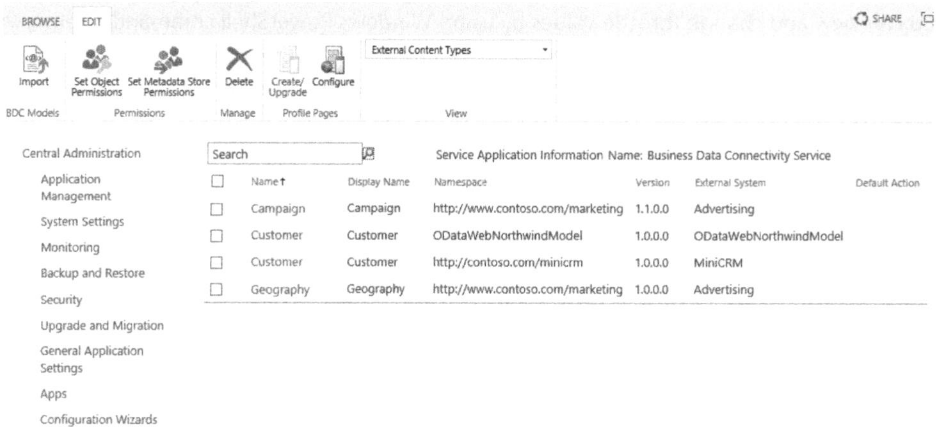

FIGURE 16-12 The BDC service application in Central Administration

From the Service Applications page, you can click the Properties button on the ribbon and view the basic service properties for the BDC service application. In the Properties dialog box, you will find the name of the database used for the ECT repository. As with all services, you can also set administrative and connection permissions for the service so that it can be used by other servers in the SharePoint farm.

Clicking the Manage button on the Service Applications page allows you to manage the ECTs in the repository. Here you will find the ECTs that you have defined along with information about the associated models and External Systems. Models can be imported and exported from this page, so you can export models from SharePoint Designer in a development environment and import them into the BDC service application in QA or production environments.

Managing the BDC service application also allows you to set permissions for the various objects in your model. Users must have permissions to access the ECT and its operations before they will see data in SharePoint. This permission is separate from the actual permissions required to access an External System. There are four different rights available for an ECT: Edit, Execute, Selectable in Clients, and Set Permissions. The Edit right grants the ability to edit models, data sources, and External

Content Types. The Execute right grants the ability to perform CRUD operations by using the ECT. The Selectable in In Clients right grants the ability to create new External Lists, use the External Data Web Parts, and pick External Content Types from the various pickers that appear in SharePoint. The Set Permissions right grants the ability to set permissions in the BDC service.

Understanding the BDC Server Runtime

The BDC Server Runtime consists of the run-time object model, the administration object model, and the security infrastructure. The run-time object model provides access to ECTs and their associated operations, whereas the administration object model provides objects for managing the ECTs and their associated models. The security infrastructure facilitates authentication and authorization for ECT operations and External System access.

Understanding the client cache

BCS uses a client cache to store information from the ECT repository and data from the External System so that Office client applications can access External Systems directly or take data offline. The client cache is a SQL Server Compact Edition database that is installed as part of the Office 2013 installation. A synchronization process called BCSSync.exe runs on the client to synchronize the cache with model information in the BDC layer. When operations are performed on data within the Office clients, the operations are queued inside the client cache and synchronized with the External System when it is available. The synchronization process also attempts to update data in the cache at various intervals from the External System depending on the user settings and availability of the External System. Conflicts between the cache and the External System are flagged for the user so that they can be resolved. When clients access External Systems, they always use the information in the cache to access the External System. There is never any case in which the client application accesses the External System through the server-side components.

Understanding the BDC Client Runtime

The BDC Client Runtime, which is also called the Office Integration Runtime (OIR), is the client-side component that complements the BDC Server Runtime. Like the server-side component, the BDC Client Runtime is responsible for the plumbing and functionality necessary to execute operations against an External System and bind the data to clients such as Outlook. The BDC Client Runtime is installed on the client as part of the Office 2013 installation process just like the cache. This means that all Office 2013 client installations will support BCS functionality.

Introduction to the Secure Store Service

The Secure Store Service (SSS) is a service application that provides for the storage, mapping, and retrieval of credential information. It is used in authentication scenarios in which the user account is either not available or not supported by the External System. To store credential sets for an External System, a new *Target Application* must be created in SSS. The Target Application acts as a container for credential sets mapped to an External System. The Target Application settings page contains a name for the application and a setting to specify whether each individual user will have a separate set of mapped credentials or whether every user will map to a single common set of credentials. Figure 16-13 shows application settings mapping a single set of credentials to an Active Directory Domain Services (AD DS) group.

Create New Secure Store Target Application ⓘ

Target Application Settings

The Secure Store Target Application ID is a unique identifier. You cannot change this property after you create the Target Application.

The display name is used for display purposes only.

The contact e-mail should be a valid e-mail address of the primary contact for this Target Application.

The Target Application type determines whether this application uses a group mapping or individual mapping. Ticketing indicates whether tickets are used for this Target Application. You cannot change this property after you create the Target Application.

The Target Application page URL can be used to set the values for the credential fields for the Target Application by individual users.

Target Application ID
`Products`

Display Name
`Products`

Contact E-mail
`administrator@wingtip.com`

Target Application Type
`Group ▾`

Target Application Page URL
○ Use default page
○ Use custom page
`_____`
◉ None

FIGURE 16-13 Creating a new Target Application in SSS

After the Target Application is defined, credential fields are defined to specify what credentials are required to access the External System. In most cases, the Target Application will save a Windows user name and password, but you could also map credentials for non-Windows authentication schemes such as SQL accounts. SSS also supports additional attributes such as personal identification numbers (PINs) for credentials. Figure 16-14 shows the field definition form for a Target Application.

Create New Secure Store Target Application ⓘ

Field Name

`Windows User Name`
`Windows Password`

Add Field

Field Type

`Windows User Name ▾`
`Windows Password ▾`

Important: The field names and field types cannot be edited later.

FIGURE 16-14 Defining credential fields

After the application and credential fields are defined, you must enter the actual credential information for a specific user. For each user or group that will access the External System, a set of credentials is stored in SSS. If a user attempts to access the system without proper credentials in SSS, then that person will be directed to a logon page so that the credentials can be entered and stored just-in-time. After the credentials are mapped, you can specify the name of the Target Application in SharePoint Designer during ECT creation. When the Target Application is specified in this way, BCS will use the SSS credentials to access the External System. Figure 16-15 shows a dialog box for setting the credentials used in a group mapping. In this case, all users are utilizing a single account.

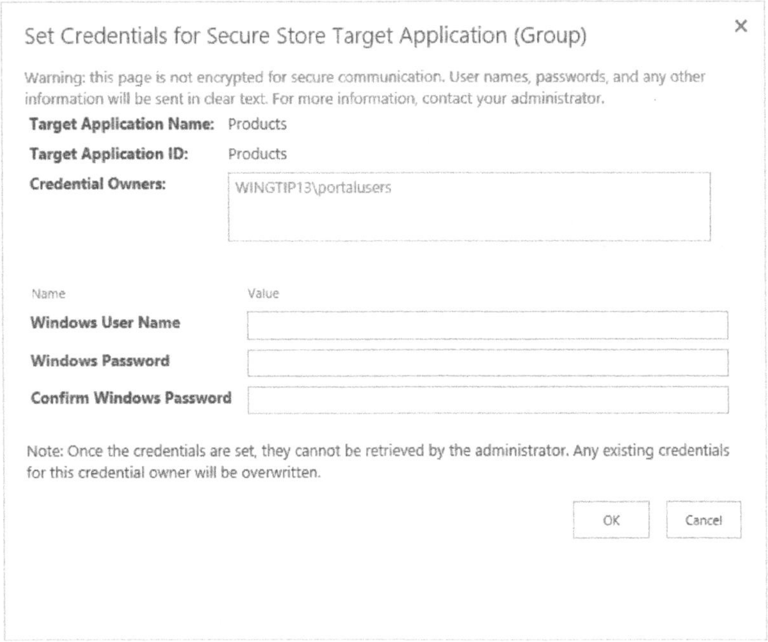

Set Credentials for Secure Store Target Application (Group)   ✕

Warning: this page is not encrypted for secure communication. User names, passwords, and any other information will be sent in clear text. For more information, contact your administrator.

Target Application Name: Products

Target Application ID: Products

Credential Owners:

WINGTIP13\portalusers

Name   Value

Windows User Name

Windows Password

Confirm Windows Password

Note: Once the credentials are set, they cannot be retrieved by the administrator. Any existing credentials for this credential owner will be overwritten.

OK   Cancel

FIGURE 16-15 Mapping group credentials to a single account

The credentials stored in SSS are accessible through a set of objects designed to support your custom solutions. By using these objects, you can create solutions, such as Web Parts, that use SSS credentials to gain access to External Systems. The *Microsoft.Office.SecureStoreService* assembly contains the main classes necessary to work with SSS. In addition, the *Microsoft.BusinessData* assembly contains supporting classes for working with BCS.

The general approach to retrieving SSS credentials in code involves getting a reference to the SSS service application through the *ISecureStoreProvider* class. The *GetCredentials* method can then be called with the name of the Target Application to return the credentials. Listing 16-1 shows how a Web Part can use this approach to build a connection string for an External System.

LISTING 16-1 Accessing the SSS programmatically

```
protected override void OnPreRender(EventArgs e) {
  string username = string.Empty;
  string password = string.Empty;

  try {
    ISecureStoreProvider p = SecureStoreProviderFactory.Create();
    using (SecureStoreCredentialCollection creds =
              p.GetCredentials(ApplicationId)) {

      // enumerate through all credentials
      foreach (SecureStoreCredential c in creds) {
        switch (c.CredentialType) {
          case SecureStoreCredentialType.UserName:
            username = ConvertToString(c.Credential);
            break;

          case SecureStoreCredentialType.Password:
            password = ConvertToString(c.Credential);
            break;

          case SecureStoreCredentialType.WindowsUserName:
            username = ConvertToString(c.Credential);
            break;

          case SecureStoreCredentialType.WindowsPassword:
            password = ConvertToString(c.Credential);
            break;
        }
      }
    }

    SqlConnectionStringBuilder cBuilder = new SqlConnectionStringBuilder();
    cBuilder.DataSource = ServerName;
    cBuilder.InitialCatalog = DatabaseName;
    cBuilder.UserID = username;
    cBuilder.Password = password;

    messages.Text = cBuilder.ConnectionString;

  }
  catch (Exception x) {
    messages.Text = x.Message;
  }
}

private String ConvertToString(SecureString s) {
  IntPtr b = Marshal.SecureStringToBSTR(s);
  try { return Marshal.PtrToStringBSTR(b); }
  finally { Marshal.FreeBSTR(b); }
}
```

Understanding package deployment

When a user elects to synchronize an External List with Outlook, BCS creates a VSTO Click-Once deployment package that contains all the elements necessary to work with the list on the client. The package is created by BCS just-in-time and stored under the list in a folder named *ClientSolution*. After the package is created, the deployment is started automatically.

The package contains the BCS model defining the External System, ECTs, operations, and security information that is necessary to access and modify data. The package also contains subscription information, which tells the client cache what data to manage and how it should be refreshed. Finally, the package contains pre-deployment and post-deployment steps that should be taken, such as creating custom forms in the client application to display the data.

After it is deployed, the add-in can use Office Business Parts on the client to help render data. Office Business Parts are Windows form controls that display a single item or list of items in a task pane to simplify the rendering process so that custom task panes do not have to be created for the client.

Understanding authentication scenarios

When connecting to back-end systems, BCS must deal with several different authentication scenarios. In the simplest case, BCS might be passing Windows credentials from the user through to the External System. However, most real-world applications have more complex requirements, such as proprietary authentication mechanisms, tokens, or claims. For BCS solutions to be secure, they must deal with these situations adequately.

Configuring authentication models

BCS supports two authentication models: *Trusted Subsystem* and *Impersonation and Delegation*. In the Trusted Subsystem model, BCS uses a single account to access the External System regardless of the user identity. Under Impersonation and Delegation, BCS attempts to impersonate the user and access the External System. The *AuthenticationMode* element in the BDC Metadata Model determines how authentication is performed and has several different options.

Understanding *Passthrough* authentication

Passthrough authentication is used in the Impersonation and Delegation authentication model. Setting the value of the *AuthenticationMode* element to *Passthrough* causes BCS to use the credentials of the current user to access the External System. You can set up *Passthrough* authentication by selecting the Connect With User's Identity option when creating a connection to an External System in SharePoint Designer. The following code shows a portion of a BDC Metadata Model connecting to the Adventure-Works database by using *Passthrough* authentication:

```
<LobSystemInstances>
  <LobSystemInstance Name="Adventureworks Data Warehouse">
    <Properties>
      <Property Name="AuthenticationMode" Type="System.String">
        PassThrough
      </Property>
      <Property Name="DatabaseAccessProvider" Type="System.String">
        SqlServer
      </Property>
      <Property Name="RdbConnection Data Source" Type="System.String">
        AWSQL
      </Property>
      <Property Name="RdbConnection Initial Catalog"
                Type="System.String">AdventureworksDW</Property>
      <Property Name="RdbConnection Integrated Security" Type="System.String">
        SSPI
      </Property>
      <Property Name="RdbConnection Pooling" Type="System.String">true</Property>
    </Properties>
  </LobSystemInstance>
</LobSystemInstances>
```

Though *Passthrough* authentication is easy to implement, it is unlikely to be useful in many situations because of a particular limitation in Windows authentication known as the *double-hop* issue. Windows authentication takes two forms: NTLM and the Kerberos protocol. NTLM is the classic challenge-response protocol used to authenticate users. The Kerberos protocol is an advanced ticket-based protocol that is much more secure. NTLM authentication is often compared to a carnival where you must pay for each ride separately. The Kerberos protocol, on the other hand, is often compared to a theme park where you pay for one ticket and then have access to all the rides. Though Kerberos authentication is considered to be a best practice for BCS, many organizations still run under NTLM authentication.

The double-hop issue describes a scenario under NTLM authentication where the web server attempts to impersonate a user through a series of "hops" involving multiple servers. When a user makes a request to view an External List, SharePoint will attempt to impersonate the user. This impersonation is done at the ASP.NET level, independent of BCS. However, when BCS subsequently attempts to access the data source, it will be prevented from continuing to impersonate the user, and the account identity will change to that of the system account. At this point, the original user identity islost and access to the data source will be denied.

The double-hop issue is not a bug; it was a built-in feature of NTLM. The limitation is designed to prevent viruses from accessing network resources if credentials are compromised. The Kerberos protocol does not suffer from this limitation because its ticketing-based protocol is more secure than challenge-response. So changing the network authentication mechanism from NTLM to the Kerberos protocol will solve this problem. Otherwise, you must use a different BCS authentication mechanism to access External Systems.

Understanding *RevertToSelf*

RevertToSelf is used in the Trusted Subsystem model of authentication. Setting the value of the *AuthenticationMode* element to *RevertToSelf* causes BCS to use the credentials of the application pool to access the External System. The following code shows a BDC Metadata Model using *RevertToSelf* authentication:

```
<LobSystemInstances>
  <LobSystemInstance Name="Adventureworks Data Warehouse">
    <Properties>
      <Property Name="AuthenticationMode" Type="System.String">
        RevertToSelf
      </Property>
      <Property Name="DatabaseAccessProvider" Type="System.String">
        SqlServer
      </Property>
      <Property Name="RdbConnection Data Source" Type="System.String">
        AWSQL
      </Property>
      <Property Name="RdbConnection Initial Catalog"
               Type="System.String">AdventureworksDW</Property>
      <Property Name="RdbConnection Integrated Security" Type="System.String">
        SSPI
      </Property>
      <Property Name="RdbConnection Pooling" Type="System.String">true</Property>
      <Property Name="ShowInSearchUI" Type="System.String"></Property>
    </Properties>
  </LobSystemInstance>
</LobSystemInstances>
```

Configuring *RevertToSelf* is accomplished by editing the connection information for the External System after it is defined. In SharePoint Designer, in the Summary View for the ECT, the connection information can be edited by clicking the hyperlink for the External System. Figure 16-16 shows the Connection Properties dialog box. *RevertToSelf* is specified by selecting the BDC Identity option for Authentication Mode.

FIGURE 16-16 Using the BDC identity to access an External System

Using *RevertToSelf* authentication eliminates the double-hop issue because BCS is no longer attempting to impersonate the user all the way to the External System. The drawback to this approach, however, is that all access is accomplished using the same account. As a result, no auditing of individual activities against the External System is possible.

In addition to the limitations imposed by *RevertToSelf* authentication, it is important to understand that the application pool identity is a powerful one whose credentials must be protected. Along with being the account under which the web application runs, the application pool identity is used to access the SharePoint content databases. Furthermore, the application pool identity is the account under which code runs when the *SPSecurity.RunWithElevatedPrivileges* method is called in SharePoint, which essentially allows code to perform any action in a SharePoint farm. For this reason, *RevertToSelf* is disabled by default and must be enabled explicitly by using the following Windows PowerShell script:

```
$bdc = Get-SPServiceApplication
 | where {$_ -match "Business Data Connectivity Service"}
$bdc.RevertToSelfAllowed = $true
$bdc.Update;
```

Understanding secure store options

SSS is a flexible credential management service that supports both the Trusted Subsystem and Impersonation and Delegation authentication models. If you map all user credentials to a single group account in SSS, then you can support the Trusted Subsystem authentication model. If you map user credentials to a unique set of credentials per user, then SSS is supporting the Impersonation and Delegation authentication model. SSS is a far superior choice to either *Passthrough* or *RevertToSelf* because you can configure access to External Systems such that auditing is still possible while still overcoming double-hop issues. SSS is capable of managing three different types of credentials: Windows, SQL, and user name/password. These three credential types, *WindowsCredentials*, *RdbCredentials*, and *Credentials*, correspond to three different settings for the *AuthenticationMode* element.

Setting the *AuthenticationMode* element to *WindowsCredentials* is used with External Systems that support Windows authentication. Setting the *AuthenticationMode* to *RdbCredentials* is used with External Systems that support SQL authentication, such as SQL Server. Setting the *AuthenticationMode* to *Credentials* is used with External Systems that support simple user name/password authentication. The *WindowsCredentials* and *RdbCredentials* are used by selecting the Impersonate Windows Identity or Impersonate Custom Identity option, respectively, in the Connection Properties dialog box. The *Credentials* setting is used exclusively with web services that do not support Windows authentication.

In addition to the primary SSS application, BCS also supports a secondary SSS application that can be used for application-level authentication. This functionality exists to support special situations in which the External System requires credentials to be passed to the system as part of each operation. The credentials held in the secondary application can be configured as a filter to restrict the results returned from the External Systems. Filters are discussed in the section "Defining filters" later in this chapter.

Accessing claims-based systems

Because SharePoint 2013 supports claims authentication, BCS can also use claims to authenticate against External Systems. To implement claims authentication, the External System must support claims and trust the claims provider used with SharePoint. Currently, there are few systems that support claims authentication.

To implement claims authentication, the *AuthenticationMode* should be set to *Passthrough*. None of the other configurations really makes sense because claims authentication is based on delegating the user's identity. For the most part, claims-based authentication happens automatically, provided that the External System accepts the token offered by BCS.

Accessing token-based systems

Today, many web-based applications use a token-based authentication system such as OAuth to secure Open Data Protocol (OData) services. BCS can support authentication against these token-based systems by using the OData Extension Provider. The OData Extension Provider allows you to attach tokens to outgoing BCS calls. In order to use the OData Extension Provider, you must create a class that implements the *ODataExtensionProvider* abstract class. This class provides a *BeforeSendRequest* method and an *AfterReceiveResponse* method. You can write custom code in these methods to query the token provider and attach the token before passing the data request to the External System.

After the assembly is created, it must be stored in the global assembly cache and registered as a new connection setting in BCS associated with the service endpoint. The assembly is registered with the *New-SPODataConnectionSetting* Windows PowerShell command. The following code shows an example:

```
New-SPODataConnectionSetting
    -Name "WingtipServiceApp"
    -ServiceContext "http://intranet.wingtip.com"
    -ServiceAddressURL "https://data.cloudapp.net/data.svc"
    -AuthenticationMode "Anonymous"
    -ExtensionProvider "WingtipExtensionProvider.Extension, WingtipExtensionProvider,
                        Version=1.0.0.0, Culture=neutral, PublicKeyToken=41bc4812ca364d35"
```

The final step is to modify the BDC Metadata Model to reference the new connection setting. This is done by adding the *ODataConnectionSettingsId* property under the *LobSystemInstance* node, as shown in the following code:

```
<Property Name="ODataConnectionSettingsId" Type="System.String">WingtipServiceApp</Property>
```

Managing client authentication

BCS clients are designed to have symmetry with the server-side functionality so that they can operate offline. The Application Model created in SharePoint Designer is synchronized with clients when External Lists are accessed through Office clients and later using subscription information. Some authentication settings, however, will not work correctly from the client because they don't make sense. For example, when you set the client *AuthenticationMode* to *RevertToSelf*, BCS is supposed to use the application pool account when accessing the External System. However, clients have no mechanism to use this account because they always access the External Systems directly. Additional problems can occur when a Trusted Subsystem authentication model maps to group credentials in SSS. In this case, BCS will prompt the user to enter credentials for the group, but the user is unlikely to know these credentials.

The *Passthrough* mode makes the most sense for clients. When you set the client *AuthenticationMode* to *Passthrough*, the client will always try to connect to the External System using the Windows credentials of the current user. This means that the External System must support Windows authentication and the current user must have rights to perform the requested operations.

Client credentials are stored not in SSS, but in the Credential Manager. The Credential Manager is a password store system that supports single sign-on (SSO) to a variety of systems, including websites and remote computers. Credential Manager is part of the client operating system, so you can open it within Windows and view and manage your credentials. If authentication fails from the client, BCS automatically deletes the credentials from the Credential Manager store and prompts you to enter them again.

Creating External Content Types

Defining External Content Types is the primary activity necessary to implement BCS solutions. The definition of an ECT includes all the information schema, data operations, relationships, filters, actions, and security descriptors necessary to bring External System data into SharePoint. All this information is defined inside a BDC Metadata Model, which is an XML file stored in the ECT repository. Although SharePoint Designer does a good job of giving you visual tools to create the model, there are times when you will want to modify the XML directly. Therefore, you should understand the basic structure of the XML model. Listing 16-2 shows part of the basic XML structure with an emphasis on the ECT definition represented by the *Entity* element.

LISTING 16-2 Partial XML model

```xml
<?xml version="1.0" encoding="utf-16" standalone="yes"?>
<Model>
  <LobSystems>
    <LobSystem Type="Database" Name="Wingtip Products">
      <LobSystemInstances>
        <LobSystemInstance Name="Wingtipdb">
        </LobSystemInstance>
      </LobSystemInstances>
      <Entities>
        <Entity Namespace="http://www.wingtip.com"
                Version="1.1.0.0"
                EstimatedInstanceCount="10000"
                Name="Product"
                DefaultDisplayName="Product">
        </Entity>
      </Entities>
    </LobSystem>
  </LobSystems>
</Model>
```

Creating operations

BCS supports a wide variety of operations designed to facilitate accessing systems and performing CRUD functions. Generally, you will be concerned with basic reading and writing to External Systems using the *Finder* (Read List), *SpecificFinder* (Read Item), *Creator* (Create), *Updater* (Update), and *Deleter* (Delete) methods. These methods are also supported in SharePoint Designer through menus in the Operations Design view. Methods that are not supported by SharePoint Designer offer additional functionality and control, but they must be created by manually editing the BDC Metadata Model or creating a .NET Assembly Connector. Manually editing the XML model requires that you export the model, edit it, and import the new model. Table 16-3 lists all the supported BCS operations.

TABLE 16-3 Supported BCS operations

Name	Description
Finder	Returns multiple records from an External System based on a wildcard
SpecificFinder	Returns a single record from an External System based on a primary key
IdEnumerator	Returns all primary keys from an External System to support search indexing
Scalar	Returns a scalar value from an External System
AccessChecker	Checks to determine what rights are allowed for a user
Creator	Creates a new record in an External System
Updater	Updates an existing record in an External System
Deleter	Deletes a record in an External System
ChangedIdEnumerator	Returns primary keys for records that have changed, to support incremental search indexing
DeletedIdEnumerator	Returns primary keys for records that have been deleted, to support incremental search indexing
AssociationNavigator	Navigates from one entity to a related entity
Associator	Associates an entity with another entity
Disassociator	Disassociates one entity from another
GenericInvoker	Used to perform operations not supported by any of the defined operations
StreamAccessor	Supports accessing binary large object (BLOB) data from an External System
BinarySecurityDescriptorAccessor	Returns a security descriptor
BulkSpecificFinder	Returns a set of records from the External System in a batch based on a set of primary keys
BulkAssociatedIdEnumerator	Returns a set of primary keys representing records associated with an entity
BulkAssociationNavigator	Supports navigation from one entity to many related entities
BulkIdEnumerator	Returns all primary keys in a batch from an External System to support search indexing
Subscribe	Allows a user or event receiver to request notification when external data changes
Unsubscribe	Allows a user or event receiver to delete a request for notification

Finder methods are used to return a result set from the External System and are one of two required operations for External Lists. You can create a *Finder* method in SharePoint Designer by selecting the option to create a *New Read List* operation from the shortcut menu. Listing 16-3 shows the definition of a *Finder* method.

LISTING 16-3 A Finder method

```
<Method Name="Read List" DefaultDisplayName="Product Read List">
  <Properties>
    <Property Type="System.Data.CommandType, [assembly name for System.Data]"
             Name="RdbCommandType">Text</Property>
    <Property Name="RdbCommandText" Type="System.String">
      SELECT TOP(@ProductID) [ProductID] , [ProductName]
      FROM [dbo].[Products] ORDER BY [ProductID]
    </Property>
    <Property Name="BackEndObjectType"
             Type="System.String">SqlServerTable</Property>
    <Property Name="BackEndObject" Type="System.String">Products</Property>
    <Property Name="Schema" Type="System.String">dbo</Property>
  </Properties>
  <Parameters>
    <Parameter Direction="In" Name="@ProductID">
      <TypeDescriptor TypeName="System.Int64" AssociatedFilter="Filter"
                     Name="ProductID">
        <DefaultValues>
          <DefaultValue MethodInstanceName="Read List"
                       Type="System.Int64">100</DefaultValue>
        </DefaultValues>
      </TypeDescriptor>
    </Parameter>
    <Parameter Direction="Return" Name="Read List">
      <TypeDescriptor
         TypeName="System.Data.IDataReader, [assembly name for System.Data]"
         IsCollection="true" Name="Read List">
        <TypeDescriptors>
          <TypeDescriptor
            TypeName="System.Data.IDataRecord, [assembly name for System.Data]"
            Name="Read ListElement">
            <TypeDescriptors>
              <TypeDescriptor TypeName="System.Int32" ReadOnly="true"
                            IdentifierName="ProductID" Name="ProductID" />
              <TypeDescriptor TypeName="System.String" Name="ProductName">
                <Properties>
                  <Property Name="Size" Type="System.Int32">50</Property>
                  <Property Name="RequiredInForms"
                           Type="System.Boolean">true</Property>
                  <Property Name="ShowInPicker"
                           Type="System.Boolean">true</Property>
                </Properties>
                ...
    </Parameter>
  </Parameters>
  <MethodInstances>
```

```
    <MethodInstance Type="Finder" ReturnParameterName="Read List" Default="true"
                Name="Read List" DefaultDisplayName="Product Read List">
      <Properties>
        <Property Name="UseClientCachingForSearch" Type="System.String"></Property>
        <Property Name="RootFinder" Type="System.String"></Property>
        <Property Name="LastModifiedTimeStampField"
                Type="System.String">LastUpdate</Property>
      </Properties>
    </MethodInstance>
  </MethodInstances>
</Method>
```

In the definition for the *Finder* method, SharePoint Designer automatically generates a SQL query to retrieve items for display in the list if the External System is a database. This is done when the methods are created in the wizard. If you want, you can use stored procedures or views instead of dynamic SQL. Also, note how the return parameters are defined so that BCS understands the data returned from the External System. In particular, note the use of the *TypeDescriptor* element. *TypeDescriptor* is used to map data types in the External System to .NET data types in BCS.

You can create multiple *Finder* methods, but one will always be designated as the default. The default *Finder* method forms the basis of the default view of an External List and provides support for indexing the External System so it can be searched. SharePoint Designer automatically adds a *RootFinder* property to the default *Finder* method. This property is used when the External System is being indexed, to specify the records in the External System that should be indexed. In addition, the method can designate a timestamp field to support incremental crawls. Designating a field as a timestamp is done in the Return Parameters section of the Operation Wizard; the field appears in the BDC Metadata Model as the value for the *LastModifiedTimeStamp* property.

SpecificFinder methods are used to return a single item from the External System and are also required to support External Lists. *Creator*, *Updater*, and *Deleter* methods are optional for External Lists. All the methods have similar XML structures in the BDC Metadata Model. You can examine these structures easily by creating models and exporting them from SharePoint Designer.

Creating relationships

BCS supports the definition of relationships between entities, which allows you to display relationships and navigate between entities within SharePoint. Within the SharePoint Designer, one-to-many, self-referential, and reverse associations are supported by the tooling. The most common type of association in BCS solutions is the one-to-many association, whereby a parent entity instance is related to many child entity instances. Self-referential associations are just like one-to-many relationships, except that a self-referential relationship uses the same ECT as both the parent and the child. Reverse associations return a single parent entity instance for a child entity instance. Reverse associations are not supported for tables and views, but they are supported for stored procedures and web services because the reverse association is not inherent in the database schema. It must be programmed explicitly through a stored procedure or web service.

To create a relationship, you select New Association from the shortcut menu in the Operations Design view. This will start a wizard to help you define the new association. The wizard will ask you to select another ECT with which to make the association. If the ECTs are based on related tables in a database, then SharePoint Designer will infer the relationship using the foreign key. If not, then you will have to specify the relationship manually by associating fields from the parent to the child ECT. Listing 16-4 shows a relationship between a *Product* entity and a *Category*.

LISTING 16-4 An entity relationship

```
<Method IsStatic="false" Name="CategoryAssociation">
  <Properties>
    ...
  </Properties>
  <Parameters>
    <Parameter Direction="In" Name="@CategoryId">
      <TypeDescriptor ... />
    </Parameter>
    <Parameter Direction="Return" Name="CategoryAssociation">
      <TypeDescriptor ...>
        <TypeDescriptors>
          ...
        </TypeDescriptors>
      </TypeDescriptor>
    </Parameter>
  </Parameters>
  <MethodInstances>
    <Association Name="CategoryAssociation" Type="AssociationNavigator"
      ReturnParameterName="CategoryAssociation"
      DefaultDisplayName="Category Association">
      <Properties>
        <Property Name="ForeignFieldMappings" Type="System.String">
        ... ForeignFieldMapping ForeignIdentifierName="CategoryId" ...
        </Property>
      </Properties>
      <SourceEntity Namespace="http://www.wingtip.com" Name="Category" />
      <DestinationEntity Namespace="http://www.wingtip.com" Name="Product" />
    </Association>
  </MethodInstances>
</Method>
```

Defining filters

When creating *Finder* and *SpecificFinder* methods, you often might want to limit the information that is returned from the External System. You might want to limit the returned data simply to prevent a large amount of data from being requested, or to support conditional queries, paging, or wildcards. The Application Model supports all these types of filters. Filters can also be thought of as input parameters to an ECT operation. Generally, their values are set by the calling client before the operation is invoked. The wizards in SharePoint Designer will help you define the most common filters when you are creating ECTs. Table 16-4 lists all the filters supported in BCS.

TABLE 16-4 Supported BCS filters

Filter	Description
ActivityId	A GUID representing the correlation ID of the current operation.
Batching	Information about the current batch operation for filtering.
BatchingTermination	Information about the current terminating batch operation for filtering.
Comparison	Filters the records returned based on a value compared to a specific field.
Input	Can be used by the operation as an input value when the operation is called.
InputOutput	Can be used by the operation as both an input and output value when the operation is called.
LastId	Identifies the ID of the last item in an operation.
Limit	Limits the total number of records returned to a fixed amount. Not compatible with the *PageNumber* filter.
Output	Can be used by the operation as an output value when the operation is called.
PageNumber	Limits the records returned using paging. Not compatible with the *Limit* filter.
Password	The password for the current operation.
SsoTicket	The ticket for use when authenticating.
Timestamp	Filters the records returned based on a specified *DateTime* field.
UserContext	Context information about the current user.
UserCulture	The current user culture.
Username	The current user name.
UserProfile	Profile information about the current user for filtering returned results.
Wildcard	Filters the records returned based on *Starts With* or *Contains* values.

Whenever you are creating *Finder* and *SpecificFinder* methods, you should define a *Limit* filter for the operation. This filter ensures that large result sets are not returned to an External List, which is critical for maintaining BCS performance. Though BCS does implement throttling at the system level, the ECT should implement its own tighter limits to ensure that query performance is maintained.

Defining filters in SharePoint Designer is done in the Operation Wizard on the Filter Parameters Configuration page. On this page, you can click Add Filter Parameter to add a new filter. After adding a new filter, you must then click the Filter hyperlink to open the Filter Configuration dialog box. Figure 16-17 shows the Filter Configuration dialog within the Operation Wizard.

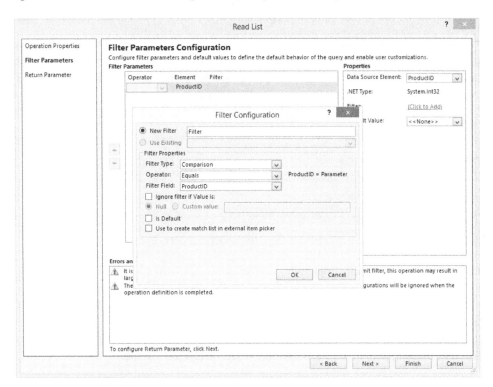

FIGURE 16-17 Defining filters

Using ECTs in SharePoint 2013

After you have created ECTs, they can be used in a variety of ways. External lists are the simplest way to use them. Beyond creating a list, you can also enhance the list with custom forms, actions, and profiles. SharePoint can also use ECTs to display data in Web Parts, to support enhancements to other lists, and as a source for custom solutions.

Creating custom forms

Although External Lists have several limitations, they also have many of the same capabilities as a standard list. When they are created from SharePoint Designer, for example, you can also select to create a Microsoft InfoPath form for editing items by clicking the Create Lists And Form button. Creating an InfoPath form allows you to customize the appearance of the form, as well as add validation logic.

After you have created the InfoPath form, you can edit it by clicking the Design Forms In InfoPath button, which is available on the List Settings tab. Clicking this button will open the form in InfoPath, where you have complete control over the appearance and functionality of the form. Figure 16-18 shows a simple item edit form that has been modified in InfoPath.

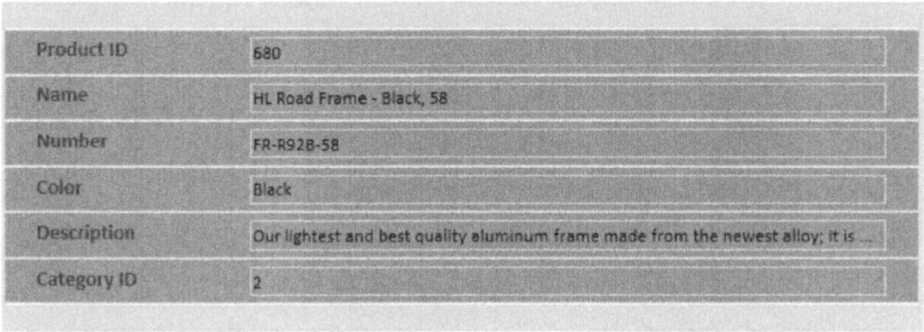

Product ID	680
Name	HL Road Frame - Black, 58
Number	FR-R92B-58
Color	Black
Description	Our lightest and best quality aluminum frame made from the newest alloy; it is ...
Category ID	2

FIGURE 16-18 An External List form in InfoPath

In addition to creating InfoPath forms, you can also create new ASPX forms for External Lists. The default forms created for the External Lists use the List Form Web Part (LFWP). The LFWP executes CAML queries against the External List to display items. Unfortunately, the LFWP does not support modifying its presentation; therefore, a new form must be created instead.

Clicking the New button above the form list in SharePoint Designer opens the Create New List Form dialog box. This dialog box is used to create, edit, and display forms that are based on the Data Form Web Part (DFWP). The DFWP uses Extensible Stylesheet Language for Transformations (XSLT) to transform list data into a display. By modifying this XSLT you can easily change the presentation of list data.

Using External Data Columns

Along with using an ECT as the basis for a list, you can use an ECT as the source for a column in another list. This capability is known as an External Data Column. When you create an External Data Column for a list, you select the ECT to use as the basis for the column. You can then select one or more of the fields available in the ECT to display alongside the column you are creating. These additional fields are known as *projected fields* because they project data from the ECT into the parent list. Figure 16-19 shows an external column definition.

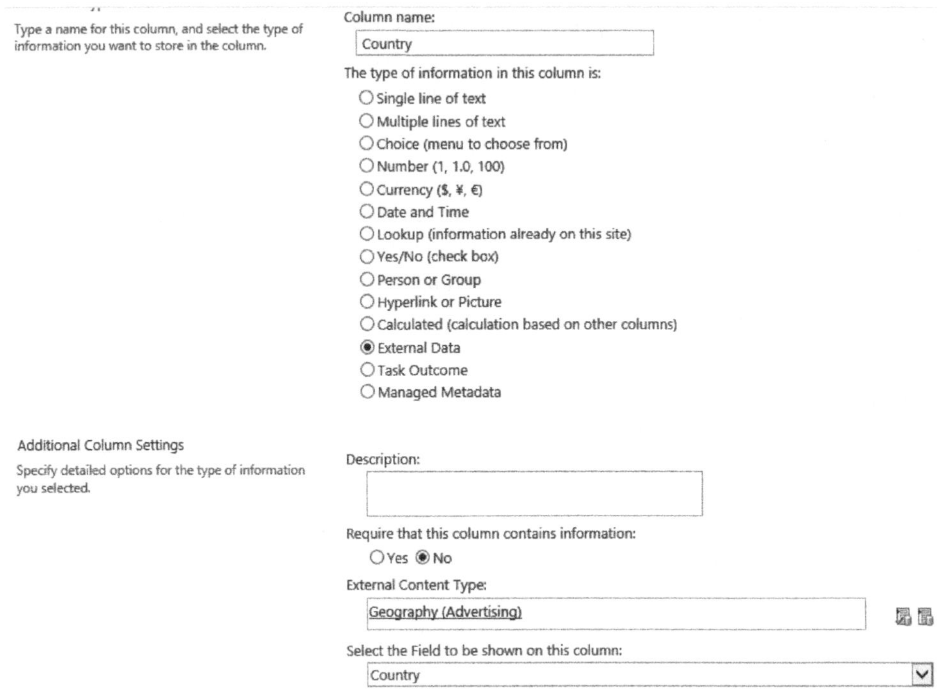

Type a name for this column, and select the type of
information you want to store in the column.

Column name:

Country

The type of information in this column is:

○ Single line of text
○ Multiple lines of text
○ Choice (menu to choose from)
○ Number (1, 1.0, 100)
○ Currency ($, ¥, €)
○ Date and Time
○ Lookup (information already on this site)
○ Yes/No (check box)
○ Person or Group
○ Hyperlink or Picture
○ Calculated (calculation based on other columns)
◉ External Data
○ Task Outcome
○ Managed Metadata

Additional Column Settings

Specify detailed options for the type of information
you selected.

Description:

Require that this column contains information:
  ○ Yes ◉ No

External Content Type:

Geography (Advertising)

Select the Field to be shown on this column:

Country

FIGURE 16-19 Defining an external column

Using External Data Web Parts

Another way you can use ECTs is through a set of Web Parts that ship with SharePoint Server 2013
known as External Data Web Parts (also called Business Data Web Parts). External Data Web Parts are
designed specifically to display ECT data and relationships. The available parts include the Business
Data List, Business Data Related List, and Business Data Item. These Web Parts display a list based on
an ECT, a list based on an ECT association, or a single item, respectively.

The Business Data List part allows you to select an ECT, and then it displays a list of data based
on a *Finder* method that you specify. In many ways, this Web Part is like an External List. You can, for
example, modify the view by selecting which columns to display. If you have filters defined for the
Finder method, the Web Part will display simple filtering controls that support operations such as keyword filtering. Finally, you can change the appearance of the list by altering the XSLT contained within
the Web Part. This XSLT is used to transform the data returned for display in the Web Part.

The Business Data Related List is meant to be used in conjunction with the Business Data List to
show data based on an association between two ECTs. After selecting an ECT for both the Business

Data and Business Data Related lists, you can use the Web Part menu to connect the two lists. When they are connected, the Business Data List Web Part acts as a filter against the Business Data Related List Web Part. This gives users a simple way to filter the list view by clicking items in the related list.

The Business Data Item Web Part is used to display a single record based on an ECT. This Web Part is configured by first selecting the ECT and then selecting the particular record to display. This Web Part is especially useful when combined with the Business Data Item Builder Web Part, which builds a business item from query string parameters in the page URL. This combination of the Business Data Item Builder Web Part and Business Data Item Web Part is used by BCS to create a profile page for an ECT. Profile pages are discussed in the next section.

Creating a profile page

When SharePoint surfaces ECT data in lists and Web Parts, it does not necessarily show all the available fields and associations. For example, when an ECT is used as the source for an external column, only a single field is required for display. When users see partial ECT data, however, they are quite often interested in being able to view the data behind it. This is where profile pages enter the picture. A *profile page* is a dedicated page that shows all the ECT data for a specific record. This way, users can jump from partial ECT data to a complete view of the record.

The Business Data Item Builder and Business Data Item Web Parts are deployed onto a dedicated profile page. The profile page is typically accessed through an action. An action is defined as a hyperlink containing query string parameters that can be used by the Business Data Item Builder Web Part to construct the profile page. Actions are typically surfaced in a drop-down menu associated with the displayed ECT data. Figure 16-20 shows a profile page.

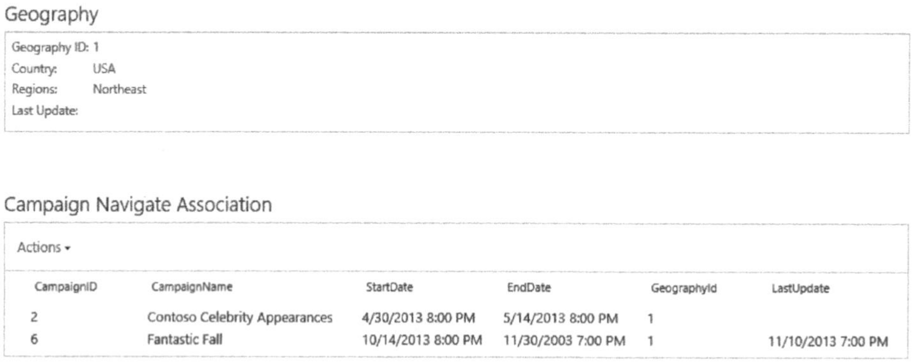

Geography

Geography ID: 1	
Country:	USA
Regions:	Northeast
Last Update:	

Campaign Navigate Association

Actions ▾

CampaignID	CampaignName	StartDate	EndDate	GeographyId	LastUpdate
2	Contoso Celebrity Appearances	4/30/2013 8:00 PM	5/14/2013 8:00 PM	1	
6	Fantastic Fall	10/14/2013 8:00 PM	11/30/2003 7:00 PM	1	11/10/2013 7:00 PM

FIGURE 16-20 A BCS profile page

Before you can create profile pages, they must be enabled through the BDC service application. On the Edit tab for the BDC service application, you can click the Configure button in the Profile Pages group. In the Properties dialog box that opens, you must specify a SharePoint site where the profile pages can be created. After that, you can simply select ECTs and click the Create/Upgrade button to make profile pages for the ECTs that you select. You can also make profile pages in SharePoint Designer when you are designing your ECT.

Searching External Systems

ECTs created with SharePoint Designer already support indexing by SharePoint Search with no additional work. However, External Systems will be indexed only if you explicitly set up a content source that includes the ECT. Content sources can be created within the Search service application, where you will have the option to create a content source associated with an External System.

When you select the option to create a new content source in the Search service application, you will be presented with a drop-down list of the available BDC service applications. When you choose a BDC service application, you will then have the option to index all External Systems associated with the selected service or to pick particular systems. Figure 16-21 shows the content source creation options.

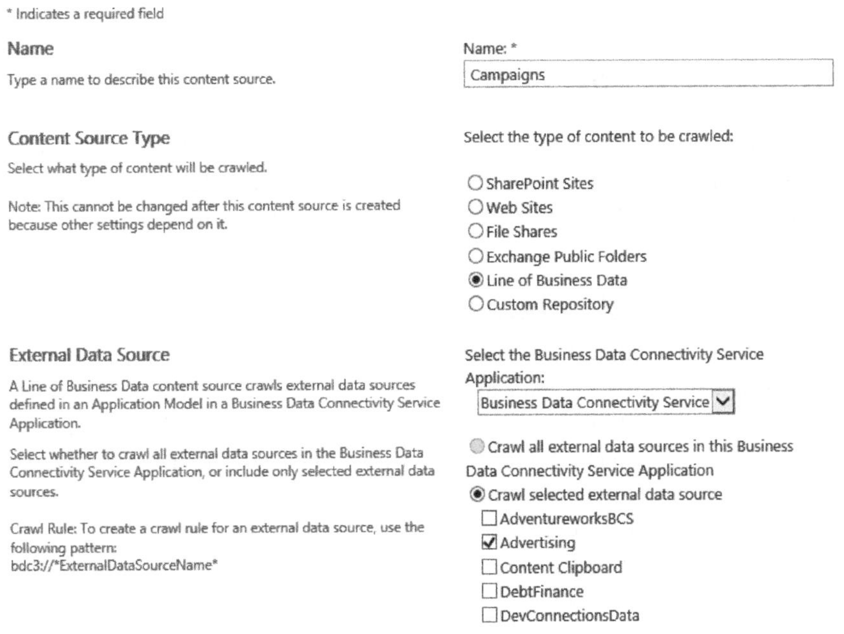

* Indicates a required field

Name

Type a name to describe this content source.

Name: *

Campaigns

Content Source Type

Select what type of content will be crawled.

Note: This cannot be changed after this content source is created because other settings depend on it.

Select the type of content to be crawled:

- ○ SharePoint Sites
- ○ Web Sites
- ○ File Shares
- ○ Exchange Public Folders
- ● Line of Business Data
- ○ Custom Repository

External Data Source

A Line of Business Data content source crawls external data sources defined in an Application Model in a Business Data Connectivity Service Application.

Select whether to crawl all external data sources in the Business Data Connectivity Service Application, or include only selected external data sources.

Crawl Rule: To create a crawl rule for an external data source, use the following pattern:
bdc3://*ExternalDataSourceName*

Select the Business Data Connectivity Service Application:

Business Data Connectivity Service ▾

○ Crawl all external data sources in this Business Data Connectivity Service Application

● Crawl selected external data source
- ☐ AdventureworksBCS
- ☑ Advertising
- ☐ Content Clipboard
- ☐ DebtFinance
- ☐ DevConnectionsData

FIGURE 16-21 Defining a content source

After a content source is created and crawled, it can be used in the standard ways. This means that you can simply go to the Search Center, type a keyword, and return records from the External System. These results include a hyperlink to the profile page so that users can view the full details of the returned records. You can also set up search scopes and use them to search only the External System data.

Supplementing user profiles

The User Profile service application is used to synchronize data from AD DS with the profile database maintained by SharePoint. The profile database contains rich information about users that can be displayed in sites. The User Profile service application maps AD DS fields to fields in the user's profile. On a scheduled basis, this information is imported from AD DS.

In much the same way that you can add search connections to External Systems through ECTs, you can add profile synchronization connections. Adding a new synchronization connection allows you to use data from External Systems to supplement the data in the profile system. This is often useful in organizations that maintain a Human Resources (HR) system but that do not have rich data in their AD DS system. In such cases, ECTs are designed against the HR system and mapped to fields in the profile database.

Using ECTs in Office 2013

Not only can ECTs be used on the SharePoint server, they can also be used in Office 2013 clients. With little effort, ECTs can be surfaced as items in Outlook or metadata columns in Word. Furthermore, Office clients can sync with SharePoint to allow External Lists to be managed offline.

Understanding Outlook integration

You can synchronize lists with Outlook by clicking the Connect To Outlook button on the List tab. Outlook allows users to work with data offline and then synchronize it with SharePoint later. When you are synchronizing External Lists, ECTs can use Outlook forms by explicitly declaring that they should be displayed as an appointment, contact, task, or post when they are designed in SharePoint Designer. Choosing to display an ECT as a particular type of Office item requires that External System fields be mapped to Outlook fields in the SharePoint Designer wizard. Generally, the SharePoint Designer wizard will prompt for the correct mapping through messages. This mapping ensures that the data is displayed correctly inside Outlook.

When you synchronize lists to Outlook, a VSTO solution is installed for working with the items. Although the synchronization behavior works out of the box, you could choose to enhance the overall solution with your own VSTO solution, which could be a full-blown custom VSTO solution created in Outlook or a special declarative solution unique to BCS. The subject of creating these advanced custom VSTO solutions is beyond the scope of this chapter.

Using Word Quick Parts

When you choose to create an External Data Column for a document library, this column appears in Word in the Document Information Panel (DIP) at the top of the document. The DIP is designed to present metadata information so that it can be filled in during the document creation process, as-opposed to prompting for metadata values when the document is saved.

In conjunction with displaying the metadata values in the DIP, document templates can also use Quick Parts. Quick Parts in Word allow you to insert fields into the document template that are bound to the metadata fields of the document. When a user fills in the field as part of the document creation process, the metadata values are set automatically. Adding Quick Parts to a document is done by selecting the appropriate metadata field from the Quick Parts list, which appears on the Insert tab in Word.

Although Quick Parts work well with all manner of document metadata, they work especially well with ECTs. This is because the Quick Parts will surface a picker dialog box for metadata that is based on an ECT. This makes it easy for users to select valid values for the metadata, improving the document creation experience.

Creating custom BCS solutions

Though BCS offers significant functionality without requiring you to write any code at all, there are advanced scenarios in which you will want to write custom code. To support custom solutions, BCS has a complete set of object models for manipulating External Data and managing ECT metadata. These models can be used on both the client and the server and have a high degree of symmetry between the two programming models. Along with coding against the client and server model, you can create your own External System connectors called .NET Assembly Connectors. These connectors are one of the most common BCS customizations because they give you a significant amount of control over the business logic applied to External Data. Finally, you can include ECTs directly in a SharePoint app, deploy them with the app, and manipulate them through the REST or CSOM APIs.

Using the BDC Runtime object models

The BDC Server Runtime and BDC Client Runtime are the server-side object models used for manipulating External Data. By using the object models, you can perform full CRUD operations on External Data through custom code. This is the programming interface used by External Lists and Outlook, which means you can create custom Web Parts, pages, and add-ins for SharePoint and Office clients.

Using the object models requires you to set references in Visual Studio 2012 to the appropriate assemblies where the programming interface is defined. Selecting the correct assemblies is first a matter of deciding whether you are creating a server-side customization or a client-side customization. For server-side customizations, you will need to set references to the assemblies *Microsoft.Business-Data.dll* and *Microsoft.SharePoint.dll*. For client-side customizations, you will need to set references to *Microsoft.BusinessData.dll* and *Microsoft.Office.BusinessApplications.Runtime.dll*.

After you set references to the appropriate assemblies, the first challenge is to connect to the appropriate catalog. If you are on the server, then you will connect to the metadata catalog associated with the BDC service application. If you are on the client, then you will connect to the client cache.

Connecting to the metadata catalog on the server can be done with or without a SharePoint context, but the code will be different. In any case, you must get a reference to *BdcServiceApplicationProxy*, which can then be used to connect with the metadata catalog, which is represented by the *DatabaseBackedMetadataCatalog* object. If your code is running with a SharePoint context, then the following code will connect to the metadata catalog:

```
BdcServiceApplicationProxy sap =
        (BdcServiceApplicationProxy)SPServiceContext.Current.GetDefaultProxy(
        typeof(BdcServiceApplicationProxy));
DatabaseBackedMetadataCatalog catalog = sap.GetDatabaseBackedMetadataCatalog;
```

If your code is running outside a SharePoint context, then you will need additional code to connect with *BdcServiceApplicationProxy*. The following code shows how to create a LINQ query to return the application proxy:

```
SPFarm farm = SPFarm.Local;
SPServiceProxyCollection spc = farm.ServiceProxies;
BdcServiceApplicationProxy sap =
(BdcServiceApplicationProxy)((from sp in spc
                             where sp.TypeName.Equals("Business Data Connectivity")
                             select sp).First.ApplicationProxies.First);
DatabaseBackedMetadataCatalog catalog = sap.GetDatabaseBackedMetadataCatalog;
```

In addition to using the *BdcServiceApplicationProxy* object to establish context, you can use the *Microsoft.SharePoint.BusinessData.SharedService.BdcService* class. The *BdcService* class is an abstraction of the BDC Service Application, and it is useful for determining whether or not a BDC Service Application is available in the farm. The following code shows how to connect to the metadata catalog:

```
BdcService service = SPFarm.Local.Services.GetValue<BdcService>;
  if (service == null)
    throw new Exception("No BDC Service Application found.");
DatabaseBackedMetadataCatalog catalog =
  service.GetDatabaseBackedMetadataCatalog(SPServiceContext.GetContext(site));
```

If your code is running on the client, then you will connect to the client cache instead of the metadata catalog. The client cache is represented by the *RemoteSharedFileBackedMetadataCatalog* object. The following code shows how to make the connection:

```
RemoteSharedFileBackedMetadataCatalog catalog = new RemoteSharedFileBackedMetadataCatalog();
```

After you make a connection to the appropriate catalog, you can read or write to the entities that it contains. These changes will be reflected in the External System, as well as any External Lists based on the ECT. Listing 16-5 shows how to retrieve an entity and print the values of its fields by using a *Finder* method.

LISTING 16-5 Retrieving an entity

```
IEntity ect = catalog.GetEntity("http://www.wingtip.com/products", "Product");
ILobSystem lob = ect.GetLobSystem;
ILobSystemInstance lobi = lob.GetLobSystemInstances["Wingtipdb"];
IFilterCollection filter = ect.GetDefaultFinderFilters;
IEntityInstanceEnumerator ects = ect.FindFiltered(filter, lobi);
while (ects.MoveNext) {
  Console.WriteLine(ects.Current["ProductName"].ToString());
}
```

If the *Finder* method defines filters (such as a limit, wildcard, or page filter), then these values must be provided in the call to the *FindFiltered* method. An *IFilterCollection* instance can be returned by calling the *GetFilters* method of the *IMethodInstance*. The values for the filters can then be set. The following code shows how to get the filter collection and set values:

```
IMethodInstance mi =
  ect.GetMethodInstance(FinderMethodInstanceName, MethodInstanceType.Finder);

IFilterCollection filters = mi.GetFilters;
(filters[0] as LimitFilter).Value = 10;
(filters[1] as PageNumberFilter).Value = 2;
(filters[3] as WildcardFilter).Value = "Bike";
(filters[4] as ComparisonFilter).Value = "CN123720";
```

Calling *SpecificFinder* is done through the *FindSpecific* method. When calling the *FindSpecific* method, you will always provide an *Identity* object, which represents the identifier for the desired entity instance. Simply create a new *Identity* object by using the appropriate value and pass the object as an argument. *Identity* objects can be created with any data type, but be aware that *String* values are case-sensitive when used as *Identifiers*. The following code shows how to call the *FindSpecific* method:

```
//Connect to BDC Service Application
BdcService service = SPFarm.Local.Services.GetValue<BdcService>;

if (service != null) {
//Get Metadata elements
  DatabaseBackedMetadataCatalog catalog =
    service.GetDatabaseBackedMetadataCatalog(SPServiceContext.Current);
  IEntity ect = catalog.GetEntity(EntityNamespace, EntityName);
  ILobSystem lob = ect.GetLobSystem;
  ILobSystemInstance lobi =
    lob.GetLobSystemInstances[LobSystemInstanceName];
}

//Execute SpecificFinder
int id = 5;
IMethodInstance mi = ect.GetMethodInstance(SpecificFinderMethodInstanceName,
                                    MethodInstanceType.SpecificFinder);
IEntityInstance item =
    ect.FindSpecific(new Identity(id), SpecificFinderMethodInstanceName, lobi, true);
```

To invoke an *Updater* method, you first use the *FindSpecific* method to return the entity to update. The field values of the return entity can then be modified, and those modifications are committed through the *Update* method of the *IEntityInstance* interface. To invoke a *Deleter* method, you first use the *FindSpecific* method to return the entity instance to delete. The entity instance can then be deleted by using the *Delete* method of the *IEntityInstance* interface.

Along with reading or updating entities, you can create new ones. As with other operations, these changes will flow all the way back to the External System. Of course, if you are writing to the client cache, the changes will be made only when the client is online. Listing 16-6 shows how to add a new record to an External System through the ECT.

LISTING 16-6 Creating an entity

```
IView v = ect.GetCreatorView("Create");
IFieldValueDictionary dict = v.GetDefaultValues;
dict["ProductName"] = "New Toy";
dict["LastUpdate"] = DateTime.Today;
Identity id = ect.Create(dict, lobi);
```

Using the Administration Object Model

Along with the Runtime Object Models, BCS has an Administration Object Model. The Administration Object Model allows you to manipulate the metadata for an Application Model. To work with the Administration Object Model, you must set references to *Microsoft.BusinessData.dll* and *Microsoft. SharePoint*.

As with the Runtime Object Models, you must first connect to the appropriate catalog before you can manipulate the data. In the case of the Administration Object Model, you must connect to the *AdministrationMetadataCatalog* object. Connecting to this catalog requires a reference to *BdcService-ApplicationProxy*, just as it did with the Runtime Object Model. Listing 16-7 shows how to connect to the catalog if your code is running outside a SharePoint context. Inside the context, you can use the *SPServiceContext* object as discussed previously.

LISTING 16-7 Connecting to the catalog outside SharePoint

```
SPFarm farm = SPFarm.Local;
SPServiceProxyCollection spc = farm.ServiceProxies;
BdcServiceApplicationProxy sap =
  (BdcServiceApplicationProxy)
    ((from sp in spc
      where sp.TypeName.Equals("Business Data Connectivity")
      select sp).First.ApplicationProxies.First);

AdministrationMetadataCatalog catalog = sap.GetAdministrationMetadataCatalog;
```

The Administration Object Model provides a set of objects that allow you to manipulate the Application Model XML. The names of the objects correspond closely with the names of the elements in the Application Model. Listing 16-8 shows a complete example of creating a simple Application Model from code and saving it into the metadata catalog.

LISTING 16-8 Creating an Application Model

```
Model model = Model.Create("MiniCRM", true, catalog);
LobSystem lob =
  model.OwnedReferencedLobSystems.Create("Customer", true, SystemType.Database);
LobSystemInstance lobi = lob.LobSystemInstances.Create("MiniCRM", true);

lobi.Properties.Add("AuthenticationMode", "PassThrough");
lobi.Properties.Add("DatabaseAccessProvider", "SqlServer");
lobi.Properties.Add("RdbConnection Data Source", "CONTOSOSERVER");
lobi.Properties.Add("RdbConnection Initial Catalog", "MiniCRM.Names");
lobi.Properties.Add("RdbConnection Integrated Security", "SSPI");
lobi.Properties.Add("RdbConnection Pooling", "true");

Entity ect = Entity.Create("Customer", "MiniCRM", true,
                           new Version("1.0.0.0"), 10000,
                           CacheUsage.Default, lob, model, catalog);

ect.Identifiers.Create("CustomerId", true, "System.Int32");

Method specificFinder =
  ect.Methods.Create("GetCustomer", true, false, "GetCustomer");

specificFinder.Properties.Add("RdbCommandText",
   "SELECT [CustomerId] ,[FullName] " +
   "FROM MiniCRM.Names " +
   "WHERE [CustomerId] = @CustomerId");

specificFinder.Properties.Add("RdbCommandType", "Text");

Parameter idParam =
  specificFinder.Parameters.Create("@CustomerId", true, DirectionType.In);

idParam.CreateRootTypeDescriptor(
    "CustomerId", true, "System.Int32", "CustomerId",
      new IdentifierReference("CustomerId",
        new EntityReference("MiniCRM", "Customer", catalog), catalog),
      null, TypeDescriptorFlags.None, null, catalog);

Parameter custParam =
  specificFinder.Parameters.Create("Customer", true, DirectionType.Return);
TypeDescriptor returnRootCollectionTypeDescriptor =
    custParam.CreateRootTypeDescriptor(
        "Customers", true,
        "System.Data.IDataReader, [full assembly name for System.Data]",
        "Customers", null, null, TypeDescriptorFlags.IsCollection, null, catalog);
TypeDescriptor returnRootElementTypeDescriptor =
```

```
        returnRootCollectionTypeDescriptor.ChildTypeDescriptors.Create(
            "Customer", true,
            "System.Data.IDataRecord, [full assembly name for System.Data]",
            "Customer", null, null, TypeDescriptorFlags.None, null);

    returnRootElementTypeDescriptor.ChildTypeDescriptors.Create(
            "CustomerId", true, "System.Int32", "CustomerId",
            new IdentifierReference("CustomerId",
                new EntityReference("MiniCRM", "Customer", catalog), catalog),
            null, TypeDescriptorFlags.None, null);

    returnRootElementTypeDescriptor.ChildTypeDescriptors.Create(
            "FirstName", true, "System.String", "FullName",
             null, null, TypeDescriptorFlags.None, null);

    specificFinder.MethodInstances.Create("GetCustomer", true,
                                    returnRootElementTypeDescriptor,
                                    MethodInstanceType.SpecificFinder, true);

    Method finder = ect.Methods.Create("GetCustomers", true, false, "GetCustomers");

    finder.Properties.Add("RdbCommandText",
                        "SELECT [CustomerId] , [FullName]FROM MiniCRM.Names");
    finder.Properties.Add("RdbCommandType", "Text");

    Parameter custsParam = finder.Parameters.Create("Customer", true,
                                            DirectionType.Return);

    TypeDescriptor returnRootCollectionTypeDescriptor2 =
        custsParam.CreateRootTypeDescriptor(
            "Customers", true,
            "System.Data.IDataReader, [full assembly name for System.Data]",
            "Customers", null, null, TypeDescriptorFlags.IsCollection, null, catalog);

    TypeDescriptor returnRootElementTypeDescriptor2 =
        returnRootCollectionTypeDescriptor2.ChildTypeDescriptors.Create(
            "Customer", true,
            "System.Data.IDataRecord, [full assembly name for System.Data]",
            "Customer", null, null, TypeDescriptorFlags.None, null);

    returnRootElementTypeDescriptor2.ChildTypeDescriptors.Create(
            "CustomerId", true, "System.Int32", "CustomerId",
            new IdentifierReference("CustomerId",
                new EntityReference("MiniCRM", "Customer", catalog), catalog),
            null, TypeDescriptorFlags.None, null);

    returnRootElementTypeDescriptor2.ChildTypeDescriptors.Create(
            "FirstName", true, "System.String", "FullName",
             null, null, TypeDescriptorFlags.None, null);

    finder.MethodInstances.Create("GetCustomers", true,
                                returnRootCollectionTypeDescriptor2,
                                MethodInstanceType.Finder, true);

    ect.Activate();
```

Creating custom event receivers

In SharePoint 2013, Business Connectivity Services introduces the ability to attach event receivers to External Lists and External Content Types. This capability is based on implementing the new *Subscribe* and *Unsubscribe* stereotypes in an ECT. Figure 16-22 shows a high-level view of the major components involved in the notification process.

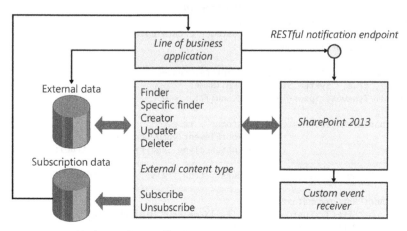

FIGURE 16-22 Understanding notifications

Custom event receivers are created in exactly the same way as standard list event receivers. This means that you simply create a class that inherits from *SPItemEventReceiver*. Custom event receivers, however, are limited to receiving only the *ItemAdded*, *ItemUpdated*, and *ItemDeleted* events. After it is created, the custom event receiver can be attached to an External List in the same way as a standard event receiver. The following code shows how to attach a custom event receiver to an external list:

```
string assembly = "4-part assembly name";
string className = "namespace.classname";
using (SPSite siteCollection = new SPSite("http://server"))
{
    using (SPWeb site = siteCollection.OpenWeb())
    {
        SPList externalList = site.Lists["ExternalList"];
        externalList.EventReceivers.Add(SPEventReceiverType.ItemAdded,
                            assembly, className);
    }
}
```

When a custom event receiver is attached to an External List, SharePoint automatically creates a RESTful endpoint to receive incoming notifications. An separate endpoint is created for each subscribed event. SharePoint then calls the *Subscribe* stereotype on the ECT associated with the External List. The *Subscribe* stereotype receives the address of the RESTful notification endpoint and is expected to save the address somewhere for use later when data changes. It is important to understand that although SharePoint creates a RESTful endpoint to receive notifications, it is the sole responsibility of the External System to call this endpoint when data changes. This means that you must create a custom solution to save the endpoints and invoke them. A typical solution is to implement the *Subscribe* method so that it saves endpoints to a database table and returns the primary key of the row. The primary key is saved by SharePoint and used when the *Unsubscribe* method is called. The *Unsubscribe* implementation uses the primary key to remove the subscription entry.

When data in the External System changes, a custom solution must call each of the saved endpoints. SharePoint receives the calls and fires any attached event handlers. The endpoint call is performed as an HTTP *POST* that can send a message back to SharePoint. This message can be read by the event receiver through the *SPItemEventProperties.ExternalNotificationMessage* property. The following code shows how to call the notification endpoint:

```
HttpWebRequest request = (HttpWebRequest)HttpWebRequest.Create({the notification endpoint});
request.Credentials = CredentialCache.DefaultCredentials;
request.Method = "POST";
request.Headers["X-RequestDigest"] = digest; //A form digest is required to call in
request.Accept = "*";
byte[] bodyBytes = Encoding.UTF8.GetBytes({a message to send});
request.ContentLength = bodyBytes.Length;
request.ContentType = "application/atom+xml";

Stream requestStream = request.GetRequestStream();
requestStream.Write(bodyBytes, 0, bodyBytes.Length);
requestStream.Flush();

using (var response = (HttpWebResponse)request.GetResponse())
{
    if (response.StatusCode != HttpStatusCode.OK)
        MessageBox.Show(response.StatusDescription);
}
```

Creating .NET Assembly Connectors

A .NET Assembly Connector associates a custom assembly with an ECT so that you can control precisely how information is accessed, processed, and returned from External Systems. The first step in developing the connector is to create a new empty SharePoint 2013 solution project and add a new Business Data Connectivity Model item. Visual Studio provides a completely coded solution when you add the new model. In fact, you can simply press F5 to start the project and then create new External Lists right away in SharePoint.

The default project provides an entity named *Entity1* along with two classes: *Entity1.cs* and *Entity-1Service.cs*. The *Entity1* class provides the properties necessary to hold data from the External System. The following code is from the *Entity1* class in the default connector project. For your own connector, you would simply create a class containing properties for the data to be returned from the External System:

```
public partial class Entity1
{
    public string Identifier1 { get; set; }
    public string Message { get; set; }
}
```

The *Entity1Service* class provides the implementation of stereotypes to perform CRUD operations against the External System. In order for a connector to support External Lists, it must implement at least a *Finder* and *SpecificFinder*. The following code shows the implementation for the default project. Notice how the *Finder* implementation returns a collection of entity class instances whereas the *SpecificFinder* returns a single entity class instance:

```
public class Entity1Service
{
    public static Entity1 ReadItem(string id)
    {
        Entity1 entity1 = new Entity1();
        entity1.Identifier1 = id;
        entity1.Message = "Hello World";
        return entity1;
    }
    public static IEnumerable<Entity1> ReadList()
    {
        Entity1[] entityList = new Entity1[1];
        Entity1 entity1 = new Entity1();
        entity1.Identifier1 = "0";
        entity1.Message = "Hello World";
        entityList[0] = entity1;
        return entityList;
    }
}
```

When you're working with the Business Data Connectivity Model item, there are three explorers/ designers available: the BDC Model Explorer, the Entity Design Surface, and the Method Details pane. The BDC Model Explorer is used to navigate the nodes of the BDC Metadata Model. The Entity Design Surface is used to design the ECT that will be associated with the .NET Assembly Connector. The Method Details pane is used to create the function signatures for ECT operations. Along with these three new elements, the Business Data Connectivity Model project template also gives you the standard windows such as the Solution Explorer and the Properties pane. Figure 16-23 shows the tooling in Visual Studio 2012.

To be successful with the tooling you must understand how the various explorers and designers relate to the underlying model XML. Furthermore, you must understand which elements of the project are affected as you make changes. In particular the BDC Model Explorer and the Method Details pane can be confusing if their relationships to the underlying XML are not well understood.

Not all of the underlying BDC Metadata Model can be represented in the BDC Model Explorer. In particular, the BDC Model Explorer shows methods, but not method instances. Methods are used in the BDC Metadata Model as prototypes, which are subsequently implemented by method instances. The Method Details pane provides the interface necessary to define the method instances.

The Entity Design Surface is also used to edit the underlying BDC Metadata Model. However, it is focused on the creation of entities. By using this tool you can create new entities, assign the Identifier, and create new methods.

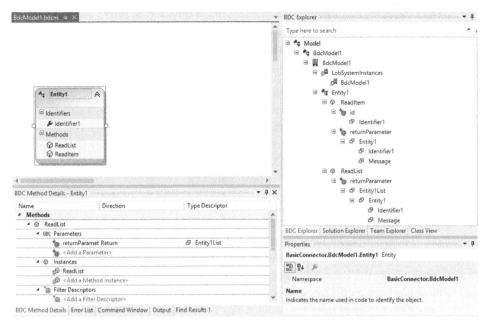

FIGURE 16-23 BCS tooling in Visual Studio 2012

Regardless of which tool you are using, the Properties pane can be used to edit the selected node. The Properties pane lists the type of node and its attributes. Although the nodes have many attributes, most of them are not required. It is not always clear, however, which attributes are required to implement any particular node. The better you understand the model, the more likely you are to create the one you need.

The tooling is all designed to edit the underlying BDC Metadata Model, with one exception. The service class is used to implement the method instances that you define in the model. This class module is created automatically and is always given the name of the entity followed by the word *Service*. If you change the name of the entity in your model, the service class name is updated automatically. If you delete the service class from the project, it is recreated the next time you make any changes to the method definitions.

The methods implemented in the service class have types defined by the input and return parameters in the BDC Metadata Model. These types can be simple types or classes. Typically, however, the *Finder* and *SpecificFinder* methods return classes that represent the ECT associated with the .NET Assembly Connector. In the Business Connectivity Model item, a class named *Entity1.cs* is created by default and is returned from the *Finder* and *SpecificFinder* methods. These methods are also created by default when you create a project with the Business Connectivity Model item.

Even though the item template includes a class that has the same name as the entity, there is actually no connection between the entity definition and the entity class as far as the tooling is concerned. Changing the name of the entity in the model does not change the name of the class, and the class is never automatically generated. The class is really just a payload returned from the .NET Assembly Connector. Its name is meaningless, but it is a best practice to keep the name of the class synchronized with the name of the entity it represents. The methods in the service class return instances of the entity class that are passed on to external lists for display. In more advanced scenarios, you might choose to implement the entity classes in a separate project so that they can be easily referenced by custom Web Parts that will display the data.

The tooling is largely focused on defining and implementing methods as opposed to defining the data returned by the entity class. In the default project template, the entity has a data field named *Message*, which is defined as a *TypeDescriptor* with a *TypeName* of *System.String*. The entity class has a corresponding property whose value is set during the execution of the *Finder* or *SpecificFinder* methods. To add or modify data fields for the ECT, you must make changes to the model in the BDC Model Explorer and add new properties to the entity class manually.

Although the Visual Studio tooling is helpful, there are times when you must access the underlying BDC Metadata Model as XML either for direct editing or simply to verify the work you have done using the tools. The BDC Metadata Model can be found in the Solution Explorer as the file with the .bdcm extension. You can open this file as XML by right-clicking it and selecting Open With from the shortcut menu. From the Open With dialog box, open the file with the XML Editor. If you make changes to the underlying model by hand, those changes will be reflected in the various Visual Studio tools. This is an excellent way to learn the relationships between the BDC Metadata Model and the Visual Studio tools.

Adding a new entity to the project can be done using the toolbox in Visual Studio. Dragging the entity object onto the Entity Design surface creates the new entity. When the new entity is created, Visual Studio automatically creates a new empty entity service class. Visual Studio does not, however, create a new entity class, which you must define manually. This class should include properties for all of the data to return from the External System, including the primary key.

After the new entity class is created, an Identifier must be defined against the primary key. In the default project, the Identifier is named *Identitier1*. You can create a new Identifier by right-clicking the entity and selecting Add, Identifier. By using the Properties pane you can subsequently set the name and data type for the Identifier.

After the entity is defined, you can create new methods for it, which is easily the most confusing process in the entire project. In the Method Details pane you can choose to create a new method. Remember that a method is just a stereotype and that you must also create a method instance to implement the method. You can create a new method instance by clicking the Add Method Instance link in the Method Details pane. After you have created the method instance, you can specify the type of the method instance in the Properties pane. Typically, your first method will be a *Finder* method.

After the method instance is defined, you must define its parameters. In the case of the default *Finder* method, you will typically define a return parameter only. Other method instances might require input parameters as well as filters. You can create a new parameter by clicking Add a Parameter in the Method Details pane. By using the Properties pane you can then change the parameter name and direction.

When a parameter is defined, Visual Studio automatically creates a *TypeDescriptor* for the parameter. The *TypeDescriptor* acts as a mapping between the data types found in the External System and the data types returned by the .NET Assembly Connector. Clicking the *TypeDescriptor* in the Method Details pane enables you to define the *TypeName* for the *TypeDescriptor*. In the case of a *Finder* method, the *TypeDescriptor* is typically a collection of entity instances. Therefore, the *IsCollection* property should be set to *True* before you select the *TypeName*. After the *TypeDescriptor* is designated as a collection, you can open the *TypeName* picker, click the Current Project tab, and select the *Product* class. Figure 16-24 shows the Type Name picker in Visual Studio.

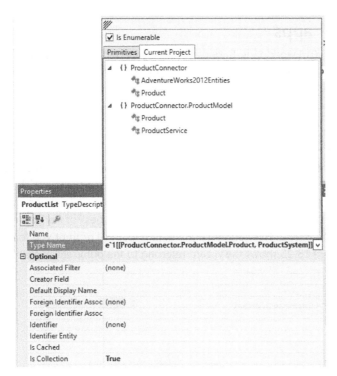

FIGURE 16-24 Picking a type name

At this point, you can open the code for the service class and see that Visual Studio has created a method whose signature is based on the method, parameter, and *TypeDescriptor* settings. However, your work is not yet done because the return *TypeDescriptor* was designated as a collection. Therefore a new *TypeDescriptor* must be added to represent the member of the collection. Additionally, each field in the collection member must be defined.

To create the additional *TypeDescriptors*, you work in the BDC Model Explorer. In the Model Explorer, you can view the *TypeDescriptor* defining the collection. You can define a collection member by right-clicking the collection *TypeDescriptor* and selecting Add Type Descriptor from the shortcut menu. Finally, you must add a *TypeDescriptor* for every property of the entity you want to return. Take care to set the *Identifier* property for the *TypeDescriptor* that represents the Identifier of the entity, in order to designate this property as the one containing the Identifier value. Finally, return to the Method Details pane and select the method instance. In the Properties pane, set Return Parameter Name and Return *TypeDescriptor* to reference the items already created. This completes the definition of the method, which can now be coded in the service class.

When the .NET Assembly Connector is complete, you can deploy and test it. As with all features created in Visual Studio 2012, you can easily debug the .NET Assembly Connector by setting breakpoints in the code and pressing F5.

Developing SharePoint apps

Along with most of the SharePoint 2013 workloads, Business Connectivity Services has been updated to work with the app model. App model enhancements include support for OData sources, app-level External Content Types, and a new client-side object model. Together, these enhancements allow you to create apps for either on-premises installation or SharePoint online.

Understanding app-level ECTs

With SharePoint 2013, BCS now supports the use of OData sources as the basis for defining an ECT. Because OData is emerging as an accepted standard for exposing data sources in the cloud, these services are an ideal source for developing BCS-based apps. When creating a SharePoint app, you can easily add an ECT based on an OData source by selecting Add, Content Types For An External Data Source from the project context menu. This action starts a wizard that will prompt you for the endpoint of the OData source. Figure 16-25 shows the wizard referring to the publically available Northwind data source.

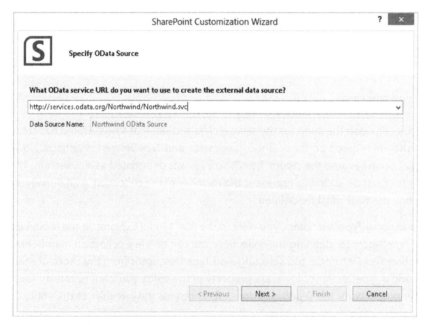

FIGURE 16-25 Selecting an OData source

After connecting to the source, the wizard prompts you to select from the available entities exposed by the service. All you have to do is select one or more entities and click Finish. Visual Studio will then generate a BDC Metadata Model and an associated external list within you app project. The BDC Metadata Model and the external list definition are packaged and deployed with the app, which uses the model at run time to connect to the source and fill the external list. Figure 16-26 shows the basic app architecture for accessing the OData source and displaying the data in an External List.

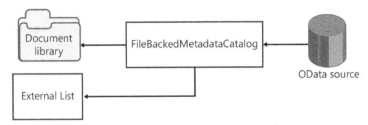

FIGURE 16-26 App-level ECT architecture

Under normal circumstances, BDC Metadata Models are stored in the BDC Service Application associated with the farm. Such an architecture would be unacceptable for apps, however, because apps are supposed to be isolated from the other farm elements. In the case of an app, the model is loaded in an in-memory BDC catalog known as the *FileBackedMetadataCatalog*. The BDC Metadata Model deployed with the app is stored in a special document library and subsequently loaded into the *FileBackedMetadataCatalog*. After it is loaded, the model is used to determine the connection to the OData source and what data to retrieve. The external list is then filled with the data in much the same way as any external list in a SharePoint farm. The only drawback is that the external list will not be immediately visible. This is because the app pages do not include a Web Part or code for displaying the list. This is where some client-side coding comes into play.

Understanding the BCS client object model

When it comes to displaying the data in the External List, you have two options. The first is to make a RESTful call to the External List. External Lists support the same RESTful access to data that standard SharePoint lists support. Therefore, there is nothing new to learn, and you can use standard techniques covered elsewhere in this book. The second option is to use the client-side object model (CSOM) through JavaScript.

CSOM access to BCS data follows the same general approach used in the server-side model discussed earlier in this chapter. Because the approaches are similar, it should be easier for developers to learn the CSOM version. The only big difference is that the CSOM version relies on asynchronous operations, so the developer must handle several callbacks to be successful.

All of the objects necessary to work with BCS in an app are contained in the sp.js library found in the LAYOUTS directory. Development begins by retrieving the standard *ClientContext* object in JavaScript. After the *ClientContext* is retrieved, it can be used to access the web associated with the app and then the in-memory *SP.BusinessData.AppBdcCatalog* object. When the catalog is accessed, the target *SP.BusinessData.Entity* object can be retrieved by using the entity name and entity namespace as shown in the following code:

```
var ctx = SP.ClientContext.get_current();
var ect = ctx.get_web().getAppBdcCatalog().getEntity(entityNamespace, entityName);
ctx.load(ect);
```

After the entity is retrieved, it can be used to execute the basic stereotypes associated with it. The JavaScript methods all have names that are similar to the ones found in the server-side object model, and you can view the complete definition for the methods by examining the sp.debug.js library found in the LAYOUTS directory. As an example, we'll walk though executing the *Finder* method using the *findFiltered* method.

The *findFiltered* method requires that you provide the name of the method instance, values for any filters associated with the method instance, and the associated *SP.BusinessData.LobSystemInstance* object. Retrieving the associated *SP.BusinessData.LobSystemInstance* object requires a round trip, so that should be done first by using the following code, which returns a *SP.BusinessData.Collections. LobSystemInstanceCollection* object:

```
var ctx = SP.ClientContext.get_current();

var ect = ctx.get_web().getAppBdcCatalog().getEntity(entityNamespace, entityName);
ctx.load(ect);

var lob = ect.getLobSystem();
ctx.load(lob);

var collection = lob.getLobSystemInstances();
ctx.load(collection);
ctx.executeQueryAsync(onLobSystemInstancesSuccess, onLobSystemInstancesError);
```

When the collection is returned, you can look through it for the associated *SP.BusinessData. LobSystemInstance* object by name. Then you can retrieve and set any required filters. Finally, you can call the *findFiltered* method, as shown in the following code:

```
var ctx = SP.ClientContext.get_current();

for (var i = 0; i < collection.get_count(); i++) {
    if (collection.get_item(i).get_name() === lobSystemInstanceName) {
        lobi = collection.get_item(i);
        break;
    }
}

var filters = ect.getFilters(methodInstanceName);
ctx.load(filters);

var results = ect.findFiltered(filters, methodInstanceName, lobi);
ctx.load(results);

ctx.executeQueryAsync(onExecuteFinderSuccess, onExecuteFinderError);
```

When the results of the operation are returned, then you can loop through them and read the property values. Typically, you will take these values and save them into an object array for use when displaying them in a webpage. The following code shows how the resulting records can be read:

```
for (var i = 0; i < results.get_count() ; i++) {
    var entityInstance = results.get_item(i);
    var fields = entityInstance.get_fieldValues();
    var v1 = fields.ProductID;
    var v2 = fields.ProductName;
    var v3 = fields.CategoryName;
    var v4 = fields.UnitsInStock;
    var v5 = fields.ReorderLevel;
}
```

Summary

Business Connectivity Services (BCS) is a powerful mechanism for connecting SharePoint to External Data. BCS solutions can be imagined to span a spectrum from simple no-code solutions to full-code solutions using run-time object models and .NET Assembly Connectors. SharePoint developers should think of these BCS components as a primary mechanism for creating solutions that require data from an external source.

## CHAPTER 17

SharePoint social enterprise features

S ocial enterprise features in Microsoft SharePoint have forever changed for the better with the release of SharePoint 2013. Many of SharePoint's new social features allow organizations and their people almost instant access to social capabilities ranging from newsfeeds, to following people and content, to taking advantage of Yammer, one of Microsoft's recent acquisitions.

The investment that Microsoft has put into these new features, along with the global trends in social components within organizations, attest to the fact that social components can be a game changer for how people collaborate and communicate with one another throughout the workplace. Efficiency and productivity can dramatically increase as a result of including social features within your organization's roadmap for your intranet, extranet, and public-facing sites. This increased attention can also be attributed to the fact that many more organizations have gone global or have a dispersed workforce than ever before, which means that social features are often viewed as the hopeful keystone for ensuring a connected workplace and team even though the individuals might be miles or countries apart.

What's new in SharePoint 2013

There have been many changes within the social space of SharePoint. Most people say that it has been rebuilt from the ground up, and in many cases this is an accurate statement. One of the primary reasons for this rebuild might have been to make the social experience with SharePoint 2013 truly people-centric. This will become more evident as you read this chapter and learn about many of these social components.

Community portals and sites are a much-needed upgrade to the discussion forums that were available in SharePoint 2010. Taking advantage of the badge and reward system found within these sites offers up new incentives and opportunities for portal users within an organization to not only help other coworkers, but to obtain merit and recognition in the form of a badge that the rest of the organization can view.

The My Sites functionality has been simplified and enhanced all at the same time. The UI and navigational elements found within personal sites have been simplified and modernized to comply with the new modern UI user experience. This has promoted the intuitive nature and experience that should exist within a personal site.

Microblogging is available within SharePoint 2013 in the form of social newsfeeds. These social newsfeeds make use of popular social features such as @ mentions, hashtags, replies, likes, and embedding links and videos within a post or reply. This is a vast improvement over the activity feed that could be used within SharePoint 2010. Yammer also makes use of the same popular social abilities of SharePoint's social feeds, but it also has the added benefit of being capable of being either a standalone solution or one that integrates with SharePoint. Yammer will be discussed in more detail in the section titled "Understanding Yammer" later in this chapter.

In addition to all these new and ready-to-use feature sets, there have been numerous enhancements to the SharePoint Object Models (OMs) and APIs, which we will discuss in detail later in this chapter, within the section titled "Working with the social APIs" and throughout this chapter.

Understanding social components

With something as new and vast as the social additions in SharePoint 2013, it is best to organize the subject into manageable pieces so that a good understanding can eventually be obtained. One of the best ways to organize these new additions is to place them into one of three major pillars or components. Figure 17-1 illustrates the breakdown of these components, which are user profiles, social feeds, and following.

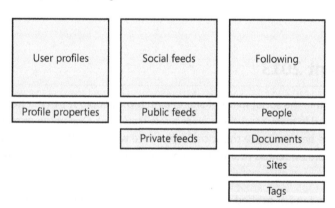

FIGURE 17-1 The SharePoint 2013 social components fall into three major categories.

The first pillar or component is user profiles. Simply put, profiles exist to allow people to be represented within SharePoint. The next logical step is to have properties within these profiles so that they can become more meaningful and useful. Properties can range in purpose and might not be visible even to the person to whom the profile belongs. Organizations have been known to use profile properties that are not visible to a typical user for operational needs, such as storing asset tag IDs for equipment that has been assigned to the person.

The second component is social feeds. Social feeds have taken the place of the activity feed found within SharePoint 2010. Social feeds at a high level can be broken down into two types: public and private. A public feed is what you would find if you went to someone's profile page and looked at the newsfeed on that page, whereas a private feed could be a feed that exists on a team site, where only those who have permissions to the team site can view the newsfeed.

The third and final social component is following. Following can be looked at as taking the place of Colleagues in SharePoint 2010, with some much-needed benefits. Some of the benefits are obvious when you look back at Figure 17-1; not only can you follow people, but you can also follow documents, sites, and tags.

These social pillars or components, in addition to Yammer, have produced the potential for a rich social ecosystem. As you continue to read through this chapter, we will examine each of these components in further detail. We will also look at how to access and extend these social components within SharePoint itself or within other line of business (LOB) applications.

Working with the social APIs

When the social components of SharePoint were rewritten, a rich set of APIs were made available to provide access to each of the primary social components previously mentioned. The server-side object model (SSOM), client-side object model (CSOM), and REST API are all available tools for accessing or extending a social component. Chapter 2, "SharePoint development practices and techniques," introduced you to these APIs, so we will not go into any further detail on what each of them are; however, we will look into the social-centric namespaces and endpoints that they offer and how they allow you to write code against the social components.

The server-side object model has been around the longest and, as such, has the most complete set of APIs and classes available. The main social namespaces for the server-side object model are:

- *Microsoft.Office.Server.Social* (social feeds and following)

- *Microsoft.Office.Server.UserProfiles* (user profiles and user profile properties)

- *Microsoft.Office.Server.SocialData* (ratings, feedback, and comments)

If you did custom development work in SharePoint 2010, you might have also used the API in the *Microsoft.Office.Server.ActivityFeed* namespace. It is important to note that this namespace and its API are deprecated, because that functionality has been replaced by newsfeeds and the APIs just listed.

The client-side object model is vastly improved over previous versions, though there are still a few core namespaces or classes that are found in the server-side object model that are absent from the client-side object model. As an example, there is no client-side accessibility to the *Microsoft.Office. Server.SocialData* namespace. The main social namespaces for the client-side object model are:

- *Microsoft.SharePoint.Client.Social* (social feeds and following)

- *Microsoft.SharePoint.Client.UserProfiles* (user profiles and user profile properties)

When comparing the server-side and client-side lists of namespaces, you can tell that there truly is more commonality then disparity between the two object models. The increased client-side functionality has also brought with it a new recommended approach for writing code against SharePoint 2013, which is that whenever possible you should use the client APIs in place of the server-side object model.

Understanding user profiles

User profiles are vital to the social experience within SharePoint, because this is where people are represented within the SharePoint environment. It is imperative that you remember that for a person to participate in the social experience he or she must have a profile and a My Site. This is a major change from what might have been typical in SharePoint 2010. In SharePoint 2010, many organizations by way of their governance committee might have elected to turn on all the profile features except the storage component, which would provision a site collection for a person. This approach still allowed profiles, the profile page, the organizational chart, and the activity feed to function, without requiring the storage for additional content databases. In SharePoint 2013, this same approach offers the ability to have profiles and the organizational chart, but social feeds and following, which take the place of the activity feed, would not be available. The primary reason for this is because the microblogging that surfaces in social feeds is now stored within the My Site Host content database, whereas in SharePoint 2010 the activity feed was stored in one of the social databases that supported the User Profile Service Application. There are many good reasons why the re-architecture is justified, but as a result you need to be more mindful in your planning of user profiles within your SharePoint implementations now and how they and My Sites can determine what social features can be used.

User profiles are also significant because of the properties that are stored within them. Everything from a user's first and last name to the user's office phone number is often available in the profile, which is easily viewable by way of the user profile page, as shown in Figure 17-2. Organizations might even elect to have user profiles with SharePoint be the single source of a user's data, because of the User Profile Service Application's ability to aggregate properties from many disparate systems (such as Personnel and Financial) and also because of the APIs that can be used to access these properties from the profile store.

FIGURE 17-2 A user profile page contains information about the user.

Retrieving user profile properties

One of the most common requirements is often to simply access a set of user profile properties for a particular purpose. This purpose could be for use within a SharePoint Web Part, to showcase the upcoming birthdays for the current month or to show office phone numbers within an LOB application that is available outside of SharePoint. It is wise to examine all of the business and functional requirements before coming up with the solution design, but after that has been done, it is time to evaluate which API is the most appropriate for the job. For example, in the case of simply needing to query for a few user profile properties, the client-side APIs would be the recommended approach; however, if you needed to write back to any of these properties, you would need to use the server-side object model. This is due to a limitation of the client-side object model that gives the API only Read access to user profile properties, with the one exception being the user profile photo property. This single-write limitation can bring a solution to a sudden halt if it is not identified and vetted against the functional requirements of the solution before code begins to be written.

Assume for this section's example that only the retrieval of user profiles properties is needed. Examples for both the CSOM and REST APIs will be shown. If you have not used CSOM or REST to perform coding tasks against SharePoint, it is recommended that you read Chapter 2 before continuing. The goal for this section's example will be to retrieve the office phone number for a user and likewise for all of that user's peers.

We will start off with the CSOM approach. You will need to have your SharePoint development environment properly configured before you begin; if you have not done so, please read the information in Chapter 3, "Server-side solution development," on how to set up a development environment.

Begin by creating a new Microsoft Visual Studio solution and project. Remember, the nice thing about using the client-side approach is that you do not have to choose one of the SharePoint project templates; you could even choose a console project template if you want. The examples throughout this chapter use a project based on the ASP.NET Empty Web Application project template, because this is more realistic than the need for a console application, as shown in Figure 17-3.

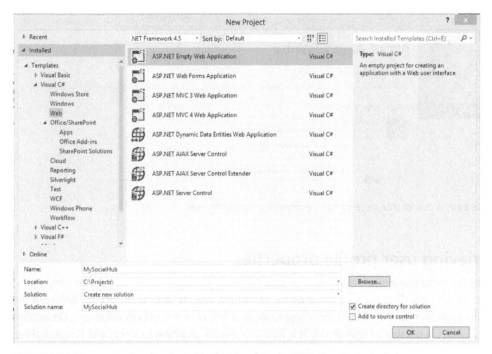

FIGURE 17-3 The new project is selected in the Visual Studio 2012 New Project window.

When the new project loads in Visual Studio, you will want to add references to the required client-side assemblies for interacting with user profiles by using C# and CSOM. They are:

- *Microsoft.SharePoint.Client*

- *Microsoft.SharePoint.ClientRuntime*

- *Microsoft.SharePoint.Client.UserProfiles*

When you have included these references, you will need to create a new page within the project, as shown in Figure 17-4.

After you have added the Web Form, you will need to add the following namespaces to the code-behind file so you can easily access the required objects for this example:

- *Microsoft.SharePoint.Client*

- *Microsoft.SharePoint.Client.UserProfiles*

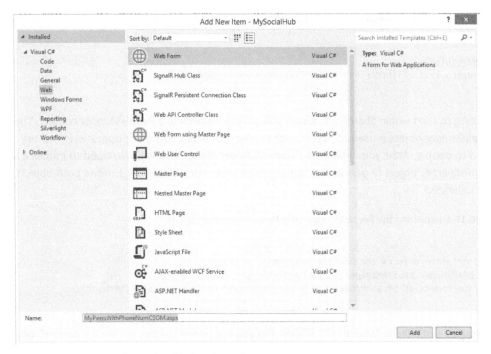

FIGURE 17-4 A new webpage is added to the project.

When that is complete, you will need to add a few variables to the code-behind of the Web Form to store the URL of a SharePoint site, so that you can get context and get the name of the user whose peers' office phone numbers we want to retrieve. The code in Listing 17-1 shows these variables set for a SharePoint site at *http://portal.contoso.com* and a user named Aaron Painter, who has a domain username of *aaronp*.

LISTING 17-1 Creating variables

```
//Variables
string siteURL = "http://portal.contoso.com";
string curUser = @"contoso\aaronp";
```

Now that you have these variables set, you can initialize the SharePoint client context by using the *siteURL* you set up to gain context within SharePoint. This is shown in Listing 17-2.

LISTING 17-2 Creating context

```
//Variables
ClientContext clientContext = new ClientContext(siteURL);
```

Having context within SharePoint allows you to now instantiate a *PeopleManager* object. The *PeopleManager* object is used to access user profile properties and other operations that are related to people. After you initialize a *PeopleManager* object, you will also need to initialize a *PersonProperties* object to gain access to the profile properties. Listing 17-3 shows both objects being initialized.

LISTING 17-3 Initializing the *PeopleManager* and *PersonProperties* objects

```
//Initialize objects for profile properties access
PeopleManager peopleManager = new PeopleManager(clientContext);
PersonProperties personProperties = peopleManager.GetPropertiesFor(curUser);
```

If you are not already familiar with CSOM and you happened to have added the *personProperties* object to a watch, you would have noticed quite a few exceptions being thrown, as shown in Figure 17-5. This is because with the client-side approach, code is sent to the SharePoint server in batches, where it is converted into server-side code, executed, and then sent back. The act of sending the code is available in both synchronous and asynchronous mode and requires an action on the client side, such as the execution of the requests registered within the *ClientContext* object by calling its *Load()* and *ExecuteQuery()* methods.

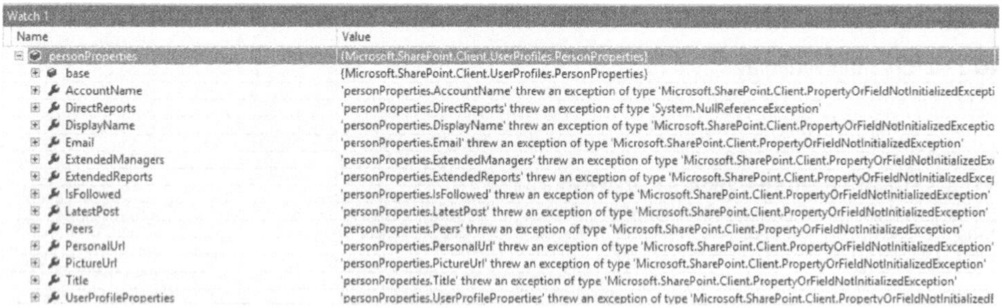

FIGURE 17-5 The *personProperties* object is shown here within a watch panel.

As you can imagine, if all of the solutions you build from this point on use the CSOM approach, that would be a lot of calls being sent to SharePoint. To be as efficient as possible, you should only request those properties that you need access to at the moment. In this case, you need to get the peers for Aaron Painter, and for good measure you will also request Aaron's display name and office phone number to display along with his peers within a list you will generate. Listing 17-4 shows the updated code to request the properties, and Figure 17-6 shows watch panel after you apply the code.

LISTING 17-4 Updated code block including *Load()* and *ExecuteQuery()* methods

```
//Get Aaron Painter's Office Phone and Peers
PeopleManager peopleManager = new PeopleManager(clientContext);
PersonProperties personProperties = peopleManager.GetPropertiesFor(curUser);
clientContext.Load(personProperties, p => p.DisplayName, p => p.UserProfileProperties
   ,p => p.Peers);
clientContext.ExecuteQuery();
```

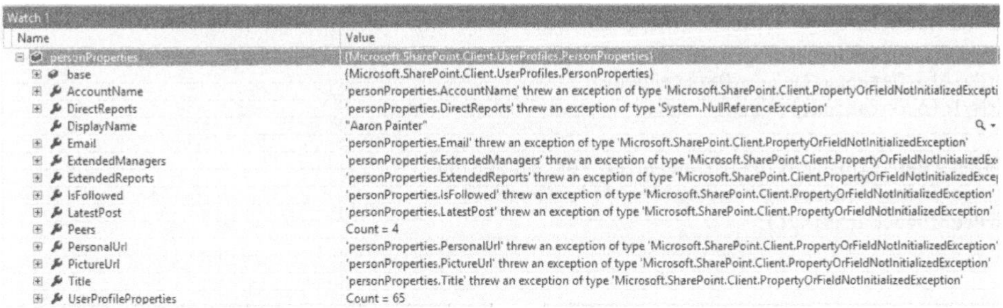

FIGURE 17-6 The updated *personProperties* object is shown within the watch panel.

After the updated code is executed, you can tell that Aaron Painter's *Display Name*, *Peers*, and *UserProfileProperties* properties are not throwing exceptions any longer and have actual values that you can use. You might be wondering where the *Office Phone* property is; it's actually stored within the *UserProfileProperties* array under the key *WorkPhone*. The *Peers* object is also an array that stores the account name for each of Aaron's peers. This proves useful because you simply need to execute the same block of code, minus the request for the *Peers* property, as you initially did for Aaron. Listing 17-5 shows the completed code needed to access both Aaron's information and the information of his peers. Listing 17-6 shows the markup necessary to complete the example.

LISTING 17-5 Updated code block for accessing the user's information and peers' information

```
//Variables
string siteURL = "http://portal.contoso.com";
string curUser = @"contoso\aaronp";
ClientContext clientContext = new ClientContext(siteURL);

//Get Aaron Painter's Office Phone and Peers
PeopleManager peopleManager = new PeopleManager(clientContext);
PersonProperties personProperties = peopleManager.GetPropertiesFor(curUser);
clientContext.Load(personProperties, p => p.DisplayName, p => p.UserProfileProperties
   ,p => p.Peers);
clientContext.ExecuteQuery();
//Get Aaron Painter's Information
Dictionary<string, string> myOfficePhone = new Dictionary<string, string>();
myOfficePhone.Add(personProperties.DisplayName,
personProperties.UserProfileProperties["WorkPhone"]);
List<string> curUserPeers = personProperties.Peers.ToList<string>();
```

```
//Get Office Phone for each of Aaron Painter's Peers
Dictionary<string,string> peersWithOfficePhones = new Dictionary<string,string>();
foreach (string peer in curUserPeers)
{
personProperties = peopleManager.GetPropertiesFor(peer);
clientContext.Load(personProperties, p => p.DisplayName, p => p.UserProfileProperties);
clientContext.ExecuteQuery();
peersWithOfficePhones.Add(personProperties.DisplayName,
  personProperties.UserProfileProperties["WorkPhone"]);
}

//Bind Aaron's Information to Repeater for Rendering

rptMyInfo.DataSource = myOfficePhone;
rptMyInfo.DataBind();

//Bind Peers Information to Repeater for Rendering
rptPeerInfo.DataSource = peersWithOfficePhones;
rptPeerInfo.DataBind();
```

LISTING 17-6 ASPX markup code

```
<div>
    <asp:Repeater ID="rptMyInfo" runat="server">
        <HeaderTemplate><div><h3>My Information</h3></div></HeaderTemplate>
        <ItemTemplate>
            <div><strong><%# Eval("Key") %></strong></div>
            <div><%# Eval("Value") %></div>
        </ItemTemplate>
        <FooterTemplate><hr /></FooterTemplate>
    </asp:Repeater>
    <asp:Repeater ID="rptPeerInfo" runat="server">
        <HeaderTemplate><div><h3>My Peers</h3></div></HeaderTemplate>
        <ItemTemplate>
            <div><strong><%# Eval("Key") %></strong></div>
            <div><%# Eval("Value") %></div>
        </ItemTemplate>
        <FooterTemplate></FooterTemplate>
    </asp:Repeater>
</div>
```

If you have success executing the code, you should find something similar to what is displayed within Figure 17-7, but probably with different names and numbers.

My Information

Aaron Painter
555-0100

My Peers

Brad Sutton
555-0110
Cesar Garcia
555-0120
David Galvin
555-0130
Terry Adams
555-0140

FIGURE 17-7 The user's information and his peers' information are displayed.

To ensure that the solution is indeed a success, you can compare the list of peers returned with those found on the user's manager's profile page. As Figure 17-8 suggests, you have successfully returned Aaron's peers within the example.

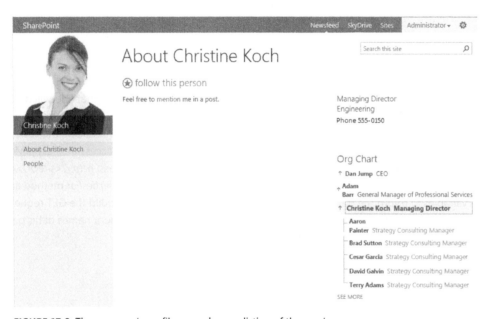

FIGURE 17-8 The manager's profile page shows a listing of the user's peers.

Next you will perform the same example, but you will use the REST API in place of CSOM. As described earlier, the REST API in SharePoint 2013 is extremely robust in comparison to its implementation in previous versions of SharePoint. To begin the REST example, you can use the same Visual Studio project that was used for the CSOM example and simply add a new HTML page to the project, as shown in Figure 17-9.

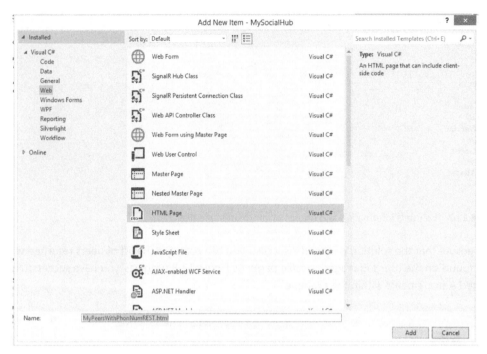

FIGURE 17-9 Add a new HTML page to the project.

The fact that you are selecting an HTML page should give you an indication that you will not be using references in the way you typically would for CSOM or SSOM. With REST, you typically make requests by sending a POST or GET request to an available endpoint. Just as with CSOM, the code will interact with a *PeopleManager* object, with the one difference being how you access the *PeopleManager* object. With REST, you access it by calling an endpoint at the following address: *http://<siteUri>/_api /SP.UserProfiles.PeopleManager*. By using this address, you can call the *GetPropertiesFor* method and pass in variables to return the desired results. Listing 17-7 shows how you can build the GET request to the *PeopleManager* endpoint to return back the user's properties and the account names of his peers.

LISTING 17-7 HTML markup and REST GET request to *PeopleManager*

```
   <html xmlns="http://www.w3.org/1999/xhtml">
<head>
    <title></title>
    <script src ="http://ajax.aspnetcdn.com/ajax/jQuery/jquery-2.0.2.min.js"></script>
    <script type="text/javascript">
        $().ready(function () {

            //variables
            var curUser = "contoso\\aaronp";
            var profileEndPoint = "http://portal.contoso.com/_api/SP.UserProfiles.
 PeopleManager/GetPropertiesFor(accountName=@v)?@v='" + curUser + "'";

            $.ajax({
                type: "GET",
                contentType: "application/json; charset=utf-8",
                datatype: "json",
                url: profileEndPoint,
                headers: { "ACCEPT": "application/json;odata=verbose" },
                success: onSuccess,
                error: onFail
            });
            function onSuccess(data) {
                var myDisplayName = data.d.DisplayName;
                var myPeers = data.d.Peers;
                $("#myDisplayName").html("<strong>" + myDisplayName + "</strong>");

                $.each(myPeers.results, function (value,key) {
                    $("#myPeers").after("<div><strong>" + key + "</strong></div>");
                });

            }

            function onFail(errorObject, errorMessage) {
                $("#errMessage").text("Error: " + errorMessage);
            }
        });
    </script>
</head>
<body>
    <div><h3>My Information</h3></div>
    <div id="myDisplayName"><strong></strong></div>
    <div id="myWorkPhone"></div>
    <hr />
    <div><h3>My Peers</h3></div>
    <div id="myPeers"></div>
    <div id="errMessage"></div>
</body>
</html>
```

Walking through the code from top to bottom, the first need is to reference the jQuery library. In Listing 17-7, this was done by using the ASP.NET Content Delivery Network (CDN). After the script reference, a script block is declared with a jQuery *document.ready()* function. For reasons of simplicity, all variables and declarations are made within this code block to avoid naming conflicts within the namespace. If you would like to learn more about namespaces, you can do so in Chapter 5, "Client-side programming." Continuing on through the code, variables are declared for Aaron Painter and for the *PeopleManager* endpoint. An Asynchronous JavaScript and XML (AJAX) method is used to execute the GET request, which passes the endpoint as the URL to which the request is to be submitted, and requests that the results be returned as a JavaScript Object Notation (JSON) object. Both a success and a failure method are used to capture either the returned JSON object or the error object. The success method accepts a data object whose top-level properties contain the *DisplayName* and *Peers* properties for the requested user profile properties. jQuery is used to render these results to the markup found with the body element of the HTML markup in Listing 17-7.

At this point, if you viewed the HTML page within the browser, you should find something similar to Figure 17-10.

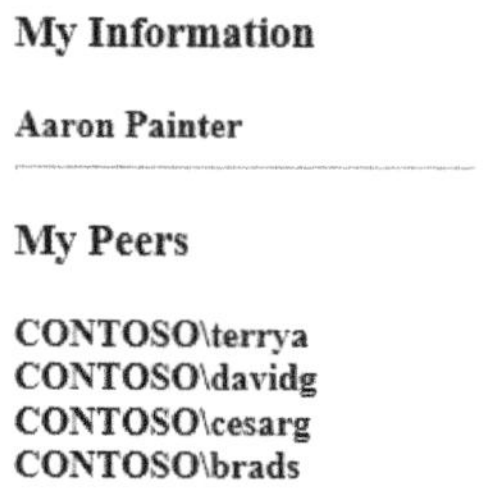

My Information

Aaron Painter

My Peers

CONTOSO\terrya
CONTOSO\davidg
CONTOSO\cesarg
CONTOSO\brads

FIGURE 17-10 The rendered results are returned from the REST call.

As you can tell, this is very close to the results that you received when using the CSOM approach. The only things missing are the display names and phone numbers for each peer in place of the account name. Listing 17-8 has a few additional utility methods that help you complete this task. The matching results to the CSOM example are shown in Figure 17-11.

```html
<html xmlns="http://www.w3.org/1999/xhtml">
<head>
    <title></title>
    <script src ="http://ajax.aspnetcdn.com/ajax/jQuery/jquery-2.0.2.min.js"></script>
    <script type="text/javascript">
        $().ready(function () {

            //variables
            var curUser = "contoso\\aaronp";
            $.ajax({
                type: "GET",
                contentType: "application/json; charset=utf-8",
                datatype: "json",
                url: buildProfileEndPoint(curUser),
                headers: { "ACCEPT": "application/json;odata=verbose" },
                success: onSuccess,
                error: onFail
            });

            function GetUserProfile(user) {
                //send GET request to SharePoint
                $.ajax({
                    type: "GET",
                    contentType: "application/json; charset=utf-8",
                    datatype: "json",
                    url: buildProfileEndPoint(user),
                    headers: { "ACCEPT": "application/json;odata=verbose" },
                    success: function (data) {
                        $("#myPeers").after("<div><strong>" + data.d.DisplayName +
                          "</strong></div><div>" + getValueByKey
("WorkPhone", data.d.UserProfileProperties.results) + "</div>");
                    },



                    error: function (errorObject, errorMessage) {
                        $("#errMessage").text("Error: " + errorMessage);
                    }
                });
            }

            function onSuccess(data) {
                var myDisplayName = data.d.DisplayName;
                var myWorkPhone = getValueByKey("WorkPhone",
                  data.d.UserProfileProperties.results);
                var myPeers = data.d.Peers;
                $("#myDisplayName").html("<strong>" + myDisplayName + "</strong>");
                $("#myWorkPhone").text(myWorkPhone);
```

```
                    $.each(myPeers.results, function (value,key) {
                        GetUserProfile(key);
                    });


            }
    function onFail(errorObject, errorMessage) {
                $("#errMessage").text("Error: " + errorMessage);
            }

            //Utility Functions
            function getValueByKey(key, results) {
                var item = jQuery.grep(results, function (e) {
                    if (e.Key === key)
                        return e;
                })[0].Value;

                return item;
            }

            function buildProfileEndPoint(user) {
                return "http://portal.contoso.com/_api/SP.UserProfiles.PeopleManager/
                    GetPropertiesFor(accountName=@v)?@v='" + user + "'"
            }

        });
    </script>
</head>
<body>
    <div><h3>My Information</h3></div>
    <div id="myDisplayName"><strong></strong></div>
    <div id="myWorkPhone"></div>
    <hr />
    <div><h3>My Peers</h3></div>
    <div id="myPeers"></div>
    <div id="errMessage"></div>
</body>
</html>
```

My Information

Aaron Painter
555-0100

My Peers

Brad Sutton
555-0110
Cesar Garcia
555-0120
David Galvin
555-0130
Terry Adams
555-0140

FIGURE 17-11 The rendering of the REST GET request is completed.

Now that you have completed an example of retrieving profile properties not only for a user but also for his peers by using both CSOM and the REST API, you have the necessary foundation to work with profiles and access properties when needed.

Understanding social feeds

As stated earlier in this chapter, social feeds for all intents and purposes have taken the place of the activity feed found in SharePoint 2010. The activity feed was a step forward from versions previous to 2010; however, with the ever-increasing demand for social features within the collaboration space, this feed would not sufficiently meet today's standards. This is why there is more than one type of social feed and why what you can do within each feed has vastly improved over the activity feed.

The important thing to remember with these feeds is that they are people-centric; even if you choose to interact with a document, the interaction itself is taken by a person or an *Actor*, which is one of the primary objects you'll be working with whenever you are coding against the user profile and social namespaces.

Another object that you'll want to become familiar with is the *SocialFeedManager*, which is similar to the *PeopleManager* in terms of how you go about accessing social feeds as with a profile.

By the end of this chapter, you will have completed examples that will be able to request the social feed for the current user, post to your feed, request the social feed for a team site, and post to a social feed for a team site.

Just as in the examples in the previous section, we will work through both a CSOM and a REST approach.

Retrieving posts from your newsfeed

The term *microblogging* is new to SharePoint and might be a mystery to some as to what it actually entails. A short description is that it is the act of posting short blocks of text or updates. These updates can be created through the SharePoint UI by a person using his personal feed, which is shown in the newsfeed found on his personal site, or from a private feed, which is a newsfeed found typically on a team site. As you can tell, these actions are very similar to those found on a full-fledged blog site, just minified in terms of the amount of content that is typically posted.

As a developer you can start to imagine all the possibilities that are available. To help you get a good idea of how microblogging works, the first example you will complete is retrieving posts from your own personal feed.

From within your Visual Studio project, create a new Web Form page similar to the one shown in Figure 17-12.

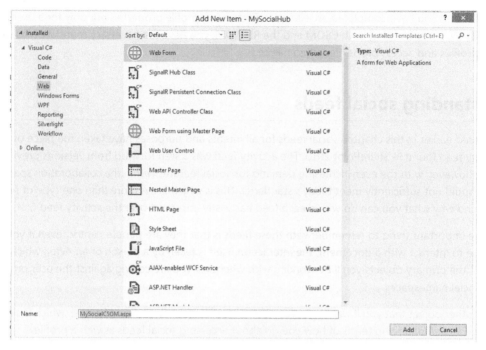

FIGURE 17-12 A new form is selected in the New Web Form dialog box.

The following namespaces need to be added to the code-behind for the newly created Web Form so that you can easily access the necessary objects:

- *Microsoft.SharePoint.Client*

- *Microsoft.SharePoint.Client.Social*

Next you will need to declare variables for a site URL to gain context within SharePoint by passing it to a *ClientContext* object. Similar to the technique you used to get the profile for a user, there is a manager class for accessing social feeds that is called the *SocialFeedManager.* By using the *SocialFeed-Manager,* you can retrieve, create, and delete posts. The methods listing here for the *SocialFeedManager* class give a good indication of what its purpose is:

- *CreateImageAttachment*

- *CreatePost*

- *DeletePost*

- *GetAllLikers*

- *GetFeed*

- *GetFeedFor*

- *GetFullThread*

- *GetMentions*

- *GetPreview*

- *GetPreviewImage*

- *GetUnreadMentionCount*

- *InitOnePropertyFromJson*

- *LikePost*

- *LockThread*

- *SuppressThreadNotifications*

- *UnlikePost*

- *UnlockThread*

As you can tell, a lot of heavy lifting is done for you via this class. For now, the method that you will want to take advantage of is the one aptly named *GetFeed*, because you want to get the current user's feed.

To use the *GetFeed* method, you first need to create an instance of *ClientContext* and then pass it to an instance of the *SocialFeedManager*, as shown in Listing 17-9.

LISTING 17-9 CSOM and C# code passing the *ClientContext* object to the *SocialFeedManager* object

```
//variables
string siteURL = "http://portal.contoso.com";
//Create instances for ClientContext and SocialFeedManager
ClientContext clientContext = new ClientContext(siteUrl);
SocialFeedManager feedManager = new SocialFeedManager(clientContext);
```

Now that you have a *feedManager* object, you can execute the *GetFeed* method. It is important to note that this method can only be used for the current user. When you use the *GetFeed* method, one of the parameters you need to specify is a feed type, which is of the *SocialFeedType* enumeration. The available types in the enumeration are:

- *Everyone*

- *Likes*

- *News*

- *Personal*

- *Timeline*

Basically what each feed type shows is a filtered version of the *Everyone* feed type, which accounts for all activity for the current user's organization. Table 17-1 shows each of the available feed types and the data that is returned by each.

TABLE 17-1 Social feed types for a user

Feed type	Description
Everyone	All recent activities by the current user's organization.
Likes	All microblog posts liked by the current user.
News	All activities by the current user; people and content that the user is following, sorted by modified date. Emphasis is on date as to what is returned.
Personal	All activities by the current user only.
Timeline	All activities by the current user, people and content that the user is following, sorted by created date. Emphasis is on the user's social graph as to what is returned.

In this example you will use the *News* type, because it will show content that you know the user would be interested in. In addition to the type of feed, you also must specify options for the feed being returned before you can request the feed. The options are based on the *SocialFeedOptions* class. There are four properties that you can use when instantiating an instance of the *SocialFeedOptions* class:

- **MaxThreadCount**   Allows you to specify the maximum number of threads to return. The default is 20 threads.

- **NewerThan**   Allows you to specify a date after which the thread must have been created.

- **OlderThan**   Allows you to specify a date before which the thread must have been created.

- **SortOrder**   Allows you to specify the order in which the threads are returned. There are only two options, passed as integers. Use 0 to sort by the modified date and 1 to sort by created date of the root post.

Now is a good time to go over how posts are constructed from an object hierarchy before we progress any further with this code example. Figure 17-13 shows a newsfeed in which Aaron Painter has started a conversation about CSAT. There are three replies by others in the organization.

FIGURE 17-13 This newsfeed shows replies.

The breakdown of this conversation from an object perspective is shown in Figure 17-14.

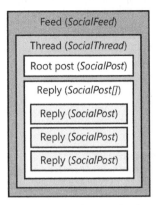

FIGURE 17-14 The newsfeed is represented as SharePoint objects.

The newsfeed is a *SocialFeed* object that contains threads that are *SocialThread* objects. From the SharePoint UI, as shown in Figure 17-13, threads are represented as conversations. Each thread has a root post, the original post or the post that started the conversation, and all the replies to the thread. Notice that all posts, regardless of whether they are the root post or one of the replies, are stored as *SocialPost* objects. The only difference is that the replies are stored in an array within the thread.

Recall that the *GetFeed* method allows you to pass into the *SocialFeedOptions* object the maximum number of threads to return, but it didn't have anything for you to specify the maximum number of replies to return. This is because the *GetFeed* method will only return the two most recent replies for the thread or conversation. Even though only two will be returned, you can read the *TotalReplyCount* property for the thread to determine if there are, in fact, more replies. If so, the *GetFullThread* method will return the thread with all of the replies, if you pass it the thread ID. You might wonder why the two-reply limit is placed on the *GetFeed* method. If you spend enough time within the SharePoint UI, you will notice that all conversations use this structure. Figure 17-15 shows the conversation Aaron Painter started before the Show All Replies link was clicked. This mechanism was put into place to be more resource-friendly and ensure that the newsfeed could render as quickly as possible. You would also be correct if you assumed that the Show All 3 Replies link within Figure 17-15 would call the *GetFullThread* method if you clicked on it, which would give you the view that is shown back in Figure 17-13.

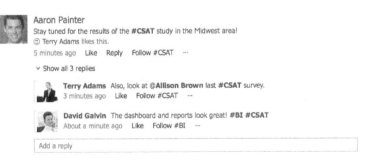

FIGURE 17-15 This newsfeed thread shows only the two most recent replies.

Now that you have a better understanding of how posts are treated in SharePoint, you can continue with the code example by executing the *GetFeed* method and displaying the results within a *Repeater* control, as shown in Listing 17-10.

LISTING 17-10 CSOM and C# code for requesting the newsfeed for the current user

```
//Code-behind
//variables
string siteURL = "http://portal.contoso.com";
//Create instances for ClientContext and SocialFeedManager
ClientContext clientContext = new ClientContext(siteURL);
SocialFeedManager feedManager = new SocialFeedManager(clientContext);
ClientResult<SocialFeed> personalFeedResults = feedManager.GetFeed(SocialFeedType.News,
new SocialFeedOptions()
{
MaxThreadCount = 5
});
clientContext.ExecuteQuery();
rptPosts.DataSource = personalFeedResults.Value.Threads;
rptPosts.DataBind();
//ASPX Markup
<%@ Page Language="C#" AutoEventWireup="true" CodeBehind="MySocialHome.aspx.cs"
Inherits="MySocialHub.MySocialHome" %>
<%@ Import Namespace="Microsoft.SharePoint.Client.Social" %>
<%@ Import Namespace="Microsoft.SharePoint.Client" %>
<%@ Assembly Name="Microsoft.SharePoint.Client.UserProfiles, Version=15.0.0.0,
Culture=neutral, PublicKeyToken=71e9bce111e9429c" %>
<%@ Assembly Name="Microsoft.SharePoint.Client.Runtime, Version=15.0.0.0, Culture=neutral,
PublicKeyToken=71e9bce111e9429c" %>
<!DOCTYPE html>

<html xmlns="http://www.w3.org/1999/xhtml">
<head runat="server">
    <title></title>
</head>
<body>
    <form id="form1" runat="server">
    <div>
        <div><h3>My Newsfeed</h3></div>
        <asp:Repeater ID="rptPosts" runat="server">
            <HeaderTemplate></HeaderTemplate>
            <ItemTemplate>
                <!-- Post Properties -->
                <div><%# ((SocialThread)Container.DataItem).RootPost.Text %></div>
                <!-- Post Replies -->
                <asp:Repeater id="rptPostReplies" runat="server"
                  DataSource="<%# ((SocialThread)Container.DataItem).Replies %>">
                    <HeaderTemplate><ul></HeaderTemplate>
                    <ItemTemplate>
                        <li><%# Eval("Text") %></li>
                    </ItemTemplate>
                    <FooterTemplate></ul></FooterTemplate>
                </asp:Repeater>
```

```
            </ItemTemplate>
            <FooterTemplate></FooterTemplate>
        </asp:Repeater>
    </div>
    </form>
</body>
</html>
```

After running this code, you can compare what is shown in Figure 17-16 with what the SharePoint UI on the newsfeed was showing and note that they match.

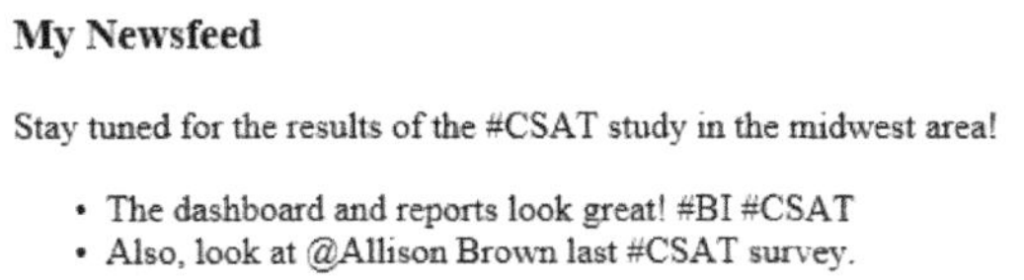

My Newsfeed

Stay tuned for the results of the #CSAT study in the midwest area!

- The dashboard and reports look great! #BI #CSAT
- Also, look at @Allison Brown last #CSAT survey.

FIGURE 17-16 The current user's newsfeed is rendered to an ASPX page by using CSOM and C#.

Now that you have successfully retrieved posts from a newsfeed by using CSOM, you will walk through the same example by using the REST API.

Start the REST API example by first creating a new HTML page within your Visual Studio project, as shown in Figure 17-17.

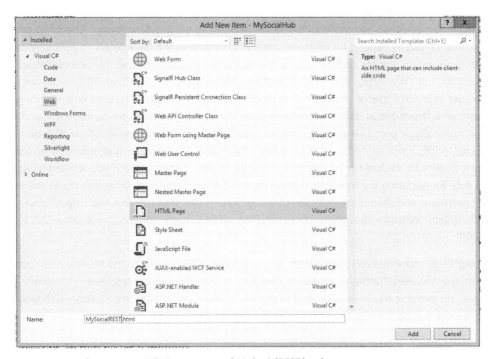

FIGURE 17-17 Create a new HTML page named MySocialREST.html.

Within the markup for the HTML page, you will want to include a script reference to the jQuery library so that you can use the AJAX method for communication with the REST API. The next step is to determine which endpoint to use when making a request for a social feed. With the CSOM example you used the *GetFeed* method to get the feed for the current user, and then specified the type that you would like returned. However, before you could use the *GetFeed* method you had to have a *SocialFeedManager* object to work with first. This is represented within the REST API by an endpoint located at *http://<site>/_api/social.feed*. When you use this endpoint, the type is determined by the endpoint you choose to append to the social feed endpoint. In Table 17-2, some of the key endpoints for use with the current user are listed, along with a description.

TABLE 17-2 Social feed endpoints for a user

Endpoint	Description
My/Feed	Activities by the current users only
My/Likes	All microblog posts liked by the current user
My/News	All activities by the current user, people and content that the user is following from the newsfeed, sorted by modified date
My/MentionFeed	All activities that mention the current user
My/Timelinefeed	All activities by the current user, people and content that the user is following, sorted by created date

You will use the *My/News* endpoint for requesting the posts for the current user for this example.

The next step is to pass feed options to the newsfeed endpoint. This is accomplished by passing parameters to the endpoint. You will use the max count of five again for the number of threads to return. Parameters can be passed to the REST endpoint in a few different ways. The appropriate approach will typically depend on what you are trying to pass as the parameters. If, for instance, you are passing a simple number such as 5, as in this case when you want to specify the max thread count, you can pass it like this: *http://<site>/_api/social.feed/my/news(MaxThreadCount=10)*. However, if you have a case in which a special character is involved, such as the backslash (\) used when passing an account name structured in domain\username style, then you might want to use something called an @ alias. An @ alias is used like this: *http://<site>/_api/social.feed/actor(item=@v)/feed?@v='domain\\ username'*. A URL is not limited as to the number of @ aliases you can use. Just make sure to use a different @ alias for each of the parameters you want to pass. For example, if you wanted to also pass a date for declaring the *NewerThan* property in addition to the username, you could still use @v for the username and @x for the date, which would have a URL structure like this: *http://<site>/_api/ social.feed/actor(item=@v)/feed(NewerThan=@x)?@v='domain\\username'&@x=datetime'2013-07-19T08:00'*.

Listing 17-11 shows the completed code for making the GET request to the *My/News* endpoint to return the newsfeed for the current user. Also, in addition to what was returned in the previous example, this example has been extended to show who the root post creator is, along with who each of the repliers is in addition to the posts.

LISTING 17-11 REST code for requesting the newsfeed for the current user

```html
<!DOCTYPE html>
<html xmlns="http://www.w3.org/1999/xhtml">
<head>
    <title></title>
    <script src="http://ajax.aspnetcdn.com/ajax/jQuery/jquery-2.0.2.min.js""></script>
    <script type="text/javascript">
        $().ready(function () {
            //variables
            var endpointURL = "http://portal.contoso.com/_api/social.feed/my/
news(MaxThreadCount=5)"

            $.ajax({
                type: "GET",
                url: endpointURL,
                headers: {
                    "accept": "application/json;odata=verbose"
                },
                success: onSuccess,
                error: onFail
            });

            function onSuccess(data) {
                var threads = data.d.SocialFeed.Threads.results;
                $.each(threads, function (value) {
                    var orgPost = threads[value].RootPost.Text;
                    var orgPoster = threads[value].Actors.results[threads[value].
OwnerIndex].Name;
                    var post = "<div><strong>" + orgPost + "</strong></div>";
                    post += "<div><i>" + orgPoster + "</i></div><br/>";
                    var replies = threads[value].Replies.results;
                    $.each(replies, function (key) {
                        var rplPost = replies[key].Text;
                        var rplPoster = threads[value].Actors.results[replies[key].
AuthorIndex].Name;
                        post += "<div class='reply'><strong>" + rplPost + "</strong>
                            </div>";
                        post += "<div class='reply'><i>" + rplPoster + "</i></div>";

                    });

                    $("#myNewsfeed").after(post);
                });
            }
            function onFail(errorObject, errorMessage) {
                $("#errMessage").text("Error: " + errorMessage);
            }
        });
    </script>
    <style>
        .reply {
            padding-left:15px;
        }
```

```
        </style>
    </head>
    <body>
        <div id="myNewsfeed"><h2>My Newsfeed</h2></div>
        <div id="errMessage"></div>
    </body>
</html>
```

When you load the HTML page, as shown in Figure 17-18, you can tell that the feed is successfully returned along with who each post was created by.

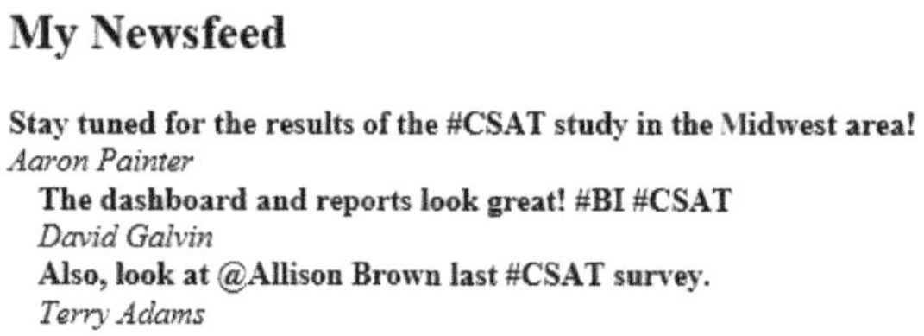

My Newsfeed

Stay tuned for the results of the #CSAT study in the Midwest area!
Aaron Painter
　The dashboard and reports look great! #BI #CSAT
　David Galvin
　Also, look at @Allison Brown last #CSAT survey.
　Terry Adams

FIGURE 17-18 The current user's newsfeed is rendered to the HTML page by using REST.

You might have noticed, if you walked through both the CSOM with C# and the REST example, that the REST example was completed with less code. This could partially be because you are using the jQuery library, so many of the functions could be abstracted, but another reason is because of how easy JSON is to work with. Because it has XML type characteristics, it can be iterated through much more easily at times than C# objects can, which can equate to less code. As developers, we should always want to write less code, because it means less to debug and sift through when it comes to maintenance.

Retrieving posts from a site feed

Retrieving posts from a site feed is very similar to retrieving posts from personal feeds. In the previous section you walked through how to retrieve the current user's feed, but if you had instead walked through how to retrieve another user's feed it would be even more similar to the example you are about to go through.

Of course, a site feed must exist on a site before you can code against it, so discussing how a site feed comes into existence is a good topic to start with. It is actually a fairly short conversation, because all the functionality required for a site feed is contained within a single web-scoped feature called Site Feed, as shown in Figure 17-19.

Site Feed
Enables the use of site feeds.

FIGURE 17-19 The Site Feed feature is a web-scoped feature.

When this feature is activated, a few items are provisioned on the site, but the more important thing for this discussion is that a microfeed feed now exists for you to code against. Figure 17-20 shows the site newsfeed for a team site that you will be coding against.

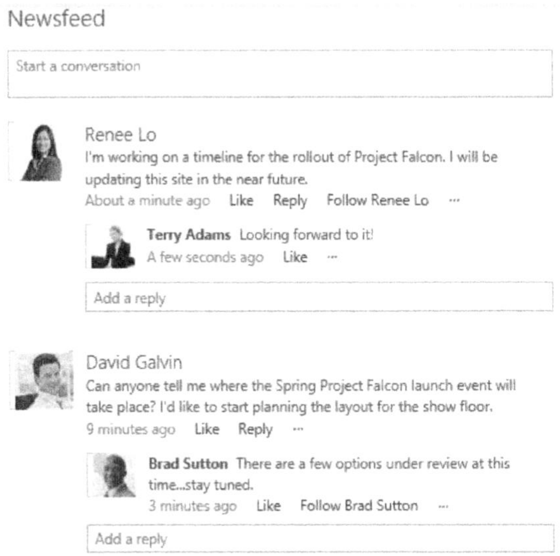

Newsfeed

Start a conversation

Renee Lo
I'm working on a timeline for the rollout of Project Falcon. I will be updating this site in the near future.
About a minute ago   Like   Reply   Follow Renee Lo   ⋯

Terry Adams Looking forward to it!
A few seconds ago   Like   ⋯

Add a reply

David Galvin
Can anyone tell me where the Spring Project Falcon launch event will take place? I'd like to start planning the layout for the show floor.
9 minutes ago   Like   Reply   ⋯

Brad Sutton There are a few options under review at this time...stay tuned.
3 minutes ago   Like   Follow Brad Sutton   ⋯

Add a reply

FIGURE 17-20 A site feed for a team site is shown within SharePoint.

Now that you have that out of the way, you can begin coding the example. You might think at first that there will be quite a few differences between site feeds and personal feeds, and in some ways there might be, but for this example, when you are trying to access each of these newsfeeds from CSOM by using C#, there are actually only two changes: you need to use the *GetFeedFor* method within the *SocialFeedManager* object, and the actor parameter that you pass is not a domain user account, but a site URL that has a social feed provisioned on it. Other than that, the objects that you interact with both from a request and a rendering perspective are identical. To start this example, you can create a Web Form page called SiteSocialCSOM.aspx, similar to the one shown in Figure 17-21. Listing 17-12 details the code-behind and the markup required to complete this example.

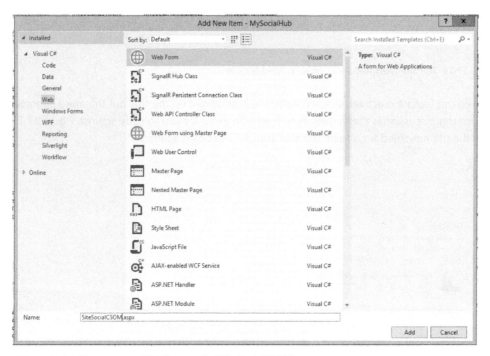

FIGURE 17-21 Create a new Web Form called SiteSocialCSOM.aspx.

LISTING 17-12 CSOM using C# code and markup for requesting a site newsfeed

```
//variables
string siteURL = "http://portal.contoso.com";

//Create instances for ClientContext and SocialFeedManager
ClientContext clientContext = new ClientContext(siteURL);
SocialFeedManager feedManager = new SocialFeedManager(clientContext);
ClientResult<SocialFeed> siteFeedResults = feedManager.GetFeedFor(
  "http://projects.contoso.com/gearsproject", new SocialFeedOptions()
{
        MaxThreadCount = 5
});

clientContext.ExecuteQuery();

rptPosts.DataSource = siteFeedResults.Value.Threads;
rptPosts.DataBind();
//ASPX markup
<%@ Page Language="C#" AutoEventWireup="true" CodeBehind="SiteSocialCSOM.aspx.cs"
Inherits="MySocialHub.SiteSocialCSOM" %>
<%@ Import Namespace="Microsoft.SharePoint.Client.Social" %>
<%@ Import Namespace="Microsoft.SharePoint.Client" %>
<%@ Assembly Name="Microsoft.SharePoint.Client.UserProfiles, Version=15.0.0.0,
Culture=neutral, PublicKeyToken=71e9bce111e9429c" %>
<%@ Assembly Name="Microsoft.SharePoint.Client.Runtime, Version=15.0.0.0, Culture=neutral,
```

```
PublicKeyToken=71e9bce111e9429c" %>
<!DOCTYPE html>

<html xmlns="http://www.w3.org/1999/xhtml">
<head id="Head1" runat="server">
    <title></title>
</head>
<body>
    <form id="form1" runat="server">
    <div>
        <div><h3>Site Newsfeed</h3></div>
        <asp:Repeater ID="rptPosts" runat="server">
            <HeaderTemplate></HeaderTemplate>
            <ItemTemplate>
                <!-- Post Properties -->
                <div><%# ((SocialThread)Container.DataItem).RootPost.Text %></div>
                <!-- Post Replies -->
                <asp:Repeater id="rptPostReplies" runat="server"
                  DataSource="<%# ((SocialThread)Container.DataItem).Replies %>">
                    <HeaderTemplate><ul></HeaderTemplate>
                    <ItemTemplate>
                        <li><%# Eval("Text") %></li>
                    </ItemTemplate>
                    <FooterTemplate></ul></FooterTemplate>
                </asp:Repeater>
            </ItemTemplate>
            <FooterTemplate></FooterTemplate>
        </asp:Repeater>
    </div>
    </f
</body>
</html>
```

And finally, Figure 17-22 shows the site newsfeed rendered out in the SiteSocialSCOM.aspx page.

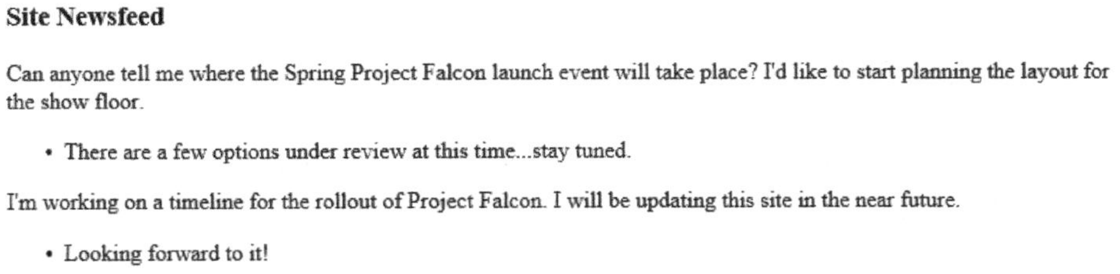

Site Newsfeed

Can anyone tell me where the Spring Project Falcon launch event will take place? I'd like to start planning the layout for the show floor.

- There are a few options under review at this time...stay tuned.

I'm working on a timeline for the rollout of Project Falcon. I will be updating this site in the near future.

- Looking forward to it!

FIGURE 17-22 The site newsfeed is rendered to the ASPX page by using CSOM.

When you want to retrieve a site newsfeed by using the REST API approach, the same holds true when it comes to the small amount of change that is necessary when compared to the previous examples. With the CSOM approach, you simply needed to use a different method and pass in the site URL; with REST this translates to a different endpoint that you pass the GET request to. In addition to the different endpoint, you also need to pass the site URL. The endpoint that you need to target is *http://<site>/_api/social.feed/actor(item=@v)/feed*. You'll notice that this endpoint uses an @ alias that you can pass at the end of the URL, like this: *http://<site>/_api/social.feed/actor(item=@v)/feed?@ v='http://<teamSite>/newsfeed.aspx'*, where the *<teamSite>* variable is the URL to the site containing a newsfeed.

To start this example, add a new HTML page called SiteSocialREST.html to the MySocialHub project, as shown in Figure 17-23.

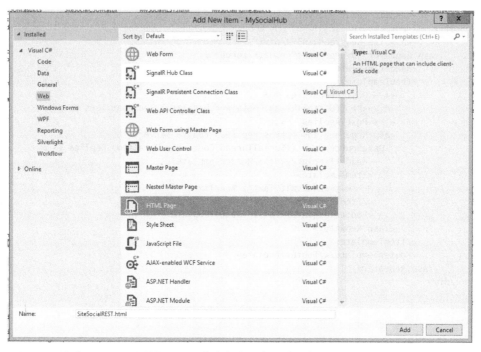

FIGURE 17-23 Create a new HTML page called SiteSocialREST.html.

At this point, you can use the code from the REST example for retrieving a personal feed, except that you need to update the endpoint that you send the GET request to. Also, because the last REST example rendered out the author of each post and used the owner index attribute to look up the author, you have another amendment to make to the code. This is because when you are working with a *SocialThread* object that is returned from a personal feed, the owner of the thread is always the author of the root post; however, when you are dealing with a site feed, the owner of the thread is always the site and, as such, has the site's title stored in it. So the way to get the true author is to always use the *AuthorIndex* property for the root post, in place of the thread's *OwnerIndex*, so that your rendering code is reusable regardless of whether it is accessing a personal feed or a site feed. Listing 17-13 contains the updated REST code for accessing the site newsfeed by using the *Author- Index*, and Figure 17-24 shows the results rendered on the HTML page.

LISTING 17-13 REST code for requesting a site newsfeed

```
<!DOCTYPE html>
<html xmlns="http://www.w3.org/1999/xhtml">
<head>
    <title></title>
    <script src="http://ajax.aspnetcdn.com/ajax/jQuery/jquery-2.0.2.min.js""></script>
    <script type="text/javascript">
        $().ready(function () {
            //variables
            var siteURL = "http://projects.contoso.com"
            var endpointURL = siteURL + "/_api/social.feed/actor(item=@v)/
              feed?@v='http://projects.contoso.com/gearsproject'"

            $.ajax({
                type: "GET",
                url: endpointURL,
                headers: {
                    "accept": "application/json;odata=verbose"
                },
                success: onSuccess,
                error: onFail
            });

            function onSuccess(data) {
                var threads = data.d.SocialFeed.Threads.results;
                $.each(threads, function (value) {
                    var orgPost = threads[value].RootPost.Text;
                    //var orgPoster = threads[value].Actors.results[threads[value].
OwnerIndex].Name;
                    var orgPoster = threads[value].Actors.results[threads[value].RootPost.
AuthorIndex].Name;
                    var post = "<div><strong>" + orgPost + "</strong></div>";
                    post += "<div><i>" + orgPoster + "</i></div><br/>";
                    var replies = threads[value].Replies.results;
                    $.each(replies, function (key) {
                        var rplPost = replies[key].Text;
                        var rplPoster = threads[value].Actors.results[replies[key].
AuthorIndex].Name;
                        post += "<div class='reply'><strong>" + rplPost + "</strong>
                          </div>";
                        post += "<div class='reply'><i>" + rplPoster + "</i></div>";

                    });
                    $("#siteNewsfeed").after(post + "<br/>");
                });
            }
            function onFail(errorObject, errorMessage) {
                $("#errMessage").text("Error: " + errorMessage);
            }
        });
    </script>
    <style>
        .reply {
```

```
                padding-left:15px;
        }
    </style>
</head>
<body>
    <div id="siteNewsfeed"><h2>Site Newsfeed</h2></div>
    <div id="errMessage"></div>
</body>
</html>
```

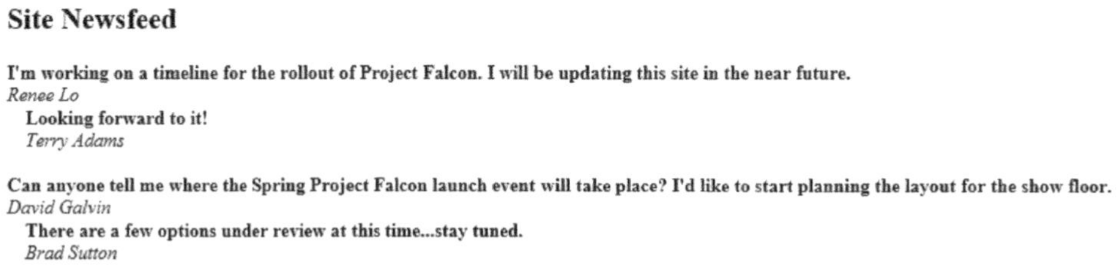

Site Newsfeed

I'm working on a timeline for the rollout of Project Falcon. I will be updating this site in the near future.
Renee Lo
  Looking forward to it!
  Terry Adams

Can anyone tell me where the Spring Project Falcon launch event will take place? I'd like to start planning the layout for the show floor.
David Galvin
  There are a few options under review at this time...stay tuned.
  Brad Sutton

FIGURE 17-24 The site feed is rendered to the HTML page by using REST.

This concludes the examples for retrieving posts from a site feed. You should now be comfortable retrieving posts from any site by using either CSOM with C# or the REST API.

Posting to your personal feed

Now that you are comfortable retrieving posts that already exist, the next logical step is to post to a social feed. You will start by posting to the current user's feed. It is important to remember that you can only post to the current user's feed, because at this time there is no administration-type functionality to post to another's feed. Even with this restriction, there are numerous possibilities that are opened up when you gain the initial knowledge required to perform a post. As with all other examples in this chapter, you will first start with the CSOM and C# approach and then finish with the REST API approach.

If you have not worked through the examples in the section "Retrieving posts from your newsfeed," it is recommended that you do so to gain an understanding of the social objects required to initially access the current user's newsfeed. The *SocialFeedManager* object is used to create posts as well as retrieve them, so this will simplify the first part of creating a post, because you are already familiar with this object. The method that is used to create a post is the aptly named *CreatePost*, which can be used to either create a root post, also known as a new thread, or reply to an existing thread. There two parameters, both of which are required, regardless of whether you want to reply to or create a new thread. The parameters are listed in Table 17-3.

TABLE 17-3 *CreatePost* method parameters

Parameter	Type	Description
targetId	String	Can be one of the following: ■ **Null** Pass *Null* to start a new thread by publishing a root post to the current user's feed. ■ **Site Feed URL** Pass the URL to a site feed for a site to post to it. ■ **Thread ID** Pass an ID to an existing post to reply to it.
creationData	SocialPostCreationData	The contents of the new post, which can be anything from an attachment (such as a video or image) to the actual text that you would like to post

Creating a post via code can be a very simple task when you are only passing text, as a new post is required to do. Listing 17-14 shows the code necessary to create a simple post with some text.

LISTING 17-14 CSOM using C# code for creating a new post

```
// Define properties for the post.
SocialPostCreationData postCreationData = new SocialPostCreationData();
postCreationData.ContentText = "Post via Code";

//Call CreatePost method
feedManager.CreatePost(null, postCreationData);

//Call ExecuteQuery
clientContext.ExecuteQuery();
```

As you can tell, there isn't much to creating a simple post. As with all the other examples in this chapter, you'll need to have *ClientContext* and *SocialFeedManager* objects, but other than that, just four lines of code will create a new post. If you dissect the code sample just shown, you'll notice that the *ContentText* property of the *SocialPostCreationData* object called *postCreationData* is what you pass the text to be included in the post to. One limitation to keep in mind is that this text is limited to 512 characters and is not permitted to have HTML tags. This restriction might seem alarming at first, because if you have spent any reasonable amount of time within the SharePoint Web UI interacting with a social feed, you'll know that links are possible in a post. So how is it that from a coded approach we have this restriction? This is merely a restriction on how links can be passed into a new post. As you have already learned, the text of the post is set by using the *ContentText* property, whereas links, tags, sites, documents, and even users are set within a post by using the *ContentItems* array. Listing 17-15 shows the previous example updated with two new items being included in the post.

```
// Create a link to include in the post.
SocialDataItem linkItem = new SocialDataItem();
linkItem.ItemType = SocialDataItemType.Link;
linkItem.Text = "SharePoint Website";
linkItem.Uri = "http://office.microsoft.com/en-us/sharepoint/";

//Create a person mention to include in the post
SocialDataItem userItem = new SocialDataItem();
userItem.ItemType = SocialDataItemType.User;
userItem.AccountName = "contoso\\terrya";

// Define properties for the post.
SocialPostCreationData postCreationData = new SocialPostCreationData();
postCreationData.ContentText = "Visit the {0}. Look for a post by {1} while you are
there.";
postCreationData.ContentItems = new SocialDataItem[] { linkItem, userItem };
feedManager.CreatePost(null, postCreationData);
clientContext.ExecuteQuery();
```

The first new block of code declares a new *SocialDataItem* object called *linkItem*. The second line in that block sets the *ItemType* to a link, by using the *SocialDataItemType* enumerator. There are, in fact, five different types available within this enumeration:

- User

- Document

- Site

- Tag

- Link

Also, including *ItemType*, there are a total of five usable properties for the *SocialDataItem* object:

- *AccountName*

- *ItemType*

- *TagGuid*

- *Text*

- *Uri*

Not all are necessary; their use depends on what you intend to use the object for. Going back to the last example, you can tell that the *linkItem* has a value set for *ItemType*, *Text*, and *Uri*. The next section in the code declares another object of the same type called *userType*, which has its type set to *User* and only sets a value for the *AccountName* property. Figure 17-25 shows how each post looks within the SharePoint UI on the current user's newsfeed. Note that a hyperlink was created by using the text for the *linkItem* and that the *Uri* is the *href.* Also, notice that even though you only used the *AccountName* property for the *userItem*, it was able to display the display name for the user and that it is also a hyperlink that links to the About page for that user.

Following   Everyone   Mentions   ...

Administrator
Post via Code
About a minute ago   Like   Reply   ...

Administrator
Visit the SharePoint Website. Look for a post by **Terry Adams** while you are there.
3 minutes ago   Like   Reply   ...

SHOW MORE POSTS

FIGURE 17-25 These posts were created by using CSOM and C#.

Posting to your personal feed by using REST is still done through the *social.feed* endpoint. Additionally, you need to add another endpoint to the end of the *social.feed* endpoint: */my/Feed/Post.* This final endpoint can be looked at as equivalent to the *CreatePost* method in the CSOM example. Also, as in the CSOM example, you need to create a *SocialPostCreationData* object. The REST API actually goes a step further and wraps this object within another object called *SocialRestPostCreationData* (note the inclusion of *REST* in the object name). Up to this point in the chapter, we have not discussed in any detail how to formulate a POST to a REST endpoint. You have, however, passed parameters to an endpoint to specify what you would like returned by the endpoint. In essence, the act of passing a parameter to an endpoint holds true for what you do in a POST request, but the parameter metadata is usually a lot more complex and is typically moved from the URI to the request body of the POST request. Listing 17-16 shows the part of the code used to send the same post you did in the final CSOM example, this time by using the REST API. The data property contains the parameter metadata.

LISTING 17-16 REST code extract for creating a new post with rich content

```
$.ajax({
        url: "http://portal.contoso.com/_api/social.feed/my/Feed/Post",
        type: "POST",
        data: JSON.stringify({
                'restCreationData': {
                        '__metadata': {
                                'type': 'SP.Social.SocialRestPostCreationData'
                        },
                        'ID': null,
                        'creationData': {
                                '__metadata': {
                                        'type': 'SP.Social.SocialPostCreationData'
                                },
                                'ContentItems': {
```

```
                                              'results': [
                                                {
                                                    '__metadata': {
                                                            'type': 'SP.Social.
SocialDataItem'
                                                    },
                                                    'ItemType': 4,
                                                    'Text': 'SharePoint Website',
                                                    'Uri': 'http://office.microsoft.com/
en-us/sharepoint/'
                                                },
                                                {
                                                    '__metadata': {
                                                            'type': 'SP.Social.
SocialDataItem'
                                                    },
                                                    'ItemType': 0,
                                                    'AccountName': 'contoso\\terrya',
                                                }
                                                ]
                                        },
                                        'ContentText': 'Visit the {0}. Look for the post by {1}
                                        while you are there.',
                                        'UpdateStatusText': false
                                    }
                                }
                    }),
                    headers: {
                            "accept": "application/json;odata=verbose",
                            "content-type": "application/json;odata=verbose",
                            "X-RequestDigest": formDigestValue
                    },
                    success: function (data) {
                            GetPersonalFeed();
                    },
                    error: function (xhr) {
                            alert("Error:" + xhr.status);
                    }
            });
```

After reviewing this code, you can tell how easy it would be to have a missing quote, colon, or comma that would result in the POST request failing. Besides advising you to be overmeticulous in checking your scripts, we will review a few noteworthy sections of the code so that you can feel comfortable moving forward with creating posts by using this approach. We will be focusing on the data property, starting with the object called *restCreationData*. This object contains an ID property that is used the same way as the *targetId* is used in the *CreatePost* method using CSOM and C#. The next object is the *creationData* object. This object contains the *ContentText* property and can optionally contain a *ContentItems* property and a few other properties. The structure of the *ContentItems* property should at first appear out of place to you, because it doesn't follow the metadata structure like the other complex properties do. In its place, you should notice that there is a results array. This is required to conform to the use of the *JSON.stringify* method requires the use of the results format when you are dealing with arrays. Inside of the results property you can begin to recognize the familiar metadata attributes again and you have the same two *SocialDataItem* objects from the previous example, with one slight difference being that you are using the numeric value for the *ItemType* enumeration. The remaining code in the listing is typical for a POST to the REST API.

Posting to a site feed

With a good understanding of how posting to your own feed is accomplished, you can extend this capability to posting to a site feed. There really isn't much of a difference between creating a post on the two types of feeds besides the fact that you can only create a root post to your own personal feed, in contrast to the fact that you can create a root post on any site's feed to which you have the correct permissions.

Another difference from the CSOM approach in posting to your personal feed is that you need to now pass the URL to a site newsfeed as the *targetId* when calling the *CreatePost* method of the *SocialFeedManager* object in place of a null. Listing 17-17 shows a code block that will create the same post from the previous section. Note the one modification to the *CreatePost* method that has the path to a site with a feed.

LISTING 17-17 The *CreatePost* method configured for a site feed

```
//Create a link to include in the post.
SocialDataItem linkItem = new SocialDataItem();
linkItem.ItemType = SocialDataItemType.Link;
linkItem.Text = "SharePoint Website";
linkItem.Uri = "http://office.microsoft.com/en-us/sharepoint/";

//Create a person mention to include in the post
SocialDataItem userItem = new SocialDataItem();
userItem.ItemType = SocialDataItemType.User;
userItem.AccountName = "contoso\\terrya";

//Define properties for the post.
SocialPostCreationData postCreationData = new SocialPostCreationData();
postCreationData.ContentText = "Visit the {0}. Look for a post by {1} while you are
there.";
postCreationData.ContentItems = new SocialDataItem[] { linkItem, userItem };
feedManager.CreatePost(feedURL, postCreationData);

clientContext.ExecuteQuery();
```

If you executed this block of code, as shown in Figure 17-26, the same post would be created with the same functionality as the post written to the personal feed.

FIGURE 17-26 This post was created on a site's feed by using CSOM and C#.

The number of differences between using the REST API for posting between each of the feed types is identical to those found in the CSOM approach. First, you of course have to use a different endpoint with the inclusion of the *social.feed* endpoint. The endpoint used for a site feed is *Actor/Feed/Post*. Inline it would look like this: *http://<site>/_api/social.feed/actor/feed/post*.

Using this endpoint, you need to pass the site URL by using an @ alias with the actor parameter, like this: *http://<site>/_api/social.feed/actor(item=@v)/feed/post?@v='http://<site>/ newsfeed.aspx'*.

Other than this simple update, you can execute the same code from the previous REST example. Figure 17-27 illustrates a site's newsfeed with two visible posts, one created with the REST example and the other with the CSOM using C# example.

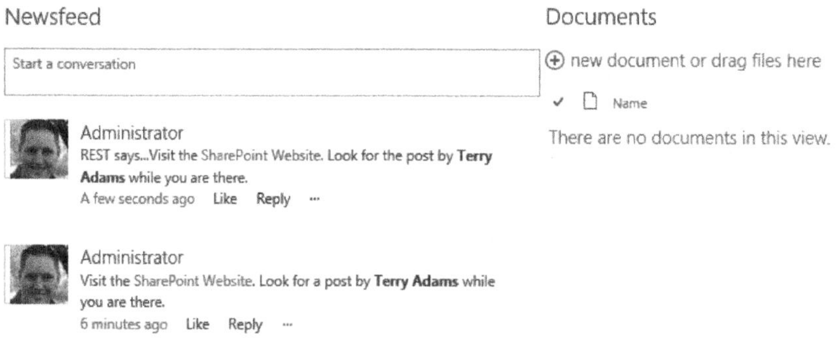

Newsfeed

Start a conversation

Administrator
REST says...Visit the SharePoint Website. Look for the post by **Terry Adams** while you are there.
A few seconds ago   Like   Reply   ...

Administrator
Visit the SharePoint Website. Look for a post by **Terry Adams** while you are there.
6 minutes ago   Like   Reply   ...

Documents

⊕ new document or drag files here

✓ ☐ Name

There are no documents in this view.

FIGURE 17-27 This post is created on a site's feed by using the REST API.

Understanding following within SharePoint 2013

The ability to follow someone or something in the social space is an expected behavior for any collaboration tool that expects to play in this space. The intent of following is to enable users to only act once when they find someone or something that they would like to be notified about when it undergoes changes. This supports the push notification model, in which users don't have to hunt around, losing precious time looking for what interests them or pertains to their daily workload. In SharePoint 2013, you can follow just about anything. To be more precise, the entities that you can follow are:

- People

- Sites

- Documents

- Tags

In the context of SharePoint, when a user choses to follow a person, for example, that person's activities, which include posts, post replies, and other social activities, will start to show up in that user's newsfeed. Also, by visiting a user's newsfeed you can view an aggregate count of each entity type that user is following, as shown in Figure 17-28.

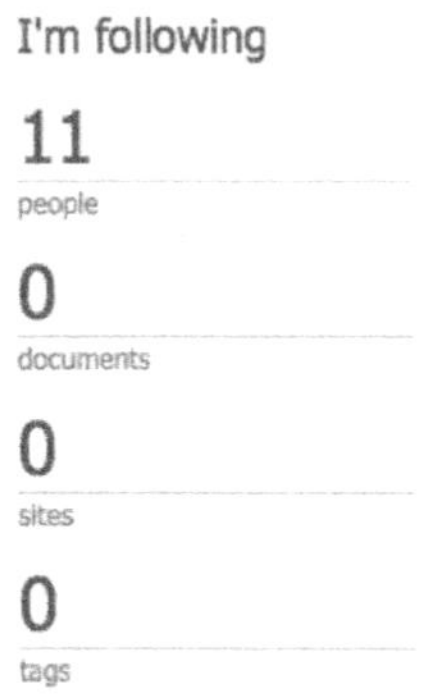

I'm following

11
people

0
documents

0
sites

0
tags

FIGURE 17-28 A user's following summary is displayed on their newsfeed page.

In the following section you will work through an example of following people by using CSOM and REST. The functionality for following content uses primarily the same objects as following people, so we will not be covering following content in any detail.

Programming for following either people or content starts with the *SocialFollowingManager* object for CSOM or the *Social.Following* endpoint for REST. By using this object, you can do any of the following:

- Have the current user start or stop following someone or an item

- Get whether the current user is following someone or an item

- Get all documents, sites, tags, and people the current user is following

- Get the count for all documents, sites, tags, and people the current user is following

- Get the people who are following the current user

- Get the people whom the current user might want to follow

- Get the URL for the site that lists the current user's followed documents or sites

Though this usage is not as common, it is important to note that the *PeopleManager* object that you used in the "Retrieving user profile properties" section can be used to access additional functionality around following people that is not available via the *SocialFollowingManager* object.

Following people

The act of following people is probably the task that users are most acquainted with due to its prevalence in most social media systems. As such, we will focus this example on following people to help acclimate you to coding tasks around following within SharePoint 2013. The exercise you will work through is that of discovering people who are following you that you are not yet following, and then adding yourself as one of their new followers.

Figure 17-29 shows a list of the current user's followers, with a star next to each that is not being followed by the current user. By the end of this example, there should be no stars, and the count for I'm Following and My Followers should both equal 4.

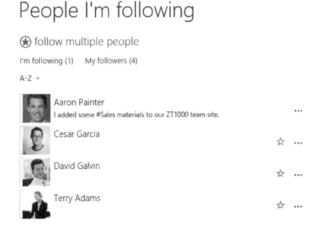

FIGURE 17-29 Four people are following the current user.

To start, create a new Web Form for your Visual Studio project named FollowingPeopleCSOM.aspx, as shown in Figure 17-30.

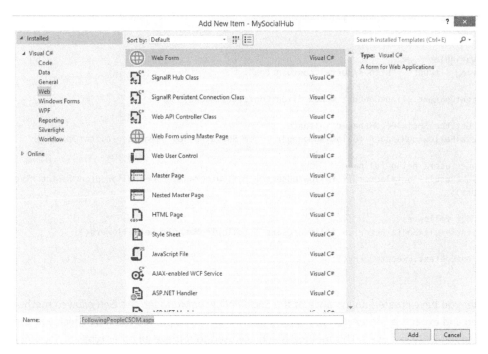

FIGURE 17-30 Add a new Web Form called FollowingPeopleCSOM.aspx.

The same namespaces that you have used throughout this chapter are still those needed to code following functionality; they are:

- *Microsoft.SharePoint.Client*

- *Microsoft.SharePoint.Client.Social*

At this point, you can start using the *SocialFollowingManager* object along with the methods to access your current followers and those users that you are also following. Listing 17-18 shows the code used to get back both your followers and those that you are followed by into two separate lists.

LISTING 17-18 Retrieving following and followed users

```
//Variables
string siteURL = "http://portal.contoso.com";

ClientContext clientContext = new ClientContext(siteURL);

// Get the SocialFeedManager instance.
SocialFollowingManager followingManager = new SocialFollowingManager(clientContext);

// Get users being followed
ClientResult<SocialActor[]> followedUsers = followingManager.GetFollowed(SocialActorTypes.
Users);

// Get followers
ClientResult<SocialActor[]> followerUsers = followingManager.GetFollowers();

clientContext.ExecuteQuery();
```

After you have created an instance of the *SocialFollowingManager*, the *GetFollowed* method is invoked and expects a *SocialActorType* enumerator for members passed within it, which you use to filter the results to just users. This method is actually used to retrieve all other types of *SocialActors* objects that the current user is also following. A full list of each of the members for the *SocialActorTypes* enumeration is found in Table 17-4.

TABLE 17-4 *SocialActorTypes* enumeration

Name	Value	Description
All	15	All actor types are included.
None	0	None of the actor types are included.
Users	1	Results are filtered to only users.
Documents	2	Results are filtered to only documents.
Sites	3	Results are filtered to only sites.
Tags	8	Results are filtered to only tags.
ExcludedContentWithoutFeeds	268435456	Results are filtered to only sites that have a site feed.

Both the *GetFollowed* and *GetFollowers* methods return a *clientResult<SocialActor[]>* object, which contains a list of each of the actors that current user is following. If in either case a following is not present, then there will be zero items in the *clientResult<SocialActor[]>* object's value. For this example, you should have a count of 1 for the *followedUsers* object and a count of 4 for the *followerUsers* object, which is illustrated in the watch panel shown in Figure 17-31.

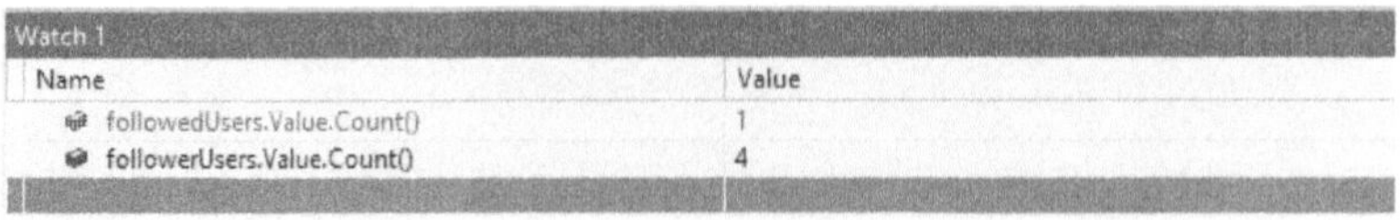

Watch 1	
Name	Value
followedUsers.Value.Count()	1
followerUsers.Value.Count()	4

FIGURE 17-31 The watch panel shows counts for following users and followers.

With this data, you can simply iterate through each one of your followers and determine if they are in the list of users that you are following, if not, you will start following them by using the *Follow* method. This can be done with the code found in Listing 17-19.

LISTING 17-19 Following users by using the *Follow* method

```
//iterate through each follower and determine if already following user
foreach (SocialActor user in followerUsers.Value)
{
        var userFound = followedUsers.Value.SingleOrDefault(u => u.AccountName ==
          user.AccountName);
        if (userFound == null)
        {
                //if not already following user, start following user
                followingManager.Follow(new SocialActorInfo()
                {
                        AccountName = user.AccountName,
                        ActorType = user.ActorType
                });
        }
}
clientContext.ExecuteQuery();
```

The *Follow* method expects a *SocialActorInfo* object as shown in the previous listing, so you need to map the attributes of the current *SocialActor* object to a new *SocialActorInfo* object that you can pass to the *Follow* method. After executing the code in this example, you can tell that you are now following each of the users that is following you, as shown in Figure 17-32.

FIGURE 17-32 The number of people in the I'm Following count now matches the number of those who are followers.

You can use REST to accomplish the same task of adding followers by using the *Social.Following* endpoint in addition to other endpoints to access who is being followed and your followers, and then another to start following others. To start, create a new HTML page similar to the one shown in Figure 17-33.

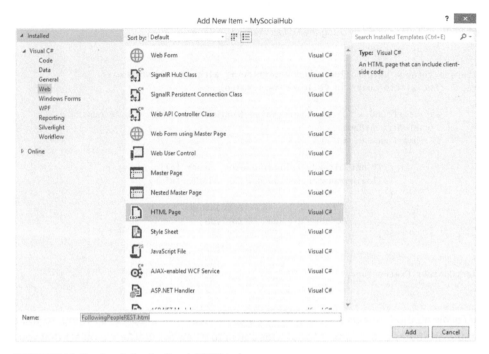

FIGURE 17-33 Create a FollowingPeopleREST.html page.

Next you can retrieve your current followers with a GET request to *http://<siteURL>/_api/ social.following/my/Followers*. To retrieve those that you are following, you need to issue a GET request to *http://<siteURL>/_api/social.following/my/Followed(1)*. Notice that you are passing a value of 1 to the *Followed* endpoint. Looking back at Table 17-4, you can tell that this is the value for the enumeration member named *User* in the *SocialActorTypes* enumeration. The only remaining endpoint needed to complete the example is *http://<siteURL>/_api/social.following/my/follow*. The *follow* endpoint, like the *Follow* method in the CSOM example, expects a *SocialActorInfo* object to be passed to it. This can be accomplished either within the URL itself or within the request body. By using the code in Listing 17-20 you can accomplish the same functionality you did in the CSOM example.

LISTING 17-20 REST code for following users who are following the user

```
window.ContosoREST = window.ContosoREST || {};

ContosoREST.FollowingPeople = {
        //variables
        EndpointURL: "http://portal.contoso.com/_api/social.following",
        FormsDigest: "",

        GetFormsDigest: function(){
                // Get form digest value
                $.ajax({
                        async: false,
                        url: "http://portal.contoso.com/_api/contextinfo",
                        type: "POST",
                        headers: {
                                "Accept": "application/json;odata=verbose"
                        },
                        success: function (contextInfo) {
                                ContosoREST.FollowingPeople.FormsDigest = contextInfo.d
.GetContextWebInformation.FormDigestValue;
                        },
                        error: function (xhr, ajaxOptions, thrownError) {
                                alert("Error:" + thrownError);
                        }
                });

        },
        GetFollowers: function () {
                var followers;
                $.ajax({
                        async: false,
                        type: "GET",
                        url: this.EndpointURL + "/my/followers",
                        headers: {
                                "accept": "application/json;odata=verbose"
                        },
                        success: function(data){
                                followers = data.d.Followers.results;
                        },
                        error: function (xhr, ajaxOptions, thrownError) {
                                alert("Error:" + thrownError);
                        }
                });
                return followers;
        },

        GetFollowed: function () {
                var followed;
                $.ajax({
                        async: false,
                        type: "GET",
                        url: this.EndpointURL + "/my/followed(1)",
                        headers: {
```

```
                                    "accept": "application/json;odata=verbose"
                            },
                            success: function(data){
                                    followed = data.d.Followed.results;
                            },
                            error: function (xhr, ajaxOptions, thrownError) {
                                    alert("Error:" + thrownError);
                            }
                    });
                    return followed;
            },

            Follow: function (accountName) {
                    $.ajax({
                            type: "POST",
                            url: this.EndpointURL + "/my/follow(ActorType=0,AccountName=@v,
                              Id=null)?@v='" + accountName + "'",
                            headers: {
                                    "accept": "application/json;odata=verbose",
                                    "X-RequestDigest": this.FormsDigest
                            },
                            error: function (xhr, ajaxOptions, thrownError) {
                                    alert("Error:" + thrownError);
                            }
                    });
            },

            GetUserByAccountName: function(key, results) {
                    var item;
                    $.grep(results, function (e) {
                            if (e.AccountName === key)
                                    item = e;
                    });

            return item;
            },

    };

    $().ready(function () {

            //Get followers and those user is following
            var followers = ContosoREST.FollowingPeople.GetFollowers();
            var following = ContosoREST.FollowingPeople.GetFollowed();

            //Get FormsDigest, so Follows can be performed
            ContosoREST.FollowingPeople.GetFormsDigest();

            //Iterate through followers
            $.each(followers, function (value,key) {
                    var userFound = ContosoREST.FollowingPeople.GetUserByAccountName(key.
    AccountName, following);
                    if (userFound == null) {
                            //Add new user to those user is following
```

```
                ContosoREST.FollowingPeople.Follow(key.AccountName);
            }
        });
    });
```

The pattern used in the previous listing for following a new person is the singleton pattern; to learn more about this pattern and others, see Chapter 5. The final section of code iterates through each of the followers and determines if they exist within the following list; if not, the *AccountName* is sent to the custom *Follow* method, which sends a POST to the *follow* endpoint and passes inline the user's account name, using an @ alias for any users who need to start being followed.

Understanding Yammer

Yammer is a social tool that allows organizations to have private social networks where their employees can connect, communicate, collaborate, and share information with one another at the organizational or group level. It can be used as a standalone application or can be integrated with any of the many applications that already exist for other purposes. The simplified hierarchy found within Yammer starts with a top-level object called a *Network*. This usually represents an organization. The next level down can either be users or groups. Groups allow conversations to be organized so that users who are not a part of the group aren't flooded with its communications. A Yammer network can be accessed by logging into Yammer by using the Yammer website or any of the mobile or desktop-based applications.

Understanding how Yammer can work with SharePoint

SharePoint is a great example of an application that can benefit from integration with Yammer for an enhanced social experience. Yammer integration was very prevalent with SharePoint 2010 because of the social shortcomings of SharePoint 2010. An advantage of being able to integrate with Yammer even with SharePoint 2013, which has a rich social experience, is Yammer's ability to be a standalone tool and at the same time have the ability to integrate with so many other applications, both mobile and web based. Because of this, Yammer is sometimes chosen as the primary social tool for an organization. As a result, the organization can choose to integrate SharePoint 2013 and Yammer so that Yammer's feed ability replaces that of the SharePoint 2013 out-of-the-box functionality and SharePoint can continue to be the primary content hub. Because of this, and because future deeper integration between these two technologies is likely, it is wise to begin to understand and use Yammer and also become acquainted with its APIs.

Retrieving followers and followings from Yammer

In the same way you learned how to access followers and those that you are following within SharePoint 2013, you can likewise access the same type of entities within Yammer.

In order to code against the Yammer APIs, you must have an account and a registered application, to name a couple of prerequisites. You can visit the Yammer developer site at *https://developer. yammer.com/connect* to learn about the different ways to authenticate to and make API requests to the Yammer platform. The quickest way to start making API requests is to create a test access token that can be passed inline or within the request body when accessing any REST endpoints. Instructions on how to do so can be found at *https://developer.yammer.com/authentication/#a-testtoken*. For the example that retrieves your followers and those you are following, it will be assumed that you have a test access token available.

The Yammer API that you will work with is the REST API. A sampling of the REST endpoints available can be found at *https://developer.yammer.com/restapi/*. It is also important to note that the list found at this URL is not exhaustive in identifying all available endpoints. For example, the two endpoints that you will use to access your followers and those you are following are not referenced on the REST API page.

To retrieve the list of users that you are following, make a GET request to *https://www.yammer. com/api/v1/users/following/<YourYammerUserID>.json*. You will need to know your Yammer ID in order to perform the GET request. If you are uncertain of what your ID is, you can access *https://www. yammer.com/api/v1/users/current.json* from any browser, passing inline the test access token as the value of a query string parameter called *access_token*. A sampling of what is returned is shown here:

```
{"show_ask_for_photo":false,"id":0000000000,"expertise":null,"mugshot_url":"https://mug0.
assets-yammer.com/mugshot/images/48x48/M2v-Z-000000000","summary":null,"contact":{"im":{"prov
ider":"","username":""},"has_fake_email":false,"email_addresses":[{"address":"aaron.painter@
contoso.com","type":"primary"}],"phone_numbers":[]},"last_name":"Painter","name":"aaronp","kids_
names":null,"network_name":"contoso.com","job_title":"Managing Consultant","url":"https://www.
yammer.com/api/v1/users/000000","settings":{"xdr_proxy":"https://xdrproxy.yammer.com"},"mugshot_
url_template":"
```

Notice that the top line contains an *"id"* property; this is your Yammer ID. With this ID, you can successfully perform a GET request to retrieve your followers. A sampling of what is returned is shown here:

```
{"more_available":false,"users":[{"url":"https://www.yammer.com/api/v1/users/000000","job_
title":" Strategy Consulting Manager","full_name":"BradSutton","stats":{"following":16
5,"updates":161,"followers":39},"state":"active","name":"bradsutton","type":"user","ac
tivated_at":"2012/07/12 18:09:56 +0000","mugshot_url":"https://mug0.assets-yammer.com/
mugshot/images/48x48/000000000","web_url":"https://www.yammer.com/contoso.com/users/
xxxxx","id":000000,"mugshot_url_template":"https://mug0.assets-yammer.com/mugshot/images/{width}
x{height}/0000000000"}
```

The first property returned tells you whether or not there are more followers than those returned by the request. Following this property is the *Users* property, which contains all the followers. There is quite a bit of useful information that will allow an application to have a rich UI, enabling it to easily access the photo for a follower, determine how many followers the user herself has, and even how long the user has had a Yammer account.

The same results are returned when you make a GET request for who you are following, though the endpoint is different. The endpoint for retrieving who you follow is *https://www.yammer.com/api/v1/users/followed_by/<YourYammerUserID>.json*.

To display both listings on an HTML page, along with each user's own count of followers and those they are following, you can use the code found in Listing 17-21. If you are successful, the output should look similar to that shown in Figure 17-34.

LISTING 17-21 REST code for listing a user's followers and those the user is following on Yammer

```
<!DOCTYPE HTML>
<html>
<head>
    <title></title>
        <script src="http://ajax.aspnetcdn.com/ajax/jQuery/jquery-2.0.0.min.js"></script>
    <script>
        window.MyYammerREST = window.MyYammerREST || {};

        MyYammerREST.Social = {

            AccessToken: "YourTestAccessToken",

            GetFollowers: function (userID) {
                var followers = "";
                $.ajax({
                    async: false,
                    url: "https://www.yammer.com/api/v1/users/following/" + userID +
".json",
                    type: "GET",
                    headers: {
                        "Accept": "application/json;odata=verbose",
                        "Authorization": "Bearer " + this.AccessToken
                    },
                    success: function (data) {
                        var users = data.users;

                        $.each(users, function (value, key) {
                            followers += "<div>" + key.full_name + "</div>" +
                                    "<div>Followers: " + key.stats.followers +
                                    "</div>" +
                                    "<div>Following: " + key.stats.following +
                                    "</div><br/><br/>"
                        });
                    },
                    fail: function (xhr, thrownError) {
                        alert("Error: " + thrownError);
                    }

                });
                return followers;
            },
```

```
            GetFollowing: function (userID) {
                var followedBy = "";
                $.ajax({
                    async: false,
                    url: "https://www.yammer.com/api/v1/users/followed_by/" + userID +
                        ".json",
                    type: "GET",
                    headers: {
                        "Accept": "application/json;odata=verbose",
                        "Authorization": "Bearer " + this.AccessToken
                    },
                    success: function (data) {
                        var users = data.users;

                        $.each(users, function (value, key) {
                            followedBy += "<div>" + key.full_name + "</div>" +
                                        "<div>Followers: " + key.stats.followers +
                                        "</div>" +
                                        "<div>Following: " + key.stats.following +
                                        "</div><br/><br/>"
                        });
                    },
                    fail: function (xhr, thrownError) {
                        alert("Error: " + thrownError);
                    }

                });
                return followedBy;
            }

        }
        $().ready(function () {
            $('#followers').append(MyYammerREST.Social.GetFollowers(YourYammerID));
            $('#following').append(MyYammerREST.Social.GetFollowing(YourYammerID));
        });
    </script>

</head>
<body>
    <div style="float:left;padding:20px;">
        <div><h2>Followers</h2></div><br />
        <div id="followers"></div>
    </div>
    <div style="float:left;padding:20px;">
        <div><h2>Following</h2></div><br />
        <div id="following"></div>
    </div>
</body>
</html>
```

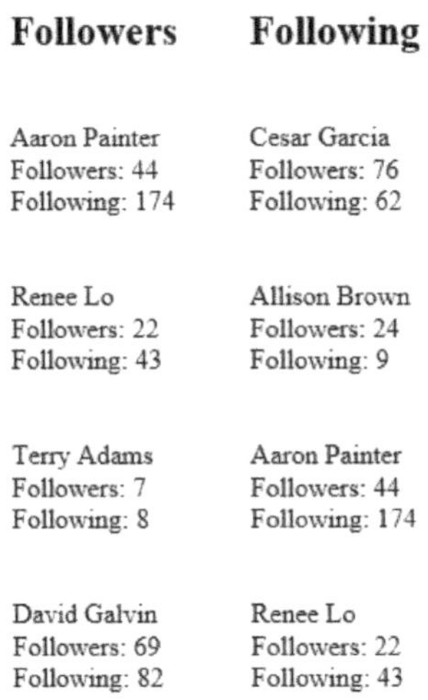

Followers	Following
Aaron Painter Followers: 44 Following: 174	Cesar Garcia Followers: 76 Following: 62
Renee Lo Followers: 22 Following: 43	Allison Brown Followers: 24 Following: 9
Terry Adams Followers: 7 Following: 8	Aaron Painter Followers: 44 Following: 174
David Galvin Followers: 69 Following: 82	Renee Lo Followers: 22 Following: 43

FIGURE 17-34 The output shows Yammer followers and followings for a user.

Working through this simple example should shed light on the potential integrations between Yammer and SharePoint, whether they are through an app for SharePoint or something as simple as a Content Editor Web Part. You can create extensive integrations, in which Yammer takes the place of the SharePoint newsfeed, or less extensive solutions, in which you merely surface parts of Yammer within parts of SharePoint.

Summary

This chapter began by examining the new social components found inside SharePoint 2013. We looked at how you can use the numerous APIs to extend or access social data stored within SharePoint. You also worked through many examples that used CSOM with C# and the REST API for getting and creating social content. You learned about the abilities and purpose of social feeds for individuals and sites. Finally, the chapter concluded by examining the art of following inside SharePoint and Yammer and how you can retrieve a list of those users you are following in addition to your own followers.

Index

Symbols

: (colon), contains operator for managed
        properties, 511
:: (colons, double), preceding class members, 31
$ (dollar sign)
    jQuery global function alias, 174
    preceding PowerShell variables, 30
.. (dots, double), range operator for managed
        properties, 511
= (equal sign), equal to operator for managed
        properties, 511
(hash sign), preceding DOM elements, 174
<> (left and right angle bracket), not equal to operator
        for managed properties, 511
< (left angle bracket), less than operator for managed
        properties, 511
<= (left angle bracket, equal sign), less than or equal to
        operator for managed properties, 511
- (minus sign), NOT operator for managed
        properties, 512
+ (plus sign), AND operator for managed
        properties, 512
> (right angle bracket), greater than operator for
        managed properties, 511
>= (right angle bracket, equal sign), greater than
        or equal to operator for managed
        properties, 511
[ ] (square brackets), enclosing class names, 31

A

AccessChecker method, BCS, 645
access control list. *See* ACL
Access Services, 14
access tokens, OAuth, 225–226, 232–234, 245–246,
        250–254

access tokens, S2S, 256
ACL (access control list), 216–217, 537–538
.action4 files, 469
action files, 469, 489–491
Active Directory, user authentication using, 10, 214–215
activities
    CompositeTask activity, 492
    custom, creating, 487–491
    DynamicValue activity, 470
    HTTPSend activity, 470
    Loop [n] Times activity, 470
    Loop with Condition activity, 470
    Sequence activity, 479, 482
    SingleTask activity, 492–494
    for workflows, 469
activity feeds, 674, 676. *See also* social feeds
ActivityId filter, BCS, 649
addClass method, jQuery, 176
<AddContentTypeField> element, 114
AdditionalPageHead delegate control, 285
Add-PSSnapin cmdlet, 32, 43, 44
administration, automating with PowerShell, 42–45
AdministrationMetadataCatalog object, 659
Administration Object Model for, 659–661
after events, 379–380
AJAX (Asynchronous JavaScript and XML), 201, 686
AjaxDelta control, 287–288
AllRolesForCurrentUser property, SPSecurableObject
        class, 223
AND operator, managed properties, 512
anonymous functions, JavaScript, 167–168
APIs (application programming interfaces), 61–68
    for apps, 163–165
    CSOM. *See* CSOM API
    REST. *See* REST APIs
    SSOM. *See* SSOM API
app catalog, publishing SharePoint apps to, 153–155

<App> element, 131
.app files, 147
AppIcon.png.config.xml file, 147
AppIcon.png file, 147
app identifier, 235
app launcher, 126
application pages, 298–302
   base classes for, 299
   creating, 299–301
   location of, 298
   navigation support for, 302
   securing, 301–302
   template files for, 87
application pool identity, 219
application pools, 268
application programming interfaces. *See* APIs
   (application programming interfaces)
ApplyChanges method, 335
<ApplyElementManifests> element, 114
App Management Service, 14
AppManifest.xml file, 58, 130–132, 147
   <AppPermissionRequest> element, 237, 240
   <AppPermissionRequests> element, 132, 524
   <AppPrincipal> element, 131, 227
   <AutoDeployedWebApplication> element, 247
   editing with visual designer, 132
   elements in, 131
   <RemoteEndpoint> element, 232
   <RemoteWebApplication> element, 247
   <StartPage> element, 229
   start page URL, 132–134, 135
app-only access tokens, 253–254
app-only permissions, 239–240
app parts (client Web Parts), 137–140, 149, 311
<AppPermissionRequest> element, 237, 240
<AppPermissionRequests> element, 132, 524
<AppPrerequisites> element, 132
<AppPrincipal> element, 131, 227
app principals, 242–243
apps. *See* Office Web Apps; Sharepoint apps
appSettings variables, 247
app web, 134–137
AppWebProxy.aspx page, 228
.ascx files, 87
.ashx files, 87
.asmx files, 87
asp:Content control, 271
asp:ContentPlaceHolder control, 271, 284
asp:Label control, 269

ASP.NET, 267–271
   applications, 268
   FBA (forms-based authentication), 10–12,
      214–215
   master pages, 270–271
   user controls, template files for, 87
   web applications using, 9
   web.config file for, 268
   Web Forms, 268–270, 282
      code-behind component, 269
      running, 269–270
      UI component, 268–269
   Web Parts, compared to SharePoint, 310–311
.aspx.cs files, 268
.aspx files, 87, 268
ASPX forms, 651
.aspx.vb files, 268
Assemblies folder, 106
association forms, 498–500
AssociationNavigator method, BCS, 645
Associator method, BCS, 645
asynchronous execution
   with JSOM, 67, 180, 188
   of Web parts, 347–350
Asynchronous JavaScript and XML. *See* AJAX
authentication for apps, 224–234
   access tokens for, 225, 226, 232
   cross-domain library for, 227–230
   external, 225, 232–233. *See also* OAuth
      authentication; S2S authentication
   flow for, 233–234
   internal, 225, 226–232
   SAML tokens for, 225, 233
   web proxy for, 231–232
authentication for BCS, 635–638, 639–644
   claims authentication, 643
   client authentication, 643–644
   Impersonation and Delegation model, 639–640
   Passthrough authentication, 644
   RevertToSelf authentication, 644
   SSS for, 642
   token-based authentication, 643
   Trusted Subsystem model, 639–642
authentication for users, 214–224
   Active Directory for, 10, 214–215
   ASP.NET FBA for, 10–12, 214–215
   challenges with, 120–121
   claims-based security for, 10–11, 214–215
   classic mode for, 10
   configuring in web applications, 215

external systems for, 10, 214–215
impersonating users, 121, 221–222
for SharePoint object access, 222–224
user credentials for, 221
User Information List for, 216
for web applications, 10–12
authoritative pages, 529
authoritative sites. *See* publishing sites
authorization code, OAuth, 245, 254–256
authorization for apps, 234–239
app identifier for, 235
default policy for, 235
permissions, 235–239, 241
authorization for users
ACLs for, 216–217
for application pool identity, 219
escalating privileges, 219, 220–221
groups, 216, 217–219
for SharePoint object access, 222–224
for SHAREPOINT\SYSTEM account, 220–221
users, 216–217
Author managed property, 512
<AutoDeployedWebApplication> element, 247
autohosted apps, 129–130, 150–152, 163–164. *See also* cloud-hosted apps
Azure ACS. *See* Windows Azure ACS

B

badge and reward system, 673
<BaseTypes> element, 442
Batching filter, BCS, 649
BatchingTermination filter, BCS, 649
BCS (Business Connectivity Services), 15, 621–624, 630–639
Administration Object Model for, 659–661
for apps, 668–671
authentication for, 639–644
claims authentication, 643
client authentication, 643–644
models of, 639–642
Passthrough authentication, 639–640, 644
RevertToSelf authentication, 640–642, 644
SSS for, 635–638, 642
token-based authentication, 643
BDC layer for, 631–635
BDC Runtime object models for, 656–659
client cache, 635
Client layer, 623

connectors for, 631
CSOM for, 669
event receivers for, 662–663
External Data Columns, 652
non-programmatic solutions using, 624–628
profile pages, creating, 653
VSTO deployment package for, 627, 639
BCS permission type, 239
BDC (Business Data Connectivity), 14, 622, 631–635
Client Runtime object model, 635, 656–659
managing, 632–634
metadata cache, 632
Metadata Model, 644–645, 664, 668
Model Explorer, 664
permissions for, 634
Server Runtime object model, 635, 656–659
Service Application, 634, 657
throttle settings, 632–634
BdcServiceApplicationProxy object, 657
before events, 379–380
BinarySecurityDescriptorAccessor method, BCS, 645
blogging. *See* social feeds
BPOS (Business Productivity Online Standard Suite), 3
branding for UI, 296–298
BreakRoleInheritance method, SPSecurableObject class, 222
BulkAssociatedIdEnumerator method, BCS, 646
BulkAssociationNavigator method, BCS, 646
BulkIdEnumerator method, BCS, 646
BulkSpecificFinder method, BCS, 646
Business Connectivity Services. *See* BCS
Business Data Connectivity. *See* BDC
Business Data Item Builder Web Part, 653
Business Data Item Web Part, 653
Business Data List Web Part, 652
Business Data Related List Web Part, 653
Business Productivity Online Standard Suite. *See* BPOS

C

C#
cloud-hosted apps using, 125, 163–165
feature receivers using, 84
managed CSOM with, 180–187
REST API with, 206–212
CAL (client access license), 3

CAML (Collaborative Application Markup
  Language), 103–104
  content types, creating, 428–430
  creating content types, 370
  creating document libraries, 372
  querying External Lists, 630
  querying lists, 185, 389–396
  site columns, creating, 428–430
CAS (code access security) policies, 102
catalogs, 617–620
Category attribute, 332
Central Administration, 7–8
  application pages in, template files for, 87
  Configure Diagnostic Logging page, 53
  Farm Configuration Wizard, 13
  Manage Service Applications page, 46, 48
  Services on Server page, 46
ChangedIdEnumerator method, BCS, 645
CheckPermissions method, SPSecurableObject
  class, 223
chrome control, 144–147
claims authentication, 643
claims-based security, 10–11, 214–215
claims mode, for web applications, 215
classic mode, for web applications, 215
client access license. See CAL
ClientContext object, 65, 179
ClientContextRuntime class, 179
ClientId variable, 247
ClientRequestException error, 181
ClientSecret variable, 247
client-side object model. See CSOM (client-side
  object model) API
Client.svc service, 177, 178, 196
<ClientWebPart> element, 138
client Web Parts (app parts), 137–140, 149, 311
closures, JavaScript, 168–169
cloud-hosted apps, 125–126
  app designs using, 163–165
  app principal for, 242
  authentication for, 227–230, 232–233. See
    also OAuth authentication; S2S
    authentication
  autohosted apps, 129–130, 163, 164
  hosting models for, 127–130
  packaging, 150–152
  provider-hosted apps, 127–129, 163, 164, 257,
    263–264
  requirements for, 164–165
cmdlets, PowerShell, 27. See also specific cmdlets

code access security policies. See CAS policies
code-behind component, Web Forms, 269
Collaborative Application Markup
  Language. See CAML
Colleagues, 675. See also following, features for
colon (:), contains operator for managed
  properties, 511
colons, double (::), preceding class members, 31
COM (Component Object Model) objects
  PowerShell scripts accessing, 31
  SharePoint objects using, 76
community portals, 673
Comparison filter, BCS, 649
comparison operators, PowerShell, 28
compatibility levels, 594
Component Object Model objects. See COM objects
CompositeTask activity, 492
configuration database, 6, 9
<Configuration> element, 444, 446
<Configurations> element, 442, 446
Configure Diagnostic Logging page, 53
connectors, 507–508
  BCS connectors, 631
  .NET Assembly Connectors, 534–539, 663–668
content aggregation, 591, 607–616
  CQWP (Content Query Web Part), 608–611
  CSWP (Content Search Web Part), 608–611
  display templates, 611–616
ContentClass managed property, 513
Content control, 271, 289
content databases, 8–10, 74, 274–275
  adding content types to, 370
  customized pages in, 278
  lists in, 396
  permissions in, 237
  sandbox solutions in, 71
  site customizations in, 24–25
  social feeds in, 676
  SPDataAccess role for, 219
  updating, 398, 402–403, 412–413
Content Organizer, 574–578
content pages, 289–295
  creating, 289
  deploying, 290–292
ContentPlaceHolder control, 271, 284
ContentPlaceHolderID attribute, 289
Content Processing Enrichment Service. See CPES
Content Search Web Part. See CSWP
<ContentTypeBinding> element, 496
<ContentType> element, 107, 370, 430, 569

Content Type Hub, 556, 558
content types, 366–371
   adding site columns to, 369
   creating, 367, 370–371
   custom, creating, 428–433
   for documents, 375–377
   enumerating through, 368–369
   standard, list of, 366–367
content types gallery, 366
content type syndication, 556–559
context objects, CSOM, 178–179
context tokens, OAuth, 244, 246, 250
Contribute site role, 224
<Control> element, 286
controls, 268–269. *See also* specific controls
   delegate controls, 285–286
   registering as safe, 280–282
control templates, 611–615
ConversionInfo class, 581
ConversionItemInfo class, 580
ConversionJob class, 580, 581
ConversionJobInfo class, 580, 581
ConversionJobSettings class, 581
ConversionJobStatus class, 580, 581
correlation ID, 53–54
CPES (Content Processing Enrichment Service), 508, 531–534
CQWP (Content Query Web Part), 608–611
crawling. *See* indexing process
CreateChildControls method, 325, 327–328, 334–336, 348–349
Created managed property, 512
CreatePost method, SocialFeedManager, 704–705, 709
Creator method, BCS, 645
Credential Manager, 644
Critical Path Training (SharePoint Server 2013 Virtual Machine Setup Guide), 13, 124
cross-domain library, 227–230
cross-site publishing, 617–620
CSOM (client-side object model) API, 63–67, 177–187
   accessing BCS data, 669–671
   app authentication, 225, 227, 233, 246, 253, 256
   context objects, 178–179
   creating content types, 371
   creating lists, 354
   JSOM (JavaScript object model), 65, 67, 164, 177, 188–195
      error handling, 190–191

      manipulating items, 192–195
      returning collections, 188–190
   Managed object model, 64–65, 164–165, 177, 180–187
      error handling, 181–184
      manipulating document libraries, 186–187
      manipulating items, 184–186
      returning collections, 180–181
   Mobile object model, 64
   people, following, 711–715
   personal feeds, posting to, 704–707
   personal feeds, retrieving, 689–695
   querying External Lists, 630
   searches using, 526–528
   Silverlight object model, 63–64
   site feeds, posting to, 709
   site feeds, retrieving, 699–702
   user profile properties, retrieving, 677–683
   workflow services with, 497–498
CSOM files, templates for, 87
CSS files, templates for, 87
css method, jQuery, 176
.csv files
   importing term sets and terms from, 545
   lists exported to, 588
CSWP (Content Search Web Part), 523, 608–611
{CurrentDisplayLanguage} token, 516
{CurrentDisplayLCID} token, 516
<CustomAction> element, 141, 302, 581
custom actions. *See* UI custom actions
CustomDocumentProperties, in display templates, 614–615
custom forms, in workflows, 498–502
   association forms, 498–500
   initiation forms, 500–502
   task forms. *See* tasks, in workflows
customized pages, 278–282
CustomizedPageStatus property, 279
custom libraries, JavaScript, 170–173
<CustomUpgradeAction> element, 98

D

.dacpac files, 152
DatabaseBackedMetadataCatalog object, 657
databases. *See* configuration database; content databases
database server, 36, 39–40
DataContext class, 398

<data> element, 316
Data Tier Application package, 151, 152
data types, JavaScript, 166
debugging, 52–55
    deactivating Web Parts after, 318–319
    Developer Dashboard, 54–61
    PowerShell scripts, 30
    tools for, 52
    ULS logs, 53–54
    web.config file settings for, 274
    Windows event logs, 53–54
DefaultMasterPage module element, 442
delegate controls, 285–286
DeletedIdEnumerator method, BCS, 645
Deleter method, BCS, 645, 659
DeltaManager object, 287
Deploy command, for projects, 78
Deployment service, for workflows, 497
Design Manager
    creating custom master pages, 296
    creating page layouts, 597
Design site role, 224
Developer Dashboard, 54–61
Developer Tools. *See* SharePoint Developer Tools
development environment, 35, 36–41
    configuring, 40–41
    hardware requirements, 38–39
    installing with PowerShell scripts, 42
    server types for, 36–38
    similarity to production environment, 40–41
    software requirements, 38–40
development farms, 7
device channel panels, 603–604
device channels, 591, 600–604
    customizing content based on, 603–604
    determining from user agent, 600–601
    properties of, 601
    redirecting to master pages, 602–603
DFWP (Data Form Web Part), 651
DIP (Document Information Panel), 656
Disassociator method, BCS, 645
discussion forums, 673
display templates, 611–616
    control templates, 611–615
    CustomDocumentProperties in, 614–615
    item templates, 611–612, 615–616
    JavaScript in, 615
DocumentIDProvider class, 564
Document ID providers, 564–567
Document IDs, 563–567

document libraries, 186, 371–379
    content types for, 375–377
    creating, 21–23, 275–276, 372
    customizing, 22–23
    Document IDs for documents in, 563–567
    document templates for, 373–375
    folders in, 378–379
document services, 559–583
    Content Organizer, 574–578
    Document IDs, 563–567
    Document Sets, 567–574
        activating, 567
        characteristics of, 567
        creating, 568–574
    records management, 584–589
        archives, site collection for, 586
        eDiscovery, 586–589
        in-place records management, 584–585
    versioning, 559–562
    Word Automation Services, 578–583
Document Sets, 567–574
    activating, 567
    characteristics of, 567
    creating, 568–574
DoCustomSearchBeforeDefaultSearch() method,
        DocumentIdProvider class, 565
DoesUserHavePermissions method,
        SPSecurableObject class, 223
dollar sign ($)
    jQuery global function alias, 174
    preceding PowerShell variables, 30
domain controller, 36
DOM elements
    binding to events, 176–177
    manipulating, 175–176
    selecting, 174–175
dots, double (..), range operator for managed
        properties, 511
.dwp files, 313
DynamicMasterPageFile attribute, Page
        directive, 299
dynamic reordering, 529
DynamicValue activity, 470

E

ECB (Edit Control Block) menu, 140, 358, 372
ECM (Enterprise Content Management), 541
    document services, 559–583

Content Organizer, 574–578
Document IDs, 563–567
Document Sets, 567–574
records management, 584–589
versioning, 559–562
Word Automation Services, 578–583
Managed Metadata Service Application, 541–559
content type syndication, 556–559
custom solution for term store, 545–556
term groups, 542–543
term sets, 543–544
term store, 541–545
ECT (External Content Type), 622, 623
in apps, 668
BDC Metadata Model for, 644–645
connection to External System, 625
creating, 624–626, 644–650
event receivers for, 662–663
exporting to XML, 626
filters for, 649–650
.NET Assembly Connector for, 663–668
Office 2013 using, 655–656
operations for, 626, 645–647
relationships between, 648–649
saving, 626
searches using, 534
eDiscovery, 586–589
Edit Control Block menu. See ECB (Edit Control Block) menu
edit mode panels, 599
Editor Parts, 333–336
EffectiveBasePermissions property, SPSecurableObject class, 223
<ElementManifest> element, 96
<Elements> element, 107, 286, 293, 302
elements.xml file, 96
for application page navigation, 302
for client Web Parts, 138–139
for custom lists, 433–435
for custom site columns, 422, 424, 428
for site templates, 458
for Web Parts, 314, 316–317, 320–321
for web templates, 451–452, 455, 457
EnsureChildControls method, 336
Enterprise Content Management. See ECM (Enterprise Content Management)
Enterprise Search. See search capabilities
entity classes, 396–400
Entity Design Surface, 664
-eq (equal to) operator, PowerShell, 28

equal sign (=), equal to operator for managed properties, 511
equal to (-eq) operator, PowerShell, 28
error handling
JSOM, 190–191
Managed object model, 181–184
error messages, 53–54. See also debugging
ETags, 205
event handling
after events, 379–380, 388–389
before events, 379–380, 387
event receivers for, 380–383, 662–663
feature receivers for, 84–86, 98–101, 344
jQuery, 176–177
life cycle events for apps, 158–162
naming events, 380
site provisioning events, 461–463
synchronization modes for, 380
for Web Part rendering, 325–327
event receivers, 380–383, 662–663. See also feature receivers
Excel Services Application, 14
ExceptionHandlingScope object, 183
exchange objects, 589
ExecuteQueryAsync method, ClientContextRuntime class, 67, 180
ExecuteQuery method, ClientContextRuntime class, 67, 180, 184
Execution Manager, 104
External Content Type. See ECT
External Data
BDC Runtime object models for, 656–659
types of, 622–624
External Data Columns, 622, 652
External Data Web Parts, 622–623, 652–653
External Lists, 622–623
accessing programmatically, 629–630
creating, 627–628
event receivers for, 662–663
forms from, creating, 651
limitations of, 628–630
synchronizing to Outlook, 655
External System, 622
connecting to, 625
searching, 654

F

Farm Configuration Wizard, 13
farm-scoped features, 80

farm solutions, 71, 76–102
    debugging, 77, 92–94
    deploying, 89–94, 121
    deploying content pages in, 290–291
    features for
        adding, 79–84
        feature receivers for, 84–86, 98–101
        lists, 81–84
        scope of, 80
        version number of, 95–96
    packaging, 89–90
    project for, creating, 77–79
    requirements for, 72
    security for, 121
    template files for, 86–89
    upgrading, 60
        features, 94–102
        to new SharePoint version, 120, 121
    Web Parts in, 313–317
    Workflow Manager farm, 468
FAST Query Language. *See* FQL
FBA (forms-based authentication), 10–12
<Feature> element, 96
feature receivers, 84–86, 98–101, 344. *See*
        also event receivers
<FeatureSiteTemplateAssociation> element, 448
Features node, for projects, 78–79
feature stapling, 448–450
feature.xml file, 96
field controls, 406, 410–420
    class for, 412–414
    for multicolumn values, 415–417
    in page layouts, 595–596
    rendering template for, 410–411
Field object, 65
<FieldType> element, 409, 417
field types, custom, 405–428
    classes for, 407–409
    creating, 405–408
    custom properties for, 417–420
    deploying, 406, 409–410
    field controls for, 406, 410–420
    JSLink property for, 420–428
    limitations of, 406
    for multicolumn values, 415–417
    validation for, 408, 427
<File> element, 293, 317, 320, 321
FileExtension managed property, 512
file formats, conversions between. *See* Word
        Automation Services

FileReader object, 373
files and folders
    accessing with SSOM, 275–277
    in document libraries, 378–379
    mapped folders, 87
    in sites, 74
Files collection object, 373
$filter operator, OData, 199–200
filters, for ECTs, 649–650
Finder method, BCS, 645–647, 658
FirstUniqueAncestorSecurableObject property,
        SPSecurableObject class, 223
FixedFormatSettings class, 581
flowchart workflow, 478
folders. *See* files and folders
following, features for, 675, 710–720
    entities that can be followed, 710–711
    people, following, 711–720
    Yammer, 720–724
foreach loops, PowerShell, 30
format handlers, 508
forms
    custom forms for workflows, 498–502
    InfoPath forms, 651
forms-based authentication. *See* FBA
FQL (FAST Query Language), 510
Full Control site role, 224
full-trust configuration, 257
    in prior SharePoint versions, 103
    uncustomized pages supported for, 278

G

-ge (greater than or equal) operator, PowerShell, 28
GenerateDocumentId() method,
        DocumentIdProvider class, 564
GenericInvoker method, BCS, 645
GetAccessToken method, TokenHelper class, 251
GetAppOnlyAccessToken method, TokenHelper
        class, 253
GetAuthorizationUrl method, TokenHelper class, 254
GetClientContextWithContextToken method,
        TokenHelper class, 249
GetContextTokenFromRequest method, TokenHelper
        class, 249
GetDocumentUrlsById() method,
        DocumentIdProvider class, 564
GetFeedFor method, SocialFeedManager, 699
GetFeed method, SocialFeedManager, 691–692, 693

GetFollowed method, SocialFollowingManager, 714
GetFollowers method, SocialFollowingManager, 714
GetFullThread method, SocialFeedManager, 693
getJSON method, jQuery, 201
Get-Process cmdlet, 27
GetS2SAccessTokenWithWindowsIdentity method,
    TokenHelper class, 263
GetSampleDocumentIdText() method,
    DocumentIdProvider class, 565
Get-SPSite cmdlet, 33
Get-SPSolution cmdlet, 45
Get-SPWebApplication cmdlet, 32
Get-SPWebTemplate cmdlet, 592–594
GetUserEffectivePermissionInfo method,
    SPSecurableObject class, 223
GetUserEffectivePermissions method,
    SPSecurableObject class, 223
ghosted pages. See uncustomized pages
global funciton, jQuery, 174
GLOBAL site definition, 442–443, 449, 454
greater than (-gt) operator, PowerShell, 28
greater than or equal (-ge) operator, PowerShell, 28
groups
    for authorization, 216, 217–219
    proxy groups, 47–48
    term groups, 542–543
-gt (greater than) operator, PowerShell, 28

H

hardware requirements, 38–39
hash sign (#), preceding DOM elements, 174
HasUniqueRoleAssignment property,
    SPSecurableObject class, 223
hide method, jQuery, 176
high-trust configuration, 257
history of SharePoint, 1, 2–4
HNSC (host-named site collection), 18–19
hosting realm. See hosting tenancy
hosting tenancy, 122–123, 235
host-named site collection. See HNSC
{HostTitle} token, 145
{HostUrl} token, 143
host web feature, 150
host web permission type, 239
"How to Create a Page Layout in SharePoint
    2013", 597
html() method, jQuery, 176
HttpModule object, 9

HTTP requests
    IIS handling, 5, 8
    MDS for, 287
    REST APIs using, 67–68
HTTPSend activity, 470

I

IdEnumerator method, BCS, 645
IFilters, 508
IIS (Internet Information Services), 5, 8
    ASP.NET applications in, 268
    SharePoint Web Applications in, 271–272
    virtual directories in, 268, 274–275
    web applications, 271
images, templates for, 87
impersonating users, 221–222, 639–640
Impersonation and Delegation model, 639–640
indexing process, 507–508
InfoPath forms, 651
initiation forms, 500–502
in-place records management, 584–585
Input filter, BCS, 649
InputOutput filter, BCS, 649
installation scopes, for SharePoint apps, 124–125
installing SharePoint apps, 155–157, 158
Install-SPSolution cmdlet, 44
Instance service, for workflows, 497
Integrated Scripting Environment,
    PowerShell. See ISE, PowerShell
Internet Information Services. See IIS
InvalidQueryExpressionException error, 181
IsCompliant property, 288
IsDocument managed property, 512
ISE (Integrated Scripting Environment),
    PowerShell, 30–31, 42
{ItemId} token, 143
items in sites, 74
    CRUD operations on
        in C#, with CSOM, 184–187
        in C#, with REST API, 207–212
        in JavaScript, with CSOM, 192–195
        in JavaScript, with REST API, 201–206
    returning collections of, 180–181
item templates, 611–612, 615–616
{ItemURL} token, 143
IWebPartField contract, 340
IWebPartParameters contract, 340
IWebPartRow contract, 340
IWebPartTable contract, 340

J

JavaScript, 165–173
  closures, 168–169
  for cloud-hosted apps, 164–165
  custom libraries, 170–173
  data types, 166
  in display templates, 615
  functions, 167–168
  jQuery library, 173–177
  namespaces, 165
  prototypes, 169–170
  REST API with, 200–206
  for SharePoint-hosted apps, 163–164
  strict, 166–167
  variables, 166–167
JavaScript object model. See JSOM
jQuery, 173–177
  DOM elements
    binding to events, 176–177
    manipulating, 175–176
    selecting, 174–175
  event handling, 176–177
  global function, 174
  methods, 175–176
  referencing in apps, 174
jQuery.ajax method, 201
JSLink property, SPField class, 420–428
JSOM (JavaScript object model), 65–67, 188–195
  error handling, 190–191
  libraries for, 177
  manipulating items, 192–195
  returning collections, 188–190
  for SharePoint-hosted apps, 164
  workflow services with, 497–498
JWT (JSON Web Token) standard, 252
.jz files, 87

K

KeywordQuery object, 526
KQL (Keyword Query Language), 510–513
  in link queries, 513–514
  managed properties for, 511–513

L

Label control, 269
LastId filter, BCS, 649

LastModifiedTime managed property, 512
LastName managed property, 513
layout pages. See application pages
_layouts directory, 298
LayoutsPageBase class, 299
left and right angle bracket (<>), not equal to operator for managed properties, 511
left angle bracket, equal sign (<=), less than or equal to operator for managed properties, 511
left angle bracket (<), less than operator for managed properties, 511
-le (less than or equal) operator, PowerShell, 28
less than (-lt) operator, PowerShell, 28
less than or equal (-le) operator, PowerShell, 28
LFWP (List Form Web Part), 651
libraries, 74
  custom, JavaScript, 170–173
  document libraries, 186, 371–379
    content types for, 375–377
    creating, 275–276, 372
    document templates for, 373–375
    folders in, 378–379
  versioning of, 559–562
licenses for SharePoint Server, 3
life cycle events for apps, 158–162
-like operator, PowerShell, 28
Limited Access site role, 224
Limit filter, BCS, 649, 650
link queries, 513–514
LinkTitle field, lists, 358
LinkTitleNoMenu field, lists, 358
LINQ to SharePoint, 396–404
  adding items to lists, 402–404
  deleting items from lists, 402–404
  entity classes for, 396–400
  querying lists, 401–402
  updating items in lists, 402–404
listdata.svc web service, 196
{ListId} token, 143
<ListInstance> element, 354
ListItem object, 65
{ListItem} tokens, 517
List object, 65
list permission type, 239
lists, 74
  adding items, with LINQ, 402–404
  adding to solutions, 81–84
  configuring
    in JavaScript, with CSOM, 356
    in JavaScript, with REST API, 356

in JavaScript, with SSOM, 356
creating, 21–23, 353–356
CRUD operations on
  in C#, with CSOM, 184–187
  in C#, with REST API, 207–212
  in JavaScript, with CSOM, 192–195, 354–355
  in JavaScript, with REST API, 201–206, 354–355
  in JavaScript, with SSOM, 354–355
custom, creating, 433–439
customizing, 22–23
deleting items, with LINQ, 402–404
document libraries, 371–379
  content types for, 375–377
  creating, 372
  document templates for, 373–375
  folders in, 378–379
in eDiscovery sets, 588
External Lists, 622, 623
  accessing programmatically, 629–630
  creating, 627–628
  event receivers for, 662–663
  forms for, 651
  limitations of, 628–630
  synchronizing to Outlook, 655
fields in, 357–362
  adding, 359–361
  content types for, 366–371
  display name of, 358, 360
  internal name of, 358, 360
  LinkTitle field, 358
  LinkTitleNoMenu field, 358
  lookup fields, 361–362
  modifying, 358–359
  properties of, 360
  site columns as alternatives to, 363–366
  Title field, 358
  types of, 357
querying with CAML, 389–396
  joined lists, 391–392
  multiple lists, 392–394
  throttling queries, 394–396
querying with LINQ, 396–402
relationships in, 361–362
types of, 353–354
updating
  with LINQ, 402–404
  with versioning, 562
versioning of, 559–562
List Settings page, 22

<ListTemplate> element, 436
<ListTemplates> element, 442
{List} tokens, 517
{ListUrlDir} token, 143
Load method, ClientContextRuntime class, 179–180
load method, JavaScript, 188
LoadQuery method, ClientContextRuntime class, 179–180
loadQuery method, JavaScript, 188
logs. *See* debugging
lookup fields, in lists, 361–362
Loop [n] Times activity, 470
Loop with Condition activity, 470
-lt (less than) operator, PowerShell, 28

M

Machine Translation Service, 14
Managed Metadata Service Application. *See* MMS Application
managed navigation, 604–607
  APIs for, 604–605
  namespaces for, 605
  navigational term sets for, 605–607
  TaxonomySiteMapProvider for, 606
Managed object model, 64–65, 164–165, 177, 180–187
  error handling, 181–184
  manipulating document libraries, 186–187
  manipulating items, 184–186
  returning collections, 180–181
managed properties, 509, 511–513
Management Shell, SharePoint 2013, 31
Manage Service Applications page, 46, 48
manifest.xml file, 90
mapped folders, 87
<%@ Master%> directive, 270–271
.master files, 270
MasterPageFile attribute, Page directive, 271, 286
Master Page Gallery, 282
  accessing files in, 594
  deploying files to, 296, 423
  display templates in, 518–520
master pages, 270–271, 282–287, 595–596
  custom, for branding, 296–298
  default master pages, 283–285
  delegate controls in, 285–286
  referencing, 286
  in site collection, 282
MdsCompliantAttribute, 288

MDSFeature folder, 288
MDS (Minimal Download Strategy), 287–289
metadata
    for ECTs, 632
    enhancing with CPES, 508
    managed by MMS. *See* MMS (Managed
        Metadata Service)
<metaData> element, 316
Method Details pane, 664
microblogging. *See* social feeds
microfeed permission type, 239
Microsoft.BusinessData.dll assembly, 656
Microsoft.Office.BusinessApplications.Runtime.dll
    assembly, 656
Microsoft.Office.Server.ActivityFeed namespace, 675
Microsoft.Office.Server.dll assembly, 62
Microsoft.Office.Server.Search.dll assembly, 528
Microsoft.Office.Server.SocialData namespace, 675
Microsoft.Office.Server.Social namespace, 675
Microsoft.Office.Server.UserProfiles namespace, 675
Microsoft.SharePoint.Client.dll assembly, 177
Microsoft.SharePoint.Client.Publishing
    namespace, 605
Microsoft.SharePoint.Client.Publishing.Navigation
    namespace, 605
Microsoft.SharePoint.ClientRuntime.dll
    assembly, 177
Microsoft.SharePoint.Client.Social namespace, 676
Microsoft.SharePoint.Client.Taxonomy
    namespace, 605
Microsoft.SharePoint.Client.UserProfiles
    namespace, 676, 678–679
Microsoft.SharePoint.dll assembly, 62, 74, 106, 656
Microsoft.SharePoint.PowerShell snap-in, 31, 43–44
Microsoft.SharePoint.SubsetProxy.dll assembly, 106
Microsoft.SharePoint.UserCode.dll assembly, 106
Minimal Download Strategy. *See* MDS
minimal.master file, 283
minus sign (-), NOT operator for managed
    properties, 512
MMS (Managed Metadata Service) Application, 14,
    541–559, 604
    content type syndication, 556–559
    term groups, 542–543
    term sets, 543–544
    term store, 541–545
        managing, custom solution for, 545–556
Mobile object model, 64
<Module> element, 290, 293, 296, 316, 320, 373,
    424, 447, 571

module pattern, JavaScript, 171–172
<Modules> element, 442, 447
multitenancy, 42, 128–129
MyAutoHostedApp project, 150
MyAutoHostedAppWeb project, 150
My Sites, 673, 676

N

namespaces
    JavaScript, 165
    for managed navigation, 605
    for REST URIs, 198
    for social enterprise features, 675–676
<NavBars> element, 442, 446
navigation
    for application pages, 302
    managed, 604–607
    structured, 606
NEAR operator, managed properties, 512
-ne (not equal to) operator, PowerShell, 28
.NET Assembly Connectors, 534–539, 631, 663–668
.NET Framework, 5, 40, 62
.NET objects, accessing, 31
New-Item cmdlet, 43
New-Object cmdlet, 31
news feed permission type, 239
newsfeeds. *See* social feeds
New-SPSite cmdlet, 33
New-SPWebApplication cmdlet, 32
not equal to (-ne) operator, PowerShell, 28
-notlike operator, PowerShell, 28
NOT operator, managed properties, 512

O

OAuth authentication, 232, 240–255
    app principals for, 242–243
    authentication server for, 242
    client app for, 242
    configuration for, 247
    content owners for, 242
    content server for, 242
    flow for, 244–246
    security tokens for, 164, 244–246, 250–254
        access tokens, 225–226, 232–233, 245, 246,
            250–254
        authorization code, 245, 254–256
        context tokens, 244, 246, 250

JWT standard for, 252
    refresh tokens, 245–246, 250
TokenHelper class for, 248–251
versions of, 240
Windows Azure ACS used by, 241–242
OData Extension Provider, 643
OData (Open Data Protocol) source, 196
    authentication for, 643
    connector for, 631
    ECTs using, 668
    querying, 199–200
Office 365
    authosted apps in, 129
    hosting tenancies with, 122–123
    sandboxed solutions with, 60
    SharePoint Online, 1
Office 2013
    BCS architecture for, 630–631
    BCS Client layer for, 623
    ECTs used in, 655–656
Office Business Parts, 639
Office Developer Tools, 73
Office Store, publishing SharePoint apps to, 152–153
Office Web Apps, 36–37
ONEAR operator, managed properties, 512
ONET.xml file, 442, 444
    for site definitions, 445–450
    for site templates, 458
    for web templates, 451–455, 457
on-premises model, 1–2
    hosting tenancies with, 123
    licenses for, 3
    SharePoint farms using, 6–7
OOBThemesV15 module element, 442
Open Data Protocol. *See* OData
operating systems, 4–6
OR operator, managed properties, 512
oslo.master file, 283
Outlook
    External Lists synchronized with, 627–628
    synchronizing lists to, 655
Output filter, BCS, 649

P

Package node, for project, 78, 90
Package.Template.xml file, 90
packaging
    farm solutions, 89–90
    SharePoint apps, 147–152

<%@ Page%> directive, 269
    DynamicMasterPageFile attribute, 299
    MasterPageFile attribute, 286
    for Web Part pages, 292
page layouts, 595–600
    creating, 596–597
    page fields in
        edit mode panels for, 599
        field controls for, 595–596
        properties of, configuring, 598–599
        RichHtmlField type, 597–599
        TextField type, 597
        Web Parts in, 599–600
page libraries, 21
Page_Load method, 269, 300
page model, 595–596
PageNumber filter, BCS, 649
PageRenderMode control, 289
pages, 267
    adding programmatically, 276–277
    application pages, 298–302
        base classes for, 299
        creating, 299–301
        navigation support for, 302
        securing, 301–302
    content pages, 289–295
        creating, 289
        deploying, 290–292
    creating, 21
    customized, 21, 278–282
    in eDiscovery sets, 589
    layouts for. *See* page layouts
    manipulating with SSOM, 275–277
    master pages, 270–271, 282–287, 595–596
        custom, for branding, 296–298
        default master pages, 283–285
        delegate controls in, 285–286
        referencing, 286
        in site collection, 282
    page model for, 595–596
    publishing pages, 295
    requesting from virtual file system, 274–275
    uncustomized (ghosted), 277–279
    Web Part pages, 292–295, 319–323
PageTitle control, 284
{Page} tokens, 517
parallel execution
    thread safety required for, 346
    of Web Parts, 345–346
parameters.xml file, 399–400

parsers, 508
Passthrough authentication, 639–640, 644
Password filter, BCS, 649
path-based site collection, 18
Path managed property, 513
people, following, 711–720
PeopleManager object, 680, 684
People term group, 542
PerformancePoint Service Application, 14
permissions. *See also* authorization
    for apps, 235–239
        app-only permissions, 239–240
        default policy for, 235
        requesting, 236–239
        types of, 239
    for BDC service, 634
    for site customizations, 19, 24
    for testing, 41
personal feeds (public), 675
    posting to, 704–709
    retrieving posts from, 689–698
    types of, 691–692
Personalizable attribute, 331–333
physical servers, 37
pipelining, in PowerShell, 28
plus sign (+), AND operator for managed
        properties, 512
PortalSiteMapProvider, 606
PowerPoint Automation Services, 14
PowerShell scripts, 26–34
    administering SharePoint, 26, 42–45
    cmdlets, 27
    COM objects, accessing, 31
    comparison operators, 28
    console for
        SharePoint 2013 Management Shell, 31
        Windows PowerShell console, 26, 42–43
    debugging, 30
    execution policy for, 29
    foreach loops, 30
    ISE for, 30–31, 42
    .NET objects, accessing, 31
    pipelining, 28
    profile for, 43–44
    service applications, creating, 51–52
    snap-in for, 31–34, 43–44
    solutions
        deploying, 44–45
        retracting, 44–45
    variables, 30

writing, 29–30
private feeds. *See* site feeds (private)
privileges. *See* authorization for users
production environment, 40–41
production farms, 7
Products Configuration wizard, 101
$profile cmdlet, 43
profile page, BCS, 653
profile synchronization connections, 655
<Project> element, 445
projects. *See also* SharePoint solutions
    creating in Visual Studio, 77–79
    Deploy command, 78
    Features node, 78–79
    Package node, 78
    Retract command, 78
    templates for, 77
<PropertyBag> element, 457
<Property> element, 317
PropertyOrFieldNotInitializedException error, 181
<PropertySchema> element, 417
prototype pattern, JavaScript, 172–173
prototypes, JavaScript, 169–170
provider-hosted apps, 127–129, 163, 164, 257,
        263–264. *See also* cloud-hosted apps
proxy groups, 47–48
.ps1 file extension, 29
PSConfig tool, 101
public feeds. *See* personal feeds (public)
Publishing feature, 295, 591
publishing pages, 295
publishing SharePoint apps, 152–155
publishing sites, 591–594
    accessing files in, 594
    content aggregation for, 607–616
    cross-site publishing, 617–620
    device channels for, 600–604
    managed navigation for, 604–607
    page layouts for. *See* page layouts
    page model for, 595–596
    templates for, 592–594

Q

query process, for searches, 509–513
    KQL for, 510–513
    managed properties, 509, 511–513
    ranking models, 510
    result sources, 510

query rules, 521
{QueryString} tokens, 517
query tokens, 516–518
Quick Parts, Word, 656

R

ranking models, 510, 530
ReadAndValidateContextToken method,
        TokenHelper class, 249
Read site role, 224
realm. *See* hosting tenancy
<Receivers> element, 384, 462
Records Center site, 586
records management, 584–589
    archives, site collection for, 586
    eDiscovery, 586–589
    in-place records management, 584–585
RefinementScriptWebPart Web Part, 529
refiners, 521–522
refresh tokens, OAuth, 245, 246, 250
Register-SPWorkflowServices cmdlet, 468
<RemoteEndpoint> element, 232
<RemoteEndpoints> element, 132
remote event receivers, 381–383
Remote Procedure Call. *See* RPC
RemoteSharedFileBackedMetadataCatalog
        object, 657
<RemoteWebApplication> element, 247
removeClass() method, jQuery, 176
Remove-SPSite cmdlet, 33
Remove-SPSolution cmdlet, 44
RenderContents method, 324, 327–328
rendering template, 410–411
Representational State Transfer APIs. *See* REST APIs
{Request} tokens, 517
ResetRoleInheritance method, SPSecurableObject
        class, 223
resource files, templates for, 87
Resource Points, 76
REST (Representational State Transfer) APIs, 67–68,
        195–212
    _api entry point for, 198
    app authentication, 225, 227, 233, 246, 251
    in C#, 206–212
    for cloud-hosted apps, 164–165
    creating content types, 371
    creating lists, 354
    in JavaScript, 200–206

people, following, 716–720
personal feeds
    posting to, 707–709
    retrieving, 695–698
querying External Lists, 630
searches using, 524–526
for SharePoint-hosted apps, 164
site feeds
    posting to, 710
    retrieving, 702–704
URIs for, 196–200
user profile properties, retrieving, 683–689
for Web Parts, 323
ResultScriptWebPart Web Part, 528
result sources, for search queries, 510, 515–518
.resx files, 87
Retract command, for projects, 78
ReusableAcl property, SPSecurableObject class, 223
RevertToSelf authentication, 640–642, 644
ribbon menu, customizing, 303–307
RichHtmlField type, 597–600
right angle bracket, equal sign (>=), greater than
        or equal to operator for managed
        properties, 511
right angle bracket (>), greater than operator for
        managed properties, 511
RoleAssignments property, SPSecurableObject
        class, 223
root directory, 86–89
RPC (Remote Procedure Call), 196
<RuleDesigner> element, 491
RunWithElevatedPrivileges method, SPSecurity
        object, 219, 220–221
Run With PowerShell command, 30

S

S2S (server-to-server) authentication, 232, 256–264
    access tokens for, 256–258
    configuring trust for, 259–263
    as high-trust configuration, 257
    for provider-hosted apps, 257, 263–264
    test certificates for, 264
    X.509 certificate for, 257–259
Safe Mode parsing, 280–282
SAML (Security Assertion Markup Language)
        tokens, 214–215, 225, 233
sample data, 41
sandboxed solutions, 71, 102–117

activating, 110, 121
CAML in, 103–104
CAS policies for, 102
code-behind in, 103
creating, 106–109
debugging, 105, 113
deploying, 109–113, 121
deploying content pages in, 291
execution environment for, 104–106
objects accessible in, 76
requirements for, 72
security for, 120–121
uncustomized pages not supported for, 278
upgrading, 60
    features, 113–117
    to new SharePoint version, 121
validator for, 110–112
Web Parts in, 311
scalability, testing, 41
Scalar method, BCS, 645
schema.xml file, 433–439
scopes, 79–81
for app installations, 124–125
farm-scoped features, 80–81
site-scoped features, 80–81
web application-scoped features, 80–81
web-scoped features, 79–81
script tags, 174
script Web Parts, 528–529
{SearchBoxQuery} token, 517
SearchBoxScriptWebPart Web Part, 529
search capabilities, 503–504
architecture of, 506–510
connectors used for, 507–508, 534–539
CSOM API for, 526–528
CSWP (Content Search Web Part), 523
indexing process, 507–508, 531–534, 539
KQL (Keyword Query Language), 510, 510–513
link queries, 513–514
list of, by SharePoint version, 503–504
managed properties, 509, 511–513
query process, 509–513
query rules, 521
ranking models, 510
refiners, 521–522
REST API for, 524–526
result sources, 510, 515–518
script Web Parts, 528–529
search-based applications, 504–506
Search Center, extending, 514–523

search results
    adding pages for, 514–515
    displaying, 518–521
    relevancy of, improving, 529–531
    security for, 537–538
    Search Results Web Part, 518, 521
    SSA (Search Service Application), 14, 506–507
Search Directories term group, 542
SearchExecutor object, 526
search permission type, 239
Search Service Application. See SSA
{SearchTerms} token, 517
seattle.master file, 283, 283–285
Secure Sockets Layer. See SSL
Secure Store Service, 14
security. See also authentication; authorization
    for application pages, 301–302
    for app web, 136
    for search results, 537–538
Security Assertion Markup Language
        tokens. See SAML (Security Assertion
        Markup Language) tokens
security principals, 213–214, 216. See also user
        authentication
    app principals, 242–243
    apps as, 224
    assigning roles to, 224
    SHAREPOINT\SYSTEM account as, 220–221
security tokens, 10, 213–215, 216
    access tokens, 225
    OAuth tokens, 244–246, 250–254
    SAML tokens, 225
Security Token Service. See STS
{SelectedItemId} token, 144
{SelectedListId} token, 143
$select operator, OData, 199
selectors, jQuery, 174–175
Sequence activity, 479, 482
sequential workflow, 476
ServerException error, 181, 183
servers, 73
    database server, 36
    domain controller, 36
    Office Web Apps server, 36
    physical, 37
    services on, determining, 46
    SharePoint server, 36
    types of, 36
    virtual, 37–38
    Workflow Manager server, 37

server-side controls. *See* Web Forms controls
server-side object model. *See* SSOM (server-side object model) API
server-to-server authentication. *See* S2S authentication
service applications, 12–13, 46–52
    configuring, 47–52
    endpoint for, 46
    instances of, 46
    platform availability of, 14–15
    proxy for, 13–14
    proxy groups of, 47–48
    for SharePoint apps, 123–124
    web service for, 46
Services on Server page, 46
Set-ExecutionPolicy cmdlet, 29
SharePoint
    compatibility levels, 594
    history of, 1–4
    on-premises model, 1–3, 6–7, 123
    operating systems supported by, 6
SharePoint 2001, 2
SharePoint 2003, 3, 214
SharePoint 2007, 3
    BPOS, 3
    root directory, 86
    user authentication, 214
SharePoint 2010, 3
    CSOM, 63
    Developer Dashboard, 54
    Developer Tools, 55
    Health Check for, 279
    Office Web Apps, 36–37
    root directory, 86
    stapling feature, 61
    upgrading solutions to SharePoint 2013, 60–61
    visual designs, 61
    Web Analytics, 60–61
    workflow host, 37
SharePoint 2013, 3–4
    component hierarchy, 73–76
    development environment for, 35–41
    hardware requirements, 38–39
    operating systems supported, 4, 5
    root directory, 86
    social enterprise features, 673–674
    software requirements, 38–40
SHAREPOINT\APP account, 254
SharePoint apps, 122–144
    APIs for, 163–165

app launcher for, 126
App Management Service, 123–124
app manifest for, 130–132, 147
app web for, 134–137
app web solution package, 148–149
authentication for, 224–234
    access tokens for, 225–226, 232
    cross-domain library for, 227–230
    external, 225, 232–233. *See also* OAuth authentication; S2S authentication
    flow for, 233–234
    internal, 225–232
    SAML tokens for, 225, 233
    web proxy for, 231–232
authorization for, 234–264
    app identifier for, 235
    default policy for, 235
    permissions, 235–239, 241
BCS for, 668–671
C# for, 163–165, 206–212
cloud-hosted, 125–126
    app designs using, 163–165
    app principal for, 242
    authentication for, 227–230, 232–233. *See also* OAuth authentication; S2S authentication
    autohosted, 129–130, 163–164
    hosting models for, 127–130
    packaging, 150–152
    provider-hosted, 127–129, 163–164, 257, 263–264
    requirements for, 164–165
code isolation for, 125–126
compared to solutions, 4
custom workflow activities for, 487–490
default content for, 58
deploying, 58
development environment for, 124
event handling in, 381–383
features, adding, 58
hosting tenancy for, 122–123, 235
icon for, 147
installation scopes, 124–125
installing, 155–158
JavaScript for, 163–173
    closures, 168–169
    custom libraries, 170–173
    data types, 166
    DOM elements, selecting, 174–175
    functions, 167–168

jQuery library, 173–177
namespaces, 165
prototypes, 169–170
REST API with, 200–206
strict, 166–167
variables, 166–167
JSOM for, 188–195
life cycle events for, 158–162
Managed object model for, 180–187
multitenancy, 128
packaging, 147–152
publishing, 133, 152–155
REST API for, 195–212
retracting, 58
server requirements for, 36
SharePoint-hosted, 125–127
app designs with, 163–164
authentication for, 227
requirements for, 164
Site Subscription Settings Service, 123–124
solution package for, building, 58
start page URL, 132–135
types of, 56–57
uncustomized pages not supported for, 278
uninstalling, 135, 158
upgrading, 157–158
user interface for, 137–144
app parts, 137–140, 149
chrome control, 144–147
link back to host web, 137, 144
UI custom actions, 140–144, 149
web templates for, 463–465
SharePoint Customization Wizard, 77
SharePoint Designer 2013
custom workflows
activities for, 490–491
creating, 470–475, 485–487
custom task outcomes for, 495–496
features of, 23–24
SharePoint Developer Tools, 55–58, 71–72
SharePoint Enterprise, 503–504. See also ECM
(Enterprise Content Management)
SharePoint farms, 4–7, 73
account for
not using for testing, 41
administration of, 7–8
configuration database for, 6, 9
development farms, 7
local, 13
on-premises farms, 6–7

production farms, 7
solutions requiring, 72
staging farms, 7
web applications in, 9
web.config files for, 272
SharePointForm control, 284
SharePoint Foundation, 4–21
history of, 2
search capabilities in, 503–504
service applications for, 14–15
SharePoint-hosted apps, 125–127
app designs with, 163–164
authentication for, 227
requirements for, 164
SharePoint objects
COM used for, 76
customizing with JSLink property, 420–428
disposing of, 76
hierarchy of, 74
iterating through, 74–76
SharePoint Online, 1–2, 3–4
search capabilities in, 503–504
service applications for, 14–15
SharePoint Portal Server, 2
SharePoint Server, 36
history of, 2–3
licenses for, 3
load on, minimizing, 59, 67
Publishing feature, 591
service applications for, 14–15
SharePoint Server 2013 Virtual Machine Setup Guide
(Critical Path Training), 13, 124
SharePoint Services, 2–3
SharePoint solutions. See also projects
best practices for, 59–60
challenges with, 120–122
compared to apps, 4
deploying with PowerShell, 44–45
farm solutions. See farm solutions
project types for, 59
retracting with PowerShell, 44–45
sandboxed solutions. See sandboxed solutions
upgrading, 59–61
upgrading to new SharePoint version, 121
SHAREPOINT\SYSTEM account, 220–221
SharePoint Team Services, 2
show() method, jQuery, 176
Silverlight object model, 63–64
Silverlight Web Part item template, 314
Simple Object Access Protocol. See SOAP

single server development installation, 36, 38–39
SingleTask activity, 492–494
singleton pattern, JavaScript, 170
Site Actions menu, 19
sitecollection permission type, 239
site collections, 15–19, 74
    authorization in, 216–219
    creating, 33, 441, 456
    host-named site collection, 18–19
    master pages in, 282
    path-based site collection, 18
    Resource Points for, 76
{SiteCollection} tokens, 517
site columns, 362–366
    adding choices to, 365–366
    in content types, 369
    creating, 364–365
    custom
        creating, 422
    custom, creating, 428–433
    enumerating through, 363–364
    field controls mapped to, 595–596
    for managed metadata, 551–553
    standard, list of, 362–363
site columns gallery, 362, 363
site definitions, 441–450
    custom code with, 458
    custom, creating, 450
    feature stapling, 448–449, 450
    GLOBAL site definition, 442–443, 449, 454
    ONET.xml file, 442–449
    order of provisioning, 449–450
    webtemp*.xml files, 443–445
SiteDeleted event, 461
SiteDeleting event, 461
<SiteFeatures> element, 447, 455
Site Feed feature, 698–699
site feeds (private), 675
    posting to, 709–710
    retrieving posts from, 698–704
Site object, 65
site pages. See content pages
site roles, 218, 224
sites, 15–19, 74
    customizations to, 19–25
    development for, 24–25
    fields in. See site columns
    provisioning, 441–466
        custom code for, 458
        events associated with, 461–463

    providers for, 459–461
    reserving URL for, 441
    site definitions for, 441–450
    site templates for, 458–459
    web templates for, 451–457
site-scoped app installations, 124
site-scoped features, 80, 314
Site Settings page, 19–20
Site Subscription Settings Service, 14
site templates, 458–459
{Site} tokens, 517
{SiteUrl} token, 143
$skip operator, OData, 200
SOAP (Simple Object Access Protocol), 196
social core permission type, 239
SocialDataItem object, 706
social enterprise features, 674–676
    APIs for, 675–676
    following, 675, 710–720
        entities that can be followed, 710–711
        people, following, 711–720
    new features, 673–674
    social feeds, 689–710
        personal feeds (public), 675, 689–698,
          704–709
        site feeds (private), 675, 698–704, 709–710
        types of, 675
    user profiles, 674, 676–689
        properties of, retrieving with CSOM, 677–683
        properties of, retrieving with REST, 683–689
    Yammer, 720–724
SocialFeedManager object, 689–691, 699, 704–705
SocialFeed object, 693
SocialFeedOptions class, 692
social feeds, 674, 689–710
    personal feeds (public), 675
        posting to, 704–709
        retrieving posts from, 689–698
        types of, 691–692
    site feeds (private), 675
        posting to, 709–710
        retrieving posts from, 698–704
    types of, 675
SocialFollowingManager object, 711, 713–714
SocialPostCreationData object, 705
SocialThread object, 693
software requirements, 38–40
Solution Gallery site collection, 102, 109
$sort operator, OData, 200
{Source} token, 143

SPBasePermissions enumeration, 224
SP.ClientContext object, 179
SPContentDatabase object, 74
SPContext object, 65
SPDisposeCheck tool, 76
SpecificFinder method, BCS, 645, 647, 658
SPEmailEventReceiver class, 380
SPFarm object, 74
SPFeatureReceiver class, 85
SPField class, 65, 360, 420–428
SPFieldMultiColumn class, 407
SPFieldNumber class, 407
SPFieldText class, 407
SPFile class, 276, 377
SPFolder class, 276, 373
SPGroup class, 216
SPHtmlTag control, 284
SPItemEventReceiver class, 380, 662
SPItem object, 74
sp.js library, 177
SPLimitedWebPartManager class, 321–323
SPList class, 358
SPListEventReceiver class, 380
SPListItem object, 65, 377, 378, 629
SPList object, 65, 74, 377, 629
SPMetal utility, 396–400
SPPrincipal class, 216
SPQuery object, 389, 394
SP.RequestExecutor object, 228
SPRequestModule, 274–275
SPRoleDefinition class, 224
SPSecurableObject class, 222–224
SPSecurity object, 219, 220–221
SPServer object, 74
SPSiteCollection object, 458
SPSiteDataQuery object, 392, 394
SPSite object, 65, 74
SPSolutionValidator class, 111
sp.ui.controls.js library, 144
SP.UI.Controls.Navigation object, 144
SPUser class, 216
SPUserToken class, 216, 221–222
SPVirtualPathProvider class, 275
SPWebApplication object, 74
SPWeb class, 363
SPWebCollection object, 458
SPWebEventReceiver class, 380, 461
SPWeb object, 65, 74, 219, 458
SPWebPartManager class, 312
SP.WebRequestInfo object, 231

SPWorkflowEventReceiver class, 380
SQL connector, 631
SQL query language, 510
square brackets ([ ]), enclosing class names, 31
SSA (Search Service Application), 14, 506–507
SSL (Secure Sockets Layer), 243
SSOM (server-side object model) API, 62
   content types, creating, 430–433
   creating content types, 370
   creating lists, 354
   files and folders, accessing, 275–277
   hierarchy of, 73–76
   objects in, CSOM equivalents for, 65
   site columns, creating, 430–433
SsoTicket filter, BCS, 649
SSS (Secure Store Service), 635–638, 642
stages, in workflows, 470, 472–475
staging farms, 7
{StandardTokens} token, 134, 137, 145
stapling. *See* feature stapling
<StartPage> element, 132–135, 229
state machine workflow, 478
State Service, 15
StreamAccessor method, BCS, 645
strict JavaScript, 166–167
structured navigation, 606
stsadm.exe utility, 26
STS (Security Token Service), 215
Subscribe method, BCS, 646
Subscription service, for workflows, 497
.svc files, 87
SyncChanges method, 335
SyncConverter class, 580–583
System term group, 542
System.Web.UI.Page class, 268

T

tasks, in workflows, 492–497
   creating, 492–494
   custom task outcomes, 494–497
TaxonomyField class, 551–553
TaxonomyFieldValue class, 555
taxonomy permission type, 239
TaxonomySession object, 605
TaxonomySiteMapProvider, 606
TaxonomyWebTaggingControl, 553–556
<Template> element, 444
templates

display templates, 611–616
document templates, 373–375
rendering templates for custom fields, 410–411
in root directory, 86–89
site templates, 458–465
tenancy. See hosting tenancy
tenancy-scoped app installations, 125, 156–157
tenant permission type, 239
term groups, 542–543
term sets, 543–544
term store, 541–545
capacity of, 544
importing term sets and terms to, 545
limitations of, 544
managing, custom solution for, 545–556
term groups in, 542–543
term sets in, 543–544
TermStores property, TaxonomySession object, 605
{Term} tokens, 517
testing, 40–41. See also debugging
Test-Path cmdlet, 43
TextField type, 597
text() method, jQuery, 176
.thmx files, 442
Timestamp filter, BCS, 649
Title field, lists, 358
Title managed property, 512
{Today} token, 517
toggle() method, jQuery, 176
token-based authentication, 643
TokenHelper class, 164, 248–251
GetAccessToken method, 251
GetAppOnlyAccessToken method, 253
GetAuthorizationUrl method, 254
GetClientContextWithContextToken method, 249
GetContextTokenFromRequest method, 249
GetS2SAccessTokenWithWindowsIdentity
method, 263
ReadAndValidateContextToken method, 249
TrustAllCertificates method, 264
$top operator, OData, 200
TrustAllCertificates method, TokenHelper class, 264
Trusted Subsystem model, 639, 640–642
TypeConverter attribute, 333

U

UI component, Web Forms, 268–269. See
also controls
UI custom actions, 140–144, 149, 302

ULS logs, 53–54
ULS Viewer, 53
uncustomized (ghosted) pages, 277–279
Uninstall-SPSolution cmdlet, 44
UnsecuredLayoutsPageBase class, 299
Unsubscribe method, BCS, 646
Updater method, BCS, 645, 658
Update-SPSolution cmdlet, 101
<UpgradeActions> element, 98, 114
upgrading SharePoint apps, 157–158
URIs, REST, 196–200
<UrlAction> element, 142
URL, reserving for sites, 441, 449
{URLToken} token, 517
user agent string, device channels from, 600–601
User and Health Data Collection Service, 15
user authentication, 214–224
Active Directory for, 10, 214–215
ASP.NET FBA for, 10–12, 214–215
claims-based security for, 10–11, 214–215
classic mode for, 10
configuring in web applications, 215
external systems for, 10, 214–215
impersonating users, 221–222
for SharePoint object access, 222–224
user credentials for, 221
User Information List for, 216
for web applications, 10–12
user authorization
ACLs for, 216–217
for application pool identity, 219
escalating privileges, 219–221
groups, 216–219
for SharePoint object access, 222–224
for SHAREPOINT\SYSTEM account, 220–221
users, 216–217
User Code Service, 104
UserContext filter, BCS, 649
user credentials, 221
UserCulture filter, BCS, 649
User Information List, 216
user information profile, 216
Username filter, BCS, 649
UserProfile filter, BCS, 650
user profiles, 674, 676–689
properties of, retrieving with CSOM, 677–683
properties of, retrieving with REST, 683–689
User Profile Service Application, 15, 468, 655
user profiles permission type, 239

{User} tokens, 518

V

v4.master file, 283
validators, for sandboxed solutions, 110–112
variables
    JavaScript, 166–167
    PowerShell, 30
var keyword, JavaScript, 166
verbs, for Web Parts, 337–339
versioning, 559–562
<VersionRange> element, 114
virtual file system, IIS, 268, 274–277
Virtual Machine Setup Guide, SharePoint 2013
        (Critical Path Training), 13
virtual path provider, 275
virtual servers, 37–38
Visio 2013, custom workflows with, 470–475
Visio Graphics Service, 15
Visual Studio
    Document Sets, creating, 568–574
    projects, creating, 77–79
Visual Studio 2010
    custom workflows using, 470
    SharePoint Developer Tools, 55
Visual Studio 2012
    configuring, 72–73
    custom workflows
        creating, 476–485
        custom task outcomes for, 496–497
    installing, 71–73
    Office Developer Tools, 73
    SharePoint Developer Tools, 55–58, 71–72
Visual Web Part item template, 314
Visual Web Parts, 329–331
VSTO deployment package, 627, 639

W

w3wp.exe file, 5
w3wp.exe process, 105
WCF (Windows Communication Foundation), 177
    connectors, 625, 631
    for custom workflows, 470
WCM (Web Content Management), 591–594
    content aggregation, 607–616
    cross-site publishing, 617–620
    device channels, 600–604

    managed navigation, 604–607
    page layouts, 595–600
    publishing files, accessing, 594
    publishing site templates, 592–594
WebAdding event, 461
web applications, 8–12, 73
    as ASP.NET applications, 9
    claims mode, 215
    classic mode, 215
    creating, 32–34
    IIS, compared to SharePoint, 271–272
    user authentication, configuring, 215
    user authentication for, 10–12
web application-scoped features, 80
WebBrowsable attribute, 332
web.config file, 9, 272–274
    for ASP.NET applications, 268, 271
    backup files for, 274
    for cloud-hosted apps, 247
    configuring for debugging, 274
    SafeMode element, 282
Web Content Management. *See* WCM (Web Content
        Management)
WebDeleted event, 461
WebDeleting event, 461
WebDescription attribute, 332
WebDisplayName attribute, 332
<WebFeatures> element, 447, 454, 457
Web Forms, 268–270, 282
    code-behind component, 269
    running, 269–270
    UI component, 268–269
WebMoved event, 461
WebMoving event, 461
WebNavigationSettings object, 606
Web object, 65
WebPart class, 310, 315–316
.webpart files, 313–314, 316
Web Part Gallery, 313
Web Part Manager, 312
WebPartPage class, 292–293
Web Part pages
    creating, 292–295
    deploying with Web Parts, 319–323
Web Parts, 21, 309–313. *See also* client Web Parts
        (app parts)
    ASP.NET compared to SharePoint, 310–311
    asynchronous execution of, 347–350
    client Web Parts (app parts), 137–140
    connections for, 340–345

consumers, 342–343
contracts, 340
providers, 341–342
control description files for, 313, 314, 316
CQWP (Content Query Web Part), 608–611
creating, 313–317
CSWP (Content Search Web Part), 523, 608–611
deactivating, 318–319
deploying, 317–323
element manifest for, 316–317, 320–321
files associated with, 314
item templates for, 314
managed metadata fields in, 553–556
parallel execution of, 345–346
properties of, 331–336
editing, with Editor Part, 333–336
persisting, 331–333
for Web Part verbs, 337
rendering of, controlling, 324–331
CreateChildControls method, 325, 327–328
event handling, 325–327
RenderContents method, 324, 327–328
Visual Web Parts, 329–331
in RichHtmlField type, 599–600
script Web Parts, 528–529
Search Results Web Part, 518, 521
site-scoped Feature for, 314
static, 312
verbs (menu options) for, 337–339
for wiki pages, 292–293, 322–323
zones for, 311–312
WebPartZone control, 311–312
Web Part zones, 599–600
web permission type, 239
Web Platform Installer tool, 468
WebProvisioned event, 461
web proxy, 231–232
web-scoped features, 79–80
web services
for service applications, 46
template files for, 87
for workflows, 470, 483–484, 485–487
website resources
"How to Create a Page Layout in SharePoint 2013", 597
MDS request and response, 288
RichHtmlField type properties, 598
SharePoint Features schema, 291
Web Platform Installer tool, 468
<WebTemplate> element, 451–452, 458

web templates, 451–457
custom code with, 458
deploying, 455–457
elements.xml file, 451–452
ONET.xml file, 451, 452–455
order of provisioning, 454
for SharePoint apps, 463–465
webtemp.xml file, 463
webtemp*.xml files, 443–445
Where-Object cmdlet, 28
WikiEditPage class, 292–293
wiki pages, Web Parts in, 292–293, 322–323
Wildcard filter, BCS, 650
Windows 8, 4, 6, 37
Windows Azure ACS, 241–242
Windows Communication Foundation. *See* WCF
Windows event logs, 53–54
Windows PowerShell scripts. *See* PowerShell scripts
Windows Server, 4, 6, 39
Windows Workflow Foundation, 37. *See also* Workflow Manager
Wingtip Toys examples, 8
Word
Document Information Panel, 656
Quick Parts, 656
Word Automation Services, 15, 578–583
WORDS operator, managed properties, 512
Worker Service, 104
Workflow Custom Activity item template, 476, 490
Workflow Foundation runtime, 467
Workflow item template, 476
Workflow Manager, 37, 467–468
Workflow Manager Configuration Wizard, 468
workflows, 467–470
activities for, 469, 487–491
custom, 470–491
arguments in, 480
flowchart workflow, 478
sequential workflow, 476
stages in, 470, 472–473, 474–475
state machine workflow, 478
templates for, 476
variables in, 480
Visio and SharePoint Designer for, 470–475, 485–487
Visual Studio for, 476–485
web services for, 470, 483–487
custom forms in, 498–502
association forms, 498–500
initiation forms, 500–502

Workflow Service Application

    Publishing Site With Workflow template, 592–593
    services for, 497–498
    status page for, 469
    tasks in, 492–497
        creating, 492–494
        custom task outcomes, 494–497
    workflow association for, 469
    workflow definition for, 469
Workflow Service Application, 15
Workflow Service Manager, 497–498
Work Management Service Application, 15
.wsp files, 78, 92, 148. *See also* packaging

X

X.509 certificate, 257–259
.xap files, 87
XRANK keyword, 512, 529

Y

Yammer, 720–724

Z

zones, for Web Parts, 311–312